T0264393

The Real MCTS
SQL Server 2008
Exam 70-432
Prep Kit

Database Implementation
and Maintenance

Mark Horninger Technical Editor
**Valentine Boiarkine, Denny Cherry,
and Steve Long** Lead Authors

Dinesh Asanka
Christian Bolton
Justin Langford

Bret Stateham
Sylvia Vargas

PUBLISHED BY
Syngress Publishing, Inc.
Elsevier, Inc.
30 Corporate Drive
Burlington, MA 01803

The Real MCTS SQL Server 2008 Exam 70-432 Prep Kit

Printed and bound in the United Kingdom
Transferred to Digital Printing, 2011

ISBN 13: 978-1-59749-420-5

Publisher: Laura Colantoni   Project Manager: Andre Cuello
Acquisitions Editor: Rachel Roumeliotis   Page Layout and Art: SPI
Technical Editor: Mark Horninger   Copy Editors: Leslie Crenna, Betty Pasagno,
Developmental Editor: Gary Byrne   Adrienne Rebello, Christina Solstad, and Jessica Springer
Indexer: SPI   Cover Designer: Michael Kavish

For information on rights, translations, and bulk sales, contact Matt Pedersen, Commercial Sales Director and Rights, at Syngress Publishing; email m.pedersen@elsevier.com.

Library of Congress Cataloging-in-Publication Data
Application submitted

Technical Editor

Mark Horninger (A+, Net+, Security+, MCSE+I, MCSD, MCAD,MCDBA, MCTS, MCITP, MCPD) is manager of database operations at Internet Pipeline, Inc. He is also the founder of Haverford Consultants, Inc. (www.haverford-consultants.com/), located in the suburbs of Philadelphia, PA. He develops custom applications and system engineering solutions, specializing primarily in Microsoft .NET technology and Microsoft SQL Server. He is a contributing author to *Securing SQL 2005, Configuring and Troubleshooting Windows XP Professional MCSE Windows 2000 Professional Study Guide* and *Designing SQL Server 2000 Databases for .NET Enterprise Servers* published by Syngress, an imprint of Elsevier Inc. Mark has also served as an adjunct professor at Kaplan University teaching Web design.

Mark has over 20 years of computer consulting experience and has passed 50+ Microsoft Certification Exams.

He lives with his wife, Debbie, and son, Robby, in the Philadelphia area.

Mark would like to thank his wife, Debbie, for her infinite patience, love, and support during this project.

Lead Authors

Valentine Boiarkine (MCSE, MCDBA, MCSD, MCT) is a founding partner at Blade Ltd., a software consulting firm based in Wellington, New Zealand. She is the lead architect of the revolutionary Blade File Transfer System file transfer technology. Valentine has over 10 years' consulting and software development experience, and she specializes in enterprise software integration, security, IT alignment, and unified communications. She has designed distributed software solutions for financial, legal, and government organizations.

Valentine is the author of numerous technical training courses, guides, and white papers for Microsoft Corp. and Quest Software, including SQL Server Microsoft Official Curriculum titles. She is also an accomplished trainer and presenter. She frequently trains support engineers at Microsoft and Microsoft partners worldwide. Her technology expertise lies in SQL Server, .NET development, Exchange Server, and Office Communications Server. Valentine resides in Auckland, New Zealand, with her husband, Keith, and children Spencer and Alexander.

Denny Cherry (MCSA, MCDBA, MCTS, MCITP) is a senior database administrator and architect for Awareness Technologies. He currently handles all database change design and implements changes to both the companies' ASP solution as well as the consumer hosted versions of the product. In addition Denny manages the Infrastructure Team, which maintains the 100-plus server environment. Denny's background includes database administration and database engineering positions at MySpace.com, IGN.com, GameSpy.com, and EarthLink Networks.

In 2008 Denny was named to the Quest Software Customer Advisory Board, and in 2009, Denny was named as a Microsoft MVP. Denny has written dozens of articles related to SQL Server, both for print magazines and various Web sites.

Steve Long is a senior software engineer/systems analyst at Wilmington Trust. Steve has over 14 years of database and application design and development experience. He currently provides database and application support to trading applications and processes using Microsoft technologies. He also serves as technical lead on significant projects in addition to lending his infrastructure, project management, and business process expertise to all initiatives. Before making a full-time switch to the information technology field, Steve spent a number of years working in the accounting field.

Steve holds a bachelor's degree from Goldey-Beacom College in Wilmington, Delaware, and a Client/Server Technology certification from Pennsylvania State University. He is currently working toward his graduate degree at Goldey-Beacom.

Steve wishes to thank his coworkers for putting up with him every day and his family for their understanding and support during his writing.

Contributing Authors

Dinesh Asanka (MVP SQL Server, B.S. [Eng], MBA [IT]) is a database architect at Exilesoft (Pvt) Ltd. He is primarily involved in designing databases in SQL Server. Dinesh has been working with SQL Server since 2000 starting from version 7.

Dinesh is a regular columnist for popular Web sites, including sql-server-performance.com, sqlservercentral.com, and sqlserveruniverse.com. Besides writing, Dinesh is actively involved in presentations for the SQL Server Sri Lankan User Group (SS SLUG).

Dinesh holds a bachelor's degree in engineering and an MBA from the University of Moratuwa, Sri Lanka.

Christian Bolton (MCA: Database, MCM: SQL Server, MVP: SQL Server) is a director and database architect for Coeo Ltd., a Microsoft Gold Partner that delivers SQL Server managed support and consulting services to organizations in the U.K. and Europe. Prior to joining Coeo, Christian worked for five years as a senior premier field engineer at Microsoft UK, working with some of Microsoft's biggest customers. He is a Microsoft Certified Architect, Certified Master and MVP for SQL Server, and coauthor of *Professional SQL Server 2005 Performance Tuning*. He works out of London and lives in the south of England with his wife and two children.

Justin Langford (MCSE, MCITP, MCDBA, SNIA, CCNA, ITIL) is a principal consultant for Coeo Ltd, a Microsoft Gold Partner in London. Coeo provides SQL Server consulting services for upgrade, performance tuning, scalability, and availability solutions for all versions of SQL Server. Coeo offers remote DBA services to customers who outsource management and 24×7 operations of their SQL Server platforms. Justin delivers and maintains SQL Server solutions for customers in many different industry sectors throughout Europe.

Prior to joining Coeo, Justin spent three years working at Microsoft UK as a premier field engineer. In this role, Justin delivered SQL Server support consulting to some of Microsoft's largest finance and government customers in Europe. Justin has also coauthored *Wrox IT Pro: SQL Server Performance Tuning*.

Bret Stateham (MCT, MCSE, MCTS, MCITP) is the owner of Net Connex Technology Training and Consulting, LLC, located just outside San Diego, CA. Net Connex provides consulting and training services that are focused primarily on Microsoft server platforms. Bret has over 20 years of experience in the industry and over 10 years as a trainer. He has been working with SQL Server since version 6.5 and has been teaching SQL Server since version 7.0. Bret has contributed to multiple Syngress SQL Server publications starting with *Designing SQL Server 2000 Databases for .Net Enterprise Server*. He stays involved with the community by helping to organize the Socal Code Camp and he is a frequent speaker at Code Camps and User Groups. Bret lives in Ramona, CA, with his wife, Lori; son, Chase; and daughter, Katie.

Sylvia Vargas has been working with information technology since 1981. Sylvia's experience in SQL Server started in 1997, although she has over 20 years' experience in other relational database technologies, including IBM SQL/DS, Digital Equipment Corp.'s RDB, and Oracle.

She has worked for state and local governments; Fortune 500 companies, such as Boeing, Disney, and Texaco; and a broad number of industries, including finance, manufacturing, Internet, and utilities.

She has been a developer, DBA, and manager on everything from a SQL/DS running on an IBM/Oracle system running UNIX to SQL Server and DB2 installations.

Sylvia has an undergraduate degree from Fordham University and an MBA from Pace University in New York. She has worked at Microsoft since 2006.

Sylvia lives in Seattle, WA, and enjoys bicycling, genealogy, and the great theatre in the Seattle area. Sylvia also teaches part-time at the University of Washington's Extension Certificate Program teaching SQL Server Development.

Contents

Companion Web Site: A more detailed answer key for the Self Test questions in this book is available on the Web.
Go to www.elsevierdirect.com/companions/9781597494205.

Chapter 1

MCTS SQL Server 2008 Exam 432

New Features in SQL Server 2008

Exam objectives in this chapter:

- New Feature Overview
- Reporting Services

Exam objectives review:

- ☑ Summary of Exam Objectives
- ☑ Exam Objectives Fast Track
- ☑ Exam Objectives Frequently Asked Questions
- ☑ Self Test
- ☑ Self Test Quick Answer Key

Introduction

Congratulations on your journey to become certified in SQL Server 2008. This book will help prepare you for your exam and give you a practical view of working with SQL Server 2008.

SQL Server 2008 is a fantastic product when you think about all it does. I've worked with SQL Server since the days of 6.5, and it's come a long way since then.

In this chapter, we will briefly review the new features in SQL Server 2008. There are quite a few enhancements to SQL Server, many of which will make the job of the DBA much easier. One of these, the new performance data management system, allows for database statistics and performance information to be automatically captured across an enterprise.

While this chapter covers the new features in SQL Server 2008, bear in mind many of the "basic" features of SQL will also be covered on the test. This book will not only cover the new features but also the topics from earlier versions of SQL Server that have not changed, as you will also need to know these items.

Head of the Class...

Know and Understand All SQL Server 2008 Features

Be sure you understand all of the topics in this book before attempting the test. It will cover old and new features, so don't limit your studying to just the new features. This will help you not only when it comes to the test, but also in using SQL Server 2008 in general.

A Word About the Test

On your testing day, make sure you arrive rested and ready to sit for the exam. Be calm and read each question carefully. Microsoft doesn't try to trick you; however, the questions and answers are presented in such a way that you should think about each question before answering it.

When you take your exam, be sure to leave no question unanswered. Most questions are multiple choice, so if you can narrow it down to two possible answers, you have a 50–50 chance at getting the question right – although this book will do an excellent job of preparing you for the exam.

If you are not sure of the answer to a question, sometimes it's good to skip that question and move on and come back to it. Another question may jog your memory, and when you come back to the first question the answer is much clearer.

When you go in for your test, don't bring pagers, laptops, cell phones, and so on. They will not allow you to bring them in. Also be sure to bring two forms of ID. Most testing centers have video cameras, and you are taped during the exam to deter cheating.

TEST DAY TIP

Be sure to read each question completely before answering! Sometimes there is a more "correct" answer than the first answer in the list. While there may be more than one correct answer, one solution may be better than another.

New Feature Overview

SQL Server 2008 has many new features for the DBA and database developer. With these features, Microsoft was able to achieve its vision of managing data more efficiently.

The following section is meant to provide a high-level overview of many of the new features found in SQL Server 2008.

TEST DAY TIP

Make certain you know which features go with which edition. You can be sure that some answers will be presented in such a manner as to test your knowledge of editions.

Installation

The new SQL Server Installation Center offers many more options. Figure 1.1 will familiarize you with the new tool.

Configuring & Implementing...

The New SQL Server 2008 Installation Center

The new SQL Server 2008 Installation Center has a different look and feel as compared to previous versions. The overall look and feel is much more user friendly than the old installation methods, and it's also more centralized.

Figure 1.1 The SQL Server Installation Center

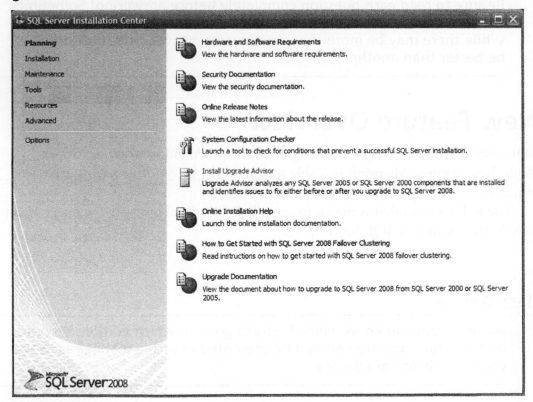

The SQL Server installation tool is used to create a new installation, or to make changes to the existing installation. Keep in mind many of the changes require you to have the installation media to complete the change.

Exam Warning

Be sure you have walked through installing SQL Server 2008 before attempting to complete the exam! The terms and questions asked will be much more familiar to you if you have.

Compressed Backups

New & Noteworthy...

Compressed Backups

Compressed backups are an exciting new feature in SQL Server 2008. While these have been available for a long time from third-party vendors such as Red Gate, Quest, and many others, they are now built into SQL Server. With compressed backups built in, I expect they will become the standard for most companies.

Compressed backup is a great new feature in SQL Server 2008. By compressing backups, you can save time and disk space. Initial thoughts may lead you to believe that compressed backups would take longer, as during the backup process the disk is usually the bottleneck; however, since less data is being written to the disk, backup time is usually reduced.

It's a relatively simple process to use compressed backups. During the backup you would select compress backup (see Figure 1.2). Bear in mind that if you are working with a SQL 2005 database this feature will not be available.

Figure 1.2 The Compress Backup Option

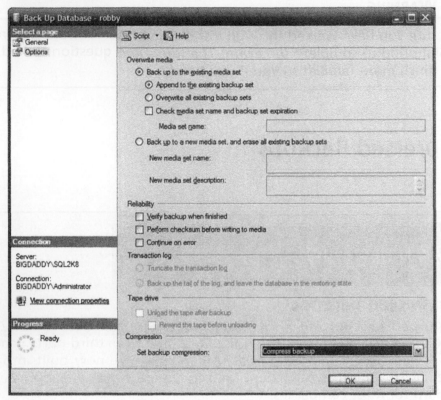

When using T-SQL to create the backup, you'd use:

```
BACKUP DATABASE [robby] TO DISK = N'C:\Backup\robby.bak' WITH
NOFORMAT, NOINIT, NAME = N'robby-Full Database Backup', SKIP,
NOREWIND, NOUNLOAD, COMPRESSION, STATS = 10
```

Either approach will produce the same result. It's a good idea to understand how to work both in the GUI and using T-SQL.

While we are on the subject of backups, it's also important to understand how *Copy Only Backup* works, and why and when you'd want to use it. The Copy Only Backup is especially useful for taking "one off" backups for development or testing – the advantage is it doesn't affect transaction log backups or differential backups. Keep in mind it also cannot serve as a base for differential or transaction log backups when restoring either.

To select Copy Only Backup, simply check the **Copy Only Backup** option in the GUI (see Figure 1.3).

Figure 1.3 The Copy Only Backup Option

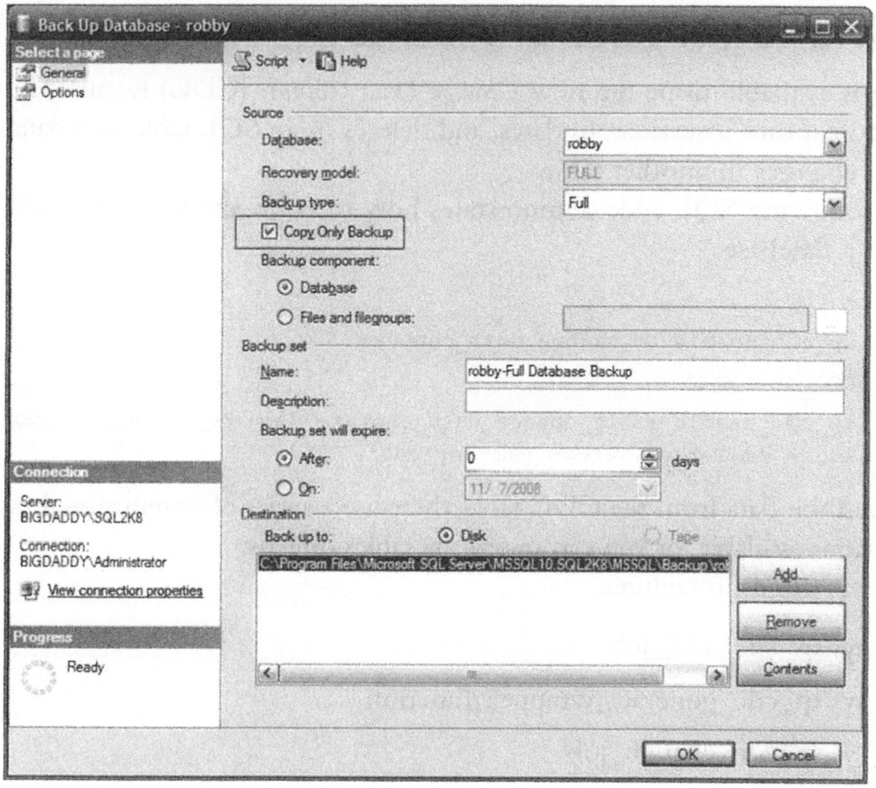

The T-SQL procedure to do a Copy Only Backup would look like:

```
BACKUP DATABASE [robby] TO DISK = N'C:\Backup\robby.bak' WITH COPY_ONLY,
NOFORMAT, NOINIT, NAME = N'robby-Full Database Backup', SKIP, NOREWIND,
NOUNLOAD, STATS = 10
GO
```

TEST DAY TIP

Be sure you are very familiar with doing backups and restores both from a T-SQL standpoint and a GUI standpoint. Since this is the bread and butter of a DBA's job, you can be sure there will be plenty of questions about backups, restores, and recovery.

Enhanced Configuration and Management of Audits

Auditing is available using the new *Change Data Capture* (CDC) feature. CDC can be used to capture insertions, updates, and deletes in an SQL table in a database and place the changes in another table.

The following SQL code demonstrates how to configure CDC for auditing of a table in a database:

```
--Activate CDC
EXEC sys.sp_cdc_enable_db_change_data_capture
--Enable CDC on table
EXEC sys.sp_cdc_enable_table_change_data_capture @source_schema = 'dbo',
@source_name = 'myTable', @role_name = 'cdc'
```

To read the data from the CDC table, there are a series of system stored procedures and functions available, or you can query the tables directly.

System stored procedures:

- sys.sp_cdc_add_job
- sys.sp_cdc_generate_wrapper_function
- sys.sp_cdc_change_job
- sys.sp_cdc_get_captured_columns
- sys.sp_cdc_cleanup_change_table
- sys.sp_cdc_get_ddl_history
- sys.sp_cdc_disable_db
- sys.sp_cdc_help_change_data_capture
- sys.sp_cdc_disable_table
- sys.sp_cdc_help_jobs
- sys.sp_cdc_drop_job
- sys.sp_cdc_scan
- sys.sp_cdc_enable_db
- sys.sp_cdc_start_job
- sys.sp_cdc_enable_table
- sys.sp_cdc_stop_job

System functions:

- cdc.fn_cdc_get_all_changes_<capture_instance>
- sys.fn_cdc_has_column_changed
- cdc.fn_cdc_get_net_changes_<capture_instance>
- sys.fn_cdc_increment_lsn
- sys.fn_cdc_decrement_lsn
- sys.fn_cdc_is_bit_set
- sys.fn_cdc_get_column_ordinal
- sys.fn_cdc_map_lsn_to_time
- sys.fn_cdc_get_max_lsn
- sys.fn_cdc_map_time_to_lsn
- sys.fn_cdc_get_min_lsn

TEST DAY TIP

You can count on questions about Change Data Capture on your exam. This new feature makes tracking down changes and auditing much easier than it has been in the past.

New Table Value Parameter

Passing tables as parameters has been a long time coming. The new table type can be passed to a stored procedure. This will solve quite a few problems!

Here's an example:

To declare a Table User Defined Type in the database:

```
create type MyTableType as table
(
    Name        varchar(150),
    City        varchar(20),
    AddressID   int
)

And here's the stored procedure that consumes it:
create procedure InsertFriends
```

```
(
        @MyTable MyTableType readonly
)
as

        insert
        into    Friends (Name, city, AddressID)
        select  Name, city, AddressID
        from    @MyTable;
--To fill create and fill the temp table:
declare @MyBestFriends_temp MyTableType
insert into @MyBestFriends_temp values ('Debbie', 'Havertown', 2)
insert into @MyBestFriends_temp values ('Chris', 'Philadelphia', 1)
insert into @MyBestFriends_temp values ('Tom', 'Garden City', 11)
insert into @MyBestFriends_temp values ('Greg', 'Lansdowne', 6)
insert into @MyBestFriends_temp values ('Steve', 'Wilmington', 6)

--And finally, to execute:
execute InsertFriends @MyBestFriends_temp
```

FileStream Data Types

FileStream data types are a new, interesting feature in SQL SERVER 2008. Basically, the database engine will store all of the data associated with the column in a disk file as opposed to the actual database. You might have used a similar home-grown scheme in earlier versions of SQL, but this integrates everything nicely into SQL Server.

In order to use FileStream, you must first enable it. This is accomplished via the *sp_FILESTREAM_configure* system stored procedure, or via the GUI in Management Studio under **advanced settings**.

Once FileStream is enabled, a file group must be added to the database in order for it to be able to use FileStream data types.

FileStream has the following limitations:

- Database mirroring cannot be configured in databases with FileStream data.

- Database snapshots are not supported for FileStream data.

- Native encryption is not possible by SQL Server for FileStream data.

EXAM WARNING

Be sure you remember the limitations of FileStream data types!

Sparse Column Support

Sparse columns are a new addition to SQL Server. Sparse columns allow for the optimized storage of null columns. Sparse columns can be a good thing, but be sure to enable them only on columns that contain sparse data, or your storage requirements may go up instead of down.

To enable a column as a sparse column, use the create statement in SQL or change the properties in the column to *Sparse* (see Figure 1.4).

Figure 1.4 Enabling a Column as a Sparse Column

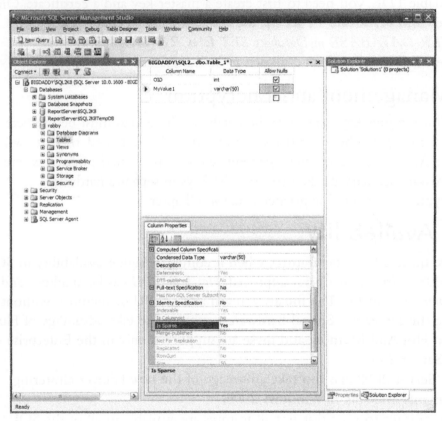

The SQL to accomplish this is as follows:

```
CREATE TABLE dbo.Table_1
    (
    OID int NULL,
    MyValue1 varchar(50) SPARSE NULL
    ) ON [PRIMARY]
GO
```

Encryption Enhancements

In the past, to use whole database encryption efficiently, it was necessary to purchase a third-party product such as NetLib. There are many other products out there that can be used for this as well.

Transparent data encryption (TDE) is available in SQL Server 2008. TDE allows you to easily encrypt the contents of your database and is designed to provide protection to the entire database. With TDE, you can encrypt the contents of your database with no changes to your application.

To enable TDE, you need to first create a master key and a certificate. Once the master key and certificate are set up, use the following to enable TDE:

ALTER DATABASE myDatabase SET ENCRYPTION ON

Once TDE is enabled, it's designed to be transparent to the application.

Key Management and Encryption

Encryption requires keys to secure the database. These keys must be protected and backed up so that in the event the system needs to be recreated, the data will still be accessible. An enterprise key management system can be incorporated where you use a hardware security module to store the keys in separate hardware.

Encryption is covered in greater detail in Chapter 5.

High Availability

There are quite a few new features when it comes to higher availability in SQL Server 2008. *Mirroring* has been improved, *Hot Add CPU* has been added, and *Hot Add Memory* is available. This means you can add a CPU or memory without switching the server off. Special hardware is required to take advantage of Hot Add CPU and Hot Add Memory, and these are supported only in the Enterprise edition of SQL Server 2008.

SQL Server 2008 can also take advantage of the new failover clustering enhancements available in Windows 2008.

It's important to note that not all features are available in all of the SQL Server editions. For example, failover clustering is not available in the Web edition or workgroup edition.

Performance

There are a number of performance enhancements in SQL Server 2008. Many of these upgrades are internal to SQL Server 2008, but there are a few worth mentioning.

Performance Data Management

Performance data management is a new tool available in SQL Server 2008. Performance data management allows you to collect performance-related data from your SQL Servers over time. Performance data management consists of a warehouse database (for storing the results) and the data collector, and collection is usually scheduled to run at specific times.

Resource Governor (similar to Query Governor)

Resource Governor is a nice new feature to help manage workload, designed to limit the resources available to a process. The way the Resource Governor works is the DBA creates a workload group and a resource pool. Workload groups are containers to hold user sessions. Workload groups are mapped to resource pools.

User sessions are mapped to workload groups based on classifier functions. The classifier functions can be by IP address, username, application name, and so on.

Figure 1.5 shows at a high level how it all fits together.

Figure 1.5 Managing a Workload with Resource Governor

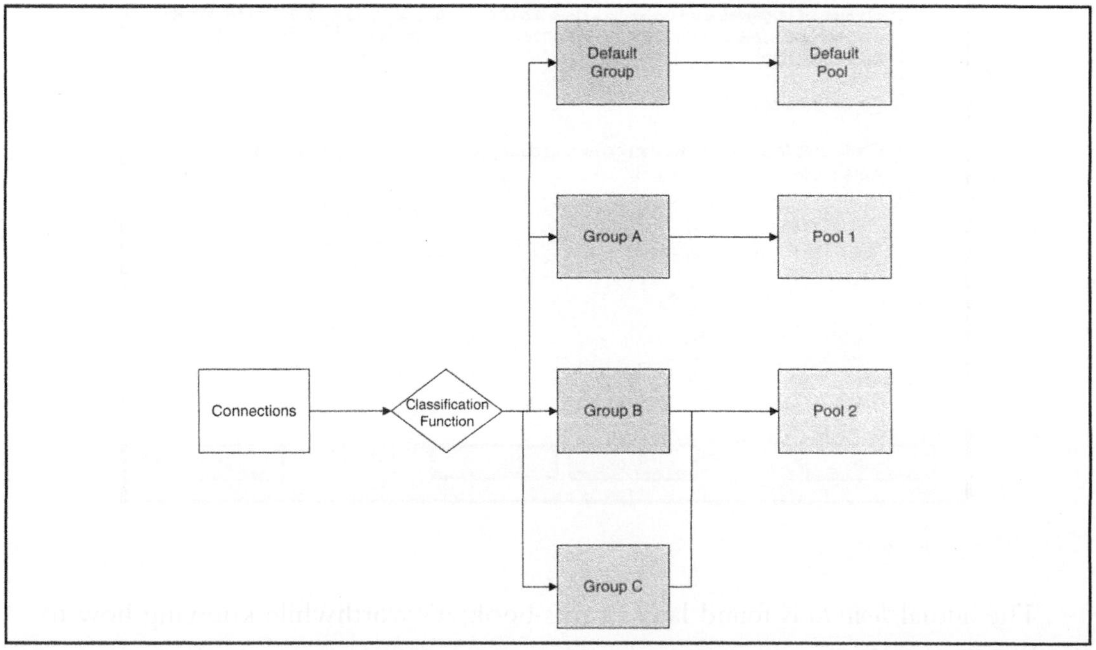

Freeze Plan

Freeze plan is a cool (pardon the pun) new feature in SQL 2008. Plan freezing is meant to offer greater predictability when it comes to executing a particular query in SQL Server 2008.

By executing a few lines of code, you can create a plan guide, which is basically a cached plan that is kept around and used for a particular query.

First, you need to create the data warehouse, which is fairly easy. There's a wizard that will guide you through the steps in the management console. The wizard's main dialog is shown in Figure 1.6.

Figure 1.6 Creating a Data Warehouse

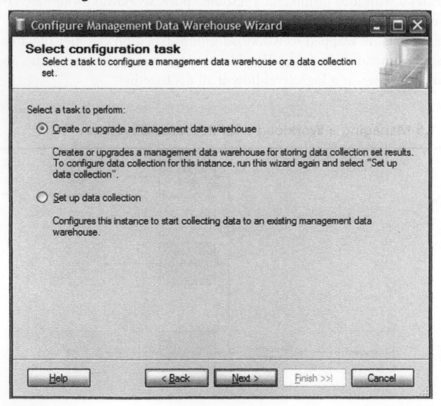

The actual *how to* is found later in this book; it's worthwhile knowing how to use this new feature.

Figure 1.7 is a sample of one of the reports available in the data collection set.

Figure 1.7 A Data Collection Report

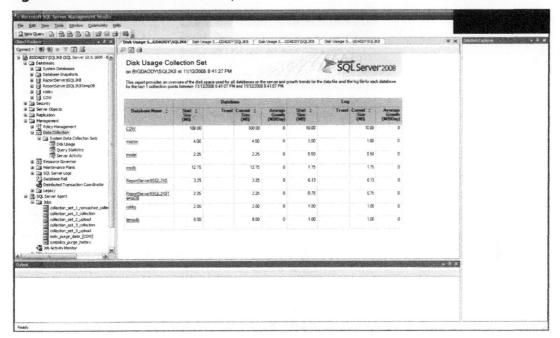

As you can see, this report can be useful. It provides quite a bit of information about your databases and their size and growth.

Unfortunately, the data collection can be used only on SQL Server 2008 servers. It will not work if you connect to a SQL 2005 or SQL 2000 database server.

SQL Server 2008 Declarative Management Framework

Another exciting new feature in SQL Server 2008 is the *Declarative Management Framework* (DMF). This is basically a new policy-based management system for SQL Server 2008.

The DMF is very similar to Windows policy; however, it's much more focused on SQL Server specifics. For example, you can enforce a particular naming convention for stored procedures and a different naming convention for tables.

There are three main components to the DMF: policies, conditions, and facets. See Figure 1.8.

Figure 1.8 DMF Components

To create or apply a policy, you would right click on the **policy node** and proceed from there. In the following screens, you'll be prompted to use facets and conditions to create a policy.

Development Improvements

Now we'll discuss a few development improvements that were made to SQL Server 2008.

LINQ Support

LINQ is a new technology. It's more of a programming language than T-SQL. It's basically a mapping of the database object to programming objects. This allows for a more object-oriented approach to dealing with database objects than in the past. This is a cool new feature and is covered in greater detail later on in this book.

MERGE Statement

The *MERGE statement* performs insert, update, or delete operations on a target table based on the results of a join to a source table.

For example, you can synchronize two tables by inserting, updating, or deleting all of the rows in one table based on differences in the other table.

Here is an example of MERGE code:

```
MERGE MyDatabase.Inventory AS target
USING (SELECT ProductID, SUM(OrderQty) FROM mySales.Orders AS o
      JOIN mySales.mySalesOrderHeader AS soh
      ON o.mySalesOrderID = soh.mySalesOrderID
      AND soh.OrderDate = @OrderDate
      GROUP BY ProductID) AS source (ProductID, OrderQty)
ON (target.ProductID = source.ProductID)
WHEN MATCHED AND target.Quantity - source.OrderQty <= 0
      THEN DELETE
WHEN MATCHED
      THEN UPDATE SET target.Quantity = target.Quantity - source.OrderQty,
            target.ModifiedDate = GETDATE()
OUTPUT $action, Inserted.ProductID, Inserted.Quantity, Inserted.ModifiedDate,
Deleted.ProductID,
      Deleted.Quantity, Deleted.ModifiedDate;
```

More on MERGE can be found in Chapters 6 and 9.

Spatial Data Type

The *spatial data type* is a new data type available in SQL Server 2008. The spatial data type is used to store location-based data. This could be a boon to applications that do geocoding.

Analysis Services Improvements

In *Analysis Services,* some of the new improvements are a better cube designer, dimension and attribute designer, and enhanced data mining structures.

ETL/SSIS Enhancements

Many of the new features carry over to SSIS, like Change Data Capture and the MERGE statement. Another good new feature is being able to script in

C# instead of only VB.NET. This will make things a bit easier for those of us who really like C#.

Reporting Services

There have been a few improvements to *SQL Server Reporting Services.* The configuration has changed; for example, it now supports rich text format.

SharePoint integration Reporting services now will integrate closely with Microsoft SharePoint.

No Longer Requires IIS

This is a key new breakthrough. In the past, IIS needed to be installed to host Reporting Services. Most of the time, this involved running IIS on the database server that had the reporting databases on it.

Better Graphing

Reporting Services supports graphing, which is great when creating dashboard style reports, charting sales, tracking growth, or anything better suited to a graph. This will make the Reporting Services reports an enterprise-class solution.

Export to Word Support

Reporting Services now has the ability to export to Word. This is a cool new feature, because in the past, you needed to purchase a third-party product such as OfficeWriter in order to export to Word.

Deprecated Features

The following is a list of deprecated features that are still available in SQL Server 2008, but will not be in future versions. Remember that while these will still work in SQL Server 2008, they are not a recommended best practice.

- BACKUP {DATABASE | LOG} WITH PASSWORD
- BACKUP {DATABASE | LOG} WITH MEDIAPASSWORD
- RESTORE {DATABASE | LOG} … WITH DBO_ONLY
- RESTORE {DATABASE | LOG} WITH PASSWORD
- RESTORE {DATABASE | LOG} WITH MEDIAPASSWORD

- 80 compatibility level and upgrade from version 80.
- DATABASEPROPERTY
- WITH APPEND clause on triggers
- Default setting of disallow results from triggers option = 0
- sp_dboption
- FASTFIRSTROW hint
- sp_addremotelogin
- sp_addserver
- sp_dropremotelogin
- sp_helpremotelogin
- sp_remoteoption
- @@remserver
- SET REMOTE_PROC_TRANSACTIONS
- sp_dropalias
- SET DISABLE_DEF_CNST_CHK
- SET ROWCOUNT for INSERT, UPDATE, and DELETE statements
- Use of *= and =*
- COMPUTE / COMPUTE BY
- sys.database_principal_aliases
- sqlmaint Utility
- The RAISERROR (Format: RAISERROR integer string) syntax is deprecated.

Exam Warning

Be sure you are aware of deprecated and removed features, as these may be the "correct" way to answer some of the questions that relate to earlier versions of SQL Server. They would not be the "correct" answer when working with SQL Server 2008.

Discontinued Features

The following is a list of features that are no longer available in SQL Server 2008:

- sp_addalias
- Registered Servers API
- DUMP statement
- LOAD statement
- BACKUP LOG WITH NO_LOG
- BACKUP LOG WITH TRUNCATE_ONLY
- BACKUP TRANSACTION
- 60, 65, and 70 compatibility levels
- DBCC CONCURRENCYVIOLATION
- sp_addgroup
- sp_changegroup
- sp_dropgroup
- sp_helpgroup
- Northwind and pubs
- Surface Area Configuration Tool
- sp_makewebtask
- sp_dropwebtask
- sp_runwebtask
- sp_enumcodepages

Summary of Exam Objectives

In this chapter, we reviewed the new features in SQL Server 2008. While most of these features will be found on your test, it's important to understand all of the content in this book. You can expect that the test will cover both the new features and some of the older features in earlier versions of SQL Server.

There are a number of deprecated features in SQL Server 2008. Know what they are and expect them to be "wrong" answers on your test, even though they still work in SQL Server 2008.

Be sure you know what features are no longer available in SQL Server 2008. Know what they are and expect them to be "wrong" answers on your test.

Exam Objectives Fast Track

New Feature Overview

☑ There are quite a few new features in SQL Server 2008, such as Change Data Capture and Declarative Management Framework.

☑ Reporting Services no longer requires IIS.

Reporting Services

☑ Deprecated features are features that will soon be removed. To that end, you should not use any of the deprecated features, for while they will work in SQL Server 2008, they will most likely be removed from the next version.

☑ Deleted features are no longer available. They may have worked with the last version of SQL Server, but they are no longer available and cannot be used.

Exam Objectives
Frequently Asked Questions

Q: Can I use the new the new Declarative Management Framework to enforce a naming convention across my mix of SQL 2005 and SQL 2008 Servers?

A: No – the DMF can only be used on SQL 2008 Servers.

Q: Can I use the new Change Data Capture feature across my mix of SQL 2005 and SQL 2008 Servers?

A: No, the Change Data Capture feature can only be used on SQL 2008 Servers.

Q: Can you use compression when backing up a SQL Server 2005 database?

A: No, compression is a new feature available in SQL Server 2008.

Q: Will backup compression take longer to complete?

A: The answer to this is complicated – in general, the disk is the bottleneck, so in most cases, backup compression will actually speed up your backups.

Q: We use an application that uses SQL 2005 DMVs. will it work with SQL 2008?

A: For the most part the DMVs remain intact. However, you should test your application to be certain.

Self Test

1. You are setting up security for your new SQL Server 2008 installation. Management is concerned about security. What approach should you take to ensure security settings are optimal?

    A. Use the Surface Area Configuration Tool to secure the installation

    B. Use the new Security Analysis tool to secure the installation

    C. Use SQL Server Configuration Manager to secure the installation

    D. Use Windows Service Manager to enable and disable the appropriate services

2. You have been tasked with setting up standards for your SQL Server 2008 installation. You need to enforce a table naming convention. What is the best way to accomplish this in your SQL Server 2008 environment?

    A. Use Windows Group Policy

    B. Create DDL Triggers

    C. Create DML Triggers

    D. Create a Declarative Management Framework policy

3. You have been asked to create a backup of your production database and restore it on a development server. Your production server is using the full recovery model. Full backups are taken Monday and Wednesday. Transaction log backups are taken every hour. Today is Friday. The backup needs to be created as quickly as possible. What's the fastest way to get the latest database copy while minimizing impact to production?

    A. Create a normal backup. Use that to restore to development.

    B. Create a Copy Only Backup. Use that to restore to development.

    C. Use the Wednesday backup. Restore the transaction log backups since Wednesday.

    D. Copy the .mdf and log files and use SP_attach.

4. You have a SQL Server 7.0 database and would like to move it to a new SQL Server 2008 instance. The database is part of an FDA-validated system and cannot be changed at all? How can this be accomplished?

    A. Restore the 7.0 database on your new server and set the compatibility mode to 7.

    B. You must upgrade the database to SQL 2005 or greater.

    C. Restore the 7.0 database on your new server and set the compatibility mode to 6.5.

    D. Copy the .mdf and log files and use SP_attach.

5. You have an application that is being upgraded from SQL Server 2005 to SQL Server 2008. You notice that some stored procedures are not working correctly. An excerpt is as follows:

    ```
    SELECT *

    FROM Territories, Region

    WHERE territories.regionid *= region.regionid
    ```

    What should you do to resolve the issue?

    A. There is no issue. The problem lies elsewhere.

    B. The join syntax is incorrect. Replace with left join.

    C. The select is incorrect. You need to enumerate the fields.

    D. The where clause should be = not *=.

6. Your disk is almost full on the transaction log drive for a database server. How can you resolve this issue?

    A. Use BACKUP LOG WITH TRUNCATE_ONLY

    B. Change the mode to simple and shrink the log

    C. Reinstall SQL

    D. Drop the database and restore from the last backup

7. You want to enforce a standard naming convention for stored procedures. What's the best way to do this in SQL Server 2008?

    A. Create a DDL trigger

    B. Use the performance data warehouse

    C. Create DML triggers

    D. Use the SQL Server 2008 Declarative Management Framework

8. You want to enforce a standard naming convention for tables and stored procedures. Your company has two SQL 2008 Servers and 60 SQL 2005 Servers. You need to use the same solution on all servers. What's the best way to do this in SQL Server 2005 and SQL Server 2008?

    A. Create a DDL trigger for all servers

    B. Use the performance data warehouse

    C. Create DML triggers

    D. Use the SQL Server 2008 Declarative Management Framework

9. You have a database table with a varchar(600) field in it. Most of the records in the table have a null value for this field. How can you save space?

    A. Move the data into a second table

    B. Use sparse columns

    C. Install a third-party tool on the machine to compress the data

    D. Use the SQL Server 2008 Declarative Management Framework

10. You have a database table with a FileStream field in it. Most of the records in the table have a null value for this field. What's the best way to save space?

    A. Move the data into a second table

    B. Use sparse columns

    C. Use the SQL Server 2008 Declarative Management Framework

    D. None of the above

11. You need to store images in for a Web site using SQL Server 2008. How can you accomplish this?

    A. Use a FileStream data type, and the images will be stored on disk

    B. Use a varchar data type and store the images in that field

    C. Use an int data type and store the images in that field

    D. Use an nchar data type and store the images in that field

12. You are responsible for a system that is used for both online transaction processing (OLTP) and reporting. When reports run on the server, the OLTP process slows way down. How can you allow reports to be run on the server and minimize impact to the OLTP processes?

    A. Use the Resource Governor

    B. Use a DDL trigger

    C. Use a DML trigger

    D. Use processor affinity masks

13. You are creating an application to track crime in different locations throughout a large city. What data type could prove useful for storing location data (longitude and latitude)?

    A. Varchar

    B. int

    C. Char

    D. Spatial

14. You are running out of space on the drive used to store backups. All of the servers use the same network location. What can you do to save space with your backups while maintaining the same number of backups?

    A. Use data compression

    B. Use compressed backups

    C. Use full backups

    D. Use a third-party tool

15. You need to store sensitive data in your SQL Server database. The application has already been written and works fine. What's the easiest way to do this without having to change your application?

    A. Modify the stored procedures to use xp_encryptstring

    B. Use transparent data encryption

    C. Use a third-party tool

    D. Use a trigger

16. Within your application, you need to log all changes to one table. DDL and DML changes must be logged. What's the best approach to solve this problem?

    A. Use the built-in auditing capability

    B. Create a DDL trigger

    C. Create a DML trigger

    D. This cannot be accomplished

17. You have a server that supports Hot Add CPU. The current CPU utilization is 95 to 100 percent most of the time. The server is mission-critical and cannot be shut down. SQL Server 2008 Standard Edition is installed. What should you do?

    A. Use the Hot Add CPU feature to add another CPU

    B. Use the Hot Add CPU feature to add two CPUs

    C. Add more memory to the server

    D. Schedule an outage and add another CPU to the server

18. You are contemplating using data compression on a table. You would like to know how much space this will save. How can you determine the savings?

    A. View the table properties

    B. Enable compression, then check the table size

    C. Use sp_estimate_data_compression_savings

    D. Use sp_check_compression

19. You have a server that supports Hot Add Memory. Performance is sluggish, and you believe adding more memory will help. The server is mission-critical and cannot be shut down. SQL Server 2008 Standard Edition is installed. What should you do?

    A. Use the Hot Add CPU feature to add another CPU

    B. Use the Hot Add CPU feature to add two CPUs

    C. Add more memory to the server.

    D. Schedule an outage and add memory to the server.

20. You have a SQL Server 2008 installation, and you want to create a high-availability solution. What are the ideal approach(es) to solve this problem?

    A. Backup and restore

    B. Replication

    C. Mirroring

    D. Clustering

Self Test Quick Answer Key

1.	C	11.	A
2.	D	12.	A
3.	B	13.	D
4.	B	14.	B
5.	B	15.	B
6.	B	16.	A
7.	D	17.	D
8.	A	18.	C
9.	A	19.	D
10.	D	20.	C and D

Chapter 2

MCTS SQL Server 2008 Exam 432

Installing SQL Server 2008

Exam objectives in this chapter:

- SQL Versions, Requirements, Features, and Differences
- Planning Your Installation
- Upgrading vs. Side-by-Side Installation
- Database Instances, Files, Locations, Filegroups, and Performance

Exam objectives review:

- ☑ Summary of Exam Objectives
- ☑ Exam Objectives Fast Track
- ☑ Exam Objectives Frequently Asked Questions
- ☑ Self Test
- ☑ Self Test Quick Answer Key

Introduction

This chapter covers the installation of SQL Server 2008. SQL Server 2008 comes in different editions, and you should be sure you understand the features and limitations of each. It's important to consider the edition during the planning stage.

In this chapter, we will review the capabilities of each of the different editions, as well as the options available when installing SQL Server 2008.

We will also review planning your installation and discuss best practices for hardware utilization when it comes to installing SQL Server 2008.

For best practices, we will discuss the tools used to install or upgrade SQL Server 2008.

SQL Versions, Requirements, Features, and Differences

A critical component of installing SQL Server 2008 is understanding the various components, editions, and versions of the SQL Server 2008 product sets to meet a specific set of business requirements. The challenge with SQL Server 2008 is in choosing between many options.

TEST DAY TIP

Make sure that you are familiar with the components and management tools with SQL Server 2008.

Similar to earlier versions, SQL Server 2008 has a number of server components and management tools that can be installed. The SQL Server 2008 includes the following components:

- *SQL Server Database Engine*, which contains the core services to store, process, manage, and secure relational and XML data, as well as services for full-text search and data replication.

- *Analysis Services*, which contains the services for creating, processing, and managing Online Analytical Processing (OLAP) analysis and data mining models for *Business Intelligence*.

- *Reporting Services*, a server-based reporting platform that provides tools and services to generate interactive, tabular, graphical, or free-form reports.

- *Integration Services,* a platform containing tools and services for building extract, transform, and load (ETL) operations for data warehousing, data integration, and workflow solutions.

SQL Server 2008 tools include:

- SQL Server Management Studio (SSMS)
- Business Intelligence Development Studio (BIDS)
- SQL Server Configuration Manager
- SQL Server Profiler
- Database Engine Tuning Advisor
- Command Prompt Utilities

SQL Server Management Studio (SSMS) is used for managing all SQL Server 2008 components, including relational database and business intelligence (BI). Examples include:

- Developing and managing SQL Server Database Engine and notification solutions
- Managing deployed Analysis Services solutions
- Managing and running Integration Services packages
- Managing report servers, Reporting Services reports, and report models

Business Intelligence Development Studio (BIDS) provides an integrated development environment for business application developers to create cubes, data sources, reports, and Integration Services packages. It is the primary environment in which to develop solutions with Analysis Services, Integration Services, and Reporting Services.

SQL Server Configuration Manager is now a Microsoft Management Console (MMC) snap-in and manages connectivity components. It replaces the following tools from pre-2005releases of SQL Server.

- Server Network Utility
- Client Network Utility
- Service Manager

SQL Server Profiler is a tool used to capture SQL Server events from a server and save them to a trace file. The trace file containing the SQL Server events can be analyzed and replayed to diagnose a specific problem arising from a series of events by correlating performance information.

The Database Engine Tuning Advisor (DTA) is a tool that analyzes a workload and the physical database implementation. After the analysis, the DTA can recommend changes to the physical database design structure to improve query performance for a given workload.

The Command Prompt Utilities are additional tools that are run from the command prompt. The tools included are:

- **bcp** Provides the ability to copy data between instances of SQL Server and a data file using a user-specified data format.

- **dta** Command line version of the Database Engine Tuning Advisor.

- **dtexec** Used to configure and execute SSIS packages.

- **dtutil** Another mechanism used to manage SSIS packages.

- **sqlcmd** Command line interface to enter and execute T-SQL statement, procedures, and script files.

- **rs** A command line tool to manage Reporting Services report servers.

- **rsconfig** Used to manage and configure a report server connection.

- **rskeymgmt** Used to manage report server encryption keys.

- **sqlagent90** Used to start the SQL Server Agent.

- **SQLdiag** Collects diagnostics for use by Microsoft Customer Service and Support.

- **sqllogship** Used for operational tasks such as backup, copy, and restore operations.

- **sqlservr** Used to start and stop the database engine for a specified instance.

- **Ssms** Command that opens SQL Server Management Studio (SSMS).

- **sqlps** Used to run PowerShell commands and scripts.

- **tablediff** Provides the capability to compare data from two tables for nonconvergence in a replication topology.

SQL Server 2008 packages the server components and features into various editions to support various usage scenarios. SQL Server 2008 editions are categorized as *Server*, *Specialized*, and *Free*. The various editions contain subsets of the SQL Server components to address specific business scenarios.

The Server Editions, which include Enterprise and Standard, are the configuration best suited to support high transaction volumes and large production environments.

- *SQL Server 2008 Enterprise Edition* provides a comprehensive data platform containing all the SQL Server components supporting the maximum number of processors that the server will allow.

- *SQL Server 2008 Standard Edition* provides a complete data platform that is targeted toward departmental or small business environments of 75 or fewer computers. Note that Standard Edition supports a maximum of only four processors on the server.

The Specialized Editions include:

- *Workgroup Edition* provides reliable data management and reporting components. This edition is best used in scenarios for small volumes of data on small servers. Workgroup Edition supports only two processors.

- *Web Edition* is designed to support highly available Web serving database applications at a low cost. One key differentiator to other editions is that only four processors are supported.

- *Developer Edition*, which is a full-featured edition like the Enterprise Edition, but is limited to development and testing only.

The Free Editions are targeted at ISV and the mobile application developer community.

- *Express Edition* provides a free and lightweight database that can be redistributed by ISVs. Note that the Express Edition is limited to one CPU and 1 GB of memory, and the database size cannot exceed 4 GB of data storage.

- *Compact Edition* is an embedded database version that provides the capability for developers to create standalone, as well as occasionally connected, applications primarily for mobile devices; however, it also supports desktops and Web clients. Similar to the Express Edition, this edition is limited to 4 GB of disk storage and one CPU but can use the maximum memory available. Unlike the Express Edition, the database engine does not have all of the programmability features of the other editions. For example, stored procedures, triggers and view, Native XML, and Service Broker are not supported.

The combination of business and hardware requirements is used in determining which edition of SQL Server 2008 to install, as well as the process by which to migrate an existing SQL Server database environment. Table 2.1 summarizes the general business usage scenarios and some of the hardware configuration requirements for the various SQL Server 2008 versions.

Table 2.1 SQL Server 2008 Editions

SQL Server 2008 Editions	Server Editions		Specialized Editions			Free Editions	
Product	Enterprise	Standard	Work group	Web	Developer	Express	Compact 3.5
Business Uses	Enterprise workloads that require high-availability, scalability, performance, data redundancy, and built-in Business Intelligence	Shared data supporting departments and small to large businesses	Remote offices that need local instances of company data	Supports Web application hosting	Full-featured edition for development and testing only	Entry-level database, ideal for learning and ISV redistribution	Embedded database for developing desktop and mobile applications
CPU Max	OS Maximum	4 CPU	2 CPU	4 CPU	OS Maximum	1 CPU	OS Maximum
Memory Min	512 MB	512 MB	512 MB	512 MB	512 MB	512 MB	512 MB
Recommended	2.048 GB or more	2.048 GB or more	2.048 GB or more	2.048 GB or more	2.048 GB or more	2.048 GB or more	2.048 GB or more
Max	OS Maximum	OS Maximum	4 GB	OS Maximum	OS Maximum	1 GB	OS Maximum
DB Size	Max: Unlimited	Max: Unlimited	Max: Unlimited	Max: Unlimited	Max: Unlimited	Max: 4 GB	Max: 4 GB

The key database engine features in the Enterprise Edition address scalability, high availability, and security.

Scalability is the ability to add more resources. In SQL Server 2008 Enterprise Edition, this is achieved by scaling up servers by adding additional CPUs, memory, or disks to a single server or by scaling out by moving certain services or databases to other servers.

The key scalability features in SQL Server 2008 database engine include:

- **Partitioning** Segmenting of data in large tables and indexes into units that can be distributed across multiple filegroups in a database to improve IO performance. Partitioning is very useful in improving the performance of very large OLTP and data-warehousing databases.

- **Data compression** Reduces the size of tables, indexes, or partitions, thereby reducing the database disk requirements.

- **Resource governor** Provides control over the amount of CPU and memory allocated to SQL Server 2008 workloads without any application changes.

- **Partition table parallelism** Improves the query processing performance on partitioned tables for parallel queries by enhancing the partitioning information in the compile-time and runtime execution plans.

- **Multi-instance support** Establishes the maximum number of SQL Server 2008 instances that can be created on a server. Enterprise Edition supports up to 50 instances on a server, Compact Edition only supports one instance, and all the other editions support up to 16 instances.

- **Log shipping** Allows you to automatically send transaction log backups from a primary database on a primary server instance to one or more secondary databases on separate secondary server instances. Log shipping supports the high availability option of database mirroring. The Express and Mobile editions do not support this feature.

- **Replication** Enables a primary database server to distribute data to one or more secondary servers.

Partitioning, data compression, and partition table parallelism are exclusive to the SQL Server 2008 Enterprise Edition. Also note that some replication features are very limited or not available in the Standard Edition.

New & Noteworthy...

Partition-Aware Seek Operation

Query performance on partitioned tables is significantly enhanced in SQL Server 2008 Enterprise Edition.

In SQL Server 2008 partitioned tables are treated like tables with an index on the partition ID column. This allows the creation and management of simpler query plans and improved performance by using the partition's column and function.

High availability refers to the availability of system resources when a component in the system fails. Please note that both log shipping and replication are considered as features of availability as well as scalability. The high availability features only available in the Enterprise Edition include:

- **Database snapshots** Provide a read–only static version of a source database on the same database instance. One of the many uses of database snapshots is creating separate databases for reporting that are separate from online transactions.

- **Fast recovery** Allows users access the database while the database is rolling back uncommitted transactions. Only the uncommitted transactions during the crash are locked till the rollback of the transaction is complete.

- **Online indexing** Allows index maintenance operations to be performed while the database is online and active.

- **Online restore** Enables the restoring of backup files using multiple filegroups while the database is still online.

- **Mirrored backups** Add redundancy of backup media, thereby increasing backup reliability.

- **Backup compression** Provides smaller backup files, thereby reducing disk space resources.

- **Hot Add Memory and CPU** Provide the ability to add memory or addition processors without a system reboot.

In the area of security, the Enterprise Edition is the only edition that supports SQL Server auditing and transparent database encryption. SQL Server auditing provides a simpler mechanism using T-SQL to trigger, store, and view audits. An example of an audit implementation is to track log-on activity of specific user accounts or groups. Transparent database encryption (TDE) encrypts the database data and log files, meeting the regulatory or corporate data security standards without requiring application changes.

In terms of replication, the Enterprise Edition supports Oracle publishing and peer to peer (P2P) transactional replication. Oracle publishing allows an Oracle database to transmit data via replication to a SQL Server instance. P2P transactional replication provides copies of data that are transaction consistent in near real-time to all servers participating in the replication topology scheme.

Integration Services in SQL Server 2008, provided in the Enterprise and Standard Editions, have the most of the Integration Services features, while the other editions have very limited features as noted in Table 2.2.

Table 2.2 SQL Server 2008 Integration Services Features by Edition

Integration Services Feature	Enterprise	Standard	Workgroup	Web	Express
SQL Server Import and Export Wizard with basic sources and destinations and Execute SQL task	Yes	Yes	Yes	Yes	Yes
Integration Services runtime	Yes	Yes	Yes	Yes	Yes
Integration Services API and object model	Yes	Yes	Yes	Yes	
Integration Services service, wizards, and command-line utilities	Yes	Yes			
Basic tasks and transformations	Yes	Yes			
Log providers and logging	Yes	Yes			
Data profiling tools	Yes	Yes			

Continued

Table 2.2 Continued. SQL Server 2008 Integration Services
Features by Edition

Integration Services Feature	Enterprise	Standard	Workgroup	Web	Express
Additional sources and destinations:	Yes	Yes			
■ Raw File source ■ XML source ■ DataReader destination ■ Raw File destination ■ Recordset destination ■ SQL Server Compact destination ■ SQL Server destination					
Advanced sources, transformations, and destinations:	Yes				
■ Data Mining Query transformation ■ Fuzzy Lookup and Fuzzy ■ Grouping transformations ■ Term Extraction and Term Lookup transformations ■ Data Mining Model Training destination ■ Dimension Processing destination ■ Partition Processing destination					

Table 2.3 lists the key Analysis Services features between the Enterprise and Standard Editions in the area of Data Warehouse creation, scale and performance, multidimensional analytics, and data mining. Analysis Services is not available in the Workgroup, Web, Express, and Compact Editions.

Table 2.3 SQL Server 2008 Analysis Services Features by Edition

Feature Group	Feature Name	Enterprise	Standard
Data Warehouse Creation	Create cubes without a database	Yes	Yes
	Auto-generate staging and data warehouse schema	Yes	Yes
	Attribute relationship designer	Yes	Yes
	Efficient aggregation designers	Yes	Yes
Data Warehouse Scale and Performance	Change data capture	Yes	
	Star join query optimization	Yes	
	Scalable read-only AS configuration	Yes	
	Proactive caching	Yes	
	Auto parallel partition processing	Yes	
	Partitioned cubes	Yes	
	Distributed partitioned cubes	Yes	
Multidimensional Analytics	SQL Server Analysis Services service	Yes	Yes
	SQL Server Analysis Services backup	Yes	Yes
	General performance/scale improvements	Yes	Yes

Continued

Table 2.3 Continued. SQL Server 2008 Analysis Services Features by Edition

Feature Group	Feature Name	Enterprise	Standard
	Dimension, attribute relationship, aggregate, and cube design improvements	Yes	Yes
	Personalization extensions	Yes	Yes
	Financial aggregations	Yes	
	Partitioned customers	Yes	
	Custom rollups	Yes	
	Semi-additive measures	Yes	
	Writeback dimensions	Yes	
	Linked measures and dimensions	Yes	
	Binary and compressed XML transport	Yes	
	Account intelligence	Yes	
	Perspectives	Yes	
	Analysis Services shared, scalable databases	Yes	
Data Mining	Standard algorithms	Yes	Yes
	Data mining tools: wizards, editors, query builders	Yes	Yes
	Cross validation	Yes	
	Models on filtered subsets of mining structure data	Yes	

Continued

Table 2.3 Continued. SQL Server 2008 Analysis Services Features by Edition

Feature Group	Feature Name	Enterprise	Standard
	Time series: ■ custom blending between ARTXP and ARIMA models ■ prediction with new data ■ cross series predictions	Yes	
	Unlimited concurrent data mining queries	Yes	
	Advanced configuration and tuning for algorithms	Yes	
	Algorithm plug-in API	Yes	
	Parallel model processing	Yes	
	Sequence prediction	Yes	
	Multiple prediction targets for naïve Bayes, neural network, and logistic regression	Yes	

Table 2.4 identifies the feature differences in editions in SQL Server 2008 Reporting Services. For further information on these features, refer to the article *Features Supported by the Editions of SQL Server 2008* at http://msdn.microsoft. com/en-us/library/cc645993.aspx.

Table 2.4 SQL Server 2008 Reporting Services Features by Edition

Feature Name	Enterprise	Standard	Workgroup	Web	Express	Express Tools	Express Advanced
Report Server	Yes	Yes	Yes	Yes			Yes
Report Designer	Yes	Yes	Yes	Yes			Yes
Report Manager	Yes	Yes	Yes	Yes (Report Manager)			Yes (Report Manager)
Role-based security	Yes	Yes	Yes (Fixed roles)	Yes (Fixed roles)			Yes (Fixed roles)
Ad-hoc reporting (Report Builder)	Yes	Yes	Yes				
Word export and enhanced text formatting	Yes	Yes	Yes	Yes			Yes
SharePoint integration	Yes	Yes					
Enhanced SSRS gauges and charting	Yes	Yes	Yes	Yes			
Export to Excel, PDF, and images	Yes	Yes	Yes	Yes			Yes
Remote and nonrelational data source support	Yes	Yes					

E-mail and fileshare delivery			Yes		
Report history, scheduling, subscriptions, and caching			Yes		
Data source, delivery, and rendering extensibility			Yes		
Infinite clickthrough			Yes		
Data-driven subscriptions			Yes		
Reporting Services memory limits	Unlimited	Unlimited	Unlimited	4 GB	4 GB	4 GB

Planning Your Installation

The planning process prior to installation is a critical component of the success of any product installation or upgrade process. In the planning process, understanding the overall architecture and the tracking all the details are critical.

- Understand the current hardware resources and budget parameters to stage, test, and perform the installations and upgrades.

- Understand the application and database architecture used in the business applications.

  - What specific functionality needs to be tested to ensure certain speed and/or security requirements?

  - Is there a test plan to support the validation process after the upgrade and installation?

- Understand the business's service level agreements for all SQL Server applications.

  - Is there a time window available for upgrading the SQL Server instances?

  - Is there disk space (or budget for additional disks) to host a side-by-side installation?

  - If the time window is insufficient for an upgrade, consider a migration process of upgrading the instance on another server or an instance on the same server.

- Document the installation components to be used in the process.

  - Create all the service and administrator accounts required by the various SQL Server components.

  - Detail the directories where the software and data directories will reside.

- Define and implement a testing process for the installation/upgrade and success criteria.

- Plan the disk layout of the new or existing environment to ensure enough storage space for backups, additional space for installation files and logs as well as the database files.

- Establish a backup and recovery plan.

  - Perform backup and recovery on test servers to ensure procedures are operable in the case of a production incident.

Head of the Class...

The Architecture in Installation Planning

One of the many times that architecture is critical is in the planning of upgrades and migrations. Prior to placing the installation disk near any disk drive, it is critical to know what the existing physical and software architecture currently is in the production and test environments. By documenting the "as-is" architecture, you'll be able to accurately (and confidently) push back those scope creep requirements of making do with less.

An example of a "problem upgrade" by a customer was communicated to me like this once:

"The production SQL Server database environment with 4 GB of memory and 100 GB of data space works fine, but when we upgraded the database to a SQL Server instance with 1 GB of memory and 20 GB of disk on a slower processor space, it is significantly slower."

After a long pause, I repeated the scenario that was described to me and noted that the difference in the system configuration would mean that the application using the production server may require more memory and disks. I then asked the key question: What type of processing does the application perform against the database?

Besides keeping up with the latest version, key questions to ask include:

- What are the goals of the upgrade?
- What is the architecture vision of the application(s) database you will be upgrading?
- Is the goal to improve performance or implement a new feature?

Understanding what the end game expectation is key to a successful upgrade.

Regardless of the intent of the upgrade, ensure that you have a repeatable process to measure and log the performance of specific business scenarios on the existing production system, the test upgrade

Continued

environment, and the post-upgrade environment. Whatever the performance metrics you are going to measure, they must be specific. Improving general system performance by 10 percent does not cut it! Identify the specific set of reports, user interfaces, jobs, and transitions that are examples of a performance to benchmark. Make sure the test on the production system and the means to execute the performance metric are reproducible.

Here is a checklist for installation planning:

Environment inventory. Document every hardware and software component your existing system has now. At a minimum identify the following:

- On what drive and in which specific directory are the SQL Server software binaries located?

- On what drive are the SQL data files located? What are the maximum sizes of the underlying disks? How much free space is on the directories/drives? Are the disks on a SCSI or a SAN device? Note the size and speed (or in the case of a SAN device, partitions) of the disks for the data.

- How many database instances are on this server?

- What are the file sizes of all the databases for each instance?

- How many processors does the server have?

- How much physical memory is on the server? How much is allocated to each SQL Server instance?

- What are the current hardware resources and budgetary restraints to stage, test, and perform the installations and upgrades?

Application and database architecture. Understand how the application and databases are used in the business applications.

- What specific functionality needs to be tested to ensure certain speed and/or security requirements?

- Is there a test plan to support the validation process after the upgrade and installation?

- What are the application dependencies to the databases to be upgraded?

Continued

Business service level. Understand what the business user's expectations for a successful upgrade are.

- What are the business hours of the application databases?
- Is there a time window available for upgrading the SQL Server instances? Is the time window sufficient for an upgrade or is a migration to another server or instance possible?
- Are there clearly defined performance metrics?

Test plan.

- Fully document and rehearse the test plan prior to the upgrade.
- Determine the testing process and success criteria.
- Design and implement verification tests for major processes in the installation/upgrade process.
- Determine the minimal downtime for the upgrade.
- Identify metrics to verify performance, so that there is no measurable performance degradation to key business processes.
- Document the upgrade process to use for testing and final implementation.
- Establish a backup and recovery plan.
- Perform test backups and the recovery process.
- Test the backup and recovery scenario again.
- How much time does the backup take? How long does it take to recover?
- Validate test plan by testing various scenarios. Log all test activities and review for any changes to test plan.
- Upgrade schedule – The timing details of the upgrade process should refine the specifics of the test plan.
- Decide dates and time schedules for the upgrade process.
- What specific skilled resources will be on-site or available to support the upgrade?
- Are the resources assigned to the upgrade experienced with the test procedures? If not, train resources with test procedure.
- What is the communication process for success or failure?

Upgrade Tools

There are a number of tools that you can leverage to help in planning for your upgrade. They include: *Best Practices Analyzer* and *SQL Upgrade Advisor*.

Running the Best Practices Analyzer (BPA) for SQL Server 2000 and SQL Server 2005 on your existing environments will help identify nonoptimal practices that can be addressed before upgrading to SQL Server 2008. The following versions of the BPA tools can be downloaded from the Microsoft download site.

- Best Practices Analyzer Tool for Microsoft SQL Server 2000 1.0
- SQL Server 2005 Best Practices Analyzer (August 2008)

The SQL Upgrade Advisor for SQL Server 2008 is essential in the planning of your SQL Server upgrade process. The SQL Upgrade Advisor analyzes your existing SQL Server 2000 and SQL Server 2005 instances and components, and then provides a detailed list of issues that are actionable.

The report generated from the SQL Upgrade Advisor is stored as an XML file in the user's default documents directory, under the subdirectory called SQL *Server 2008 Upgrade Advisor Reports.* More important, the Upgrade Advisor report provides a detailed list of issues. Each issue is identified as ***advisory*** or required. The required issue identifies a corrective action to be done before or after the database upgrade to the database or to the calling applications.

In addition to being included in the SQL Server 2008 installation CDs, the SQL Upgrade Advisor is a free download from the Microsoft download Web site – www.microsoft.com/downloads/ and enter **SQL Server 2008 Upgrade Advisor** in the **Search** box. Save the downloaded SQLUA.msi file to disk. Run the appropriate executable version of SQLUA.msi on every server that contains a SQL Server 2000 or 2005 instance and component to analyze. Also note that the Upgrade Advisor requires Microsoft .NET Framework 2.0 and Windows Installer 4.5, and can be downloaded from www.microsoft.com/downloads.

Once installed, the SQL Update Advisor can be executed from the **Start** menu: Click **Start**, point to **Programs**, point to **Microsoft SQL Server 2008**, and then click **SQL Server 2008 Upgrade Advisor**.

Configuring & Implementing...

Reporting Services and Upgrade Advisor

If you have Reporting Services instances on a separate server from your database instance, be sure to install the Upgrade Advisor on the report server as well!

Hardware Requirements: CPU, Memory, and Disk

SQL Server 2008 supports three different hardware platforms: 32-bit and two 64-bit technologies. 32-bit technology has been around for a number of years. Most SQL Server databases on the 32-bit platform are used for small and mid-size databases with limited number of users.

In the 64-bit space, there are two different hardware implementations: x64 and Itanium (IA64). IA64 refers to support of the Itanium processor. x64 supports the following processors:

- AMD Opteron
- AMD Athlon 64
- Intel Xeon with Intel EM64T support
- Intel Pentium IV with EM64T support

There are several reasons to use 64-bit CPU technology over 32-bit. The first is the ability to use more memory. The additional memory supported by 64-bit is highly desirable for all Analysis Services as well as online transaction processing (OLTP) applications with a large number of concurrent users. Another reason is the ability to handle larger floating point numbers, from which scientific and engineering calculations benefit. 64-bit chips can directly use precision up to 2^{64} versus 32-bit chips that are limited to 2^{32}. 64-bit environments also have the capability of supporting up to 64 processors.

64-bit performance is also highly leveraged in scenarios where there is a high volume of concurrent users and large amount of data processing, which is the ideal scenario for SQL Server Enterprise and Standard Editions.

Note that management tools such as SQL Server Management Studio (SSMS) and Business Intelligence Developer Studio (BIDS) are supported in WOW64, a feature of 64-bit editions of Windows that enables 32-bit applications to run natively in 32-bit mode. Applications function in 32-bit mode, even though the underlying operating system is running on the 64-bit operating system.

In determining which edition of SQL Server 2008 to install and use, understanding hardware requirements from existing or new servers is critical (see Table 2.5).

Table 2.5 SQL Server 2008 Enterprise Edition Hardware Requirements

SQL Server 2008 Editions	Server Editions		
Product Version	**Enterprise (32-bit)**	**Enterprise (64-bit – IA64)**	**Enterprise (64-bit – x64)**
Processor Type	Minimum: Pentium III- compatible processor or faster	Itanium	Minimum: ■ AMD Opteron ■ AMD Athlon 64 ■ Intel Xeon with Intel EM64T support ■ Intel Pentium IV with EM64T support
Processor Speed	Min: 1.4 GHz Better: 2.0 GHz or faster	Min: 1.4 GHz Better: 2.0 GHz or faster	Min: 1.4 GHz Better: 2.0 GHz or faster
Max CPUs	OS Maximum	OS Maximum	OS Maximum
Memory	2.048 GB or more	2.048 GB or more	2.048 GB or more
Min	512 MB	512 MB	512 MB
Max	OS Maximum	OS Maximum	OS Maximum
DB Size	Max: Unlimited	Max: Unlimited	Max: Unlimited

The Standard Edition supports a maximum of four CPUs for both the 32-bit and 64-bit hardware (see Table 2.6). The CPU maximum of four is one of the key hardware limitations of the Standard Edition compared with the Enterprise Edition in the areas of scalability and high availability. Table 2.7 lists the hardware requirements for SQL Server 2008 Workgroup and Web editions.

Table 2.6 SQL Server 2008 Standard Edition Hardware Requirements

SQL Server 2008 Editions	Server Editions	
Product Version	**Standard (32-bit)**	**Standard (64-bit)**
Processor Type	Pentium III-compatible processor or faster	Minimum: ■ AMD Opteron ■ AMD Athlon 64 ■ Intel Xeon with Intel EM64T support ■ Intel Pentium IV with EM64T support
Processor Speed	Min: 1.4 GHz Better: 2.0 GHz or faster	Min: 1.4 GHz Better: 2.0 GHz or faster
Max CPUs	4 CPU	4 CPU
Memory	2.048 GB or more	2.048 GB or more
Min	512 MB	512 MB
Max	OS Maximum	OS Maximum
DB Size	Max: Unlimited	Max: Unlimited

Table 2.7 SQL Server 2008 Workgroup and Web Edition Hardware Requirements

SQL Server 2008 Editions	Specialized Editions			
Product Edition	Workgroup (64-bit) x64	Workgroup (32-bit)	Web (64-bit) x64	Web (32-bit)
Processor Type	Minimum: • AMD Opteron • AMD Athlon 64 • Intel Xeon with Intel EM64T support • Intel Pentium IV with EM64T support	Pentium III-compatible processor or faster	Minimum: • AMD Opteron • AMD Athlon 64 • Intel Xeon with Intel EM64T support • Intel Pentium IV with EM64T support	Pentium III-compatible processor or faster
Processor Speed	Minimum: 1.4 GHz Better: 2.0 GHz or faster	Minimum: 1.0 GHz Better: 2.0 GHz or faster	Minimum: 1.4 GHz Better: 2.0 GHz or faster	Minimum: 1.0 GHz Better: 2.0 GHz or faster
Max CPUs	2 CPU	2 CPU	4 CPU	4 CPU
Memory Suggested	2.048 GB or more	2.048 GB or more	2.048 GB or more	2.048 GB or more
Min	512 MB	512 MB	512 MB	512 MB
Max	4 GB	4 GB	OS Maximum	OS Maximum
DB Size	Max: Unlimited	Max: Unlimited	Max: Unlimited	Max: Unlimited

SQL Server 2008 Developer Edition includes all the functionality of the Enterprise Edition, but it is licensed only for development, test, and demo purposes. In addition, the Developer Edition provides all the support for the 32-bit and both 64-bit processors. The difference between the hardware configurations is the maximum number of CPUs supported (see Table 2.8).

Table 2.8 SQL Server 2008 Developer Edition Hardware Requirements

SQL Server 2008 Editions	Developer		
Product Edition	IA64 (64-bit)	X64 (64-bit)	32-bit
Minimum Processor Type	Itanium processor or faster	AMD Opteron, AMD Athlon 64, Intel Xeon with Intel EM64T support, Intel Pentium IV with EM64T support	Pentium III-compatible processor or faster
Processor Speed	1.0 GHz or faster	Minimum: 1.4 GHz Better: 2.0 GHz or faster	Minimum: 1.0 GHz Better: 2.0 GHz or faster
Max CPUs	2 CPU	4 CPU	OS Maximum
Memory Suggested	2.048 GB or more	2.048 GB or more	2.048 GB or more
Min	512 MB	512 MB	512 MB
Max	OS Maximum	OS Maximum	OS Maximum
DB Size	Max: Unlimited	Max: Unlimited	Max: Unlimited

In terms of disk space for the installing the SQL Server components, the following are the minimum disk requirements for the various SQL Server components.

- Database engine, replication, and full-text search and default data files use 280 MB

- Analysis Services engine and data files require 90 MB

- Reporting Services and Report Manager require a total of 120MB

- Integration Services require 120MB

- Client components require 850MB

- SQL Server Books Online and SQL Server Compact Books Online require 240MB

Operating System Requirements

The operating system minimum requirements for a SQL Server 2008 upgrade or installation is dependent on the hardware, as well as on which version of SQL Server 2008 is being installed. Table 2.9 shows most of the operating system options for the Enterprise and Standard Editions of SQL Server 2008.

SQL Server Books Online on MSDN contains a detailed list of operating systems for all the SQL Server Editions. Search for SQL Server 2008 Software Requirements on the MDSN home page at http://msdn.microsoft.com for more details.

Table 2.9 Operating System Requirements for SQL Server 2008 Editions

Operating System Requirements	Enterprise x64	Enterprise IA64	Standard x64	Standard x64 for Small Business	Enterprise x32	Standard x32
Windows XP Professional x64			√			
Windows Server 2003 SP2 64-bit x64 Standard	√ - WOW64		√ - WOW64			
Windows Server 2003 SP2 64-bit x64 Data Center	√ - WOW64		√ - WOW64			
Windows Server 2003 SP2 64-bit x64 Enterprise	√ - WOW64		√ - WOW64			
Windows Server 2003 SP2 64-bit Itanium Data Center		√ - WOW64				
Windows Server 2003 SP2 64-bit Itanium Enterprise		√ - WOW64				
Windows Server 2008 x64 Web			√ - WOW64			
Windows Server 2008 64-bit x64 Standard	√		√ - WOW64			

Continued

Table 2.9 Continued. Operating System Requirements for SQL Server 2008 Editions

Operating System Requirements	Enterprise x64	Enterprise IA64	Standard x64	Standard x64 for Small Business	Enterprise x32	Standard x32
Windows Server 2008 64-bit x64 Standard without Hyper-V	√		√ - WOW64			
Windows Server 2008 64-bit x64 Data Center	√		√ - WOW64			
Windows Server 2008 64-bit x64 Data Center without Hyper-V	√		√ - WOW64			
Windows Server 2008 64-bit x64 Enterprise	√ - WOW64					
Windows Server 2008 64-bit x64 Enterprise without Hyper-V1	√ - WOW64					
Windows Server 2008 64-bit Itanium		√ - WOW64				
Windows Vista Ultimate x64			√			

Windows Vista
Enterprise x64

Windows Vista
Business x64

Windows Small
Business Server 2008

Windows Server 2008
for Windows Essential
Server Solutions

Windows Server 2008
for Windows Essential
Server Solutions
without Hyper-V

NOTE

Enterprise IA64 is not available in the localized versions of Italian, Spanish, Portuguese (Brazilian), or Russian. WOW64 indicates that the Management Tools are supported in WOW64, a feature of 64-bit editions of Windows that enables 32-bit applications to run natively in 32-bit mode.

Software Requirements

As part of the SQL Server 2008 software installation wizard, a validation process performed by System Configuration Check routinely scans the server for conditions that might block the setup or installation process.

Pre-installing .NET Framework 3.5, Microsoft Installer 4.5, and Windows PowerShell 1.0 will minimize or avoid a system reboot or errors on installation. All of these can be downloaded from the Microsoft download site, www.microsoft. com/downloads.

Microsoft Internet Explorer 6 SP1 or later will be required for the installation process. Internet Explorer is required by SSMS, BIDS, Reporting Services' Report Designer, HTML Help, and Microsoft Management Console (MMC).

Establishing Service Accounts

The selection of the installation account and the service accounts is part of the installation planning. The most common scenarios for the installation account privileges include:

- For local installations, the installation account must have Administrator privileges.

- For installs where the installation software is on a remote share, the installation account must be a domain account with Administrator privileges, and read and execute permissions on the remote share.

- For installations on clusters, the installation account must be a local administrator on the cluster with permissions to log in as a service on the cluster.

Each service in SQL Server must have an account configured during installation. Service accounts used to start and run SQL Server can be built-in system accounts, local user accounts, or domain user accounts. Microsoft recommends that service accounts be configured such that SQL Server services are granted the minimum permissions to complete their tasks. SQL Server 2008 service accounts are described in the following list:

- **Domain user account** If the service must interact with network services, access domain resources such as file shares, or use linked server connections to other computers running SQL Server, you might use a minimally privileged domain account. Many server-to-server activities require a domain user account. The domain accounts must exist prior to the installation process, unlike when using local accounts.

- **Local user account** A local user account without Windows Administrator permissions is recommended if the computer is not part of a domain.

- **Local service account** An account that is a built-in account (also known as an *"NT AUTHORITY\Local Service account"*) and has the same level of access to resources and objects as members of the Users group. These restricted privileges help safeguard the system if individual services or processes are compromised, but they are not supported for SQL Server or SQL Server Agent services.

- **Network service account** (*"NT AUTHORITY\NetworkService"*) The network service account is a built-in account that has more access to resources and objects than members of the Users group. Services that run as the network service account access network resources by using the credentials of the computer account.

- **Local system account** (*"NT AUTHORITY\System"*) A very high-privileged built-in account that has extensive privileges on the local system and acts as the computer on the network.

In addition to having user accounts, every service has three possible startup states that users can control:

- **Disabled** The service is installed but not currently running.

- **Manual** The service is installed, but will start only when another service or application needs its functionality.

- **Automatic** The service is automatically started by the operating system.

The administrator account used during the installation process enables the setup process to create local service user groups for the different SQL Server services, and assigns the service account or service SIDs to the appropriate local service group. The service user groups help secure the SQL Server files, as well as simplify the process of granting permissions required by the service.

Table 2.10 summarizes the account types that can be used for each SQL Service, as well as user groups and permissions created by the SQL Server installer.

Table 2.10 SQL Server 2008 Service Accounts and Privileges

SQL Server Service Name	Optional Accounts	User Group	Default Permissions Granted by SQL Server Setup
SQL Server	SQL Server Express: Domain User, Local System, Network Service All other editions: Domain User, Local System, Network Service1	Default instance: SQLServerMSSQLUser$ComputerName$MSSQLSERVER Named instance: SQLServerMSSQLUser$ComputerName$InstanceName	■ Log on as a service (SeServiceLogonRight) ■ Log on as a batch job (SeBatchLogonRight) ■ Replace a process-level token (SeAssignPrimaryTokenPrivilege) ■ Bypass traverse checking (SeChangeNotifyPrivilege) ■ Adjust memory quotas for a process (SeIncreaseQuotaPrivilege) ■ Permission to start SQL Server Active Directory Helper ■ Permission to start SQL Writer ■ Permission to read the Event Log service ■ Permission to read the Remote Procedure Call service
SQL Server Agent	Domain User, Local System, Network Service **Note:** *SQL Server Agent Service is disabled on instances of SQL Server Express and SQL Server Express with Advanced Services.*	Default instance: SQLServerSQLAgentUser$ComputerName$MSSQLSERVER Named instance: SQLServerSQLAgentUser$ComputerName$InstanceName	■ Log on as a service (SeServiceLogonRight) ■ Log on as a batch job (SeBatchLogonRight) ■ Replace a process-level token (SeAssignPrimaryTokenPrivilege) ■ Bypass traverse checking (SeChangeNotifyPrivilege) ■ Adjust memory quotas for a process (SeIncreaseQuotaPrivilege)

Analysis Services	Domain User, Network Service, Local Service, Local System	Default instance: SQL-ServerMSOLAPUser$*ComputerName*$MSSQLSERVER Named instance: SQL-ServerMSOLAPUser$*ComputerName*$-*InstanceName*	Log on as a service (SeServiceLogonRight)
Reporting Services	Domain User, Local System, Network Service, Local Service	Default instance: SQL-ServerReportServer-User$*ComputerName*$MSRS10.MSSQLSERVER Named instance: SQL-ServerReportServer-User$*ComputerName*$MSRS10.*InstanceName*	Log on as a service (SeServiceLogonRight)
Integration Services	Domain User, Local System, Network Service, Local Service	Default or named instance: SQL-ServerDTSUser-$*ComputerName*	■ Log on as a service (SeServiceLogonRight) ■ Permission to write to application event log. ■ Bypass traverse checking (SeChangeNotifyPrivilege) ■ Impersonate a client after authentication (SeImpersonatePrivilege)

Continued

Table 2.10 Continued. SQL Server 2008 Service Accounts and Privileges

SQL Server Service Name	Optional Accounts	User Group	Default Permissions Granted by SQL Server Setup
Full-Text Search	Use an account different than the account for the SQL Server service. The account will default to Local Service on Windows Server 2008 and Windows Vista.	Default instance: SQL-ServerFDHostUser-$ *ComputerName*-$MSSQL10.MSSQL-SERVER Named instance: SQL-ServerFDHostUser-$*ComputerName*-$MSSQL10.*Instance-Name*	Log on as a service (SeServiceLogonRight)
SQL Server Browser	Local Service	Default or named instance: SQLServer-SQLBrowserUser-$*ComputerName*	Log on as a service (SeServiceLogonRight)
SQL Server Active Directory Helper	Local System, Network Service	Default or named instance: SQL-ServerMSSQLServer-ADHelperUser-$*ComputerName*	None
SQL Writer	Local System	N/A	None

Upgrading vs. Side-by-Side Installation

Once the user requirements and expectations are discovered in the installation planning process, it is easier to decide which type of upgrade strategy to use. The two installation scenarios are upgrade and side-by-side installation.

The upgrade scenario updates an existing SQL Server installation while preserving the user data. The advantages of an upgrade include no additional hardware, and applications do not require any changes due to new server or database instance names.

The disadvantages of the upgrade scenario include:

- All databases in the instance remain unavailable to users while the upgrade is in progress.

- The rollback scenario is more complex. Since the SQL Server software and database will need to be restored on the same server this extends the downtime of the database application to the users in the case a recovery scenario is required.

In the upgrade scenario, SQL Server 2008 requires that SQL Server 2000 instances have service pack (SP) 4 installed. For SQL Server 2005 instances on a Windows 2008 Server, SP 2 or greater is required, otherwise SQL Server 2005 RTM or greater is supported. For the latest information, refer to the MSDN article, *SQL Server 2008 Upgrade Technical Reference Guide*.

Side-by-side installation requires that there be sufficient disk and memory resources on the server hosting the SQL Server 2000 or 2005 instance, or a separate server on which to install the SQL Server 2008 software and new database. By having both database instances available, it provides the users and administrators to verify that all applications work the same on both versions.

While the side-by-side installation process is more costly in terms of hardware and application changes, to change the database instance and/or server name, the existing database software and instance provides a straightforward rollback/recovery strategy for the database and system administrator. To recover to the previous version, the application setting would be changed to the legacy version.

A side-by-side installation is done with the following:

1. Install the SQL Server 2008 software on new disks or server hardware.

2. Create a new SQL Server 2008 instance on new disks or server hardware.

3. Copy database data and log files or backup files to the new SQL Server 2008 disks or server.

4. Create the SQL Server database using via detach/attach database method, backup and restore, or by using the copy database wizard.

5. Change applications to reference the new SQL Server 2008 databases.

Both upgrade and side-by-side installations require that the post–upgrade activities described in the next section be completed.

The best reference for detailed installation procedures is *Quick Start Installation of SQL Server 2008* on the MSDN site: http://msdn.microsoft.com/en–us/library/ bb500433.aspx.

For side–by–side installations, verify that your existing SQL Server installation is supported in Table 2.11.

Table 2.11 Side-by-Side Upgrade Support

Existing Instance of SQL Server 2008	Side-by-Side Support
SQL Server 2008 (32-bit)	SQL Server 2000 (32-bit) SQL Server 2000 (64-bit) x64 SQL Server 2005 (32-bit) SQL Server 2005 (64-bit) x64
SQL Server 2008 (64-bit) IA64	SQL Server 2005 (64-bit) IA64
SQL Server 2008 (64-bit) x64	SQL Server 2000 (32-bit) SQL Server 2000 (64-bit) x64 SQL Server 2005 (32-bit) SQL Server 2005 (64-bit) x64

Clustered Installation Considerations

Server cluster configuration is outside the objective of this book. However, please be aware of the following for clustered installations and upgrades of SQL Server 2008.

- Install the SQL Server on the active node of an existing Windows cluster and then use the SQL Server setup program to add the additional nodes to the failover cluster configuration.

- Verify that the disk technology to be used, SAN or iSCSI, is supported by the operating system and the particular version of SQL Server 2008.

- Ensure the network between the server cluster nodes follows the hardware and SQL Server compatibility list requirements.

- Nodes configured as domain controllers are not supported in a SQL Server 2008 failover cluster configuration.

- Mounted disk drives are not supported in an installation of SQL Server 2008 in a clustered configuration.

- .NET Framework applications such as Microsoft Management Studio require that the cluster have access to the Internet.

Prior to performing a SQL Server 2008 upgrade to an existing SQL Server clustered environment, collect and save the list of resources associated to the SQL Server clustered instance. Run **"cluster.exe resource"** on one of the nodes of the cluster and save the output. As part of the upgrade process you may need to remove these accounts. This list will provide you with the information to restore the account information.

Unattended Installations

As in SQL Server 2005, SQL Server 2008 does not have an unattended installation mechanism, but a command line interface that provides parameters and the ability to use a configuration file to develop scripts to install, update, and repair scenarios. The command-line interface provides a robust set of keywords and parameters for customizing and creating repeatable processes for installations.

For more details on the command line options, refer to *How to: Install SQL Server 2008 from the Command Prompt* on the MSDN Web site at http://msdn. microsoft.com/en-us/library/ms144259.aspx.

Configuring & Implementing...

Command-Line Install Tips

To reduce the logging and prompting of the installer, you have a couple of options. To suppress messages, use the **/Q** command-line switch for quiet mode. Use **/QS** parameter, in conjunction with the **/Action=install** command parameter, for quiet simple mode. This option will show progress, but does not accept any input and displays no error messages if errors are found.

In either case, this will require review of the installation log upon completion of the process to ensure that the installation was successful.

Post-Upgrade Activity

Once the upgrade or side-by-side installation is complete, there are several required post-upgrade activities.

1. Review all upgrade/installation log files.

    Review the Summary.txt file in the directory <drive>:\Program Files\ Microsoft SQL Server\\100\Setup Bootstrap\LOG\Files\ for any error messages.

    Even if no errors are indicated in the Summary.txt file, review file SQLSetup[xxxx].cab in the same directory.

    Search for the text "UE 3," indicating an error, in the following files:

    ■ Recently modified core log file named SQLSetup[xxxx]_ [ComputerName]_Core.log

    ■ Recently modified Windows user interface log SQLSetup[xxxx][s]__ [ComputerName]_WI.log

    ■ Component installation files: SQL Setup[xxxx]_{ComputerName]_ SQL.log

2. Ensure that the component services installed are running. Use SQL Server Configuration Manager to view and start services (see Figure 2.1).

Figure 2.1 SQL Server Configuration Manager

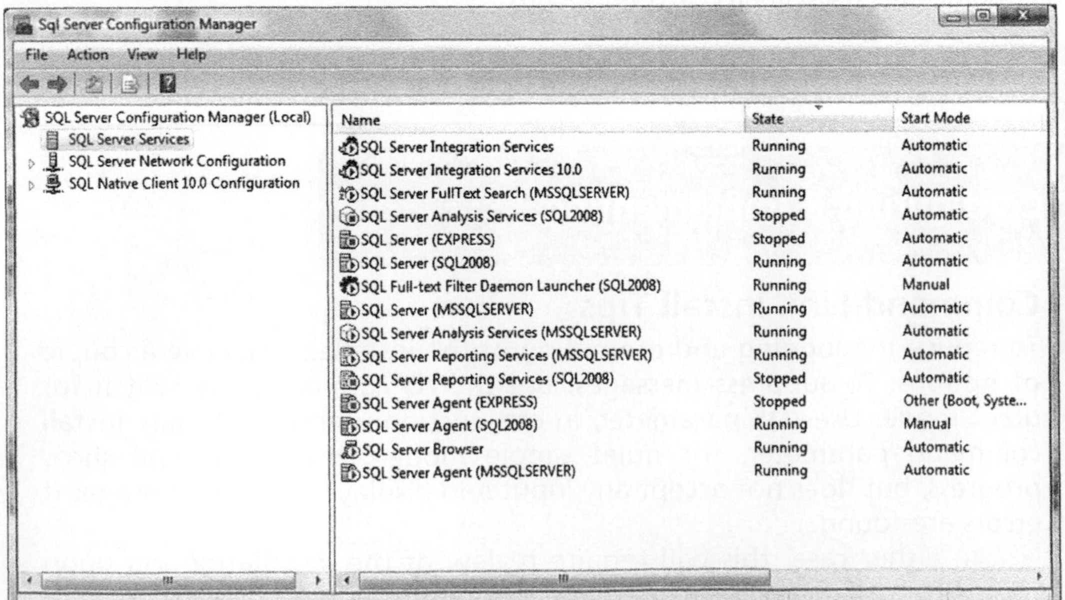

3. Perform a full backup.

4. Verify that the database compatibility level is set to 100 by performing the following query in SQL Server Management Studio or connect via *sqlcmd* utility (see Figure 2.2). You can perform the following query from the *sqlcmd* or the query window in SQL Server Management Studio once connected to the target upgraded/installed instance.

```
select name, compatibility_level from master.sys.databases
```

Figure 2.2 Compatibility Versions

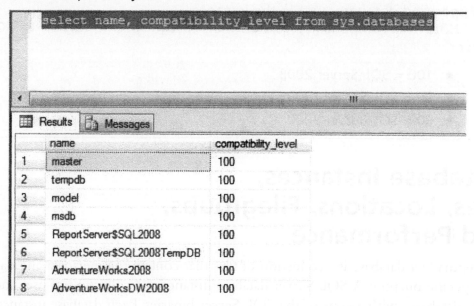

5. Update statistics to ensure query performance.

6. If full-text search was implemented in the previous version, the full-text catalog and indexes need to be rebuilt.

7. Verify that all jobs and maintenance tasks (i.e., database backups) are activated.

8. Review and verify security settings in the database.

Configuring & Implementing…

Compatibility Versions

Compatibility version sets a specific database behavior within an instance to be compatible with a specific version of SQL Server. Note that the compatibility version does not affect the whole server instance, but only the specified databases within the instance.

Note the compatibility version map to the specific version of SQL Server.

- 100 = SQL Server 2008
- 90 = SQL Server 2005
- 80 = SQL Server 2000

Database Instances, Files, Locations, Filegroups, and Performance

Conceptually a database is a collection of files that contain the metadata and data for a specific purpose. A SQL Server database instance is a collection of user and system databases with a copy of the SQL Server binaries. Each database instance contains five system databases.

The *master* database is the central repository for the database instance responsible for tracking the location of, for example, other database files, login accounts, system configurations, endpoints, and linked servers. The *model* database is used as a template for creating user databases. The *msdb* database is used by the component service SQL Server Agent for scheduling alerts and jobs including backup and recovery history. The *tempdb* database is used as a resource for all databases in an instance to perform temporary operations such as sorting, aggregation, and intermediate operation storage, as well as for rolling back transactions using row versioning or snapshot isolation. The *resource* database is hidden in SQL Server Management Studio and is used only to physically persist a read-only version of system objects, which are then accessible by every database's sys objects, such as *sys.sysobjects*.

SQL Server databases consist of data files and log files. *Data files* contain data and database objects such as tables and indexes. *Log files* contain the transaction log for recovering the database.

Data files are further subtyped into primary and secondary data files. The primary data file is used to reference the starting point of the database and key metadata. The metadata contains references to the other files associated with the database, as well as system tables for tables, indexes, columns, and users.

The file suffix of *.mdf* is recommended. The secondary data files contain data not in the primary data file. For database and query performance, the secondary data files can be moved to separate disks. The file name suffix *.ndf* is used for secondary data files.

Each database must contain one data file and one log file (see Table 2.12). Although the file name suffixes for the data and log files are not enforced by SQL Server, it is a best practice to use these filename extensions so administrators can easily identify the file types in their environments.

Table 2.12 System Database File Locations

System Database	File Directory Location	Data File Name	Log File Name
master	*<drive>*:\Program Files\ Microsoft SQL Server \MSSQL10.*<instance_name>* \Data	master.mdf	mastlog.ldf
msdb	" "	MSDBData.mdf	MSDBLog.mdf
model	" "	model.mdf	modellog.ldf
tempdb	"	tempdb.mdf	Templog.ldf
resource	*<drive>*:\Program Files\ Microsoft SQL Server \MSSQL10.*<instance_name>* \Binn	mssqlsystem- resource.mdf	mssqlsystem- resource.ldf

Binary File Locations

The installation directory, located under Program Files by default, contains the binaries as well as the location of the installation and system log files. The common files directory for SQL Server 2008 follows the same directory conventions as previous versions, with 100 indicating SQL Server 2008-specific components (see Table 2.13).

Table 2.13 SQL Server Software Directory Location for SQL Server Versions

SQL Server Version	Common File Directory
2008	\<drive\>:\Program Files\Microsoft SQL Server\100\
2005	\<drive\>:\Program Files\Microsoft SQL Server\90\
2000	\<drive\>:\Program Files\Microsoft SQL Server\80\

The data directory naming conventions have changed and are more intuitive in SQL Server 2008. The default SQL Server 2008 installation directories have the prefix **MSSQL10** in the instance name, which is used in the component directory names (see Table 2.14).

Table 2.14 SQL Server 2008 Instance Naming for Various Components

SQL Server Component	Instance Name Format	Default Instance Name	Named Instance Example:*InstanceA*
Database Engine	MSSQL + Major Version +. + instance name	MSSQL10.MSSQLSERVER	MSSQL10.InstanceA
Analysis Services	MSAS+ Major Version +. + instance name	MSAS10.MSSQLSERVER	MSAS.InstanceA
Reporting Services	MSRS+ Major Version +. + instance name	MSRS10.MSSQLSERVER	MSRS10.InstanceA

The default data file locations for a default instance would be as follows:

- \<drive\>:\Program Files\Microsoft SQL Server\MSSQL10. MSSQLSERVER\Data – Default instance of SQL Server

- \<drive\>:\Program Files\Microsoft SQL Server\MSAS10. MSSQLSERVER\Data – Default instance of SQL Server Analysis Services.

Configuring & Implementing...

Invalid instance ID characters

Instance IDs must not begin with an underscore (_), a pound sign (#), or a dollar sign(sign). These characters are not supported in instance ID names.

Filegroups

Filegroups are structures by which administrators logically organize data files to optimize database performance. For example, specific tables and indexes can be associated to specific filegroups, thereby isolating the data storage of the specified tables or indexes from others. This separation enables the administrator to move theses files on separate disk devices, and ideally on separate RAID controllers, to optimize I/O for the queries and other database operations in tables on the filegroup.

SQL Server supports two filegroup types: primary and user-defined. The primary filegroup is the default location for all primary data files and other files for which a filegroup is not specifically defined. All the system tables are created in the primary filegroup. Log files are never part of a file group.

The user-defined filegroups are created via the CREATE DATABASE or ALTER DATABASE commands specifying the FILEGROUP name, file directory, file name, and initial and max size, as well as filegroup, as shown in Figure 2.3.

Figure 2.3 Filegroup Examples

```
CREATE DATABASE Research on PRIMARY
(NAME = ResearchPrimary, FILENAME =' D:\SQL\FG\ResearchPrimary.mdf'
, SIZE = 500MB, MAXSIZE = 700, FILEGROWTH=20);

ALTER DATABASE Research on FILEGROUP RESEARCH1
(NAME = ResearchPrimary, FILENAME =' D:\SQL\FG\Research1.ndf'
, SIZE = 500MB, MAXSIZE = 700, FILEGROWTH=20);
```

Disk Planning Best Practices

For all enterprise database servers requiring high availability, it recommended to place both data and log files on RAID 10 disk devices. For implementations not requiring high availability, or if cost is an issue, use RAID 5 for data files, while keeping the log files on RAID 10.

Database servers not using RAID disks should use filegroups to distribute data files across disks to distribute I/O and maximize performance. Specifically, place log files on disks other than data files to reduce I/O contention.

Other best practices include:

- Do not place data and log files on the disk drives that contain the operating system binary files.

- Avoid placing the SQL Server binaries and database files on the c: drive.

- Place the tempdb system database on a separate disk drive, preferably on a RAID 5 or RAID 10 system.

Head of the Class…

Calculating the Real Cost

A rule of thumb in determining which hardware or disk architecture to use is to determine the cost of an outage for a database recovery versus the cost of the server and application. Outage costs can include:

- Cost of labor during the outage, which would include the number people affected by the outage multiplied by the average costs of those resources during the outage
- Lost revenue during the outage

Use these costs in discussion with business owners to help gauge their risk profile and their ability to invest in their disk and hardware architecture.

The moral to this story is the least expensive hardware is not always the least expensive to the business.

Summary of Exam Objectives

SQL Server 2008 comes in different editions, and you should understand the capabilities and limitations of each of these editions. You also should have an understanding of the options available when installing SQL Server 2008. The planning process prior to installation is a critical component of the success of any product installation or upgrade process. In the planning process, understanding the overall architecture and the tracking all the details are critical.

Once the user requirements and expectations are discovered in the installation planning process, it is easier to decide which type of upgrade strategy to use. After reading this chapter, you should have an understanding of the two installation scenarios: upgrade and side-by-side installation.

In this chapter we reviewed planning your installation and discussed best practices for hardware utilization when it comes to installing SQL Server 2008. We discussed the tools used to install or upgrade SQL Server 2008 to ensure that your enterprise is in line with recommend best practices.

Exam Objectives Fast Track

SQL Versions, Requirements, Features, and Differences

- ☑ SQL Server 2008 editions are categorized as Server, Specialized, and Free. The various editions contain subsets of the SQL Server components to address specific target business scenarios.

- ☑ SQL Server 2008 consists of the SQL Server database engine, Analysis Services, Reporting Services, and Integration Services.

- ☑ Resource Governor provides control of the amount of CPU, and memory is allocated with SQL Server 2008 workload without any application changes.

- ☑ Enterprise and Standard Editions have all or most of the Integration Services features, while the others have very limited features.

Planning Your Installation

☑ Review and document the existing hardware and software configurations and compare to the SQL Server 2008 hardware and software requirements.

☑ Understand the business' service level agreements for all SQL Server applications.

☑ Plan the disk layout of the new or existing environment to ensure enough storage space for backups, and additional space for installation files and logs, as well as the database files.

☑ Establish a backup and recovery plan and rehearse backup and recovery scenarios prior to upgrading.

☑ Use tools such as SQL Upgrade Advisor for SQL Server 2008 and Best Practice Analyzer for SQL Server 2000 and 2005 to identify issues that can be corrected prior to the upgrade.

Upgrading vs. Side-by-Side Installation

☑ The upgrade scenario is the least complex process; however, it requires that the database instance be unavailable during the upgrade process, and the rollback scenario is more complex and lengthy.

☑ The side-by-side installation process requires additional disk space and possibly additional servers, but provides the least downtime from the end user's perspective.

☑ SQL Server 2008 does not have an unattended installation mechanism, but rather a command line interface that provides parameters and the ability to use a configuration file to develop scripts to install, update, and repair scenarios. Use SQL Server Configuration Manager to view and start component services after the upgrade process.

☑ Inspect the installation log files Summary.txt, *SQLSetup[xxxx].cab*, SQLSetup*[xxxx]*_[ComputerName]_Core.log, SQLSetup*[xxxx]* *[s]*__[ComputerName]_WI.log, SQL Setup[xxxx]_{ComputerName]_SQL. log. located in the *<drive>:\Program Files\Microsoft SQL Server\\100\Setup Bootstrap\Log* for any error messages.

☑ Compatibility version sets specific database behavior within an instance to be compatible with a specific version of Microsoft SQL Server, and each database in an instance can be set differently.

Database Instances, Files, Locations, Filegroups, and Performance

☑ A SQL Server database instance is a collection of user and system databases with a copy of the SQL Server binaries.

☑ *Data files* contain data and database objects such as tables and indexes. *Log files* contain the transaction log for recovering the database.

☑ Filegroups are structures by which administrators logically organize data files to optimize performance.

Exam Objectives
Frequently Asked Questions

Q: How much time should I invest in planning for the SQL Server 2008 upgrade?

A: The answer is, how much time and money can you afford if the upgrade is not successful? Careful planning and testing not only guarantees a successful upgrade, but it is also an opportunity for you and your team to become experienced in the various SQL Server 2008 products and features before going to production.

Q: How should I prepare for the upgrade process?

A: First run the SQL Server 2008 Upgrade Advisor to identify any issues and provide guidance on resolving any problems. Rehearsing the upgrade process on a test environment repeatedly for several weeks prior to the upgrade will provide confidence in the basic procedures. The testing of the backup and recovery scenarios is an opportunity to train less experienced individuals. Training and building a team benefit the upgrade investment.

Q: What business requirements should drive the upgrade process?

A: The customer's budget and sensitivity to application database outage are the key drivers to the upgrade process. The amount of downtime will steer the selection process toward upgrading a database instance or performing a side-by-side install.

Q: What are the key requirements selecting the SQL Server version?

A: The business usage and requirements of the database application's scalability, availability, and security in coordination with the hardware constraints are essential in the determining the SQL Server version.

Self Test

1. Which SQL Server 2008 edition supports IA64?

   A. Web and Compact Editions

   B. Standard and Workgroup Editions

   C. Enterprise and Developer editions

   D. All of the above

2. How many instances can be created in SQL Server 2008 Standard Edition?

   A. 1

   B. 4

   C. 16

   D. Unlimited

3. How many SQL Server default instances can be installed on a single, nonclustered server?

   A. 1

   B. 4

   C. 16

   D. Unlimited

4. Which of the following editions has all the features and functionality but is not licensed for production?

   A. Compact Edition

   B. Web Edition

   C. Developer Edition

   D. Workgroup Edition

5. Which SQL Server 2008 edition is best suited for mobile applications?

   A. Compact Edition

   B. Web Edition

   C. Developer Edition

   D. Workgroup Edition

6. Which SQL Server 2008 edition provides the most Analysis Services features?

   A. Enterprise Edition

   B. Standard Edition

   C. Workgroup Edition

   D. Web Edition

   E. Express Edition

7. Which tool should be on an existing SQL Server 2000 or 2005 database instance prior to upgrading to SQL Server 2008?

   A. Integration Services

   B. Reporting Services

   C. Analysis Services

   D. Upgrade Advisor Tool

8. Which of the following is a command line utility used to run PowerShell command and scripts?

   A. sqlcmd

   B. SQLdiag

   C. Ssms

   D. sqlps

9. Which of the following editions does not support any Reporting Services features?

   A. Enterprise Edition

   B. Standard Edition

   C. Workgroup Edition

   D. Web Edition

   E. Express Edition

10. Which of the following accounts has the least privilege when used as a service account?

   A. Domain user account

   B. Local user account

    C. Local service account

    D. Administrator account

    E. Local system account

11. Which of the following accounts should be used to perform a SQL Server 2008 installation or upgrade?

    A. Domain user account

    B. Local user account

    C. Local service account

    D. Administrator account

    E. Local system account

12. In which of the following directories are the default instance database data and log files located?

    A. <drive>:\Program Files\Microsoft SQL Server\\100\Setup Bootstrap\ LOG\Files\

    B. <drive>:\Program Files\Microsoft SQL Server\MSSQL10. MSSQLSERVER\Data

    C. <drive>:\Program Files\Microsoft SQL Server\MSSQL9.DEFAULT\Data

    D. <drive>:\Program Files\Microsoft SQL Server\MSAS10. MSSQLSERVER\Data

    E. <drive>:\Program Files\Microsoft SQL Server\MSRS10. MSSQLSERVER\Data

13. What additional software is required for SQL Server's Business Intelligence Developer's Tool?

    A. .NET Framework 2.0

    B. Microsoft Installer 4.5

    C. Microsoft Internet Explorer 6 SP1 or later

    D. Windows PowerShell 2.0

    E. Windows Vista Enterprise SP1 or greater

14. Which of the following is the SQL Server component that provides the services for creating, processing, and managing OLAP and data mining?

    A. Business Intelligence Developer Studio

    B. SQL Server Management Studio

    C. Windows PowerShell 2.0

    D. SQL Server Database Engine

    E. Analysis Services

15. Which of the following is a scalability feature in SQL Server Enterprise Edition?

    A. Partitioning

    B. Data Mining Queries

    C. Binary and compressed XML transport

16. In which directory are the installation log files found?

    A. *<drive>:\Program Files\Microsoft SQL Server\\100\Setup Bootstrap\LOG\Files*

    B. *<drive>:\Program Files\Microsoft SQL Server\\90/Data*

    C. *<drive>:\Program Files\Microsoft SQL Server\\Binn*

    D. *<drive>:\Program Files\Microsoft SQL Server\\logs*

17. Which system database is hidden to SQL Server Management Studio and is used to persist a read-only version of system objects?

    A. Master

    B. Resource

    C. Tempdb

    D. System

18. Which is the compatibility version associated with SQL Server 2008?

    A. 80

    B. 90

    C. 100

    D. 200

19. Which SQL Server tool is used to check that SQL Server component services are running?

    A. SQL Server Management Studio (SSMS)

    B. Business Intelligence Development Studio (BIDS)

    C. SQL Server Configuration Manager

    D. SQL Server Profiler

    E. Database Engine Tuning Advisor

20. Which type of file contains data and database objects such as tables and indexes?

    A. Data files

    B. Log files

    C. File groups

    D. Binary files

    E. Summary.txt

Self Test Quick Answer Key

1. **C**

2. **C**

3. **A**

4. **C**

5. **A**

6. **A**

7. **D**

8. **D**

9. **E**

10. **B**

11. **D**

12. **B**

13. **C**

14. **E**

15. **A**

16. **A**

17. **B**

18. **C**

19. **C**

20. **A**

Chapter 3

MCTS SQL Server 2008 Exam 432

Configuring SQL Server 2008

Exam objectives in this chapter:

- Instances vs. Default Instance
- SQL Server Configuration Manager
- sp_configure and SQL Server Management Studio
- Database Mail
- Full-Text Indexing

Exam objectives review:

- ☑ Summary of Exam Objectives
- ☑ Exam Objectives Fast Track
- ☑ Exam Objectives Frequently Asked Questions
- ☑ Self Test
- ☑ Self Test Quick Answer Key

Introduction

This chapter explores using multiple SQL Server instances and managing connection protocols and service accounts with Configuration Manager. You'll learn about some key configuration options and how to set them using sp_configure and Management Studio as well as how to set up and use Database Mail and manage Full-Text Indexes.

Instances vs. Default Instance

A SQL Server installation is referred to as an instance. Up to and including SQL Server 7.0, only one installation of SQL Server was possible on a server, but that restriction didn't suit a number of deployment scenarios that customers required, including high-availability and consolidation.

With the release of SQL Server 2000, multiple installations of SQL Server were possible on a single server and were known as SQL Server instances. SQL Server 2008 continues with this model and with very few changes.

A *default instance* has much the same profile that SQL Server installations have had in past; you install SQL Server and then connect using the computer name of the server. Your Windows Server can only have one computer name, so you can only use it to connect to one SQL Server instance. This is called the default instance.

If you install additional instances of SQL Server, these are referred to as named instances. You connect to them using the <computername>\<instancename> format. For example, if you have a server named PLUTO and you install a named instance named SQL1, you would connect to that instance using PLUTO\SQL1. If you installed another named instance called SQL2, you would connect using PLUTO\ SQL2. If you had a default instance installed, you would connect using PLUTO.

Each instance is completely independent of any other instance and has its own set of services, databases, and configuration settings. All the components of a single instance are managed together, and service packs and patches are applied to all components within an instance.

During the installation process you have to specify a unique instance ID, which is used to define the directory structure, registry structure, and service names for that instance. This is new in SQL Server 2008. By default, the instance name that you specified is used as the instance ID. For the default instance, MSSQLSERVER is used as the instance ID.

In Figure 3.1 you can see the installation screen for a default instance showing the instance ID. You can also see that two named instances are already installed: PLUTO\SQL1 and PLUTO\SQL2. You don't have to have a default instance installed to install or use named instances.

Figure 3.1 Installation Screen for Default
Instance with Two Named Instances Already Installed

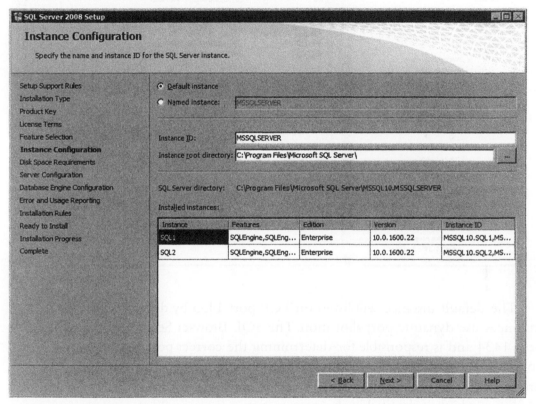

If you take a look at the directory structure after the installation in Figure 3.2, you'll see separate directories for each instance as well as each installation of Analysis Services and Reporting Services. There are also three directories called 80, 90, and 100, which contain components that are shared across all instances such as the Management Tools. 80 and 90 hold SQL Server 2000 and SQL Server 2005 components for backward compatibility, and 100 contains the SQL Server 2008 shared components, including SQL Server Integration Services if it's installed. SQL Server Integration Services is not instance aware, so you can only have one installation on a server.

Figure 3.2 Directory Structure for Three
Instances with Analysis Services and Reporting Services

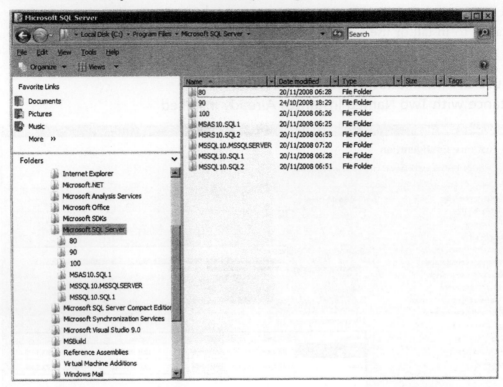

The default instance will listen on TCP port 1433 by default, and named instances use dynamic port allocation. The SQL Browser Service listens on UDP port 1434 and is responsible for determining the correct port when you try to connect. If the SQL Browser Service isn't running, you will need to specify a unique TCP port for each instance to listen on using SQL Server Configuration Manager, which is detailed in the next section.

Once you know which port your instance listens on, you can specify it in your connection string. For example, if you configured PLUTO\SQL1 to listen on port 53000 you would connect using PLUTO\SQL1:53000. You don't normally have to do this because the SQL Browser Service is installed and runs automatically, but it is sometimes disabled to tighten security.

Instance Limitations

Microsoft has officially tested and supports a limited number of instances per server. These limits are detailed in Table 3.1.

Table 3.1 Number of Supported SQL Server Instances per Server by Edition

SQL Server Edition	Supported Instances
Developer	50*
Enterprise	50*
Standard	50*
Workgroup	16
Express	16

* Only 25 instances are supported on a Windows failover cluster

Performance Considerations

We have already discussed how each instance is completely independent of any other instance. This gives you the advantage of being able to run multiple SQL Servers on the same server with different instance level requirements, such as development and production instances, or separating international instances with different collation requirements.

The downside to using multiple instances are the resources required to run each instance. They all run separate services, have their own system databases, and require memory and disk space before you've even started using them. They have no knowledge of each other so they can't dynamically share resources. PLUTO\SQL1 sees PLUTO\SQL2 as it would any other application that was installed on the server.

Typically, a single instance will provide the best performance because SQL Server is very good at managing all its own resources. Multiple instances require additional resources and can therefore impact the performance of a server if its resource constrained.

Using multiple instances is acceptable if you have enough resources available, but there are very few scenarios where they would give you a performance benefit; use them instead when you are forced to run separate, independent SQL Servers and want to utilize the resources on an existing server.

You can follow Exercise 3.1 to practice installing and connecting to multiple SQL Server instances.

EXERCISE 3.1

INSTALL AND CONNECT TO MULTIPLE INSTANCES

1. Perform a stand-alone installation of SQL Server with the following attributes:

   - **Components** For the components select **Database Engine Services, Analysis Services, and Management Tools**
   - Named Instance with Instance ID = SQL1
   - Default file paths

2. Perform a stand-alone installation of SQL Server with the following attributes:

   - **Components** For the components select **Database Engine Services and Reporting Services**
   - Named Instance with Instance ID = SQL2
   - Default file paths

3. Review directory structure at C:\Program Files\Microsoft SQL Server\. On a clean server you will see subdirectories for:

   - 80,90,100 (Shared Components)
   - MSAS10.SQL1 (Analysis Services SQL1 Instance)
   - MSSQL10.SQL1 (Database Engine SQL1 Instance)
   - MSRS10.SQL2 (Reporting Services SQL2 Instance)
   - MSSQL10.SQL2 (Database Engine SQL2 Instance)

4. Launch **SQL Server Management Studio from the All Programs | Microsoft SQL Server 2008** menu.

   In the **Connect to Server** dialogue box type **<YourComputer Name>\SQL1** for the server name and click the **Connect** button. When connected you will see an **Object Explorer** window on the left. Click on the **Connect** drop down button and select **Database Engine.** For the SQL2 instance, go to the **Connect to Server** dialogue box again and type **<YourComputerName>\SQL1** for the server name and click the **Connect** button.

   You have just installed two named instances with no default instance and connected to them both in SQL Server Management Studio. Your screen should now look like Figure 3.3.

Figure 3.3 SQL Server Management
Studio Connected to PLUTO\SQL1 and PLUTO\SQL2

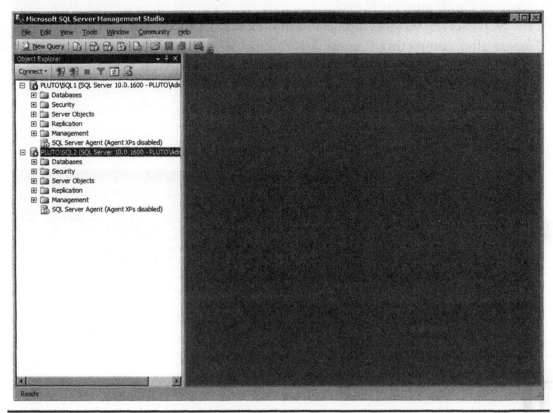

SQL Server Configuration Manager

The SQL Server Configuration Manager is used to perform the following actions:

- Start and stop SQL Server services

- Change service account passwords

- Enable and disable FileStream

- Enable and disable protocols

- Change TCP ports

- Manage connection aliases

We'll be exploring each of these in this section.

Managing Services

Launching Configuration Manager connects you to the local server and displays all of the SQL Server Services installed locally. Figure 3.4 shows Configuration Manager after completing Exercise 3.1. You can see the two instances that are installed as well as the Analysis Services and Reporting Services installations, and can start, stop, and restart the services by right-clicking on the appropriate instance.

Figure 3.4 SQL Server Configuration Manager

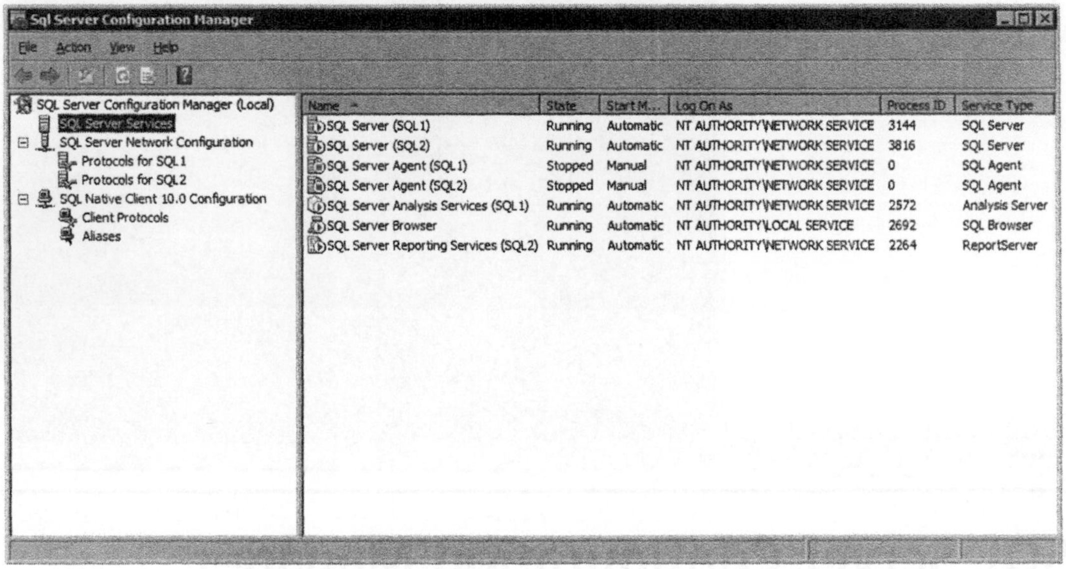

Note that the two SQL Server Agent Services are stopped and set to start manually.

Right-clicking on a **service** and selecting **Properties** gives you access to four tabs, the first of which allows you to change the account that the service logs on with. In Figure 3.5 you can see that SQL1 is currently running using the *Network Service* account, and you can change it here to run using a dedicated Windows account. It's a Microsoft best practice for SQL Server to run using a dedicated Windows account.

Figure 3.5 Changing the Service Account

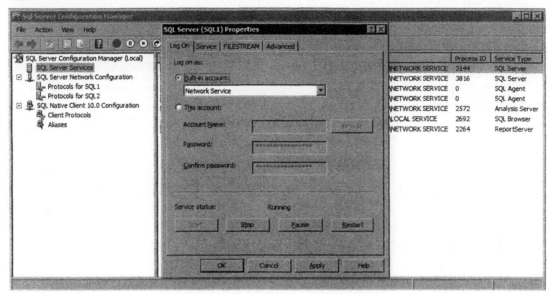

If you need to change the service account for any of the SQL Server services, then this is the only supported method to do it. SQL Server Configuration Manager assigns additional advanced user rights to the accounts when the service is configured, which won't get assigned if you just use the **Services** applet in control panel.

The **Service** tab allows you change the startup type of the service to *Automatic, Manual,* or *Disabled.* They work the same way as any other Windows service, but it's worth noting that if you are running SQL Server 2008 on a Windows failover cluster you will see all the services set to start manually. This is because the failover cluster software manages when the services get started and stopped; they don't get started in the normal way by Windows during startup. They will be stopped on passive nodes and started on active nodes.

The **Advanced** tab provides access to change whether or not you want to automatically provide feedback or errors to Microsoft; where SQL Server should store memory dumps in the event of failure; and most importantly, the startup parameters to use when starting the SQL Server Service. In Figure 3.6 you can see an expanded view of the default startup parameters as well as a trace flag that has been set to run on startup.

Trace flags enable different behaviors in SQL Server, and different flags can be enabled on startup by using the *−T switch.* In this example trace flag 1222 has been enabled on startup, which will dump detailed data to the error log in the event that a deadlock has been encountered on the server.

Figure 3.6 Viewing and Changing Startup Parameters

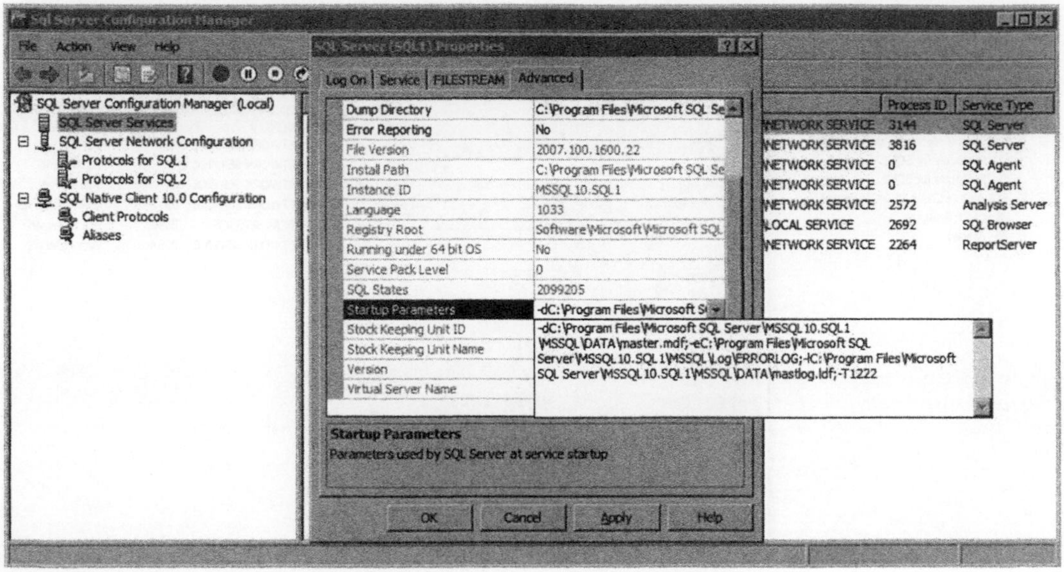

Enabling FileStream

FileStream is a new feature in SQL Server 2008 that allows applications to store unstructured data, such as documents and images, in the file system rather than directly in SQL Server. This allows applications to take advantage of the optimizations that Windows has for dealing with files rather than forcing it all to be stored directly in the database. Using FileStream is outside the scope of this exam but you will need to know how to enable it.

Enabling FileStream is done in two parts: one for Windows and one for SQL Server. However, if you enable FileStream during the SQL Server installation process, then both parts are done for you.

To enable FileStream after installation you first need to enable it for Windows, and this is done through SQL Server Configuration Manager. If you look at the properties of the SQL Server Service you'll see a new tab for SQL Server 2008 called **FILESTREAM.**

On the new tab, the first option you have is to **Enable FILESTREAM for Transact-SQL access** and is mandatory for any level of FileStream access. This allows you to work with FileStream data using Transact-SQL statements.

The second option enables the use of file I/O streaming access. What this means is FileStream access through other programming languages using the Win32 APIs. This option requires a fileshare to be created to access the files and has an additional option of whether to allow remote clients to access the FileStream data. In Figure 3.7 you can see that FILESTREAM access has been enabled on SQL1 for Transact-SQL access and file I/O streaming using a fileshare called SQL1.

Figure 3.7 Enabling FILESTREAM in SQL Server Configuration Manager

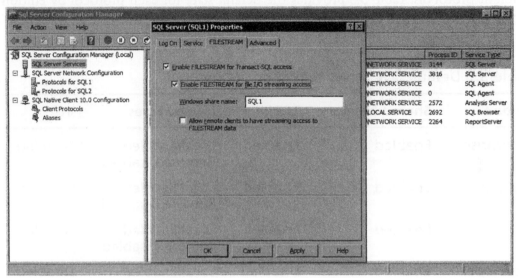

Once the SQL Server Service is configured to allow FileStream access, you need to enable it within SQL Server itself using the *filestream_access_level* option. This is modified using the *sp_configure* command, valid values for which can be found in Table 3.2. sp_configure is covered in more depth later in this chapter.

Table 3.2 Values for sp_configure filestream_access_level

Value	Description
0	Disables FILESTREAM support for this instance
1	Enables FILESTREAM for Transact-SQL access
2	Enables FILESTREAM for Transact-SQL and Win32 streaming access

If you enabled FILESTREAM during the SQL Server installation process, this option will have been configured for you. You will only need to modify it to make a change post installation.

Managing Connections and Protocols

The network protocols used to communicate with SQL Server are managed using SQL Server Configuration Manager but depend on the protocols being configured already at the operating system level. SQL Server 2008 can communicate using four different protocols. Table 3.3 provides the default state for each protocol by edition of SQL Server.

Table 3.3 Default SQL Server Network Configuration

Edition	Shared Memory	TCP/IP	Named Pipes	VIA
Enterprise	Enabled	Enabled	Local:Enabled, Remote:Disabled	Disabled
Standard	Enabled	Enabled	Local:Enabled, Remote:Disabled	Disabled
Workgroup	Enabled	Enabled	Local:Enabled, Remote:Disabled	Disabled
Developer	Enabled	Disabled	Local:Enabled, Remote:Disabled	Disabled
Evaluation	Enabled	Disabled	Local:Enabled, Remote:Disabled	Disabled
Express	Enabled	Disabled	Local:Enabled, Remote:Disabled	Disabled

Shared Memory

Simple and fast, *Shared Memory* is the default protocol used to connect from a client running on the same computer as SQL Server. It has no configurable properties and is always tried first when connecting, but it can be disabled to help troubleshoot connectivity issues with other protocols.

For example, you have remote applications that can't connect to SQL Server via TCP/IP, so you logon to the server, ensure that TCP/IP is configured properly, disable Shared Memory, and connect using SQL Server Management Studio. If you can connect locally using TCP/IP you know that SQL Server is configured correctly, which helps to rule out a SQL Server configuration issue as the cause of the problem.

Named Pipes

TCP/IP and *Named Pipes* are comparable protocols in the architectures that they can be used in. Named Pipes was developed for Local Area Networks (LANs) but can be inefficient across slower networks such as Wide Area Networks (WANs).

To use Named Pipes, you first need to enable it in SQL Server Configuration Manager (if you'll be connecting remotely) and then create a SQL Server Alias, which connects to the server using Named Pipes as the protocol.

Named Pipes uses TCP port 445, so make sure the port is open on any firewalls between the two computers, including Windows Firewall.

VIA

Virtual Interface Adapter (VIA) is a protocol that enables high-performance communications between two systems. It requires specialized hardware at both ends and a dedicated connection.

Like Named Pipes, to use the VIA protocol you first need to enable it in SQL Server Configuration Manager and then create a SQL Server Alias, which connects to the server using VIA as the protocol.

TCP/IP

The most common access protocol for SQL Server allows you to connect to SQL Server by specifying an IP address and port number. Typically, this happens automatically when you specify an instance to connect to. Your internal name resolution system resolves the hostname part of the instance name to an IP address, and you will connect to the default TCP port number 1433 for default instances, or the SQL Browser Service will find the right port for a named instance using UDP port 1434.

You can also connect directly to the instance by specifying the **<IP Address>: <Instance Port>** in the connection string. For example, **10.0.0.1:50000** will connect you to server 10.0.0.1 and the instance listening on port 50000.

Changing the TCP Port

To change the TCP port on which an instance listens, open **SQL Server Configuration Manager** and expand **SQL Server Network Configuration**. Now select **Protocols** for **<instance name>** for the instance you want to change, and right-click on **TCP/IP** to get the **Properties** window. You can change the port for each IP address that SQL Server is listening on individually, or you can scroll down and specify a fixed port for all IP addresses. In Figure 3.8 you can see that port 50000 has been specified for all IP addresses on the SQL1 instance. Note that the TCP Dynamic Ports value has been deleted.

Fixed ports are most often specified for named instances or port 1433 changed for the default instance to provide additional security measures. If you use fixed ports and specify them in the connection string, then you don't need to run the SQL Browser Service, which will reduce the visible network presence of your SQL Servers.

Figure 3.8 Changing the TCP Port for an Instance

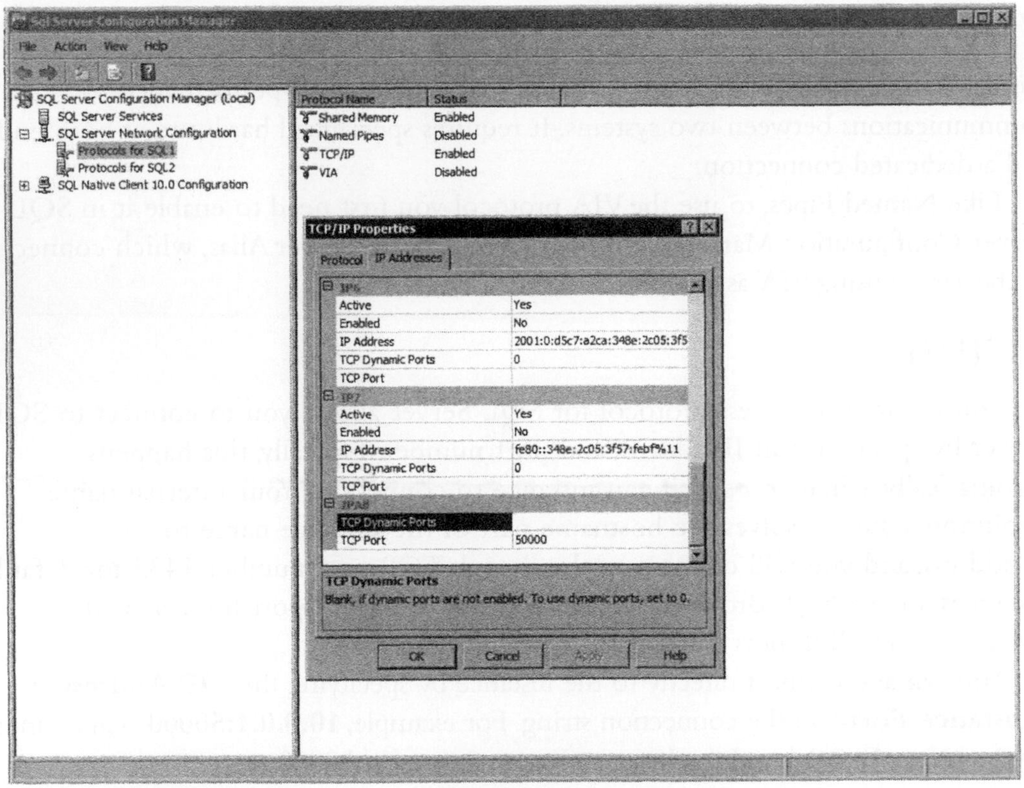

Configuring & Implementing...

SQL Server and Windows Firewall on Windows Server 2008

The most common connectivity issue arising when installing SQL Server 2008 on Windows Server 2008 is that the default configuration of Windows enables Windows Firewall, which blocks SQL Server from being accessed across the network and suppresses error messages to say that SQL Server has been blocked. You need to manually add the SQL Server Services to the firewall exception list before you can connect to SQL Server across the network.

Aliases

A SQL Server Alias is effectively a *shortcut* to a SQL Server instance for which you can specify alternative connection information. Once created, you can use the Alias to connect to a SQL Server rather than the specifying the full instance name. For example, I could create an Alias called SQL1 that connects to PLUTO\SQL1, and then I would only have to specify SQL1 as the computer name in any connection string on that server.

Now imagine that you've changed the TCP port on the SQL Server to 50000 and stopped the SQL Browser Service. To connect to SQL1 you now have to specify the port number in the connection information, or you add port 50000 to the alias definition.

Aliases are managed under **SQL Server Native Client 10.0 Configuration** in the **SQL Server Configuration Manager** tool. In Figure 3.9 you can see that an alias has been created called SQL1 that will connect to instance PLUTO\SQL1 using TCP/IP and port 50000. The protocol property in the window has a drop down list where you could select Named Pipes or VIA as an alternative protocol.

Figure 3.9 Creating a SQL Server Alias

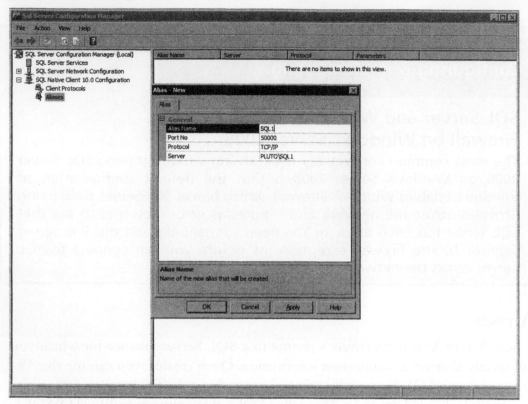

Exercise 3.2 steps you through changing the service account, TCP port number, disabling dynamic port detection and creating an alias using Configuration Manager.

EXERCISE 3.2

USING SQL SERVER CONFIGURATION MANAGER

1. First, you're going to change the SQL Server Service account. Create a local Windows user account with the following attributes:
   - Name: SQLService
   - Local Groups: Users

2. Launch SQL Server Configuration Manager from the **All Programs | Microsoft SQL Server 2008 | Configuration Tools** menu.
   Right-click on the **SQL Server (SQL1) Service** and select **Properties**. Under **Log on as:** select the **This account** radio button. Type **SQLService** as the account name and the **account password** in the password and confirm password boxes and click **OK**.

Click **Yes** to continue and restart the service. You have successfully changed the SQL Service account, and this is reflected in the SQL Services view where you'll now see **.\SQLService** under the **Log On As** column for SQL Server (SQL1).

3. Now let's change the default TCP port for SQL1. Stay in SQL Server Configuration Manager and expand **SQL Server Network Configuration.**

   Select **Protocols for SQL1,** right-click on **TCP/IP,** and select **Properties**. Select the **IP Addresses** tab and scroll down to the **IPAll** section. As this is a named instance it will have been dynamically assigned a high-range port. Delete the value for **TCP Dynamic Ports** and enter **50000** for the **TCP Port** value. Click **OK** to close the dialog box but don't restart SQL Server yet. Right-click **Shared Memory** and select **disable.** Click **OK** to clear the dialog box. Select **SQL Server Services** in the left menu. Right-click on **SQL Server (SQL1)** and select **restart.** You have just changed the TCP port for SQL1 and disabled the Shared Memory protocol to force local connections to use TCP/IP. Launch **SQL Server Management Studio.** You should still be able to connect to your instance without specifying the TCP port name.

4. You're now going to stop the SQL Browser Service and create a SQL Server Alias.

   Go back to **SQL Server Configuration Manager** and select **SQL Server Services**. Right-click on **SQL Server Browser** and select **Properties**. Under the **Service** tab change the **start** mode from **automatic** to **manual** and click **OK**. Right-click **SQL Server Browser** and stop the service. Launch **SQL Server Management Studio** and try to connect to **<computername>\SQL1**. The connection should fail with *A network-related or instance-specific* error message. The connection fails because you have disabled dynamic port detection on the server. Go back to **SQL Server Configuration Manager,** expand **SQL Native Client 10.0 Configuration,** and select **Aliases**. Right-click in the **right** pane and select **New Alias**. Create an alias with the following attributes:

   Alias Name: '<computername>\SQL1' (insert your computer name)
   Port No: 50000
   Protocol: TCP/IP
   Server: '<computername>\SQL1'

Launch **SQL Server Management Studio** and try to connect to
<computername>\SQL1. You should now be able to connect.
You have just changed the SQL Server Service account,
changed the TCP port to a fixed nondefault value, stopped
dynamic port detection, and created a client connection alias
specifying the TCP port to which to connect.

Configuring & Implementing...

Stopping Dynamic Port Detection

Some companies require that dynamic port detection and being able
to browse to SQL Servers on their network must be disabled to tighten
security. They do this by stopping the SQL Browser Service on all their SQL
Servers and manually configuring each SQL Server instance to listen on
a fixed TCP port.

All the applications that connect to the SQL Server instances either
specify the port number in the connection string or have a SQL Server Alias
configured on the application server which contains the port number.

---

sp_configure and
SQL Server Management Studio

We've covered installing and configuring the different SQL Server Services so far.
Now we'll move on to configuring SQL Server itself.

SQL Server Management Studio is the central tool for managing SQL Server,
and you will need to be very familiar with it for the exam. Fortunately, most of the
exam objectives require the use of this tool so you will get plenty of practice with
it as you read through the book. For this section we're going to be focused on the
Server Properties that can be changed through the Management Studio interface and
by using the sp_configure command in a *query* window.

sp_configure provides far more configuration options than the Management
Studio interface, and you will need to be familiar with it for the exam. Because of
this, we're going to focus on sp_configure and its options, highlighting where a
particular option is also available in Management Studio.

To run sp_configure simply type it into a **query** window and click **execute.**
In Figure 3.10 you can see the results of executing sp_configure on an instance with
default values. To access the **Server Properties** in Management Studio, right-click
on a **registered server** in the **Object Explorer** window and select **Properties.**

Figure 3.10 sp_configure Output With Default Values

Advanced Options

As you can see in Figure 3.10, when you run sp_configure you'll get a list of
16 options. One of the first things you'll typically do as a DBA is to expand that list
to show all of the configuration options. You do this by enabling **show advanced
options** using the following command:

```
sp_configure 'show advanced options', 1
go
reconfigure
```

This is the format for changing all of the options; you pass the option name in single quotes followed by a comma and then the value you want to change it to. When you change a configuration option, typically only the *config_value* changes, and then you need to run **reconfigure** to tell SQL Server to reload all the values. After this is executed you'll see the new values in both the *config_value* and *run_value* columns in the sp_configure output, indicating that SQL Server is using the new values. There are some settings, however, that require SQL Server to be restarted..

When you run **sp_configure** again you'll see an extended list of 68 options. This is a persisted instance-wide change, so all administrators will now see the advanced options.

We'll now take a look at some of the most commonly changed options and requirements, highlighting where the change can also be made in Management Studio.

AWE

On a 32-bit system SQL Server is limited to using 2GB of memory. To use more than 2GB of memory you need to enable the **Address Windowing Extensions (AWE)** option in SQL Server. AWE allows a 32-bit application, built to support it, to access as much memory as the underlying operating system. Windows Server 2008 Enterprise supports as much as 64GB of RAM. AWE has two valid values, 0 or 1.

To enable AWE to run:

```
sp_configure 'AWE', 1
go
```

This setting is only visible after enabling **show advanced options.** It requires you to restart SQL Server before it takes effect and can also be configured in SQL Server Management Studio. You should always set **max server memory** when using AWE to prevent SQL Server taking too much RAM from Windows.

Setting the Maximum and Minimum Memory for SQL Server

By default, SQL Server will grow its memory usage to take advantage of as much memory on the server as possible. This can very often leave only 100 to 200 MB of memory free on a server, causing problems when Windows requires more memory for something and SQL Server is too slow to give some back.

Max Server Memory (MB)

Max server memory (MB) controls the maximum size of the *buffer pool,* which is the pool of memory that SQL Server uses for most of its requirements. Setting the maximum server memory is strongly recommended if you are using AWE or if you're running a 64-bit version of SQL Server. To set max server memory (MB) to 6 GB run:

```
sp_configure 'max server memory (MB)', 6144
go
reconfigure
```

This setting is only visible with sp_configure after enabling **show advanced options,** but you can also change this setting in SQL Server Management Studio on the *Memory* page.

Min Server Memory (MB)

Min server memory works hand in hand with max server memory but isn't as important to as many scenarios. It provides a minimum value that SQL Server will attempt not to go under once it has reached that value.

For example, you set min server memory to 2GB. When SQL Server first starts it takes the minimum amount of memory required for it to start and then grows its memory usage as it needs to. Once it has grown to be more than 2GB, SQL Server will attempt to keep the buffer pool above that value. This setting is most useful when running multiple instances on a single server or if there are other memory-intensive applications running on the server. To set min server memory (MB) to 2GB run:

```
sp_configure 'min server memory (MB)', 2048
go
reconfigure
```

You can also change this setting in SQL Server Management Studio on the *Memory* page.

Head of the Class...

32-bit, 64-bit, and Memory

32-bit (or x86 as it's sometimes known) systems have a limitation of 4 GB of virtual address space, so if you have more than 4 GB of RAM in a server without AWE enabled, then SQL Server won't be able use the extra memory. 64-bit (or x64 as the most common platform is known) has a limitation of 8TB of virtual address space, so you get access to more RAM without having to switch on AWE.

The Standard and Enterprise Editions of SQL Server both support as much RAM as the Windows version that they run on, and they come with licenses to run either the x86 or x64 version of SQL Server at no additional cost.

Maximum Degree of Parallelism

If SQL Server determines that a query that has been executed is expensive enough in terms of resource consumption, it may try to break down the work into several units and execute them on separate CPUs. This is called *parallelism* and is a very intensive operation, where SQL Server assumes that this query is important enough to run as quickly as possible at the expense of additional CPU usage.

By default SQL Server will use up to all of the available CPUs on a server for a parallel operation. This can cause problems with all the CPUs running at 100 percent for a period and slowing down other operations.

The *max degree of parallelism* option allows you to control how many CPUs can be used for parallel operations. A common best practice is to set this value to half the number of CPU cores on your server. For example, if you have four dual-core CPUs, you will see eight cores in Windows, so you should set **max degree of parallelism** to 4. You will not be tested on what the formula should be to calculate the optimal value, but you may be tested on what it does.

To set max degree of parallelism to 4 run:

```
sp_configure 'max degree of parallelism', 4
go
reconfigure
```

The max degree of parallelism is also known as *MAXDOP* and can be specified at the query level using the **MAXDOP** keyword, as well as the server level.

The default value of 0 means *use all available processors.* You can also change this setting in SQL Server Management Studio on the **Advanced** page.

Security Certifications

SQL Server 2008 can be easily configured to support requirements to meet certain compliance standards. You should be aware of these and how to enable them for the exam.

C2 Auditing

This is a standard developed by the U.S. government that determines how system usage is audited. It is enabled by running:

```
sp_configure 'c2 audit mode', 1
go
reconfigure
```

This will start a SQL Trace that runs continually and stores the output in a trace file in the default data directory. Because of the stringent requirements set out by the C2 standard, if SQL Server can't write that trace file (if you run out of disk space for example) it will stop the SQL Server Service, in other words, nothing happens unless it's audited.

You can also enable this setting in SQL Server Management Studio on the **Security** page.

Common Criteria Compliance

This a security standard developed in Europe and adopted worldwide that supersedes the C2 standard. There are several levels of Evaluation Assurance Levels (EAL) within the Common Criteria and SQL Server 2008 is certified to level EAL4+, which is the most widely adopted.

It is enabled by running:

```
sp_configure 'common criteria compliance enabled', 1
go
```

Common Criteria Compliance requires a SQL Server Service restart to take effect, and it can also be enabled in SQL Server Management Studio on the **Security** page. To be fully EAL4+ compliant, you need to download and run a script from Microsoft.

New Features

You'll notice a couple of new configuration options if you're upgrading your skills from SQL Server 2005.

Backup Compression Default

SQL Server 2008 has a new feature that enables compressed backups to be taken, which saves time and storage requirements. It is an Enterprise Edition-only feature that is switched off by default. When you take a SQL Server backup it will not be compressed unless you specifically asked it to be. You can control this default behavior by configuring the **backup compression default** option with **sp_configure**. It is enabled by running:

```
sp_configure 'backup compression default', 1
go
reconfigure
```

The backup compression default cannot be controlled through the SQL Server Management Studio interface.

FileStream Access Level

We've already looked at this option earlier in the chapter. It is configured the same way as all the other options, and you can refer back to Table 3.2 for a list of valid values and what they correspond to. You can also control this setting through the Management Studio interface on the **Advanced** page.

Database Mail

Database Mail is a solution that enables you to send email messages from SQL Server. It is disabled by default and uses the SMTP standard to deliver messages, so there is no need to have a MAPI client such as Outlook installed on the server.

It runs as an isolated process outside of SQL Server to ensure it doesn't affect the availability of your database, it can be configured with multiple SMTP servers for redundancy, and is fully supported to run on a Windows failover cluster.

Database Mail uses SQL Server Service Broker to provide asynchronous message delivery, and you must be a member of the DatabaseMailUserRole in msdb to be able to send email messages. It is not supported in SQL Server Express.

Scenarios where Database Mail is often used include:

- Sending a basic message on completion of a SQL Server Agent job
- Executing a query and emailing the results automatically as an attachment

You can also send emails in HTML format.

Configuring Database Mail

Before you configure Database Mail you'll need to have access to an existing SMTP server. Microsoft IIS, which comes with Windows, has an SMTP service that you can configure easily if you don't have an existing SMTP server on your network.

The easiest way to configure Database Mail is by using the **Configure Database Mail** wizard accessible by right-clicking **Database Mail** under the **Management** section of a SQL Server that you have connected to in Management Studio.

You also use the same wizard to manage the Database Mail configuration after you've initially set up. When you run the wizard for the first time, you'll need to select **Set up Database Mail by performing the following tasks:**

Next you'll need to specify a **Profile** name and create new SMTP accounts through which to send emails. You can add multiple SMTP accounts on different servers to a Profile. If the first account fails then Database Mail will try the next account and server in the list. In Figure 3.11 in the active window, you can see a second email account and SMTP server being added to a Database Mail profile (seen in the inactive window).

Figure 3.11 Adding a Database Mail Account to a Profile

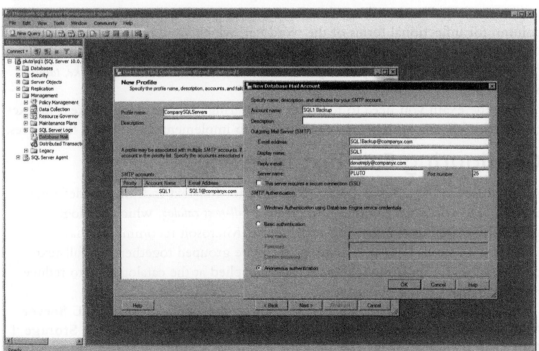

Once you've created a profile, the next screen will prompt you to configure **profile security,** where you can setup your profile to be *Public* and accessible to all users, or *Private* and accessible to a specific user.

The last screen allows you to configure parameters such as retry attempts, but generally you can just leave the defaults.

Once you've run through the wizard you'll now be able to use Database Mail by calling the sp_send_dbmail stored procedure. Here is sample code that sends a basic email to an address using the CompanySQLServers profile that was created using the Database Mail wizard:

```
EXEC msdb.dbo.sp_send_dbmail
  @profile_name = 'CompanySQLServers',
  @recipients = 'DBA@companyx.com',
  @body = 'Output from procedure X was not as expected',
  @subject = 'Procedure X execution';
```

Full-Text Indexing

Full-text indexing is a feature of SQL Server 2008 that allows you to carry out sophisticated searches of text-based data called a *full-text search*. A full-text search is different from a normal search of data through a normal index because it enables you to use linguistic-based searches. For example, you could search a text-based column for inflectional forms of the word *run,* which would return results including *running* and *ran.* You could also search for similar words using the thesaurus feature, so searching for *bicycle* might return results including *bike, pushbike, tandem* and *tricycle.*

For the exam you need to focus on configuring and managing full-text indexes to support full-text searches rather than how to implement the searches themselves.

Configuring Full-Text Indexing

All databases in SQL Server 2008 are enabled for full-text indexing by default, so the first step you need to make is to create a *full-text catalog,* which is a logical object for grouping together full-text indexes. Microsoft recommends that full-text indexes with similar update activity patterns are grouped together in a full-text catalog, so that population schedules can be applied at the catalog level to reduce resource usage during population.

Full-text catalogs can be created from the **right-click** menu in **SQL Server Management Studio** at **<instance>** | **Databases** | **<database>** | **Storage** | **Full Text Catalogs** or by executing the following T-SQL:

```
CREATE FULLTEXT CATALOG <name>
```

Before you can create a full-text index for a table, you'll need to make sure it has an existing unique, single column, nonnullable index. The full-text index will base its index keys on this.

Once you've fulfilled all the requirements you can create a full-text index using the CREATE FULLTEXT INDEX t-sql command, or use Management Studio by navigating to the table and selecting **Full-Text Indexes** from the **right-click** menu.

Managing Full-Text Indexes

Once you've created a full-text index, the process of filling it is referred to as *populating* the index. This is done initially when you create it, and by default the index will stay up to date as the underlying data changes. There are scenarios, however, where this default behavior is undesirable. As the population process is resource intensive, if you have frequent updates to your underlying text data, it might be prohibitive for you to keep the index automatically updated.

In this scenario, you can modify the default behavior of *change tracking,* which is to automatically track changes and populate the index. You can configure it to **manual,** which specifies that changes will be tracked but not propagated until you run or schedule the **ALTER FULLTEXT INDEX ON <tablename> START UPDATE POPULATION** t-sql command or set it to **off,** in which case changes will not be tracked or propagated until you run a **FULL** or **INCREMENTAL** population. An incremental population will update the index with changed rows since the last population, but it requires a column with the *timestamp* data type to be present on the underlying table.

Summary of Exam Objectives

In this chapter you've looked in-depth at the difference between default and named instances, seen how to change the default TCP port and the SQL Server service accounts, learned how to add startup parameters to SQL Server, and learned when to use Server Aliases—all with SQL Server Configuration Manager.

You've also seen how to view and change serverwide options with sp_configure and SQL Server Management Studio, looked at the benefits of Database Mail over SQLMail and how to configure it, and learned how to create and manage full-text indexes in SQL Server.

Exam Objectives Fast Track

Instances vs. Default Instance

☑ A default instance is accessed by using the servername, and a named instance is accessed using servername\instancename.

☑ You can have only one default instance per server, and by default it will use TCP port 1433.

☑ Each instance is completely independent of any other instance and has its own set of services, databases, and configuration settings.

SQL Server Configuration Manager

☑ You need to use Configuration Manager to change the SQL Server Service account to ensure that the correct permissions are assigned.

☑ To configure FILESTREAM after installation, you need to enable it in Configuration Manager *and* by using **sp_configure filestream_access_level.**

☑ You can change the TCP port an instance listens on by using Configuration Manager.

sp_configure and SQL Server Management Studio

☑ You need to enable **show advanced options** using sp_configure to view all of the sp_configure options.

☑ Only a subset of configuration options can be changed using Management Studio; most can only be changed with sp_configure.

☑ AWE is used to enable SQL Server to access more than 2GB of RAM on 32-bit systems.

Database Mail

☑ Database Mail replaces SQLMail found in versions prior to SQL Server 2005.

☑ It uses SMTP rather than MAPI, so you don't need to install a mail client.

☑ You can specify multiple SMTP accounts on different servers for redundancy.

Full-Text Indexing

☑ All new databases are enabled for full-text indexing by default.

☑ Once you've defined an index, filling it is referred to as *populating* the index.

☑ A full-text catalog is a logical grouping of full-text indexes.

Exam Objectives
Frequently Asked Questions

Q: Do I have to install a default instance?

A: No. You can install named instances on a server without having a default instance.

Q: If a named instance uses dynamic port allocation how will I know which port to connect to each time?

A: The SQL Browser service needs to be running on the SQL Server. It will automatically return the correct port to your connection without you having to specify anything.

Q: Why shouldn't I change a SQL Server service account using the services applet?

A: Changing the service account using SQL Server Configuration Manager will assign all the file system permissions and advanced user rights needed for SQL Server to work properly. Using the services applet won't do this and could cause problems when the service is next started.

Q: Should I change SQL Server configuration settings using the Management Studio interface or with sp_configure?

A: The end result is the same so it doesn't really matter. However, sp_confgure has many more options than the interface and is easy to script so it tends to be the popular choice with DBAs.

Q: I've enabled AWE on my 32-bit SQL Server but still can't see more than 2 GB of RAM. What should I do?

A: First, check that you're running the Enterprise or Datacenter version of Windows. Then check in c:\boot.ini for the /PAE switch which enables Windows to see the extra RAM. If that all looks fine then check that the service account has the 'lock pages in memory' user right. If it doesn't there will be an error logged to the SQL Server errorlog on startup.

Q: I'm upgrading from SQL Server 2000 where I have SQLMail configured and Microsoft Outlook installed on the server. Why don't I need Outllook installed for Database Mail in SQL Server 2008?

A: Database Mail uses Simple Mail Transport Protocol (SMTP) which doesn't need a client install like the older SQLMail that uses the Mail API (MAPI) and requires a mail client like Outlook to be installed.

Self Test

1. You've just started as a DBA at a company that has recently installed a dedicated server running both a SQL Server 2008 default instance and the database for the company's ERP system. You want to implement a process to test the database with new SQL Server patches and service packs before they are applied to the live database. There is no budget to buy any new servers, but the existing hardware is under-utilized and you're confident it will suffice for your short-term needs. Which of these options would meet your needs?

   A. Restore a copy of the live database as *test* on to its own disk array. Apply patches and service packs to the new database and test them before applying them to the live database.

   B. Install a named instance for testing. Create a database snapshot on the named instance pointing to the live database on the default instance. Apply patches and service packs to the named instance and test before applying them to the default instance.

   C. Install another default instance for testing and restore a copy of the live database. Apply patches and service packs to the second instance and test before applying them to the live instance.

   D. Install a named instance for testing and restore a copy of the live database. Apply patches and service packs to the named instance and test before applying them to the default instance.

2. Last month your company went through an exercise to standardize service accounts while you were on holiday. You've just restarted SQL Server after applying a service pack, and now the instance won't start. You check the Windows Event Log and see lots of errors about not being able to open the error log. What is the most likely cause?

   A. The SQL Server Service account was not changed using SQL Server Configuration Manager

   B. The service pack failed

   C. Data corruption

   D. You don't have the right permissions to the error log

3. You have a default instance and a named instance installed on your server. The developers are complaining that they can't connect to the named instance from

their workstations using Management Studio anymore. You log on to the server through Terminal Services and can connect to each instance without issue. What could the cause of this behavior be?

A. The developers haven't created a SQL Server Alias to the named instance using the Shared Memory protocol.

B. The SQL Browser Service has been started

C. The SQL Browser Service has been stopped

D. The IP addresses of the developers' workstations have been added to the Exclude list in the TCP/IP properties of the named instance in Configuration Manager.

4. Your security administrator has determined that all the SQL Servers in your organization need to listen on nondefault TCP ports, and she doesn't want network users to see the SQL Servers in a browse list. Which *two* actions would achieve this goal?

A. Stop and disable the browser service on each SQL Server

B. Use Configuration Manager on each server to change each instance to listen on port 50000

C. Use Configuration Manager on each server to change each instance to listen different ports

D. Configure the SQL Browser Service to hide each instance

E. Enable **Show Advanced Options** using sp_configure and use the **Default TCP port** option to configure the port for each instance

5. The company you work for has just merged with another company that uses Novell Netware as their network operating system. The new company's developers are struggling to connect to your SQL Server. What could be the problem?

A. SQL Server 2008 doesn't support the Banyan Vines protocol

B. You haven't enabled the IPX/SPX protocol

C. You haven't enabled the Banyan Vines protocol

D. SQL Server 2008 doesn't support the IPX/SPX protocol

6. You have just upgraded your databases from a SQL Server 2005 default instance to a SQL Server 2008 named instance called Phobos on a server named MARS. The application that uses the SQL Server sits on its own server,

and you've just found out that you can't change the connection string in the application to point to the new instance. How can you fix it?

A. Add a CNAME record on your DNS server for MARS that points to MARS\Phobos

B. Install SQL Server Client Tools on the application server and create a SQL Server Alias called MARS that points to MARS\Phobos

C. Install SQL Server Client Tools on the application server and create a SQL Server Alias called MARS\Default that points to MARS\Phobos

D. Add a PTR record on your DNS server for MARS that points to MARS\Phobos

7. You install a default instance of SQL Server 2008 Developer Edition with default configuration options. The developers complain that they can't connect to the server using SQL Server Management Studio. Which of these options is the most likely cause?

A. A firewall is blocking port 1433

B. The SQL Browser Service isn't running

C. The SQL Server tools on the developer workstations haven't been service packed

D. TCP/IP is disabled by default in Developer Edition

8. A SQL Server recently suffered from all CPUs running at 100 percent, which you found to be caused by a missing index. You fixed the problem, but you want to stop any new occurrences from saturating all CPUs. Which of these options would achieve this?

A. Use sp_configure to set **max degree of parallelism**
B. Use Configuration Manager to configure the SQL Server Service to use fewer CPUs

C. Run the Database Tuning Advisor and apply any recommendations

D. Use sp_configure to set cost threshold for parallelism

9. A developer has contacted you because he wants to enable AWE memory on his Developer Edition instance, but he says that he can't see the option with sp_configure. What is the most likely cause?

A. AWE is not supported with Developer Edition

B. The developer is connecting with a low-privilege user and doesn't have enough permissions

C. He hasn't enabled **show advanced options** with sp_configure

D. He hasn't enabled /PAE in boot.ini

10. You're running SQL Server 64-bit and want to make sure that SQL Server doesn't take too much memory. Which of these options would achieve that?

A. Set "Maximum Server Memory (MB)" using sp_configure

B. Assign the SQL Service account the "Lock Pages in Memory" privilege

C. Set "Maximum Server Memory (MB)" using SQL Server Management Studio

D. Start SQL Server with the -g switch passing the maximum memory as a parameter.

11. One of your DBAs is setting up SQLMail and has asked you for a license key for Outlook. You suggest he enables Database Mail instead. Which *two* of these options are features of Database Mail?

A. Received e-mails are stored in msdb

B. It doesn't require a MAPI client

C. It is Windows failover-cluster aware

D. It is available in all SQL Server editions

12. A business user has just phoned to say that his data wasn't updated overnight. You check SQL Server and see that a SQL Server Agent job that runs a data load failed last night. You want to be automatically notified via email if it happens again. Which of these options will provide the most efficient, supported solution?

A. Implement SQLMail

B. Implement Database Mail

C. Install a 3rd-party SMTP mailer

D. Implement Service Broker

13. You've just upgraded to SQL Server 2008 from SQL Server 2000, and you've dropped SQLMail in favor of Database Mail. The IT Manager wants to know if Database Mail has redundancy if a mail server goes down. How would you reply?

    A. Yes, you can configure multiple SMTP servers in a Database Mail Profile

    B. Yes, you can configure SQLMail as a backup

    C. No, you would have to reconfigure it to use a different mail server

    D. Yes, Database Mail is supported on a failover cluster

14. You've been investigating deadlocks on your server using trace flag 1222, and you'd like to enable it permanently to capture extra information if deadlocks occur again, even if SQL Server gets restarted. What is the easiest way to do this?

    A. Execute DBCC TRACEON (1222,-1)

    B. Create a startup stored procedure containing DBCC TRACEON (1222,-1) and use sp_configure to enable **scan for startup procs**

    C. Use Configuration Manager to add −T1222 as a startup parameter for the SQL Server service

    D. Execute DBCC TRACEON (1222)

15. You've been told that you need to make your SQL Server compliant with EAL4+. What is the first step you need to do in this process?

    A. Use sp_configure to enable **c2 audit mode**

    B. Use sp_configure to enable **common criteria compliance enabled**

    C. SQL Server 2008 is automatically EAL4+ compliant

    D. SQL Server 2008 does not support EAL4+ compliance

16. Some of your full-text indexes are consuming a lot of server resources. You investigate and discover that the index causing the problem is on a text-based field that is updated frequently. You've spoken to the business, and the updates don't affect their search results. What could you do to reduce the overall impact on the server while keeping the index fairly up to date?

    A. Set change tracking on the index to AUTO

    B. Move the index to a filegroup on its own drive

    C. Set change tracking on the index to MANUAL and schedule a nightly population update.

    D. Set change tracking on the index to OFF

17. You have installed a default and two named instances called Phobos and Deimos on a server called Mars. How would you connect to each instance?

    A. Mars, Mars\Phobos, Mars\Deimos

    B. Mars, Mars1\Phobos, Mars2\Deimos

    C. Default, Phobos, Deimos

    D. Default, mars\phobos, mars\deimos

18. Your developers complain that they can't connect to the server using SQL Server Management Studio. You've used Terminal Services to log on to the server, and you've confirmed that TCP/IP is enabled. You now want to test it with a local connection. What should you do?

    A. Nothing, just connect

    B. Disable Shared Memory in Configuration Manager

    C. Move TCP/IP above Shared Memory in the connection protocol order

    D. Disable Shared Memory using sp_configure 'shared memory enabled'

19. You are responsible for a large-capacity server that has a default instance of SQL Server 2008 installed and hosts databases for multiple applications belonging to several of your customers. A new database needs to be moved to the server, which has a different collation, and the collation of TempDB needs to match it. You can't change the collation for your existing TempDB because it will affect all the applications. What could you do?

    A. Create another TempDB with the right collation and configure the new database to use it

    B. Configure the database to use a different TempDB on a remote server

    C. Install a new instance for the database with a default collation the same as the database

    D. A separate server with a separate instance is the only option

20. You're implementing a database backup strategy and you have full-text indexes that took 12 hours to build, so you need to make sure that they are backed up to avoid a long recovery time. What should you do?

    A. Nothing extra, they're backed up with the databases

    B. Add WITH FULLTEXT to the database backup command

    C. Switch on **fulltext backup default enabled** with sp_configure

    D. Configure the full-text indexes for AUTO

Self Test Quick Answer Key

1.	**D**	11.	**B** and **C**
2.	**A**	12.	**B**
3.	**C**	13.	**A**
4.	**A** and **C**	14.	**C**
5.	**D**	15.	**B**
6.	**B**	16.	**C**
7.	**D**	17.	**A**
8.	**A**	18.	**B**
9.	**C**	19.	**C**
10.	**A** and **C**	20.	**A**

Chapter 4

MCTS SQL Server 2008 Exam 432

Managing Security

Exam objectives in this chapter:

- Principals
- Roles
- The "Principle of Least Privilege"
- Users
- Schemas
- Permissions
- Auditing
- The SQL Server Configuration Manager
- Security and SQL Agent

Exam objectives review:

- ☑ Summary of Exam Objectives
- ☑ Exam Objectives Fast Track
- ☑ Exam Objectives Frequently Asked Questions
- ☑ Self Test
- ☑ Self Test Quick Answer Key

Introduction

Security is an often overlooked factor when designing an application. In this chapter, all aspects of security will be discussed.

Logins and Users will be covered, as well as SQL Server 2008's built-in roles. Some new features are available for policy management.

This chapter will also review user roles and schemas, as well as the pros and cons of granting access to objects. The tradeoff between more granular security and less granular security will be discussed.

SQL Authentication will be covered in great detail, along with the pros and cons of each method.

The SQL Server Surface Area Configuration tool will be covered as well as the provisioning of the accounts used for SQL Server Services.

Principals

As we begin to look at SQL Server 2008 security management, a good place to start is to define what SQL Server considers a principal. Principals are entities that can request SQL Server resources and their scope of influence depends on the definition scope of the principal. Windows-level principals have a Windows permission scope, SQL Server-level principals have server-level permissions and Database-level principals have database-level permissions. A Security identifier (SID) is assigned to every principal. The following shows the hierarchy of SQL Server 2008 principals and how logins and database users can be mapped to security objects. Fixed server and database roles are not shown here but are discussed in the next section.

TEST DAY TIP

Make sure that you are familiar with this hierarchy and how the principals can be mapped.

Windows-level principals

- Windows domain login
- Windows local login
- Windows group

SQL Server-level principals

- SQL Server login
- SQL Server login mapped to a Windows login
- SQL Server login mapped to a certificate
- SQL Server login mapped to an asymmetric key

Database-level principals

- Database user
- Database user mapped to SQL Server login
- Database user mapped to a Windows login
- Database user mapped to a certificate
- Database user mapped to an asymmetric key
- Database role
- Application role
- Public role

The hierarchy of securable objects in SQL Server 2008 is as follows:

Server

- Database
- Endpoint
- Remote Binding
- Route
- SQL Server Login

Database

- Application Role
- Assembly
- Asymmetric Key
- Certificate
- Database User
- Fixed Database Role

- Full-Text Catalog
- Message Type
- Service
- Service Contact
- Symmetric Key

Schema

- Default
- Function
- Procedure
- Query Stats
- Queue
- Rule
- Synonym
- Table
- Trigger
- Type
- View
- XML Schema Collection

EXAM WARNING

Make sure that you are familiar with the principals listed above regarding their scope and how they fit into the SQL Server 2008 hierarchy.

Roles

Like Windows groups, SQL Server provides two roles, server- and database-level roles into which logins and users can be added. Server-level roles are fixed roles that have a serverwide permission scope. Each built-in role serves a specific purpose and have the required permissions associated with them. Although you are limited to the built-in server-level roles, you can create new database-level roles in addition to those available to suit more specific needs.

SQL Server logins, Windows accounts, and Windows groups can be added to server-level roles. Server-level roles are as follows:

- sysadmin – Perform any activity in the server. By default, the BUILTIN\ Administrators group and the local administrator's group are members of the sysadmin role.

- serveradmin – Change server-wide configuration options and shut down the server.

- securityadmin – Manage logins and their properties. They will be able to reset passwords for SQL Server logins and GRANT, DENY, and Revoke database-level and server-level permissions.

- processadmin – End processes running in an instance of SQL Server.

- setupadmin – Add and remove linked servers.

- bulkadmin – Run the BULK INSERT statement.

- diskadmin – Manage disk files.

- dbcreator – CREATE, ALTER, DROP, and restore any database.

You can find the following objects in the master database that can help when working with server-level roles:

- sp_helpsrvrole – Returns a list of server-level roles.

- sp_helpsrvrolemember – Returns information about the members of a server-level role.

- sp_srvrolepermission – Displays the permissions of a server-level role.

- IS_SRVROLEMEMBER – Indicates whether a SQL Server login is a member of the specified server-level role.

- sys.server_role_members – Returns one row for each member of each server-level role.

- sp_addsrvrole_member – Adds a login as a member of a server-level role.

- sp_dropsrvrole_member – Removes a SQL Server login or a Windows user or group from a server-level role.

There are two types of database-level roles, fixed database roles that are predefined in the database and flexible database roles that you can create.

The fixed database-level roles are:

- db_owner – Can drop the database as well as permission to perform all configuration and maintenance tasks.

- db_security_admin – Can modify role membership and manage permissions. Please be careful when adding principals to this role; an unintended privilege escalation could result.

- db_accessadmin – Can add or remove database access for Windows logins, Windows groups, and SQL Server logins.

- db_backupoperator – Can back up the database.

- db_ddladmin – Can run any Data Definition Language command.

- db_datawriter – Can add, delete, or change data in all user tables.

- db_datareader – Can read all data from all user tables.

- db_denydatawriter – Will deny permission in the database to add, modify, or delete any data in the user tables.

- db_denydatareader – Will deny permission in the database to read any data in the user tables.

These objects can be helpful when working with Database-level roles:

- sp_helpdbfixedrole – Returns a list of the fixed database roles.

- sp_dbfixedrolepermission – Displays the permissions of a fixed database role.

- sp_helprole – Returns information about the roles in the current database.

- sp_helprolemember – Returns information about the members of a role in the current database.

- sys.database_role_members – Returns one row for each member of each database role.

- IS_MEMBER – Indicates whether the current user is a member of the specified Microsoft Windows group or Microsoft SQL Server database role.

- CREATE_ROLE – Creates a new database role in the current database.

- ALTER_ROLE – Changes the name of a database role.

- DROP_ROLE – Removes a role from the database.

- sp_addrole – Creates a new database role in the current database.

- sp_droprole – Removes a database role from the current database.

- sp_addrolemember – Adds a database user, database role, Windows login, or Windows group to a database role in the current database.

- sp_droprolemember – Removes a security account from a SQL Server role in the current database.

EXAM WARNING

Understand the difference between Server-level and Database-level Roles as well as their permissions scope.

Figure 4.1 shows the fixed server roles. Figure 4.2 shows the predefined database roles.

Figure 4.1 Fixed Server-Level Roles

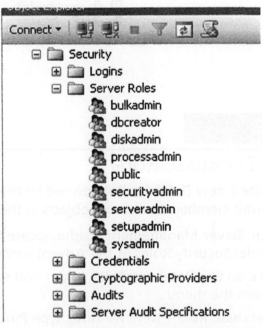

Figure 4.2 Database-Level Roles

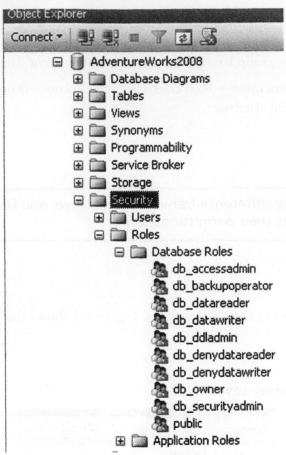

EXERCISE 4.1

CREATE A NEW DATABASE ROLE

You need to create a new Database Role owned by the HumanResources role that will permit members to also use objects in the purchasing schema.

1. In the SQL Server Management Studio, locate the Database Roles folder under Security/Roles in the AdventureWorks2008 database.

2. Right-click on the Database Roles folder and select **New Database Role...** from the menu.

3. In the Database Role – New window, type **Purchasing** into the Role name text box.

4. In the Owner text box, browse and select **HumanResources** as the Owner.

5. In the Owned Schemas section, locate and select the **Purchasing** schema.

6. Your window should look like Figure 4.3. By creating your new role, notice the schemas owned by your new role by default.

7. Click **OK**. Your newly created database role will appear in the database role folder.

Figure 4.3 Database Role Properties

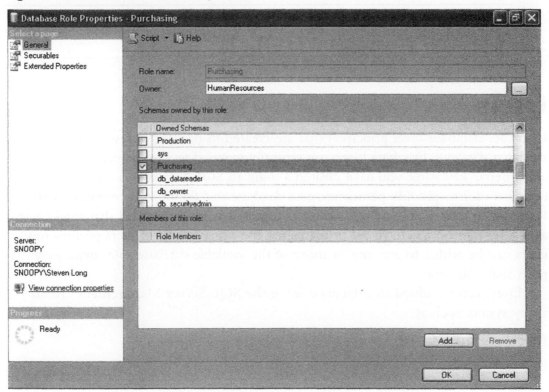

The "Principle of Least Privilege"

In order to maintain a secure SQL Server environment it is important to take the approach of granting the minimum amount of permissions possible to any entity requesting a SQL Server resource. So it is very important to do your due diligence when adding a user to a specific role or granting any additional permissions. If you are not familiar with what access you are granting, you may inadvertently elevate a user's access, thus posing a significant security risk. Make sure that you are familiar with what access has been granted to that role or what that permission enables a user to do. If the user does not need to do sysadmin tasks, the user should not be added to the sysadmin group. The same goes for the database-level roles; if they only need to select data from a table, the db_datareader should be sufficient. Not every user needs to be at the db_owner permission level. If a user is granted permissions beyond the scope of their specific need, this principle has been violated.

Test Day Tip

Be familiar with the "Principle of Least Privilege" and how that applies to granting permissions to SQL Server resources.

Users

Users are database-level principals that are created in order to access resources within a database. Database Users are typically mapped to a login, certificate, or asymmetric key. After you have created a login to SQL Server, you create a database user in order to provide permission to a database and the objects contained within. In order to more easily tie users back to logins, it is recommended that the Log-in and User names match. To aid in managing the organization of users permissions, users can be added to any one or more of the available database roles or to new roles that you create.

Users can be added to a database using the SQL Server Management Studio or by syntax such as:

```
CREATE USER user_name
    [ { { FOR | FROM }
      {
        LOGIN login_name
        | CERTIFICATE cert_name
        | ASYMMETRIC KEY asym_key_name
      }
      | WITHOUT LOGIN
    ]
    [ WITH DEFAULT_SCHEMA = schema_name ]
```

See Figure 4.4.

Figure 4.4 Database Users

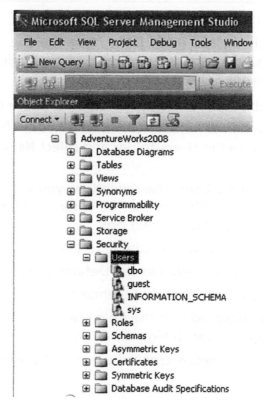

Schemas

Database schemas are collections of objects such as tables, views, and procedures that enable a powerful way to manage permissions. As demonstrated in the AdventureWorks2008 database, schemas have been set up for business areas such as Human Resources, Sales, and Purchasing. Although all the objects associated with each business area are contained within the same database, the objects are logically grouped within the respective schemas, enabling greater control through permissions. As seen in the User section, one schema or multiple schemas can be granted to a user making it unnecessary to permission each object individual to the user. The user is limited to the schemas to which they have been granted access, preventing a user from being able to access objects owned by another user. Schemas must be transferred to a different user or role if the schema owner needs to be deleted.

EXERCISE 4.2

ADD A NEW USER

You need to explicitly add a SQL Server Login to the AdventureWorks2008 database so that a user can select data from all the user tables in the Sales schema.

1. In the SQL Server Management Studio, locate the Users folder in the Security folder for the AdventureWorks2008 database.

2. Right-click on the **Users folder** and select **New User** from the menu.

3. In the Database User – New window, you will be mapping your Login to create this new user, so enter your **instancename\your name** in the User name text box.

4. Browse to your Login to complete the Login name text box.

5. Select the **Sales** schema as the Default schema.

6. Select **Sales** in the Owned Schemas section.

7. Select **db_datareader** in the Role Members section. Your window should look similar to Figure 4.5.

8. Click **OK**. Your newly created user will appear in the Users folder.

Figure 4.5 New Database User Properties

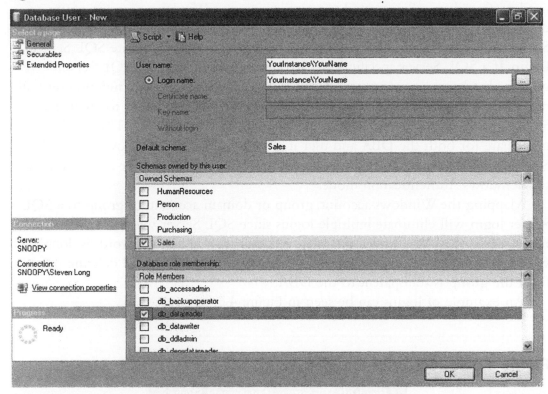

Users versus Logins

We have already touched on the definition of both Users and Principals. We will now take a look at Logins and how they relate to users and other instance and database securables.

When you are setting up users and logins it is important to distinguish between Authentication: identifying users and determining if they are who they say they are, and Authorization: what level of access should the user have, what permissions do they have, and to which resources do they have access.

Logins are created at the instance level and can be mapped to a Windows user account, a domain account, a Windows group, a domain group, or an isolated login contained within SQL Server. Setting up a SQL Server Login provides a user access to the SQL Server instance. While setting up a login, you can provide access to one or more databases. Logins do not provide access to the objects contained within the database. Permissions to access database objects are at the database user level.

When the SQL Server instance has been set up to use Windows Authentication mode, referred to as "integrated security," mapping a Windows account, group or domain account, or group to a login enables a Windows user to login into SQL Server using their Windows credentials. They do not need a separate SQL Server Login. If a SQL Server specific login has been created when the SQL Server instance has been set up to use mixed mode authentication, the Windows user will need to log in into their Windows account and then be prompted to enter their SQL Server user name and password when accessing SQL Server. This can be a nightmare for both the DBA and user if attempting to keep Windows and SQL Server Logins in sync. SQL Server logins cannot not be used if the server is using the Windows Authentication mode.

Mapping the Windows account, group or domain account, or group to a SQL Server login will eliminate multiple logins since SQL Server will validate the user by checking their Windows credentials. Maintenance of user passwords is done within Windows and if mapping groups to a login, the adding and deleting of users from the group is transparent to the DBA.

An example of logins can be seen in Figure 4.6.

Figure 4.6 SQL Server-Level Logins

EXERCISE 4.3

CREATE A SQL SERVER LOGIN

You need to add a new SQL Server Login and it will be mapped to a domain account and be set up to access the AdventureWorks2008 database.

1. In the SQL Server Management Studio, locate the security folder at the instance level.

2. Under the security folder you will see a folder named Logins. Right-click on **Logins** and select **New Login** from the menu.

3. In the "Login – New" window in the general section locate the domain account that you need to map to the login. Make sure that Windows authentication is selected.

4. For the Default Database, select **AdventureWorks2008**.

5. Now switch sections and select **User Mapping**.

6. In the User Mapping section, locate **AdventureWorks2008** in the "Users mapped to this login" section and check the Map column. Your entries should look similar to Figure 4.7 and Figure 4.8.

7. Click on **OK** and you have completed creating a new SQL Server login.

Figure 4.7 General Section

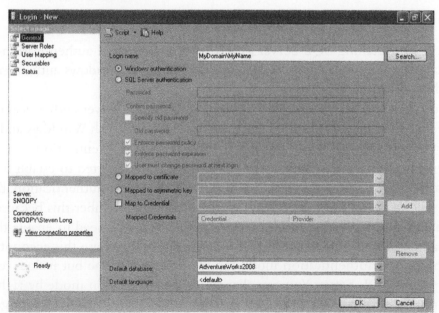

Figure 4.8 User Mapping Section

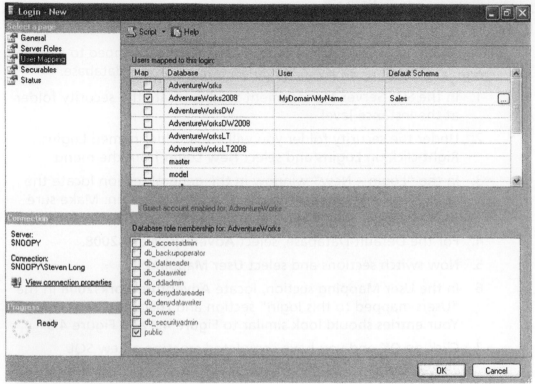

Authentication Mode

When you are installing SQL Server 2008, the selection of an authentication mode for the database engine is required. The choices are either Windows authentication or mixed mode authentication.

If you select the Windows authentication mode, SQL Server authentication will be disabled. Selecting mixed mode authentication enables both Windows and SQL Server authentication. You cannot disable Windows authentication.

When selecting mixed mode authentication you are required to establish a strong password for the sa account. If you selected Windows authentication, the sa account will be created but disabled. It is important to remember this because if you change authentication modes at a later time, you will need to enable this account and establish a password at that point if you wish to use this account.

Changing the authentication mode can be done at anytime but it does require that you restart SQL Server. You can change the authentication mode by right clicking on the server in the SQL Server Management Studio and the change can be made under security in the Server Authentication section. See Figure 4.9.

TEST DAY TIP

Make sure that you know what you need to do to change the
Authentication mode.

Figure 4.9 SQL Server – Server Authentication Properties

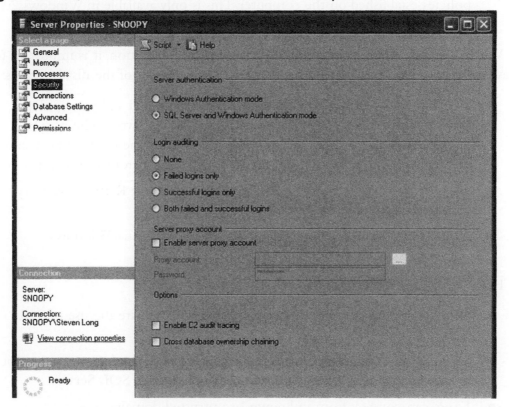

Using Windows Authentication (integrated security) is recommended and
considered to be more secure than using SQL Server logins or mixed mode.
Windows accounts are subject to the built-in security features in Windows and are
sometimes considered to be Trusted connections to SQL Server since Windows
handles the authentication.

If you are using mixed mode, Any SQL Server Logins created that are not based
on Windows user accounts are required to follow strong password guidelines.
Database users using SQL Server logins will need to login using a user name and
password every time they connect.

SQL Server logins offer the following password policies:

- User must change password at next login – Established in the Log-in properties in the SQL Server Management Studio.

- Enforce Password Expiration – Based on the maximum password age policy of the computer.

- Enforce Password Policy – SQL Server enforces Windows password policies established on the computer. This is only available in Windows 2003 Server and later.

When you are establishing using SQL Serving authentication, it is important to be aware of the disadvantages and advantages. Here are some of the disadvantages:

- A Windows domain user who has a Windows user id and password will have to also enter their SQL Server user id and password. The user will have to present the SQL Server credentials every time they connect, and maintaining multiple user ids and passwords can be troublesome for users.

- SQL Server Logins cannot not take advantage of the Kerberos security protocol that is used by Windows.

- SQL Server Logins cannot offer many of the additional Windows password policies.

Here are some of the advantages:

- SQL Server can support older applications that require the use of SQL Server Logins.

- Users in an environment of mixed operating systems where users are not authenticated by a Windows domain can connect to SQL Server.

- Users can connect from unknown or untrusted domains.

- Users can connect when creating their own identities in Web-based applications.

- Software developers can distribute applications based on specific SQL Server Logins.

EXAM WARNING

You will need to understand the advantages and disadvantages of the Authentication Modes.

EXERCISE 4.4

CHANGE THE AUTHENTICATION MODE

You selected mixed mode authentication when you installed SQL Server 2008. You have done some research and have found that none of the applications connected to SQL Server are depending on SQL Server Logins so you want to make your environment more secure and have decided to switch the Authentication Mode to Windows Authentication exclusively.

1. In the SQL Server Management Studio, right-click on the server and select Properties from the menu.

2. In the Security Authentication section of the screen, select **Windows Authentication**. Your screen should look like Figure 4.10.

3. Click on **OK** to save the change.

4. Restart SQL Server.

Figure 4.10 Changing the Authentication Mode

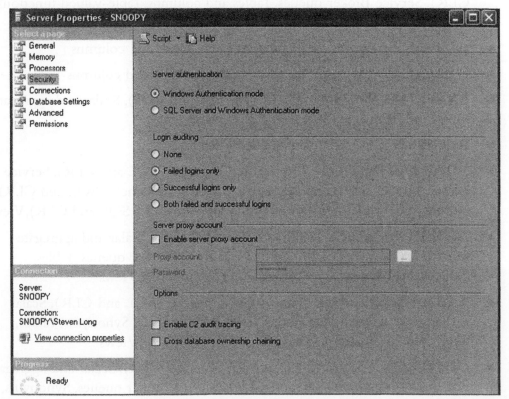

Permissions

Designing a permissions strategy is important when properly securing database objects. Considering the hierarchy of securables—a database, a schema, or an object—you have options of applying permissions by either granting permissions on the database, on each schema within the database, or on each individual table or view.

The permissions that can be granted and to which securables they can be applied are as follows:

- **SELECT** Synonyms, Tables and columns, Table-valued functions, Transact-SQL and common language runtime (CLR), and columns, Views and columns

- **VIEW CHANGE TRACKING** Tables and Schemas

- **UPDATE** Synonyms, Tables and columns, Views and columns

- **REFERENCES** Scalar and aggregate functions (Transact – SQL and CLR), Service Broker queues, Tables and columns, Table-valued functions (Transact – SQL and CLR), and columns, Views and columns

- **INSERT** Synonyms, Tables and columns, Views and columns

- **DELETE** Synonyms, Tables and columns, Views and columns

- **EXECUTE** Procedures (Transact – SQL and CLR), Scalar and aggregate functions (Transact – SQL and CLR), Synonyms

- **RECEIVE** Service Broker queues

- **VIEW DEFINITION** Procedures (Transact – SQL and CLR), Service Broker queues, Scalar and aggregate functions (Transact – SQL and CLR), Synonyms, Tables, Table-valued functions (Transact – SQL and CLR), Views

- **ALTER** Procedures (Transact – SQL and CLR), Scalar and aggregate functions (Transact   SQL and CLR), Service Broker queues, Tables, Table-valued functions (Transact – SQL and CLR), Views

- **TAKE OWNERSHIP** Procedures (Transact – SQL and CLR), Scalar and aggregate functions (Transact – SQL and CLR), Synonyms, Tables, Table-valued functions (Transact – SQL and CLR), Views

- **CONTROL** Procedures (Transact – SQL and CLR), Scalar and aggregate functions (Transact – SQL and CLR), Service Broker queues, Synonyms, Tables, Table-valued functions (Transact – SQL and CLR), Views

Cross-Database Ownership Chaining

Enabled at the instance level, cross-database ownership enables setting permissions on one database object such as a view which retrieves data from two or more tables, or databases in the same instance. This approach does provide a slight performance increase since permission checks are skipped on subsequent objects in the chain; taking this approach has major implications when managing security. Question 14 in the Self Test section of this chapter includes a cross-database ownership chaining scenario.

EXERCISE 4.5

GRANTING PERMISSIONS

You need to add a new login and grant Execute permissions on the AdventureWorks2008 database.

1. Create a new SQL Server login named Test432 and set the default database to AdventureWorks2008 database.

2. Create a new database user in the AdventureWorks2008 database, mapping it to the SQL Server login Test432. Do not give the user any permissions.

3. Execute the following code:

   ```
   GRANT EXECUTE ON DATABASE::AdventureWorks2008 TO Test432
   ```

4. Once you see, "Command(s) completed successfully", user Test432 will have to execute permissions on all the objects in the AdventureWorks2008 database.

5. To test what you've done, log in to SQL as Test432 and run the following code:

   ```
   exec dbo.uspGetEmployeeManagers 2
   ```

If you do not get an error, your grant worked properly.

Head of the Class…

The Correct Match of Permissions

It can seem like every request brings a new challenge for determining the best match for permissions when adding a new user to a database. When business areas consolidate or the responsibilities or business areas span across multiple business areas such as accounting, where they are often involved in supporting every other business area in an organization, it is necessary to construct a list of permissions requirements before just dropping the user into a role or granting a permission that looks like it might work.

You should always be able to justify the choice that you have made. You may need to explain in significant detail what permissions a user or users have been granted. Taking the time to gain a thorough understanding of the SQL Server security hierarchy will greatly help you not only make the best decisions when designing access, you will have a more secure instance and be able to speak with confidence when answering questions in regard to permissions.

Object Permissions

Modules can be marked with an execution context. This enables the code to be run under a specific security context other than whom or what may be calling it. As long as the appropriate permissions exist for context in which the module is run, users only need to be granted permission to the module. Granting explicit object permissions to the module reference objects for the module's users is not necessary.

The following arguments are available when specifying an Execution Context:

- **CALLER** Statements inside the module are executed in the context of who called the module. Appropriate permissions must be applied to the module being called as well as all objects referenced by the module.

- **SELF** Equivalent to EXECUTE AS user_name, the specified user is the person creating or altering the module.

- **OWNER** The module is executed in the context of the current module owner or if an owner is not specified on the module then the owner of the schema of the module is used.

- **'user_name'** The module is executed in the context of the user specified in user_name.

- **'login_name'** The module is executed in the context of the SQL Server login specified in login_name.

EXAM WARNING

Be sure to understand the purpose for each Execution Context and what permissions are necessary for the objects in the chain.

Log-in Permissions (As Related to Roles)

Logins can be added to server-level roles which are used to grant server-wide privileges to a user added to any of the fixed server-level roles. It is important to remember to make sure that a user is not being granted more permissions then they need. The server-level roles generally have the ability to perform tasks beyond the scope of users other than a DBA or server administrator.

EXERCISE 4.6

ADD A SQL SERVER LOGIN TO A SERVER-LEVEL ROLE

You will add a SQL Server login to the db_creator server-level role.

1. Logged in as sysadmin, Execute the following code (any SQL Server login can be specified that does not already exist in the db_creator role):

```
exec sp_addsrvrolemember @loginame= 'test432', @rolename =
'dbcreator'
```

2. Verify that the log-in name you specified is now shown as a member of the db_creator server-level role.

Auditing

Available in SQL Server 2008 Enterprise, automatic auditing can be set up by using SQL Server Audit. The Audit object can capture activity in the database server and save it to a log. Audit information can be stored in a File, Windows Application Log, or Windows Security Log.

In order to create an Audit object you need to first use the CREATE SERVER AUDIT statement. The following is an example of creating a server audit that is saved to a file:

```
CREATE SERVER AUDIT HIPAA_File_Audit
      TO FILE ( FILEPATH='\\SQLPROD_1\Audit\' );
```

The resulting filename generated takes the form of: "AuditName_AuditGUID_nn_TS.sqlaudit."

After you have created the Audit object, events can be added to the server audit that you created by creating a server audit specification. The syntax for that looks like the following:

```
CREATE SERVER AUDIT SPECIFICATION Failed_Login_Spec
FOR SERVER AUDIT HIPAA_File_Audit
    ADD (FAILED_LOGIN_GROUP);
```

Database Audits can also be created to track and CREATE, ALTER, or DROP actions in the database or any INSERT, UPDATE, or DELETE activities performed on database objects.

An example of creating a database audit specification looks like the following:

```
CREATE DATABASE AUDIT SPECIFICATION Sales_Audit_Spec
FOR SERVER AUDIT HIPAA_AppLog_Audit

    ADD (DATABASE_OBJECT_CHANGE_GROUP),
    ADD(INSERT, UPDATE, DELETE
      ON Schema:: Sales
      BY SalesUser, SalesAdmin);
```

EXAM WARNING

Be sure to understand the difference between server-level and database-level audits and your options for storing the audit activity.

EXERCISE 4.7

SET UP A DATABASE AUDIT SPECIFICATION

You need to set up a database audit specification on the HumanResources.
Employee table to monitor any SELECT or DELETE statements. Start setting
up your server audit, enabling the server audit, and then creating the
database audit specification. Your code should resemble the following:

```
USE MASTER

GO

-- You are creating the server audit with this statement

CREATE SERVER AUDIT Employee_Security_Audit

   TO FILE ( FILEPATH =

'C:\Program Files\Microsoft SQL Server\MSSQL10.MSSQLSERVER\
MSSQL\DATA' );

GO

-- You need to then enable the server audit

ALTER SERVER AUDIT Employee_Security_Audit

WITH (STATE = ON) ;

GO

-- Now you need to set up the database audit by switching to the
target database.

USE AdventureWorks

GO

-- Now create the database audit specification for the Employee
table.

CREATE DATABASE AUDIT SPECIFICATION Employee_Table

FOR SERVER AUDIT Employee_Security_Audit

ADD (SELECT, DELETE

        ON HumanResources.Employee BY dbo )

WITH (STATE = ON)

GO
```

You have now completed setting up database auditing for the
HumanResources.Employee table in the AdventureWorks2008 database.

Change Data Capture (CDC)

New in SQL Server 2008 and only available in the Developer, Enterprise, and Evaluation additions, Change data capture (CDC) can be implemented to capture INSERT, UPDATE, and DELETE activity applied to SQL Server tables from the SQL Server transaction log. CDC captures column information along with the metadata, such as the action being taken, that is required to apply the changes to a target environment for rows affected. The data capture information is stored in change tables that resemble the column structure of the tracked source tables.

New & Noteworthy...

Change Data Capture (CDC)
CDC functionality is new in SQL Server 2008, providing the capability to capture INSERT, UPDATE, and DELETE activity from the SQL Server transaction logs.

Before CDC can be used it must be enabled; the following SQL code shows how to do this.

```
use testDatabase
--Activate CDC
EXEC sys.sp_cdc_enable_db_change_data_capture
--IsDatabaseEnabled?
SELECT is_cdc_enabled FROM sys.databases WHERE name = 'testDatabase'
--Enable CDC on table
EXEC sys.sp_cdc_enable_table_change_data_capture @source_schema = 'dbo',
@source_name = 'Table_1', @role_name = 'cdc_test'
--IsTableEnabled?
SELECT is_tracked_by_cdc FROM sys.tables WHERE name = 'table_1'
```

Using DDL Triggers

DDL triggers are a great way to keep track of any structural changes to the database schema. DDL triggers fire after DDL language events and are fully transactional.

Changes can roll back and, besides running Transact-SQL code, Common Language Runtime (CLR) code can be executed as well.

Providing an audit of schema changes can be very helpful when you want to make sure that column data types tied to data loads are not inadvertently changed or production tables are not dropped, resulting in data load or application failures.

DDL triggers can be set up at the database-level and at the server-level. An example of a database-level trigger would be a trigger that tracks or prevents DDL changes to tables. A server-level DDL trigger could track such changes as Logins being added to SQL Server.

Once created, you can see DDL and DML triggers using the database-level catalog view, *sys.triggers*, or the server-level view, *sys.server_triggers*.

The syntax for creating a DDL trigger is:

```
CREATE TRIGGER trigger_name
ON { ALL SERVER | DATABASE }
[ WITH <ddl trigger_option> [,... n ] ]
{ FOR | AFTER } { event_type | event_group } [,...n ]
AS { sql_statement [ ; ] [,...n ] | EXTERNAL NAME < method specifier > [ ; ] }
```

<ddl_trigger_option> ::=

```
    [ ENCRYPTION ]
    [ EXECUTE AS Clause ]
```

Here is an example of a database-level DDL that prevents a table from being altered or dropped:

```
CREATE TRIGGER DONOTCHANGEIT
ON DATABASE
FOR DROP_TABLE, ALTER_TABLE
AS
    PRINT 'You must contact a DBA before dropping or altering tables!'
ROLLBACK
;
```

TEST DAY TIP

Make sure that you are familiar with the difference between database-level and server-level DDL triggers.

EXERCISE 4.8

IMPLEMENTING A DATABASE-LEVEL DDL TRIGGER

You have an application vendor that supports their application and the supporting SQL Server database remotely. When support issues or maintenance requests arise, this vendor can log in securely and make database schema changes. Unfortunately, the vendor is not aware of any of the in-house custom development so you want to make sure that you are aware of the changes that they are making so that you can head off any problems arising from table changes.

Write a DDL trigger that will keep track of any table changes and the User who has made the change. You will want to save this table audit information to an audit table.

The SQL Server Configuration Manager

In SQL Server 2005, The Surface Area Configuration Tool was used to manage SQL Server features such as Database mail and xp_cmdshell. In SQL Server 2008, the Surface Area Configuration Tool no longer exists; it has been replaced with the SQL Server Configuration Manager. Available as a Facet at the server instance level, Database mail, CLR integration, and xp_cmdshell, as well as a few other features, can be enabled or disabled through this new interface.

Configuring & Implementing...

Secure by Default

Many SQL Server 2008 features are installed in a disabled state requiring that they be manually enabled when needed.

Following the "secure by default" philosophy of SQL Server, many features are installed in a disabled state so that potential attackers cannot exploit them. In order to use functions such as the Service Broker, database mail, xp_cmdshell, and CLR they have to be enabled by using the Surface Area Configuration Tool. This tool can be accessed by **Right Clicking** on the Server and selecting **Facets**. Then by selecting **Surface Area Configuration** from the drop-down menu, you will see a screen that looks like Figure 4.11.

Be aware of what features are automatically set up to run when SQL Server 2008 is installed and which functions need to be enabled, as well as their purpose.

Figure 4.11 Surface Area Configuration Facet

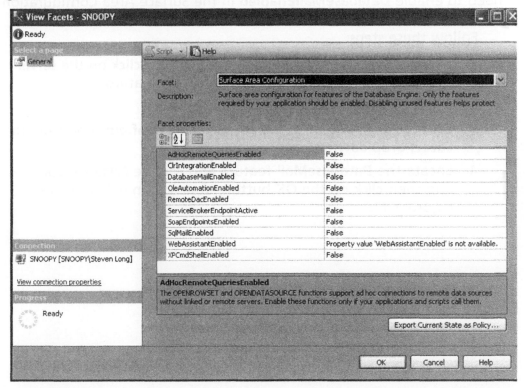

Keep in mind that you only want to enable what you know you need. Enabling unused functions will leave your server vulnerable to potential attack.

Using sp_configure will display configuration settings for the current server. Changes can also be made using sp_configure. Configuration settings can be viewed by executing the following:

```
USE Master;
GO
EXEC sp_configure;
```

EXERCISE 4.9

ENABLING DATABASE MAIL

You have just installed SQL Server 2008 and you are upgrading databases from SQL Server 2005. Many of the databases that you administer contain stored procedures that produce email alerts or emails containing reports.

Since the Database mail feature is installed in a disabled state, we need to enable **DatabaseMailEnabled** in the Surface Area Configuration tool.

Follow these steps:

1. In the SQL Server Management Studio, **right-click** on the server that you wish to enable the DatabaseMail feature.

2. Select Facets from the menu

3. On the Facets screen, select **Surface Area Configuration** from the Facets drop down.

4. Locate the DatabaseMail feature and change **False** to **True** and then click on the **OK** button. Your screen will look like Figure 4.12.

Figure 4.12 Enabling the DatabaseMail Feature

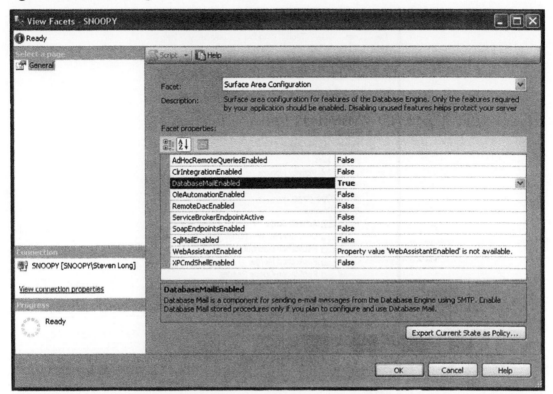

Security and SQL Agent

SQL Server job steps often need to do more than just execute Transact-SQL.
In order to perform tasks such as operating system commands (*CmdExec*), executing
Integration Services packages, and PowerShell scripts, various credentials often
associated with Windows logins are necessary. SQL Server Agent Proxies mapped to
the appropriate credentials necessary can be created and associated with one or
more SQL Server Agent subsystems. You can associate one or more proxies with the
available SQL Server Agent subsystems. See Figure 4.13 for the SQL Server Agent
subsystems that you can associate to proxies.

Figure 4.13 SQL Agent Proxies

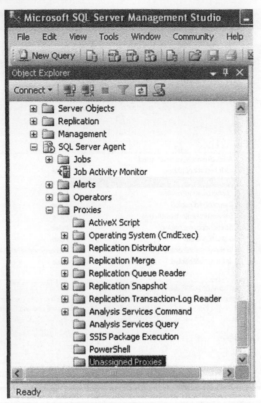

EXAM WARNING

Make sure that you understand how the SQL Server Agent uses Proxies and how the credentials used need to have sufficient permissions to perform the required task but not in excess of what is needed.

EXERCISE 4.10

CREATE A SQL SERVER AGENT PROXY

You need to set up a Proxy so that SQL Server Agent can create a file in a Windows directory. We need to set up a credential for the Proxy to use and then set up the Proxy that can work with the SQL Server Agent Operating System (CmdExec). Make sure that SQL Server Agent has been started before attempting this exercise.

1. In the SQL Server Management Studio expand the Security folder.

2. Right-Click on the Credentials folder and select **New Credential**.

3. In the New Credential window assign a Credential name, select a User or Built-in security principal as the Identity, then provide and confirm a password.

4. Click the **OK** button to create the Credential.

5. Now locate the Proxies folder under SQL Server Agent, right-click on the Operating System (CmdExec) folder and select **New Proxy**.

6. In the General section enter a Proxy name in the Proxy name: textbox.

7. In the Credential textbox, enter the Credential that you created in Step 3.

8. In the Subsystem section, make sure that Operating System (CmdExec) is checked.

9. Click **OK** to create the Proxy.

Service Accounts and Permissions

A few changes have taken place in SQL Server 2008 starting with the Windows local groups that have been a component of SQL Server installs prior to SQL Server 2008. The groups are still created but rights are no longer granted in SQL Server for them. Accounts selected during the SQL Server install process for service startup are the only accounts that are granted rights in SQL Server.

To maintain a secure environment you should always run SQL Server services using the minimum amount of user rights. Additional permissions should not be granted to these accounts. It is recommended that a specific user account or domain account should be used for SQL Server services. Shared accounts should not be used. A Domain User account that does not have permissions as a Windows administrator is more appropriate for use with SQL Server services. Using the Network Service account for SQL Server services is not recommended since it is shareable. A Network Service account should only be considered if it can be ensured that no other services that use the account are installed on the computer.

EXAM WARNING

Make sure that you are aware of which types of accounts are recommended for use with SQL Server services.

Figure 4.14 shows the SQL Server Services in the SQL Server Configuration Manager.

Figure 4.14 SQL Server Configuration Manager—Service Properties

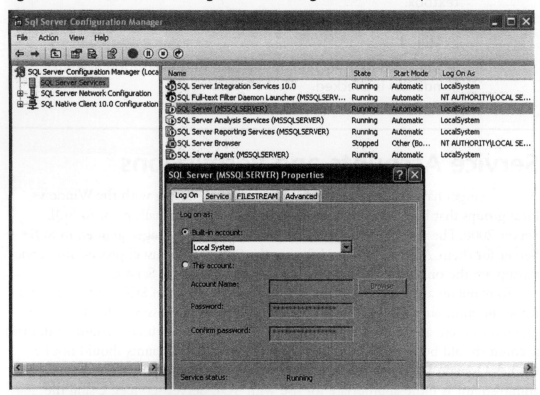

EXERCISE 4.11

GET FAMILIAR WITH THE SQL SERVER CONFIGURATION MANAGER

We do not want to modify anything at this point but it is a good time to get familiar with the SQL Server Configuration Manager. Let's take a look around:

1. Open up the SQL Server Configuration Manager.

2. Click on **SQL Server Services** as in Figure 4.14.

3. Right-click on **SQL Server Agent** and click **Properties**.

4. In the properties window on the Log-on tab click on the drop-down menu for **Built-in account:** and take a look at the available accounts.

5. Now take a look on the Service tab and locate the Start Mode. Remember that at the time of install this service is disabled. This is where you would change the Start Mode in order to enable SQL Server Agent.

6. Select the **Cancel** button to exit Properties.

7. Exit the SQL Server Configuration Manager.

Domain Service Accounts versus Local Service Accounts

There are a few restrictions to which account types can be used by SQL Server services. There are a couple things to consider when selecting an account type to use with a SQL Server service.

If the service must access file shares or use link server connections to other SQL servers, using a minimally privileged Domain user account is the best option.

The Local service account is a built-in account with the same level of access to resources and objects as members of the Users group. The limited access of the local service account can help safeguard the system if individual services or processes are compromised.

You cannot use a Local Service account for SQL Server or SQL Server Agent.

Summary of Exam Objectives

The key to securing SQL Server is understanding the security hierarchy and the elements involved. The security of how principals connect to SQL Server and how the numerous features that require access to resources beyond SQL Server should be managed using The Principle of Least Privilege.

SQL Server security is managed through Logins, Database users, Server-level Roles, Database-level Roles, and the service accounts needed by the various SQL Server features. It is very important to carefully consider the level of permissions needed for each user and establish the most precise match in order to reduce security risk exposure. If a user has access to SQL Server resources that they will not use or do not need, the policy has been violated.

Doing your due diligence to understand what a specific permission or role has access to will help you best fit the user's permissions to their specific needs and establish the best secured SQL Server possible.

Exam Objectives Fast Track

Principals

- ☑ Windows-level principals are a Windows Domain Login, Windows local login, and Windows group.

- ☑ SQL Server-level principals are a SQL Server login, SQL Server login mapped to a Windows login, SQL Server login mapped to a certificate, and SQL Server login mapped to an asymmetric key.

- ☑ Database-level principals are a Database User, Database user mapped to a SQL Server login, Database user mapped to a Windows login, Database user mapped to a certificate, Database user mapped to an asymmetric key, Database Role, Application Role, and Public Role.

Roles

- ☑ Like a Windows group, SQL server provides two roles, fixed server-level and database-level roles.

- ☑ Fixed Server-level Roles have a serverwide scope.

- ☑ Database-level Roles have a database-level scope and custom database-level roles can be created.

The "Principle of Least Privilege"

☑ Do not grant more permissions than necessary.

☑ Be familiar with what each specific permission enables a user to accomplish.

☑ Inadvertently elevated permissions can pose a significant security risk.

Users

☑ Users are database-level principals and are created to access resources within a database.

☑ User and Log-in names should match.

☑ Users can be added to any one or more of the available database roles.

Schemas

☑ Schemas are collections of database objects such as tables, views, and procedures.

☑ Permissions can be granted to individual schemas within a database, providing a powerful way to manage permissions.

☑ It is not necessary to grant access to each object within a schema when granting permission to the schema.

Permissions

☑ Designing a permissions strategy is important when properly securing database objects.

☑ Permissions can be granted on the database, on each schema within the database, or by granting permissions on each individual table or view within the database.

☑ Grantable permissions include SELECT, VIEW CHANGE TRACKING, UPDATE, REFERENCES, INSERT, DELETE, EXECUTE, RECEIVE, VIEW DEFINITION, ALTER, TAKE OWNERSHIP, and CONTROL.

Auditing

☑ Automatic auditing is available in SQL Server 2008 Enterprise, and can be enabled using SQL Server Audit.

☑ Auditing can be enabled at the Server level and Database level.

☑ CDC and DDL triggers are methods of tracking data changes and structural changes to the database schema.

The SQL Server Configuration Manager

☑ Properties for SQL Server services can be managed in the Surface Area Configuration Facet.

☑ SQL Server features such as Database mail and CLR integration are not enabled by default.

☑ Disabling unnecessary features helps secure SQL Server.

Security and SQL Agent

☑ SQL Server Agent Proxies are set up and mapped to the appropriate credentials to perform the required tasks.

☑ Credentials can be associated with one or more SQL Server Agent subsystems.

☑ One or more Proxies can be associated with the available SQL Server Agent subsystems.

Exam Objectives
Frequently Asked Questions

Q: What is considered to be a Principal in SQL Server 2008?

A: Any entity that requests SQL Server Resources.

Q: What is the definition of "The Principle of Least Privilege"?

A: Only give permissions that are needed. Giving more access violates this principle.

Q: Can you modify Server-level Roles?

A: No, Server-level Roles are fixed and cannot be modified.

Q: Can you create your own Database-level Roles?

A: Yes, Database-level Roles can be created to better fit a user's security requirements.

Q: What is the most secure Authentication Mode and why?

A: The Windows Authentication Mode is more secure because it is managed by the Windows operating system and subject to additional Windows password policies.

Q: What SQL Server tool is used to enable the DatabaseMail feature in SQL Server 2008?

A: The Surface Configuration Tool.

Q: When working with SQL Server services such as SQL Server Agent, which tool do you use?

A: SQL Server Configuration Manager.

Q: When setting up SQL Server services that need to perform tasks outside of the local server, which account type should you use?

A: Domain Service Accounts.

Self Test

1. Which of the following is considered a Principal?

    A. SQL Server

    B. SQL Server Integration Services

    C. SQL Server Login

    D. SQL Server Agent

2. Which of the following is a securable object in a database schema?

    A. Database User

    B. Database

    C. Service

    D. Procedure

3. Which of the following fixed server-level roles enables a member to add and remove linked servers?

    A. Securityadmin

    B. Setupadmin

    C. Serveradmin

    D. Dbcreator

4. You have a team member who needs the ability to manage SQL Server logins and you do not want them to have permissions to perform any task on the server. Their responsibilities include resetting logins as well as granting, denying, and revoking database-level and server-level permissions. Which of the following server-level roles best fits their permissions requirement?

    A. Serveradmin

    B. Sysadmin

    C. Securityadmin

    D. Processadmin

5. Which of the following can be added to a server-level role?

    A. Windows group

    B. Database User

    C. Database-level role

    D. Domain server account

6. Which of the following database-level roles limits a user's permissions to reading all data from all user tables?

    A. db_owner

    B. db_datareader

    C. db_datawriter

    D. db_securityadmin

7. You have a user that requires the permissions to drop a database and perform any configuration and maintenance tasks. Which of the following actions would violate "The Principle of Least Privilege"?

    A. Adding the user to the db_datareader role

    B. Adding the user to the db_owner role

    C. Adding the user to the sysadmin role

    D. Giving the user permission to modify tables

8. Which of the following can be mapped to a database User?

    A. Windows account

    B. Login

    C. Windows group

    D. Domain account

9. Although T-SQL can be used to create database users, which of the following SQL Server management tools can also be used?

    A. SQL Server Configuration Manager

    B. The Surface Area Configuration Fact

    C. Microsoft Visual Studio

    D. SQL Server Management Studio

10. Which of the following defines mixed mode authentication?

    A. Connections can only be made using Windows accounts.

    B. Connections to SQL Server can be made with either Windows accounts or with SQL Server Logins.

C. Connections can only be made using SQL Server Logins.

D. Connections can only be made using database Users.

11. Which of the following is an advantage to using mixed mode authentication?

A. Users can connect from unknown or untrusted domains

B. The Kerberos security protocol

C. Windows password policies

D. Windows accounts are maintained outside of SQL Server

12. Which SQL Server tool is changed in the Authentication Mode?

A. SQL Server Configuration Manager

B. Visual Studio

C. SQL Server Management Studio

D. The Surface Area Configuration Facet

13. When you change the Authentication Mode, what action do you need to perform before the mode change takes effect?

A. Reboot the server operating system.

B. Lock out all the database users.

C. Restart SQL Server Agent.

D. Restart the SQL Server Instance.

14. Jose has ownership of database tables in database A and database B, both of which reside in the same instance of SQL Server where cross database ownership chaining has been enabled. Jose uses a database view in database A to join both tables in order to retrieve the needed data. Jose grants Jack permission to use her database view. What other permissions need to be granted in order for Jack to retrieve data using Jose's view?

A. Jack needs to be granted read permissions to the table in database B that is used by the view.

B. Since cross database ownership chaining is enabled in this instance, no additional permissions need to be granted.

C. The tables used by the view in database A and B need read permissions granted to Jack.

D. Jack cannot use Jose's view since she is the owner. Jack will need his own view and permissions.

15. Which of the following is an Execution Context?

   A. Execute sp_srvrolepermission

   B. Execute sp_dbfixedrolepermission

   C. Execute sp_addrole

   D. Execute AS user_name

16. Which of the following is captured when using CDC?

   A. SELECT

   B. ALTER

   C. EXECUTE

   D. UPDATE

17. You want to prevent changes to tables in one of the databases in your SQL Server instance since changes to any of the tables can cause the associated client application to stop functioning. What can be implemented to prevent any tables from being changed?

   A. A stored procedure

   B. A database-level DDL trigger

   C. A DML trigger

   D. A server-level DDL trigger

18. Which tool is used to enable SQL Server features not automatically enabled, such as Database Mail, when SQL Server is installed.

   A. SQL Server Configuration Manager

   B. Visual Studio

   C. Surface Area Configuration Facet

   D. SQL Server Installation Center

19. What is used to apply appropriate subsystem permissions to SQL Server Agent tasks?

   A. Database-level roles

   B. Proxies

    C. Server-level roles

    D. Credentials

20. Which SQL Server tool is use to manage SQL Server services such as the SQL Server Agent and SQL Server Integration services?

    A. Surface Area Configuration Manager Facet

    B. SQL Server Management Studio

    C. Visual Studio

    D. SQL Server Configuration Manager

Self Test Quick Answer Key

1.	**C**	11.	**A**
2.	**D**	12.	**C**
3.	**B**	13.	**D**
4.	**C**	14.	**B**
5.	**A**	15.	**D**
6.	**B**	16.	**D**
7.	**C**	17.	**B**
8.	**B**	18.	**C**
9.	**D**	19.	**B**
10.	**B**	20.	**D**

MCTS SQL Server 2008 Exam 432

Managing Data Encryption

Exam objectives in this chapter:

- **Understanding Transparent Data Encryption**
- **Encryption Keys**
- **Cell- and Column-Level Encryption**
- **EFS Encryption (Through the OS)**
- **Third-Party Tools**

Exam objectives review:

- ☑ Summary of Exam Objectives
- ☑ Exam Objectives Fast Track
- ☑ Exam Objectives Frequently Asked Questions
- ☑ Self Test
- ☑ Self Test Quick Answer Key

Introduction

Many enhancements have been made to SQL Server 2008 in area data encryption. These enhancements are covered in detail in this chapter. We'll explain encryption keys along with encryption and encryption key management. It's important to understand *when* and *why* to use different forms of encryption as well as *how* to implement.

In SQL Server 2008 there are a number of different options available. In this chapter, we will touch on some of the benefits of using encryption. Finally, we'll talk about some other types of encryption that are available, such as Windows built-in Encrypting File System (EFS).

Understanding Transparent Data Encryption

With overall concern for data privacy as well as the increase in regulatory compliance in the area of data security, encryption is used as a method for protecting data. Encryption is a way of keeping data confidential and unreadable by unauthorized users.

SQL Server 2008 introduced transparent data encryption (TDE) to provide the ability to encrypt entire databases, data, and log files without the requirement of application changes and with minimal performance impact. TDE protects data files at rest by encrypting the data and log files for a specific database on disk. When a transaction requires data from data or log files, the specific data pages are decrypted in memory. Once a TDE is enabled on a database, all the database's backups are encrypted. Also, tempdb will be encrypted. It's interesting to note that filestream data (the new filestream data types) will be encrypted as well.

In the past, it was necessary to either use a third-party tool, or if you were using cell-based encryption, you would need to change the data type of the column to varbinary. This would on occasion require changes to foreign keys and make searching more complex. The application needed to make an additional call to encrypt and decrypt the data. Transparent data encryption will allow you to apply encryption to a database without having to change the application that accesses the database. All data types, keys, indexes, and so on can be used to their full potential without sacrificing security or leaking information on the disk when using transparent data encryption.

Test Day Tip

Be sure to understand which features are available in which editions, especially when it comes to encryption!

Head of the Class...

Encryption and Security

But why use encryption if my database server and facilities are physically secure?

While this may be true for your organization, the reality is the backups of the data and log files are susceptible to loss or theft. Often the backups are stored off site. Ideally they should be stored in a physically secure location. More importantly, without TDE or another post-backup encryption method, the backup data and log files can be restored on another server and information can be stolen.

More often than not, the use of backup files and tapes used for disaster recovery at remote sites as focused more for availability and the security concerns of the media are not as rigid.

The economic realities of outsourcing and downsizing have increased the real threat of losing data to theft. Regulations to maintain data privacy and integrity have created a key operational requirement in the data management business. While database encryption is not required to protect information as such as credit card, Social Security numbers, and other personally identifiable information (PII) to meet the government regulations per Sarbanes-Oxley and the Health Insurance Portability and Accountability Act of 1996 (HIPAA), it is an easier and more cost-effective solution for a growing international business problem.

Requirements

The SQL Server 2008 Enterprise and Developer editions only support TDE. TDE-encrypted databases cannot be attached/used by other editions.

Enabling TDE

The steps to enable TDE on a database consist of the following:

1. Creating a service master key at the database instance.

2. Creating a database master key and associated certificate in the master database.

3. Creating a database encryption key in the user database to be encrypted.

4. Setting the user database to use the encryption.

Before describing the mechanics of creating the components of the TDE, let's review the SQL Server 2008 cryptography scheme.

At its core TDE uses the Windows Data Protection application program interface (API) to encrypt and decrypt keys and data. In Microsoft Window 2000, the Data Protection API (DPAPI) was introduced to encrypt and decrypt data. Since SQL Server 2005, DPAPI is used to generate a key for the database instance, also known as the service master key (SMK). At the time the database instance is created, the SMK is generated by using the DPAPI functions and the Windows credentials of the SQL Server service account. The SMK is then encrypted using local machine credentials. The SMK can only be decrypted by the service account used during the SQL Server setup processing at installation or by an account that has access to the SQL Server service account's Windows credentials or belongs to the same security group.

The SMK is used to encrypt and decrypt all other keys within the SQL Server instance.

Table 5.1 describes the key hierarchy in TDE to enable the encryption of a user database.

Table 5.1 The Hierarchy in TDE

Step	SQL Server Key	Dec	SQL Command
| 1 | Service master key (SMK) | Created by SQL Server at the time of setup, the SMK is encrypted using Windows Operating System's Data Protection API (DPAPI) and the local computer key that is derived from the Windows credentials of the SQL Server service account and the computer | ```
BACKUP SERVICE MASTER
KEY TO FILE =
'<complete path and
filename>' ENCRYPTION
BY PASSWORD =
'<password>';
``` |
| 2 | Master database's database master key (DMK) and certificate | The DMK is created and stored in the *master* database.

The DMK is a symmetric key used to protect the private keys of certificates and asymmetric keys that are present in the database. When it is created, the DMK is encrypted by using the Triple Data Encryption Standard (DES) algorithm and a user-supplied password.

Please note it is best practice to back up the DMK in a safe location. | USE master
GO
CREATE MASTER KEY ENCRYPTION BY PASSWORD = 'some password';
CREATE CERTIFICATE *tdeCert* WITH SUBJECT = *'TDE Certificate'*;
BACKUP CERTIFICATE *tdeCert*
TO FILE = 'path_to_ file'
WITH PRIVATE KEY (FILE = 'path_to_ private_key_file', ENCRYPTION BY PASSWORD = ' TDE cert p@sswurd'); |

Continued
```

Table 5.1 Continued. The Hierarchy in TDE

Step	SQL Server Key	Dec	SQL Command
3	Database encryption key (DEK)	The DEK is stored in the boot record of the encrypted database and is created by using the DMK certificate.	CREATE DATABASE ENCRYPTION KEY WITH ALGORITHM = AES_256 ENCRYPTION BY SERVER CERTIFICATE tdeCert

TDE encrypts the data and log files using the database encryption key (DEK) and the specified encryption algorithm defined for the target TDE database. The complexity of encryption in TDE arises from the SQL Server encryption hierarchy to create and use the DEK as well as the specified encryption algorithm.

SQL Server supports a number of encryption algorithms including 3 Key Triple DES, AES with 128-bit, 192-bit or 256-bit key. The definition or best practices of encryption keys are beyond the scope of this book, but as a general rule strong encryption algorithms require more CPU resources and in generally are slower.

Configuring & Implementing...

Backup Service Master Key

Creating a backup of the SMK is the first activity that should be done after an SQL Server installation. The SMK backup should be stored in a secure, off-site location. It's important to protect and have a backup of the SMK, as it's the "Master Key" to encryption for the SQL database.

```
BACKUP SERVICE MASTER KEY TO FILE = '<pathname>\<filename>'
ENCRYPTION BY 'password'
```

Continued

Note that the password specified in the T-SQL commands are subject to password complexity checks.

The complexity checks include the following:

- Must be eight characters long with a maximum of 128 characters
- Does not contain all or part of the user account name
- Contains characters from three of the following:

Uppercase Latin letter (A thru Z)

Lower case Latin letters (a thru z)

Numeric digits 0 thru 9

Non-alphanumeric characters: ! (exclamation point), $ (dollar sign), # number sign, % (percent sign).

How Data Is Encrypted

Using the DEK and encryption algorithm, TDE encrypts the database files at the database page level. Before the data page is written to disk, each page is encrypted and decrypted when the page is read into memory. The page is encrypted and decrypted using the DEK.

When TDE is enabled for a database, the is_crypted column in the sys.databases view is changed to 1, indicating the database is set for encryption. The encryption scan process then starts and scans all the database files associated to the database and encrypts the database files using the specified encryption algorithm specified when creating the DEK. The encryption process takes a shared lock on the database and encrypts each page in the specified database.

During this process, detaching the database or file structure changes is denied. Data existing in the log file is not encrypted. Entries in the log file are encrypted entries after the encryption process is complete.

Once the database encryption is complete, all database encryption and decryption is performed in memory. Each page is decrypted when the page is read into memory and each page is encrypted before the data page is written to disk. The page is encrypted and decrypted using the DEK.

Encryption Keys

Keys are the basis of cryptography, the science of obfuscating/hiding information. There are two types of keys used in SQL Server for encryption, symmetric and asymmetric.

Symmetric keys use the same password to encrypt and decrypt data, whereas asymmetric keys use one password (public key) to encrypt the data and another (private key) to decrypt the data. While the symmetric key processing is faster than asymmetric keys, the limitation is that using the same password for encryption and decryption is not as secure as asymmetric keys.

Certificates and asymmetric keys are both used in asymmetric encryption.

A certificate, also known as public key certificate, is a digital object that binds a digital signature to a person or organization. Certificates are generally used to identify a person or organization. In other words, a certificate is an electronic form of an id card. Often used as containers for asymmetric keys, certificates have addition attributes such as issuer and expiration information as specified in the Internet Engineering Task Force (IETF) X.509v3 standard.

Within SQL Server 2008, certificates provide several purposes. Certificates can be used for the following tasks:

- To encrypt connections and data transmitted across a network between SQL Server and a client application
- To support database mirroring
- To encrypt Service broker conversations
- To sign Integration services packages to sign the source.

Certificates in SQL Server are securable objects, meaning permissions can be granted or denied to them, just as with tables and views.

SQL Server can use internally generated certificates or externally generated ones.

Key Management

Key management provides the ability to:

- Create new database keys
- Back up and restore server and database keys
- Restore, delete, and change keys.

By default, TDE locally stores all encryption keys with SQL Server, and provides the ability to export keys to files to be archived.

As more information is encrypted, the management of these keys becomes challenging. External key management (EKM), new in SQL Server 2008, provides organizations with hardware-based security modules (HSM) or external software based-security modules to interface with SQL server to externally manage the encryption keys as well as enable encryption and decryption.

TEST DAY TIP

Understand that TDE is not a form of access control. If someone has permission to access the database, TDE will not prevent them from accessing the data. Note that they do not need permission to the DEK or a password.

Database Encryption Keys

Note that there are a number of encryption algorithms you may choose when you create the DEK. Not all operating systems support all types of encryptions, so be sure you select an encryption scheme that is supported by the operating system you'll be using.

The algorithms supported by SQL Server are: WITH ALGORITHM = {AES_128 | AES_192 | AES_256 | TRIPLE_DES_3KEY}

Best Practices for Managing Database Keys

Managing SQL Server keys consists of creating, deleting, and modifying database keys, as well as backing up and restoring database keys.

To manage symmetric keys, you can use the tools included in SQL Server to do the following:

- Back up a copy of the server and database keys so that you can use them in the event a server needs to be reinstalled, or for a planned migration.

- Restore a previously saved key to a database to a new server instance. This enables a new server instance to access existing data that it did not originally encrypt.

- Re-create keys and re-encrypt data in the unlikely event that the key is compromised. As a security best practice, you should re-create the keys periodically to protect the server from attacks that try to decipher the keys.

Cell- and Column-Level Encryption

Introduced in SQL Server 2005, cell-level encryption provides developers with a granular level of encryption for their applications that have specific data security requirements. While this provides the application development much flexibility, it has additional performance and space costs.

First of all, cell- and column-level encryption require that the column to be encrypted in the table schema be stored as a *varbinary* object. This requires additional processing and disk space overhead. Specifically, most data is usually a character or numeric field. So there is an additional performance cost of converting the data to and from a *varbinary* type in addition to the processing required to encrypt and decrypt each cell in a table.

Column-level encryption is established in the same manner as cell-level encryption. The main difference between cell- and column-level encryption is that the expense of column-level encryption is magnified by the number of rows in the table.

Let's look at an example of encrypting social security numbers in an *Employees* table (see Figure 5.1). For demonstration purposes, we have a plaintext (*Customer_SSN*) and an encrypted column (*Customer_SSN_asym*) to contain social security information.

Figure 5.1 A List of Employees

Customers	
Column Name	Data Type
🔑 Customer_id	int
Customer_first_name	varchar(50)
Customer_last_name	varchar(50)
customer_SSN	varchar(20)
customer_SSN_asym	varbinary(MAX)
customer_address	varchar(50)
customer_address_2	varchar(50)
customer_city	varchar(50)
customer_state	char(2)
customer_zip	int
customer_zip_ext	int

First let's create the asymmetric key to use for encrypting the *customer_SSN_asym* column. For simplicity we have created a simple asymmetric key with password that is used for decryption.

```
CREATE ASYMMETRIC KEY dboAsymKey AUTHORIZATION dbo
  WITH ALGORITHM = RSA_2048
ENCRYPTION BY PASSWORD =N'SylviaP@zzwurd';
```

Now let's load a couple of records.

```
DECLARE @ssn1 VARCHAR(100) = '111-11-1111'
DECLARE @ssn2 VARCHAR(100) = '222-22-2222'
INSERT into Customers (Customer_first_name, Customer_last_name, Customer_SSN,
Customer_SSN_asym, customer_city, customer_zip)
VALUES
('Jane', 'Smith' , @ssn1, EncryptByAsymKey(AsymKey_ID('dboAsymKey'),@ssn1),
'Redmond', 98052),
('John', 'Doe', @ssn2, EncryptByAsymKey(AsymKey_ID('dboAsymKey'),@ssn2),
'Redmond', 98054);
```

Now let's decrypt the column *Customer_SSN_asym* to ensure that it is the same as the column *Customer_SSN* (see Figure 5.2).

Figure 5.2 Decrypting Employees' Social Security Numbers

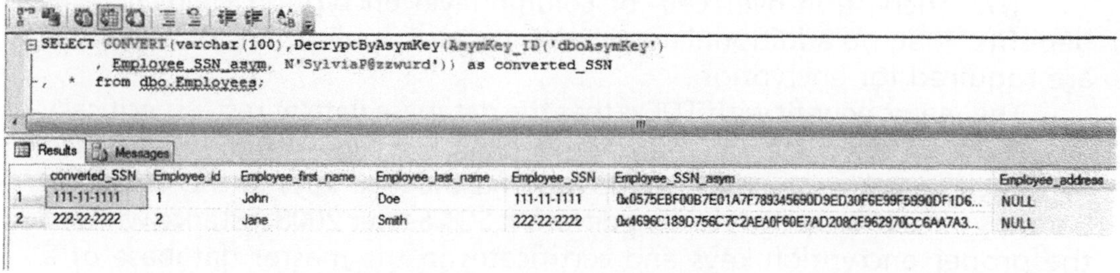

This example illustrates the breakdown of an encryption chain in that a key requires input of a password. The key problems here include the following:

- How and where to store the password for decrypting asymmetric keys.
- The built-in functions **CONVERT** or **CAST** are needed to format the data properly.
- Although not applicable to the social security numbers, per se, column encryption does not allow for the field to be used as an index and can not be used in a search (WHERE) clause.

These issues can be solved with an investment of software architecture design and programming resources.

Head of the Class...

Pros and Cons of Data Encryption

Which form of encryption is the best for my situation?

Well the answer is, it depends!

Data encryption provides a great security benefit, but it also has performance, disk, and administrative costs.

Asymmetric key encryption algorithms are more compute intensive than symmetric key algorithms. In general, it is more efficient to encrypt large datasets using a symmetric key, while encrypting the symmetric key with an asymmetric key.

Although TDE encryption overhead is low, there is a small overhead cost in the operational performance and additional disk space for the encrypted database. Most of the encryption impact is at the time of encrypting the database.

TDE encryption over cell- or column-level encryption yields various benefits. First, no additional application code or application code changes are required for encryption.

The major benefit with TDE is that the database data at rest—specifically any copies of the database's data, log, and backup files—cannot be accessed without the proper security permissions via the TDE keys in the database. Backups cannot be recovered to a different SQL Server 2008 instance without the proper encryption keys and certificates in the master database of a different SQL Server instance.

EFS Encryption (Through the Operating System)

Windows 2000 introduced Encrypting File System (EFS), which provides file- and folder-level encryption using the Windows operating system. Generally, EFS is used to protect user data on a single computer used by a single user. Both EFS and TDE protect *data at rest*. Data at rest refers to data on a disk. The security issues arise when files containing personal (or organizational) identifiable information are susceptible to access to nonauthorized users.

Currently TDE does not support encryption of the system databases (master, model, msdb, and resource). However, in some scenarios EFS can be used to encrypt the system databases. One of the disadvantages of using EFS is that SQL Server will experience decreased performance. Since EFS does not support asynchronous input/output (I/O), I/O will be serialized and become the bottleneck. Synchronous I/O is a key database management system requirement to support high-concurrent transactions on enterprise database and applications.

In most cases, EFS is not a good idea; certainly with SQL Server 2008, TDE will be a better choice.

Another issue to using EFS on database files is in the area of administration. Although key management is simpler with the use of the Windows certificate store and offers a data recovery path if keys are lost, database administration would require file administration privileges on the operating system level. Most organizations do not provide this operating system privilege to a database administrator.

Head of the Class...

Concurrency and the Use of EFS

Although it is possible to implement EFS on SQL Server databases, the concurrency requirement makes EFS an unattractive option for encryption. The whole point of using SQL Server over a flat file or an Excel file is concurrency. The primary job of a database is to ensure that database transactions are processed concurrently while maintaining data integrity. The cost of application and database bottleneck and performance degradation would be greater than the savings and safety of using EFS.

EFS in a Clustered Environment

Special care must be taken to use file encryption in a clustered environment. All cluster computer accounts and the virtual computer account must be trusted for delegation. The cluster needs to be configured to support Kerberos authentication. The files need to be encrypted on the cluster's drive.

Configuring & Implementing...

Effect on Backups

Once a SQL database is encrypted via TDE, all the backups are also encrypted. That's the easy part.

Backups and secure storage of the SMK, certificates, and DMKs are critical. If these keys are lost, the backups are not recoverable. It is recommended best practice to back up the keys and certificates in SQL Server. As part of the database backup process, store the certificate and private key backup files in a physically safe location but separate from the database backup files.

Backing up these keys to a secure location is critical; if the keys fall into the wrong hands they could be used to access your data. If it's worth encrypting, it's important to keep the keys safe. The following example illustrates the SQL command to back up the DEK and certificate.

```
BACKUP CERTIFICATE [TESTDB_TDE]
TO FILE = 'SAFE_LOCATION\TESTDB_TDE.2009.01.01.cer'
WITH PRIVATE KEY
   (FILE = 'SAFE_LOCATION\ TESTDB_TDE.2009.01.01.pvk',
   ENCRYPTION BY PASSWORD = 'TESTDB TD3 P@sswurd')
```

Restoring Encrypted Backups to Another Server or Instance

If you attempt to restore an encrypted backup to a server that doesn't have the correct server certificate, you'll get the following error:

```
Msg 33111, Level 16, State 3, Line 1
Cannot find server certificate with thumbprint
'0xCA741797B81ED8D1305EAFF5A747BA51E1DAB80D'.
Msg 3013, Level 16, State 1, Line 1
RESTORE DATABASE is terminating abnormally
```

On the new server you need to create the server certificate from the backup of the server certificate from the server where the database originated from. The syntax for restoring is as follows:

```
USE master
GO
-- create database master key if it doesn't exist
CREATE MASTER KEY ENCRYPTION BY PASSWORD = 'sleepyguyjn$&adsg12345'
GO
--create TDE certificate from backup
CREATE CERTIFICATE Cert1
FROM FILE = 'c:\Cert''
WITH PRIVATE KEY (FILE = 'c:\MyCertPrivKey',
DECRYPTION BY PASSWORD = 'this#is#a$ecret')
GO
```

Once the key has been restored, you may restore the database normally, and you should see no errors.

```
RESTORE DATABASE MarksEncryptedDB
FROM DISK = 'c:\MarksEncryptedDB_11_14_2008.bak'
WITH move 'MarksEncryptedDB' TO 'e:\data\MarksEncryptedDB.mdf',
move 'MarksEncryptedDB_log' TO 'f:\logs\MarksEncryptedDB.ldf',
recovery
GO
```

Third-Party Encryption Tools

SQL Server 2008 introduced Extensible Key Management (EKM). EKM provides an interface for third-party vendors to manage and store encryption keys outside of the database. EKM also enables third-party vendors to register their modules in SQL Server. Once registered, SQL Server can use the third party encryption tools as well as key management functionality.

A number of third-party tools are available, such as NetLib's Encryptionizer SQL Server encryption. These tools are not necessarily on the test, but it's a good idea as a DBA to be aware they exist and they do have their place in the encryption scheme.

HSM devices provide a central system that is dedicated to performing symmetric and asymmetric cryptography to one or multiple servers on a network, thereby providing better performance. In essence, it offloads the encryption and decryption processing as well as provides a remote key management solution

Important Note: In SQL server 2008, EKM does not support certificates.

Summary of Exam Objectives

Encryption is a way of keeping data confidential and unreadable by unauthorized users. SQL Server 2008 includes several enhancements in the area of encryption, including Transparent Data Encryption (TDE). Without TDE or another post-backup encryption method, backup data and log files can be restored on another server and information can be stolen.

Keys are the basis of cryptography, and SQL Server 2008 uses symmetric and asymmetric keys for encryption. Symmetric keys use the same password to encrypt and decrypt data while asymmetric keys use one password (public key) to encrypt the data and another (private key) to decrypt the data.

Cell-level encryption, a form of encryption that was introduced in SQL Server 2005, provides developers with a granular level of encryption for their applications that have specific data security requirements. Encrypting File System (EFS) provides file and folder-level encryption using the Windows. Generally, EFS is used to protect user data on a single computer used by a single user.

Extensible Key Management (EKM) is a feature introduced in SQL Server 2008. EKM provides an interface for third-party vendors to manage and store encryption keys outside of the database as well as provide the ability to register their modules in SQL Server. In SQL Server 2008, EKM does not support certificates. Once registered, SQL Server can use the third party encryption tools as well as key management functionality.

After reading this chapter, you should have an understanding of why and when you should use the various types of encryption that SQL Server 2008 offers.

Exam Objectives Fast Track

Understanding Transparent Data Encryption

- ☑ SQL Server 2008 introduced transparent data encryption (TDE) to provide the ability to encrypt entire databases, data, and log files without the requirement of application changes and with minimal performance impact.

- ☑ Without TDE or another post-backup encryption method, the backup data and log files can be restored on another server and information can be stolen.

- ☑ At its core TDE uses the Windows Data Protection application program interface (API) to encrypt and decrypt keys and data.

Encryption Keys

☑ Two types of keys are used in SQL Server for encryption, symmetric and asymmetric.

☑ Symmetric keys use the same password to encrypt and decrypt data, whereas asymmetric keys use one password (public key) to encrypt the data and another (private key) to decrypt the data.

☑ External key management (EKM), new in SQL Server 2008, provides organizations with hardware-based security modules (HSM) or external software based-security modules to interface with SQL server to externally manage the encryption keys as well as enable encryption and decryption

Cell- and Column-Level Encryption

☑ Introduced in SQL Server 2005, cell-level encryption provides developers with a granular level of encryption for their applications that have specific data security requirements.

☑ Cell- and column-level encryption require that the column to be encrypted in the table schema be stored as a *varbinary* object.

☑ The main difference between cell- and column-level encryption is that the expense of column-level encryption is magnified by the number of rows in the table.

EFS Encryption (Through the OS)

☑ Windows 2000 introduced Encrypting File System (EFS), which provides file- and folder-level encryption using the Windows operating system.

☑ One of the disadvantages of using EFS is that SQL Server will experience decreased performance. Since EFS does not support asynchronous input/output (I/O), I/O will be serialized and become the bottleneck.

☑ Although it is possible to implement EFS on SQL Server databases, the concurrency requirement makes EFS an unattractive option for encryption.

Third-Party Encryption Tools

☑ SQL Server 2008 introduced Extensible Key Management (EKM)

☑ EKM provides an interface for third-party vendors to manage and store encryption keys outside of the database. EKM also enables third-party vendors to register their modules in SQL Server.

☑ A number of third-party tools are available, such as NetLib's Encryptionizer SQL Server encryption.

Exam Objectives
Frequently Asked Questions

Q: What is DPAPI and how is it used in TDE architecture?

A: DPAPI (Data Protection Application Programming Interface) is a set of cryptographic program interface introduced with Microsoft Windows 2000 and later Microsoft Windows operating systems. The API consists of two functions: CryptProtectData (used to encrypt data) and CryptUnprotectData (to decrypt data). DPAPI is the top level of the TDE encryption hierarchy and is used by SQL Server to protect the service master key (SMK) for the database instance. In TDE, the SMK is used to protect the next level of the SQL Server encryption hierarchy, specifically the database master key (DMK), and is stored in the master database. The last encryption level for TDE is the database encryption key (DEK). Using a certificate created for the DMK, the DEK is encrypted using the DMK certificate from the master database and then stored in the specified user database.

Q: What is Transparent Data Encryption?

A: Transparent Data Encryption (TDE) provides the ability to encrypt entire databases, data, and log files without the requirement of application changes and with minimal performance impact.

Q: What edition of SQL Server is required to use TDE?

A: TDE is only available on SQL Server 2008 Enterprise and Developer editions.

Q: When is the Service Master Key created?

A: The SMK is created during SQL Server setup of the instance. It uses the DPAPI and the SQL Server service credential to generate the SMK.

Q: What is the Service Master Key used for?

A: The SMK is at the core of SQL Server encryption. An SMK is generated on a SQL Server instance when an instance is first started. The SMK is used to encrypt various components on the database instance including linked server passwords, database master keys, and credentials. The SMK is encrypted by using the local computer. By default, the SMK is created by the Windows service account using the Windows data protection API and the local server key.

Q: Where are the certificates stored?

A: By default all keys and certificates are stored in the SQL Server. With EKM and HSM vendors, keys can be stored outside of SQL Server.

Q: What is the difference between cell- and column-level encryption?

A: Cell- and column-level encryption require that the column to be encrypted in the table schema be stored as a *varbinary* object. The main difference between cell- and column-level encryption is that the expense of column-level encryption is magnified by the number of rows in the table.

Self Test

1. What level of protection does transparent data encryption (TDE) provide?

    A. Cell-level

    B. File-level

    C. Database-level

    D. Drive-level

2. Which of the following best describes transparent data encryption (TDE)?

    A. Data in specific columns is encrypted.

    B. Encrypts everything, such as indexes, stored procedures, functions, keys, etc, without sacrificing security or leaking information on the disk.

    C. Once data types have been changed to varbinary, everything will be encrypted.

    D. Once database schemas have been changed to accommodate data encryption, everything will be encrypted.

3. Which edition of SQL Server 2008 offers transparent data encryption (TDE)?

    A. SQL Server 2008 Express

    B. SQL Server 2008 Standard

    C. SQL Server 2998 Web

    D. SQL Server 2008 Enterprise

4. Which SQL Server permissions are required to enable transparent data encryption (TDE)?

    A. Permissions associated with creating the user database.

    B. Permissions associated with making server-level changes.

    C. Permissions associated with creating a database master key and certificate in the master database and control permissions on the user database.

    D. Permissions associated with the operating system administrator's account.

5. The first step to enabling TDE on a database is to create a database master key (DMK). Which of the following is the correct syntax for creating a DMK?

    A. CREATE MASTER KEY ENCRYPTION BY PASSWORD = 'somepassword';

    B. ALTER DATABASE tdedatabase SET ENCRYPTION ON;

    C. CREATE CERTIFICATE tdeCert WITH SUBJECT = 'tdeCertificate';

    D. CREATE DATABASE ENCRYPTION KEY WITH ALGORITHM = AES_256 ENCRYPTION BY SERVER CERTIFICATE tdeCert;

6. It is very important to back up the Certificate with the private key once it has been created and to copy it to a secure location other than on the server that it was created on. Which of the following is the correct syntax to back up a Certificate?

    A. CREATE CERTIFICATE tdeCert WITH SUBJECT = 'tdeCertificate';

    B. BACKUP CERTIFICATE tdeCert TO FILE = 'path_to_file' WITH PRIVATE KEY (FILE = 'path_to_private_key_file', ENCRYPTION BY PASSWORD = 'cert password');

    C. CREATE DATABASE ENCRYPTION KEY WITH ALGORITHM = AES_256 ENCRYPTION BY SERVER CERTIFICATE tdeCert;

    D. ALTER DATABASE tdedatabase SET ENCRYPTION ON;

7. Which sys catalog view is used to monitor the progress of an encryption scan?

    A. Sys.configurations

    B. Sys.certificates

    C. Sys.key_encryptions

    D. Sys.dm_database_encryption_keys

8. When transparent data encryption (TDE) is enabled, which of the following system catalog views will the database show as encrypted?

    A. Sys.databases

    B. Sys.all_objects

    C. Sys.all_columns

    D. Sys.configurations

9. When transparent data encryption (TDE) is enabled, database backups are encrypted. If you cannot locate the associated Certificate and private key files, what happens to the data if you need to restore the encrypted database?

    A. Everything will be readable since the Certificate and private key can be recreated.

B. The data will not be readable since the Certificate and private key files are lost.

C. Only encrypted columns will not be readable.

D. Everything will be readable once the database encryption has been turned off in the master database.

10. In which edition of SQL Server 2008 is cell-level encryption available?

A. Only in the Enterprise edition

B. Only in the Web edition

C. Only in the Workgroup edition

D. All SQL Server 2008 editions

11. When using cell-level encryption which data type is required in order to encrypt the data?

A. VARCHAR

B. No special data type is necessary

C. BINARY

D. VARBINARY

12. What is the query performance impact when using cell-level encryption?

A. There is a positive query performance impact since there are only specific columns that are encrypted.

B. There is a negative query performance impact since data types have to be converted from varbinary to the correct data type and primary keys and indexes are not used, resulting in full table scans.

C. There is a negative query performance impact unless TDE has been enabled.

D. There is a positive query performance impact as long as TDE has been enabled.

13. Cell-level encryption is best used in which of the following?

A. Performance sensitive situations

B. All situations

C. Limited access control through the use of passwords situations

D. Situations when a password is not needed to access the encrypted data

14. Which of the following best describes the difference between symmetric and asymmetric keys?

    A. An asymmetric key uses the same password to encrypt and decrypt the data and a symmetric key uses a public key to encrypt the data and a private key to decrypt the data.

    B. An asymmetric key uses the same password to encrypt and decrypt the data and a symmetric key uses a private key to encrypt and a public key to decrypt the data.

    C. A symmetric key uses the same password to encrypt and decrypt the data and an asymmetric key uses a public key to encrypt and a different password/ private key to decrypt the data.

    D. A symmetric key uses the same password to encrypt and decrypt the data and an asymmetric key uses a private key to encrypt and a different password/ public key to decrypt the data.

15. Which of the following best describes EFS encryption?

    A. Encryption occurs at the file-level.

    B. Encryption occurs at the database-level.

    C. Encryption occurs at the cell-level.

    D. Encryption occurs at the server-level.

16. When you are using Encrypting File System (EFS) with SQL Server, which SQL server account must have access to file encryption keys encrypting any database files?

    A. SQL Server agent account

    B. Database server, service account

    C. SA account

    D. SQL executive account

17. In which of the following is EFS best used?

    A. Web server

    B. Database server

    C. Workstation

    D. Application server

18. Which of the following best describes SQL Server 2008 Extensible Key Management?

    A. Enables third-party EKM/HSM vendors to register their modules in SQL Server

    B. Enables easy management of Encrypting File System (EFS) encryption

    C. Enables easy creation of an EKM key with another EKM key

    D. Enables easy back up of a database encryption key

19. In which of the following editions of SQL Server 2008 is Extensible Key Management available?

    A. Workgroup edition

    B. Web edition

    C. Enterprise edition

    D. Express edition

20. Which system stored procedure is used to enable Extensible Key Management?

    A. Sys.dboption

    B. Sys.sp_configure

    C. Sys.sp_helpdb

    D. Sys.sp_addextendedproc

Self Test Quick Answer Key

1. **C**

2. **B**

3. **D**

4. **C**

5. **A**

6. **B**

7. **D**

8. **A**

9. **B**

10. **D**

11. **D**

12. **B**

13. **C**

14. **C**

15. **A**

16. **B**

17. **C**

18. **A**

19. **C**

20. **B**

Chapter 6

MCTS SQL Server 2008 Exam 432

Managing High Availability

Exam objectives in this chapter:

- Defining High Availability
- SQL High-Availability Options
- Expandability

Exam objectives review:

- ☑ Summary of Exam Objectives
- ☑ Exam Objectives Fast Track
- ☑ Exam Objectives Frequently Asked Questions
- ☑ Self Test
- ☑ Self Test Quick Answer Key

Introduction

This chapter focuses on how high availability ensures that your application is always available. High availability incorporates such technologies as clustering, log shipping, and replication. These will all be covered in detail, along with the pros and cons of each, in the following chapter. Clustering has improved in SQL 2008, and these improvements are discussed in this chapter.

It's important to have a good understanding of the differences between each technology, as each has its own advantages and disadvantages.

Hot-add CPU support and hot-add memory support will also be explained in this chapter.

We will also touch on fault tolerant disk subsystems, like RAID 5 and mirroring. It's important to understand the performance implications of using different disk systems.

Defining High Availability

The basic definition of high availability is a solution that allows for a hardware or software failure but continues to run. Simple high-availability solutions include using redundant hard drives, redundant memory, or redundant CPUs in your server. As you get into more advanced solutions you will have redundant servers to provide redundancy in the event of a software problem on one of the servers. In this case the backup server will take over for the failed server either manually or automatically.

When you are dealing with redundant hard drives you have several options. When you configure redundant hard drives you can create what is called a RAID array—a Redundant Array of Inexpensive Disks (or Redundant Array of Independent Disks). The exact array depends on the number of disks you have, the protection level you want, and the performance that you want to get from the system.

All RAID levels require at least two disks, and some require three or four disks. Each RAID level has its strengths and weaknesses. Understanding these strengths and weaknesses is key in deciding which RAID level you should select.

RAID 0 (also called a stripe set) is where all the disks are written to at the same time. The upside to this RAID level is that it is very fast, and you get the most amount of storage for your money. The downside to this system is that there is no redundancy. Because there is no redundancy in a RAID 0 array, if any disk in the RAID array fails then all data on the RAID array is lost.

RAID 1 (also called a mirror set) is where you have two disks, and as data is written to the first disk, it is also written to the second disk at the same time.

Although there is no performance benefit when using this RAID level, the data is fully protected since if either hard drive fails the data is still available by the use of the hard drive that has not failed. This is one of the most expensive RAID options available to you because you are paying for two hard drives and only getting the space and speed of one hard drive. When the failed hard drive is replaced all the data is copied from the working hard drive to the new hard drive.

RAID 5 is the most common RAID level in use. It provides the best of both RAID 0 and RAID 1, but at a lower cost per gigabyte. A RAID 5 array requires at least three hard drives. RAID 5 writes data to all the disks except for one. The last disk is used to store parity information for the data on the other disks in the array. This allows the system to continue to function in the event of a disk failure. It also allows the system to re-create the missing information once the failed hard drive is replaced. Because this parity data must be calculated for each write operation the writes to a RAID 5 array will be slower than some of the other RAID levels that are available.

RAID 6 is a new RAID level that is really starting to show itself in the database world. A RAID 6 array requires at least four hard drives. RAID 6 is very similar to RAID 5, except that it uses two separate parity drives. This allows the RAID array to survive two different disk failures without running the risk of losing any data on the array. Like the RAID 5, array a RAID 6 array will be slower than some of the other RAID levels that are available because of this parity calculation.

RAID 10 is the highest performing, highest redundancy, most expensive RAID solution that is available to you. A RAID 10 array requires at least four hard drives. A RAID 10 array is in essence two RAID 0 arrays for performance that are then mirrored together for redundancy. Because of the mirroring that is being done this is the most expensive RAID level available per gigabyte. Because of this cost many people will prefer to use RAID 5 or RAID 6.

Exam Warning

Microsoft has started putting RAID questions on the exams. A basic understanding of the RAID levels is key to passing those questions.

When dealing with the storage for many of the high-availability solutions, we will be looking at a high-end storage solutions such as a SAN. Some of these solutions require these high-end storage solutions. When using these high-end solutions keep in mind that your hard drives could be sharing the physical spindles on the SAN with other systems in your environment. When you are troubleshooting systems using these SAN solutions, make sure that you know what else is using the hard drives, even if it not a SQL Server. If you have a file server on the same spindles as a SQL Server, that can be fine, unless the file server is defragging the hard drive, in which case the disks will perform poorly without no indication on the SQL Server as to the problem.

When selecting the hardware for your backup server, you can usually cut a few corners to save a couple of bucks. The goal of your backup server is to run the system. It doesn't have to run it at the same speed as your production environment does, it just needs to keep it running while the primary or active system is being repaired or rebooted. As an example, if your system runs fine on two processors but runs great on eight, get a two-processor server for the backup machine. This will help keep the costs of the backup server a bit more reasonable.

The licensing costs are different for each technique that we will be discussing; therefore the license ramifications will be covered in each section throughout this chapter.

SQL High-Availability Options

There are many different high-availability options that are available to you as a production database administrator. Each of these various options has its strong points and its weak points, and in addition to knowing how to use each method, it is very important that you know when each method should be used.

Log Shipping

SQL log shipping is a tried-and-true method of keeping your SQL Server online. Microsoft has supported log shipping within SQL Server since at least SQL Server 2000. By using standard T/SQL backup and restore commands you could have set up log shipping back in the SQL 7 and prior days.

Log shipping (also known as transaction log shipping) is the process by which you take a full backup of your database and restore it to the destination machine. You then back up the transaction log every few minutes (usually between 5 and 15 minutes) and then copy the log backup to the remote machine. After the file has been copied you then restore the transaction log to the remote machine or machines, rolling forward any transactions that are in the transaction log. This gets you an exact duplicate of the primary database.

Log shipping does not require special hardware, nor does it require that the backup server be configured like the production server. However it does make it much easier when the two servers are using like hardware, and most specifically when the hard drives are laid out exactly the same.

SQL Server 2008 includes log shipping in all the Editions of SQL Server that you have to pay for—in other words, Web, Workgroup, Standard, and Enterprise Editions. This is a big change from SQL Server 2000 when log shipping was an Enterprise-only feature.

TEST DAY TIP

Unless a question specifically mentions the Edition of SQL Server that you are using, licensing or features that are missing between editions are not going to be the answer. Unless stated otherwise you can usually assume that you have the Enterprise Edition of all products involved in the question.

To begin log shipping, connect to the server you wish to be the source of the log shipping in the Object Explorer. Right-click the database to bring up the context menu and select **Tasks**, then **Ship Transactions Logs** as shown in Figure 6.1. You can also get to this Transaction Log Shipping menu by selecting Properties from the first context menu.

Figure 6.1 Database Context Menu

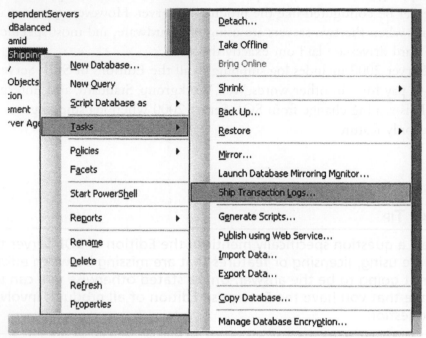

On the screen that appears, check the check box at the top of the window that says **Enable this as a primary database in a log shipping configuration**. This will enable the **Backup Settings** button. Click this button and specify the two paths listed, as well as file deletion settings. These folders must exist before you can click **OK** on the main settings page. Keep in mind that SQL will delete these log files even if they have not been restored to the backup server so don't set them too short. The backup job name will be the name of the SQL Agent job with which the backups are taken. In the example shown in Figure 6.2 the backups will be made to the C drive of the SQL1 server, which is the primary server. The backups will be kept for 72 hours with an alarm raised if no backup is taken within an hour. You can enable backup compression on the transaction log backups; however this usually is not needed unless your backup server is across a WAN.

TEST DAY TIP

The exams are designed to make sure that you know the official way to perform tasks, which is not always the quickest or easiest way. This is a key distinction that you should be aware of when you are taking the exams.

Figure 6.2 Transaction Log Backup Settings

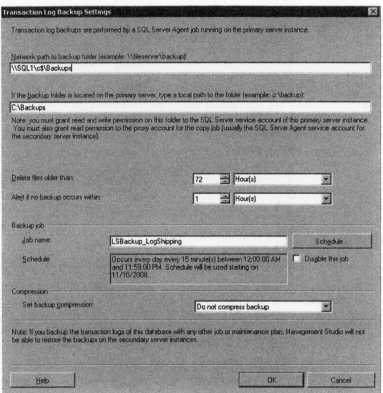

After you complete the backup settings, you can tell the database server to which Instances you want to ship the logs. Single-click the **Add** button in the middle of the window, then click **Connect** on the new window. On the first of three tabs on this window you can tell SQL Server if you want SQL to handle the full backup automatically, use an existing full backup, or whether you have manually restored the full backup. On the second tab you give SQL Server the folder on the backup server to which you wish to have it copy the files. You also give it the name of the SQL Agent job that will copy the files from the primary system to the backup system. On the third tab you tell SQL Server which state to leave the database in—No Recovery or Standby. You can also tell it how long to wait before restoring a log file, and when to raise an alert if no log has been restored. You also name the restore job that the SQL Server Agent will run. After clicking **OK** you are taken back to the Log Shipping page of the database properties as shown in Figure 6.3.

Figure 6.3 Transaction Log Shipping Page Filled Out

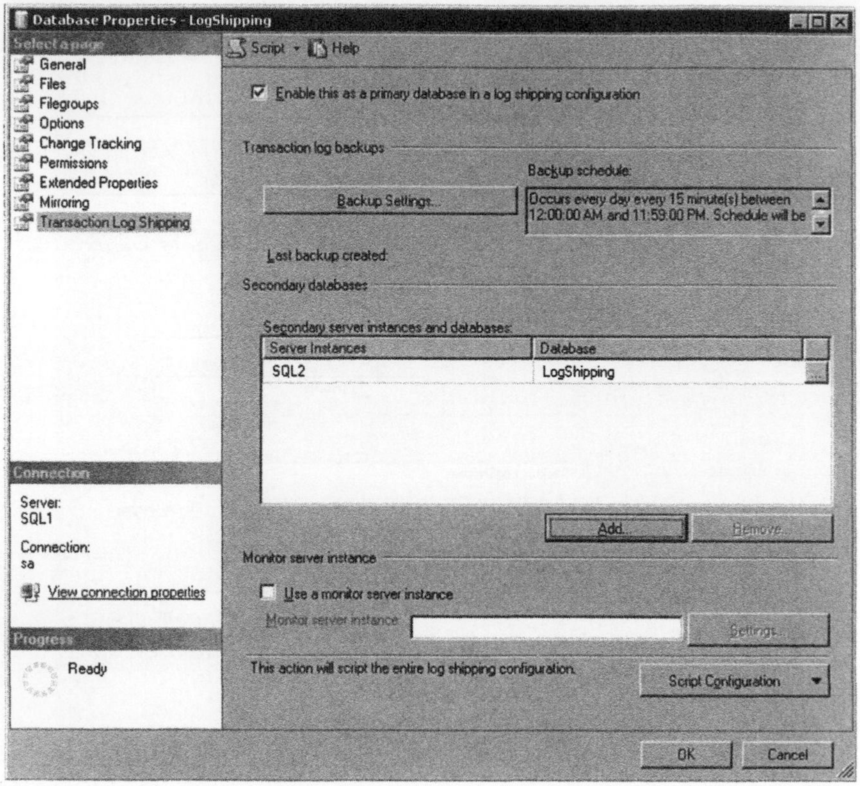

If you wish to configure a remote instance to monitor the log shipping then check the **Use a monitor server instance** check box (which is unchecked in Figure 6.3) and click the **Settings** button. On the Log Shipping Monitor Settings page that appears, select the **Instance to Monitor Log Shipping** and click **OK**.

For additional redundancy you can ship your logs to several servers by clicking the **Add** button in the middle of the Log Shipping properties page of the Database Properties as shown in Figure 6.3.

EXERCISE 6.1

SETTING UP LOG SHIPPING

1. Set up log shipping between two instances of Microsoft SQL Server 2008.

2. You want to ship the logs every 15 minutes and wait at least one hour before restoring them to your backup server.

3. Be sure to review the code by clicking the **Script Configuration** button so that you are also familiar with the T/SQL stored procedures that are used.

All this log shipping can be done via T/SQL code as well. Before clicking OK you can script out the commands to the clipboard, a new file, or a new query window. This will produce a several hundred line set of scripts with about 100 lines of T/SQL code to be run against each database server involved.

There is no quick and easy way to fail over a log shipping database. To fail over the database, disable the log shipping jobs on the backup server and the primary server. Copy any uncopied backup files from the backup share to the destination folder on the backup server. Restore these logs to the backup server. If the primary server is still available, back up the transaction log and restore it to the backup server. You can then bring the backup database online by either selecting the *WITH RECOVERY* option when restoring the last transaction log or by running the *RESTORE LOG* command with the *WITH RECOVERY* option without specifying a log file to restore as shown here. After you have put the backup database into read/write mode you can configure your clients to connect to the now active server.

```
RESTORE LOG LogShippingDB WITH RECOVERY
```

To fail the log shipping back to the primary server, go through the configuration process using the backup server as the primary server, and the normal production server as the backup server. Once the servers are in sync repeat the failover process to bring the primary server online and reset the log shipping with the backup server as the destination once again.

When considering log shipping as an option for your high-availability solution keep in mind that each server that you are using for log shipping must be licensed for use. If you have a production server and a backup server both machines will need to be licensed.

Mirroring

Database mirroring is a relatively new technique that can be used for high availability. Microsoft introduced database mirroring in SQL Server 2005, and it went live as a production-ready product with SQL Server 2005 SP1. Because database mirroring was not ready when SQL Server 2005 was released, this turned many people off of database mirroring. However, since then, database mirroring has proven itself to be a very reliable solution.

Database mirroring can be configured in a few different ways. The first option you have is whether you want to run it in synchronous mode, or in asynchronous mode. Synchronous mode most typically is used when the two database servers are relatively close to each other. This is because when using synchronous mode, changes are written to the primary server, then written to the mirrored server. Once the mirrored server has completed the write it sends an acknowledgment back to the primary server, which then sends an acknowledgment back to the client. Because of this double processing that must be done, all transactions will take longer to process. This increase in time will be at least double the amount of time. If the servers are far away from each other and the transaction contains a lot of data then the amount of time will be more than double because you have to wait for the data to be transmitted from one server to the other.

When running in asynchronous mode commands are written to the first server, and then an acknowledgment is sent back to the client. After the transaction is committed the transaction then is sent to the mirror server. The mirror server then sends an acknowledgment back to the active server.

When you are running in synchronous mode you have another choice to make. You can run it in either automatic failover or manual failover. Manual failover is exactly that; the administrator manually tells the SQL Server to fail back to the mirror system from the active system. With automatic failover you configure a third SQL Server to monitor the two SQL Servers, called the Witness. In the event that the active SQL Server fails or is rebooted the Witness tells the backup server to take over as the active server. If you are using database mirroring to provide high availability between sites you should run your witness at the backup site. This way if the primary site goes offline the witness is still online to tell the backup server to come online.

Asynchronous mode is also called high performance mode, and synchronous mode is also called high safety mode. This is because the asynchronous mode will perform faster than synchronous mode; synchronous mode guarantees that the mirror database will always have the exact same transactions written to it.

EXAM WARNING

Make sure that you are clear about asynchronous and synchronous modes, as well as which one is high performance mode and which one is high safety mode. In the exams Microsoft will use both names.

Like most Microsoft technologies, database mirroring comes with its own set of terminology to learn. When working with database mirroring the server that is currently writeable is called the Principal. The server that is receiving the new transactions from the Principal is called the mirror. The server that monitors the Principal and the mirror, and that decides if auto-failover is required, is the witness.

Head of the Class...

Selecting the Correct Solution

When you are deciding which high-availability solution to select keep in mind that not every solution is right for every situation. All too often companies select the wrong high-availability solution, which they then get locked into. One company I worked for, which was in the mortgage industry, insisted on using Double Take for replicating data to the backup site. Now, don't get me wrong—Double Take is a great product, just not in this case.

We had a very slow network connection between the two sites, a single T1 was the total WAN link we had to work with, and all of IT had to replicate everything from our office in Southern California to our backup facility in the Midwest somewhere. No matter how many times Double Take would overload its cache and tell the SQL Server to stop accepting new transactions, management would not let us use another technology to move the data. It turns out that there was a press release several years ago that had said that we were using Double Take to move all our data, and they didn't want to look like they had made a mistake.

In this case (this was SQL 2000 at the time) log shipping or replication would have been a much better option for us to use. If we had used replication and we had replicated all our stored procedures then we would have needed to transmit only the commands and not all the block level changes, and our WAN footprint would have been much smaller.

Database mirroring can be configured via the wizard in the SQL Server Management Studio, or manually via T/SQL. Database mirroring is a database-by-database high-availability solution. This means that each database must be configured individually. Only user databases can be configured for database mirroring. This is because both servers involved in database mirroring must be active at the same time. Because of this, when you are mirroring your databases you must create your logins, SQL Jobs, and SSIS packages on both servers manually. However for the flexibility that database mirroring gives you, this is a small price to pay.

Whether you use the automatic failover or manual failover you will want to make sure that all your clients are using the SQL Server 2005 driver or newer. If you use the SQL Server 2005 driver or newer you can include the Failover Partner setting within the connection string. This will allow the client to automatically know when the database has been failed over and automatically connect to the correct server.

```
Single Server Connection String: Data Source=YourServer;Initial
Catalog=AdventureWorks;Integrated Security=True;
```

```
Mirrored Server Connection String: Data Source=YourServer;Initial
Catalog=AdventureWorks;Integrated Security=True;Failover Partner=BackupServer;
```

EXAM WARNING

Make sure that you are familiar with telling the clients how to connect to both the primary database and the mirror.

In the event that the primary server is offline, and you have failed over to the backup server, your users will notice a slight delay when connecting to the SQL Server because the connection to the first server must fail before the driver will automatically connect to the backup server. Once you bring the primary server back online the connection speed will go back up to the normal speed. This is because the client will connect to the primary server, which will then inform the client that the database is the mirror. The client will then automatically connect to the backup server and begin running its command.

To configure Database Mirroring, right-click on the database you wish to mirror and select **Tasks** then **Mirror** as shown in Figure 6.4. You can also right-click on the database you wish to mirror and select **Properties** then select the Mirroring option from the page list. Before you can configure database mirroring you must take a full backup of your database and restore it to the backup server with the NORECOVERY option enabled.

Figure 6.4 Database Mirroring Menu

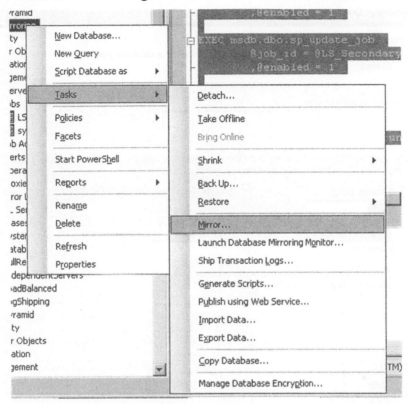

Once you get the Database Mirroring page on the screen, the first thing you must do is click the **Configure Security** button. This button will present you with a wizard, which will walk you through the process. The key screens will be shown here, the others merely described. After clicking **Next** on the introduction page, you are asked if you wish to configure security to include a witness server instance.

After clicking **Next** you are prompted with a page with the Principal and Mirror checked and grayed out with the Witness server either checked or grayed out. If you select No on the first page then this page is skipped.

On the next page you are asked to configure the Database Mirroring Endpoint as shown in Figure 6.5. This is the endpoint that will be created on the Principal server that the Mirror instance (and Witness instance) will use to contact the Principal instance. Port 5022 is the default TCP port number, however this port number can be changed to another port number if required. You can also change the Endpoint name if you so desire.

Figure 6.5 Database Mirroring Principle Server Endpoint Configuration

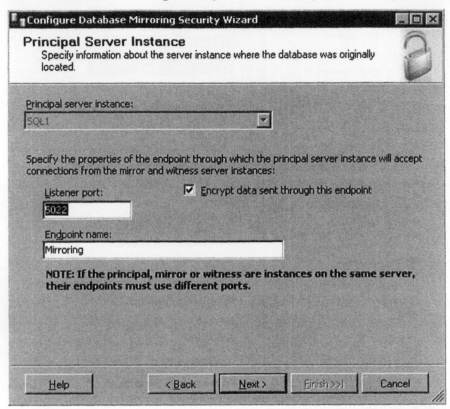

The next page asks you to select the Mirror server instance and set its port number and Endpoint name. If the instances are on different physical servers it is recommended that you use the same port number because this keeps your configuration less complex. If the instances are on the same physical server then you will need to select different port numbers since only one instance at a time can use a single port number.

If you have selected to use a Witness then the next page lets you select the instance to use as the Witness instance as well as the port number and name of the endpoint. The same rules about port numbers apply.

The next page asks you for the service accounts of the SQL Servers. If the machines are on the same domain, or the domains are trusted, then fill out these fields. If the machines are not on trusted domains, or the machines are not on a domain then leave the fields all blank. If the instances are all on the same machine and are running under a local machine account enter the machine account here. Because our lab machines are on a Windows 2003 domain and the instances are running under domain accounts we enter these accounts in the boxes as shown in Figure 6.6. If you are not configuring a Witness then that field will not appear. From this screen you can click **Next** or **Finish** since you have completed the wizard. Doing so will configure the Endpoints and grant the remote instances accounts rights to connect to that Endpoint. Confirm any messages that the wizard gives you.

Since you will have the SQL Servers connecting to each other it is recommended that you run the SQL Servers and SQL Server Agents under a domain account. Although this is not required it is recommended, and it makes database mirroring easier to set up and manage.

Figure 6.6 Database Mirroring Service Accounts Page

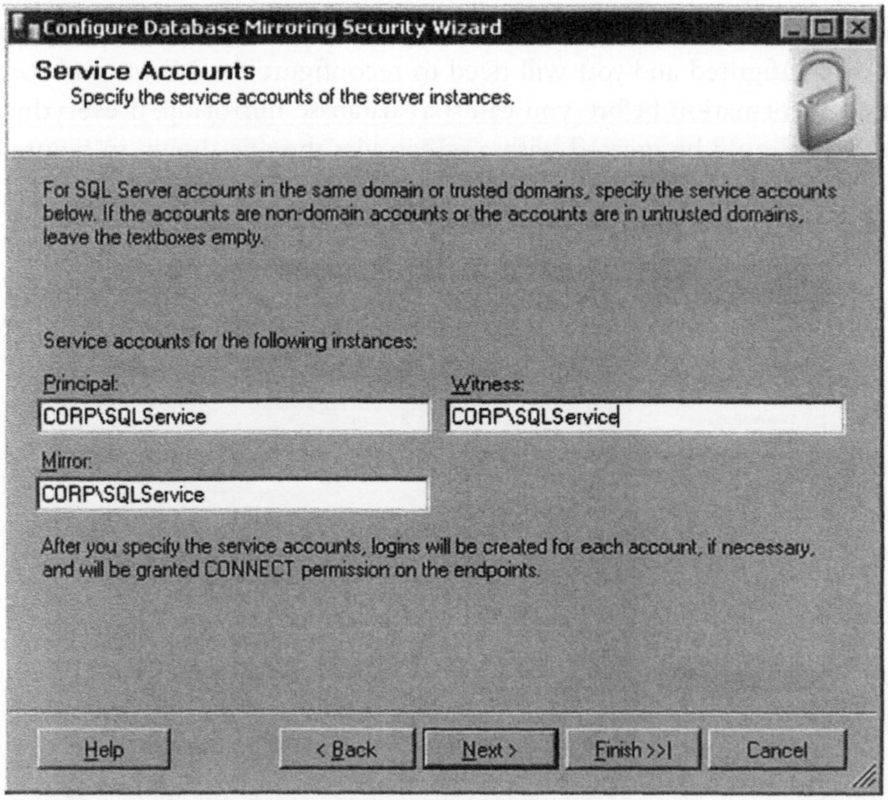

After completing the wizard you will be prompted with a screen similar to the one shown in Figure 6.7.

Figure 6.7 Database Mirroring Confirmation Window

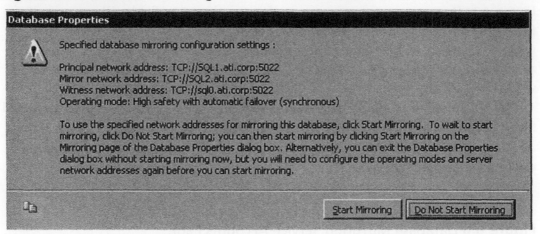

If you select the Do Not Start Mirroring button then database mirroring will not be configured and you will need to reconfigure the Mirror and Partner connection information before you can start database mirroring. If everything goes correctly you should be greeted with a screen like the one shown in Figure 6.8.

Figure 6.8 Database Mirroring Running Correctly

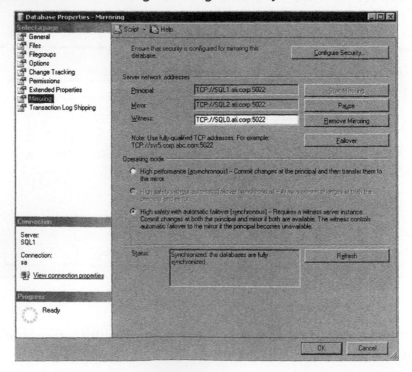

EXERCISE 6.2

SETTING UP DATABASE MIRRORING

1. Set up a database in one instance of SQL Server.
2. Configure database mirroring in High Performance mode.

Once database mirroring is running you will notice some additional information in the object explorer when you are connected to the servers that are being mirrored. The Principal database will show the word Principal, and the Mirror will show "Restoring…" next to it. The Principal will also tell you the status of the mirror. In Figure 6.9 we can see that the mirror is synchronized to the Principal. If the mirror is receiving its log updates the principle will report this as well.

Figure 6.9 Object Explorer Showing Mirrored Databases

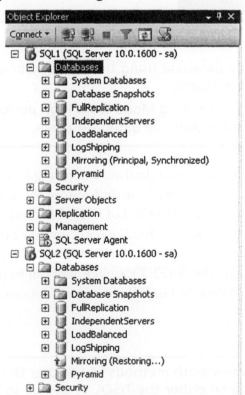

TEST DAY TIP

The exam loves to use syntax questions with T/SQL. This helps gauge if you know the keywords to the commands, or if you can get them in the correct order as well. You might see an answer with SET FAILOVER PARTNER and SET PARTNER FAILOVER and be asked which one is correct.

There are two ways to manually fail over a database. You can either bring up the database mirroring properties (see Figure 6.8) and click the **Fail over** button, or you can use the *ALTER DATABASE* command to failover the database as shown here. If the mirror is completely caught up with all the transactions then the database will fail over. If there are transactions missing from the destination then an error will be returned.

```
ALTER DATABASE Mirroring
    SET PARTNER FAILOVER;
```

EXERCISE 6.3

WORKING WITH DATABASE MIRRORING

1. Fail over the database using the T/SQL command and the Management Studio.

2. Change the Operating Mode from high performance to high safety, then fail over the database again.

You can also configure the entire database mirroring by using the *ALTER DATABASE* command. After you back up and restore the database to the backup server as you did earlier, run the *ALTER DATABASE* command with the *SET PARTNER = 'TCP://SQL2.ati.corp:5022'* parameter. You can then run the *ALTER DATABASE* command with the *SET WITNESS = 'TCP://SQL0.ati.corp:5022'* parameter. Using the *SAFETY* switch you can figure if the database mirroring will use High Safety or High Performance options.

EXAM WARNING

Ensure that you know both methods to fail over the database. The exams can test you on either the T/SQL or the UI, so knowing only one is not enough.

When considering database mirroring as an option for your high-availability solution keep in mind that both the primary server and the mirror must be licensed for use.

Clustering

Windows Clustering via the Microsoft Cluster Service (MSCS) is one of the most effective ways of setting up a high-availability solution. Windows Clustering allows for automatic failover of services in their entirety from one physical server to another. The basic concept of Windows Clustering is that you have a single set of hard drives configured for both servers to access. You then install and configure the Microsoft Cluster Service on both servers in the cluster. When you install the SQL Server on the cluster you will select the option to install on a cluster. This tells the installer to display the additional screens needed for a clustered configuration as well as to register the SQL Services as clustered resources.

When you are running the SQL Server on a cluster the SQL Server Service runs on one and only one node of the cluster at any one time. In the event that you fail the service manually or the service fails over automatically the cluster service simply starts the SQL Server service on the second node of the cluster. This provides you with an incredible amount of uptime. Because the entire SQL Server Instance is clustered you have only a single set of system databases, which means that you need to create logins, SQL Jobs, and SSIS packages only once. And since the entire instance is clustered, not just the individual databases like with database mirroring, every database that you create on the instance is created as part of the cluster and therefore is protected by the high-availability solution.

When setting up a Windows Cluster you are going to set up what is called a quorum drive for the cluster. The quorum drive is used by the cluster to store the cluster-specific settings, as well as some log data. This drive needs to be a shared drive on the cluster created from the storage solution as it needs to be available to all nodes of the cluster. This drive does not need to be very large, 512 megs or 1 gig will work just fine for a quorum drive.

Each service, drive, network share, IP address, host name, and such that are set up to be clustered are called resources. A resource is mapped to the actual service or drive that is controlled by it. The resources can be chained together so that the cluster service knows in what order the resources should be brought online. This is done through what is called dependency chaining. This is done to ensure that resources that are required to run other resources are available. For example, SQL Server will be dependent on the SQL Server Network Name, which is the host name used to access the SQL Server. The SQL Server will also be dependent on hard drives that are required by the SQL Server. The SQL Server Network Name will also be dependent on the SQL Server IP Address resource. This resource is the actual IP address used to connect to the SQL Server Service. Because of this dependency, if any of the drives do not come online or if there is an IP address conflict the SQL Server will not attempt to start.

These resources are then put into a collection called a Resource Group. A Resource Group is a set of resources that fail over from one node of the cluster to another. When you fail over a clustered resource you are actually failing over the entire Resource Group. Each Resource Group is completely independent of each other and no dependencies can be made between Resource Groups. Each SQL Server instance is placed into its own Resource Group. This is done so that if one instance fails over it will not cause other instances to fail over. This also means that you have to set up each instance with its own host name, IP address, and hard drives.

The cluster works by the servers constantly polling each other, looking to see if any of the resources have failed or if a server has gone offline. If the service goes offline the quorum tells another server that has the capability to run the service to start the service on itself. All the machines track whether the machine that is running the quorum is running. In the event that the quorum fails the machines take a vote as to who should begin running the quorum. The winner of this vote then starts the quorum and decides which machines should begin running any other resources that are not running but should be.

When installing SQL Server in a clustered environment, you must first cluster the Windows Servers. Walking through clustering Windows is beyond the scope of this book. Once Windows has been clustered, installing the SQL Server as a Clustered Resource requires launching the SQL Server installer just as you normally would.

Once the initial installer launches and installs the various hotfixes that are required, from the installation screen where you normally click the **New SQL Server Stand-Alone Installation** link, click the link directly below that says **New SQL Server Failover Cluster Installation** as shown in Figure 6.10. This will launch the clustered installer.

Figure 6.10 SQL Server Installation Center—Installation Menu

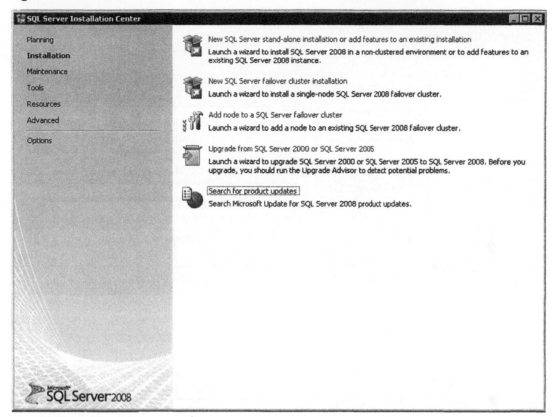

After the install launches the first few screens will be the same as the normal installer. When you get to the page that asks for the instance name, a new field will ask you for the cluster name. This is the host name, which will be unique for this SQL Server instance on the cluster as shown in Figure 6.11.

Figure 6.11 Instance Naming Screen

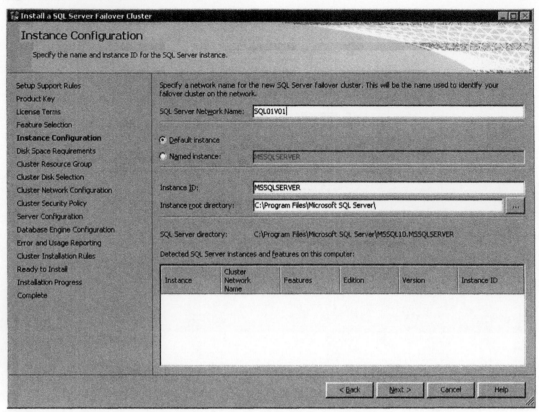

After this you will see the normal Disk Space Requirements screen, after which you will see four new screens to configure the cluster information. The first of these is the screen in which you select the Resource Group in which the SQL Server will be placed. You can select an existing Resource Group, or unlike SQL Server 2005 you can create a new Resource Group.

New & Noteworthy...

Creating Clustered Resource Group During Installation

The ability to create the cluster resource group and select the disks for the Resource Group during the SQL Server 2008 installation is a new feature. In prior versions of Microsoft SQL Server you had to manually create the Resource Group and move the hard drives into the resource group. This addition of this feature into the SQL Server installer is a huge plus for SQL Server.

By placing this functionality directly into the SQL Server installer as DBAs we now need to rely less on the system administrators who assemble the servers and cluster the Windows operating system to set up the resource groups and hard drives. We can now, without having any additional knowledge of the Windows Cluster Administrator tool, set up the SQL Server quickly and easily in a Windows Cluster.

In the example shown in Figure 6.12 an existing Resource Group was selected. This Resource Group was created before the SQL Server 2008 installer was launched and this Resource Group has the disks already located in it.

Figure 6.12 Cluster Resource Group Screen

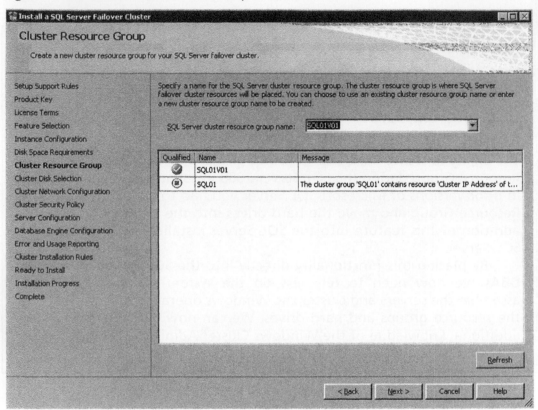

On the next screen select the disks that you wish to use for the SQL Server. You should select any and all hard drives that you will be using for the SQL Server. Additional hard drives can be added later through the Cluster Manager. As you can see in Figure 6.13 only disks that do not have other resources dependent on them are available for use by the SQL Server. In this case the Q drive is in use as the quorum and by the MSDTC service. The Q drive can be used by both of these because both of them are in the same Resource Group.

EXAM WARNING

Microsoft loves to test on new technology and features. The fact that this is new means that it is more likely to be on the exam.

Figure 6.13 Cluster Disk Selection

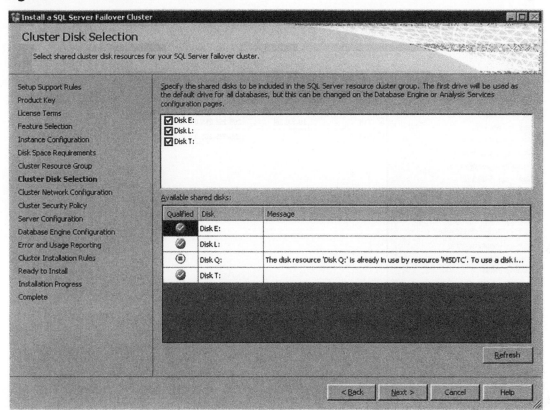

On the next screen you select the IP addresses you will be using for the clustered SQL Server instance. You can select each network that is set up on the cluster and configure a separate IP address for each network. In the example shown in Figure 6.14 there are two networks shown. One is the public network, which is the network that the client computers will connect to the instance. The other is the private network, which is the network that the nodes in the cluster use to talk to each other. The names that are shown are the names of the network connections in the network control panel.

Figure 6.14 Cluster Network Configuration

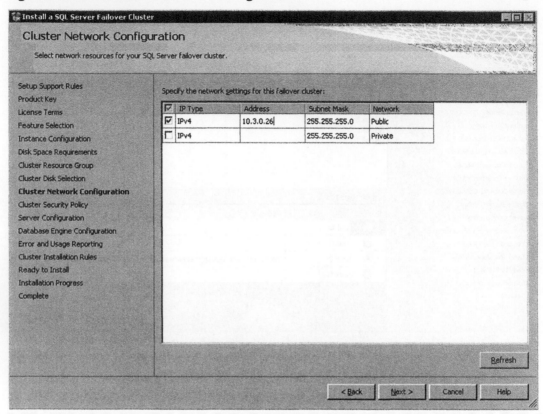

The final cluster page is the Cluster Security Policy screen. This screen will be different depending on the operating system installed, and the domain functional level of your Windows domain. If you are installing SQL Server 2008 on a Windows 2008 operating system and the domain functional level is above Windows 2000 mixed, then you will see the screen as shown in Figure 6.15. If you are installing on a Windows 2003 operating system or a Windows 2008 operating system and your domain functional level is Windows 2000 mixed mode or lower, then the radio buttons will not be displayed as your only option will be to use the domain groups. If you are using Windows 2008 to host your cluster you have the option of using DHCP for your SQL Server. If this option is available to you, a check box will be shown in the grid which allows for DHCP. If the installer determines that DHCP is not an option for you, then it will not show you the check box.

The options allow you to select how you will control which accounts are able to run the SQL Services. It is recommended to use the new service SIDs functionally, but the legacy option of using domain groups is still available as an option.

Figure 6.15 Cluster Security Policy

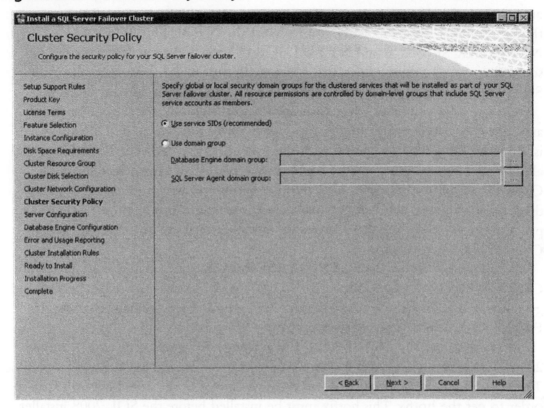

If you are using the domain groups option and you have just created the domain groups shortly before running the SQL Server installer, you may receive an error saying that the domain group or groups do not exist when they do. This is normal as the domain group simply has not replicated to all the domain controllers in the domain. An example of this error is shown in Figure 6.16. Depending on how your domain is configured it could take from a few minutes to over an hour for the domain groups to replicate to all your domain controllers.

Figure 6.16 Cluster Security Policy Error Message

It is recommended that the domain accounts that will be running the services are put into the domain groups before you run the SQL Server installer. Even though the SQL Installer allows you to select the NT AUTHORITY\ NETWORK SERVICE and NT AUTHORITY\SYSTEM accounts to run the services under, the only service that can actually run under these accounts is the SQL Server Browser. All clustered services must run under a domain account.

On the next page you select your authentication mode, set your sa password, and specify yourself as a member of the fixed server role. The Data Directories tab is the same for a clustered install with the exception that the Data Root Drive and all the other folders listed will be based on the first drive letter selected on the Cluster Disk Selection screen. Although the UI will allow you to select from any drive on the system, you will get a validation warning if you attempt to continue past this screen using any drive letters for any fields that are not selected on the Cluster Disk Configuration.

If you enable use of the FILESTREAM you will notice that the Allow Remote Clients To Have Streaming Access To FILESTEAM Data check box is checked and grayed out. It is disabled because having this access is a requirement of using the FILESTREAM in a clustered environment.

In order to use the FILESTREAM in a clustered environment on a Windows 2003 Cluster you must install hotfix KB937444 from the Microsoft Knowledge Base. This is not a public hotfix so you will need to open a ticket with Microsoft CSS in order to get the hotfix. This hotfix must be installed before the SQL 2008 installer is run because the hotfix requires a reboot. The need for this hotfix is detected only on the Cluster Installation Rules page and not at the beginning of the process.

The final difference you will see when installing SQL Server 2008 in a clustered environment is that the Installation Rules page is called Cluster Installation Rules. This will check various requirements against the system to ensure that you meet all the required items. At this point in the installer the process is the same as the stand-alone installer.

After you have completed the installer on the first node of the cluster you must then complete the installation on the other nodes of the cluster. Launch the installer from the SQL Server 2008 DVD and return to the screen shown in Figure 6.10. Then select the Add node to a SQL Server failover cluster **option** on the menu selecting the correct instance you wish to install the second node for (if there are multiple instances installed on the primary node). This will install the binaries and registry settings on the other node. This action should be taken on all the other nodes of the cluster.

Unlike SQL Server 2005 and prior, SQL Server 2008 no longer pushes the installers to each node in the cluster. Along these same lines the hotfixes and service packs will also need to be manually installed on each server of the cluster. When patching this gives the advantage of being able to perform what is called a rolling upgrade. This allows you to patch the cluster with only two to three minutes of downtime as each instance is patched separately.

The recommended method for installing patches on a SQL Server 2008 cluster is to patch your active node, test the patch giving you the option of failing over to an un-patched node if there is an issue. Once you are sure that the active node is working as you expect it to, you can continue to patch the other nodes in the cluster. This new technique gives you the obvious advantage of being able to test the hot fixes and service packs on one node before deploying them to all the nodes in the cluster. The downside to this technique is that much more work is required when patching a large multinode cluster.

Special Hardware Requirements

Using the Microsoft Cluster Service is a very high-end solution. It requires some fairly specialized equipment, which has a very high buy-in price because of the costs involved in setting up the shared storage solution. There are some less expensive solutions available but they are far less flexible in the number of servers that can be attached to them, and the number of machines that you can put in each cluster. The operating system you select also has a large impact on the number of nodes that you can set up in each cluster.

If you use a SCSI storage solution for Windows 2003, you can configure only a two-node cluster. Windows 2008 no longer supports clustering using SCSI disks. If you are using a local fiber channel storage solution or SAN solution, Table 6.1 will show you the maximum number of nodes supported in a Windows Cluster.

Table 6.1 Nodes Supported in a Windows Cluster

Operating System	Maximum Number of Nodes
Windows 2003 Enterprise Edition	4 nodes
Windows 2003 Data center Edition	8 nodes
Windows 2008 Itanium	8 nodes
Windows 2008 ×86 / ×64	16 nodes

Special Software Requirements

Not all Editions of SQL Server can be clustered using the Microsoft Cluster Service. Until SQL Server 2005 only the Enterprise Edition of SQL Server supported clustering. Starting with SQL Server 2005 clustering was available under the Standard Edition. The ability to cluster SQL Server using the Standard Edition has been extended into SQL Server 2008 as well. This greatly reduces your software licensing costs while still giving you the option to cluster your SQL Server.

If you wish to increase your Standard Edition cluster to a three-node cluster or higher, then you will need to upgrade the software version to the Enterprise Edition of SQL Server before you can increase the size of the cluster.

Beyond the two-node limit of SQL Server standard edition, most of your design choices when designing your cluster will be dictated by the version of the operating system you select. When configuring your Windows 2003 cluster, you must use static IP addresses, which are all on the same subnet. When configuring a cluster under Windows 2008, you may use a DHCP address. While Windows 2008 clusters support having the nodes of different subnets, the SQL Server 2008 installer does not have room for a second set of IP addresses, so it is recommended to use a single subnet for your cluster.

EXERCISE 6.4

SET UP SQL SERVER IN A CLUSTER

If you have access to a SAN, VMware, or Hyper-V, set up two Windows 2003 Enterprise or Windows 2008 Enterprise servers and cluster them. Install SQL Server in a clustered configuration.

If you are using VMware and Windows 2003 guest OSes to host your Windows Cluster, there is an excellent walkthrough that will help you set up the shared server stored in the virtual environment without needing access to a SAN. This site assumes that you have ESX server available, but this technique should work with VMware Server, which is a free download at http://exchangeexchange.com/blogs/bkeane/archive/2007/07/30/mscs-clustering-invmware.aspx.

If you are using Windows 2008 guest OSes to host your Windows cluster, you will need to present iSCSI LUNs to your guests OSes. You can either present LUNs to your guest OSes through a physical iSCSI solution of by using a software iSCSI target such as Starwind iSCSI target by RocketDivision.

When you are installing SQL Server in a clustered environment, special attention must be paid to the SQL Server Integration Service (SSIS). If you wish to use SSIS on your cluster you will need to manually install SSIS on each node of the cluster.

After you install SSIS on each node of the cluster you will need to edit the configuration file for SSIS to tell it where the MSDB database is. By default SSIS looks for the default local instance for the location of the MSDB database to which it wants to connect. Because the location of the SQL Instance is a different name, or possibly has an instance name, you will need to edit the MsDtsSrvr.ini.xml file. By default it is found in the C:\Program Files\Microsoft SQL Server\100\DTS\Binn folder. Open the file in your favorite XML editor (NOTEPAD will do fine) and find the branch with the *xsi:type = "SqlServerFolder"* and change the ServerName child from "." to your virtual host name that you configured during the SQL Server Installation. The relevant portion of the XML file is shown here.

```
<Folder xsi:type="SqlServerFolder">

    <Name>MSDB</Name>
    <ServerName>.</ServerName>

</Folder>
```

Test Day Tip

Be familiar with the name of this configuration file. The editing of this file was left out of the SQL Server 2005 exams, but there are questions about it in the SQL Server 2008 exams.

Manually moving an instance of SQL Server from one node of a cluster to another is a very simple procedure. Simply open the Cluster Administrator and connect to the cluster. Right-click on the Resource Group or any resource within the group and select the Move option. This will **Move** all the resources within the Resource Group to another node in the cluster. (Do not do this on a production cluster as there is a short outage while the service is started on the remote machine.)

If you will be using MSDTC in a clustered environment some changes should be made to the MSDTC configuration within the Component Services applet in the Administrative Tools menu. Navigate to My Computer and right-click on it and select **Properties**. Select the **MSDTC** tab, and click the **Security Options** button. In order for MSDTC to work correctly in a clustered environment be sure to select the **No Authentication Required** option. Each server that will be performing a distributed transaction must be set in this way. This will not allow users to connect to the database without providing authentication credentials, it simply allows a machine to begin a distributed transaction with the coordinator without authenticating against the machine. This is a requirement of a cluster only.

If you will be using MSDTC on a server, through a firewall you will need to specify the number of TCP ports that RPC can use by following MSKB 250367 (http://support.microsoft.com/kb/250367). In a clustered environment when following this MSKB article you will need to increase the number of TCP ports available to RPC. This setting not only sets the number of ports that MSDTC used to talk through the firewall, but it restricts all RPC communication to the server to these ports. The MSDTC monitoring page of the Component Services uses RPC to query the MSDTC services, and the Cluster Administrator also uses RPC to manage the cluster, as does the SQL Server Instance when communicating with the MSDTC service. It is recommended that in a clustered environment you increase this number to at least 100 (from the 20 shown in the MSKB article) if not higher.

When considering clustering for your high-availability solution, you need to license only the nodes of the cluster that are actively running SQL Server. If you have a two-node cluster and are running a single instance then you need to purchase licenses for only a single node (whichever one has more CPUs if the number of CPUs is different between the nodes). If you have a four-node cluster with three instances and each instance is running on a separate node then you would need licenses for three of the nodes. You do not need to license the passive node because it is considered a cold standby, because the services are not actively running on the machine at the time. When the cluster fails over, since it is a single instance that is failing over, Microsoft considers the license to transfer to the now active machine from the formally active machine.

Geo-Clustering

Geo-Clustering is a special setup of Windows Clustering where you are spreading the nodes of your Windows cluster between two different data centers usually in two different cities. Setting up a geographically dispersed cluster requires extremely expensive storage solutions to configure. This is because your storage solution must be able to automatically replicate the data from the storage solution at the local site to the storage solution at the remote site. This data transfer not only needs to be done, but it must be done in an asynchronous manner in order to keep both sites completely up to date.

Under Windows 2003 and prior, setting up a geographically dispersed cluster was even more complex. This is because each node of the cluster had to be on the same IP address subnet. This creates a problem in most facilities because typically each data center will have a different IP address subnet assigned to them. The technique of setting up the same IP address subnet in two different data centers is extremely complex. With Windows 2008 you now have the option to set up a cluster using different IP address subnets for each site. This makes the process much easier to set up.

Configuring & Implementing…

Combining Solutions

In the real world setting up a geographically dispersed cluster is extremely difficult even with the advancements that have been made the clustering software in Windows Server 2008. You may in fact find it easier to combine two of these solutions instead.

If you needed to replicate data from a west coast data center to an east coast data center, but still maintain a high-availability solution at your primary West Coast data center, one configuration you may choose is a cluster on the WEST COAST, then use database mirroring to replicate your data from the WEST COAST to the EAST COAST. This would allow you to satisfy the requirements of having a local high-availability solution on the west coast (your Windows cluster); and still giving you the option of replicating your data to the east coast using database mirroring.

In this case you would probably want to use database mirroring in the high performance mode so that your front end application is not slowed down by the WAN link latency between the two sites. When deciding on how to replicate data between sites over a WAN, keep in mind that no matter the solution you use data takes approximately three microseconds for every kilometer of fiber cable. A 100 kilometer distance will have a round trip time of approximately 600 microseconds (0.6 milliseconds).

Going from a data center in New York to a data center in Los Angeles and back will take approximately 26 milliseconds. This is in addition to any latency that is added by firewalls, encryption devices, and the time it takes the storage to actually write the data to the hard drive. To us 26 extra milliseconds is not much, but to the SQL server this amount of time is a very long wait, which will be shown within the local SQL server as blocking while you wait for the data to be transmitted and the acknowledgment to be returned.

When you set up a geographically dispersed cluster you do not use a quorum drive. This is because you can't replicate the quorum drive from site to site and have the cluster work correctly. Instead you use what is called a Majority Node Set. When you use a Majority Node Set whenever a node fails or the cluster is told to fail over a service, all the nodes take a vote as to which node should start the service. The node that wins then starts the service. A majority node set requires an odd number of servers so that there cannot be a tie—for example if you have three nodes at your primary site and two nodes at your backup site as shown in Figure 6.17.

Figure 6.17 A Majority Node Set

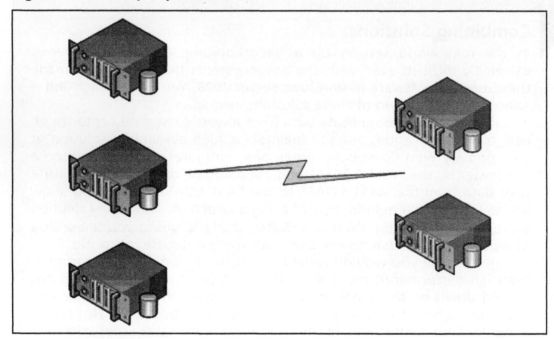

In the event that your primary site fails and the two servers on the right cannot connect to the three servers on the left they will take a vote between themselves and decide if the remote servers are offline. Once they decide that the three servers at the primary site are offline they will take control of the clustered resources and begin starting the clustered resources such as the SQL Server Service and the SQL Server Agent Service.

Once the primary site comes back online, the storage arrays at each site will begin replicating back the changes that have been made. Once this process is completed the cluster will be ready to move the services back to the original site.

If you have automatic failback enabled then the cluster will take a vote as to which servers should control everything. The site with three nodes will win the vote and the services will be automatically moved back. If you do not have automatic failback enabled then you will need to manually trigger the failback when it is most convenient to do so.

Troubleshooting a clustered installation of SQL Server can be a bit trickier than troubleshooting a stand-alone SQL Server installation. This is because of the clustered component. In the event that SQL Server is not starting, check the ERRORLOG file for information. This will tell you if the SQL Server service is starting or not. If the SQL Service is not starting check the application log and system log for errors about the cluster. If the ERRORLOG file shows that the SQL Server is starting and stopping then your issue is probably not going to be related to the cluster.

If you recently have changed the resource dependencies of the cluster and the SQL Server will no longer start, make sure that the SQL Server is dependent on all the correct hard drives and on the network name. If the SQL Service is not dependent on the hard drives the SQL Server will not start.

Changing the IP Address of a clustered SQL Server is not as easy as simply changing the IP Address of the SQL Server IP address resource in the cluster administrator. You will also need to search the registry and change any references from the old IP address to the new IP address, or the SQL Server will start, but not listen correctly.

If you have multiple instances of SQL Server installed in a clustered environment make sure that the instances are configured to listen on their own IP address only or that each instance uses a different TCP port number. If you do not, the SQL Service will attempt to listen on all the IP addresses on the node of the cluster on which it is being hosted. If all SQL Services have the same port number, only the first SQL Server to start will actually be able to listen on that port since only a single Windows Service can use any one port number. If you use the default of dynamic port numbers for the named instances this will not be a problem because the SQL Server will pick a port number at random of the ports that are not in use.

If you are using the SQL Server Maintenance plans to back up the database, and you are backing up the database to a disk that is a clustered resource, but is in a different Resource Group than the SQL Server, be sure to create a network share via the cluster administrator and back up the database over the network to that network share. If you do not, and the Resource Group that holds the hard drive you are backing up to is hosted by a different node of the cluster than your SQL Server Resource Group, the backups will fail as the hard drive cannot be accessed locally.

In the example cluster shown earlier, you would want to host the hard drive in the SQL01 Resource Group where the SQL Server is hosted in the SQL01V01 Resource Group. You would then want to create a network share \\SQL01\ SQLBackups that points to a folder on that new hard drive. You would then set up the backups to point to the network share instead of a local drive.

Replication

Replication is another technique that can be used for high availability. By replicating the data from one system to another you can easily redirect your clients to the secondary system in the event that your primary system fails. Since you are going to want the changes that are made to the backup system replicated back to the primary system after it is brought back online, you will want to use merge replication so that the subscriber can replicate its changes back to the publisher. Refer to Chapter 9 for information on setting up SQL Server Replication.

When using Merge replication, failover and failback are relatively easy. Simply redirect your clients to connect to the subscriber. Once the publisher is back online and in sync you can configure your clients to connect back to the publisher.

If you are using transaction replication then you will need to set up your subscriber as a publisher, and publish the data back to your original publisher. After the two servers are in sync, stop all client connections and remove the replication. Point all your clients to the publisher and configure that server to publish its data back to the subscriber.

Replication typically does not make a good high-availability solution because new objects are not replicated to the subscriber automatically. It is also difficult to make schema changes since replication limits what can be done to the table schemas. It also requires that you manually deploy procedures, views, functions, and such to the subscribers whenever they are updated.

The upside to using SQL Server Replication for your high-availability solution is that is you are using merge replication and your database is designed without having the requirement of unique columns that are not part of your primary key. You can use your high-availability solution to spread the load of your database between multiple SQL Servers.

If your database has a table that requires uniqueness as shown in the following example then it is not a good candidate for running both machines actively because you could create a record in one server, then create a second record with the same value for the unique column on the other server before the data is able to replicate. Even with a unique index or constraint on this column, uniqueness cannot be guaranteed since the unique index or constraint can be enforced only after the data has been replicated to the other server. If you have a unique index on the UserName column then your replication will fail because it cannot successfully add the row to the other server.

```
CREATE TABLE Authentication
        (UserId INT PRIMARY KEY IDENTITY(1,1),
        UserName NVARCHAR(50) /*This column must be unique*/,
        Password NVARCHAR(100),
        Active BIT)
```

Troubleshooting replication when used for a high-availability solution will be the same as when using normal SQL Server replication. This is discussed in Chapter 9.

When using SQL Server Replication for your high-availability solution like log shipping and database mirroring you will need to license each machine to which the database is being replicated.

Recovery Model

Depending on Which high-availability model you select will determine which recovery models are available to you for your database. Database mirroring, clustering, and replication will support any of the available database recovery models. When using log shipping you should use the full recovery model. This is because you have to keep the transaction log available and every transaction needs to be logged so that it can be backed up and shipped to the backup server.

All recovery models log most or all transactions to the transaction log. The bulk logged recovery model is different from the simple and full recovery models in that all transactions are fully logged with the exception of bulk insert tasks. These bulk insert tasks are only minimally logged. With the simply recovery model the transactions are purged from the transaction log file every few minutes at most.

Expandability

In addition to having the redundant hardware some systems will allow you to add CPUs and RAM to the system on the fly. These are Enterprise class features, but as more time goes on these features will make their way into more and more systems.

Hot Add CPU

The ability to add CPUs into the server is a hardware and operating system function as well as a function of the SQL Server. This gives you the ability to physically add physical CPUs to the server without powering down the system. This typically is done when the system needs to be expanded. By having this ability when you need to add new CPUs to the server you do not have to take a system outage to increase the system's processing power.

Most of the top-tier hardware vendors support the Hot Add CPU function. If the server hardware does not support this feature then it is disabled at both the operating system and the SQL Server levels.

In order to ensure your hardware supports this feature check with your hardware vendor. This feature is supported only by the Data center or Itanium Edition. The ability to hot replace CPUs also requires Data center or Itanium Edition.

Hot Add Memory

The ability to add RAM into the server is also a hardware and operating system function as well as a function of the SQL Server. Like the Hot Add CPU feature this gives you the ability to add RAM into the server without taking the server offline.

In order to ensure your hardware supports this feature check with your hardware vendor. Only the Enterprise, Data center, and Itanium Editions of Microsoft Windows support this feature. In Windows 2003 this feature is not available in the 64-bit builds of Windows. The ability to hot replace RAM also requires Data center or Itanium Edition.

Summary of Exam Objectives

We have set up a database mirror, using both the SQL Server Management Studio as well as T/SQL code. We also have failed over a database mirror, using both the SQL Server Management Studio as well as T/SQL code.

We have configured and failed over a Clustered installation of SQL Server, log shipping from one server to another, and a high-availability solution using SQL Server replication.

Exam Objectives Fast Track

Defining High Availability

- ☑ Selecting the right storage options is critical to the proper design on your high-availability solution.

- ☑ High-availability solutions can be directly attached storage or SAN storage.

- ☑ The goal of the high-availability solution is to keep the system online after some key piece of hardware has failed.

SQL High-Availability Options

- ☑ Clustered solutions most often are used to keep databases online within a single site due to the complexity of setting up a geographically dispersed cluster.

- ☑ Database mirroring is the newest of the solutions and can be used within a single site, or from site to site over a WAN.

- ☑ Log shipping is the oldest of the high-availability technologies that are available. However, this solution is still in use today.

Expandability

- ☑ Hot add CPU and RAM requires special hardware to add hardware while the server is still online.

- ☑ Hot add CPU and RAM requires at least Windows Enterprise Edition if not the Data center Edition.

- ☑ Hot installation of RAM is available only on the 32-bit Edition of Microsoft Windows.

Exam Objectives Frequently Asked Questions

Q: Which is better, RAID 5 or RAID 10?

A: RAID 5 is better for systems that have mostly reads. RAID 10 is better for systems that have mostly writes. You will need to evaluate the specific system for which you are designing the storage before you can decide on a RAID level.

Q: Why not use RAID 10 all the time?

A: RAID 10 is an extremely expensive solution to use all the time. Part of the responsibility of the DBA is to ensure that you are using the right solution for the right situation.

Q: Since my hard drives are backed up to other hard drives, does this mean that I don't need to back up my database anymore?

A: No, you should still back up your database as you did before. It is possible that more than one hard drive will fail at the same time. Without a good database backup you would lose all the data in the database.

Q: What is the best high-availability solution for moving data long distances?

A: When you have to move data long distances database mirroring in high performance mode, and log shipping will be your best bet. These solutions allow for a small amount of data loss, but will not impact the performance of your production database when transmitting data across the WAN like database mirroring in high safety mode or using a Windows Cluster.

Q: How does clustering provide a high-availability solution when the servers are sharing the storage?

A: The storage systems that are used behind a Windows Cluster (typically a SAN) are very high-end systems that are designed to survive a hardware failure within themselves. They will often detect that a hard drive is starting to go bad before it actually does and take that drive out of service before it fails so that the drive can be replaced before the system is running in an unprotected state.

Q: When setting up database mirroring when the primary and mirror are in different data centers, which data center should the witness be in?

A: The witness should be in the backup data center along with the mirror server. This way if the primary server or data center fails the witness will still be online and can tell the mirror that it needs to become active.

Self Test

1. You are designing a new database server for your company. You wish to store the database's MDF file and NDF files on the most cost efficient storage possible, while providing a redundant storage solution. Your database will be 95% reads, and 5% writes. What RAID level should you use for your MDF and NDF files?

   A. RAID 0

   B. RAID 1

   C. RAID 5

   D. RAID 10

2. You are configuring log shipping on your OLTP database from one data center to another. You need to ensure that the minimum amount of bandwidth is used when moving the logs from your primary site to the backup site. When configuring the log backups, which option should you select to meet your goal?

   A. Use the default server setting

   B. Compress backup

   C. Do not compress backup

3. You are setting up log shipping for a database between two instances of SQL Server 2008. You want to ensure that your users have access to the database when the logs are not actively being restored so that they can read the updated data for reporting purposes. In what state should you leave the database?

   A. RECOVERY

   B. NO RECOVERY

   C. STANDBY

4. Which of the following database mirroring modes requires the use of a witness instance?

   A. High Performance with automatic failover

   B. High Performance

    C. High Safety

    D. High Safety with automatic failover

5. You are setting up your deployment scripts to create your database mirroring endpoints on your production SQL Server. Each server has a single instance on it. Which script will correctly create the database mirroring endpoint?

    A.
```
CREATE ENDPOINT MyEndpoint
STATE = STARTED
AS HTTP (PATH=/sql/MyEndpoint, AUTHENTICATION=BASIC)
FOR DATABASE_MIRRORING;
```

    B.
```
CREATE ENDPOINT MyEndpoint
STATE = STARTED
AS TCP (LISTENER_PORT=5022)
FOR DATABASE_MIRRORING;
```

    C.
```
CREATE DATABASE_MIRRORING ENDPOINT MyEndpoint
STATE=STARTED
AS TCP (LISTENER PORT=5022);
```

    D.
```
CREATE ENDPOINT MyEndpoint
STATE = STARTED
AS TCP (LISTENER PORT=1433)
FOR DATABASE_MIRRORING;
```

6. You are designing your high-availability solution. Because of the importance of the database system you are required to have more than one independent backup server running at all times. Which high-availability solution fits these requirements?

    A. Database mirroring

    B. Log shipping

    C. Clustering

    D. Replication

7. You have installed SQL Server 2008 in a clustered environment. You are installing SSIS on the SQL Server. You have installed SQL Server 2008 as a named instance and need to tell SSIS that it needs to connect to the named instance. What file should you edit?

    A. C:\Program Files\Microsoft SQL Server\100\DTS\Binn\msdtssrvr.exe.
       config

    B. C:\Program Files\Microsoft SQL Server\100\DTS\Binn\MsDtsConfig.
       ini.xml

    C. C:\Program Files\Microsoft SQL Server\100\DTS\Binn\DTExec.exe.
       config

    D. C:\Program Files\Microsoft SQL Server\100\DTS\Binn\MsDtsConfig.
       ini.config

8. You are selecting your high-availability solution for your production environment. You have a single data center that houses all your servers. Which high-availability solution requires administrative overhead after the initial setup is complete?

    A. Database mirroring

    B. Replication

    C. Clustering

    D. Log shipping

9. You are considering the licensing costs for your new high-availability solution. You will be using the Standard Edition of Microsoft SQL Server. Which solution has the lowest licensing costs?

    A. Database mirroring

    B. Replication

    C. Clustering

    D. Log shipping

10. You need to upgrade the CPUs in your SQL Server. You want to add new CPUs without taking the system offline. Your hardware supports this feature. What operating system or systems support this feature?

    A. Web Edition

    B. Standard Edition

    C. Enterprise Edition

    D. Data center Edition

11. You need to upgrade the RAM in your SQL Server. You want to add more RAM without taking the system offline. Your hardware supports this feature. What operating system or systems support this feature?

    A. Web Edition

    B. Standard Edition

    C. Enterprise Edition

    D. Data center Edition

12. When you are setting up your clients to connect to a clustered SQL Server database, to which host name should they be connecting?

    A. The host name of the node that is actively running the SQL Service

    B. The host name of the node that is not actively running the SQL Service

    C. The host name that was used when setting up the Windows Cluster

    D. The host name that was used when installing SQL Server

13. You are using merge replication to make your user authentication database highly available. The database has a single table that is shown in Example A. The replication has been running for several months without issue. Your replication has begun failing, giving a unique index violation. What should you do to correct the problem? Your business processes require that each username remain unique within the system, and that users use their e-mail address for their username.

Example A: Merge Replication

```
CREATE TABLE Authentication
(UserId INT PRIMARY KEY IDENTITY(1,1),
UserName NVARCHAR(255),
Password NVARCHAR(100),
Active BIT)
GO
CREATE UNIQUE INDEX IX_Authentication_UserName ON dbo.Authentication
(UserName)
INCLUDE (Password, UserId, Active)
WITH (FILLFACTOR=60)
GO
```

A. Mark the subscriber for reinitialization, and run the snapshot agent.

B. Identify the rows that are causing the violation and delete both rows from the servers.

C. Identify the rows that are causing the violation, then identify which UserId is being used by the customer within the rest of your business processes, then modify the UserName value of the invalid row to a different value.

D. Delete the subscriber and re-create the subscription.

14. You are administrating a SQL Server cluster that is running three instances of Microsoft SQL Sever 2008. Each instance uses SQL Service Broker to send messages to other instances both on the cluster and on other machines in the Enterprise. After patching and rebooting the host machines you see that one of the instances is not getting its service broker messages. One of the instances is using TCP port 1433, and the other two are using dynamic port numbers. The server that is not receiving SQL Service broker messages is using a dynamic TCP port number. You examine the SQL Server ERRORLOG and find the following relevant messages:

```
2008-11-05 23:14:23.64 Server   Server is listening on [ 'any'
<ipv6> 49237].

2008-11-05 23:14:23.64 Server   Server is listening on [ 'any'
<ipv4> 49237].

2008-11-05 23:14:23.64 Server   Server is listening on [ ::1 <ipv6> 49551].

2008-11-05 23:14:23.65 Server   Server is listening on [ 127.0.0.1
<ipv4> 49551].
```

You know that the SQL Service Broker Endpoint is configured on port 5200. How should you resolve this issue with the least impact to the users of the databases hosted by this instance?

A. Move one or more instances to the other node, then restart this instance so that the endpoint can take the TCP port number it has been assigned.

B. Change the port number of the ENDPOINT to a free TCP port number that is not configured for use by the other instances by using the *ALTER ENDPOINT* command, changing the state from stopped to started at the same time. Reconfigure the routes on the machines that send SQL Service Broker messages to this server to use the new TCP port number.

C. Restart the problem instance hoping that it gets access to its port number.

D. Use the Cluster Administrator to move the problem instance to its own node so that the service can gain access to the port number in question.

15. You have installed SQL Server 2008 in an Active Passive environment running on the servers SQL01A and SQL01B. You have several SSIS packages within your database environment. You have installed SQL Server as the default instance using the default configuration on your cluster using the name SQL01V01 as the clustered resource name. When your SQL Server's Resource Group is running on SQL01B the SSIS packages work without error. When your SQL Server's Resource Group is running on SQL01A the SSIS packages fail to start. All the SSIS packages are run from SQL Agent Jobs. How should you correct this problem?

    A. Fail the SQL Server back to SQL01B and always run the SQL Server on that node.

    B. Reconfigure the SQL Agent Jobs that run the SSIS jobs to use SQL01B as the SSIS repository instead of SQL01V01.

    C. Install the SQL Server Integration Services service on the SQL01A and apply the same patches and hotfixes that are in use by the SQL Server service.

    D. Configure another SQL Server to be the SSIS repository instead of SQL01V01.

16. You are installing a new SQL Server that will be used to store the WEBLOGS from your IIS WEB FARM. The database will be 99% write, and 1% read. Data will be read from the system only in the event of a system problem or legal investigation. You need to store the data on the most efficient solution possible, while providing redundancy, so that writes to the database are not slowed down. What RAID level should you use?

    A. RAID 0

    B. RAID 5

    C. RAID 6

    D. RAID 10

17. You are administrating a clustered SQL Server solution in a shared storage environment. You are seeing disk performance problems weekly on Saturday nights. You VPN in on Saturday night in order to attempt to troubleshoot the problem. You see nothing out of the ordinary on the SQL Server except that the SQL Server is reporting that the hard drives are not responding quickly enough. You open performance monitor and see that the disk queues are less

than five, and you are averaging 80 operations per second. When you look at the Avg Disk Sec/Read you see you are averaging 0.8 seconds with a max of 7 seconds. What is the most likely cause of this kind of performance problem?

A. The server is not sending the commands to the storage correctly to do weekly maintenance, and because the commands have to be sent over and over they are taking too long to be completed.

B. Part of the SAN is powered down on weekends to save power as part of the company's Green policies.

C. Another server using the same spindles is performing some very heavy workload against the disks every week—something like a tape backup or a defrag.

D. Your SAN is under-licensed and performs periodic workload slowdowns in order to bring this to the attention of the SAN administrator so that they will correct the SAN licensing.

18. You are troubleshooting distributed transaction problems on your clustered SQL Server. Your SQL Server is on your internal network, and there are several servers in the DMZ that use MSDTC to use distributed transactions with the SQL Server. These machines are receiving sporadic messages about not being able to connect to the MSDTC service on the SQL Server cluster. You manually begin a distributed transaction and query a remote system and it works correctly most of the time, sometimes failing with a message saying that the local MSDTC service cannot be contacted. What action should you perform to correct this problem?

A. Restart the MSDTC service.

B. Move the MSDTC service to the same node on which the SQL Service is running.

C. Configure RPC to use more TCP ports.

D. Reinstall MSDTC from the Programs and Features Control Panel Applet.

19. You are installing SQL Server 2008 on a new Windows 2008 cluster. You get to the disk configuration screen and are unable to configure the tempdb database to be placed in the C:\MSSQL\MSSQL\Data folder as per your IT policy. How should you resolve this issue?

A. Add the C drive as a clustered resource using the Windows cluster administrator. Rerun the SQL Server 2008 installed, selecting the C drive as a disk resource.

B. Install SQL Server with the TEMPDB database on a clustered drive. After installing SQL Server 2008, change the location of the TEMPDB database to the C drive and restart the SQL Server.

C. Add a new drive to the cluster as a clustered resource. Use this drive to host the TEMPDB database.

20. You are designing your high-availability solution. You have decided to use SQL Server replication in order to move data from server to server. You need a bidirectional replication solution so that you can use either server as your active server. What replication topology should you use?

A. Snapshot

B. Merge

C. Transactional

Self Test Quick Answer Key

1.	C	11.	C and D
2.	B	12.	D
3.	C	13.	C
4.	D	14.	B
5.	B	15.	C
6.	B and D	16.	D
7.	B	17.	C
8.	C	18.	C
9.	C	19.	C
10.	D	20.	B

Chapter 7

MCTS SQL Server 2008 Exam 432

Maintaining Your Database

Exam objectives in this chapter:

- Understanding Data Collation
- Maintaining Data Files
- Backing Up and Restoring Data
- Performing Ongoing Maintenance
- Performance Data Collection

Exam objectives review:

- ☑ Summary of Exam Objectives
- ☑ Exam Objectives Fast Track
- ☑ Exam Objectives Frequently Asked Questions
- ☑ Self Test
- ☑ Self Test Quick Answer Key

Introduction

Ongoing maintenance, preventative monitoring, and fine-tuning are key to the health of your SQL Servers and the ongoing operation of your organization. Plan maintenance tasks thoroughly and perform them regularly. In this chapter, you will learn about the most critical database maintenance tasks and the factors that influence them: storing and maintaining international data; optimizing data files; and daily operations like backups, restores, and gathering performance data for preventative monitoring.

A key task of any database administrator is to implement a robust disaster recovery strategy. This strategy ensures business continuity. A clearly defined disaster recovery strategy formalizes your requirements, procedures, and expectations related to data protection. Backup is a critical part of any disaster recovery strategy. Choosing the correct backup parameters like type, frequency, and media allows you to meet the data recovery objectives set by your organization. Backup strategies are implemented so that at some point you can perform adequate data recovery. SQL Server allows you to perform recovery at several levels, from individual corrupt data pages to the entire database or server settings.

SQL Server 2008 is designed to deliver the best possible performance by allowing administrators to fine-tune the system to meet their organization's specific needs. The Data Collector feature is a new feature that allows you to systematically collect and analyze performance related and other data. The centralized performance data repository allows you to better understand the performance of your SQL Server as a whole, as well as examine its interactions with environmental dependencies.

Understanding Data Collation

In today's global economy, many organizations need to store data in different languages in addition to sorting and querying it based on culture-specific rules. SQL Server 2008 fulfills this need. SQL Server 2008 allows you to store data from multiple languages in a single database column. It also allows you to define specific languages for individual server instances, databases, and database columns. *Collation* is the set of rules for storing, sorting, and comparing text data. Collation affects most database operations. Collation can affect query results, the ability to import and export data, as well as backup and restore operations. To be able to effectively maintain SQL Server 2008 databases in a multilingual environment, you must understand data collation.

When you perform a fresh install of SQL Server, you are asked to select a data collation, as shown in Figure 7.1. The collation you choose becomes the collation of the Model database as well as the default collation for all new databases. What determines the suggested default collation? If you are performing a fresh install, i.e., SQL Server has never been installed previously on this computer, the most appropriate collation based on the Windows regional settings will be suggested.

Figure 7.1 Selecting a Default Server Collation during Installation

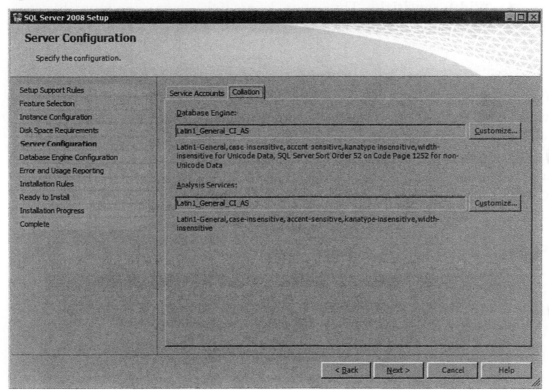

A collation defines the bit pattern that represents each character in the data set. Usually, the collation name starts with the language or character set, for example Latin1_, Thai100_, Arabic100_. The collation also defines the following rules regarding data comparison and sorting:

- **Case sensitivity** This option defines if the comparison or sort is case sensitive. For example, in a case sensitive comparison 'Banana' = 'banana' will return true. When sorted, 'banana' will always come before 'Banana'.

- **Accent sensitivity** This option defines if the comparison is accent sensitive. For example, in an accent sensitive comparison 'Valentine' will not be equal to 'Válentine'.

- **Kanatype sensitivity** This option defines if the comparison is sensitive to the type of Japanese kana characters used. Two types of kana characters are available: Hiragana and Katakana. When a comparison is kana-insensitive, SQL Server will consider equivalent Hiragana and Katakana characters as equal for sorting purposes.

- **Width sensitivity** This option defines if the comparison treats characters represented as a single byte as equivalent to the same character represented as a double byte.

Suffixes _CS, _AS, _KS, and _WS are used in collation set names to show that the collation is case, accent, kana, or width sensitive. Alternatively CI, AI, KI, and WI can be used for case, accent, kana, or width insensitive collations. Unless specifically specified, width insensitivity and kanatype insensitivity is assumed. For example, the collation Latin1_General _CI_AS_KS_WS is case-insensitive, accent-sensitive, kanatype-sensitive and width-sensitive. As another example, the collation SQL_Latin1_General_CP1_ CS_AS is case-sensitive, accent-sensitive, kanatype-insensitive, and width-insensitive. Figure 7.2 shows the collation options when specifying a server collation.

Figure 7.2 Customizing Collation Options

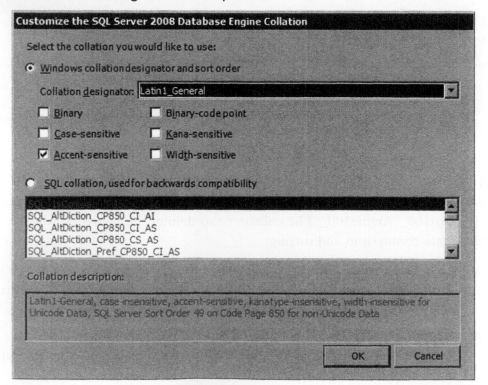

We can see from Figure 7.2 that we can choose either a Windows collation or a SQL collation. The Windows collation is based on the language and rules specified by the Windows locale. This is defined in the Regional Settings Control Panel applet. One key attribute of Windows collations is that Unicode and non-Unicode data will be sorted the same way for the language specified. This avoids inconsistencies in query results, specifically, if you are sorting the same data in varchar and nvarchar type columns. You may receive different results here if you are not using a Windows collation.

EXAM WARNING

Always choose to use the default Windows collation, unless you have a very specific reason not to. For example, if you need to store non-Unicode data in a single language that is different from the language of your computer, you will have to select a collation for that language. Another exception is when you need to run distributed queries or replicate with an instance of SQL Server that has a different collation. You should maintain consistency between multiple interoperating systems as far as possible.

SQL Server Collations

SQL Server collations provide comparing and sorting compatibility with earlier versions of SQL Server, specifically SQL Server 6.5 and SQL Server 7. If you are intending to interoperate with these versions of SQL Server, you need to pick an appropriate SQL Server collation. SQL Server collations have differing rules for Unicode and non-Unicode data. This means that if you are sorting the same data in varchar and nvarchar type columns, you are likely to receive different results. Additionally, the sort order of non-Unicode data in the context of a SQL collation is likely to be different to a sort order of non-Unicode data performed by the Windows operating system. Names of SQL Server collations are prefixed with SQL_.

Binary Collations

Binary collations are collations that sort and compare data based on the binary values representing each character. Binary collations are intrinsically case sensitive. Performing binary comparison and sort operations is simpler than performing the same operation using a non binary collation. This means that you can use binary collations to improve the performance of your queries if they suit your requirements. Binary collations have a suffix of _BIN or _BIN2. The _BIN2 binary collation is known as binary-code point collation. This type of collation is newer and should be used at all times whenever a binary collation is required. The _BIN collation should be used for backwards compatibility only.

New & Noteworthy...

New Collation Features of SQL Server 2008

SQL Server 2008 introduces 80 new collations that are aligned with the new Windows Server 2008 language features. Windows Server 2008 is the latest server operating system from Microsoft, and it includes many enhancements to support multiple languages. Most of the new collations in SQL Server 2008 provide more accurate ways of sorting data for specific cultures. Specifically, the new features include the following:

- Unicode 5.0 case tables
- Weighing for some non weighed characters
- Chinese minority scripts
- Support for linguistically correct surrogates
- Support for new East Asian government standards

Additionally, some collations have been deprecated, like Macedonian_ CI_AS, SQL_ALTDiction_CP1253_CS_AS, Hindi_CI_AS and several others. These collations are still supported, but only for backwards compatibility purposes. These collations are not displayed in the list of available collations when you install SQL Server 2008, nor are they returned by the ::fn_helpcollations( ) system function.

Using Collations

You have already learned that when SQL Server 2008 is installed, you are required to select a server level default collation. As well as the server-level default, a collation can be specified at the following levels:

- **Database-level collation** You can specify a collation for each individual database. If you don't explicitly specify a database-level collation, the server-level default collation will be used. The database collation is used as a default collation for new columns in the database tables. Additionally, the database collation is used when running queries against the database.

- **Column-level collation** You can specify a collation for columns of type char, varchar, text, nchar, nvarchar, and ntext. If you don't explicitly specify a column-level collation, the database-level default collation will be used. Example 7.1 demonstrates the use of column-level collations.

- **Expression-level collation** Sometimes you wish to use a collation different from the database default in your query when sorting or comparing data. You can specify the collation to be used using the COLLATE clause.

Database-level collations and column-level collations are specified using the COLLATE clause for the CREATE DATABASE and CREATE TABLE statements. You can also select a collation when creating a new database or table using SQL Server Management Studio. Expression-level collation is specified using the COLLATE clause at the end of the statement. Example 7.1 demonstrates the creation of a new database, table, and column as well as the effect of collation on query results.

Example 7.1 Demonstrating Database-Level and Column-Level Collations

```
CREATE DATABASE ExampleDB2
COLLATE Latin1_General_CS_AS
GO

USE ExampleDB2
GO

CREATE TABLE TeamMembers
(MemberID int PRIMARY KEY IDENTITY,
MemberName nvarchar(50) COLLATE Latin1_General_CI_AI)
GO

INSERT TeamMembers(MemberName)
VALUES
(N'Valentine'),
(N'Peter'),
(N'Matthéw'),
(N'valentine'),
(N'Matthew')
GO

SELECT * FROM TeamMembers ORDER BY MemberName
-- Results:
-- MemberID      MemberName
-- ----------    ----------------------------------------------
-- 3             Matthéw
-- 5             Matthew
```

```
-- 2              Peter
-- 1              Valentine
-- 4              valentine

SELECT * FROM TeamMembers ORDER BY MemberName COLLATE Latin1_General_CS_AS
-- Results:
-- MemberID       MemberName
-----------       ----------------------------------------------
-- 5              Matthew
-- 3              Matthéw
-- 2              Peter
-- 4              valentine
-- 1              Valentine

SELECT * FROM TeamMembers WHERE MemberName = 'Matthew'
-- Results:
-- MemberID       MemberName
-- ----------     ----------------------------------------------
-- 3              Matthéw
-- 5              Matthew

SELECT * FROM TeamMembers WHERE MemberName = 'Matthew' COLLATE
Latin1_General_BIN
-- Results:
-- MemberID       MemberName
-- ----------     ----------------------------------------------
-- 5              Matthew

DROP DATABASE ExampleDB2
GO
```

Configuring & Implementing...

Selecting the Appropriate Collation

Given that your choice of collation has a profound effect on query results, how do you choose the correct collation? To answer this question, first consider your multilingual requirements. Will you store data in other languages? Will you integrate with other SQL Server systems that run under a different language? If the answer to these is 'no', you should

Continued

> keep the default Windows collation suggested by the SQL Server Setup program. You can choose collation options like case sensitive or binary-code page, if you require case sensitive sorts and comparisons.
>
> If you are upgrading from SQL Server 6.5 or SQL Server 7, your collation will be set to the SQL collation of the system you are upgrading from, and no collation-related choices will be offered. If you need to replicate or synchronize data with SQL Server 6.5 or SQL Server 7 systems, you should choose the SQL collation of the target system.
>
> Finally, if you are going to be working with data from many languages, choose the most used or the most compatible language for the server-level default collation. You can then create language-specific databases and columns with collations that differ from the server default.

Collation
Considerations for Backup and Restore

SQL Server allows you to restore databases to a different server. If a server is rendered inoperable by a disaster, you can immediately start restoring important databases from backup onto an existing server. The server that hosted the database before the disaster is referred to as the source server, while the server you plan to restore the database to is referred to as the target server. The collation of the source server may not be the same as the collation of the target server.

When a database is restored to a target server that has a different collation from the source server, the database will always retain its original collation settings. For example, you have a SQL Server with the server-level default collation set to French_CI_AI. You create a database on this server without specifying a collation. The database will inherit the French_CI_AI collation. You take a backup of this database and restore it to another server that has the collation of Latin1_General_CS_AS. The database will retain its original collation of French_CI_AI. If you need to sort or compare data in this restored database using rules of the Latin1_General_CS_AS target server collation, you must use the COLLATE Latin1_General_CS_AS clause in your queries.

As a more permanent solution, you may need to use the ALTER TABLE statement to change the collation of the column. However, ALTER TABLE cannot be used if a constraint, computed column, index, or any manually created statistics reference the column you are altering.

EXAM WARNING

You are likely to be asked about the impact of collations on backup and restore. Ensure that you understand how collations are affected by the restore operation, i.e., the restored database will retain its original collation. Ensure that you understand how to use the COLLATE clause with the SELECT statement and have practiced using it.

EXERCISE 7.1

USING COLLATIONS

In this exercise, we will practice working with the COLLATE clause. Before you begin, you must have the following software installed on your computer:

- SQL Server 2008 – a free trial is available for download
- AdventureWorks sample database

We will be querying the Person.Contact table in the AdventureWorks database using various collations.

1. Open SQL Server Management Studio. To do this click **Start | All Programs | Microsoft SQL Server 2008 | SQL Server Management Studio**.

2. Create a new query against the AdventureWorks database.

3. Use the SELECT…INTO statement to retrieve a distinct list of first names into a temporary table named "#Names".

```
SELECT DISTINCT FirstName

    INTO #Names

    FROM AdventureWorks.Person.Contact
```

4. Sort the data using the Latin1_General_CS_AI case sensitive collation. In order to see how case sensitivity affects query results, union the table to itself by casting join columns upper and lower case. Take note of the sort order (lower case before upper case).

```
SELECT UPPER(CAST(FirstName AS nvarchar(50)) COLLATE
    Latin1_General_CS_AI) AS FirstName

    FROM #Names

UNION ALL
```

```
SELECT LOWER(CAST(FirstName AS nvarchar(50)) COLLATE
   Latin1_General_CS_AI) AS FirstName
 FROM #Names
 ORDER BY FirstName
```

5. Perform a self-join using a case sensitive collation. In order to see how case sensitivity affects joining, we cast one side of the join all in upper case. Will any rows be returned here?

```
SELECT a.FirstName, UPPER(b.FirstName)
   FROM #Names AS a
   INNER JOIN #Names AS b

-- Matching using case sensitive comparison, but ignoring accent
ON CAST(a.FirstName AS nvarchar(50)) COLLATE Latin1_General_CS_AI =
   UPPER(CAST(b.FirstName AS nvarchar(50))) COLLATE
Latin1_General_CS_AI

-- Sorting by a case sensitive collation
   ORDER BY CAST(a.FirstName AS nvarchar(50)) COLLATE
Latin1_General_CS_AI
```

6. Sort the data using an accent sensitive collation. In order to see how accent sensitivity affects sorting, use another self-join to find all those cases where the only difference between the two names is in accented characters.

```
   SELECT a.FirstName
FROM #Names AS a
INNER JOIN #Names AS b

-- We match ignoring case and accent
ON CAST(a.FirstName AS nvarchar(50)) COLLATE Latin1_General_CI_AI =
   CAST(b.FirstName AS nvarchar(50)) COLLATE Latin1_General_CI_AI

-- We find rows that do not match on accent.
AND CAST(a.FirstName AS nvarchar(50)) COLLATE Latin1_General_
CI_AS <>
   CAST(b.FirstName AS nvarchar(50)) COLLATE Latin1_General_CI_AS

-- We sort by a case sensitive collation
   ORDER BY CAST(a.FirstName AS nvarchar(50)) COLLATE
Latin1_General_CI_AS
```

7. Using a similar self-join as in the previous step, view name matches side by side. Force the matches with accents to one side

of the join using an OR operator. Review the results of this statement and how it is affected by collation.

```
SELECT a.FirstName,
    b.FirstName
    FROM #Names AS a
    INNER JOIN #Names AS b
-- We match ignoring case and accent
ON CAST(a.FirstName AS nvarchar(50)) COLLATE Latin1_General_CI_AI =
    CAST(b.FirstName AS nvarchar(50)) COLLATE Latin1_General_CI_AI
-- We find rows that do not match on accent.
AND CAST(a.FirstName AS nvarchar(50)) COLLATE Latin1_General_CI_AS >
    CAST(b.FirstName AS nvarchar(50)) COLLATE Latin1_General_CI_AS
DROP TABLE #Names
```

Maintaining Data Files

Database objects, like tables and indexes, are physically stored in data files sometimes across multiple filegroups. In production databases, you must perform ongoing maintenance on these data files, as well as optimize database performance and disk space used. The key techniques to optimize disk space usage are data compression, sparse columns, and the shrinking of database and log files using the Database Console Commands (DBCC) DBCC SHRINKFILE option. Performance is optimized by the creation and ongoing maintenance of indexes. In this section, you will learn how to use data compression, maintain indexes, and use the DBCC commands to validate and fix errors in your databases.

Implementing Data Compression

You can enable data compression to reduce the amount of disk space that your database uses. Data compression is a new feature of SQL Server 2008 and can be enabled at two levels: *row compression* and *page compression*. The decision to enable data compression should not be taken lightly as it is very likely to reduce the performance of your database applications. The performance reduction is caused by the additional work your server must do to compress the data. Consequently, the decision to enable data compression is a trade-off between disk space and performance.

Data compression is only available in SQL Server 2008 Enterprise Edition or SQL Server 2008 Developer Edition. Data compression can be applied to tables and indexes.

As you have learned from earlier chapters, tables can be stored as a heap, where rows are stored in no particular order; or as a clustered index, where rows are stored in the order defined by the index. You can use compression on both types of table. Nonclustered indexes are stored separately from the table on which they are defined. Nonclustered indexes can also be created on views, a situation referred to as "indexed views". You can use compression on nonclustered indexes for tables and views. Finally, data compression can be configured for individual partitions that tables and indexes are stored across. For example, if a table is partitioned into current and historical partitions, you can choose to enable data compression on the historical partition only.

To enable compression on a table or index, use the CREATE TABLE or CREATE INDEX statement with DATA_COMPRESSION = ROW | PAGE option. If you are enabling compression on an existing table or index, use the DATA_COMPRESSION option with the ALTER TABLE or ALTER INDEX statement. Enabling compression will cause a rebuild of the object and is, therefore, a highly time and resource consuming operation. Enabling data compression on a table will have no effect on that table's non clustered indexes. Each non clustered index can be compressed separately. The syntax for enabling data compression is shown in Examples 7.2 through 7.6.

Example 7.2 Enabling Data Compression on a New Table—Syntax

```
CREATE TABLE [database_name].[schema_name].table_name
(<Column Definition List>)
WITH (DATA_COMPRESSION = ROW | PAGE)
Example 7.3 Enabling Data Compression on an Existing Table—Syntax
ALTER TABLE [database_name].[schema_name].table_name
REBUILD WITH (DATA_COMPRESSION = ROW | PAGE | NONE)
Example 7.4 Enabling Data Compression on a New Nonclustered Index—Syntax
CREATE NONCLUSTERED INDEX index_name
ON table_name (<Column List>)
WITH (DATA_COMPRESSION = ROW | PAGE)
Example 7.5 Enabling Data Compression on an Existing Nonclustered
Index—Syntax
ALTER INDEX index_name
ON table_name
REBUILD WITH (DATA_COMPRESSION = ROW | PAGE | NONE)
Example 7.6 Enabling Data Compression on a Partitioned Table—Syntax
ALTER TABLE partitioned_table_name
REBUILD PARTITION = 1 WITH (DATA_COMPRESSION = ROW | PAGE | NONE)
```

Row versus Page Compression

Row compression attempts to reduce disk space by storing all fixed-length data types as variable length, including numeric data types. This can reduce the size of each individual row, allowing you to fit more rows on a page. Row compression uses compression metadata to describe the offset of each value within the row. However, this space saving is not always achieved. For example, when values stored in columns of fixed length data type consume the entire length of the column, no space saving occurs. In fact, in this scenario more space is used as the overhead compression metadata must still be written to the page.

Row compression has no effect on the smallest possible data types like tinyint, smalldatetime, date and uniqueidentifier data types. It also has no effect on data types that are already stored as variable-length like varchar, nvarchar, and varbinary. Finally, special data types like text, image, xml, table, sql_variant, and cursor are not affected by row level compression. The bit data type is always negatively affected because, together with the metadata overhead, it requires four bits of storage as opposed to the one byte usually required for up-to-eight–bit columns.

Page compression applies the following compression techniques to each data page:

- Row compression
- Prefix compression
- Dictionary compression

These techniques are applied in order when the data page becomes full. This is why page compression has a profound negative effect on write performance. Page compression goes further than row compression when attempting to save space. When you enable page compression, row compression is automatically enabled.

Prefix compression identifies repeating values in each column and stores the repeating value once in the compression information (CI) structure in the page header. The repeating value throughout the column is then replaced by a reference to the value in the page header. The reference can also indicate a partial match.

Dictionary compression is applied after prefix compression. This type of compression identifies repeating values anywhere on the page and then stores these values, once in the CI structure, in the page header. Repeating values throughout the page are replaced by a reference. Dictionary compression is not limited to a single column; it is applied to the entire page.

Estimating Space Savings
Using sp_estimate_data_compression_savings

It can be difficult to decide whether or not to implement data compression. To take the guesswork out of this decision, SQL Server 2008 provides a handy stored procedure: sp_estimate_data_compression savings. This stored procedure takes the name of the table or indexed view, optional index number (specify NULL for all indexes or 0 for the heap), optional partition number, and the type of data compression to calculate the estimate for. This stored procedure is also useful if you have a compressed table and want to know how much space the table would consume uncompressed. The following columns are included in the results of the sp_estimate_data_compression_savings stored procedure:

- **Object_name** This is the name of the table or the indexed view for which you are calculating the savings.

- **Schema_name** The schema that this table or view belongs to.

- **Index_id** Index number: 0 stands for the heap, 1 for the clustered index, other numbers for nonclustered indexes.

- **Partition_number** Number of the partition: 1 stands for a nonpartitioned table or index.

- **Size_with_current_compression_setting (KB)** Current size of the object.

- **Size_with_requested_compression_setting (KB)** Estimated size of the object without fragmentation or padding.

- **Sample_size_with_current_compression_setting (KB)** Size of the sample using the existing compression setting.

- **Sample_size_with_requested_compression_setting (KB)** Size of the sample using the requested compression setting.

In Example 7.7, we will use the sp_estimate_data_compression_savings with the Purchasing.PurchaseOrderDetail table.

Example 7.7 Estimating Compression Savings

```
Use AdventureWorks;
GO
execute sp_estimate_data_compression_savings Purchasing, PurchaseOrderDetail,
null, null, Page
```

Using Sparse Columns

Sparse columns reduce the amount of space taken up by null values. However, sparse columns increase the time it takes to retrieve values that are not null. Most columns that allow nulls can be marked as sparse. The best practice is to use sparse columns when the technique saves at least 20 to 40 percent of space. You are not concerned about read performance reduction for non-null values. Columns are marked as sparse within the CREATE TABLE or ALTER TABLE statements, as shown in Examples 7.8 through 7.10.

Example 7.8 Creating a Sparse Column in a New Table—Syntax

```
CREATE TABLE [database_name].[schema_name].table_name
(Column1 int PRIMARY KEY,
Column2 varchar(50) SPARSE NULL)
Example 7.9 Marking an Existing Column as Sparse—Syntax
ALTER TABLE [database_name].[schema_name].table_name
ALTER COLUMN Column2 ADD SPARSE
Example 7.10 Marking an Existing Column as Non-Sparse—Syntax
ALTER TABLE [database_name].[schema_name].table_name
ALTER COLUMN Column2 DROP SPARSE
```

New & Noteworthy...

Using Column Sets

Sparse columns are often used with a new feature of SQL Server called column sets. A column set is like a calculated column that, when queried, returns an XML fragment representing all values stored in all sparse columns within a single table. A column set, similar to a calculated column, consumes no storage space except for table metadata. Unlike a calculated column, you can update a column set by updating the XML returned by the column set. This makes column sets especially useful for storing a large number of properties that are often null.

Consider using column sets when it is difficult to work with a large number of columns individually, and many of the values in these columns are null. Column sets can offer improved performance except in situations where many indexes are defined on the table. Example 7.11 demonstrates the use of column sets:

Example 7.11 Using Column Sets

```
CREATE TABLE Planets
(PlanetID int IDENTITY PRIMARY KEY,
PlanetName nvarchar(50) SPARSE NULL,
PlanetType nvarchar(50) SPARSE NULL,
Radius int SPARSE NULL,
PlanetDescription XML COLUMN_SET FOR ALL_SPARSE_COLUMNS);
GO

INSERT Planets (PlanetName, PlanetType, Radius) VALUES
('Earth', NULL, NULL),
('Jupiter', 'Gas Giant', 71492),
('Venus', NULL, 6051);
GO

SELECT PlanetDescription FROM Planets
-- Results:
-- PlanetDescription
-- ------------------
-- <PlanetName>Earth</PlanetName>
-- <PlanetName>Jupiter</PlanetName><PlanetType>Gas Giant
</PlanetType><Radius>71492</Radius>
-- <PlanetName>Venus</PlanetName><Radius>6051</Radius>

UPDATE Planets
SET PlanetDescription = '<PlanetName>Earth</PlanetName><PlanetType>Terrestrial
Planet</PlanetType><Radius>6371</Radius>'
WHERE PlanetName = 'Earth';
GO

SELECT * FROM Planets
-- Results:
-- ------------------------------
-- PlanetID    PlanetDescription
-- ---------   -------------------
-- 1           <PlanetName>Earth</PlanetName><PlanetType>Terrestrial Planet
            </PlanetType><Radius>6371</Radius>
-- 2           <PlanetName>Jupiter</PlanetName><PlanetType>Gas Giant
            </PlanetType><Radius>71492</Radius>
-- 3           <PlanetName>Venus</PlanetName><Radius>6051</Radius>

DROP TABLE Planets;
GO
```

The use of sparse columns is especially appropriate with filtered indexes. Filtered indexes are indexes that are optimized for querying data based on certain criteria. A filtered index on a sparse column can index only the rows that have non-null values. Filtered indexes created on sparse columns consume less disk space and improve performance.

Maintaining Indexes

Index maintenance is an important part of looking after databases. As you have learned from earlier chapters, indexes are structures that speed up data retrieval significantly. Indexes are stored on disk as physical structures. Indexes are automatically updated when underlying table data is modified. However, with time and data usage analysis, you may want to create new or drop existing indexes. You may also need to defragment indexes on frequently modified tables as they can be highly fragmented.

TEST DAY TIP

Sometimes very large indexes become difficult to maintain. As an alternative, consider partial indexes created with a filter (WHERE) clause. For partial indexes, the index structure is created only for a subset of data that is frequently searched for. For example, if you store a decade's worth of data in a table and only ever query the last year's worth of data frequently, there is no reason to maintain the index for the portion of the data that is accessed infrequently. An index with a WHERE clause helps overcome the situation by creating a small and efficient index structure that covers the current data only.

Dynamic Management Views (DMVs) is a feature introduced in SQL Server 2005 that allows you to view useful information about indexes. The following DMVs are available for index maintenance:

- sys.dm_db_missing_index_details Lists missing indexes

- *sys.dm_db_index_operational_stats* Shows index usage statistics

- *sys.dm_db_index_physical_stats* Shows fragmentation information on each index

As shown in Example 7.12, when the sys.dm_db_missing_index_details includes equality_columns, the DMV lists potential index suggestions.

Example 7.12 Finding Missing Indexes

```
SELECT DB_NAME(Database_id) AS DbName,
OBJECT_NAME(object_id, Database_id) AS ObjName, *
FROM sys.dm_db_missing_index_details

-- Results (no indexes are missing in this case):
-- DbName ObjName index_handle database_id object_id
equality_columns
inequality_columns
included_columns
statement
-- ------- -------- ------------ ----------- ----------- -----------------
-- (0 row(s) affected)
```

To identify any unused indexes that can be dropped, query the sys.dm_db_index_usage_stats DMV. This view explains when an index was last used, and how it was used (the number of seeks, scans, and bookmark lookups). The dm_db_index_usage_stats DMV is emptied every time the SQL Server service is restarted. In order to see the name of the index, you need to join the sys.dm_db_index_usage_stats DMV to the sys.indexes table, as shown in Example 7.13.

Example 7.13 Viewing Index Usage Statistics

```
SELECT indexes.name, IndexStats.*
    FROM sys.dm_db_index_operational_stats
    (DB_ID(N'AdventureWorks'),
      OBJECT_ID(N'AdventureWorks.Person.Address'),
      NULL,
      NULL) AS IndexStats
    INNER JOIN AdventureWorks.sys.indexes
    ON IndexStats.object_id = indexes.object_id
    AND IndexStats.index_id = indexes.index_id
```

Indexes become fragmented over time due to underlying data changes. There are two types of fragmentation: external and internal. In order to understand the difference, you must understand how SQL Server stores data. Rows are stored in 8KB pages, which are stored in extents. An extent can contain up to 8 pages. SQL Server always accesses data by extent, not by page or row. When a clustered index exists on a table, the actual table data is stored in the order of the index within each page. When the clustered index was first created, SQL Server arranged those pages so that contiguous pages were on the same extent.

However, if there's no room on the page to insert new rows, SQL Server splits the page, moving half of the data to a new page. This creates space to keep rows in logical sequence. If there is no space on the extent, SQL Server moves the new page to a different extent. In order to read a sequence of rows covering these two pages, SQL Server must load the two extents, or 16 pages, into memory. This can also occur when updating data, i.e., when the updated row no longer fits the page on which it was originally stored. In this case, the operation results in a split page.

When the logical order of pages becomes scattered across multiple extents, the situation is referred to as external fragmentation. When a table has external fragmentation, SQL Server spends more time accessing the drives. This is a problem because disk activity is the most resource consuming task SQL Server performs.

Internal fragmentation refers to empty space within data pages. Empty space within pages is created when data is deleted. Empty space within tables and indexes improves write performance because SQL Server can insert new records into the empty space without rearranging page structure. However, empty space decreases read performance, because SQL Server must load more extents into memory to read a data set. Allocating intentional empty space within a clustered or nonclustered index is called fill factor. The FILLFACTOR option can be used when creating new or rebuilding existing indexes. The FILLFACTOR option can be specified with the CREATE INDEX or ALTER INDEX WITH REBUILD statements (see Example 7.14). The FILLFACTOR is an integer between 0 and 100. For example, a FILLFACTOR of 80 means that the index pages will be 80 percent full. When values 0 or 100 are specified, no fill factor is used. Regularly defragmenting indexes can maintain the fill factor and optimize performance.

Example 7.14 Using the ALTER INDEX Statement with FILLFACTOR

```
USE AdventureWorks;
GO
ALTER INDEX IX_Contact_LastName ON Person.Contact.LastName
REBUILD WITH (FILLFACTOR = 80);
GO
```

Rebuilding an index is a resource intensive operation. Users cannot access the index while it is being rebuilt, unless the ONLINE option is used with the ALTER INDEX statement. As a best practice, you should rebuild all indexes that are reporting over 30 percent fragmentation. If the fragmentation reported is between 10 and 30 percent, it is recommended that you reorganize the index instead. Reorganizing indexes is a less intensive operation than a rebuild (see Example 7.15). The table and all of its indexes remain online and can be accessed by users while they are being reorganized. You can cancel reorganization without causing a rollback and without losing any of the defragmentation that has already taken place. However, reorganizing indexes takes longer and is not as thorough as rebuilding them.

Example 7.15 Reorganizing an Index

```
USE AdventureWorks;
GO
ALTER INDEX IX_Contact_LastName ON Person.Contact.LastName
REORGANIZE;
GO
```

TEST DAY TIP

Remember that you should rebuild an index when fragmentation is reported at 30 percent or more and reorganize when fragmentation is reported between 10 and 30 percent. Less than 10 percent fragmentation is normal. It would be counterproductive to try to defragment an index with less than 10 percent fragmentation. Also, ensure that you understand the implications of FILLFACTOR on read and write performance.

DBCC Explained

Database Console Commands, or DBCC, is a set of Transact SQL commands that allow you to perform table, index, and database maintenance tasks. DBCC can be used to validate the integrity of a database or its individual tables, indexes, tables, filegroups, or page allocation. Useful fragmentation information for tables and databases can be provided by DBCC. Maintenance tasks like shrinking database files or forcibly emptying caches can be performed by DBCC statements. Table 7.1 lists the options that can be used with DBCC.

Table 7.1 DBCC Options

Informational Statements	
INPUTBUFFER	Shows the contents of the current input buffer for a specific session.
OUTPUTBUFFER	Shows the contents of the current output buffer for a specific session.
OPENTRAN	Shows information about the last open transaction.
PROCCACHE	Shows information held in procedure cache.
SHOW STATISTICS	Shows query optimization statistics.
SHOWCONTIG	Shows information about the fragmentation of tables and indexes.
SQL PERF	Shows transaction log statistics for all databases.
TRACESTATUS	Shows which diagnostic trace flags have been set.
USEROPTIONS	Shows the connection options.
Validation Statements	
CHECKALLOC	Checks the integrity of disk space allocation for a database.
CHECKCATALOG	Checks catalog integrity.
CHECKCONSTRAINTS	Checks constraint integrity.
CHECKDB	Checks database integrity.
CHECKFILEGROUP	Checks the integrity of all tables and indexes in a filegroup.
CHECKIDENT	Shows the last identity value for a specified table. Can reseed the identity value.
CHECKTABLE	Checks table integrity.
Maintenance Statements	
CLEANTABLE	Reclaims space in a table after a variable length column has been dropped.
DROPCLEANBUFFER	Removes clean buffers from the buffer pool.

Continued

Table 7.1 Continued. DBCC Options

FREEPROCCACHE	Removes plans from the execution plan cache.
SHRINKDATABASE	Shrinks database files and log files for a database by a specified percentage.
SHRINKFILE	Shrinks database and log files.
UPDATEUSAGE	Shows and corrects page count and row count inaccuracies in catalog views.
DBREINDEX	Rebuilds indexes in a database. This option is deprecated and should be used for backwards compatibility only.
INDEXDEFRAG	Defragments indexes. This option is deprecated and should be used for backwards compatibility only.
Other Statements	
Dllname (FREE)	Frees the memory used by the specified extended stored procedure (xp) dll.
FREESESSIONCACHE	Flushes the distributed query cache for the current connection.
FREESYSTEMCACHE	Flushes all caches by releasing unused cache entries. Note that SQL Server cleans caches automatically in the background.
HELP	Shows the syntax for the specified DBCC command.
TRACEON	Enables trace flags used for diagnostic tracing.
TRACEOFF	Disables trace flags used for diagnostic tracing.

Most DBCC commands do not affect the live database. Instead, they are performed on a database snapshot. The snapshot is created, used for the command, and then dropped. Sometimes the snapshot cannot be created, for example, when the DBCC statement is run against the Master database. In this case, the statement is executed against the actual database. Using the snapshot instead of the actual database avoids congestion or locking through the DBCC affecting your live environment.

However, it is important to remember that most DBCC commands are processor intensive and should not be performed when the server is under a heavy load.

TEST DAY TIP

Don't spend a lot of time memorizing the syntax of every DBCC option. Instead, perform the DBCC CHECKTABLE, DBCC CHECKDB, and DBCC SHRINKFILE examples to become familiar with more commonly used DBCC options.

Some of the most powerful and frequently used DBCC commands are those that allow you to check data file fragmentation, validate the integrity of tables or databases, and reclaim space used by your databases and logs. Let's examine these commands in more detail. Performing the examples will familiarize you with how these statements can be used.

Using DBCC CHECKTABLE to Verify Table Integrity

DBCC CHECKTABLE examines and optionally repairs the structural integrity of all pages in a specified table. Any inconsistencies in table structure are reported. Use the syntax shown in Example 7.16 to run DBCC CHECKTABLE.

Example 7.16 Using DBCC CHECKTABLE—Syntax

```
DBCC CHECKTABLE (table_name | view_name,
{ NOINDEX | index_id } |,
{ REPAIR_ALLOW_DATA_LOSS | REPAIR_FAST | REPAIR_REBUILD }
)
[WITH ALL_ERRORMSGS, EXTENDED_LOGICAL_CHECKS, NO_INFOMSGS, TABLOCK,
ESTIMATEONLY, PHYSICAL_ONLY | DATA_PURITY}
```

When running DBCC CHECKTABLE, you can specify various options to alter the command behavior. The NOINDEX option specifies that checks should not be run on nonclustered indexes. This reduces the time it takes for the command to complete. Alternatively, you can specify the ID of the specific nonclustered index you wish to examine as the *index_id*. The table itself, whether stored as a heap or a clustered index, is always examined.

You can choose to repair the errors found by the DBCC by using the REPAIR_ALLOW_DATA_LOSS, REPAIR_FAST and REPAIR_REBUILD options. REPAIR_FAST is used for backwards compatibility only; it does not actually do anything. REPAIR_ALLOW_DATA_LOSS option specifies that data loss is acceptable during the repair operation. REPAIR_REBUILD does not allow data loss. The database must be in single user mode for any repair to occur.

The ALL_ERRORMSGS option specifies that all error messages must be shown, otherwise only the first 200 are shown. The NO_INFOMSGS specifies that no informational messages are to be shown.

The EXTENDED_LOGICAL_CHECKS option is a new option in SQL Server 2008. It instructs the DBCC to verify the logical structure of indexed views, XML indexes, and special indexes. This option is only available when the database compatibility level is set to SQL Server 2008 (100).

The TABLOCK option instructs the DBCC not to create a database snapshot. Instead, the DBCC will obtain a table lock on the table. This reduces the time it takes for the DBCC CHECKTABLE statement to complete. However, it also means that other users cannot write to the table while DBCC is running.

Running DBCC CHECKTABLE is a resource intensive task, and it consumes space in the tempdb database. By specifying ESTIMATEONLY, you will be shown the amount of space the operation will require in tempdb.

The PHYSICAL_ONLY option forces the DBCC to perform only checks on the physical structure integrity of pages, row headers, and B-tree structures. This check is quicker than the full run of DBCC CHECKTABLE because it omits the extensive logical checks that are normally run. The PHYSICAL_ONLY check can detect common hardware failures that result in table corruption and torn pages.

The DATA_PURITY option checks the validity of the data according to its data type. For example, the DATA_PURITY check will show all values that are not valid dates stored in columns of DateTime data type or values that are not valid integers stored in a column of int data type. SQL Server 2005 and 2008 perform this checking automatically. However, databases upgraded from SQL Server 2000 or earlier could contain such invalid column data. In this case, you must execute the DBCC CHECKTABLE WITH DATA_PURITY, manually correct all errors reported, and run DBCC CHECKTABLE WITH DATA_PURITY again to enable automatic column level integrity checking.

Example 7.17 demonstrates the use of the DBCC CHECKTABLE.

Example 7.17 Using the DBCC CHECKTABLE

```
USE AdventureWorks;
GO
-- Perform default checks
DBCC CHECKTABLE ("Person.Contact");
GO
-- Results:
-- DBCC results for 'Person.Contact'.
-- There are 19982 rows in 567 pages for object "Person.Contact".
-- DBCC results for 'sys.xml_index_nodes_341576255_256000'.
-- There are 195 rows in 3 pages for object
"sys.xml_index_nodes_341576255_256000".
-- DBCC execution completed. If DBCC printed error messages, contact your
system administrator.

-- Perform physical checks without creating a snapshot. Do not check
nonclustered indexes.
DBCC CHECKTABLE ("Person.Contact", NOINDEX)
WITH PHYSICAL_ONLY, TABLOCK;
GO
-- Results:
-- DBCC execution completed. If DBCC printed error messages, contact your
system administrator.

-- Generate estimate of tempdb space that would be consumed by the DBCC
CHECKTABLE operation.
DBCC CHECKTABLE ("Person.Contact")
WITH ESTIMATEONLY;
GO
-- Results:
-- Estimated TEMPDB space needed for CHECKTABLES (KB)
-- --------------------------------------------------
-- 8425
-- (1 row(s) affected)
-- DBCC execution completed. If DBCC printed error messages, contact your
system administrator.

-- Repair the Contact table, without losing data.
ALTER DATABASE AdventureWorks
SET SINGLE_USER;
GO
DBCC CHECKTABLE ("Person.Contact", REPAIR_REBUILD);
GO
-- Results:
-- DBCC results for 'Person.Contact'.
-- There are 19982 rows in 567 pages for object "Person.Contact".
-- DBCC results for 'sys.xml_index_nodes_341576255_256000'.
-- There are 195 rows in 3 pages for object "sys.xml_index_
nodes_341576255_256000".
```

```
-- DBCC execution completed. If DBCC printed error messages, contact your
system administrator.
ALTER DATABASE AdventureWorks
SET MULTI_USER;
GO
```

Using the DBCC CHECKDB to Verify Database Integrity

DBCC CHECKDB verifies the physical and logical integrity for all objects in a specified database and optionally attempts to repair integrity errors. DBCC CHECKDB runs DBCC CHECKALLOC, DBCC CHECKTABLE, and DBCC CHECKCATALOG on every applicable object in the database. If enabled DBCC CHECKDB validates the link between tables and FILESTREAM access, DBCC CHECKDB validates Service Broker data, if any. The syntax used to run DBCC CHECKDB is the same as DBCC CHECKTABLE, and all DBCC CHECKTABLE options apply to DBCC CHECKDB (see Example 7.18).

Example 7.18 Using the DBCC CHECKDB - Syntax

```
DBCC CHECKDB ( database_name | database_id | 0, [NOINDEX], [ REPAIR_ALLOW_
DATA_LOSS | REPAIR_FAST | REPAIR_REBUILD ])
WITH [ ALL_ERRORMSGS, EXTENDED_LOGICAL_CHECKS, NO_INFOMSGS, TABLOCK,
ESTIMATEONLY, PHYSICAL_ONLY | DATA_PURITY ]
```

Study the options used with DBCC CHECKTABLE as these apply to DBCC CHECKDB also. DBCC CHECKDB checks every table in the database. If 0 is specified for the *database_name* or the *database_name* is not specified, the current database is used. Example 7.19 demonstrates the use of DBCC CHECKDB:

Example 7.19 Using the DBCC CHECKDB

```
-- Repair any errors in the AdventureWorks database, allowing data loss.
ALTER DATABASE AdventureWorks
SET SINGLE_USER;
GO
DBCC CHECKDB ('Adventureworks', REPAIR_ALLOW_DATA_LOSS)
WITH EXTENDED_LOGICAL_CHECKS;
GO
-- Results:
-- DBCC results for 'AdventureWorks'.
```

```
-- Service Broker Msg 9675, State 1: Message Types analyzed: 14.
-- Service Broker Msg 9676, State 1: Service Contracts analyzed: 6.
-- Service Broker Msg 9667, State 1: Services analyzed: 3.
-- Service Broker Msg 9668, State 1: Service Queues analyzed: 3.
-- Service Broker Msg 9669, State 1: Conversation Endpoints analyzed: 0.
-- Service Broker Msg 9674, State 1: Conversation Groups analyzed: 0.
-- Service Broker Msg 9670, State 1: Remote Service Bindings analyzed: 0.
-- Service Broker Msg 9605, State 1: Conversation Priorities analyzed: 0.
-- DBCC results for 'sys.sysrscols'.
-- There are 1483 rows in 17 pages for object "sys.sysrscols".
-- -- DBCC results for 'sys.sysrowsets'.
-- There are 286 rows in 3 pages for object "sys.sysrowsets".
-- DBCC results for 'sys.sysallocunits'.
-- There are 334 rows in 5 pages for object "sys.sysallocunits".
-- DBCC results for 'sys.sysfiles1'.
-- (Truncated for brevity)
ALTER DATABASE AdventureWorks
SET MULTI_USER;
GO
```

Using the DBCC SHRINKFILE Option to Reclaim Database Space

DBCC SHRINKFILE shrinks a database file or a log file by rearranging data in the file to reclaim empty space. It can also move all data from a data file to another data file in the same filegroup, allowing you to remove the empty file. Using DBCC SHRINKFILE, you can shrink the file to a smaller size than its minimum size setting. The minimum size setting will then be reset to reflect the actual size. Use the syntax shown in Example 7.20 to run DBCC SHRINKFILE.

Example 7.20 Using the DBCC SHRINKFILE—Syntax

```
DBCC SHRINKFILE ( file_name | file_id, [EMPTYFILE],
[target_size], [NOTRUNCATE | TRUNCATEONLY] )
[ WITH NO_INFOMSGS]
```

When running DBCC SHRINKFILE, you can specify various options to alter the command behavior. You must specify the logical file name or file ID of the database or log file you wish to manipulate. When the EMPTYFILE option is specified, the DBCC moves all data from the specified file to other files in the same filegroup. SQL Server will no longer write to the file you have just emptied, allowing you to remove the empty file using the ALTER DATABASE statement.

You can specify the *target_size* in megabytes. The DBCC will then attempt to shrink the file to the target size. It does so by moving all data from throughout the end pages to free space earlier in the file. The file shrinkage will only be achieved if enough free space is available in the file.

The NOTRUNCATE option specifies that although the data in the file will be rearranged, the free space will not be released back to the operating system. This means that the actual file size of the file will not change. On the other hand, TRUNCATEONLY will rearrange the data and reclaim the free space to the operating system, thereby shrinking the file. TRUNCATEONLY ignores the target_size, reclaiming all possible space. Both NOTRUNCATE and TRUNCATEONLY are applicable only to database files.

The NO_INFOMSGS specifies that no informational messages are to be shown by the DBCC.

Example 7.21 demonstrates the use of DBCC SHRINKFILE.

Example 7.21 Using the DBCC SHRINKFILE

```
USE AdventureWorks;
GO
SELECT file_id, name
FROM sys.database_files;
GO
-- Reclaim all available free space from the data file
DBCC SHRINKFILE ('AdventureWorks_Data', TRUNCATEONLY);
-- Results:
-- DbId     FileId       CurrentSize  MinimumSize UsedPages   EstimatedPages
-- ------   -----------  -----------  ----------- ----------- --------------
-- 5        1            21760        21760       21432       21432
-- (1 row(s) affected)
-- DBCC execution completed. If DBCC printed error messages, contact your
system administrator.
-- Shrink the log file to 5 MB
DBCC SHRINKFILE (AdventureWorks_Log, 5);
GO
-- Empty a file
ALTER DATABASE AdventureWorks
ADD FILE ( NAME = NewData, FILENAME = 'C:\temp\newdata.ndf', SIZE = 5MB);
GO
-- Empty the data file.
```

```
DBCC SHRINKFILE (NewData, EMPTYFILE);
GO
-- Remove the data file from the database.
ALTER DATABASE AdventureWorks
REMOVE FILE NewData;
GO
-- Results:
-- DbId    FileId        CurrentSize MinimumSize UsedPages    EstimatedPages
-- ------  -----------   ----------- ----------- -----------  --------------
-- 5       3             640         640         0            0
-- (1 row(s) affected)
-- DBCC execution completed. If DBCC printed error messages, contact your
system administrator.
-- The file 'NewData' has been removed.
```

Backing Up and Restoring Data

Every organization that values its databases must have a disaster recovery strategy that works when needed. The disaster recovery strategy defines procedures for backing up and restoring SQL Server databases. Defining and adhering to the disaster recovery strategy is a primary task of any database administrator. In this section, you will learn about various types of backup available with SQL Server, best practices for performing backups, and restoring databases from backup.

Understanding Database Recovery Models

The database recovery model determines how transaction logs are used by SQL Server for a specified database. Your choice of recovery model affects which operations are performed as nonlogged and whether the database can be recovered to a point in time. Three recovery models are available for SQL Server 2008 databases:

- Simple recovery model
- Full recovery model
- Bulk-Logged recovery model

When the database recovery model is set to Simple, log files are reused as soon as they become full. This means that very little space is consumed by the transaction logs, and you don't need to worry about log file management. However, when a database is set to Simple recovery model and the database file is lost, you will not be able to recover any changes made after the last full backup. You will also not be able to recover to a point in time as transaction details are stored in transaction logs that have been overwritten in this case.

The Full recovery model could be said to be the opposite of the Simple recovery model. Transaction logs are kept, and all transactions without exception are written to the logs. This includes nonlogged operations like TRUNCATE TABLE and SELECT…INTO. Although you lose the performance advantages of nonlogged operations with this recovery model, all data is recoverable provided transaction logs are intact. You can also restore to a point-in-time if necessary.

The Bulk-Logged recovery model is similar to Full recovery model, except that nonlogged operations are performed as nonlogged. This provides a performance advantage for Bulk-Logged operations. However, if a Bulk-Logged operation has occurred since the last full backup, you will not be able to recover any changes made since the last full backup. The Bulk-Logged recovery model does not support point-in-time recovery.

In production environments, the full database recovery model is generally used as it ensures maximum recoverability. However, if the administrator wishes to perform a high performance nonlogged operation, they would temporarily switch the recovery model to Bulk-Logged, perform the operation, switch the recovery model back to Full, and perform a full backup. The Full recovery model is the default when creating databases in SQL Server.

Backup Types

SQL Server databases can be backed up using the Backup Database Wizard or the BACKUP DATABASE Transact-SQL statement. By specifying a particular backup type, you designate what data should be backed up. For example, you may choose to back up all data in a database or only the differences from the last full backup. All SQL Server backups are performed *online*. This means that users can continue to read and write to and from the database while the backup is being performed. However, backup is a resource and time intensive operation, especially for large databases. Therefore, backups should be scheduled at off-peak times to avoid performance degradation. Table 7.2 describes the types of backup available with SQL Server 2008.

Table 7.2 SQL Server 2008 Backup Types

Backup Type	Functionality	Purpose
Full Backup	Backup all data stored in data files and a small part of the transaction log generated while the backup operation was taking place.	To back up an entire database that can be restored as a whole. The most disk intensive and time consuming backup type.
Differential Backup	Backup the extents that were modified since the last full backup.	Provides the ability to create a frequent, incremental backup which can then be restored into an earlier version of a database restored from full backup.
Partial Backup	Backup of the primary filegroup, all writeable filegroups, and optionally specified read-only filegroups. Also available in differential partial backup, which backs up only the extents changed since the last full or partial backup of the corresponding filegroup.	Perform a more efficient, full or differential backup affecting only change-able data. Especially useful for large partitioned databases consisting of historical data that does not change and current data that does. Using partial backup, you can back up historical data only once and perform frequent partial backups of the current data.
File or Filegroup	A full backup of a specified database file or filegroup.	Allows you to granularly back up specific files or file groups for databases consisting of multiple files. When database files are distributed across mul-tiple disks, you can restore the data file to the failed disk only, which is more efficient than restoring the entire database.

Continued

Table 7.2 Continued. SQL Server 2008 Backup Types

Backup Type	Functionality	Purpose
Copy Only	Same as the full backup, however, the copy-only backup does not mark the database as having been backed up. You cannot take differential backups based on a copy backup.	Take an additional database backup without interfering with normal backup sequence.
Transaction Log	Back up all log entries since the last full backup. Multiple continuous log backups can be restored or "replayed" into a restore of a full backup, bringing the database up-to-date.	Perform a fast and efficient backup of all changes since the last full backup. Unlike differential backup, you can restore or "replay" a log backup to a particular point-in-time. This allows you to roll back unwanted activity like malicious deletions. This also truncates the log file.
Tail-Log Backup	Backup of the transaction log performed just before a restore operation.	If a database file is lost but the log file is still intact, replaying the tail-log backup into the restored database allows you to bring the database up-to-date and eliminate the loss of transactions that occurred after the backup.

TEST DAY TIP

Study the various types of backup available and ensure that you understand the differences between them. Remember that although differential and transaction log backups are quicker to perform, they take a longer time to be replayed into a restored database. On the other hand, while backing up the entire database is time consuming, restoring it as a whole is faster than replaying numerous differential and transaction log backups into an initial restored database.

Choosing a Database Backup Strategy

Choosing the appropriate database backup strategy depends on your organization's individual business continuity requirements, the size of your database, and the amount of time allocated for backup operations. The data loss tolerance is a measure defining how much data your organization is prepared to lose in the worst case scenario. For example, if your organizations data loss tolerance is one day, you must take some form of backup at least every day. If the data loss tolerance is six hours, you must take some form of backup at least every six hours.

The challenge of any disaster recovery strategy is balancing the data loss tolerance against the amount of time it takes to perform a backup. For example, a full backup of a large database can take 24 hours or longer. This means that you cannot conduct full backups every six hours. In this situation, you may wish to settle for a full backup every weekend and a differential or log backup every six hours.

Use the following best practices as your guide when selecting a backup strategy:

- For small databases, you can choose to take full backups only. Perform a full backup as often as your data loss tolerance dictates, e.g., every day or every weekend. Restoring a full backup is the most complete and time-effective way to restore a database. Tail-log backups can be used in conjunction with a restore from a full database backup in the event that the database file is lost but the log file is not.

- Full + transaction log backup strategy is suitable to larger databases. For example, you can choose to backup the database every weekend and trans-action logs every day. This achieves a reduction in backup time and a reduction in the space consumed by the backup while providing you with the complete backup of the daily database activity. The trade-off is in the restore time. It takes longer to replay every single log backup into the database than simply restoring the entire database from a full backup. When recovering the database protected by this backup strategy, you must first restore the latest full database backup. You must then restore every log backup, including the tail-log backup if desired. This is the only strategy that allows you to recover to a point-in-time.

- Full + differential backup strategy is suitable for very large databases, where certain extents are updated more frequently than others. For example, you can choose to backup the database every weekend, and back up the differences every day. This gives you a complete backup of daily database activity as well as a reduction in backup time and a reduction in space con-sumed by the backup. Again, the trade off is in the restore time. It takes longer to replay all the daily differentials into a database than to restore the entire database from a full backup. When recovering the database protected by this backup strategy, you must first restore the latest full database backup. You can then restore the latest differential backup. Finally, you can restore any transaction log backups (including the tail–log backup) taken since the last differential backup. This strategy consumes less restore time than an equivalent full + log backup but more restore time than the full backup only.

■ File or filegroup backup strategy consists of alternately backing up each read/write file or filegroup that comprises the database. Additionally, the transaction log grown between file or filegroup backups is also backed up. This strategy is suitable for large partitioned databases. Although this strategy consumes less backup time than a full backup, it is more complicated.

New & Noteworthy...

Backup File Compression

Compressing backups is a new feature of SQL Server 2008. Performing compressed backup is only available in the Enterprise edition of SQL Server 2008. All editions of SQL Server 2008 and later can restore compressed backups. Compressed backup offers performance advantages as the backup file is smaller. However, performing compressed backups is more processor intensive than performing uncompressed backups.

Compressed backups cannot reside on the same media set (file or tape) with uncompressed backups or non-SQL Server backups. Compressed backups cannot be read by earlier versions of SQL Server.

TEST DAY TIP

Remember that only a transaction log backup can be used to restore a database to a point-in-time. You can only replay a transaction log backup into a restored database. For example, if you took a full database backup on 15 February at 1:00 a.m. and log backups every day until 20 February, you can restore the database from the full backup then bring it forward to any point in time between 15 February 1:01 a.m. and 20 February. You cannot, however, roll the database back to 14 February or any time before the full database backup.

Configuring & Implementing...

Performing Test Restores

Disasters strike unexpectedly. To be prepared for disaster recovery, you must perform regular test restores. Performing a test restore can help you determine whether the recovery procedures defined in your disaster recovery strategy meet your organization's objectives for data recovery. Test restores also help administrators understand the course of action to take in the event of a disaster. If a disaster occurs, they will be able to act in a competent manner.

Test restores also validate the backup procedures. Only a successful test restore can assure that the backup is functioning, the backup hardware is working correctly, and the backup media is intact.

When performing a test restore, you should consider doing so on a separate lab server. Alternatively, if this is not possible, you can restore the database under a different name onto the existing server.

Restoring Databases

When you wish to recover database data, you must restore the database from backup to an operational state. During a restore, the database is copied from backup, but the restore operation is not marked complete. At this point, any contiguous transactions recorded in the log can be applied to the restored database. This process is known as "roll forward", because it advances the database state to a target recovery point. The recovery point is usually all available data. However, in certain circumstances you may wish to roll the database forward to a specific point in time. Once the restore is marked complete, no subsequent differential or log backups can be rolled forward into the database.

There are multiple possible restore scenarios. The restore scenario you choose depends on your restore requirements and the type of backup you are restoring from. The restore scenarios are dependent on the database recovery model and the SQL Server edition.

When you restore a database from a database backup, SQL Server re-creates the database. All database and log files are placed in their original location, unless new locations are explicitly specified. SQL Server databases are inherently portable. You can restore databases from backup on any SQL Server or even restore a copy of the database under a different name on the same server.

Performing Online Restore

During a full restore, the database is normally rendered inaccessible, and users cannot connect to or use the database. However, sometimes you may be restoring only a small part of the database like a file, filegroup, or individual page. In this case, it is possible to leave the database online, and all parts of the database, except the ones you are restoring, will be accessible to users. Online restore is the default when performing file, filegroup, or piecemeal (multiple filegroup) restores.

To perform an online restore, follow these steps:

1. Restore the data file, filegroup, or page.

2. Restore the log. Use the WITH RECOVERY option for the last log restore (see Example 7.22).

3. The restored data will become accessible once the log has been replayed successfully.

Example 7.22 Performing an Online Restore

```
-- First, restore the filegroup A and C
RESTORE DATABASE adb FILEGROUP='A',FILEGROUP='C'
FROM partial_backup
WITH PARTIAL, RECOVERY;
-- Next, restore the filegroup B. At this point filegroups A and C are
accessible to users.
RESTORE DATABASE adb FILEGROUP='B' FROM backup
WITH RECOVERY;
```

Restoring Individual Pages

Sometimes data corruption can result in "suspect" pages. These are pages that cannot be read by SQL Server or that result in errors when accessed. You can view the list of suspect pages for all databases by querying the suspect_pages table in the MSDB database. If the suspect page occurs in a nonclustered index, you can repair the index by rebuilding it. If the suspect page contains table data, you will have to restore it from backup. Page restores are performed online. Example 7.23 demonstrates the proper use of PAGE parameter with RESTORE DATABASE.

Example 7.23 Restoring a Damaged Page Online

```
-- First, restore the filegroup A and C
RESTORE DATABASE AdventureWorks PAGE='1:57, 1:202, 1:916, 1:1016'
    FROM DBFile2_Backup
    WITH NORECOVERY;
RESTORE LOG AdventureWorks FROM LogFile1_Backup
    WITH NORECOVERY;
RESTORE LOG AdventureWorks FROM LogFile2_Backup
    WITH NORECOVERY;
BACKUP LOG AdventureWorks TO TailLog_Backup
RESTORE LOG AdventureWorks FROM TailLog_Backup WITH RECOVERY;
GO
```

Head of the Class...

Disaster Recovery Considerations for System Databases

SQL Server stores important configuration information in system databases. Unfortunately, the backup of system databases is often overlooked. This oversight results in difficulties when SQL Server is rendered inoperable by a disaster, and you must restore it to the last known state. When you are restoring an entire server, always restore the system databases before user databases.

The following system databases must be backed up for production servers:

- Master
- Model
- MSDB
- Configuration/Distribution

The recovery model is set to Simple for all system databases except MSDB. The recovery model for the MSDB database can be configured to Full or Bulk-Logged.

If you notice that system databases are damaged, you have a choice of restoring the databases from backup or rebuilding them to their initial state. If you can start the SQL Server service, it is recommended that the system databases be restored from the most recent backup. If you cannot start the SQL Server service, you must rebuild the system databases first then attempt to restore the databases. Perform the following steps to restore the Master database:

1. Configure SQL Server to run in single user mode.

2. Restore the Master database from backup using the RESTORE DATABASE statement.

3. After the restore, SQL Server service will disconnect your connection.

4. Configure SQL Server to run in multiple user mode and restart the service.

Performing Ongoing Maintenance

Many repetitive administrative tasks are critical to maintaining your SQL Server's health and performance. These tasks include database validation, index maintenance, and backup. SQL Server 2008 makes it easy to follow best practices for ongoing maintenance. The SQL Server Agent feature allows you to schedule administrative routines by creating multi step jobs. The SQL Server Agent feature can also notify people when a certain event occurs. You can use the Maintenance Plans feature to visually create, schedule, and monitor ongoing maintenance tasks. Maintenance Plans allow you to consolidate all individual administrative tasks into a coherent strategy. Policy-Based Management allows administrators in large organizations to monitor and configure any number of SQL Servers and databases for configuration settings and compliance. Using this feature, you can also enforce compliance rules and standards on the naming and configuration of SQL Servers and SQL Server objects.

Using SQL Server Agent

SQL Server Agent is a service installed with SQL Server 2008. This service allows you to schedule activities to run at certain times. SQL Server Agent is widely used by administrators to schedule database backups, performance data collection, policy applications, and other routine tasks. SQL Server agent has the ability to notify people by e-mail of certain events, a feature known as notifications.

Let's examine the three key concepts behind SQL Server Agent:

- **Jobs** Jobs are the tasks you wish to execute on a schedule. Jobs consist of job steps, which define the individual task to run and what happens if the step fails. Steps are defined using Transact-SQL; however, multiple wizards generate the required Transact-SQL statements from a friendly interface.

When defining job steps, you can specify their order and which step to execute next on success or failure of the previous jobs. Jobs are associated with flexible schedules. Figure 7.3 shows the types of schedules you can configure.

Figure 7.3 SQL Server Agent Schedule Options

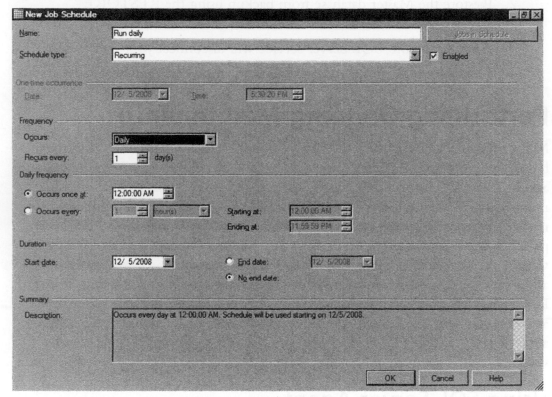

- **Alerts** Alerts are actions that SQL Server will perform when a particular event occurs. Alerts consist of conditions and actions. Conditions can be specific error codes, error severities or object states like databases files growing to a certain size. Actions performed by an alert are notifying a person, or running a job.

- **Operators** Operators are people who will be notified of alerts or job completion. SQL Server Agent can notify operators through e-mail, pager, or a net send network command.

SQL Server Agent stores the configuration for jobs, schedules, alerts, and operators in the MSDB system database. This is why it is very important to backup the MSDB system database in production environments. If you don't back up this database, you risk losing the entire maintenance related configuration you have spent countless hours implementing.

EXAM WARNING

SQL Server Agent is widely used by system activities like Maintenance Plans and replication. Therefore, if you are using any of these features, you must ensure that the SQL Server Agent service is running. Ideally, you should set the Startup Type for this service to Automatic to ensure the service is not accidentally stopped during server restart.

Also remember that there is a separate SQL Server Agent service for every instance of SQL Server installed on the computer.

In order to enable SQL Server Agent to notify users by e-mail, the Database Mail feature of SQL Server must be configured. Database Mail uses a Simple Mail Transfer Protocol (SMTP) server to relay its e-mail. It is recommended that you turn off the Database Mail feature if you are not going to be notifying operators by e-mail. This is to avoid the risk of your server being compromised and used as a relay point for unauthorized bulk e-mail. If you wish to enable Database Mail settings, use the Database Mail Configuration Wizard accessible from the Object Explorer. To configure it, expand **Management**, right-click **Database Mail** and then click **Configure Database Mail.** This feature is not reliant on the availability of SQL Server service as it caches the e-mail profile and credentials. Therefore, SQL Server Agent can notify you of a server outage by e-mail.

Using Database Maintenance Plans

Database Maintenance Plans are a wizard-based way to perform recommended tasks on your SQL Server 2008 servers. The Maintenance Plan Wizard allows you to select from a set of best practice based tasks and will create and schedule SQL Server Agent jobs to perform these tasks on a specified schedule. It is strongly recommended that you start with the guidance offered by the Maintenance Plan Wizard and set up the core administration tasks. You can later customize the plans by adding extra tasks or modifying the tasks themselves. You can schedule Maintenance Plans or run them manually. You can also target linked servers with your maintenance plans if you wish.

TEST DAY TIP

Your user account must belong to the sysadmin fixed server role to view, create, or modify Maintenance Plans. If you are connected with an account that is not a member of sysadmin, the Maintenance Plans item will not appear in Object Explorer.

Let's examine the important routine management tasks that can be created easily using the Maintenance Plan Wizard:

- Maintain indexes by reorganizing or rebuilding them with a Fill Factor. Routinely rebuilding indexes prevents overall performance degradation due to fragmentation. Routinely enforcing a Fill Factor ensures that write performance is optimal. This plan option uses the ALTER INDEX WITH REBUILD | REORGANIZE statement.

- Maintain indexes by updating index statistics to ensure optimal query performance. This plan option uses DBCC UPDATESTATISTICS command.

- Keep used disk space to a minimum by data in database files so that any empty space is moved to the end of the file. Then, the maintenance plan can physically shrink the file by truncating empty space. This plan option uses DBCC SHRINKFILE command.

- Validate database integrity, detect database corruption, and attempt to repair it. This plan option uses DBCC CHECKDB command.

- Backup the databases and transaction logs customized for your backup strategy. This plan option uses BACKUP DATABASE command.

- Run any SQL Server Agent job.

As you can see, although you can use SQL Server Agent to create and schedule these tasks manually, it is quite complicated and easy to view and change. Database Maintenance Plans allow you to configure and schedule these vital tasks using a simple user interface. When maintenance plans execute, they produce log records that are written to a file-based report, which by default is stored in the *%Program Files%\Microsoft SQL*
Server\MSSQL.1\MSSQL\LOG folder and is named starting with the Maintenance Plan name followed by the execution date and time. Execution results are always written to Sysmaintplan_log and sysmaintplan_logdetail tables stored in MSDB.

The configuration of maintenance plans is stored in MSDB also. Again, you must back up MSDB to avoid the risk of losing your maintenance plan configuration.

To configure Maintenance Plans, expand **Management**, right-click **Maintenance Plans,** and then click **Maintenance Plan Wizard.** To view the execution history of a particular maintenance plan, right-click on it in the Object Browser, then click **View History**.

Policy-Based Management

Many database administrators work for large organizations that keep many SQL Servers—for example, a customer organization that maintains over 50 SQL Servers in different locations. As you can imagine, it is difficult to report on and apply configuration changes to that many servers individually. Keeping the configuration standardized becomes a laborious task, and, with individual management, mistakes are inevitable. This is why the Policy-Based Management feature has been introduced in SQL Server 2008. Policy-Based Management allows you to view and configure settings on multiple instances of SQL Server 2008. Using Policy-Based Management you can apply a configuration change to a group of servers with one administrative action. Furthermore, Policy-Based Management allows you to enforce standards on your SQL Server, for example, object naming standards. This is known as *Explicit Administration*. SQL Server Management Studio provides Policy-Based Management wizards. These are accessible from the Object Browser under **Management | Policy Management.**

Let's examine the key components of Policy-Based Management and how they relate to each other:

- *Managed targets* are the objects you will be managing with Policy-Based Management. Instances of SQL Server, databases, tables, indexes, and other database objects can be targeted for Policy-Based Management. Targets are presented in a logical hierarchy. You can create *target sets* by filtering all managed targets using a filter criterion; for example, all database names starting with 'MOSS_' or all non system tables in a database named 'HR_Database'.

- Facets are essentially a logical group of properties that apply to a particular target. For example, the facet Server Information applies to targets of type Server. This facet contains many properties including Collation, IsClustered, and IsSingleUser. All these represent SQL Server properties. Another example is the Index facet. Not surprisingly, this facet applies to Index targets and contains properties like PadIndex, FillFactor, and SpaceUsed.

■ Conditions are expressions that represent what states are allowed for a particular target or target set. The expression is generally represented by a formula such as facet property <comparison operator> value. An example is Table facet, Name LIKE 'tbl_'. This condition states that table names must start with 'tbl_'. Figure 7.4 shows a policy condition that checks that all views in user databases are prefixed with vw_.

Figure 7.4 Policy Condition

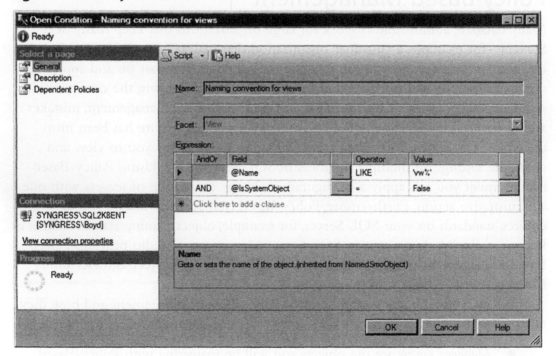

■ Policies are a unit of management that can be enabled or disabled. A policy links a condition with an applicable evaluation mode, filter, schedule, and target set. One policy represents one condition only. Policies can be grouped into categories for ease or administration. Databases and servers are subscribed to policy categories, and policies from those categories apply to the database subscribed. You can also subscribe a server to a policy category. In this case, the policies from this category apply to every database on that server. Policies can be evaluated to examine all targets that are not compliant, or, in some cases, they can be applied to reconfigure the targets to be in compliance.

■ Any of the four *evaluation modes* can be linked to the policy: *"on demand," "on change: prevent," "on change: log only,"* and *"on schedule."* These modes are used to check whether the target complies with the policy. The "on change: prevent" and "on change: log only" policies are enforced using recursive DDL triggers. The "on schedule" evaluation is performed using SQL Server Agent. Not all policies support "on change: prevent" and "on change: log only" evaluation modes. When the policy is evaluated automatically by "on change: prevent" and "on change: log only" or "on schedule" evaluation modes, an event is written to the event log. You can subscribe to these events if you wish and create a SQL Server agent alert that notifies you automatically.

You can create and apply policies using SQL Server Management Studio by performing the following high-level steps:

1. Choose a facet that contains the properties you wish to use in your policy.

2. Create a policy condition on this facet.

3. Create a new policy and link it to the condition you have just defined.

4. Specify the filter criteria that define which target sets this policy will apply to.

5. Specify the policy evaluation mode: "on demand," "on change: prevent," "on change: log only," or "on schedule."

6. Evaluate the policy to identify if any targets are not compliant with the policy.

7. Apply the policy to reconfigure the noncompliant targets so that they are compliant. This may not be possible for all types of properties, for example, you cannot reconfigure the ServerVersion property, but you can change the LoginMode property.

8. If a policy has failed, the noncompliant target will be marked with a red warning icon in Object Explorer. This icon will also be displayed next to all the parent nodes of this target, so you can easily find it.

Examples of Using Policy-Based Management

Why would you want to use Policy-Based Management? When you must examine the configuration of several SQL Servers or several databases, Policy-Based Management makes this task a lot easier than doing this individually or creating elaborate scripts. Policy-Based Management also allows you to apply the change to multiple servers or databases at once, saving a great deal of administrative effort. Finally, the automatic evaluation modes can enforce compliance by either not allowing people to make configuration changes that would violate policies or by raising an administrative alert when a violation takes place.

Let's examine some examples of how organizations have implemented Policy-Based Management.

- For security reasons, your organization prohibits SQL Server Authentication mode on any of its 27 SQL Servers. You create a policy with a condition for the Server Security facet, LoginMode = Integrated. You create a policy linking this condition with a policy and identify servers that don't comply with it. Unfortunately, you cannot use Policy-Based Management to apply this policy.

- Your organization is a software development company, and it creates many databases for customers. You are tired of junior developers not applying a naming convention to stored procedures and wish to stop it. You create a policy with a condition on Stored Procedure facet, Name LIKE sp_%. You apply the policy in "on change: prevent" mode to ensure that developers must follow the naming convention for stored procedures or they will not be able to create them.

- You wish to quickly check which SQL Servers have a certain service pack applied. You create a policy condition Server Information facet, VersionNumber >= <your required version>. You apply the policy on demand and quickly identify all servers that have not had the required service pack applied.

Using the Data Collector to Collect Performance Data

SQL Server 2008 includes a Data Collector feature: a powerful set of scheduled SQL Agent jobs, data structures, and tools designed for collecting and analyzing data from various sources. The Data Collector is often used to collect and consolidate performance data, but this is not the only use of this feature. Data collected by the Data Collector is stored in a relational database referred to as the management data warehouse. You can define how long data should remain in the management data warehouse. SQL Server Reporting Services can be used to create reports, then view and analyze the collected data. Default reports are available for the most common data analysis tasks.

The Data Collector comprises the following components:

- **Data Providers** These are compliant sources of data that the Data Collector can connect to and retrieve data from. Common data providers are SQL Server Trace, Performance Monitor (Perfmon), and custom query results.

- **Collection Items** A collection item defines the pieces of data you wish to collect and retain. For example, you may wish to only retain one or two columns from a query or only a specific performance counter. When you define a collection item, you also specify how often the item should be collected. Collection items are grouped logically into collection sets.

- **Management Data Warehouse** This relational database stores diagnostic information and data collected by the data collector.

- **Data Collector Reports** These SQL Server Reporting Services reports display the collected data. Some commonly used reports are installed by default, or you can create your own custom reports. Figure 7.5 shows one example of the many default Data Collector reports included with SQL Server 2008.

- **Proxy Accounts** These accounts are used to access data sources and must have sufficient permissions to collect data from these sources.

Figure 7.5 Example: Default Data Collector Report

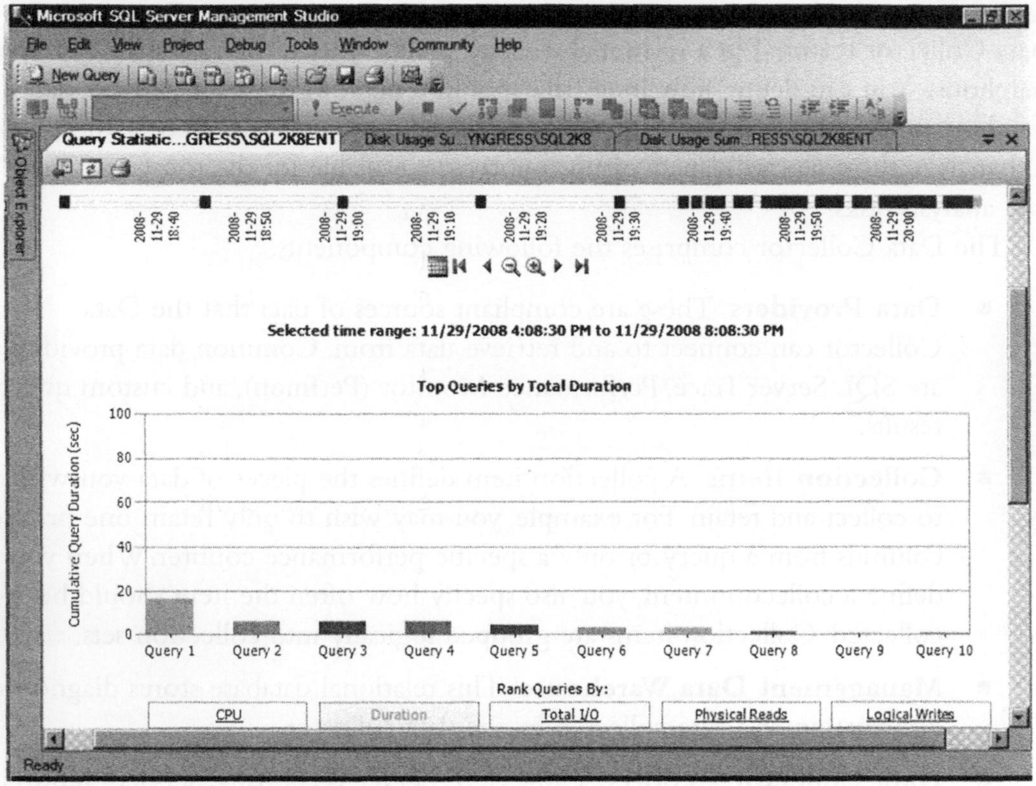

EXERCISE 7.3

USING THE DATA COLLECTOR

In this exercise, you will configure the Data Collector feature of SQL
Server 2008, enable performance data collection, and, finally, view Data
Collector reports.

Before you begin, you must have the following software installed on
your computer:

- SQL Server 2008: a free trial is available for download

- SQL Server 2008 Reporting Services (optional)

- AdventureWorks2008 sample database

- SQL Agent must be started

Once you have met these requirements, you may begin.

1. Open SQL Server Management Studio. To do this click **Start | All Programs | Microsoft SQL Server 2008 | SQL Server Management Studio**.

2. In the Object Explorer pane on the left, expand **Management**, right-click **Data Collection,** then click **Configure Management Data Warehouse Wizard**. On the Welcome page, click **Next**.

3. In the **Configure Management Data Warehouse Wizard** ensure that **Create or upgrade a management data warehouse** is selected, then click **Next**.

4. Configure the data warehouse to be stored on the local server using a new database named **DataCollectorDW**. Click **Next | Finish**. Wait for the configuration to complete, then click **Close**.

5. In the Object Explorer pane on the left, expand **Management**, right-click **Data Collection,** then click **Configure Management Data Warehouse Wizard**. On the Welcome page, click **Next**.

6. In the **Configure Management Data Warehouse Wizard,** ensure that **Set up data collection** is selected, then click **Next**.

7. Choose to use the **DataCollectorDW** database on the local server you have just created. Choose to use **C:\Temp** as the cache directory. Click **Next | Finish**. Wait for the configuration to complete, then click **Close**.

8. In the Object Explorer pane, expand **Data Collector | System Data Collection Sets**.

9. If you have SQL Server 2008 Reporting Services, right-click **Disk Usage | Reports | Historical | Disk Usage Summary** and view the report data. Close the report.

10. Double-click **Disk Usage** and review the data collection set properties.

11. Close SQL Server Management Studio.

Summary of Exam Objectives

In this chapter you have learned about ongoing maintenance tasks you must perform to keep your databases functioning well.

Data collation defines how text data is stored, sorted, and compared. Specifically, data collation defines the code page to use with non-Unicode (char, varchar, text) text data types. It also defines whether sort and comparison operators are case sensitive, accent sensitive, kana sensitive, and/or width sensitive. Collation names provide clues to the functionality of data collation, for example, French_CS_AI data collation uses French character codepage and is case sensitive and accent insensitive. Binary collations are always case and accent sensitive. You can assign data collation at server, database, and column level. Use the *COLLATE collation_name* clause with the SELECT statement to select a specific collation for sort, comparison, or join.

You must maintain your database by regularly checking for data validity, managing disk space, and optimizing database performance. Data validation and repair is performed using the Database Console Commands (DBCC). Although many commands are available, you should learn about DBCC CHECKDB and CBCC SHRINKFILE in detail. You have also learned about page and row level compression, which can be used to maximize the utilization of disk space by your tables. Mark columns as sparse to reduce the space used by storing null values. Sparse columns can be efficiently used with column sets and filtered indexes.

Maintenance tasks, including database validation, index maintenance, and backup are key to the health of your SQL Server. To automate these tasks, use SQL Server Agent to create multi step jobs and run them on a schedule. For proactive monitoring, use SQL Server Agent alerts to notify operators when an error occurs. The Maintenance Plans feature allows you to visually consolidate many individual administrative tasks into a coherent strategy based on proven best practices. Finally, the new Policy-Based Management feature of SQL Server 2008 allows administrators in large organizations to monitor and configure any number of SQL Servers and databases for configuration settings and compliance. Using this feature, you can also enforce compliance rules and standards on the naming and configuration of SQL Servers and SQL Server objects.

Creating and executing a disaster recovery strategy is a key part of any database administrator's job. The disaster recovery strategy consists of a backup strategy that encompasses the type and frequency of backup and a restore strategy that specifies how data is to be restored in the event of a disaster. SQL Server offers many backup and restore types to meet your organization's needs. You can back up an entire database as a whole or only the changes since the last backup. You can also back up the log file and then replay it into a database restored from a full backup. Restoring databases is a highly flexible operation in SQL Server 2008, allowing you to restore a full backup, merge differential backup changes into the full backup, and replay logs to a point-in-time to roll the database forward. Backup compression is a new feature of SQL Server 2008 Enterprise Edition that delivers faster, smaller backups. Importantly, you can restore parts of a database while the unaffected parts remain accessible to users through an online restore.

The Data Collector feature of SQL Server 2008 uses scheduled SQL Agent jobs, data structures, and tools designed to collect and analyze data from various sources. The Data Collector can be used to collect and consolidate performance data, custom collection items, and sets from compatible data providers. Data collected by the Data Collector is stored in the management data warehouse. You can create SQL Server Reporting Services reports to view and analyze the data. Some reports are available by default.

Exam Objectives Fast Track

Understanding Data Collation

☑ Data Collation defines the code page for multilingual data and rules for sort, and comparison of this data (case, accent, kanatype and width sensitivity).

☑ The server-level default collation applies to all new databases unless a different database-level collation is specified. The database-level collation applies to all new table columns unless a different column-level collation is specified.

☑ If a database is restored to a server with a different collation, the database-level and column-level collations will remain as they were originally specified.

☑ You can use the COLLATE collation_name option in a SELECT statement to explicitly specify a collation to use in the ORDER BY, WHERE or JOIN clauses.

Maintaining Data Files

☑ To reduce the disk space used by your database, consider implementing data compression. Data compression can be set at the row level and page level. Additionally, you can implement sparse columns to decrease the space it takes to store null values.

☑ You can view index usage statistics and new index suggestions by querying dm_db_missing_index_details, dm_db_index_operational_stats and dm_db_index_physical_stats Dynamic Management Views (DMVs).

☑ You can rebuild and reorganize indexes by using the ALTER INDEX statement with the REBUILD or REORGANIZE clause. You can also specify a FILLFACTOR to determine how much free space should be allocated for future inserts on index pages.

☑ The Database Console Commands (DBCC) are a useful set of commands that allow you to view and manipulate your databases. For example, you can verify the integrity of all tables in a database using DBCC CHECKDB, or shrink a database or log file using DBCC SHRINKFILE.

Backing Up and Restoring Data

☑ The Database Recovery Model defines how transaction logs are used for a database. Simple recovery model overwrites the transaction log as needed. The Full recovery model forces all transactions to be written to the log without exception. Bulk- Logged recovery model records most transactions, except the Bulk-Logged operations like TRUNCATE TABLE. The Full recovery model should be used in production, and is the only recovery model that guarantees the ability to restore transaction logs into a database.

☑ SQL Server allows you to backup an entire database (known as full backup), individual files and filegroups, changes to database extents since the last backup (known as a differential backup) or create a copy-only backup that does not interfere with normal backup schedule.

☑ Transaction log backup can be taken, and then replayed into the database when restored. Backing up and restoring a salvaged transaction log after a restore operation is known as Tail-Log backup and restore.

☑ You can roll the database forward to a specified point in time by replaying transaction logs into a database during restore.

☑ An online restore is a way of restoring individual files, filegroups and even pages into an existing database, while the rest of the database remains accessible by users.

Performing Ongoing Maintenance

☑ SQL Server Agent is a service that can create multi step jobs, notification alerts, and notify operators by e-mail, pager or NET SEND command.

☑ SQL Server Agent service must be running for jobs and alerts to execute. It is also key to system functionality like replication, Policy-Based Management and data collector.

☑ The Database Maintenance Plan wizard allows sysadmins to create, modify, schedule and run customized maintenance plans. A Maintenance Plan is a sequence of ongoing maintenance tasks like rebuilding indexes, validate databases, and perform backup.

☑ Policy-Based Management is a new feature of SQL Server 2008 that allows you to create and apply policies to multiple target servers or database objects. A policy consists of a set of conditions that must be met by the object for it to be compliant with the policy. Objects that do not comply with the policy are reported to you when the policy is evaluated.

☑ Policies can be evaluated manually or automatically. This is known as "on demand", "on change: prevent", "on change: log only" and "on schedule" policy evaluation modes. These modes are used to check whether the target complies with the policy, and possibly prevent a change that will cause the object to become noncompliant. The "on change: prevent" and "on change: log only" policies are enforced using recursive DDL triggers. The "on schedule" evaluation is performed using SQL Server Agent.

Performance Data Collection

☑ The Data Collector is a feature of SQL Server 2008 that allows you to systematically collect data from various sources and store it in a data warehouse.

☑ The Data Collector can be used to collect performance data, but it is not limited to this use.

☑ The Data Collector uses SQL Agent jobs to collect data, and SQL Agent must be running for the Data Collector to work.

☑ SQL Server Reporting Services reports are created on collected data. Built-in reports are available, or you can create custom reports.

Exam Objectives
Frequently Asked Questions

Q: What happens to the database collation when a database is restored from backup to a server that has a different data collation?

A: The database collation remains as it was on the source server.

Q: How do I change collation settings at column and database level once they have been assigned?

A: Use ALTER TABLE and ALTER DATABASE statements with the COLLATE clause. Unfortunately, there are many restrictions preventing this operation.

Q: What happens when I join two tables, but the join keys have different collations?

A: You will receive an error message similar to 'Cannot resolve collation conflict between 'Latin1_General_CS_AS' and 'Greek_CI_AS' in equal to operation.'

Q: Which is more efficient: row-level compression or page-level compression?

A: Page-level compression results in more efficient disk space usage as it enables row-level compression, prefix compression, and dictionary compression. However, page-level compression also results in higher performance overhead.

Q: Can I create a column set on the entire table and update each row as an XML fragment?

A: No, because column sets are defined on sparse columns and the primary key column cannot be marked as sparse. You must always have a primary key column in a table.

Q: Is the Fill Factor of an index automatically maintained by SQL Server?

A: No, the Fill Factor is only an initial setting. This is why you must rebuild your indexes as an ongoing task.

Q: What is the overhead of Policy-Based Management on my SQL Server?

A: Unless the policy is currently being evaluated, there is no overhead on SQL Server. Two exceptions are the "On Change: Prevent" and "On Change: Log

Only" evaluation modes. These modes use DDL Triggers, which execute to perform a check every time an object in the policy's target set is altered. This results in some overhead.

Q: Can you manage earlier versions of SQL Server using Policy-Based Management?

A: Yes, except not all settings are applicable to all versions of SQL Server.

Q: When a SQL Server Agent job executes, what credentials are used?

A: The credentials used are those of the SQL Server Agent service account, unless a proxy is explicitly configured or the statement is performing custom impersonation.

Q: Is it better to create Maintenance Plans or individual SQL Server Agent jobs to perform my routine management and maintenance tasks?

A: It is recommended that you use Maintenance Plans because they are easier to view and edit. Additionally, the Maintenance Plan Wizard will not let you misconfigure a task, which cannot be said for complicated homegrown Transact-SQL scripts.

Q: Differential and log backups both record changes from the last full backup, so what is the difference between them?

A: The difference between these backup types is in the way changes are backed up. The differential backup records all database extents that have changed since the last backup. When a differential backup is restored, all changes must be restored as there is no order or sequence of data changes. This makes the differential backup faster to restore than a log backup. Log backups record transactions in sequence. Replaying the log means redoing all transactions recorded in it. This is a time consuming operation, but it does allow you to roll forward to a point-in-time, provided all sequential log file backups are available.

Q: I am missing a log file backup from the middle of a log sequence. Is it possible to restore all the other logs I have and roll the database forward, losing only the transactions recorded in the lost log?

A: No, logs can only be restored in sequence. In this case, you can only roll the database forward to the point of the lost log.

Q: How often should I back up the Master database?

A: The Master database stores much of the server configuration information including security settings, database configuration, and logins. You should back it up regularly in the live environment. The exact frequency depends on your organization's tolerance for loss of configuration data and how often this configuration changes.

Q: I have configured the performance Data Collector, but it has collected no data. Why?

A: The most likely reason that the Data Collector is not collecting data is that the SQL Agent is not running. The Data Collector uses SQL Agent jobs to perform data collection.

Self Test

1. You have a large centralized line of business database used by hundreds of users all around the world. One of the key tables is the Orders table. This table is frequently updated and frequently searched. A nonclustered index named IX_Orders_CustomerID exists on the Orders table, CustomerID column. Recently your company has experienced record sales, and many new customers have been added. You have received several user reports of degraded performance when trying to search for orders by a specific customer. After running some diagnostics, you are convinced that the reason for the performance degradation is index fragmentation. You wish to resolve the problem for your users, but, due to the 24-hour nature of your business, you are not allowed to take the index offline. Additionally, you wish to be able to interrupt reindexing operations without losing progress, in case the maintenance operation affects performance severely while it is running. What is the best way to resolve the problem while meeting your objectives?

    A. Run ALTER INDEX _Orders_CustomerID ON Orders.CustomerID REBUILD

    B. Run ALTER INDEX IX_Orders_CustomerID ON Orders.CustomerID REORGANIZE

    C. Run CREATE INDEX IX_Orders_CustomerID ON Orders. CustomerID WITH DROP EXISTING

    D. Run DBCC INDEXDEFRAG (LOBDatabase, "Orders", IX_Orders_ CustomerID)

2. You have recently removed a lot of historical data from your SQL Server 2008 database named HR by archiving it to a different server. However, you notice that the disk space consumed by the database file remains unchanged and the .MDF file is taking up the majority of space on the drive. How can you decrease the size of the database file?

    A. Run DBCC CHECKDB ('HR', REPAIR_ALLOW_DATA_LOSS)

    B. Run DBCC SHRINKFILE ('HR_Data', TRUNCATEONLY)

    C. Run DBCC SHRINKFILE ('HR_Data', NOTRUNCATE)

    D. Use the Copy Database Wizard to copy the database, then delete the original database. Finally, rename the new database you have just copied to the same name as the original database.

3. You have a very large table named PhoneSurvey. The table contains a Question column and an Answer column, both of type char(1000). Many questions are similar or the same. Many answers are very similar. Many questions re-phrase the answers. Additionally, many values in the answer column are null. The table resides on a high-performance system, and you are not concerned about query performance. What is the best way to reduce the size of this table as much as possible (choose all that apply)?

   A. ALTER TABLE PhoneSurvey REBUILD WITH DATA_ COMPRESSION = ROW

   B. ALTER TABLE PhoneSurvey ALTER COLUMN Answer ADD SPARSE

   C. ALTER TABLE PhoneSurvey ALTER COLUMN Question ADD SPARSE

   D. ALTER TABLE PhoneSurvey REBUILD WITH DATA_ COMPRESSION = PAGE

4. Your organization is worried about the security risks of Database Mail and SQL Mail. You are asked to verify that all servers in your organization have these features disabled. If not, you must disable the feature on those servers that don't have it enabled as soon as possible. What is the best way to accomplish this task with minimum administrative effort?

   A. Use Policy-Based Management to create a policy condition for the Server Configuration facet, SQLMailEnabled = False OR DatabaseMailEnabled = False. Create a policy linking this condition with a target set. Evaluate the policy to identify servers that don't comply with this policy. After evaluating the policy, apply the policy to reconfigure any noncompliant servers.

   B. Use Policy-Based Management to create a policy condition for the Server Configuration facet, SQLMailEnabled = False AND DatabaseMailEnabled = False. Create a policy linking this condition with a target set. Evaluate the policy to identify servers that don't comply with this policy. After evaluating the policy, apply the policy to reconfigure any noncompliant servers.

   C. Use Policy-Based Management to create a policy with no conditions. Choose to apply this policy to a target set defined by the filter SQLMailEnabled = True OR DatabaseMailEnabled = True. Evaluate the policy to identify servers that don't comply with this policy. After evaluating the policy, manually change the SQL Mail and Database Mail settings to reconfigure any noncompliant servers.

D. Use Policy-Based Management to create a policy condition for the Server Configuration facet, SQLMailEnabled = False AND DatabaseMailEnabled = False. Create a policy linking this condition with a target set. Evaluate the policy to identify servers that don't comply with this policy. After evaluating the policy, manually change the SQL Mail and Database Mail settings to reconfigure any noncompliant servers.

5. You have created a multi step job to prepare data for an important weekly production report. The job consists of several steps: getting data from multiple servers, consolidating it into a single table, and producing a report. Your users have complained that several times no report was created because certain servers were unavailable. They tell you that they would rather see a report based on last week's data than not see a report at all. What should you do to satisfy your users?

A. Change Step 2: Create Report runs only On Failure of Step 1: Consolidate Data.

B. Change Step 2: Create Report runs On Success and On Failure of Step 1: Consolidate Data.

C. Rearrange the job steps so that Create Report is Step 1 and Consolidate Data is Step 2.

D. Rearrange the job steps so that Step 1: Consolidate Data runs on failure of Step 2: Create Report.

6. You have been asked to produce a report comparing sales activity between the London and São Paulo offices. You restore a backup of the São Paulo sales database on the London SQL Server. You write a query to show sales by product, ordered by product name, and execute it against both databases. You notice that the report based on the São Paulo database is sorted differently. The sales department requires your report in 15 minutes. What is the quickest way to make the sort results of both reports consistent?

A. Use the Import / Export data wizard to copy the table from the São Paulo database to the London database.

B. Use the ALTER TABLE statement to change the collation of the Product Name column in the Product table to the collation used in the London database.

C. Use the copy database wizard to copy the database to a new database on the London server, specifying the new collation.

     D. Use the COLLATE Collation_Name option with the ORDER BY clause for the SELECT statement that the report is based on. Specify the collation of the London server as Collation_Name.

7. You have created a maintenance plan named BasicDBMaint and scheduled it to run every Sunday at 10:00 a.m. When you come back to work on Monday, you wonder whether the plan has executed successfully. What are the easiest ways to do this (choose all that apply)?

     A. In SQL Server Management Studio, expand SQL Server Agent | Maintenance Plans. Right-click BasicDBMaint Maintenance Plan, and click View History.

     B. Examine the contents of C:\Program Files\Microsoft SQL Server\ MSSQL.1\MSSQL\LOG\ BasicDBMaint_<DateTime> file.

     C. In SQL Server Management Studio, expand Management | Maintenance Plans. Right-click BasicDBMaint Maintenance Plan, and click View History.

     D. Examine the contents of C:\Program Files\Microsoft SQL Server\ MSSQL.1\MSSQL\LOG\ SQLAGENT.OUT file.

8. Your organization has recently hired a new DBA named Keith. You ask Keith to optimize the maintenance plan you have configured for the ERP database. A few hours later, Keith calls you and explains that he cannot see the Maintenance Plans option in the Management folder in SQL Server Management Studio. What is likely to be the problem?

     A. Keith is not a member of the db_owner role for the ERP database.

     B. Keith is not a member of the sysadmins server role.

     C. Keith is not a member of the serveradmins server role.

     D. Keith is connected to SQL Server with a SQL Server login not a Windows Integrated login.

9. A flood in the server room has rendered your primary SQL Server in Washington inoperable, and you must wait at least a week for replacement hardware. In the meantime, you must prepare a customer activity report based on the Sales database. You restore the Sales database to a SQL Server in Moscow. You know that the collation of the Washington server was set to Latin1_General_CI_AI, while the Moscow server's collation is Cyrillic_General_CS_AS. Unicode is used in all databases in your organization.

What must you do to ensure that the customer activity report based on the restored database is sorted in the same way as it was before the disaster?

A. Use the COLLATE Latin1_General_CI_AI clause with the ALTER DATABASE statement after the restore.

B. Use the COLLATE Latin1_General_CI_AI clause with the SELECT statement in the report.

C. Do nothing. The results will be sorted the same way as they were before the restore operation because the database collation will not change.

D. Use the COLLATE Latin1_General_CI_AI clause with the RESTORE DATABASE statement.

10. During some electrical maintenance work in your server room, someone has mistakenly pressed the emergency power down button, which caused the entire server room to lose power. After bringing all servers and devices back online you still feel uneasy about the state of your main SQL Server 2008 database. What should you do to check the entire database for corruption and repair the corruption if possible?

A. Connect to the database and execute SELECT * on every table. If the results are displayed, the database is uncorrupted; if not, the database must be restored from backup.

B. Run DBCC CHECKTABLE on every table in the database.

C. Run DBCC CHECKDB on the database.

D. Run DBCC DBREINDEX on the database.

11. You are a part-time database administrator for a small company that relies on its 3GB database for all business needs. You decide to implement a backup strategy of performing a full backup at 1:00 a.m. every night. What is the easiest way to implement your strategy?

A. Open NTBACKUP from **Start | Programs | Accessories | System Tools.** Create the backup and schedule it to recur every day at 1:00 a.m.

B. Use the BACKUP DATABASE Transact-SQL statement to create and schedule the backup job to recur every day at 1:00 a.m.

C. Use the Backup Database wizard from SQL Server Management Studio to create the backup job and schedule it to recur every day at 1:00 a.m.

D. Use the SQL Server Agent New Job wizard to create the backup job and schedule it to recur every day at 1:00 a.m.

12. Your organization has recently hired a new DBA named Keith. You wish to notify Keith by e-mail when your SQL Server 2008 experiences an error of severity 025 – Fatal Error. What are the steps you must take to enable this action (choose all that apply)?

A. Create a SQL Server Agent operator to represent Keith. Assign Keith a valid e-mail address.

B. Use the Database Mail wizard to configure Database Mail.

C. Create a SQL Server Agent alert to be raised when an error of severity 025 – Fatal Error occurs. In the alert settings, choose to notify Keith by e-mail when this alert is raised.

D. Start the SQL Server Agent Service and set its startup type to Automatic.

E. Create a SQL Server Agent job. For the first step, create a command that parses the server log for the error of severity 025 – Fatal Error. The second step should notify Keith on success of the first step.

13. Your organization wishes that any user-defined functions that developers create in the ERP database are prefixed with "udf_". You wish to prevent developers from creating functions that do not adhere to the convention. What is the best way to accomplish this task with minimum administrative effort?

A. Use Policy-Based Management to create a policy condition for the User Defined Function facet, Name Like 'udf_%'. Create a policy linking this condition with a target set of the database named ERP. Set the evaluation mode of the policy to On Change: Log Only.

B. Use Policy-Based Management to create a policy condition for the User Defined Function facet, Name Like 'udf_%'. Create a policy linking this condition with a target set of any server, any database. Set the evaluation mode of the policy to On Schedule.

C. Use Policy-Based Management to create a policy condition for the User Defined Function facet, Name Like 'udf_%'. Create a policy linking this condition with a target set of any server, any database. Set the evaluation mode of the policy to On Change: Prevent.

D. Use Policy-Based Management to create a policy condition for the User Defined Function facet, Name Like 'udf_%'. Create a policy linking this condition with a target set of the database named ERP. Set the evaluation mode of the policy to On Change: Prevent.

14. You have a database named Procurement. A full backup runs on Procurement every day at 1:00 a.m. The data file for the Procurement database is placed on the D: drive, while the log file for the Procurement database is placed on the L: drive. Unfortunately, the RAID disk hosting the D: drive volume corrupts, and the data on this disk becomes unreadable. The database recovery model was set to FULL. What should you do after you replace the damaged disk to bring the database back online and recover as much data as possible (choose all that apply)?

A. Back up the tail-log that resides on the L: drive.

B. Restore the latest full backup to the D: drive using the NORECOVERY option.

C. Restore the tail-log you have just backed up and replay it into the Procurement database to bring the database forward using the RECOVERY option.

D. Restore the latest full backup to the D: drive using the RECOVERY option.

15. Your organization has headquarters in Auckland, New Zealand, and branch offices in most countries around the world. Recently, you have centralized all SQL Servers on to a single server in Auckland. The main database is accessed by users from every office. The database is large and takes around 20 hours to perform a full backup. Additionally, the full backup is detrimental to performance and should be minimized during business hours of any of the offices. You are also aware that your organization cannot afford to lose more than one day's data. Your task is to create a backup strategy that produces the fastest possible restore time, meets the recovery point objective, and has minimal impact on performance experienced by users. What will you recommend?

A. Perform a copy-only backup every Sunday and a differential backup every day at the least busy time.

B. Perform a full backup every Sunday and a log backup every day at the least busy time.

C. Perform a full backup every Sunday and a copy-only backup every day at the least busy time.

D. Perform a full backup every Sunday and a differential every day at the least busy time.

16. Your company headquarters are in London, United Kingdom. Your company also has a branch office in Paris, France. Most customers are registered with both the head office and the branch office. You are tasked with finding out which customers are registered with both offices. To do this, you obtain a backup of the Paris database and restore it onto the London server. You the print a report of all customers sorted by last name from the London and Paris databases. You notice that the same names are sorted differently from each database. You must quickly produce a report from the Paris database that is sorted in the same way as the London database. What is the quickest way to produce this report?

A. Use the ALTER TABLE statement along with the COLLATE option to change the Customers table in the Paris database to have the same collation as the London database.

B. Use the COLLATE clause with your SELECT statement to enforce the same collation as the London database.

C. Use the Copy Table wizard to move the Customers table from the Paris database to the London database.

D. Use the b\cp utility to copy data from the Customers table from the Paris database to the London database.

17. You are tasked to identify all SQL servers that are running SQL Server 2005 or earlier within your organization. What is the best way to accomplish this task with minimum administrative effort?

A. Use Policy-Based Management to create a policy condition for the Server Information facet, VersionMajor >= 9. Create a policy linking this condition with a target set of all servers. Evaluate the policy to identify servers that don't comply with this policy.

B. Use Policy-Based Management to create a policy condition for the Server Information facet, VersionMajor <= 9. Create a policy linking this condition with a target set of all servers. Evaluate the policy to identify servers that don't comply with this policy.

C. Run the SELECT @@Version statement against every SQL Server in the organization.

D. Run the SELECT Version from sys.ServerInfo.

18. You are a part-time database administrator for a small company that relies on its 3GB database for all business needs. Unfortunately, disk space is at a

premium and recovery model for this database is set to SIMPLE. What should you do to protect the database so that their maximum data loss objective of 12 hours is met? What should you tell the company's owner about the risks of having their primary business database set to a SIMPLE recovery model (choose all that apply)?

A. Perform a full backup every 12 hours. Explain that the SIMPLE recovery model means that should you lose the database due to hardware failure or corruption, you will not be able to recover any transactions that have happened after the last full backup.

B. Perform a full backup every day and an incremental log file backup every 12 hours. Explain that the SIMPLE recovery model means that should you lose the database due to hardware failure or corruption, you will not be able to recover any transactions that have happened after the last incremental log file backup.

C. Perform a full backup every day and a differential backup every 12 hours. Explain that the SIMPLE recovery model means that should you lose the database due to hardware failure or corruption, you will not be able to recover any transactions that have happened after the last differential backup.

D. Perform a full backup every 12 hours. Explain that the SIMPLE recovery model means that should you lose the database due to hardware failure or corruption, you may be able to recover all transactions that have happened after the last full backup as long as the log file is intact.

19. You have decided to use the new SQL Server 2008 Data Collector feature to collect performance data from several servers in your organization. You install a SQL Server 2008 on a new server and run through the Configure Management Data Warehouse Wizard to set up data collection. One week later you view the performance reports and see that no data has been collected all week. What should you do to troubleshoot this issue (choose all that apply)?

A. Check that SQL Server Agent service is running and is configured for Automatic startup.

B. Check that SQL Server Data Collector service is running and is configured for Automatic startup.

C. Check that the recovery model on Management Data Warehouse is not set to SIMPLE.

D. Check that you have configured Data Collector proxy accounts so that they have permissions on the servers you are collecting data from.

20. You work for a large organization in a regulated industry. Currently, you adhere to a backup strategy, as shown in Figure 7.6.

Figure 7.6 Current Backup Schedule

Backup Schedule			
Backup Time	Backup Type	Backup Duration	Light User Activity Window
Mon 1 a.m.	Incremental	3 hours	1am – 6am.
Tue 1 a.m.	Incremental	3 hours	1am – 6am
Wed 12 a.m.	Differential	5 hours	12 am – 6am
Thu 1 a.m.	Incremental	4 hours	1am – 6am.
Fri 1 a.m.	Differential	5 hours	1am – 6am
Sat 12:00 a.m.	Incremental	5 hours	12 am – 6am
Sun 4:00 a.m.	Full	8 hours	4a.m – midnight

A recent change in applicable regulatory requirements states that you must provide a backup of your database to a compliance officer every week. This backup must be performed to special media provided by the agency. The compliance officer must be able to easily restore the backup whenever they wish and be able to search through the entire database. The compliance related backup must not interfere with user activity or the existing backup mechanism. The compliance related backups cannot be used in a disaster recovery restore as they are not kept within your reach. What is the best way to meet these compliance requirements without interfering with the existing backup mechanism and avoiding impact on users?

A. Take a full backup written to the special media on Sunday at 1:00 p.m. Give this backup to the compliance officer.

B. Take a copy-only backup written to the special media on Sunday at 1:00 p.m. Give this backup to the compliance officer.

C. Take an incremental backup written to the special media on Sunday at 1:00 p.m. Give this backup to the compliance officer.

D. Take a partial backup written to the special media on Sunday at 1:00 p.m. Give this backup to the compliance officer.

Self Test Quick Answer Key

1. **B**

2. **B**

3. **B** and **D**

4. **B**

5. **B**

6. **D**

7. **B** and **C**

8. **B**

9. **C**

10. **C**

11. **C**

12. **A, B, C,** and **D**

13. **D**

14. **A, B,** and **C** (in that order)

15. **D**

16. **B**

17. **A**

18. **A** and **C**

19. **A** and **D**

20. **B**

Self Test Quick Answer Key

1.	B	11.	C
2.	B	12.	A, B, C, and D
3.	B and D	13.	D
4.	B	14.	A, B, and C (in that order)
5.	B	15.	B
6.	D	16.	B
7.	B and C	17.	A
8.	B	18.	A and C
9.	C	19.	A and D
10.	C	20.	B

Chapter 8

MCTS SQL Server 2008
Exam 432

ETL Techniques

Exam objectives in this chapter:

- Bulk Copying Data
- Distributed Queries
- SQL Server Integration Services
- Alternative ETL Solutions

Exam objectives review:

- ☑ Summary of Exam Objectives
- ☑ Exam Objectives Fast Track
- ☑ Exam Objectives Frequently Asked Questions
- ☑ Self Test
- ☑ Self Test Quick Answer Key

Introduction

The ETL (extract/transform/loading) process is generally done using SQL Server Integration Services (SSIS). Other methods for ETL in SQL Server are available, such as BCP, Select/Into, and insert/select. You can also write custom code using ASP.Net or other languages.

This chapter covers all of the aspects and methods for performing ETL with SQL server, from BCP to SQL Server integration Services.

Distributed queries and transactions are also covered in this chapter, as well as setting up and using a linked server for cross-server communications and/or queries. Setting up systems to work correctly with distributed queries can be difficult, and this chapter will help to demystify the process.

Understanding ETL

Organizations often have more than just one database. Organizations also often need to share data between those databases in-house as well as to exchange data with business partners. Therefore, organizations need tools to move data between databases, across platforms, and often even between different businesses. As the data moves from one database to another, there is also often a need to perform some manipulation or transformation on the data. The process of extracting data from a data source, transforming the data to meet your needs, and loading the data into a destination is known more generally as extract, transform, and load, or more simply, ETL.

SQL Server provides a wide array of tools to move data. Exactly what data these tools move and how they do it varies significantly. The data could be an entire database, such as the Copy Database Wizard; a specific set of rows, such as the BCP, BULK INSERT, and OPENROWSET commands; or an extremely complex set of data movements as defined by an SSIS package. In this section, we will review all of these tools. We'll start by looking at tools for bulk copying data.

Bulk Copying Data

When you want to move a lot of data into or out of SQL server, you will likely find that the most efficient and best-performing tools are those that facilitate the bulk loading of data. The bulk loading tools are typically used to move data between flat files (e.g., a .csv file) and SQL Server, but it is possible to use the bulk copy operations with data sources other than flat files by using certain programming techniques. Regardless of what the data source is, though, the whole point of using the bulk copy tools is performance. Organizations use bulk loading techniques when they want to move a large number of rows as quickly as possible, and with as little impact on their servers as possible. Optimizing that performance can be a bit of an art, but we'll talk about some performance techniques at the end of this section. Before we get into performance, however, let's look at the first of the bulk load tools, BCP.

Using BCP

BCP (short for Bulk Copy Program) is a command line utility that you can use to import data from a file into SQL Server, export data from SQL Server into a file, and generate format files for use by BCP and other bulk copy tools. BCP has been available in many versions of SQL Server. Before tools like SSIS existed, BCP was the only available means for easily getting data into or out of SQL Server.

BCP is limited to working with flat files and SQL Server. If you want to get data from another data source (e.g., and Oracle database) into SQL Server, BCP is not the most direct means for this type of data transfer. SSIS would be a better tool for this type of transfer. BCP is a useful tool, however, if you have flat files (delimited, fixed format, etc.) to either extract data from or load data into.

Exam Warning

Remember that BCP can work with only text files and SQL Server. It can't be used to move data directly from one SQL Server to another. The data must first be exported from one database to a flat file and then imported to the destination from the flat file.

So let's start with the basic structure of the BCP utility:

```
bcp {dbtable | query} {in | out | queryout | format} datafile [option,..n]
```

You can find explanations of these in Table 8.1.

Table 8.1 Required BCP Syntax Arguments

Syntax Element	Description
dbtable	If you will be importing or exporting data from a SQL Table or View, this is the qualified object name. For example, to import into the Person table in the Person schema of the AdventureWorks2008 database, this would be:
	[AdventureWorks2008].[Person].[Person]
	The bcp command allows you to tell it which SQL Server instance to connect to, but does not allow you to specify which database. If the table you wish to work with is not in the connections default database, you will need to qualify the object name using the database.schema.object format.
	If you will be importing to a view, you need to make sure that the view supports inserts.
	dbtable can be used with the in, out, or format options. This means that you can import to the table (in) or export from it (out).
query	You can export from a query rather than a specific table or view. You need to enclose the query in double quotes (") and use single quotes for any character literals inside the query.
	query can be used with the queryout and format options. You *cannot* import to a query.
in	Use this option when you will be importing data into the dbtable specified.
out	Use this option when you will be exporting data from the dbtable specified.
queryout	Use this option when you will be exporting data from the specified query.

Continued

Table 8.1 Continued. Required BCP Syntax Arguments

Syntax Element	Description
format	Use this option to generate a format file. When format is used, no import or export is performed. Use this option with the –f and or –x parameters to specify the path of the generated format file. We will discuss format files later.
datafile	The path of the data file that you will be importing from or exporting to.
Optional arguments	There are number of additional arguments that can be used with the BCP utility. They are optional overall, but certain options may be required depending on what kind of operation you are performing. For example, if you use the format argument to generate a format file, you must also use the –f argument to specify the path of the file. See Table 8.2 for a list of some additional common bcp arguments.

In addition to the required arguments, there are a number of options that can be used to control BCP's behavior. You can get a complete list from the SQL Server 2008 documentation. Table 8.2 lists some of the options we will discuss in this chapter. Pay attention to the uppercase/lowercase nature of the options. They are case sensitive.

TEST DAY TIP

The list of options available for BCP can be overwhelming at first. It is worth your time to be familiar with them, but don't stress on them. You won't likely be tested on specific command-line switches.

Table 8.2 Optional BCP Arguments

Option	Description
-S *instancename*	Specifies which instance of SQL Server BCP should connect to. If the –S option is not specified the local default instance is assumed.
-T	Indicates that you wish BCP to connect using a trusted connection (aka Windows authentication).
-U *loginname*	Used to specify a SQL authentication login name when not using –T.
-P *password*	Used to specify the password associated with the –U login name.
-N	Use a Unicode native data file type.
-n	Use a native data file type (use only when you don't have Unicode data).
-c	Use a character data file type.
-w	Use a Unicode data file type.
-t *fieldterminator*	Specifies the field terminator that should be used in delimited data files. If special characters are needed, or a space is part of the delimiter, surround the delimiter in double quotes ("). If no field terminator is specified, the tab character is used.
-r *rowterminator*	Specifies the row terminator that should be used in delimited data files. As with the field terminator, if special characters are needed or a space is used in the delimiter, you can enclose the terminator in double quotes ("). If no row terminator is specified, a line feed (or new line) character is used ("\n").
-F *firstrownum*	Specifies the row number of the first row of data. This can be used to skip over header rows. It can also be used with the –L argument to specify a range of rows to process if the same data file is being processed on multiple workstations.
	If you are using a source file that has the column names in the first row, you need to make sure to use the –F parameter to tell BCP to start processing the file at the second row (-F 2). Otherwise, it will try to read the column names as field values.

Continued

Table 8.2 Continued. Optional BCP Arguments

Option	Description
-L *lastrownum*	Specifies the row number of the last row of data to process. This can be used if the data file has a footer that you don't want to process. It can also be used with the –F argument to specify a range of rows to process if the same data file is being processed on multiple workstations.
-b *batchsize*	Specifies the number of rows to include in a single batch. Each batch then ends up as a separate commit operation. The entire file is treated as a single batch by default. By using the –b option you can break the load up in multiple batches to help manage the load on the transaction log and possibly restart a load at a certain point if it fails partway through.
-f *formatfile*	Specifies the path to the format file to use.
-x	Used to generate an XML-formatted format file. Use this in conjunction with the "format" operation and the –f option to specify the path of the file.
-h	Allows you to specify a number of "hints" that mainly affect the performance of the BCP option. We will discuss some of them when we talk about performance.
Others	Again, there are other options available. You should review the information on BCP in the SQL Server 2008 documentation.

So taking the information listed in Tables 8.1 and 8.2, let's try a quick sample. You will export data from the AdventureWorks2008.Person.Person table to a file named person.txt. You will ask BCP to store the data in SQL Server Unicode native format (-N), and you will connect using a trusted connection (-T). Since no instance is specified (no –S parameter) the default local instance is assumed. So this is what it looks like:

```
bcp AdventureWorks2008.Person.Person out person.txt -N -T
```

The output from the preceding statement looks something like this:

```
Starting copy...

1000 rows successfully bulk-copied to host-file. Total received: 1000

1000 rows successfully bulk-copied to host-file. Total received: 2000

1000 rows successfully bulk-copied to host-file. Total received: 3000

...

1000 rows successfully bulk-copied to host-file. Total received: 19000

19972 rows copied.

Network packet size (bytes) : 4096

Clock Time (ms.) Total : 4807 Average: (4154.77 rows per sec.)
```

If you were to open the resulting person.txt file in notepad, you would likely be able to see some information, but the majority of it would be illegible. The reason for this limited legibility of this information is because you asked BCP to use a native data file type. We'll talk more about data file types and the formatting of the data later. For now, let's discuss importing the sample data.

To test this data file, create a sample table that you can load the data back into. After opening a query window connected to your SQL Server instance inside SQL Server Management Studio (SSMS), you could run the following statement to create a table with the same structure as the AdventureWorks2008.Person.Person table, but without any data:

```
USE AdventureWorks2008;

SELECT TOP 0 * INTO Person.PersonCopy FROM Person.Person;
```

You will be testing with this table in various situations. To make sure the table is ready for a load, you could truncate any data in it by running the following Transact-SQL (T-SQL) statement inside SQL Server Management Studio:

```
TRUNCATE TABLE AdventureWorks2008.Person.PersonCopy;
```

So now that you have a place to load the data back into, try loading the data file you just created back into SQL Server. You should notice that the syntax looks very similar to the command line you used for the export. The only differences is the destination table name, AdventureWorks2008.Person.PersonCopy, and "in" instead of "out," indicating that you will be importing from the file rather than exporting to it.

```
bcp AdventureWorks2008.Person.PersonCopy in person.txt -N -T
```

If you were to run the preceding statement, the output would look similar to the following:

```
Starting copy…
1000 rows sent to SQL Server. Total sent: 1000
1000 rows sent to SQL Server. Total sent: 2000
1000 rows sent to SQL Server. Total sent: 3000
…
1000 rows sent to SQL Server. Total sent: 19000
19972 rows copied.
Network packet size (bytes) : 4096
Clock Time (ms.) Total : 15252 Average: (1309.47 rows per sec.)
```

If you now go back to your query window in SQL Server Management Studio and run the following query, you will see that the AdventureWorks2008.Person.PersonCopy table now has data in it.

```
SELECT * FROM AdventureWorks2008.Person.PersonCopy;
```

In the previous two examples, you exported data to a file and imported it back in using BCP. By using the Unicode native file type for the data (-N), you increased the likelihood that BCP would be able to parse the data files correctly and that the data would be compatible with SQL Server. Using the Unicode native data file type is great when you are moving data from SQL Server to SQL Server. Other data file types are also available, though. We'll talk about those next.

Using BCP Data File Types

Often, you need to import data that you get from sources other than SQL Server. As we discussed in the earlier example, native data files types are great as an intermediate format moving data between to SQL Server databases. When you receive data files from business partners or internal systems other than SQL Server, however, the files will more likely be in a nonnative character or Unicode format.

Native data files are best used for moving data between two SQL Server instances. However, two "flavors" of native files are available: regular native files (-n) and Unicode native files (-N). The Unicode native files provide the highest likelihood that the characters in the source database get transferred properly to the target system because the native mode can't represent all the characters that are possible in nchar and nvarchar fields.

BCP also can work with nonnative character and Unicode data files. When the native file type is used, BCP knows how to parse the files correctly, so you don't need to describe the structure of the file to BCP. When you use character or Unicode files, however, you must describe the structure of the data in the file to BCP. For example if it is a delimited file, the delimiters need to be specified for BCP to recognize them.

Head of the Class...

Dealing with Characters and Collations

The file storage type that is used can be a common problem when sharing data between different database systems, operating systems, and organizations. If you receive a data file that has the data stored as character data, the way those characters are encoded can be an issue. In SQL Server you describe the encoding of the character data as well as how that data can be sorted and compared using collations.

The Unicode character set is able to represent thousands of possible character symbols. The Unicode character set is sufficient for representing characters from all the major languages, alphabets and cultures in the world.

However, non-Unicode character sets typically can represent only 256 possible symbols. So when you create SQL Server instances, databases, and character columns, you need to specify the character set that has the 256 characters you want.

When you are transferring data between two systems, it is possible that the two systems may have elected to use different sets of characters for their non-Unicode data. BCP gives you a number of ways to deal with the differences. You can use the command line arguments to let bcp know that the data file contains either character (-c) or unicode (-w). You can also specify the specific code page (or character set) that the data file was encoded with by including the –C argument. Finally, you can do column-specific collation assignments using bcp format files.

You have probably worked with either comma–separated value (csv) or tab–separated value (tsv) files in the past. They store data as values with a delimiter (a comma, a tab, or something else) between each of the values. The rows typically end with a line feed ("\n") or a carriage return and a line feed ("\r\n"). The following example exports the same data that you got before from the AdventureWorks2008.

Person.Person table, but this time you'll use a nonnative Unicode format (–w) for the data, and you will specify a comma as the delimiter (-t ",").

```
bcp AdventureWorks2008.Person.Person out person.csv -w -t, -T
```

If you were to open the person.csv file that is created by the preceding statement, it would look similar to the following (the output has been trimmed for readability). Notice that the field values are separated by commas as was specified in the command line:

```
1,EM,0,,Ken,J,Sánchez,,0,,<IndividualSurvey...
2,EM,0,,Terri,Lee,Duffy,,1,,<IndividualSurvey...
3,EM,0,,Roberto,,Tamburello,,0,,<IndividualSurvey...
...
```

Now try to import the data back into the same AdventureWorks2008.Person. PersonCopy table that you used before. Because it already has data in it, you will truncate the table first. To do that you can run the following statement in a query window in SQL Server Management Studio:

```
TRUNCATE TABLE AdventureWorks2008.Person.PersonCopy;
```

Next, you'll try to load the data into the newly truncated table. Review the script and the output. Notice that you receive an error:

```
bcp AdventureWorks2008.Person.PersonCopy in person.csv -w -t, -T
Starting copy...
SQLState = 22005, NativeError = 0
Error = [Microsoft][SQL Server Native Client 10.0]Invalid character
value for cast specification
```

The cause of the error is that actual data has commas in it (this is common in fields that contain human-entered notes or comments). BCP reads the comma in the data as if it were the delimiter of the field. This messes up the reading of the file and causes errors.

If you had to stay with a nonnative file, you could specify an alternate field terminator. When picking either field or row terminators, you want to select a character, or a character sequence, that doesn't occur in the data itself. In this case you could try a tab ("\t") or something like a pipe character (|) that almost never occurs in human-entered data. If you ran the preceding example with no –t option, the default tab delimiter would have been used to delimit the fields, and because there are luckily no tabs in the actual data, it should work. Here is what that command would look like:

```
bcp AdventureWorks2008.Person.Person out Person.tsv -w -T
```

The data file produced by the preceding statement would be tab delimited. You could then successfully import it into your Person.PersonCopy table using a very similar statement:

```
bcp AdventureWorks2008.Person.PersonCopy in Person.tsv -w -T
```

You can see where getting BCP to work with your data could be problematic. It has already become a problem pulling data from one of your own SQL tables. It can get even more troublesome when you have to make data that has come from business partners to load successfully into your own tables. As the data formatting specification becomes more complex, you need the power of format files. In the next section we'll talk about format files.

Using Format Files

Format files allow you to more explicitly describe the structure of the data file and how it maps to the corresponding SQL Server table or view. For native data files or simple character or Unicode data file types, you can probably specify all the information that BCP needs to parse the files just using the command line switches. However, if the files use fixed field widths rather than delimiters, or if different fields use different delimiters, the command line options fall short. There are also times when the data file you are using has a different number of columns than the target table you want to load the data into. In those situations format files become a requirement.

A common situation where format files are needed is when the target object has an identity column that generates primary key values, but the data file does not include the values for the column. There will be a mismatch between the number of columns in the data file and the target table.

Creating a format file is easiest when you have BCP do the initial work for you. There are a number of ways you can do this task. You could run the bcp command with insufficient input and have it prompt you for the details, or you could specify the details needed on the command line, but ask that it generate a format file for you by using the "format" and "-f" options. Finally, you could have it produce a newer XML format file by including not only the "format" and "-f" options but also the "-x" option.

To demonstrate using format you will start with a simple table that has three columns in it. The following script would generate the table and load it with some sample data:

```
USE AdventureWorks2008;

CREATE TABLE dbo.Presidents
(PresidentID int IDENTITY(1,1) NOT NULL PRIMARY KEY,
   FirstName varchar(50) NOT NULL,
   LastName varchar(50) NOT NULL);

INSERT INTO Presidents VALUES ('George','Washington')
INSERT INTO Presidents VALUES ('John','Adams')
INSERT INTO Presidents VALUES ('Thomas','Jefferson')
```

Next, you will have BCP create a format file named character type data file and have it name the format file Presidents.fmt. Because you are only generating a format file and not really moving any data, there is no data file. That explains the "*nul*" where the data file path would normally be:

```
bcp AdventureWorks2008.dbo.Presidents format nul -T -c -f Presidents.fmt
```

The file that is produced by the preceding command looks like this:

```
10.0
3
1 SQLCHAR 0 12 "\t"    1 PresidentID   ""
2 SQLCHAR 0 50 "\t"    2 FirstName     SQL_Latin1_General_CP1_CI_AS
3 SQLCHAR 0 50 "\r\n"  3 LastName      SQL_Latin1_General_CP1_CI_AS
```

Let's break the preceding format file down. The first row states the version of BCP that the format file is from (v10.0 is SQL Server 2008's BCP utility). The second row lists how many fields there are in the data file. In this case there are three columns. The next three rows describe each of the data fields, and the corresponding SQL table column they map to.

Table 8.3 explains each of the elements of the format file field definitions for the second field definition in the format file:

Table 8.3 Format File Field Definition

Purpose	Sample Value	Description
Host File Field Order	2	Indicates the ordinal position of the field as it is in the data file
Host field data type	SQLCHAR	The storage type of the data in the data files. In our example everything is just SQLCHAR because the file is a character file.
Host field prefix length	0	Can be zero unless the field contains NULLs. Learn more in the SQL Server 2008 documentation.
Host field data length	50	The length of the host file data field in bytes. The firstname field in the original table was 50 characters, or 50 bytes wide.
Host file field terminator	"\t"	The character that will be used in the data file to indicate the end of the field. The "\t" value here means that the "tab" character is the field terminator.
Server Column Num	2	The position of the destination column in the target database object
Server column name	FirstName	The name of the destination column in the target database object
Server column collation	SQL_Latin1_General_ CP1_CI_AS	The collation of the destination column in the target database object.

So now that you have a format file, use it during an export from the AdventureWorks2008.dbo.Presidents table (the following command is printed in the book on two lines, but should be entered as a single line:

```
bcp AdventureWorks2008.dbo.Presidents out Presidents.tsv -T
-f Presidents.fmt
```

When the preceding command is run, it produces a data file named
Presidents.tsv that looks like this:

```
1.   George  Washington
2.   John  Adams
3.   Thomas  Jefferson
```

You could turn around and import the data right back into the same table with
the command (again, the command should be entered on a single line):

```
bcp AdventureWorks2008.dbo.Presidents in Presidents.tsv -T
-f Presidents.fmt
```

Of course, the problem would be that the data file has PresidentIDs in it that
conflict with the PresidentIDs of the same records already in the table. What would
happen? Well, SQL Server would just ignore the identity values in the data file and
generate new identity values. Three new rows would be added with the same names
as before, but with new PresidentIDs.

If you wanted to override the identity behavior of the PresidentID field, you
could use the –E option of BCP to keep the identity values in the data file. In this
case the load would fail because that column also has a primary key constraint on it,
and as the rows were inserted with the same PresidentID values as the existing rows,
the primary key violation would keep the import from succeeding.

What if the source file didn't have any values for the PresidentIDs? If you were
to edit the Presidents.tsv file that was produced from your earlier output, you could
manually remove the ID values to make the file look like this:

```
George Washington
John Adams
Thomas Jefferson
```

To make this work, you would then need to edit the Format file as well.
The format file would need to indicate that there are now only two fields in the
data file rather than three, and that the data file fields map to the FirstName and
LastName fields in the AdventureWorks2008.dbo.Presidents table. Your edited
Presidents.fmt file would look like this:

```
10.0
2
1 SQLCHAR 0 50 "\t"     2 FirstName   SQL_Latin1_General_CP1_CI_AS
2 SQLCHAR 0 50 "\r\n"   3 LastName    SQL_Latin1_General_CP1_CI_AS
```

Notice in the preceding format file that the first field in the data file is mapped
to the second column in the table (FirstName) and that the second field in the data

file is mapped to the third column in the table (LastName). You completely ignore the first column in the table (PresidentID). SQL Server will use the IDENTITY property on that field to generate those values.

You could finally run the same bcp command to import the data file as before, and SQL Server would use the identity property to generate the PresidentID values automatically.

```
bcp AdventureWorks2008.dbo.Presidents in Presidents.tsv -T
-f Presidents.fmt
```

No discussion on BCP format files would be complete without looking at BCP's new XML format files. These files were introduced in SQL Server 2005, and although they can be much easier to work with than the traditional format files, they still don't appear to be as widely used. The following command generates a format file just like the first example in this topic, but this time it uses the –x option to produce an XML format file:

```
bcp AdventureWorks2008.dbo.Presidents format null -T -c
-f Presidents.fmt.xml -x
```

The format file that is produced by the preceding command looks like the following example:

```
<?xml version="1.0"?>
<BCPFORMAT

    xmlns="http://schemas.microsoft.com/sqlserver/2004/bulkload/format"
    xmlns:xsi="http://www.w3.org/2001/XMLSchema-instance">

<RECORD>
  <FIELD ID="1"
    xsi:type="CharTerm"
    TERMINATOR="\t"
    MAX_LENGTH="12"/>

  <FIELD ID="2"
    xsi:type="CharTerm"
    TERMINATOR="\t"
    MAX_LENGTH="50"
    COLLATION="SQL_Latin1_General_CP1_CI_AS"/>

  <FIELD ID="3"
    xsi:type="CharTerm"
    TERMINATOR="\r\n"
```

```
    MAX_LENGTH="50"
    COLLATION="SQL_Latin1_General_CP1_CI_AS"/>
  </RECORD>
  <ROW>
    <COLUMN SOURCE="1" NAME="PresidentID" xsi:type="SQLINT"/>
    <COLUMN SOURCE="2" NAME="FirstName" xsi:type="SQLVARCHAR"/>
    <COLUMN SOURCE="3" NAME="LastName" xsi:type="SQLVARCHAR"/>
  </ROW>
</BCPFORMAT>
```

After our description of the traditional format file, the preceding options should make sense. If you are looking at creating format files for new systems and don't need to maintain backward compatibility with older SQL server versions, the XML format files may actually be easier to work with and work better with future versions.

The BCP command can be a little difficult to work with, but once you get the command line switches and format files right, it can be an extremely efficient way to import or export data from SQL Server. BCP is a command line utility, however, and runs outside of the SQL Server process. Consequently, the data has to be sent, or "marshaled," between the client and the server. If there is a lot of data to load, this might be a good thing. Why? Well, because the bcp command could be run multiple times in parallel from multiple workstations and the load could be distributed across many machines. However, if the data file is manageable enough for a single process to handle, it might be more efficient to do it from within SQL Server itself. The BULK INSERT statement enables you to do just that. Before we get into BULK INSERT, though, give BCP a try yourself.

EXERCISE 8.1

USING BCP

In this exercise, you will export data from the AdventureWorks2008. Person.Person table to a data file using BCP. This exercise assumes that you have administrative privileges on the SQL Server instance you are working with, that you have the AdventureWorks2008 sample database installed on your SQL Server instance, and that you are running the exercise from the same computer where the SQL Server instance is installed.

1. Create a folder off the root of the C: Drive named BCP (C:\BCP).
2. Open a command prompt in windows and change to the C:\BCP directory.
3. Use the following command to export the AdventureWorks2008. Person.Person table data to a file:

```
bcp AdventureWorks2008.Person.Person out C:\BCP\Person.tsv -w -T
```

4. View the file the C:\BCP\Person.tsv file in notepad.

Using the BULK INSERT Statement

The BULK INSERT Transact-SQL statement closely mimics the BCP command line utility. There are some differences, though. The BULK INSERT statement can only import data into SQL Server. It won't export data to a file like BCP. Moreover, because it is executed by the SQL data engine, you don't have the ability to run multiple loads in parallel from different machines to optimize performance.

EXAM WARNING

Remember that the BCP command line utility can import and export data from SQL server. The BULK INSERT Transact-SQL statement, however, can only *import* data into SQL Server.

The basic syntax for a BULK INSERT in SQL Server looks like this:

```
BULK INSERT {dbtable} FROM {datafile} [WITH (option,..)]
```

As with BCP the *dbtable* states the target of the load. The *datafile* parameter specifies the path to the data file. Remember that you are submitting a statement that the server will execute, so the path used must be resolvable by the server. A number of options can be specified. They mirror very closely to a similar option in BCP. Table 8.4 shows some common BULK INSERT statement options.

Table 8.4 Common BULK INSERT Options

BULK INSERT WITH Option	BCP Equivalent	Description
DATAFILETYPE	-c -w –n -N	Specifies the data file type of the source file. This can be 'char', 'widechar','native', or 'widenative.'
FIELDTERMINATOR	-t	Specifies the field terminator character or characters.
ROWTERMINATOR	-r	Specifies the row terminator character or characters.
FORMATFILE	-f	Specifies the path to a format file. As with the datafile, the path must be relative to the server.

There are other options, and we will discuss some of them in the section of this chapter on performance.

So let's look at a quick example. Earlier you exported a Unicode, tab-delimited set of data from the Person.Person table. Assume the path to the data file is "C:\bcp\Person.tsv". In the following script you will first truncate (or clear) the AdventureWorks2008.Person.PersonCopy table, and then you will import the data file contents into the table using the BULK INSERT statement:

```
--Clear the table from previous loads
TRUNCATE TABLE AdventureWorks2008.Person.PersonCopy;
--Bulk insert new data into the table
BULK INSERT AdventureWorks2008.Person.PersonCopy
FROM 'C:\bcp\Person.tsv' WITH (DATAFILETYPE='widechar');
```

Remember that BCP is a command line tool, so you run BCP statements from a Windows command prompt. BULK INSERT, however, is a Transact-SQL statement, so you need to run the preceding statement in a query window in SQL Server Management Studio (or some other tool like sqlcmd).

After running the statement, however, you get a simple report back from SQL Server:

```
(19972 row(s) affected)
```

Of course, you could use the same format files (either traditional, or XML) that we discussed earlier. So as you can see the BULK INSERT statement is very similar in functionality to the BCP command line utility. From the previous two sections you should have a pretty good idea about the mechanics of bulk inserting data.

You may be wondering what all the parameters we haven't discussed are for. Mostly, they have to do with performance. In the next two sections, well discuss a few pointers on maximizing the performance of your bulk loads. We'll start by looking at how the transaction log is used during bulk operations. But first, get your hands dirty and try a BULK INSERT.

EXERCISE 8.2

USING BULK INSERT

In this exercise, you will export and import the data file that you created previously in Exercise 8.1 back into SQL Server. This exercise assumes that you have administrative privileges on the SQL Server instance you are working with, that you have the AdventureWorks2008 sample database installed on your SQL Server instance, and that you are running the exercise from the same computer where the SQL Server instance is installed.

1. Launch SQL Server Management Studio and open a new query window in the AdventureWorks2008 database.

2. Create the target table by running the following T-SQL statement:

   ```
   SELECT TOP 0 * INTO AdventureWorks2008.Person.PersonCopy
   FROM AdventureWorks2008.Person.Person;
   ```

3. Use the following T-SQL statement to load the data from the data file into the new table:

   ```
   BULK INSERT AdventureWorks2008.Person.PersonCopy
   FROM 'C:\bcp\Person.tsv'
   WITH (DATAFILETYPE='widechar');
   ```

4. Run the following query to view the imported data:

   ```
   SELECT * FROM AdventureWorks2008.Person.PersonCopy;
   ```

Recovery Model and Bulk Operations

Every SQL Server database has an option that determines its *recovery model*. The recovery model of the database determines how the transaction log can be used for backups, and how much detail is recorded in the live log for bulk operations. A database's recovery model can be set to FULL, BULK_LOGGED, or SIMPLE.

The FULL recovery model specifies that all transactions, including bulk operations, will be fully logged in the transaction log. The problem with having the FULL recovery model turned on when you are doing bulk operations is that every record that is inserted gets completely logged in the databases transaction log. If you are loading several records, you might end up with a problem. It can fill the databases transaction log up, and the logging activity itself can slow down the bulk operation. The FULL recovery model does make it possible to do point-in-time restores, even partway through a bulk operation, using the transaction log in the event of a failure.

The BULK_LOGGED recovery model records all regular transactions fully just liked the FULL recovery model. Bulk operations are minimally logged, however. What does that mean? Rather than recording the details of every row that was written, the transaction log tracks only which data pages and extents were modified by the bulk operation. The upside is that you don't bloat the log with a large number of inserts, and because less I/O is being performed against the log, performance can increase. The downside is that the transaction log alone no longer has all the information required to recover the database to a consistent state.

When you back up the transaction log that contains information about bulk operations, the actual data extents that were modified by the bulk operation are included in the log backup. That sounds weird, but it's true. The log backup actually contains extents from the data files, thereby making it possible to restore the transaction log backup and get all the data that the bulk operation inserted back as well. You should also note that the live log can remain small (because it doesn't have to log every insert performed as part of the bulk load), but the log backup will be large because the log backup contains the actual database extents that were modified.

However, when you are using the BULK_LOGGED recovery model, there is some exposure to loss. If a catastrophic failure were to occur after the bulk operation completed, but before you had a chance to back up the log, or the database, you could lose the data that was loaded. This implies that when you are using the BULK_LOGGED recovery model, you must perform at least a transaction log backup of the database immediately after the bulk operation completes. A transaction log backup is enough, but it doesn't hurt to do full or differential database backups as well.

Regardless of whether you are using the FULL or BULK_LOGGED recovery model, SQL Server will keep all entries in the transaction log until they are backed up using a BACKUP LOG statement, thereby ensuring that you can back up a contiguous chain of all transactions that have occurred on your database and that you can then restore the database using the transaction log backups. This is true even with the BULK_LOGGED recovery model, as long as you back up the log immediately after a bulk operation occurs.

The SIMPLE recovery model is not typically recommended for production databases. The big reason is that SQL Server can clear entries from the log, even though they may not have been backed up yet. However, as far as how the log works with bulk operations, SIMPLE is the same as BULK_LOGGED. After a bulk operation is performed, however, you have no choice of doing a log backup. You must follow up with a full or differential database backup.

So what recovery model should you be using? SIMPLE isn't a viable option for critical production databases because it doesn't allow you to back up the transaction log. FULL is the best option in terms of recoverability because it allows you to back up the log, and the log contains all the details. BULK_LOGGED, however, can offer performance and maintenance benefits when doing bulk operations.

The answer then is really a mixture of FULL and BULK_LOGGED. It is generally recommended that you leave your production databases with a FULL recovery model. When doing a bulk operation you would first run a statement to change the recovery model to BULK_LOGGED, do the bulk load, run another statement to change the recovery model back to FULL, and then back up the transaction log.

A couple of other requirements must be met for minimal logging to occur. Minimal logging requires that the target table not be replicated and that a TABLOCK be placed on the table by the bulk operation. It also requires that the target table not have any indices on it, unless the table is empty. If the table already has data in it and it has one or more indices, it may be better to drop the indices before the load, and then rebuild them after. Of course, this should be tested in your own environment.

The following sample code shows an example of a minimally logged BULK INSERT:

```
ALTER DATABASE AdventureWorks2008 SET RECOVERY BULK_LOGGED;

BULK INSERT AdventureWorks2008.Person.PersonCopy

FROM 'C:\bcp\Person.tsv' WITH (DATAFILETYPE='widechar', TABLOCK);

ALTER DATABASE AdventureWorks2008 SET RECOVERY FULL;

BACKUP LOG AdventureWorks2008 To DISK='C:\…\SomeFile.bak'
```

Note that the preceding code is only a sample. The AdventureWorks2008 database actually uses the SIMPLE recovery model by default. Although the code shown in this example would work, it assumes that the full database backup has already been performed. Log backups can't be run unless a full backup has been performed. If you do try the preceding code, you might want to set the recover model back to SIMPLE when you are done.

Using the right recovery model and bcp options to enable minimal logging can help improve performance by not writing as much detail to the live transaction log for a database. These steps reduce the amount of work the hard drives must do and can accelerate the performance of your bulk loading. It can also make the load more manageable by not bloating the transaction log with a large amount of data. This bloat alone could actually cause a bulk load to fail if the log filled to capacity. Figure 8.1 shows a performance monitor chart of the Percent Log Used counter for the AdventureWorks2008 database. The chart shows the log utilization for two bulk loads. The first load was not minimally logged. The second load was. You can see the dramatic difference in performance between the two modes.

Figure 8.1 Minimal Logging Performance Impact

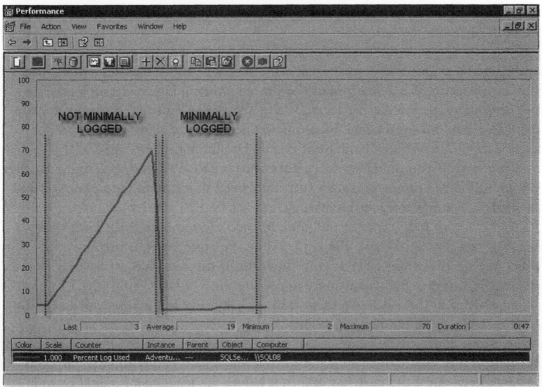

There are other ways to optimize performance, though. In the next section we will cover some ways to optimize the performance of bulk load operations.

Optimizing Bulk Load Performance

The whole point of performing bulk loads is performance. Well, performance and convenience, but performance is probably the critical part. You want to get as much data into the server as fast as you can, and with as little impact on the server as possible. As we discussed in the previous topic, configuring your bulk loads to be minimally logged can significantly improve the performance and decrease the negative impacts of bulk loads. However, you have other options that you can use to help manage bulk loads as well as improve their performance. These options include breaking the data into multiple batches, and presorting the data to match the clustered index on the target table.

Both BCP and BULK INSERT support breaking the load of large files down into smaller batches. The default behavior is that a single batch is used. Each batch equates to a transaction. Therefore, the default is that the bulk operation is performed as a single transaction. One big problem with this option is that the entire load succeeds, or the entire load fails. It also means that the transaction log information that is maintained for the bulk load can't be cleared from the log until the bulk operation completes.

You can optimize the loading of your bulk data by breaking it down into smaller batches. This allows you to fail only the batch rather than the whole load if an error occurs. When you restart the process, you could restart (using the first row options) with the specific batch. It also allows the log to be cleared if backup operations run during the bulk load time frame. Finally, it allows you to break a larger data file into pieces and have it be run by multiple clients in parallel.

Of course, if you didn't have a performance problem to start with, using batches can actually make things worse. So you really need to test with the options to find the optimal settings for your situation.

You can also help improve the performance of your bulk loads by making sure that the data in the data file is sorted by the same order as the clustered index key on the target table. If you know this is the case, you can specify to the bulk operation that the data is presorted using the ORDER hint of the BCP utility or BULK INSERT statement. This can improve the performance of bulk loads to tables with clustered indexes.

In addition, it may be beneficial to drop nonclustered indices on the table before the load, and re-create them after the load. If the table is empty to start with, this may not help, but if the table has data in it before the load, then it could provide a performance improvement. Of course you should test this with your own databases.

In the last few sections we have discussed a broad range of bulk load operations. The BCP and BULK INSERT statements both assume that you will be working with flat files, and SQL Server. Sometimes the data you want is already in another database engine somewhere else, however, and you would like to get it straight from that database rather than having to go through a flat file as an intermediary. Distributed queries are one way to do that, and we'll talk about those next.

Distributed Queries

Distributed queries make it possible for you to have SQL Server work with data in external data sources. The external data sources could be other SQL Server instances, or they could be an Oracle instance, or an Excel file, and so on. There are a number of methods available to working with data in external data sources. You can specify the data source as part of the query using functions like OPENROWSET or OPENDATASOURCE. Because these methods specify the data connection with the query, and not as a preconfigured server object, we call them "ad hoc distributed queries." You can also formally define the external data sources before you use them by defining linked servers. These linked servers can be used in four-part, fully qualified object names to directly reference tables and views in the external data sources. We will talk about ad hoc distributed queries and linked server, but first let's quickly cover the use of fully qualified names.

Understanding Fully Qualified Object Names

The fully qualified name of an object in SQL Server is actually made up of four parts with each part separated by a period. The format of a fully qualified name is:

```
[InstanceName].[DatabaseName].[SchemaName].ObjectName
```

The [InstanceName] is optional. If you don't specify it, it assumes the instance that the client is connected to. In fact, initially you can use the name of only the SQL Instance to which you connected. However, through the use of Linked Servers or the OPENDATASOURCE function, you can provide information about another instance to use in your fully qualified names. SQL Server then can use that information to connect to that other instance on your behalf.

The [DatabaseName] is also optional. It defaults to the database the connection is currently in. However, you can specify an alternative database name if the object you need to access is in another database on the same instance.

The [SchemaName] is optional as well. It defaults to the default schema for the user account the connection is connected as. If the object isn't found in the user's default schema, SQL Server will make a second check to see if there is an object with the same name in the dbo schema. Schema can be used in databases to help organize objects for security purposes. They also help to organize objects into different namespaces. This allows you to have to objects with the same name in the same database, as long as they belong to different schema. If your database uses schema heavily (like AdventureWorks and AdventureWorks2008 do), then you should be in the habit of always including the schema name in your object identifiers.

Actually, schema qualifying your object identifiers is a best practice even if you don't use schemas to organize your objects. Even if you stick every object in the dbo schema, you would still benefit from always including the dbo schema reference in your identifiers. There are a couple of reasons for this. The most important is that you will get better reuse of cached plans. Because your object references are specific, the optimizer knows exactly what objects are being referenced and can create shareable copies of the plan in the procedure cache. If you don't schema qualify, it makes plans that are cached and reusable only by your connection. Furthermore, it gets you in the habit of schema qualifying your objects. This is a good habit to have with the increased dependency on schemas in SQL environments, as well as in other platforms like Oracle.

Finally, you must specify the object name. This is the only piece that is not optional. If the object name, or any other component (instance, database or schema) contains nonstandard characters, then you must enclose the element in either square brackets ([ ]) or double quotes (") if the quoted identifiers setting is turned on.

For example, if your SQL Server instance is named "SQL08," and on the instance there is a database named "AdventureWorks2008," and in the database there is a schema named "HumanResources," and in that schema there is a table name "Employee," the fully qualified name of the Person table is:

```
[SQL08].[AdventureWorks2008].[Person].[Person]
```

The preceding name is written using the square brackets to delimit the identifiers. However, none of them have any special characters and therefore the square brackets are not required. So you could have just written:

```
SQL08.AdventureWorks2008.Person.Person
```

Remember that you don't have to specify a component of the fully qualified identifier if the default is appropriate. The following example shows querying data from a table in the AdventureWorks2008 database even though our connection is in the Master database:

```
USE master;
SELECT * FROM AdventureWorks2008.Production.Product;
```

Finally, here is an example of querying a data from a table named Demo in the dbo schema in the AdventureWorks2008 database. Because the dbo schema is always checked if the object isn't found in the user's default schema, you could just not specify it and rely on the default.

```
USE master;
SELECT * FROM AdventureWorks2008..Demo;
```

Notice the double dots ("..") in the identifier in the preceding example. Those have to be there so that SQL Server knows that you have given it the database name and object name, but not the schema name. SQL Server always parses the object identifiers from the right to the left. The right-most name is the object, the next name to the left is the schema, then the database, and then the instance.

Great, so now you know how to fully qualify an object name. Let's start looking at how we can get data from other systems in SQL Server.

Enabling Ad Hoc Distributed Queries

Allowing clients to submit ad hoc queries that access external data has a number of security implications. What is the external data they are accessing? Whom do they access it as? Are there any issues that could be destabilizing the SQL instance? Starting with SQL Server 2005 Microsoft started implementing a "secure out-of-the-box" installation model. This means that while there are a massive number of features in the SQL Server platform, a large number of them are turned off by default. This allows administrators to safely configure the ones they want to use and enable only those features. The other features that you don't need can be left off. This helps reduce the number of features that hackers can attempt to break into. When many features in SQL Server are enabled it is a big target; when fewer features are enabled, SQL Server is a smaller target. That is where the term "Surface Area" comes from. The smaller you are, the smaller your surface area, and the harder you are to attack.

Ad hoc distributed queries are one of those features that need to be turned on if you want to use them. The following code shows you how to use the sp_configure system store procedure to enable ad hoc queries or to disable them if necessary. You must have sysadmin (or CONTROL) permissions on the instance to set these options. Also the option is an "advanced" option, so you must first enable the viewing of advanced options. Here is the code to use:

```
--Turn on AdHoc Queries…
EXEC sp_configure 'Show Advanced',1;
RECONFIGURE;
EXEC sp_configure 'Ad Hoc Distributed Queries',1;
```

```
RECONFIGURE;
--Turn off AdHoc Queries…
EXEC sp_configure 'Show Advanced',1;
RECONFIGURE;
EXEC sp_configure 'Ad Hoc Distributed Queries',0;
RECONFIGURE;
```

In addition to enabling ad hoc distributed queries in general, each OLE DB provider can be set to either allow or disallow ad hoc access. If you set an OLE DB provider to not allow ad hoc access, only non–sysadmin users are limited. Connections that run with sysadmin privileges will still be allowed to perform ad hoc distributed queries using the provider. This makes it possible for you to allow ad hoc queries using specific OLE DB providers while preventing ad hoc access with others. To prevent a specific provider from allowing ad hoc access, you can use the **Object Explorer** in SSMS. Here are the basic steps:

1. Connect to your SQL Server instance in the SSMS Object Explorer.

2. Expand **Server Objects | Linked Servers | Providers**

3. You will see a list of the OLE DB providers on your system.

4. Right click on the provider you wish to configure ad hoc access for and select **Properties**.

5. In the list of **Provider Options**, set the **Disallow adhoc access** to meet your requirements.

Exam Warning

Notice that the Disallow adhoc access is a negative property. Turning the property *on disables* ad hoc access, while turning it *off enables* ad hoc access.

For example, an OLE DB provider allows access to any ODBC data source. It is rather dangerous because any ODBC data source can be configured as long as it exists on the server. If you want to prevent users who are not system administrators from using ad hoc queries to access ODBC data sources, you could disable ad hoc access for the OLE DB provider. The MSDASQL Provider is the OLE DB Provider for ODBC Drivers. Figure 8.2 shows an example of the provider properties for the MSDASQL Provider.

Figure 8.2 The Disallow Ad Hoc Access Property

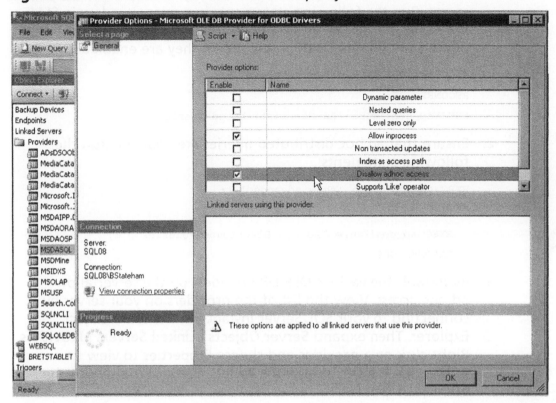

Once you have set the preceding property, any users who are not system administrators attempting to perform an ad hoc query using the MSDASQL provider would receive the following error:

```
Msg 7415, Level 16, State 1, Line 1
Ad hoc access to OLE DB provider 'MSDASQL' has been denied. You must access
this provider through a linked server.
```

EXERCISE 8.3

ENABLING AD HOC DISTRIBUTED QUERIES

In this exercise, review and set the Ad Hoc Distributed Queries server configuration option. This option must be enabled for ad hoc distributed queries functions like *OPENROWSET()* and *OPENDATASOURCE()* to work. This exercise assumes that you have administrative privileges on the SQL Server instance you are working with and that you are running the exercise from the same computer where the SQL Server instance is installed.

1. Determine if ad hoc queries have already been enabled on your server. Run the following statements in a query window in SSMS. A zero in the run_value column in the result set means ad hoc queries are disabled, and a one means they are enabled.

```
EXEC sp_configure 'show advanced',1;
RECONFIGURE;
EXEC sp_configure 'Ad Hoc Distributed Queries';
```

2. Ensure that ad hoc distributed queries are enabled. Run the following statements:

```
EXEC sp_configure 'show advanced',1;
RECONFIGURE;
  EXEC sp_configure 'Ad Hoc Distributed Queries', 1;
  RECONFIGURE;
```

3. By default the various OLE DB providers on the server allow ad hoc access. View the list of the providers on your server by connecting to your SQL Server instance in the SSMS Object Explorer. Then expand **Server Objects | Linked Servers | Providers**. Right click on a provider and choose **Properties** to view its properties. Is it set to disallow ad hoc access? What about the other providers?

Using the OPENROWSET Function

The OPENROWSET function can be used to access data from data sources external to SQL Server. This can be a great way to interact with data in external sources without requiring administrators to first configure a linked server. The OPENROWSET function can also be used as yet another way to bulk load data into SQL Server.

OPENROWSET is a table-valued function. That means that the result of the call to the function is actually a table. The implication is that you use the OPENROWSET( ) function call in place of a table reference in statements that work with tables (like SELECT, INSERT, UPDATE, and DELETE).

Start by seeing how to use SQL Server to access external data.

The basic syntax of the OPENROWSET Function looks like this:

```
OPENROWSET
(
'provider_name',
{ 'datasource'; 'user_id'; 'password' | 'provider_string' },
{ [ catalog. ] [ schema. ] object | 'query'
)
```

The "provider_name" is the name of the OLE DB provider you wish to use when connecting to the external database. For SQL Server, you can use SQLNCLI. You can find out what the names of your other available providers are by looking at the documentation for the providers, looking in the registry (HKLM\SOFTWARE\ Microsoft\Microsoft SQL Server\MSSQL10.MSSQLSERVER\Providers), and, of course, searching the Internet for resources.

The provider will need to know where and as whom to connect. There are two ways to do this. You can use a canonical format of 'datasource'; 'user_id'; 'password'" or we can specify a "provider_string."

The "'datasource'; 'user_id'; 'password'" is a single parameter that has semi-colon delimited elements. This method of providing connection details is the easiest to use, but requires that you use SQL Authentication (assuming the target is another SQL instance). This means the credentials are entered as clear text in the syntax. That's alarming.

The "provider_string" method is a little harder to get right, but makes it possible to use a trusted connection (Windows Authentication) to the external data source. This can be tricky to get right, but once you get it configured, it is a much more secure way to connect. You can also use additional information in your connection strings to further control the behavior of the connection.

Once you have specified how to connect, you finally need to specify what data to retrieve. You again have a choice. You can either state a database.schema.object qualified object identifier, or you can write a query to be executed by the external data source.

If you use the database.schema.object identifier to name an object to return data from, the referenced object needs to be a valid table or view, and the identity the connection is made with must have permissions to the object. In the documentation of the statement you see the word "catalog" used instead of "database." Again, catalog is just what the ANSI specification calls a database.

EXAM WARNING

Remember that ad hoc queries are disabled by default. The administrator has to have enabled them using sp_configure.

Querying Data with OPENROWSET

Let's see how to use the OPENROWSET function to query some data from a remote instance of SQL Server. Assume there is another instance of SQL Server named WebSQL. You want to query (SELECT) data from the WebSQL.AdventureWorks2008. Sales.SalesOrderHeader table. The following statements show a number of variations, all of which would work. Pay attention to how the OPENROWSET() function call is placed where you would normally find a table name in a SELECT statement:

```
--Using the 'datasource';'loginname';'password' format
--and referencing an object
SELECT * FROM OPENROWSET(
    'SQLNCLI',
    'WEBSQL';'sa';'P@ssw0rd',
    AdventureWorks2008.Sales.SalesOrderHeader);

--Using the 'datasource';'loginname';'password' format
--and supplying a query
SELECT * FROM OPENROWSET(
    'SQLNCLI',
    'WEBSQL';'sa';'P@ssw0rd',
    'SELECT * FROM AdventureWorks2008.Sales.SalesOrderHeader');

--Using the 'provider string' format
--and passing a query
SELECT * FROM OPENROWSET(
    'SQLNCLI',
    'Server=WEBSQL;Trusted_Connection=Yes;Database=AdventureWorks;',
    'SELECT * FROM AdventureWorks2008.Sales.SalesOrderHeader');
```

In the examples where the canonical format is used you see that you can read the credentials used to connect in clear text. That is a major security issue. Of course, in the samples above the "sa" account is being used to connect as well, and that is another big no-no. It is shown that way in this example to highlight how much of a security risk these types of queries can be if they are not written and reviewed carefully.

The "provider_string" version of the preceding query was able to use a "Trusted Connection," but that string can be difficult to configure. It requires that the servers interact properly with Active Directory and takes some configuration by the Windows administrator to make it work. However, once it is properly configured it is a much more secure and controllable way to connect.

EXERCISE 8.4

Using OPENROWSET

In this exercise, you will create a text file with some sample data in it. You will then use the OPENROWSET() function to query data from the text file from within SQL Server. This exercise assumes that you have administrative privileges on the SQL Server instance you are working with, that you have the AdventureWorks2008 sample database installed on your SQL Server instance, and that you are running the wizard from the same computer where the SQL Server instance is installed. *You must have completed Exercise 8.3 to enable ad hoc distributed queries as well.*

1. Create a directory off the root of the C: Drive named C:\BCP (if it doesn't already exist from before).

2. Using Notepad create a new text file named C:\BCP\Presidents.csv. Enter the following text into the file and save it:

```
PresidentID,FirstName,LastName
1,George,Washington
    2,John,Adams
    3,Thomas,Jefferson
```

3. In a query window in SSMS enter the following query to select the data from the text file:

```
SELECT * FROM OPENROWSET (
    'MSDASQL',
        'Driver={Microsoft Text Driver (*.txt; *.csv)};
        DBQ=c:\bcp;',
            'SELECT * from presidents.csv');
```

4. Try creating some different text files to query from. How about a tab-delimited file?

Modifying Data with OPENROWSET

OPENROWSET can be used with INSERT, UPDATE, and DELETE statements as well. Just as you could query data in a remote data source using a SELECT statement with OPENROWSET, you can also *change* data in a remote data store. The trick is to place the OPENROWSET(…) function call where the table reference would normally exist.

Here is an example of change data in the WebSQL.AdventureWorks.Person. Person table:

```
UPDATE OPENROWSET(
  'SQLNCLI',
  'Server=WEBSQL;Trusted_Connection=Yes;Database=AdventureWorks;',
  AdventureWorks2008.Person.Person)
  SET FirstName = 'Ken'
  WHERE BusinessEntityID = 1;
```

We will talk a little more about this in a later section.

Copying Data with OPENROWSET

Another powerful thing to do with that is to store the data you query from the external data source as data in your own SQL server instance. You can do this with the SELECT…INTO or INSERT…SELECT statements.

The following example shows both methods to copy data from the WebSQL. AdventureWorks2008.Sales.SalesOrderHeader table to a local table called AdventureWorks2008.Sales.SalesOrderHeaderCopy:

```
--Create a local table as a result of the copy
SELECT * INTO AdventureWorks2008.Sales.SalesOrderHeaderCopy
FROM OPENROWSET(
  'SQLNCLI',
  'Server=WebSQL;Trusted_Connection=Yes;Database=AdventureWorks;',
  AdventureWorks2008.Sales.SalesOrderHeader);

--Insert the selected data into an existing table
INSERT INTO Sales.SalesOrderHeaderCopy
SELECT *
FROM OPENROWSET(
  'SQLNCLI',
  'Server=WebSQL;Trusted_Connection=Yes;Database=AdventureWorks;',
  AdventureWorks2008.Sales.SalesOrderHeader);
```

Using OPENROWSET (BULK,…)

OPENROWSET can also be used to BULK load data, just like the BCP and BULK INSERT statements. We have already covered bulk loading in some detail, so we will leave this topic up to your own research. One comment on using OPENROWSET as an alternative to BCP or BULK INSERT is that parsing the external data file property OPENROWSET (BULK,…) *requires* that you use a format file. Format files are optional with BCP and BULK INSERT if the command arguments can describe the formatting of the file, but OPENROWSET(BULK,…) must have a format file.

However, using the BULK option of OPENROWSET does allow you to do something that you can't do with BCP and BULK INSERT—read the entire external data file as a single value. This can be useful if you are trying to populate a large data type field (varchar(max), nvarchar(max), varbinary(max), or xml) with the contents of the file. You can do this by using the *SINGLE_BLOG*, *SINGLE_CLOB*, and *SINGLE_NCLOB* options. When you use any of those options, OPENROWSET reads the external file and returns it as a single column, single row rowset (in other words, a single value) that is either a large binary data type (SINGLE_BLOG), character value (SINGLE_CLOB), or Unicode character value (SINGLE_NCLOB).

Here is an example, if you had an XML file with the following contents:

```
<?xml version="1.0" ?>
<Presidents>
  <President ID="1" FirstName="George" LastName="Washington"/>
  <President ID="2" FirstName="John" LastName="Adams"/>
  <President ID="3" FirstName="Thomas" LastName="Jefferson"/>
</Presidents>
```

And if you had a table with the following structure:

```
CREATE TABLE SomeXML
(
  RowID int IDENTITY(1,1) PRIMARY KEY,
  TheXML xml
);
```

You could use the OPENROWSET() function to read the contents of the XML file into the SomeXML.TheXML column like this:

```
INSERT INTO SomeXML(TheXML)
SELECT * FROM OPENROWSET(
```

```
BULK N'C:\sample\Presidents.xml',

SINGLE_BLOB) AS XMLFile;
```

The following example shows a query of the SomeXML table and the results:

```
SELECT * FROM SomeXML;
--Results:
RowID        TheXML
----------   ----------------------------------------------------

1            <Presidents><President ID="1" FirstName="George"...
```

TEST DAY TIP

OPENROWSET(BULK,...) is one of the more obscure bulk-loading mechanisms. It is good to know that it is possible, but you likely won't find many questions on the exam related to this topic.

Using the OPENDATASOURCE Function

OPENDATASOURCE is another function that you can use to perform ad hoc distributed queries. It is different from OPENROWSET in that you use the OPENDATASOURCE in place of an instance name in a fully qualified name, rather than in place of a table reference. Like OPENROWSET, however, the OPENDATASOURCE function can be used in SELECT, INSERT, UPDATE, and DELETE statements.

The basic syntax for the OPENDATASOURCE function is:

```
OPENDATASOURCE ( provider_name, provider_string )
```

Just like OPENROWSET, the *provider_name* is the name of the OLE DB provider that you wish to use. Again, "SQLNCLI" is the provider you should use for a SQL 2008 instance. The *provider_string* is similar to the *provider_string* in OPENROWSET.

What you don't see in OPENDATASOURCE that was in OPENROWSET is an object identifier or a query. As we mentioned earlier, OPENDATASOURCE doesn't represent a table (or a set of rows) like OPENROWSET. Instead, it represents a data source or an instance of data source to connect to. With OPENROWSET you have the ability to pass a query through to the external data source in a syntax it understands. It can then process that query and return the results. That process is called a "pass-through" query.

With OPENDATASOURCE SQL Server uses the OLE DB provider to dynamically construct a query to retrieve the data object specified in the four-part name. Let's show you an example of using OPENDATASOURCE to query the same WebSQL.AdventureWorks2008.Sales.SalesOrderHeader data you saw with OPENROWSET:

```
SELECT *
FROM OPENDATASOURCE(

  'SQLNCLI',

  'Server=WEBSQL;Trusted_Connection=Yes;'

  ).AdventureWorks2008.Sales.SalesOrderHeader;
```

The preceding code had to be wrapped to fit on the page. It runs as it is shown, but can be confusing. In fact, at first glance it may not seem any different than the OPENROWSET version. Take some time to compare them both side by side, though, and you will see the difference. Exercise 8.5 gives you a chance to do just that.

EXERCISE 8.5

COMPARING OPENROWSET AND OPENDATASOURCE

1. Type the following two statements into a query window in SQL Server Management Studio:

```
--OPENROWSET QUERY
SELECT * FROM OPENROWSET(

    'SQLNCLI',

    Server=WEBSQL;Trusted_Connection=Yes;Database=AdventureWorks;',

    'SELECT * FROM AdventureWorks2008.Sales.SalesOrderHeader');
--OPENDATASOURCE QUERY
SELECT * FROM OPENDATASOURCE(

    'SQLNCLI',

    'Server=WEBSQL;Trusted_Connection=Yes;'

).AdventureWorks2008.Sales.SalesOrderHeader;
```

2. Study them carefully until you see the differences between them.
3. If you have access to another SQL Server instance, try modifying the statements and run them to access your external data.

Using Linked Servers

Linked servers provide a more formal mechanism for defining external data sources as well as controlling who can access them. Linked servers can be extremely powerful tools for integrating data. Because it sits on top of OLE DB, you can use most any provider when creating linked servers (or any of the distributed query methods discussed in this chapter). That means you can link to Access, Excel, Oracle, MySQL, and so on. And because you can use linked servers so conveniently via four-part names, it makes it trivial to perform joins across multiple platforms in a single query. We call these heterogeneous queries. If you work in an environment where multiple database platforms or even just multiple servers exist, you can really expand your reach with linked servers.

The OPENROWSET and OPENDATASOURCE functions may be of interest to a developer because they can control what provider is used and how they connect. From an administrative point of view, though, those functions can become quite problematic. Imagine a situation where a developer used OPENROWSET in a number of different views and procedures. If the target database location or credentials changed, each one of those views and procedures would have to be manually edited, retested, and redeployed to accommodate the change.

Linked servers provide administrators with a way to centrally define the external data sources available to an instance. Link servers also enable administrators to control how the connection to the external data is made and which logins are allowed to access it. When you create a linked server in SQL Server, you define a name for the linked server that can then be used in place of an instance in a four-part name. Thus, writing queries that access data from linked servers is much cleaner than their OPENROWSET or OPENDATASOURCE counterparts.

Configuring & Implementing...

Enabling OLE DB Providers

Linked servers are not ad hoc. They are preconfigured server-side objects that can then be used in queries of any type. Administrators might still like to control exactly what types of data are available via linked servers. You can manage that by enabling only the OLE DB providers you wish in SQL Server Management Studio's Object Explorer.

Continued

> To learn more about configuration of the OLE DB providers, you can look up "Configuring OLE DB Providers for Distributed Queries" in the SQL Server 2008 documentation.

You can create linked servers using SQL Server Management Studio or using a set of stored procedures. We will discuss the stored procedures here. Once you have a handle on those, using SQL Server Management Studio to do the same thing should be a snap. Figure 8.3 shows you an example of the New Linked Server dialog box in SSMS.

Figure 8.3 New Linked Server Dialog Box

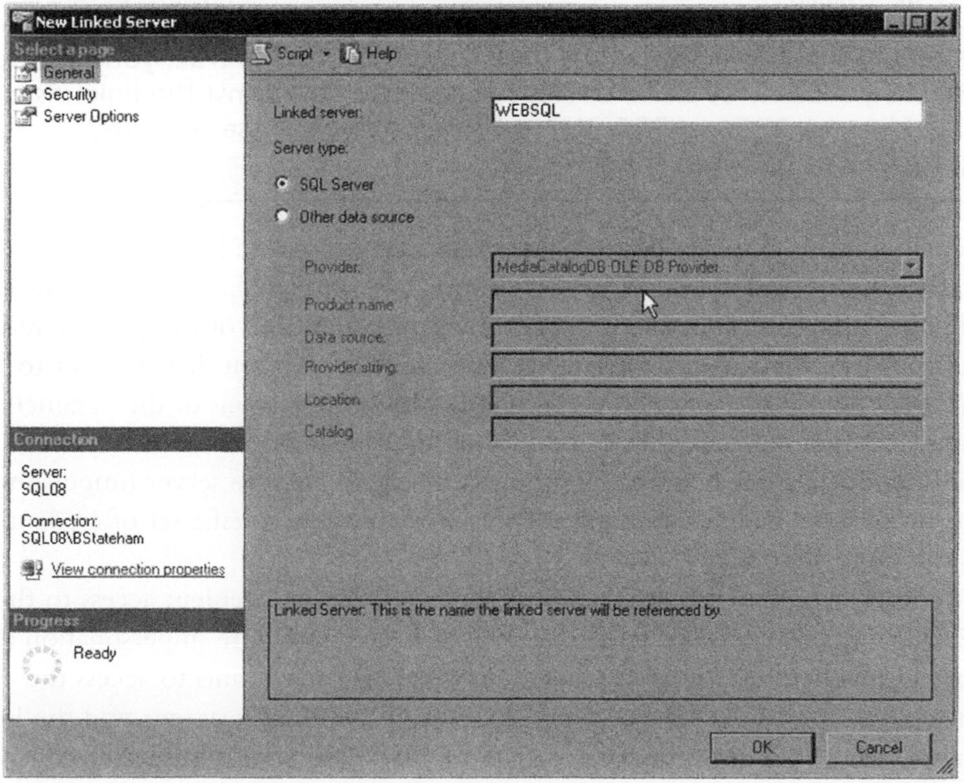

There are far too many procedures to cover in detail in this chapter. However, you can get all the details you want from the documentation. To see all the following procedures and more in a single place, look for "Distributed Queries Stored Procedures" in the SQL Server 2008 documentation.

To create a linked server, you use the sp_addlinkedserver stored procedure. This procedure allows you to specify the name of the linked server, which OLE DB provider should be used, and some basic information about the linked server. This procedure has to be run before you can configure the linked server further.

Once the linked server exists, you can set some options on it using the sp_serveroption stored procedure. The sp_serveroption stored procedure allows you to specify which collations are to be used when dealing with character data, connection time outs, and more. By setting the Data Access option to true, you enable SELECT, INSERT, UPDATE, and DELETE statements with the linked server. The RPC and RPC OUT options allow remote procedure calls (RPCs) with the linked server.

EXAM WARNING

Remember that if the Data Access option isn't set to true, you can't run SELECT, INSERT, UPDATE, or DELETE statements against the linked server. Also the RPC and RPC OUT options enable the use of stored procedures between the linked servers.

Finally, you have to decide how users will connect via the linked server. You do that using the sp_addlinkedsrvlogin procedure. It is through the @rmtsrvname, @useself, @locallogin, @rmtuser and @rmtpassword parameters of this procedure that you can control who users on a local system connects as when they attempt to connect to the remote server. You can use various combinations of the parameters to imply a default account that is used for all local users on the remote system, require that local users have matching accounts on the remote server (imperson-ation), or perform individual mapping of a local user to a specific set of credentials for the remote system.

The following script creates a linked server to allow convenient access to the WebSQL server you worked with earlier. It will then configure impersonation as the log-in mechanism. That means that any local user who wants to access the remote system has to have a matching account on the remote system, and the local user also must specify that the two servers use the same collation for character data. Finally, it runs a query against the linked server using a simple four-part name:

```
EXEC master.dbo.sp_addlinkedserver
   @server = N'WebSQL',
   @srvproduct=N'SQL Server';

EXEC master.dbo.sp_addlinkedsrvlogin
```

```
  @rmtsrvname = N'WebSQL',
  @locallogin = NULL,
  @useself = N'True';
EXEC master.dbo.sp_serveroption
  @server=N'WebSQL',
  @optname=N'collation compatible',
  @optvalue=N'true';
SELECT * FROM WebSQL.AdventureWorks2008.Sales.SalesOrderHeader;
```

The result of the script would be that the WebSQL.AdventureWorks2008.Sales.
SalesOrderHeader data would be retrieved. Notice how clean the final query is.
Developers need to know only the name of the linked server as it was defined in
the sp_addlinkedserver procedure. They can then use that name as the instance
name in their four-part identifiers.

Linked servers can be used in SELECT, INSERT, UPDATE, and DELETE
statements, and you can use the same SELECT..INTO and INSERT..SELECT
methods discussed earlier to copy data from a linked server to the local instance.

Using the OPENQUERY Function

OPENQUERY is a rowset function similar to OPENROWSET. You might recall
that we explained how OPENROWSET supported "pass-through" queries by
allowing you to send syntax through a connection to the remote server. That can
be a powerful thing. The problem with OPENROWSET is that you had to define
all the connection information as part of the function call every time you used it.

OPENQUERY, on the other hand, allows you to use a linked server definition
to point to the remote data source, and then allows you to specify a pass-through
query that can be sent through the connection to the linked server. The result is
that you get the same pass-through query capabilities that you got with
OPENROWSET, but without all the mess and security concerns.

You use OPENQUERY in place of a table reference in a statement, just like
OPENROWSET. The basic syntax of the OPENQUERY function is:

```
OPENQUERY ( linked_server,'query' )
```

In the syntax of the preceding example, the "linked_server" is the name of the
linked server you wish to send the query to, and "query" is the actual query itself.
Remember that you have the ability to use syntax appropriate for the remote
system in that query. This capability can be helpful if you know how to express
a query on the remote system that is difficult to do in Transact-SQL.

The following example queries data from the WebSQL server:

```
SELECT * FROM OPENQUERY(
  WebSQL,
  'SELECT * FROM AdventureWorks2008.Sales.SalesOrderHeader');
```

As with the other distributed query function, OPENQUERY can be used not only with SELECT statements but also with INSERT, UPDATE, and DELETE statements.

Using Distributed Transactions

Distributed transactions enable you to perform changes on remote systems as well as on the local system as part of a single transaction. You've seen that through the use of the distributed query functions and linked servers, you have the ability not only to SELECT data from remote systems but also to INSERT, UPDATE, or DELETE data in remote systems. Anytime we mention making changes in SQL Server, though, we have to also think about transactions. All change on SQL Server occurs as part of a transaction. When you want to make changes on both a remote system and SQL Server in a single transaction, you need to use distributed transactions.

Distributed transactions occur between two resource managers. The transaction is managed by a transaction manager. If you had two instances of SQL Server that you wanted to perform a distributed transaction across, the two instances would each be a resource manager. SQL Server can then use the Distributed Transaction Coordinator (DTC) in Windows as the transaction manager. The DTC is compliant with the Open Group XA specification for distributed queries. Therefore, you can use resource managers other than just SQL Server (like Oracle, and others) in your distributed transactions.

Distributed transactions use what is known as a two-phase commit (2PC). The two phases are prepare and commit. In the prepare phase the resource managers do all the work that would be required to commit, but they keep a hold of the locks on resources. The resource managers all report back to the transaction manager. If any reports a failure, the transaction manager tells them all to abort the transaction. Because they still have a hold of the locks, they can roll everything back and exit the transaction. If all the resource managers report a successful prepare, the transaction manager can instruct them all to commit. The resource managers then commit the transactions and release the locks.

To begin a distributed transaction you have to first make sure the Distributed Transaction Coordinator service is running on both resource managers. It should be started automatically for you on your server platforms, but you want to confirm it. Then, you can use syntax similar to the following example:

```
BEGIN DISTRIBUTED TRANSACTION;
    --Do whatever work should be done as part of the transaction
    --This could include INSERT, UPDATE or DELETE operations on
    --both the local and remote instances.
COMMIT TRANSACTION;
```

You would then perform the operations that you want to occur as part of the transaction and either COMMIT or ROLLBACK the transaction as normal.

SQL Server Integration Services

SQL Server Integration Services (SSIS) is a powerful set of tools for performing what the industry calls extract, transform, and load", or just ETL for short. SSIS isn't just one program; it is a collection of wizards, development tools, command line utilities, and a Windows service that provides a framework for moving data around between systems. The purpose of this section is to give you an overview of the SSIS landscape and to address specific issues that administrators need to know about and that you may be tested on.

Any data import or export process involves a number of elements. There is a data source you want to get data from, a destination for that data to go to, and possibly some conversion or transformation of the data that has to occur. There also are typically a set of tasks that are involved in the process. For example, you might first need to get the source file from your business partner via FTP. Once you have the file, you can do the import to your server. You might then need to validate the data. Finally, you probably want to archive the source file and maybe send an e-mail message to those interested about the success of the load. Of course, that all assumes things go according to plan. There may be an alternative sequence of tasks to follow should an error occur. That is a lot of stuff to do. It would be helpful if you could tell SSIS how to do all that once, and then have it reuse that set of instructions every time you need to run the process. Well, that is exactly what an SSIS package allows you to do.

The package is the heart of SSIS. It is in a package that you can define all the information that SSIS needs to complete a data import or export process on your behalf. An SSIS package is, at its simplest, an XML file that contains all the information needed to connect to the data sources and destinations, to move the data, to run the tasks in their proper sequences, log the results, and handle the errors.

You can create SSIS packages in a variety of ways. The simplest way is to use either the Import and Export Wizard or the Copy Database Wizard. These wizards prompt you for information, build SSIS packages based on your inputs, and then either schedule those packages to be executed at a later time, or actually run them for you. The SSIS packages created by the wizards, while functional, are relatively basic. If you have very complex processes that need to be implemented, you can have developers create custom SSIS packages using Business Intelligence Development Studio (BIDS). For totally customized solutions, developers can even create SSIS packages on the fly by writing code.

Actually, there is another way to create an SSIS package, and that is by creating a maintenance plan. Maintenance plans are really just SSIS packages that have specific tasks in use. Because maintenance plans don't really perform ETL operations for you, though, we won't discuss them further in this chapter.

If developers are creating packages on their workstations, you need to "deploy" those packages up to a server that has SQL Server Integration Services installed. There are a number of ways to deploy packages, and we will cover them later in this chapter.

Finally, once the packages have been deployed to your SSIS server, you can then execute the packages in the production environment. You do execute packages manually, or you could even schedule them to be run for you using the SQL Server Agent. Again, we will cover the various execution methods later in this chapter.

So to review, the basic flow of working with SSIS is:

1. Create the package
2. Deploy the package
3. Run the package

We'll walk through this a step at time, starting with ways to create SSIS packages.

Creating SSIS Packages

As we discussed in the preceding section, an SSIS package contains all the information that is needed for an ETL process. We also saw that there are four ways to create an SSIS package:

- Copy Database Wizard
- Import and Export Wizard
- Business Intelligence Development Studio
- Programmatically creating packages

Creating packages programmatically is way beyond the scope of this book, so we won't be talking about that option at all. Just know that it is possible if you need it. We will look at the two wizards, however, and take a brief look at using BIDS to work with packages. Let's start by looking at the Copy Database Wizard.

Using the Copy Database Wizard

The Copy Database Wizard gives SQL administrators an easy way to copy an entire database between two SQL Server instances. The obvious goal of the Copy Database Wizard is to make a copy of an *entire* database. Normally, this is going to be between two instances of SQL Server; however, you can use it to copy a database within a single instance.

You can think of a database two different ways; *physically* or *logically*. Physically, a database is a collection of.mdf, .ndf, and .ldf files on disk. Logically, a database is made up of a bunch of objects (like tables, indices, views, procedures), data (the rows in the tables), and metadata (object definitions, permissions, and so on).

Given those two possible views of a database, you then have two different models for copying a database. You could copy the.mdf, .ndf, and .ldf files that make up the physical database. Alternatively, you could create new, empty files on the destination server, and logically copy the database by running statements to create copies of every object in the target database, copying the data into those objects, and then copying all the metadata. The Copy Database Wizard supports both models. It performs physical copies through the "detach-and-attach" method. It performs logical copies via the "SQL Management Object" method.

The "detach-and-attach" method is the most efficient method of copying an entire database. This method physically copies the entire database by detaching the database from the source instance; copying the .mdf, .ndf, and .ldf files to the destination; and then attaching them to the destination SQL Server instance. It does have some constraints, though. First, the source database must be taken offline while the physical data files are being copied. Second, the SQL Server agent on the target server must have permissions to the file system on the source server via some share. If you can meet those requirements, you'll probably find the "detach-and-attach" method to be the method of choice.

The "SQL Management Objects" (SMO) method of transferring the database is slower, but it doesn't require that the SQL Server Agent job run as an account with access to the file system on the source server. This method may help you accomplish a copy between servers when you don't have as much control over the source server's Windows permissions. The SMO method is slower because it uses the SMO object model to programmatically re-create each source object in the destination database. It then copies the data over to the new objects as well as all the metadata.

Configuring & Implementing...

Working without Active Directory

If you are trying to practice for these exams on your own machines, you would benefit from configuring a test network complete with an Active Directory domain. You can certainly work without it, and for home, dev, and test purposes that is acceptable. However, many of the features in SQL Server, like the Copy Database Wizard, assume you are working in a multiserver environment. In a production environment that almost certainly means that there will be some centralized security mechanism. In Windows networks, that means Active Directory. To truly grasp the implementation of SQL Server as it would be used in a production environment, you need Active Directory.

Working with multiple systems and without Active Directory can be a problem because computers won't recognize each other's user accounts. This can be a problem when you are trying to use tools that need to talk to both systems, like the Copy Database Wizard. You can attempt to create user accounts on all systems that have the same names and passwords, but as much as that seems as if it should work, it still doesn't in some cases.

If you are having problems using the Copy Database Wizard because of authentication problems, you can test it by just copying a database to the same instance. This won't show you all the possible options in the wizard, but it will give you the overall sense of the process. The wizard is smart enough to recognize that the source and destination instances are the same, and it doesn't prompt you to synchronize instance level objects like logins, SQL Server Agent Jobs, and so on. It also automatically names the database with a "_new" at the end, as well as renames the target database file names so that they won't overwrite the original database files.

Regardless of which method you choose to use, some things that exist outside of a given database, will still be required for the database to be functional on the target server. These include:

- Logins
- User-defined error messages

- Stored procedures created by in-house developers, but stored in master (not very common)

- SQL Server Agent job definitions

- SQL Server Integration Services Packages

- Endpoints for things like the Service Broker, HTTP access, and so on

When you are copying a database between two instances, the Copy Database Wizard will prompt you for the aforementioned classes of objects you may want to copy and then allow you to specify exactly which of the objects you wish to have copied.

That is a basic overview of what the Copy Database Wizard can help you do. Rather than showing you screen shots, we will do an exercise to get a feel for the Copy Database Wizard. To make sure that everybody can do it, we will test copying a database to the same instance. If you have multiple instances available to you, you can try it yourself by copying between two instances.

EXERCISE 8.6

USING THE COPY DATABASE WIZARD

In this exercise, you will use create a database named CopyMe and load it with some data. You will then use the Copy Database Wizard to copy the database to the same SQL Server instance. Finally, you will verify that the copy worked by looking at the data in the copied database as well as viewing the SSIS package and SQL Server Agent job that the wizard creates. This exercise assumes that you have administrative privileges on the SQL Server you are working with.

1. In SQL Server Management Studio, open a new query window that is connected to your instance of SQL Server.

2. Run the following statement to create the database we will copy:

```
CREATE DATABASE CopyMe;
```

3. Run the following statement to populate the database with some data. This way, you can make sure the copy worked by ensuring the same data is in the copied database:

```
SELECT *
INTO CopyMe.dbo.Product
  FROM AdventureWorks2008.Production.Product;
```

4. Connect to the SQL Server instance in the SSMS Object Explorer.

5. Expand the Databases node and right click on the **CopyMe** database.

6. From the pop-up menu select **Tasks | Copy Database...**

7. On the **Copy Database Wizard** first page click "**Next.**"

8. On the **Select a Source Server** page, in the **Source Server** field enter the name of your SQL Server Instance and select **Windows Authentication**. Click **Next**.

9. On the **Select a Destination Server** page, in the **Destination Server** field, leave the value at **(local)**, and again select **Windows Authentication**. Click **Next**.

10. On the **Select the Transfer Method** page, select **Use the detach and attach method**. Leave the **If a failure occurs, reattach the source database** checkbox checked. Note: you can ignore the warning about the SQL Server Agent needing a proxy account. Because the source and destination servers are the same, the permissions should be valid. Click **Next**.

11. On the **Select Databases** page make sure the **Copy** checkbox is enabled for the **CopyMe** database. All other checkboxes should be cleared. (Note that in the Status column for the CopyMe database that it sees the database already exists. That's all right; you'll copy it to a new name). Click **Next**.

12. On the **Configure Destination Database (1 of 1)** page, review and leave everything at their default values. Notice that the wizard has automatically named the copy CopyMe_new to make sure the copy doesn't overwrite the original database. Review the paths of the data files as well. Select **Stop the transfer if a database or file with the same name exists at the destination**. Click **Next**.

13. On the **Configure the Package** page, leave the package name unchanged, but remember it so that you can look it up later. Turn on the **Save transfer logs?** checkbox. Select **Text file** from the drop down menu, and leave the log path at the default (record the path so that you can look at the log after the copy). Click **Next**.

14. On the **Schedule the Package** page, leave the option set to **Run immediately**. Even though you are running it immediately, it will still create a SQL Server Agent Job to run the copy for you. Leave the **Integration Services Proxy Account** set to **SQL Server Agent Service Account**. Click **Next**.

15. On the **Complete the Wizard** page, review the list of actions and then click **Finish**.

16. On the **Performing operation** page, watch as the package is created and run. If all is well, each item in the list should complete with **Success**.

17. Back in the SSMS Object explorer, right click the **Databases** node and choose **Refresh**. You should now see a **CopyMe_new** database in the list.

18. Expand the **CopyMe_new** database and then expand **Tables**. You should see the **dbo.Product** table in the list of tables. Right-click the **dbo.Product** table and select **Select Top 1000 Rows**. Review the data in the query window that opens. Close the query window when you are done.

19. In Object Explorer under your SQL Server instance, Expand **SQL Server Agent** and then expand **Jobs**. You should see a job listed with the same name as the package (you were supposed to have remembered that name back in step 13). This is the SQL Server Agent Job that got created to run the package. Open the job and review its details, but don't change anything.

20. In the **Object Explorer**, from the **Connect** menu, select **Integration Services...** Enter the name of your SQL Server Instance for the **Server name:** and click **Connect**.

21. Expand **Stored Packages | MSDB | <YOUR INSTANCE NAME> | DTS Packages | Copy Database Wizard Packages**. You should see a package there with the name you recorded in step 13. This is the actual package. It has been saved into the MSDB database on your local instance. Later, you'll open the package up in BIDS to see what is inside it.

Using the Import and Export Wizard

While the Copy Database Wizard copies an entire database, the Import and Export Wizard provides you with a more granular copy mechanism. The Copy Database Wizard was also limited to using only SQL Server as both the source and destination. The Import and Export Wizard, however, can connect to most any database engine as either the source or the destination.

The Import and Export Wizard allows you to export data from the source database by either selecting the specific tables and views you want to export, or by writing a query to extract specific data from the source. Of course, to write a query the source must support queries when the source has multiple tables or support queries. If you are pulling from a flat file (like a .csv file), you can get only the data that is in the file. If, however, you were importing data from another SQL Server, you could select one or more tables or views, or write a query to pull just the data you want.

The paths you can take through the wizard vary greatly with the data sources and destinations you choose. The general flow, however, is:

1. Launch the Wizard. You can Launch the wizard by clicking the **Start** menu | **All Programs** | **Microsoft SQL Server 2008** | **Import and Export Data**. You can also run dtswizard.exe, or right click a database in SSMS's Object Explorer and choose **Tasks** | **Import Data**... or **Tasks** | **Export Data**....

2. Choose a Data Source. You can use the wizard to import data from flat files, Excel files, Access databases, or any database that you can access via an ODBC, OLE DB, or .Net provider. Each provider will need to be configured differently. You will need to have the information that your selected data source requires. For example, if you were pulling from a flat file, you would need to know the path of the file, how it was delimited (comma, tab, etc.), and whether or not there was a header row, etc.

    You can also configure the data source. For example, if the source is a flat file, you can use the Advanced page to set appropriate data types for the fields in the text file.

3. Choose a Data Destination. Just like the data source, this could be a flat file, Excel files, Access databases, or some backend database you connect to using ODBC, OLE DB, or .Net providers. Again, you will configure the destination provider according to the properties of your target.

    You can then also configure the destination. For example, if the destination is SQL Server, you can choose which database to import data into, or you can even create a new database by using the options in the wizard.

4. Select the Source Tables and Views. Depending on what kind of source you selected, there may be multiple tables or views in the source that you can import from. The wizard will allow you to select one or more of the specific tables and views. Or if the data source is support queries, you could instead write a query to extract just the data you want from the source.

Once you have selected the source objects you can map them to destination objects. If the destination tables already exist, you can select them, or you can define new tables for the data to be loaded into. The wizard will help to generate the SQL statement to create the target table. You can also select options regarding whether existing data in the destination table should be kept or cleared, how values for identity columns should be handled, and so on.

5. Review Data Type Mappings. There may be some issues with the data types used for the source and destination columns. If there is, the wizard will show you the Review Data Type Mappings page. It will flag the tables and columns that have problems with a warning icon if there are mapping issues.

Where the data types don't match, you may want to go back and review the options you selected in the wizard to make sure that you are mapping the right source columns to the right destination columns. If the source is a flat file, you can also use the advanced properties on the data source to indicate the correct data types to use as it pulls data from the source file.

You can also use the Review Data Type Mapping page to specify how the import process should deal with errors that occur. You can choose to ignore the error (which probably means you will get a null for the value that was invalid), or you could choose to have the error fail the package. You can set global responses for both errors and truncations (the data in the source is too large for the destination). You can also set the error handling specifically for each column if needed.

6. Save and Run the Package. You can run and/or save the information you just configured in the wizard. If you choose to save it, the wizard will create an SSIS package and save it based on the options you choose in the wizard. You can save it as a .dtsx file in the file system (this is one of those XML package files mentioned earlier), or you can save it as data into the MSDB database on a SQL Server instance. When saving it, you also get to choose how and at what level to encrypt the package. If you choose to save it, the next screen in the wizard will prompt you for the location to which you want to save the package.

The preceding list of steps is a generalization of the process you use as you go through the wizard. You should run through the wizard a few times, selecting different types of sources and destinations each time so that you can get a feel for how the wizard works in each situation.

Again, it is probably better to have you try the wizard than to just fill this book up with screen shots. So give the following exercise a try.

EXERCISE 8.7

USING THE IMPORT AND EXPORT WIZARD

In this exercise, you will use the Import and Export Wizard to export data from the AdventureWorks2008 database to a flat file. This exercise assumes that you have administrative privileges on the SQL Server instance you are working with, that you have the AdventureWorks2008 sample database installed on your SQL Server instance, and that you are running the wizard from the same computer where the SQL Server instance is installed.

1. Since you will be exporting to a file, you need a directory in the file system for the file to be placed into. Create a directory off the C: Drive named C:\Wizard.

2. In SQL Server Management Studio, connect to your instance in the Object Explorer. Expand the **Databases** folder then right click **AdventureWorks2008**. From the menu select **Tasks | Export Data....**

3. On the wizard's welcome page, click **Next**.

4. On the Choose a Data Source page ensure the values match the ones shown in the following example and then click **Next**:

   - **Data Source** SQL Server Native Client 10.0
   - **Server Name** SQL08
   - **Authentication** Use Windows Authentication
   - **Database** AdventureWorks2008

5. On the Choose a Destination page, enter the information shown in the following example and then click **Next**.

   - **Destination** Flat File Destination
   - **File Name** C:\Wizard\Product.csv
   - **Locale** (whatever your default value is)
   - **Code Page** (whatever your default value is) Format Delimited
   - **Text qualifier** <none>
   - **Column names in the first data row** Checked

6. On the **Specify Table Copy or Query** page, select **Copy data from one or more tables or views** and then click **Next**.

7. On the **Configure Flat File Destination** page, set the value to match those shown in the following example. After you have set the values, click the **Edit Mappings...** and **Preview...** buttons to view the information in them. Finally, click **Next**.

   - Source table or view [Production].[Product]
   - Row delimiter {CR}{LF}
   - Column delimiter Comma {,}

8. On the **Save and Run Package** page, set the values to match those shown in the following example and then click **Next**.

   - **Run immediately** Checked
   - **Save SSIS Package** Checked
   - **SQL Server** Selected
   - **Package protection level** Rely on server storage and roles for access control

9. On the **Save SSIS Package** page, set the values to match those shown in the following example and then click **Next**.

   - **Name** Export Product Data
   - **Description** Exports Production.Product to C:\Wizard\Product.csv
   - **Server name** (you SQL Server instance name)
   - **Use Windows Authentication** Selected

10. On the **Complete the Wizard** page, review the list of actions and then click **Finish**.

11. In the SQL Server Import and Export Wizard window, watch as the process runs. It should take only a few seconds. When it is done, you should have a "Success" result. You should also see an action titled "Copying to C:\Wizard\Product.csv" with a status of "Success" and a message similar to "504 rows transferred." If there was a problem, use the information in the window to go back through the wizard and fix any problems.

12. Verify that the export worked properly by opening the **C:\Wizard\Product.csv file** in notepad or Excel and viewing the data.

13. In the **Object Explorer** in SSMS, click **Connect | Integration Services....** In the **Connect to Server** window enter the name of your SQL Server in the **Server name:** box and then click **Connect**.

14. To verify that the package was saved correctly, in Object Explorer expand the node for your server's Integration Services instance, then click **Stored Packages | MSDB | Export Product Data**. As long as you see it, it was saved. If it isn't there, you may have selected a different name or location in the wizard.

Using Business Intelligence Development Studio

The ultimate way to create SSIS packages is by using Business Intelligence Development Studio (BIDS). The Copy Database Wizard and the Import and Export Wizard both allow you to create and save SSIS packages that perform specific actions. As your data movement needs become more complex, however, you'll likely find that the wizards are too limited in what they can do. Enter BIDS. BIDS is actually the same Visual Studio 2008 development environment that VB. Net and C# developers use. When you install BIDS as part of your SQL Server installation, you get the Visual Studio development environment (if it isn't already on your workstation), and a number of "Business Intelligence Projects" project templates that you can use.

BIDS is a developer tool and is normally run from a developer's workstation, not from the server itself. As this book is focused on administrators, not developers, it isn't worth digging deep into BIDS. However, we will give a quick overview because no discussion of SSIS is complete without covering BIDS. As an administrator, you may want to open a package up in BIDS from time to time to learn more about what it does or why problems may be occurring.

Let's look at creating an Integration Services Project in BIDS. To get started, follow these steps:

1. Launch BIDS by going to **Start menu | All Programs | Microsoft SQL Server 2008 | SQL Server Business Intelligence Development Studio**.

2. In BIDS, you will then create a new project from the menu bar by clicking **File | New | Project…**.

3. In the **Project Types** list select the left **Business Intelligence Projects** and then in the **Templates** list on the right, select **Integration Services Project**.

4. Finally, you can complete the New Project window by giving your project a name, selecting the location of the parent folder that the project will be created under, and creating a solution for the project to belong to.

Head of the Class...

BIDS Projects and Solutions

Remember that Business Intelligence Development Studio (BIDS) is really Visual Studio. Visual Studio is the development environment that developers use when working with a variety of technologies. With the right products installed, Visual Studio could be used by Windows developers writing programs in Visual Basic.Net, by Web developers creating Web sites in C#, or by business intelligence developers working with Integration Services, Analysis Services, or Reporting Services.

Each different type of work, or development, that can be done in Visual Studio is represented by a project template. When working with SQL Server Integration Services, for example, you would choose from the Integration Services Connection Project, or the Integration Services Project templates. Again, it depends on what products you have installed on your workstation as to what project templates will appear when creating a new project in BIDS.

Each project will have files that need to be stored on the developer's workstation. For SSIS projects, the package files will be stored locally on the developer's workstation. Projects use a folder structure to organize the files related to each project. So when you are naming a project in BIDS, you are naming not only the project but also the folder in which the projects resources will be stored. When creating a project you also need to choose under which parent folder, your project's folder will be created. By default this will be under your My Documents folder in a Visual Studio 2008\Projects subfolder. However, you can store them wherever you like.

Continued

> Solutions allow developers to work with multiple projects at once. Often developers need multiple project types to complete a business requirement. For example a developer may be using C# to create a custom task to be used in SSIS. The developer would benefit from having both the C# project and SSIS project open at the same time in BIDS. That's where solutions come in. A solution is a container of one or more projects. Whenever you work with a project in BIDS, it is always a part of a solution. Most of the solutions you work with will have only a single project; however it is possible to add multiple projects to a solution. The benefit is that when the developer opens the solution, all the projects that are part of the solution are available within BIDS. The developers can then seamlessly move between projects as they complete their development work.

If you use BIDS to create a new project, you will find two projects related to Integration Services in the Business Intelligence Projects category. The Integration Services Connections Project template starts a new project, but it runs a wizard to prompt you for the connection information for the various data sources to which you will need to connect. This configures a package with the connection managers for the data sources you specify already set up. This may be helpful if you are new to creating packages in BIDS, but it configures only one package with the connection managers. Any additional packages will have to be created from scratch. The other project template is just the Integration Services Project template. This template starts you out with a single empty package. You build up from there.

Integration Services projects can have *multiple* packages. Each package is stored in the project folder as an XML file with the .dtsx extension. Developers can create new packages or edit existing ones. When you open a package in BIDS, the package designer is displayed. Figure 8.4 shows BIDS with a package open.

Figure 8.4 BIDS Package Designer—Control Flow

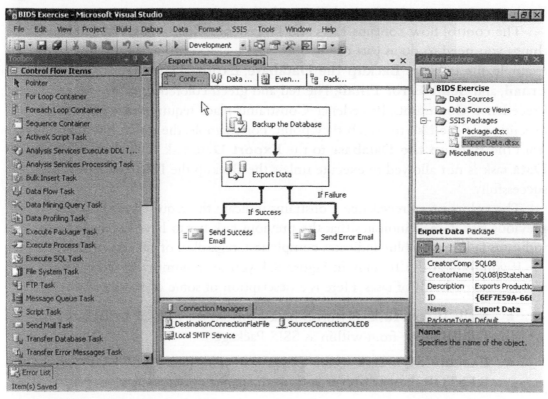

The screen shot shown in Figure 8.4 shows you a number of important elements, BIDS, and an SSIS Package. As you look at the screenshot in Figure 8.4, you see that it is broken into a number of windows. The left-most window is the **Toolbox**. Depending on what tab developers are on in the package designer, the toolbox changes to show items that are appropriate for that tab. Currently, the toolbox is showing the tasks that are available to place in a package. The largest section in the middle of the screen is the package designer, and you can see that the **Export Data.dtsx** package file has been opened for editing. The various boxes and lines in the package designer represent tasks and how they are sequenced. The window at the top right is the **Solution Explorer**. It displays all the projects in the current solution, and all the resources in those projects. Finally, the window in the lower right is the **Properties** window. The properties window shows all the properties of whatever is currently selected in the package designer.

If you focus on the package designer in the middle of the screenshot, you can see it is broken down into some subtabs, although you can't read their full names in this screen shot. It's hard to fit all the stuff into a screen shot that fits nicely in a book! The subtabs are Control Flow, Data Flow, Event Handlers, and Package Explorer. Currently, the Control Flow subtab is selected.

The control flow contains Tasks and Precedence Constraints. The tasks are things you need to do as part of the SSIS package's execution. In the preceding example, the tasks are **Backup the Database**, **Export Data**, **Send Success Email**, and **Send Error Email**. The red and green colored lines are called Precedence Constraints. Precedence Constraints place requirements on the execution of the task to which they point. For example, the green line that points from the **Backup the Database** to the **Export Data** task implies that the **Export Data** task is not allowed to execute unless the Backup the Database task runs successfully.

The colors of a Precedence Constraint indicate the required result of the previous task. Green indicates that the previous task has to have succeeded, red indicates failure, and blue indicates completion, regardless of success or failure.

If you look at the Toolbox in Figure 8.4, you see a number of icons that represent type kinds of tasks. Here is a description of some of those tasks:

- **Bulk Insert Task** Performs bulk loads similar to BCP or BULK INSERT, but from within as SSIS Package

- **Execute SQL Task** Runs a SQL statement (like a BACKUP, RESTORE, or whatever you need) against a database

- **FTP Task** Could be used to send or receive files from a server using FTP

- **Script Task** Allows developers to write their own code in Visual Basic. Net or C# as part of an SSIS package

- **Data Flow Task** The Data Flow Task is the true ETL task. It allows you to specify any source, any destination, and any set of transformations that you need as part of a data movement.

The Data Flow Task can require a lot of configuration. It could have multiple sources, multiple destinations, multiple paths for the data to flow through, multiple transformations to perform on the data, and so on. The task could have such a complex definition that it has its own design surface in the Package Designer. Figure 8.5 shows an example of the "Export Data" Data Flow Task show in Figure 8.4.

Figure 8.5 BIDS Package Designer—Data Flow

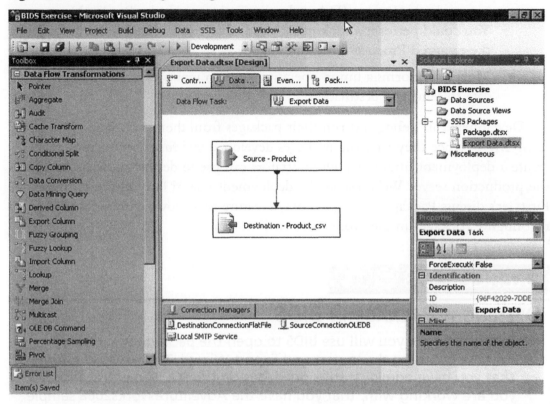

In Figure 8.5, you can see the data connections that represent the source and destination of your data flow, and the green arrow represents the set of "good" rows from the source that make it into the destination. You can also take rows that have errors (not shown in the screen shot) and send them down their own paths to either log the errors or possibly even fix them and route them back into the destination.

The "Toolbox" in Figure 8.5 shows a sampling of the transformations that can be performed on the data as it moves from the source to the destination. The screen shot doesn't show any transformations in use, but the following list describes some of the common transformations that can be applied:

- **Character Map** Used to convert strings to all upper or lower case, convert between character and Unicode formats, and so on.

- **Conditional Split** Could direct rows down different paths based on the data in the records.

- **Data Conversion** Converts data to different types. For example, Data Conversion could convert a datetime to an nvarchar.

- **Lookup** Can perform lookups on data. For example, the source might have only the ProductID, but the destination needs the ProductName. You could perform a lookup against a table that has both values to capture the required ProductName and include it.

- **Merge** Performs a union operation on two inputs to create a single set of data to send to a destination.

Developers can debug and run their packages from their own workstations using BIDS. Once they have the packages developed and functioning, they can create a deployment utility that administrators can use to deploy those packages to the production server. We'll discuss the deployment wizard later in this chapter. First, let's discuss Package Configurations, a feature that allows administrators to reconfigure packages in the production environment.

EXERCISE 8.8

OPENING A PACKAGE IN BIDS

In this exercise, you will use BIDS to open the package you created in Exercise 8.7 using the Import and Export Wizard. This exercise assumes that you have administrative privileges on the SQL Server instance that you are working with, that you have the AdventureWorks2008 sample database installed on your SQL Server instance, that BIDS is installed, and that you are running the exercise from the same computer where the SQL Server instance is installed.

1. Start BIDS by clicking the **Start menu | Microsoft SQL Server 2008 | SQL Server Business Intelligence Development Studio**.

2. In the BIDS menu bar select **File | New | Project…**.

3. In the **Project Types** list on the left select **Business Intelligence Projects** and then in the **Templates** list, select **Integration Services Project**. Enter **BIDS Practice** as the **Name:**. Leave everything else at the default values and click **OK**.

4. If the **Solution Explorer** window is not open, from the menu bar select **View | Solution Explorer**.

5. In the **Solution Explorer** window right click the **SSIS Packages** folder and select **Add Existing Package**.

6. In the **Add Copy of Existing Package** window, complete the fields as follows and click **OK**.

- **Package Location** SQL Server
- **Server** (local)
- **Authentication Type** Windows Authentication
- **Package Path** /Export Product Data

7. In the Solution Explorer double click the **Export Product Data.dtsx** package to open the package designer.

8. Switch between the Control Flow and Data Flow tabs to view the package contents. Select items and view their properties in the properties window. When you are done, close BIDS.

Using Package Configurations

Developers build the SSIS packages on their workstations. Therefore, the paths to data files, the connection information to the development servers, and any number of other settings often can be significantly different from those that are needed when the package runs in production. Developers can facilitate the simple management of this problem by implementing package configurations. Package configurations make it possible for the SSIS runtime to dynamically read alternative values for these properties and use the new values rather than the values that are hardcoded in the package.

The package configuration values can be saved in XML Files, SQL Tables, environment variables, and registry settings. By working with the developers, administrators can easily reconfigure packages to work correctly in production environments without have to open and edit the packages themselves. Ideally, developers will design and configure the package configurations as part of the package development process. However, even if developers did not facilitate package configurations, you can manually override almost any property in a package when using the various execution utilities.

Exam Warning

Remember that package configurations allow you to change the definition of a package's connections, variable values, and so on. If a package that ran in development is having problems working in a production environment, package configurations may well be the answer!

Managing SSIS

SSIS actually includes a Windows service named SQL Server Integration Services 10.0. This service is responsible for managing the storage of SSIS packages on the server, enforcing the security of those packages, and managing the packages while they are running. The SSIS Service is a shared instance; that is, even if you install multiple instances of SQL Server on a single computer, there will be only a single SQL Server Integration Services 10.0 instance.

To manage the SQL Server Integration Services instance, you can connect to it in SQL Server Management Studio using the Object Explorer. To connect to the SSIS Instance, you can use the **Connect** drop down in the **Object Explorer** window and select **Integration Services...**. Once you have connected, the Object Explorer shows a tree view of any packages that are currently running, as well as a tree view of the SSIS file system and MSDB storage. Figure 8.6 shows you how to connect to an Integration Services instance using the Object Explorer.

Figure 8.6 Connecting Object Explorer to an SSIS Instance

Once you select the option, you will be prompted with a standard connect dialog box. Notice that the only option you can change in the connect dialog box is the **Server name:**. You can connect to an SSIS instance only by using Windows Authentication. Once you have connected, the Object Explorer allows you to interact with the SSIS instance by managing both running as well as stored packages. Figure 8.7 shows the Object Explorer when it is connected to an SSIS instance.

Figure 8.7 Working with SSIS in Object Explorer

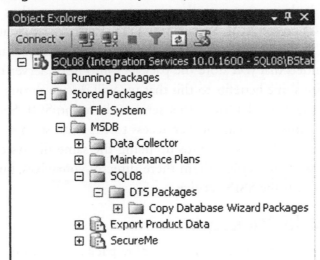

We showed you before that an SSIS package is actually an XML file. And after reading about BIDS, you know that the package files themselves can actually exist on a developer's workstation when they are being created. Once developers have completed a package (or a set of packages), they need to get them deployed to the server where the SQL Server Integration Services service is installed for execution. There are actually a number of choices for how a package should be stored. Figure 8.7 shows two containers under the **Stored Packages** folder. You could store packages as files in the **File System**, or as records in the **MSDB** database on a SQL Server. As you can see from Figure 8.7, SSIS can access packages in both storage areas. We'll discuss your storage options in the next section.

Understanding SSIS Package Storage

Where a package is saved, or stored, really doesn't have anything to do with where it is used or executed. An analogy would be that it doesn't matter where you save a Word document; as long as you can get to it across the network, you can open and use it from anywhere. The idea is the same with a package. Where you store a package impacts where it lives only when the package isn't being used. Typically, however, you will store the packages physically on the same server where they will be run.

When developers are done building a package, they either deploy them to a production server themselves (not recommended) or the give them to an administrator for deployment to the production server (better). Regardless, when you "deploy" a package, you are really just copying the package to either the file system or to the SQL Server MSDB database on the target system.

SSIS supports storing packages as files in the file system or as records in SQL Server. When you deploy packages to the file system on a server, they should go to C:\Program Files\Microsoft SQL Server\100\DTS\Packages by default. When you deploy them to SQL Server, they end up in the msdb.dbo.sysssispackages table. It is typically recommended that you store the packages into SQL Server rather than to the file system. There are some benefits to this that we will discuss throughout this section.

When the packages are deployed to a server where the SQL Server Integration Services service is running, it can broker access to the local storage through what is called the SSIS Package Storage. It ends up being the same file system and MSDB locations as if you were to deploy them there directly yourselves, but it formalizes access to them through the SSIS service.

Deploying SSIS Packages

There are a number of ways that you can deploy packages to your servers. Table 8.5 explains the common deployment mechanisms:

Table 8.5 SSIS Package Deployment Tools

Tool	Description
Deployment Wizard	Developers can use a feature of BIDS to produce what is called a deployment utility. The deployment utility produces a file with the SSISDeploymentManifest extension in the same directory as the package files and configuration files extension. The developer can zip the file up and send it to the administrator. The administrator simply double clicks the **SSISDeploymentManifest** file and follows the prompts. If the packages were designed with configurations, the deployment wizard even allows the administrator to provide the alternative configuration values as part of the deployment.
Object Explorer	In SQL Server Management Studio's Object Explorer, you can connect directly to an Instance of the SQL Server Integration Services Instance. From there, you can import and export packages from the SSIS Package Store on the server simply by right clicking an item and choosing either **Import Package...** or **Export Package...**

Continued

Table 8.5 Continued. SSIS Package Deployment Tools

Tool	Description
DTUtil	DTUtil is a command-line utility that can be used to perform imports and exports of packages from the SSIS package storage on the server in addition to a number of other package management tasks.

Securing SSIS Packages

Once a package is deployed you can control who has the ability to run it and change it. For packages saved to the file system, you can simply use NTFS permissions to control security. For packages saved to SQL Server, though, you have a role-based security model. Regardless of how access to the packages is handled, however, the sensitive information needed in a package (like credentials for databases) is never stored in clear text. This information is either not stored or it is encrypted.

Using Package Protection Levels

When you save a package you can choose from a number of protection level options. These protection levels specify how much data is encrypted if any and how it is encrypted. You can decide how much of a package to encrypt and how to encrypt it when saving a package. You could not encrypt anything, encrypt just the "sensitive" data (like passwords, or specific variable values), or encrypt the entire package. When you encrypt data, you can choose between a key that can be used by only yourself or a password that you can share with others. You also can let the server encrypt the package if you are saving it to SQL Server. Table 8.6 lists the available package encryption options.

Table 8.6 Package Encryption Options

Protection Level	Description
Do not save sensitive data	Any content in the package that is sensitive (like clear text credentials) will *not* be saved in the package. Any users who want to work with the package will have to provide that information themselves.
Encrypt sensitive with password	Sensitive data is encrypted using the supplied password. You can share that password with others to allow them to open the package with the sensitive data intact. Any users who do not know the password will have to supply the sensitive values themselves.
Encrypt all with password	The entire package is encrypted with the shared password. Users must know the password to work with the package in any way.
Encrypt sensitive user key	The sensitive data in the package is encrypted with a key that is unique to the person saving the package. Only that person can open the package with the sensitive data intact. Other users will have to resupply the sensitive data.
Encrypt all with user key	The entire package is encrypted with the unique user key. Only the person who saved the package can open it.
Reply on server storage for encryption	This option is only available when a package is being saved to SQL Server. This option allows SQL Server to encrypt the package using its own key and limit who can access the package using package roles. This option is the preferred protection level when deploying packages to a production environment.

MSDB Database Roles and SSIS Package Roles

When a package is saved to SQL Server and the "Rely on server storage for encryption" protection level is used, access to the package is based on a combination of some database roles in the MSDB database and the package roles assigned to the package. Three specific roles exist in the MSDB database for the purpose of controlling access to packages: db_ssisadmin, db_ssisltduser, and db_ssisoperator. Table 8.7 lists the roles and their level of access.

Table 8.7 MSDB Database Roles
and Default SSIS Package Role Assignments

Database Role	Default Access
db_ssisadmin	Full control over packages. If you are a system administrator, you don't need any of these roles. However, this role can be used to delegate SSIS administrative tasks to an individual or Windows group.
db_ssisltduser	You can see all packages, but can work only with your own. You can import packages and delete or change your own packages. This may be a good role for developers on development servers.
db_ssisoperator	You can view, execute, and export all packages as well as schedule packages to run in the SQL Server Agent. You can't modify or delete packages. This role would be useful for a SQL Server operator to have.

It should be noted that Windows administrators can view all of the running packages and stop all packages that are running, but they don't have the ability to start, modify, import, export, or delete packages.

There are also two "package roles" that imply a level of access on each package: the reader role and the writer role. By default, the roles on each package are assigned as follows:

- **Reader Role** db_ssisadmin members and the creator of the package can read the package.

- **Writer Role** db_ssisadmin, db_ssisoperator, and the creator of the package can read the package.

You could create your own roles in MSDB and assign them specifically to the Reader or Writer roles; however, this isn't really recommended except in rare cases. Ideally, the default database roles will meet your needs.

Executing SSIS Packages

Once a package has been deployed to the server there are a variety of ways you can run the package. The SSIS runtime is installed with Business Intelligence Development Studio as well as with SQL Server Integration Services. You can legally run the packages only in BIDS or on a computer where SQL Server Integration Services is installed. Table 8.8 lists the various utilities that you can use to execute an SSIS package.

Table 8.8 SSIS Package Execution Methods

Utility	Description
DTExec	The DTExec command-line utility can be used manually from the command line or from within a batch file. The command line utility can retrieve a package from wherever it is stored, assign package configurations, override package properties, assign variable values, and so on. With all these possibilities, the command line can be a little confusing to get right. Another major concern with DTExec is that any passwords required to access the package will be shown in clear text in the command line.
DTExecUI	The DTExecUI utility offers the same capabilities as DTExec, but it provides you with a Windows program and a graphical user interface. You can point and click to supply the various options needed rather than having to know the command line switches. The DTExecUI utility can also generate a DTExec command line for you based on the options you have selected.
Object Explorer	In the SSMS Object Explorer, you can connect to your Integration Services instance, right click on a package, and choose **Run Package**.... You will be presented with the same interface as DTExecUI with which you can run the package.

Continued

Table 8.8 Continued. SSIS Package Execution Methods

Utility	Description
SQL Server Agent	The SQL Server Agent has a SQL Server Integration Services Package step type. Again, it offers the same options available via the DTExecUI utility. If you want to schedule your package's execution, this is the best way to do it. The SQL Server Integration Services Package job step also makes it possible to run packages that require passwords, but have the passwords not be stored as clear text. This is much more secure than using DTExec for scheduled operations when passwords are needed.
Programmatically	Developers can cause packages to run programmatically.

Logging Package Execution

Finally, we should mention that SSIS has an extremely flexible logging framework. Developers configure the logging in the SSIS packages. You can override the logging configuration manually when you run a package, but it would be beneficial to have a consistent model for logging packages arranged with developers.

SSIS supports logging the results of package execution to the following destinations:

- Windows Event Log
- Text Files
- XML Files
- SQL Server tables
- SQL Server Profiler trace files

By working with the package developers, you can ensure that the right amount of detail about the execution of your packages is recorded in a place where you can find it easily.

EXERCISE 8.9

EXECUTING AN SSIS PACKAGE

In this exercise, you will use the DTExecUI utility to execute the package that you created in Exercise 8.7 using the Import and Export Wizard. This exercise assumes that you have administrative privileges on the SQL Server instance that you are working with, that you have the AdventureWorks2008 sample database installed on your SQL Server instance, that BIDS is installed, and that you are running the exercise from the same computer where the SQL Server instance is installed.

1. Start the DTExecUI utility by clicking **Start menu | Run....** Enter **dtexecui** in the **Open:** box. Click **OK**.

2. On the General page enter the following values. *DO NOT* click **Execute** yet:

   ■ **Package Source** SQL Server

   ■ **Server** (local)

   ■ **Logon to the Server** Use Windows Authentication

   ■ **Package** \Export Product Data

3. View the options on the other pages in the utility. Don't change anything (yet).

4. Click **Execute** and watch the status as the package executes.

5. Verify that the C:\Wizard\Product.csv was just re-created (check the date and time stamp).

6. Close the **Package Execution Progress** window by clicking **Close**.

7. This time, when you run the package, you will have it write to a different output file. Back in the **Execute Package Utility** select the **Connection Managers** page.

8. Turn on the checkbox next to the **DestinationConnectionFlatFile** connection manager.

9. Click into the **Connection String** field for the DestinationConnectionFlatFile connection manager and change the path to **C:\Wizard\NewProduct.csv**.

10. Click the **Execute** button and again watch the execution status in the **Package Execution Progress** window.

11. Verify that there is now a new file at C:\Wizard\NewProducts.csv. You successfully change the destination of the package!

Alternative ETL Solutions

As you can see, Microsoft provides a variety of methods that you can use to move data both in and out of your SQL Server instances. However, there are still more ways that you can perform ETL operations. These include writing custom code and using third-party solutions.

Coding Solutions

The SQL Server Native Client OLE DB provider offers a programmatic interface named IRowsetFastLoad. Developers who need to bulk load data into a SQL Server instance can write programs that consume the SQL Server Native client OLE DB provider. The developers can then use the IRowsetFastLoad interface to perform bulk load operations from within their applications. This isn't a common need, but it is important to know that it is an option when applications need tight integration with SQL Server and the ability to quickly load a large number of rows into the database engine.

Third-Party Solutions

Numerous solutions exist from companies other than Microsoft to move data around in your organization. Commercial tools from companies like Informatica and Pervasive, as well as open source tools like Pentaho, provide you with a wide range of alternatives to Microsoft's tools. One of the biggest benefits of Microsoft's tools, however, is that they are included with the SQL Server database engine. When you buy SQL Server, you get these solutions in the box.

Why use a third-party tool then? Well, a third-party tool may offer specific features for transferring data between SQL Server and an external database. When you use SSIS, you abstract all the non-SQL sources through OLE DB. That often means that you lose some of the subtleties of the remote database. A third-party tool written for specific platforms may not only transfer the data between the two databases but also provide a higher fidelity transfer of the structure, metadata, and perhaps even code objects.

Summary of Exam Objectives

The topics in this chapter cover the various means by which you can move data around between your systems. The industry acronym for the process of extracting data from a source, transforming the data to meet your needs, and loading the data into a destination is ETL. SQL Server has a number of methods that you can use to perform ETL operations.

The tools that can perform bulk copy operations allow you to move between flat files and SQL Server. The benefits you get from bulk copying data include better performance and a lighter impact on the server. The BCP command line tool and the BULK INSERT Transact-SQL statement both allow you to import a large number of records from an external data file into SQL Server. By properly configuring the database's recovery model, preparing indices, and using the right locking options, you can optimize the performance and minimize the impact of the bulk operation.

Distributed queries provide you with a way to directly reference external data sources other than just using data files from within SQL Server. The OPENROWSET( ) and OPENDATASOURCE( ) Ad Hoc Distributed Query functions allow you to specify the database provider and connection information as part of a query. However, the security concerns implied by having connection information and credentials in clear text as part of a query tend to keep these functions from being used commonly in production environments. Linked Servers on the other hand give us a very configurable and secure way to define external data connections. Once the connections are in place, you can use fully qualified names to reference the objects in the remote databases, or you can use the OPENQUERY function to send passthrough queries.

Distributed Transactions enlist both the local and remote database engines into a single transaction through the use of the Distributed Transaction Coordinator. The power of Distributed Transactions is that you can perform changes against multiple databases as part of a single transaction that can be committed or rolled back as a unit.

Finally, this chapter discussed SQL Server Integration Services (SSIS). SSIS is an entire framework for moving data around. The SQL Server Integration Services 10.0 Windows service gets installed on your servers. You can create packages that define the data import export process to be run and store those packages as XML files (.dtsx) in the file system or as data in the MSDB database. You can use tools like the Copy Database Wizard or the Import and Export Wizard to create the packages, or you could have developers create highly customized packages using Business Intelligence Development Studio. Finally, you can run those packages manually using tools like DTExec and DTExecUI, or you can schedule the packages to be run for you by the SQL Server Agent service.

Exam Objectives Fast Track

Bulk Copying Data

☑ The BCP command line tool can import data from flat files into SQL Server, as well as export data from SQL Server into a flat file.

☑ The BULK INSERT Transact-SQL statement can only import data from flat files. It does not export.

☑ Both the BCP command line tool and the BULK INSERT Transact-SQL statement support character, Unicode, native, and Unicode native file types.

☑ Both the BCP command line tool and the BULK INSERT Transact-SQL statement can work with delimited files (like .csv files) as well as fixed field width files.

☑ Simple file formats can be defined using the command arguments.

☑ Complex file formats require the use of a format file.

☑ To optimize performance the database should be set to the BULK_ LOGGED recovery model, and the bulk command should use TABLOCK to lock the entire table.

Distributed Queries

☑ The four parts of a fully qualified object name are *instance*, *Database*, *Schema*, and *object*.

☑ Ad hoc distributed queries are disabled by default. They must be enabled using the sp_configure statement.

☑ OPENROWSET( ) and OPENDATASOURCE( ) are both ad hoc distributed query functions.

☑ OPENROWSET( ) sends a pass-through query to the remote instance and treats the result set as a table.

☑ OPENDATASOURCE( ) acts as an instance and can be used in place of an instance in four-part, fully qualified names.

☑ Linked servers allow you to predefine the connection information needed to connect to a remote instance.

☑ The name of a linked server can be used in place of an instance name in a four-part, fully qualified name.

☑ The OPENQUERY( ) function can be used to perform pass-through queries on linked servers.

☑ The BEGIN DISTRIBUTED TRANSACTION statement can be used to begin a distributed transaction.

SQL Server Integration Services

☑ Packages contain the information needed to run an SSIS package.

☑ The Copy Database Wizard and the Import and Export Wizard can be used to create simple packages.

☑ Business Intelligence Development Studio (BIDS) can be used to create custom packages.

☑ Packages can be saved as .dtsx files in the file system or as data in the MSDB database in SQL Server.

☑ Packages can be deployed to the server by using the deployment utility created by BIDS, the DTUtil command line tool, or the Object Explorer in SSMS.

☑ The SQL Server Integration Services service must be running on the production systems where you want to run your packages.

☑ You can connect to the SQL Server Integration Services instance in SQL Server Management Studio's Object Explorer to manage the service.

☑ Packages can be run using the DTExec, DTExecUI, Object Explorer, or SQL Server Agent's SQL Server Integration Services Package step type.

☑ Package configurations allow you to override the values (like connection information) in a package at runtime.

☑ Package execution can be logged to the Windows Event Logs, text files, SQL Server Tables, XML files, and SQL Server profiler trace files.

Alternative ETL Solutions

☑ The SQL Server Native Client OLE DB provider offers a programmatic interface named IRowsetFastLoad. Developers who need to bulk load data into a SQL Server instance can write programs that consume the SQL Server Native client OLE DB provider.

☑ One of the biggest benefits of Microsoft's tools, however, is that they are included with the SQL Server database engine. When you buy SQL Server, you get these solutions in the box.

☑ A third-party tool written for specific platforms may not only transfer the data between the two databases but also provide a higher fidelity transfer of the structure, metadata, and perhaps even code objects.

Exam Objectives
Frequently Asked Questions

Q: When I use BCP to export data to a csv file, the column names are not shown in the header row. Is there a way to do this?

A: No, BCP does not support exporting to data files with a header row. You can import from a file with a header row, however, by using the −F switch to skip the first row.

Q: I need to create a format file for my import to work. Should I use a non-XML format file or an XML format file?

A: If you need to maintain compatibility with an older version of BCP, you should use a non-XML format file. Otherwise, the XML format files are often easier to work with, and they are the new format file type.

Q: When I open my source file in notepad, I can see the data. There are spaces between the letters, but it is readable. However, when I try to import the data, BCP fails. What might be the problem?

A: The source data file is likely a Unicode data file. Try running the BCP import command with the −w command argument to specify a Unicode file type.

Q: I want to write a report that shows data from both SQL Server and Oracle in a single query. Should I use the ad hoc query functions or create a linked server?

A: If this is a report that will be long running, not just a onetime deal, then you should create a Linked Server to run the report against.

Q: I use Oracle's syntax when I query my Oracle instance using a linked server. However, when I try to enter that syntax in SSMS, I get errors. What should I do?

A: To use Oracle's own syntax, you need to send it using a pass-through query. The OPENQUERY( ) function allows you to submit a query to be processed by the remote instance.

Q: While trying to run a distributed transaction across to SQL Server instances, I receive an error with the number 8501, stating that the "MSDTC on server '....' is unavailable". What do I need to do to fix the problem?

A: Distributed transactions between two SQL Server instances on separate machines require each machine to have the Distributed Transaction Coordinator service started. Ensure that the service is started on both machines and try the transaction again.

Q: I need to export data from one production system between 10:00 p.m. and 12:00 a.m., but I can't import the data into the destination server until after 2:00 a.m. What should I do?

A: You could create two SSIS packages. One package would export from the source system to an intermediate file (csv, or better yet use SSIS's RAW file format). Schedule that package to run at 10:00 p.m. The second package would import from the intermediate file to the destination server. Schedule that package to run at 2:00 a.m.

Q: I created a package in BIDS. The package ran successfully on my workstation. When I deployed it to the production server, it failed. What could be the problem?

A: When you run a package in BIDS on your workstation, it runs with your credentials and uses data paths that are relative to your workstation. When you deploy it to a production environment, it is normally being run with the SQL Server Agent service. Ensure that the SQL Server Agent Job is being run with a proxy that has access to the databases the package connects to, and that the connection strings to the databases are correct for the production environment.

Q: I want to create a package that imports data daily from a text file that has a file name based on the date and time the file was created. Can I do that with the Import and Export Wizard?

A: Unfortunately, no. This is an example of where you would need to create a custom package using BIDS. You could create the custom package using a sample file with the Import and Export Wizard, but you would have to open the package in BIDS to implement the dynamic file name and redeploy the package.

Self Test

1. You want to export data from a SQL Server instance to a text file. This operation needs to be scheduled to run at night without human intervention. Select the best option from the following possibilities:

   A. Use BCP in a SQL Server Agent Job

   B. Use BULK INSERT in a SQL Server Agent Job

   C. Use SQLCMD in a SQL Server Agent Job

   D. Use OSQL in a SQL Server Agent Job

2. You want to use BCP to transfer data between two instances of SQL Server 2008. The table that you will be transferring data for has some columns that use the nvarchar( ) data type, and has. To ensure that the data is transferred without any corruption of the character data, which data file type should you use?

   A. Character

   B. Unicode

   C. Native

   D. Unicode native

3. You need to import data from a data file that has a different number of fields than the target table. What could you do to import the file (select all that apply)?

   A. Create a format file to map the columns

   B. Create an XML format file to map the columns

   C. Run BCP without a format file

   D. Run BULK INSERT without a format file

4. You need to export data based on a join of two tables into a single flat file. Which of the following bcp command line arguments supports this kind of operation?

   A. in

   B. out

   C. queryout

   D. format

5. When doing a BULK INSERT operation you receive an error stating that the transaction log for the database is full. What can you do to make the BULK INSERT succeed (Select all that apply)?

    A. Set the database's recovery model to BULK_LOGGED

    B. Run the BULK INSERT with the TABLOCK option

    C. Set the database's recovery model to FULL

    D. Use BCP instead of BULK INSERT

6. A BULK INSERT operation you run weekly takes too long to execute. You have been asked to optimize the performance of the operation. Which of the following options could help (select all that apply)?

    A. Break the file into smaller pieces and run multiple BULK INSERT statements in parallel

    B. Break the file into smaller pieces and run multiple BCP commands in parallel

    C. Ask for the source file to be sorted in the same order as the clustered index on the target table, and use the ORDER option.

    D. Drop any non-clustered indexes from the table before the load

7. When you are performing a minimally logged bulk operation against a database using the BULK_LOGGED recovery model, what must you do after the bulk operation completes to ensure your ability to recover the database?

    A. Change the database recovery model to FULL

    B. Change the database recovery model to SIMPLE

    C. Truncate the transaction log

    D. Backup the transaction log

8. You have created a linked server to your Oracle instance to control access to the data in the Oracle instance via SQL Server. You now want to prevent your users from performing distributed ad hoc queries against your Oracle instance. However, there are situations where developers need to perform distributed ad hoc queries against SQL Server instances. What could you do to prevent ad hoc access to only the Oracle instances?

    A. Use sp_configure to set "Ad Hoc Distributed Queries" to 0

    B. Enable the "Disallow adhoc access" property on the Oracle OLE DB provider

    C. Un-install the Oracle providers from the server

    D. Create a linked server to the Oracle instance

9. You need to write a query that joins data from your local SQL Server Instance with data from an Oracle instance. You need to be able to submit specific syntax to the Oracle instance to get the correct results by using a pass-through query. No linked servers currently exist for the remote Oracle instance. You are not an administrator on the system. Which one of the following choices meets your needs?

    A. Use OPENQUERY( )

    B. Use OPENDATASOURCE( )

    C. Use OPENROWSET( )

    D. Create a Linked Server

10. You need to provide support for distributed queries to a remote SQL Server instance, but you need to allow it only for selected users. Which one of the following solutions meets the requirements?

    A. Grant execute permissions on the OPENROWSET function to the selected users

    B. Create a linked server and assign the selected users credentials to use when connecting to the remote instance

    C. Enable the "disallow adhoc access" on the SQL Server OLE DB to prevent ad hoc access

    D. Use sp_configure to set the "Ad Hoc Distributed Queries" to 1

11. Developers complain that they are receiving errors when trying to perform ad hoc distributed queries against Oracle, although they are able to run distributed ad hoc queries against SQL Server. What must you do to solve the problem?

    A. Install the Oracle client libraries on the developer workstations.

    B. Use sp_configure to set the "Ad Hoc Distributed Queries" to 1

    C. Enable the "disallow adhoc access" property on the Oracle OLE DB provider

    D. Disable the "disallow adhoc access" property on the Oracle OLE DB provider

12. You need to transfer a database to another server for testing purposes. You want to ensure that you get the entire database as well as any logins and SQL Server Agent Jobs related to the database. You want to perform the transfer as easily as possible. Which one of the following tools best meets your needs?

    A. Import and Export Wizard

    B. Copy Database Wizard

    C. Business Intelligence Development Studio

    D. BCP

13. You need to import data from an Access database into a database in SQL Server. You want to perform the import as simply as possible. Which one of the following options best meets the requirements?

    A. Import and Export Wizard

    B. Copy Database Wizard

    C. Business Intelligence Development Studio

    D. BCP

14. You need to deploy an SSIS package to a production server. You want to use package roles to control access to the packages. When the developer creates the package, which protection level should they use?

    A. Encrypt sensitive with password

    B. Encrypt all with user key

    C. Rely on server storage and roles for access control

    D. Encrypt all with password

15. Your company implements formal development, test, and production environments. Packages are using servers in the development environment, tested on servers in the test environment, and finally run in the production environment. You need to point the packages to the correct servers depending on the environment without having to edit the packages themselves. Which of the following options best supports changing the properties of a package at runtime?

    A. Package Configurations

    B. DTExec command line options

    C. "SQL Server Integrations Services Packages" step in a job.

    D. DTExecUI options

16. You receive a data file each day from a business partner. You need to import the file each morning after it is received. Your developers have created a package to properly import the file, and have deployed the package to your SSIS instance. When they saved the package, they used the "Encrypt all with Password" protection level. You need to make sure the password can't be seen in the scheduled job's definition. What should you do to schedule the package?

    A. Create a SQL Server Agent job and use an "Operating System (cmdExec)" step to run the DTExec utility

    B. Create a SQL Server Agent job and use a "SQL Server Integration Services Package" step

    C. Use the "Scheduled Tasks" in windows to run the DTExec utility nightly

    D. Use the "Scheduled Tasks" in windows to run the DTExecUI utility nightly

17. You are a sysadmin on your SQL Server instance. You are trying to manage the package roles on the "Export Product Data" package shown in Figure 8.8, but receive an error. What must you do to allow the package roles to be used?

Figure 8.8 Exporting Product Data

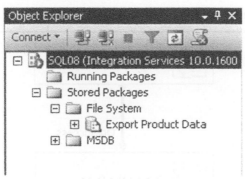

    A. Use the "Encrypt all with user key" protection level

    B. Use the "Encrypt all with password" protection level

    C. Save the package to the MSDB database rather than the file system.

    D. Add your user to the db_ssisadmin database role

18. Your developers and created and successfully tested a package. You have deployed it to your production server and scheduled the package to run using the SQL Server Agent. However, when you look at your SQL Server Agent job history, you see errors on the SQL Server Integration Services Package step. The errors indicate that the connection to the database failed inside the package. Which of the following should you check to find the problem (select all that apply?)

   A. Verify that the SQL Server Agent Service account has access to the remote database

   B. Make sure that the SQL Server Agent service is running

   C. Make sure that the package was saved with the "Rely on server storage and roles for access control" protection level

   D. Check the package configuration to ensure it is pointing at the right database

19. Review the SSIS package control flow shown in Figure 8.9. What is the simplest way to receive an e-mail message after the "Import the Data" task has run, but regardless of its status?

Figure 8.9 SSIS Package Control Flow

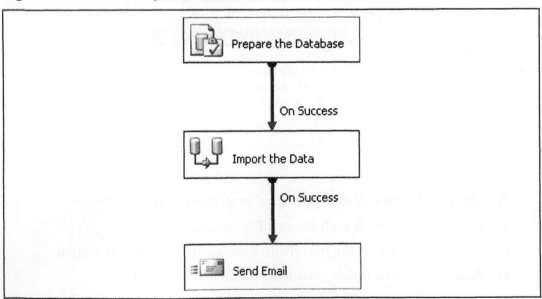

A. Change the "Send Email" tasks precedence constraint to be on completion rather than success.

B. Remove the precedence constraint from the "Send Email" task.

C. Add a second precedence constraint between the "Import the Data" and "Send Email" tasks and set the status to Failure.

D. Make a copy of the "Send Email" task and add a failure precedence constraint to it from the "Import the Data" task.

20. You need to create a single package that imports data from multiple data files. Which of the following tools could you use to create the package (select all that apply)?

A. Import and Export Wizard

B. Copy Database Wizard

C. Business Intelligence Development Studio

D. Maintenance Plan Wizard

Self Test Quick Answer Key

1. **A**

2. **D**

3. **A** and **B**

4. **C**

5. **A** and **B**

6. **B, C,** and **D**

7. **D**

8. **B**

9. **C**

10. **B**

11. **D**

12. **B**

13. **A**

14. **C**

15. **A**

16. **B**

17. **C**

18. **A** and **D**

19. **A**

20. **C**

Chapter 9

MCTS SQL Server 2008 Exam 432

Managing Replication

Exam objectives in this chapter:

- Replication Scenarios
- Replication Types
- Replication Configuration
- Conflict Resolution
- DDL Replication
- Security Considerations
- Replication Performance
- Monitoring

Exam objectives review:

- ☑ Summary of Exam Objectives
- ☑ Exam Objectives Fast Track
- ☑ Exam Objectives Frequently Asked Questions
- ☑ Self Test
- ☑ Self Test Quick Answer Key

Introduction

Replication technology has been with SQL Server for several versions now. With each new version of SQL Server Replication you will see improvements; the same applies to SQL Server 2008 as well.

Replication is copying and distributing data between databases and then synchronizing them to maintain consistency and integrity.

Head of the Class...

Why Replication and Which Replication Type

Because there are several methods for disaster recovery in SQL Server, most of the time, users are confused about which method to use when. Most of the users are more aware of replication than the other types (i.e., clustering, mirroring and log shipping) available to them, so they will decide to use replication without knowing its features and limitations.

However, replication has several configurations to do compared with other disaster recovery methods. More importantly, there are three main types of replication, and users may not know which type of replication will be better suited for their problem.

Replication is one of four methods available for high availability of your SQL Server:

- Clustering
- Mirroring
- Log shipping
- Replication

Replication has the advantage over the other technologies because it has the ability to filter rows or columns in a given table. Unlike mirroring and log shipping, replication has the ability to provide readability in the primary and secondary databases.

You can implement replication for the following scenarios:

- **Improving Performance** By implementing replication, data is distributed among several database servers. You can point your applications to these servers to distribute load. For example, you can use read-only databases for reporting and analysis and therefore, the main database will handle only the transactions.

- **Improving Availability** In case of disaster, you need to have an additional database so that it takes the load. Replication can be used for such scenarios. However, unlike in database mirroring, in replication you need to find a mechanism to change the connection of application from the failed database node to the active database node.

- **Connecting with Mobile Devices** In case you have users who are using mobile devices, you can use replication. For example, mobile users can connect to database and synchronize data, then discount from the database. After doing his normal activities (i.e., quotations, sales), the user can connect to the replicated database and synchronize it again.

- **Transferring Data between Database Servers** In today's business environment, you need to transfer data between servers. For example, the Financial Division needs sales information of all the retail locations, the HR division needs employees' attendance of all the factories around the country, and so on.

- **Using Replication as a Staging Database Server in a Data Warehouse** In a data warehouse application, most of the time you are not allowed to modify schema in the source system. In this type of situation, you can use replication to load source data into a staging server and apply any schema changes you need to the staging database.

Test Day Tip

Replication is not only a disaster recovery (DR) method—you can use replication as load balancing as well. Therefore when selecting replication as a technology, you should consider the other options available with replication.

Replication is analogous to the publishing industry. A publisher can collect a set of articles and create any type of publication, and has the sole rights to decide on the content. There is no rule to prevent a publisher from creating any publication he or she wants.

After the publication is done, publisher will transfer the publications to the distributor, and it is distributor's duty to ensure that the relevant publication has passed to the subscriber depending on the subscriber's subscription.

Replication Scenarios

In replication, there are few concepts and scenarios we need to know before jumping into configuring replication in SQL Server 2008.

Article

Article is a database object that you want to replicate; it can be a Table, View, or Store procedure, or other objects.

In some cases of replication, Article can be subset of a database object. For example, you can replicate a selected number of columns instead of all columns. Moreover, you can replicate a selected number of rows by adding a where clause.

Publication

Publication is a collection of articles. Article is a database object that you want to replicate. Database object can be a Table, View, Store procedure or other objects. One article can be in one or more publications. Publication can be treated as a logical grouping for the articles. For example, if you want to replicate only the employee master data, you can include employee table article, address article, and any other relevant views and stored procedures relevant can be added to the publication.

Subscription

Subscription is a request for a copy from the publication. Subscription defines where to receive the publication, what the frequency for the receiving is, and whether data is pulled from the subscriber end or data is pushed from publisher end.

Publisher

Publisher is a database instance that holds publications for other database instances to receive. There can be several different types of publication in one publisher.

Distributor

Each publisher has a distributor to store replication status data, and metadata about the publication. Sometimes the distributor acts as a data queue for data moving from the publisher to the subscribers and vice versa. There are two types of distributors, local and remote. Local distributor is where the publisher and distributor are in one database server instance.

Subscriber

Subscriber is a database instance that receives replicated data from the publisher. In some replication types the subscriber also passes data to the publisher.

Replication Types

Unlike other disaster recovery methods, replication itself has several configuration types. You can select the correct replication type to suite your requirement.

Snapshot

As the name specifies, Snapshot Replication distributes data as it appears in the publisher at a specific moment of time. Whenever the Subscriber called for subscription, it will send the snapshot of the current Publisher and send it to the Subscribers.

Because of the fact that every time Snapshot Replication sends the entire snapshot, there are limitations for using Snapshot Replication.

Following are the scenarios where you can use Snapshot Replication:

- Replicating a small volume of data. If you want to replicate less data volume (like system data, which is less than 100 rows of data), you can use snapshot replication.

- Infrequently changing data. Sometimes there are data that rarely change. For example, some organizations won't change their price list frequently, maybe just once a year. For those cases, you can configure snapshot replication.

- When it is acceptable to have out-of-data copy at the subscriber end. Every time you don't need subscriber data you are allowed to have out-of-data at the subscriber end.

- Replicating table that does not have a primary keys. Snapshot replication does not require primary article tables. Though it is very rare that you will not see a primary key in your tables, if there is no primary key, you can implement Snapshot Replication.

Components

Two agents are used in Snapshot Replication, snapshot and distribution.

- **Snapshot Agent** This agent is a shared agent for all replication types. For any kind of replication it needs to have initial schema and data scripts. The snapshot agent's job is to generate data scripts for the objects you are replicating. These scripts are written to a folder in the file system called a *snapshot folder*. Apart from writing scripts to snapshot folder, the snapshot agent will write commands to the distribution databases.

- **Distribution Agent** This agent will read from a snapshot folder and distribution database to propagate to the subscriber end.

In snapshot replication, the subscription database is not read only, which means that you have the option of modifying the data at the subscriber database. However, your changes will be reverted back when the publisher snapshot agent runs.

Transactional

Transactional replication is the most used replication type out of the three available replication types. The most valuable feature of the transactional replication is the ability to replicate incremental changes rather than applying the all-data set.

Transactional replication uses transactional log to generate transactions for replication. However, you don't need your database recovery model to be either *Full* or *Bulk-Logged*. Transactional replication works with every database model.

You need to have a primary key for all the tables that you are going to replicate.

Transactional replication is much more scalable than snapshot replication, mainly due to the fact that transactional replication takes less time than snapshot replication.

Here are the scenarios where you can use transactional replication:

- Replicate huge volumes of data. As transactional replication propagates incremental data to the subscribers, it can handle large volumes of data.

- For real-time application. For real-time applications you need to replicate data with minimum latency. Because transactional replication uses transaction log, latency between the time changes are made at the publisher and the changes arrive at the subscriber.

- Replicate data between non-SQL Server databases. Transactional replication allows you to replicate data between Oracle and SQL Server. Oracle

Server instance can be a publisher or subscriber. However, Oracle publishing is available only in the Enterprise and Developer versions of SQL Server 2008.

Components

Transactional replication uses three components; snapshot agent, log reader agent, and distribution agent. The snapshot agent was described in a previous section.

The log reader agent's task is to monitor the changes in the transaction log and propagate this data to the subscriber. When the log reader captures data from the transaction log, it will update the *dbo.MSrepl_transactions* table in the distribution table. Then it will generate commands, which need to be run at subscriber at the *dbo.MSRepl_Commands* table in the distribution database.

These commands are stored in binary format; in case you need to read them you can use the *sp_browsereplcmds* stored procedure in the distribution databases.

The distribution agent's task is to propagate distribution commands to all subscribers. After delivering all the commands to all subscribers, this agent makes sure that those commands are removed from the distribution database.

There are two additional replication mechanisms that come under transactional replication, with updatable subscriptions and peer-to-peer-replication.

Updatable Subscription

With SQL Server 2005, a new replication type was introduced called *Transactional publication with updatable subscriptions*. This is another transactional replication type that has an option of having updatable subscribers. This feature is possible with two options in the transactional replication (when this replication is configured, a new column of *uniqueidentifier* type and a trigger is added to the table):

- Allow immediate updating subscriptions. Changes occurring at subscriber are written to the publisher using MS Distributed Transaction Coordinator (MS DTC). Therefore, you need to make sure that MS DTC service is started.

- Allow queued updating subscriptions. Changes occurring on the subscriber are replicated to the publisher using the queue reader agent. Transactional replication with queued updating is much better when there are less numbers of subscribers and changes at the subscriber are infrequent.

Peer-to-Peer Replication

Peer-to-peer replication is an option with transactional replication. All nodes in a peer-to-peer replication topology subscribe and publish from and to all other nodes. A transaction originating at one node will be replicated to all other nodes, but not replicated back to originator. This replication model is intended for use in applications to have multiple databases or database servers participating in a scale-out solution. Refer to Figure 9.1.

Figure 9.1 Layout of Peer-to-Peer Replication

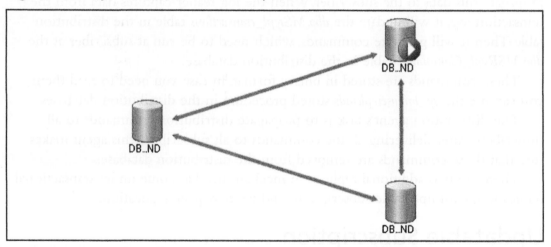

Clients may connect to one of many databases, which typically have the same data. One of the databases or database servers can be removed from the bank of servers participating in the scale-out solution and the load will be distributed among the remaining servers.

New & Noteworthy...

Peer-to-Peer Replication Configuration and Features

In SQL Server 2008 Peer-to-Peer Replication dialog is introduced to enhance the easiness of configuring Peer-to-Peer replication. In the previous version of SQL Server, you need to type the server name and database and you

Continued

don't have a chance to visualize the Peer-to-Peer replication configuration. Also, with SQL Server 2008, you have the privilege of dropping the connection between two servers. Configuration of Peer-to-Peer replication will be discussed later in the chapter.

In earlier versions of SQL Server, you can add a node to a topology and connect the new node to one existing node. To connect the new node to more than one existing node, you must suspend all activity in the topology and then make sure that all pending changes are delivered to all nodes. In SQL Server 2008, you can connect the new node to any number of existing nodes without stopping it. This is made possible in the Configure Peer-to-Peer Topology Wizard or by specifying a value of *init from lsn* for the *@sync_type* parameter of *sp_addsubscription*.

Peer-to-Peer Replication in SQL Server 2008 has the ability to detect conflicts during synchronization. This option is enabled by default and this enables the Distribution Agent to detect conflicts and to stop processing changes at the affected node.

However, Peer-to-Peer Replication is available only with SQL Server Enterprise and Developer Editions, which is a drawback of Peer-to-Peer Replication. Also, after configuring Peer-to-Peer Replication you cannot disable it. Another major disadvantage in Peer-To-Peer Replication is that you cannot have filtering for it.

Merge

Merge Replication, like other replication technologies, will start from the initial snapshot. Afterward, changes at both publisher and subscriber(s) are tracked with triggers. Merge Replication does not propagate intermediate data; instead it will propagate net changes of data. For example, if a row changes three times at a Subscriber before it synchronizes with a Publisher, the row will change only once at the Publisher to reflect the net data change. This will enhance the performance of the Merge Replication.

EXAM WARNING

There can be questions about selecting correct data types when there are updates in both publisher and subscriber. Most users may have used replication in SQL Server 2000 and since there is no possibility in subscriber to update, most users will think that the only relevant replication type is Merge Replication. However, you need to remember that in Transactional Replication there is an option for updatable subscribers.

Here are the scenarios where you can use Merge Replication:

- **Working offline** If you have a system where you want to download a data set while you are working offline and then connect to the publisher to synchronize data, Merge Replication is the most suitable method.

- **When the subscriber requires a different partition of data**

- **When there are other SQL Server versions** With Merge replication you have the option of replicating data between SQL Server 2008, 2005, and 2000 versions.

Head of the Class...

Difference between Merge and Peer-to-Peer Replication

Most users are confused with the differences and usage of Merge and Peer-to-Peer Replication because both replication types allow users to update/insert data at any Subscriber or at Publisher. Apart from that, both features support conflict resolution. However, Peer-to-Peer Replication does not support filtering, which is supported by Merge Replication. When you are considering Peer-to-Peer Replication, do not configure with more than 10 nodes, because it will have degrade performance.

After you configure merge replication, new objects will be created in the dbo schema.

- Insert, update, and delete triggers are added to published tables to track changes. The triggers are named in the form *MSmerge_ins_<GUID>*, *MSmerge_upd_<GUID>*, and *MSmerge_del_<GUID>*. The GUID value is taken from the entry for the article in the system table *sysmergearticles*.

- Stored procedures are created to handle inserts, updates, and deletes to published tables, and to perform a number of other replication-related operations.

- Views are created to manage inserts, updates, deletes, and filtering.

- Conflict tables are created to store conflict information. The conflict tables match the schema of the published tables: each published table is scripted, and then the script is used to create the conflict table in the publication database. Conflict tables are named in the form *dbo.MSmerge_conflict_ <Publication>_<Article>*.

Components

Merge replication uses two components, Snapshot Agent and Merge Agent. If the publication is unfiltered or uses static filters, the Snapshot Agent creates a single snapshot. If the publication uses parameterized filters, the Snapshot Agent creates a snapshot for each partition of data. The Merge Agent applies the initial snapshots to the Subscribers. It also merges incremental data changes that occurred at the Publisher or Subscribers after the initial snapshot was created, and detects and resolves any conflicts according to rules you configure.

Replication Configuration

Though there are several replication types, which we discussed earlier, configuration of those types are almost similar. Therefore, in this chapter we will look at how to configure Merge Replication. Later we will discuss how to configure Peer-to-Peer Replication.

Configuration of Distributor

Before configuring any replications on your server, you need to configure your distribution. If no distribution is available when configuring publication, the publication wizard will ask for relevant information to configure the distribution.

EXERCISE 9.1

CONFIGURING DISTRIBUTOR

1. Launch Open SQL Server Management Studio from **Program Files| SQL Server 2008**.

2. Supply the correct authentication for you to login to the SQL Server in which you are going to configure the distribution.

3. In the SQL Server Management Studio, navigate to Replication node in the Object Explorer. Right-click the **Replication** node and select **Configure Distribution** in the context menu.

4. After the start page you will be taken to the screen shown in Figure 9.2. From this screen, you can decide where your distribution server is. It can be either on the same database server instance where your publication is or on some other server that must already be configured as a distributor.

Figure 9.2 Configuring Distributor Server

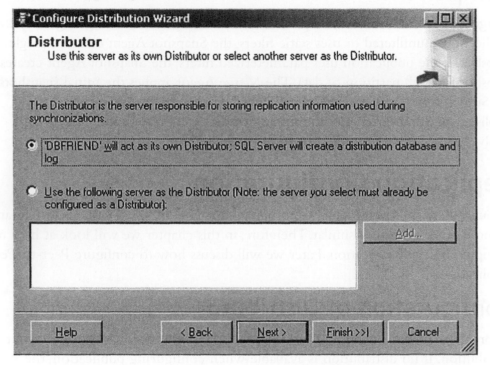

5. Configure the snapshot folder. To support both push and pull subscriptions, use a network path to refer to this folder.

6. Configure the distribution database. Supply the database name, database data file path and name, and database log file path and name. By default the database name is distribution.

7. Next you can add who can use this distributor when they become publishers.

Configuration of Publisher

After configuring distribution, the next step is to configure publisher, which is the major configuration in Replication. Exercise 9.2 will help you create a publisher.

EXERCISE 9.2

CONFIGURING PUBLISHER

1. Launch Open SQL Server Management Studio from **Program Files|
   SQL Server 2008**.

2. Supply the correct authentication for you to login to the SQL
   Server in which you are going to configure the publisher.

3. Navigate to Local Publication leaf under the Publication leaf and
   right-click the Local Publication leaf. Select **New Publication....**

4. After the starting screen, the next screen asks you to select the
   database you want to publish. All the user databases will be
   listed, which means that you cannot replicate system databases.

5. After selecting the database, select the Replication type you want
   to implement, as seen in Figure 9.3.

Figure 9.3 Selecting Publication Type

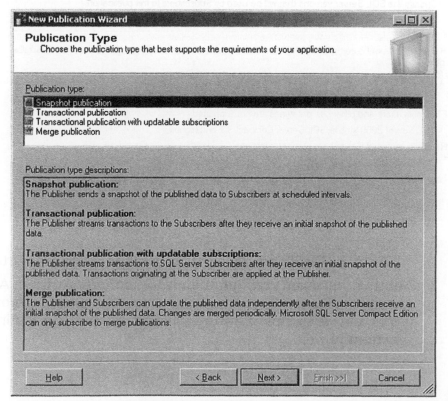

Four replication types are shown and Peer-to-Peer Replication is missing here. We will see how we can configure Peer-to-Peer Replication later. When configuring replication, the most difficult part is to select which replication you want. Figure 9.3 gives you a short description about each replication so that you can be sure before selecting a replication type.

In this example, we are going to configure Merge Replication, so we will select the last option.

6. Next, you will be asked what the database versions are for subscribers. This is Merge Replication specific configuration, and will not be seen for other replication configurations. In Figure 9.4, you can see that Merge Replication supports SQL Server versions after 2000.

Figure 9.4 Subscriber Types

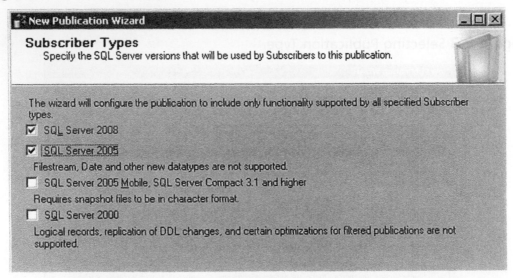

Also, in SQL Server 2000, DDL replication is not supported.

7. Another important configuration is to configure Articles. As you can see in Figure 9.5, you have the luxury of replicating not only tables and views, but also stored procedures and user-defined functions as well.

Figure 9.5 Publisher Articles

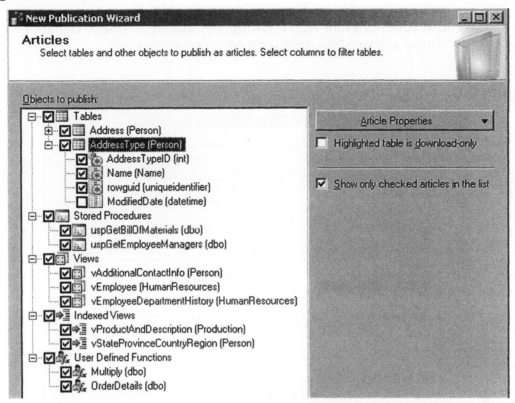

SQL Server requires that all tables referenced by published views and indexed views be available at the Subscriber. If the referenced tables are not published as articles in this publication, they must be created at the Subscriber manually.

In case of transactional replication you are not allowed to select tables without primary keys to select as articles.

8. The next screen is an issue screen of the previous selected articles. For example, in the case of Merge Replication, tables without *rowguid* will be listed. Also, if you have selected views and have not selected referenced tables, which are referred by views again, a warning will be raised here.

9. The next screen lets you set filters (Figure 9.6). By clicking **Add**, you can set filters. You can create either static filters or dynamic filters. Static filters are straightforward; a simple where clause filters data. Dynamic filters filter which different subscribers receive different portions of data. For example, you may have

a centralized employee master database, and for each location, relevant employee data will be replicated. To do this, you can use functions like *HOST_NAME()* or *SUSER_NAME()*. Dynamic filters are possible only with Merge Replication.

Figure 9.6 Adding Filters

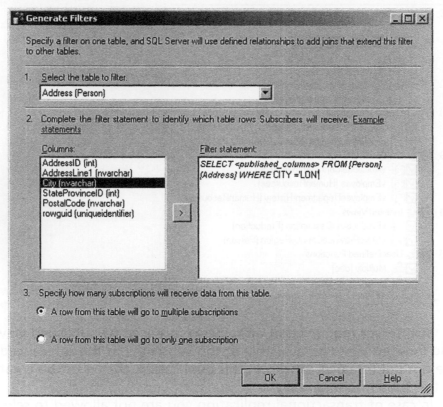

10. The next screen sets schedules for the snapshot; it is better if you can schedule the snapshot during off-peak hours of the database.

11. Next is the security setting, which will be discussed in detail later.

12. Finally you have to assign a name for the publication.

Configuration of Subscriber(s)

After the configuration of Publisher, the next task is to configure Subscriber to access data in the publications of Publisher. There can be one or more Subscribers to one Publisher. Exercise 9.3 will help you to create a Subscriber.

EXERCISE 9.3

CONFIGURING SUBSCRIBER

1. Launch Open SQL Server Management Studio from **Program Files| SQL Server 2008**.

2. Supply the correct authentication for you to login to the SQL Server in which you are going to configure the subscriber.

3. Navigate to the Replication node in the SQL Server Management Studio. In the Replication node, select **Local Subscription** and right-click the node and select **New Subscription...** from the Context menu.

4. In the new subscription wizard, after the starting page you will see the image shown in Figure 9.7. In this you can select the Publisher from the drop-down menu, and it will list the databases and their publications. You have the option of selecting one Publisher from the list.

Figure 9.7 Choosing Replication for Subscriber

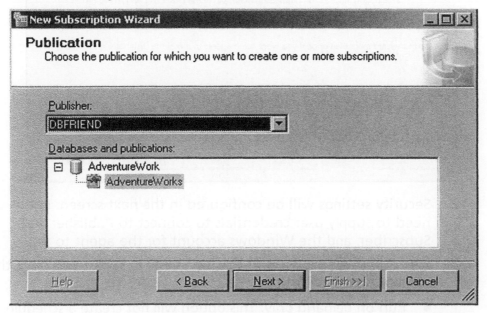

5. Next you need to specify whether the subscription is Pull or Push. This simply defines when the agents should run. If it is a Push subscription, all agents will be run at the distributor. This option makes it easier to administer the synchronization of subscriptions

centrally. Pull subscription will run the agents at the subscriber and will reduce the load.

6. At the next screen (Figure 9.8), you can configure more subscribers. Also you have the option of allocating the subscriber database. If the database does not exist, you can create a new database from this screen itself by selecting the <new database...> option.

Figure 9.8 Choosing Replication for Subscriber

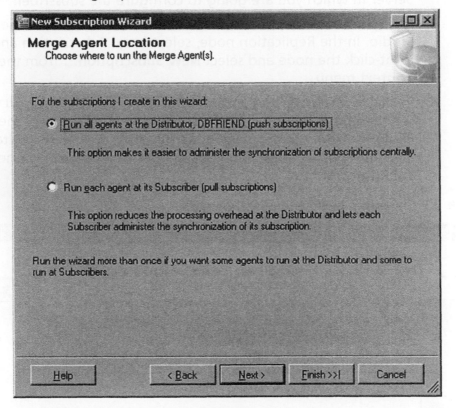

7. Security settings will be configured in the next screen. In this you need to supply user credentials to connect to Publisher and Subscriber, and the Windows account for the agent to run.

8. Scheduling will be done in the next page in which you have three options for scheduling:

   ■ Run on demand only: This option will not create a schedule; instead it will need manual execution of the agent jobs when required.

   ■ Run continuously: This will update the data subscriber continuously. In the case where you need near real-time data, you can configure the scheduling as Run continuously.

- <Define Schedule...>: This will allow you to define your own schedule.

9. Next is to define when you want to synchronize the subscriber database, whether immediately or at the first synchronization. It is better if you can select the first option when there are fewer loads in the publisher database server.

10. The next screen (Figure 9.9) gives you the option of assigning priorities for the conflicts. This option is available only with Merge Replication. If the Subscription Type is server then you can configure the priorities. 0 means lowest priority and 99.99 is the highest priority.

Figure 9.9 Choosing Replication for Subscriber

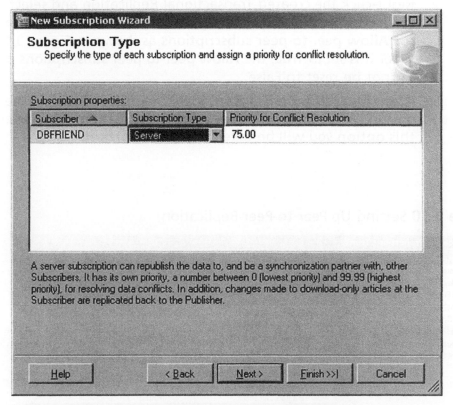

11. The next couple of screens will give you the option of creating scripts of the subscriber(s) you created.

Configuration of Peer-to-Peer Replication

Most users are puzzled when they want to configure the Peer–to–Peer Replication since there is no replication type seen when you are selecting a replication type.

EXERCISE 9.4

CONFIGURING PEER-TO-PEER REPLICATION

1. To configure Peer-to-Peer Replication you need to configure Transactional Replication first.

2. Right-click the created Transactional Replication and select **Properties**. In the dialog select **Subscription Options** and set True for **Allow peer-to-peer subscriptions** as shown in Figure 9.10. After it is set to **True**, the **Allow peer-to-peer subscriptions** property cannot be reset to False.

3. If you right-click the Transactional Publisher you will see new option called Configure Peer-to-Peer Replication. After selecting this option you will be taken to another wizard.

Figure 9.10 Setting Up Peer-to-Peer Replication

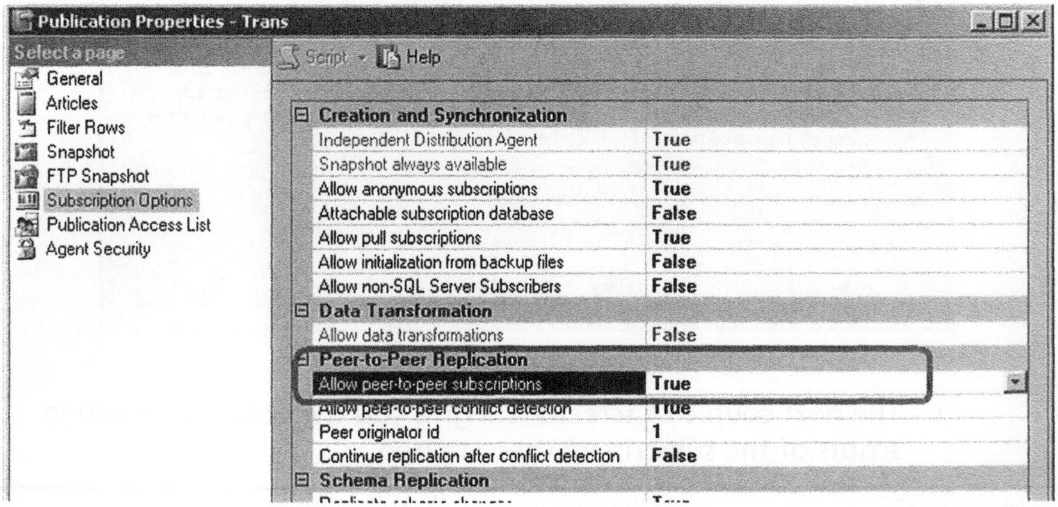

4. In this wizard, after the starting page, you will be asked about the publisher you want to select.

5. Next, you will see the Configure Topology, which is the new addition in SQL Server 2008. Right-click the window to add the databases you need to add to the Peer-to-Peer Replication and peer originator id. The peer originator id should be unique across the Peer-to-Peer topology. After configuring Peer-to-Peer Replication, in all tables there will be hidden column to store the peer originating id.

6. The beauty of this feature is that, in case of an expansion, you can add few more nodes to the topology without much trouble.

Conflict Resolution

In Merge Replication, if the row is modified on two or more ends, the merge agent will detect this change, which is called a conflict. Conflict resolution is based on a set of rules. By default, Publisher will win most conflicts. However, you have the option of customizing conflict resolution. To configure conflict resolution, you need to use the steps in Exercise 9.5.

EXERCISE 9.5

ENABLING CONFLICT RESOLUTION

1. Launch Open SQL Server Management Studio from **Program Files| SQL Server 2008**.

2. Supply the correct authentication for you to login to the SQL Server in which you are going to enable conflict resolution.

3. Navigate to Replication node in the SQL Server Management Studio. In the Replication node, select **Local Publication** node and expand it.

4. Right-click the publication you want to configure for conflict resolution and choose **Properties** from the menu.

5. Select **Articles**.

6. Click the **Article Properties** button and select **Set properties of Highlighted Table Article**. You will be taken to the screen in Figure 9.11 after you select the **Resolver** tab.

Figure 9.11 Conflict Resolvers for Merge Replication

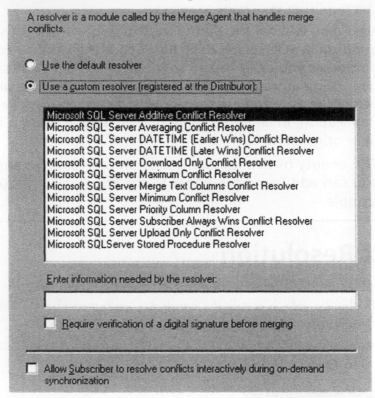

The default resolver is the publisher or the subscriber with the highest priority wins.

- Microsoft SQL Server Additive Conflict Resolver: Values of the column defined in the text box ("Enter information needed by the resolver") are summed together for conflicting values.

- Microsoft SQL Server Averaging Conflict Resolver: Values of the column defined in the text box are summed and averaged for conflicting values.

- Microsoft SQL Server DATETIME (Earlier Wins) Conflict Resolver: The row with the earlier value for the column defined in the text box wins the conflict.

- Microsoft SQL Server DATETIME (Later Wins) Conflict Resolver: The row with the later value for the column defined in the text box wins the conflict.

- Microsoft SQL Server Download Only Conflict Resolver: The data downloaded wins.

- Microsoft SQL Server Maximum Conflict Resolver: The row with the highest value in the column defined in the text box wins the conflict.

- Microsoft SQL Server Merge Text Columns Conflict Resolver: Data in the text column defined in the text box wins the conflict.

- Microsoft SQL Server Minimum Conflict Resolver: The row with the lowest value in the column defined in the text box wins the conflict.

- Microsoft SQL Server Priority Conflict Resolver: The row with the highest priority wins the conflict.

- Microsoft SQL Server Subscriber Always Win Conflict Resolver: The subscriber always wins the conflict.

- Microsoft SQL Server Upload Only Conflict Resolver: The row uploaded from the subscriber wins the conflict.

- Microsoft SQL Server Stored Procedure Conflict Resolver: The conflict is based on the stored procedure defined in the text box.

Conflict Resolution Mechanism in Peer-to-Peer Replication

In previous versions of SQL Server there was no conflict resolution in Peer-to-Peer Replication. When there is conflict in Peer-to-Peer replication, replication will fail and you need to fix it manually before starting the replication again.

However, in SQL Server 2008 there is a mechanism for conflict resolution in Peer-to-Peer Replication. Conflict detection is managed by each row having a hidden column listing the peer originator ID. The Distribution Agent on each node will detect conflicts by comparing the hidden column. The highest value of peer originator ID publisher wins in a conflict.

DDL Replication

Database schemas are not static—schemas will change as customers' requirements change. However, there is a problem when you want to change the schema of a table that is a published article in SQL Server 2000. From SQL Server 2005, by default DDL changes will replicate to the subscribers. You can easily find this option under Subscription Options in the Publication Properties dialog box. The option is called Replicate schema changes (shown in Figure 9.12), which is set to *True* by default for all publications.

Figure 9.12 DDL Replication Option

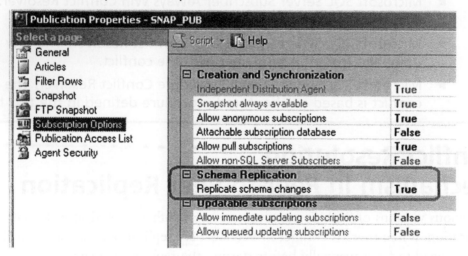

To propagate DDL changes in replicated environment, you need to make sure those DDL statements run at the Publisher, not at the Subscriber. Also, schema changes to tables must be made by using Transact-SQL or SQL Server Management Objects (SMO). When schema changes are made in SQL Server Management Studio, Management Studio attempts to drop and recreate the table. You cannot drop published objects, therefore the schema change fails.

Merge Replication can be implemented between SQL Server 2008 or 2005 and SQL Server 2000 versions. If there is SQL Server 2000 instance in the replication configuration, altering the table *will not* reflect at the SQL Server 2000; instead *sp_repladdcolumn* and *sp_repldropcolumn* will reflect at the subscriber.

Security Considerations

Security is one of the most neglected topics in SQL Server Replication. There are a few measures that need to be taken in order to prevent any security flaws.

Snapshot Agent

When defining Snapshot agent security, you have the option of specifying which SQL Server Agent service account to use for the snapshot agent or specifying separate windows domain accounts. Specifying the SQL Server Agent service is the easier one. In a normal production environment, SQL Server Agent account has more privileges because it is responsible for many operations like database backup, SQL Server Agent Job, and so on. Therefore, if you specify the SQL Server Agent service account for the Snapshot Agent account you are indirectly giving more privileges to the snapshot agent. So, best practice is to select a lower-privilege account to run the snapshot agent.

Connect to Publisher

You have the option of selecting an account to connect to the Publisher. The recommended method is to use a Windows Account as it uses high level of encryption and you can enable you password policies for better use of the passwords.

Replication Performance

Performance is an important factor in replication. There are various steps you can take in order to improve the performance of replication.

- The initial snapshot can be replicated from the replication. If you have a large database this will take lot of time. Instead of using replication, you can back up the existing publication database and restore it to the subscriber server. So that initial snapshot will be lighter.

- Try to avoid replicating unnecessary database objects and columns. Most of the time, users replicate all the columns though it is unnecessary. This will reduce the network traffic and the overall replication performance.

- In transactional replication, a transactional log reader is used to read the transactional log. To improve the performance of this reader, you can move the transactional log to a different hard disk to the data file.

■ The distribution database plays a vital role in replication, therefore for better performance it is recommended to have it in a separate database server instance. This will reduce publisher loading however; by separating *distributor* databases, overall network traffic will increase.

■ The snapshot agent bulk copies data from publisher to the distributor. When scheduling the snapshot agent, try to schedule it when the CPU is idle and during low production periods.

■ You have the option of scheduling replication for continuous instead; to improve the performance try to schedule it at a regular intervals.

■ Though you have the option of replication, *text,ntext*, *varchar(max)*, *nvarchar(max)*, *FileStream*, and *image* data types, it is recommended to avoid replicating these data fields because these data types require more storage space.

■ As specified before, pull subscription will move the processing to subscriber from distributor.

■ Sometimes, you may use articles with filtered rows. In that case, it will be better to include indexes for those fields to improve the performance.

Monitoring

In case replication failed, you need to take prompt actions as it would lead to critical issues. To avoid these issues, you need to monitor your replication. To monitor replication, there are three options with SQL Server 2008.

Replication Monitor

Replication monitor is separated monitoring, which can run directly by executing **sqlmonitor.exe** in **\Program Files\Microsoft SQL Server\100\Tools\Binn** folder.

New & Noteworthy...

Replication Monitor Features

In Replication Monitor grids, you can select which columns to view, sort by multiple columns, and filter rows in the grid based on column values

Continued

to improve the usability of replication monitor. Right-click a grid, and then select Choose Columns to Show, Sort, Filter, or Clear Filter. Filter settings are specific to each grid. Column selection and sorting are applied to all grids of the same type, such as the publications grid for each Publisher.

The Common Jobs tab for the Publisher node has been renamed to Agents. The Agents tab now provides a centralized location to view information about all the agents and jobs that are associated with publications at the selected Publisher. Agents and jobs that are associated with publications include the following:

- The Snapshot Agent, which is used by all publications.

- The Log Reader Agent, which is used by all transactional publications.

- The Queue Reader Agent, which is used by transactional publications that are enabled for queued updating subscriptions.

- Maintenance jobs, which are used by all publications.

Follow Exercise 9.6 to launch Replication Monitor.

EXERCISE 9.6

LAUNCHING REPLICATION MONITOR

1. Launch Open SQL Server Management Studio from **Program Files| SQL Server 2008**.

2. Supply the correct authentication for you to login to the SQL Server in which you are going to enable conflict resolution.

3. Navigate to Replication node in Object Explorer of the SQL Server Management Studio.

4. Right-click the Replication node and select **Launch Replication Monitor**.

5. Expand the server node and you will see the available Publishers in the current server as shown in Figure 9.13.

Figure 9.13 Replication Monitor

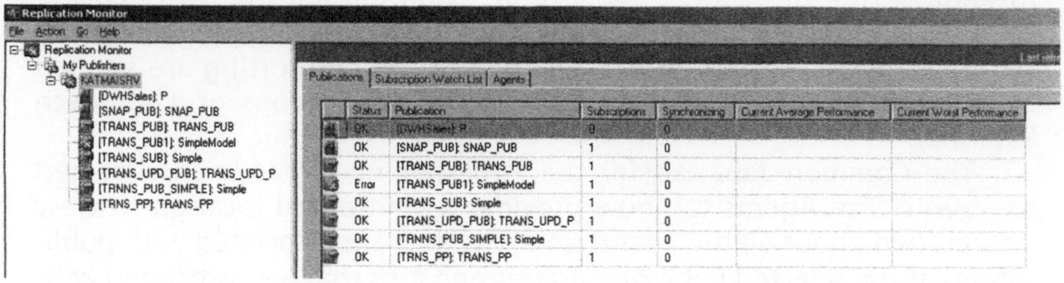

6. You can right-click the **My Publishers** and add any other Publishers.

7. If you click the Publisher server, in the right-hand side you will see all the Publishers and other information relevant to the Publisher.

8. If you select the **Subscription Watch List** tab, you will see all information about Subscribers. You can view subscription information, which is grouped by the replication type.

9. The next tab is the **Agent** tab, where you will get information about Snapshot, Log reader, and Queue reader agents.

10. In the left-hand side, under the publisher there are subscribers. Click any subscriber you want to monitor.

11. You will see three tabs: All Subscription, Agents, and Warning. In case of a Transactional Replication, you will see an additional tab called Tracer Tokens. Tracer tokens and Warning are discussed later in the chapter.

12. You can use the Replication monitor to find the performance of the subscribers, which depends on the Latency. Excellent, Good, Fair, Poor, and Critical (Transactional Replication only) are the values available for the performance, as shown in Figure 9.14.

Figure 9.14 Performance Monitoring from Replication Monitor

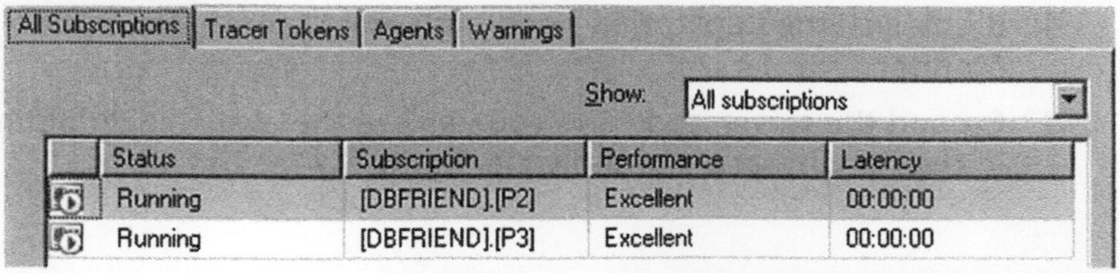

Tracer Tokens

Tracer tokens are to measure the latencies in transaction replication. Tracer tokens measure how much time has elapsed between the following actions:

- A transaction being committed at the Publisher and the corresponding command being inserted in the distribution database at the Distributor

- A command being inserted in the distribution database and the corresponding transaction being committed at a Subscriber

Basically Tracer Tokens can be used to find out which Subscribers are take the most time to receive a change from the Publisher. Also Tracer Tokens can be used to find out which Subscribers expected to receive the tracer token, and which, if any, have not received it.

EXERCISE 9.7

CREATING TRACER TOKENS

1. Launch Open SQL Server Management Studio from **Program Files| SQL Server 2008**.

2. Supply the correct authentication for you to login to the SQL Server in which you are going to enable conflict resolution.

3. Navigate to Replication node in Object Explorer of the SQL Server Management Studio.

4. Right-click the Replication node and select **Launch Replication Monitor**.

5. Expand the server node and you will see the available publishers in the current server; select a transactional publication in which you want to create a tracer token.

6. From the right-hand side select the Tracer Token Tab as shown in Figure 9.15.

Figure 9.15 Replication Monitor Tracer Tokens

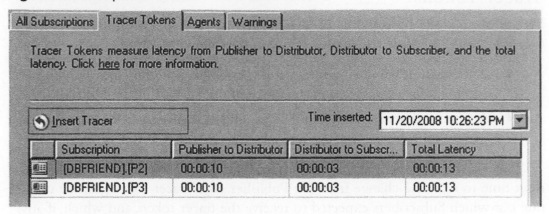

7. Click the Insert Tracer button; you will get a record for each subscriber with the latency time for Publisher to Distributor and Distributor to Subscriber.

8. You can create several tracer tokens and view them by selecting relevant time stamp from the Time inserted drop-down menu.

Alerts

Alerts are needs to make proactive decisions. In replication you can create alerts and can be directed to relevant operators by using relevant medium, email, pager, and so on.

EXERCISE 9.8

CREATING ALERTS

1. Launch Open SQL Server Management Studio from **Program Files| SQL Server 2008**.

2. Supply the correct authentication for you to login to the SQL Server in which you are going to enable conflict resolution.

3. Navigate to Replication node in Object Explorer of the SQL Server Management Studio.

4. Right-click the Replication node and select **Launch Replication Monitor**.

5. Expand the server node; you will see the available publishers in the current server. Select any publication in which you want to create an alert.

6. Select the **Warnings** tab (see Figure 9.16).

Figure 9.16 Replication Monitor Warnings

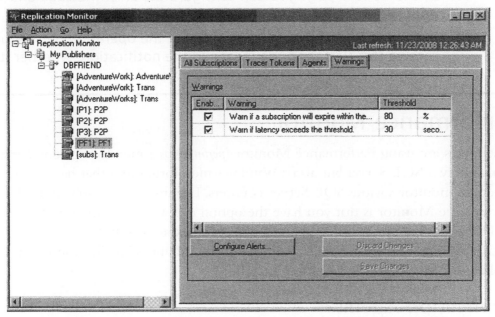

7. Click the **Configure Alerts...** button and you will see the screen in Figure 9.17.

Figure 9.17 Configure Replication Alerts

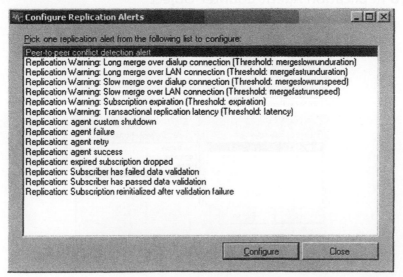

8. Select the alert you want to configure and click the **Configure** button.

9. You will be taken to the Alert configuration windows.

10. In the General page you can configure the Error Message and enable the alert.

11. In the Response tab, you can configure the operation, who should receive this alert, and the means of the notification, whether it is an email, pager, or net-sent message.

Performance Monitor

Most DBAs are using Performance Monitor (*perfmon*) as a monitoring tool. *Perfmon* is a not only a SQL Server but also a Windows monitoring tool that has counter objects to monitor various SQL Server counters. The important thing about the Performance Monitor is that you have the option of using integrating with Profiler.

There are five performance counter objects to monitor SQL Server replication using *perfmon*: Replication Agents, Replication Distribution, Replication Log Read, Replication Merge, and Replication Snapshot.

Replication Agents

There is only one counter in this counter object—*Running*. *Running* can be used to measure the number of replication agents currently running. You can select the specific agent as shown in Figure 9.18.

Figure 9.18 Replication Agent Counter Object

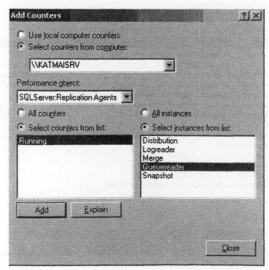

You can see from the image in Figure 9.18 that you have the option of selecting the following replication agents: **Distribution, Logreader, Merge, Queuereader,** and **Snapshot.** This counter is important when you want to measure whether all the replication agents are running.

Replication Distribution

This counter object provides information about the data delivery between distribution and subscriber (Figure 9.19).

Figure 9.19 Replication Distribution Counter Object

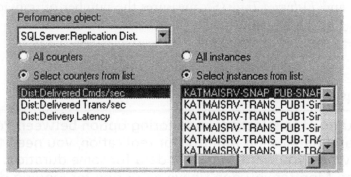

There are three counters for the *Replication Distribution. Delivered Cmds* measures the number of commands per second delivered to the subscriber. *Delivered Trans/Sec* measures the number of transactions per second delivered to the subscriber. *Delivery Latency* measures current amount of time, in milliseconds, elapsed from when transactions are delivered to the Distributor to when they are applied at the Subscriber. You can select the needed subscriber from the instance list. This counter is important to measure the performance between distributor and subscriber.

Replication Logread

This counter group is to monitor transactional replication. This counter has the same counters as the Replication Distribution Counter group but it measures from Publisher to Distributor.

Replication Merge

This counter group consists of three counters, *Conflicts/Sec, Downloaded Changes/Sec,* and *Uploaded Changes/Sec. Conflicts/Sec* measures the number of conflicts per second occurring during the merge process. Conflicts will happen if you haven't configured conflict resolution. This counter is to measure the conflicts. *Downloaded Changes/Sec* measures the number of rows per second merged from the Publisher to the Subscriber, and *Uploaded Changes/Sec* measures the number of rows per second merged from the Subscriber to the Publisher. The last two counters are to measure the load of the merge replication. By integrating Performance Monitor with profiler, you can find the queries from when the merge replication load was high.

Replication Snapshot

This counter group consists of two counters, *Delivered Cmds/Sec* and *Delivered Trans/Sec*. *Delivered Cmds/Sec* measures the number of commands per second delivered to the Distributor and *Delivered Trans/Sec* measures the number of transactions per second delivered to the Distributor.

TEST DAY TIP

When you need to select the monitoring option between Performance Monitor and Replication Monitor for replication, you need to choose *perfmon* when you want to gather data for some duration. Also, in Replication Monitor you don't have an option for logging data, which is available with *perfmon*.

DMVs

DMVs were introduced with SQL Server 2005. There are few DMVs that are related to Replication. The sys.dm_os_performance_counters DMV will list the performance counters with their current values. By including a like operator to object_name field as listed here, you can view the current values for all replication counters and for their instances.

```
SELECT *
FROM sys.dm_os_performance_counters
WHERE object_name LIKE '%replication%'
```

There are four DMVs that are related to replication. They are *sys.dm_repl_articles*, *sys.dm_repl_schemas*, *sys.dm_repl_tranhash*, and *sys.dm_repl_traninfo*. You can use these DMVs to gather information about replication.

Summary of Exam Objectives

In this chapter we discussed Replication in SQL Server 2008. We covered the roles of Publisher, Subscriber, and Distributor. There are three main different types of replication, Snapshot, Transactional, and Merge. We compare them with the features and usages of each replication type. Replication monitoring is important because you need to monitor whether your replication is responding to your configurations.

Exam Objectives Fast Track

Replication Scenarios

☑ Publication consists of articles that are database objects that need to publish.

☑ Distributor is responsible for distributing data between Publisher and Subscriber.

☑ Subscriber can be considered as the end user who will receive the data of the article that Publisher publishes.

Replication Types

☑ There are three main types of replication; Snapshot, Transactional, and Merge replication are used in different situations.

☑ Peer-to-Peer Replication is a transactional replication that can be used when you need to replicate the entire contents of the database. With SQL Server 2008, Peer-to-Peer Replication has the feature of conflict resolution.

Replication Configuration

☑ You need to create an initial snapshot for all replications.

☑ All the main configuration for replication is almost identical; each has minor changes.

☑ When you are configuring Peer-to-Peer Replication, first you have to configure Transactional Replication and enable the Peer-to-Peer Replication.

Conflict Resolution

☑ In Merge Replication, you can set Publisher to win when a conflict exists. Also, you have the option of setting the priorities for subscribers.

☑ Apart from default settings, you can customize the conflict resolution for date, time, and values.

☑ In Peer-to-Peer Replication, conflict resolution is introduced with SQL Server 2008, and the highest number of peer originator id wins when there is a conflict.

DDL Replication

☑ DDL Replication is enabled by default.

☑ DDL Replication will be failed at SQL Server 2000 when it is a subscriber for Merge Replication.

Security Considerations

☑ Recommended practice is to use a unique domain user account to connect to publishers and distributors rather than using a SQL Server Agent account.

☑ A better option is to run the agent service account using the domain user account.

Replication Performance

☑ Always try to limit replication objects as much as possible. You can ignore the unnecessary database objects and columns.

☑ Pull subscriber will reduce the load of the distributor when there are lots of subscribers.

☑ Try to schedule creating snapshots during an off-peak time of the database load.

Monitoring

☑ Replication Monitor is a SQL Server in-built monitoring tool.

☑ Performance Monitor (perfmon) also is used for replication monitoring.

☑ You can create alerts so that operators can take proactive decisions.

Exam Objectives
Frequently Asked Questions

Q: What is the difference between replication and clustering?

A: Clustering is for entire database server, and you can implement replication for database objects level and filter horizontally (rows) and vertically (columns). In clustering cost is higher than the replication.

Q: What is the difference between replication and mirroring or log shipping?

A: Mirroring or log shipping is for the entire database. You can implement replication for database objects level and filter horizontally (rows) and vertically (columns). In mirroring or log shipping, you will not have the option of accessing the database while data is in synchronizing mode, which is a possibility in replication.

Q: Do I need a separate database server for distribution?

A: No you can configure Distributor in the publication server. However, for the performance benefits, it is recommended to have a separate database server.

Q: When there is a failure of one database that has connection to the replicated subscriber, is it possible to configure connection string so that it will be pointed to the other subscriber?

A: No, You need to transfer it manually.

Q: For transactional replication, do you need your database to be in full or bulk-logged recovery method?

A: No. Recovery method can be anything in your database to support transaction replication.

Q: How do you stop the trigger from being triggered when data is inserted from replication?

A: You can write a trigger with the NOT FOR REPLICATION option so that the trigger will not execute for replicated data.

```
CREATE TRIGGER trg_I_Code ON tblCODE
AFTER INSERT
```

```
NOT FOR REPLICATION
AS
<Trigger Code>
```

Q: Is it possible to have two Insert/Update/Delete triggers on a table—*FOR REPLICATION* and *NOT FOR REPLICATION*?

A: Yes. You can have more than one trigger with *FOR REPLICATION* and *NOT FOR REPLICATION* settings.

Q: Is it possible to replicate a SQL Server 2008 database with a SQL Server 7 database?

A: No. The database should be at least SQL Server 2000 to enable Merge Replication.

Q: If you configure replication with a continuous scheduling option, will data be at the subscriber immediately?

A: No. Though data should be replicated at Subscriber immediately, there can be latency that is governed by your network capabilities.

Q: Is it possible to configure replication with both Publisher and Subscriber in the same server?

A: Yes. Unlike mirroring or log shipping there are no such restrictions.

Q: Do I need to take backups of a distribution database?

A: Yes. The distribution database can be restored to the last backup without reconfiguring replication or reinitializing subscriptions. Usually, the Log Reader Agent connects to the publication database, scans the log, retrieves the next set of N transactions that need to be replicated, propagates them to the distribution database, and then indicates to the publication database that the transactions have been successfully committed at the distribution database.

At this point, the publication database can truncate the part of the log that contains these transactions (provided they have been backed up). If the distribution database fails at this point and is restored to a previous backup, it will not be possible for the Log Reader Agent to deliver the missing transactions because the part of the log containing them may have been truncated.

Q: What are the steps you need to enable logging in Merge Replication when there is an error?

A: You should follow five steps:

1. Right-click on your merge agent for this publication. Select **Agent Properties**.

2. Select job steps and then select the **Run Step** option. Click **Edit**.36

3. At the end of your string type the following command:

   -OutputVerboseLevel 3 -Output C:\temp\repllog.txt

4. Click **OK**, and restart your merge agent.

5. If you get any errors, check the log for details in *repllog.out*.

Q: How can I configure automatic redirect for my connection string when there is a failure in the replication?

A: There is no automatic configuration for redirection in replication. You need to write your own code inside your application.

Q: Is it possible to replicate different SQL Server versions in a replication topology?

A: For all types of replication, the Distributor version must be no earlier than the Publisher version. For Transactional Replication, a Subscriber to a transactional publication can be any version within two versions of the Publisher version. For example, a SQL Server 2000 Publisher can have SQL Server 2008 Subscribers, and a SQL Server 2008 Publisher can have SQL Server 2000 Subscribers. For merge replication, a Subscriber to a merge publication can be any version no later than the Publisher version.

Self Test

1. You have a database and it was decided to implement load balancing technology so that it will reduce the current load in the existing database. However, after analyzing the existing database, it was found that you cannot have some columns like Salary or Credit card numbers in the secondary server. What technology are you going to use?

   A. Clustering

   B. Log Shipping

   C. Mirroring

   D. Replication

2. You are a DBA of an organization whose prime business is selling goods. The organization has several branches around the country. Prices of the goods are controlled by the central location and it needs to be propagated to all branches. Price change occurs once every two years. What replication type are you going to implement?

   A. Snapshot

   B. Transactional

   C. Peer-to-Peer

   D. Merge

3. You are a DBA of an organization whose main business is selling goods around the area. You have sales representatives who have PDAs with them. Before they travel to their clients, they need to download data from the server and at the end of the sales, they need to connect to the network and synchronize their data with the system. What replication type are you going to implement?

   A. Snapshot

   B. Transactional

   C. Peer-to-Peer

   D. Merge

4. You are a database architect in a data warehouse and you have a source system that is running in SQL Server 2005. You are referring to this database instance to generate Customer Slowly Changing Dimensions (SCD). The customer

table has a million records; hence, you need to capture only the changes. You cannot change the source system. What is the technology you use to create a copy of customer table?

A. Clustering

B. Log Shipping

C. Mirroring

D. Replication

5. You are working in an organization where there are retail shops in several locations. Each location is running a SQL Server database and the end of each day there is a requirement to transfer a subset of data from all locations to the main server at the head office. What technology can you use to implement this scenario easily?

A. Linked Server

B. Service Broker

C. Transactional Replication

D. SQL Server Integration Services (SSIS)

6. You are a DBA of an organization that has real-time data. This data has a high volume of inserts and updates at the head office. It was decided to expand the business to other locations and those locations need information at the head office. Replication mechanism was selected as the method of data distribution. What replication type are you going to implement?

A. Snapshot

B. Transactional

C. Peer-to-Peer

D. Merge

7. You have asked to implement Disaster Recovery (DR) to your SQL Server 2008 database. In addition to the DR, you are looking into options for using the DR instance as reporting database. What technology can you implement?

A. Log Shipping

B. Transactional Replication

C. Merge Replication

D. Mirroring

8. You have configured Transactional Replication and you have not disabled DDL Replication. What is the T-SQL statement that will not be replicated to subscribers, if you run it in a Publisher?

   A. ALTER TABLE statement on a table that is a published article

   B. ALTER VIEW statement on a view that is a published article.

   C. DROP TABLE statement on a table that is a published article.

   D. ALTER TRIGGER statement on a table that is a published article and the trigger is a DML trigger statement.

9. You have implemented replication between SQL Server 2008 and a SQL Server 2005 database server instance. Because of the system expansion, there are some modifications to be done to the existing article. What step can you take?

   A. Since DDL replication is enabled by default, there is nothing you have to do.

   B. Drop the article and recreate them.

   C. Recreate the Publisher.

   D. Recreate the Subscriber.

10. What action will result in schema changes in Subscriber where DDL replication is enabled?

    A. Changing column type smalldatetime to date

    B. Adding a new table

    C. Modifying DDL trigger

    D. Adding Stored procedure

11. You have table named tblSETTINGS, which takes the following format:

    ```
    CREATE TABLE tblSETTINGS
    (SETTINGNAME VARCHAR(150))
    ```

    This table changes frequently. What replication type can you include to replicate the preceding table?

    A. Snapshot Replication

    B. Transactional Replication

    C. Merge Replication

    D. Cannot implement any replication type

12. You are a DBA at an organization with several locations, and each location has a SQL Server 2008 instance. Employee records from all the locations are at also at the head office, and each employee record needs to be replicated to each location. What scalable method can you use to implement this?

    A. Implement many publishers and each publisher has a filter with hardcoded location name.

    B. Implement Merge Replication with dynamic filters.

    C. Implement this using Peer-to-Peer Replication with dynamic filters.

    D. You cannot implement this using replication.

13. You have enabled Peer-to-Peer Replication and later found that you want filter some data in the replication. How can you do this?

    A. Modify the initial publication and filter data.

    B. Disable the Peer-to-Peer Replication and filter data.

    C. Create a new database, and restore the current database and recreate Peer-to-Peer Replication.

    D. You cannot have filtering for Peer-to-Peer Replication.

14. You have more than 20 subscribers; what is the subscription method are you going to use to improve the performance?

    A. Push

    B. Pull

    C. Both Push and Pull

    D. Nothing will change the performance

15. You are going to propose buying SQL Server 2008 version to support replication. Currently you have Oracle Servers and they may be included for publication. What SQL Server edition are you going to purpose?

    A. Enterprise

    B. Standard

    C. Workgroup

    D. Express

16. You are a DBA of an organization where several replications are configured. In this configuration you have noticed that some agents suddenly stopped;

you are not aware of the reason or when the agent was down. What is the monitoring tool you can use to find that information?

A. Replication Monitor

B. DMVs

C. Performance Monitor

D. Profiler

17. Oracle Servers can be included in your replication topology. How can an Oracle server function in SQL Server Replication?

A. As a Subscriber only

B. As a Publisher only

C. As a Subscriber or Publisher

D. As a Subscriber, Publisher, or Distributor

18. You have implemented replication of a SQL Server database server, but are concerned about the additional load of having 100 PDAs running SQL Server Compact Edition subscribing to read-only publications. You have monitored that there are performance issues in the replication. What step can you take to improve the performance?

A. Move the Publisher duties to another SQL Server to lessen the load on the main server.

B. Move the Distributor duties to another SQL Server to lessen the load on the main server.

C. Move the Subscriber duties to another SQL Server to lessen the load on the main server.

D. There is nothing you can do to lower the load if you have that many clients.

19. You have SQL Server 2005 replication and decided to upgrade it to SQL Server 2008. In which order do you perform an upgrade to SQL Server 2005 for replicated databases to SQL Server 2008?

A. Distributor, Publisher, then Subscriber

B. Publisher, Distributor, then Subscriber

C. You cannot upgrade SQL Server 2005 to SQL Server 2008

D. Any order

20. What can tracer tokens measure in SQL Server 2005 Transactional Replication?

    A. The time duration between a transaction being committed on the publisher and it being written to the distribution database

    B. The amount of time a transaction is in the distribution database before all subscribers receive it

    C. The amount of time elapsed between a command being written to the distribution database and being committed on a subscriber

    D. A and C

Self Test Quick Answer Key

1. D
2. A
3. D
4. D
5. C
6. B
7. B
8. C
9. A
10. A

11. C
12. B
13. D
14. B
15. A
16. C
17. C
18. B
19. A
20. D

Chapter 10

MCTS SQL Server 2008 Exam 432

Monitoring and Troubleshooting

Exam objectives in this chapter:

- Service Troubleshooting
- Concurrency Issues
- Agent Issues
- Error Logs
- SQL Server Profiler
- Performance Monitor

Exam objectives review:

- ☑ Summary of Exam Objectives
- ☑ Exam Objectives Fast Track
- ☑ Exam Objectives Frequently Asked Questions
- ☑ Self Test
- ☑ Self Test Quick Answer Key

Introduction

There are quite a few "moving parts" when it comes to SQL Server, and lots of things can go wrong. This chapter is meant to help you understand many of the issues and how to fix them. This chapter also shows you how to monitor your SQL Server to spot problems before they occur.

Service Troubleshooting

When dealing with a SQL Server that won't start, the first place to look is the SQL ERRORLOG file. The ERRORLOG is misnamed as it doesn't just hold error information. It also holds all sorts of informational messages that the SQL Service writes out. If the SQL Service won't start, most of the time the reason is written into the ERRORLOG file. The SQL Server also writes errors into the Windows Application log. In the event that the SQL Server cannot write to the ERRORLOG file, it will still write to the Application log.

Failure to read the ERRORLOG or Windows Application log is the most common mistake that people make when troubleshooting a SQL Service that won't start. The data in these logs isn't usually cryptic, and it usually spells out the problem in plain English (or the assigned system language). If a log says that the service can't find the path to the master.mdf file, then you have moved the master database. If it can't find the path to the ERRORLOG file, you'll need to recreate the path to the log file. If the server can't access one or more data files, it will be indicated in the ERRORLOG file and you just need to restore access rights to the file.

After the SQL Server is up, probably the most common problem that stops the service from running is that the tempdb database has been moved to a new folder or there is a typo in the path name for one or more of the database files. When you move the tempdb database, you have to restart the SQL Service to complete the database move and avoid problems.

EXAM WARNING

Be sure to be familiar with the data logged in the ERRORLOG file and the file's location. Remember that when taking the exam, unless you are told otherwise, all files and folders will be the defaults. By default the ERRORLOG and SQLAGENT.OUT files are in C:\Program Files\Microsoft SQL Server\MSSQL10.{Instance Name}\MSSQL\Log.

To fix a database server where you have a typo in the path to the tempdb database, you have to get the database server restarted in order to move the tempdb database. If you have typed in an incorrect drive letter or an incorrectly formatted file path, this can be very tricky to do. The easiest way at this point is to start the SQL Server in what is called minimal configuration mode, which allows the database instance to be started without having the tempdb database up and running. This is done by starting the SQL Server from the command line with a few switches after it. Open a command prompt and navigate to the default location of the folder that has the SQL Server binary in it: "C:\Program Files\Microsoft SQL Server\MSSQL\MSSQL\Binn". Then run **sqlservr.exe** with the **–c, –f,** and **–m** switches. Your DOS command should look like the one shown in Figure 10.1.

Figure 10.1 Command to Run SQL Server
in Minimal Configuration Single User Mode

The –c switch tells the SQL Server instance to start up and run from the command prompt instead of running as a service. This will output what is normally written to the ERRORLOG to the console instead. The –f switch tells the SQL Server instance to startup in the minimal configuration mode. The –m switch tells the SQL Server instance to start in single user admin mode. Single user mode allows only a single session at a time to connect to the instance, and the user must be a member of the sysadmin fixed server role. After the database has been started with these switches, you can connect to the SQL Server using **sqlcmd.** Then use the **ALTER DATABASE** command to correct the path to the tempdb database. After the database path is corrected, restart the database normally.

TEST DAY TIP

Remember these switches and what they do. The exam may try to trip you up by giving you an incorrect definition for them.

The second most common problem that prevents a database from starting is when a systems administrator accidentally changes the rights on SQL Server file folders in the process of securing the server and changing drive permissions. The tricky part is that you won't see the problem until the SQL Server instance is restarted. Since the SQL Server instance already has access to the database files, it keeps running. When the instance is restarted, the SQL Server tries to access the database files (even though it no longer has access to their path), and it isn't able to start. Restoring access to the SQL Server's databases files and paths corrects the problem.

If you are using named instances and are not able to connect to them, check that the SQL Service Broker is up and running. The SQL Service Broker is used to inform the client machine which TCP port number to connect to in order to access the named instance. The SQL Service Broker is accessed on UDP port 1434; therefore, that UDP port must be open from your clients to your SQL Server. If you are unsure which TCP port number your named instance is using, you can find this toward the top of the ERRORLOG file, which is created when the instance first starts up.

Concurrency Issues

Concurrency issues arise when a database developer makes changes to the database without verifying that the value being used for the calculation is the newest version of the value. A typical example is an inventory system for a retail book store. You have two different cashiers checking out customers at the same time. When the checkout software sells the merchandise, the inventory system queries the quantity in stock and shows it to the cashier. When the sale is completed, it removes the inventory from the stock in hand and uploads the new value to the database. While this works fine if the cashiers are selling different products, if they are selling the same product, you have a problem.

Cashier 1 starts ringing in the first customer. The first customer buys
books 1, 2, and 3. Each book shows 10 copies in stock. The customer is
purchasing 1 copy of each book.

Cashier 2 starts ringing in the second customer. The second customer buys
books 1, 3, and 4. Each book shows 10 copies in stock. The customer is
purchasing 1 copy of each book.

Cashier 1 finishes the sale and the system updates the in stock amount to
show 9 copies in stock.

Cashier 2 finishes the sale and the system updates the in stock amount to
show 9 copies in stock.

The problem is that even though there were two copies sold, the system only shows one copy sold. Now the in-stock amount is out of sync with what is actually in the store.

There are a couple different solutions to this problem. One removes the concurrency issues without causing a work slowdown for the cashiers. Another removes the concurrency issue but causes a work slowdown. In the first, there is a good deal of code change, which has to be made to the client and the database; in the second, the solution requires minimal code change to the client and no change to the database.

In the first solution, instead of passing the ending total back to the database as "9", the system passes back that "1" has been sold. The database code must be changed to take the value being passed in and subtract it from the stored stock in hand.

In the second solution, you configure the cashiers' computers and the server to support distributed transactions. Then you set the isolation level to a higher level of transaction from the default. This will cause the SQL Server to take a lock on the record that contains the stock data. The stock can then updated using the current technique. When the transaction is committed, the system completes the update and commits the transaction to the database. The problem with this technique is that when the second cashier tries to ring up the second customer, the cash register won't respond until the first cashier has completed the sale.

Agent Issues

The SQL Server Agent is a pretty robust system. It has its own log file, SQLAGENT.OUT, which writes to the same folder as the SQL Server ERRORLOG. Any issues the SQL Server Agent has are logged into the SQLAGENT.OUT file. If the SQL Agent isn't starting or nothing is being logged to the SQLAGENT.OUT file, ensure that the account the SQL Agent is running under has full control of the folder and log files being written to. In order for the SQL Server Agent to work correctly, the account the SQL Agent is running under should be a member of the sysadmin fixed server role. If the agent doesn't have these rights, it won't have access to view all the jobs nor will it have the ability to perform scheduled database maintenance tasks.

TEST DAY TIP

Don't get confused by which service logs data into which log file. The ERRORLOG is used by the SQL Server engine, and the SQLAGENT.OUT file is used by the SQL Server Agent.

With the release of SQL Server 2005, we were introduced to the concept of proxy accounts. Proxy accounts allow a user who creates a SQL Server Agent job to run individual steps of the job as another domain or local user. This is especially useful when SQL Server Agent jobs need access to network resources but the SQL Server Agent is running under a local user account or a system account. This concept of proxy accounts adds another layer of complexity to configuring and managing SQL Server Agent jobs.

EXAM WARNING

Credentials and proxies, while not new in SQL Server 2008, were new to SQL Server 2005, which means that you have a greater chance of seeing questions about them on the exam.

All SQL Server Agent job step types support running under a proxy account with the exception of the T/SQL job step type. In order to create a proxy account, you must first create a credential. (See Chapter 4 for more information about creating a credential.) After the credential is created, you can create a proxy account either within the SQL Server Management Studio in the Object Explorer or via T/SQL by using the sp_add_proxy system stored procedure, which can be found in the msdb database. In Figure 10.2, you can see a proxy account called "Sample_Proxy," which is based on the credential "Sample_Credential". This proxy account has access to be used only for job step types of the operating system type.

TEST DAY TIP

Credentials are created based on domain or local Windows accounts. Proxies are made from credentials. You cannot create a proxy until a credential has been created. To create a credential, you must have the current password of the Windows account that the credential will be based on. If the password for the Windows account is ever changed, the credential must be manually updated before the proxy account will begin working again.

Figure 10.2 Creating a SQL Server Agent Proxy

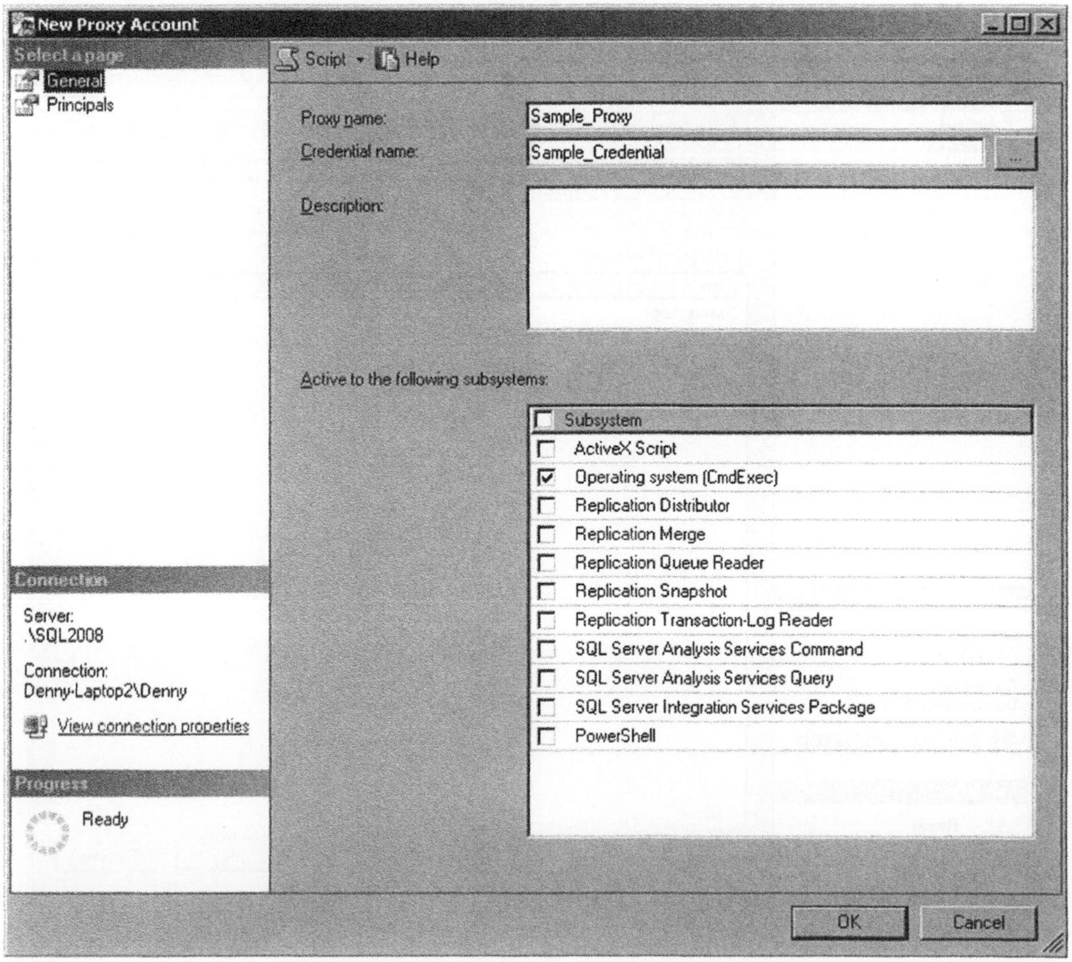

On the second tab of the New Proxy window, you can assign local, domain, or SQL Server logins, which all have the right to use the proxy account. Even if the account used to create the credential (that is, mapped to the proxy) is the login that will be running, the job will not have access to use the credential. For example, let's say you have a domain user named CONTOSCO\bob, and this login needs to run a job. However, the SQL Server doesn't have access to a folder that holds the application that needs to be launched, and you create a credential and proxy based on the CONTOSCO\bob account. The login CONTOSCO\bob will not have access to the proxy unless you add CONTOSCO\bob as a principal on the second screen. Logins that are members of the sysadmin fixed server role have access to all proxy accounts on the server, and these rights cannot be removed. Figure 10.3 shows a SQL Server login being granted rights to the SQL Server Agent proxy.

Figure 10.3 Granting SQL Server Logins Access to the Proxy

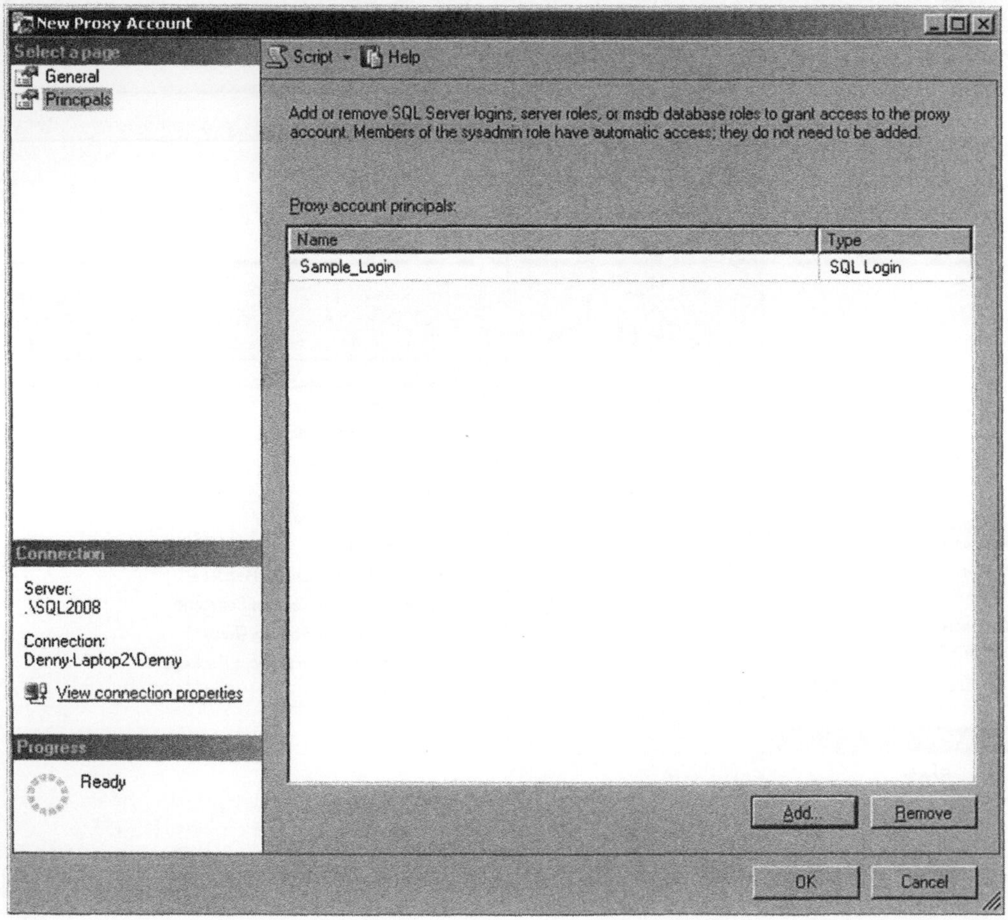

After you have created the proxy and granted the correct login the right to the proxy, you can use the proxy within your job step as shown in Figure 10.4. When you have selected the job step type, additional options appear in the "Run as" drop down box. Simply select the proxy account you wish to use and Click **OK**.

Figure 10.4 Creating a Job Using a Proxy Account

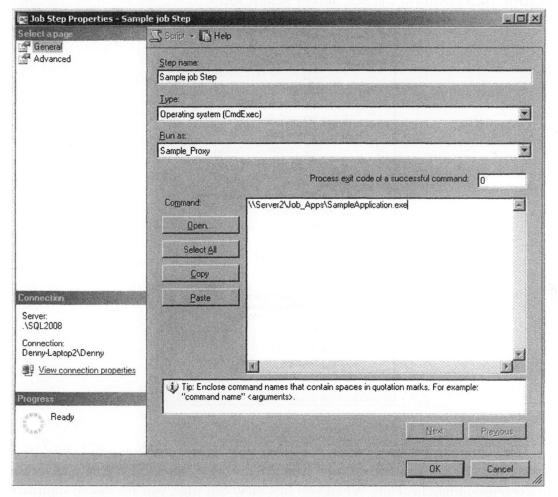

If there is a problem with the SQL Server Agent's proxy account, you will see it listed in the history of the SQL Server Agent job. To access the job history, you can right click on the job in the Object Explorer and select **View History** (see Figure 10.5). Because the proxy is mapped to a credential, which is mapped to a domain or local Windows account, there are several things that can cause problems with the proxy account. The account's password might have expired or been changed, the account might have been disabled by a domain administrator, or the account might have expired and auto-disabled itself. All of these issues require that you as the database administrator work closely with domain administrators to find the cause of the issue and resolve it.

Figure 10.5 Locating the SQL Server Agent Job

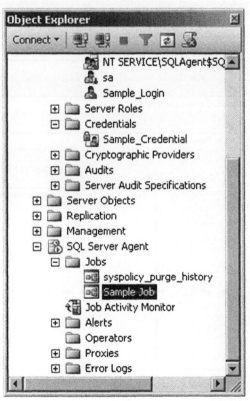

The window that opens when you select View History, as shown in Figure 10.6, shows you the job's history. You can view the history of any job by simply checking its corresponding checkbox. When you first view this page, you are shown summary information for each time a job was run. As you can see in Figure 10.6, our sample job was run twice and both executions were successful. By clicking the plus sign for each execution, you can view the output from each step of the job.

Figure 10.6 Job History

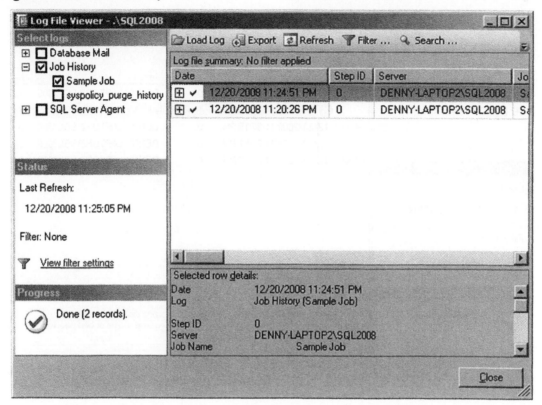

While you can view the history of the job steps, if the output is long, you will not get the full output. This is because the field that the job step history is logged into has a data type of NVARCHAR(4000) limiting the field to 4000 characters.

As you can see from Figure 10.7, the fourth time the job was run there was a problem with execution. By expanding the failed job execution, we can see the failure reported by job step. If we scroll down in the lower right pain of the window, we can see the error message that was reported when the command was run. As shown in Figure 10.7, there was a login failure for this account because the account was either deleted or the password stored within the credential is no longer correct. In order to resolve this issue, you would need to work with the domain administrator to see if the password for this account was changed or deleted.

Figure 10.7 Failed Job Execution

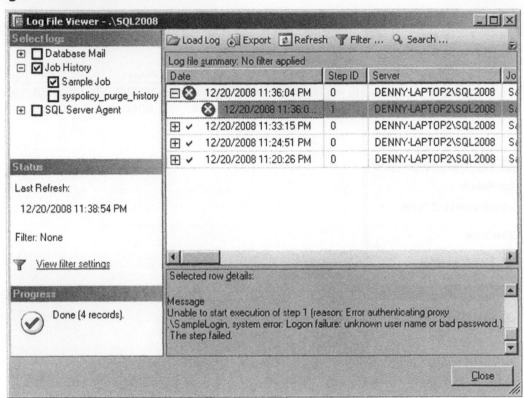

Head of the Class...

Practical Uses for Proxy Accounts

SQL Server Agent proxy accounts are something that you really don't see a practical use for until you need them. Once you get into an environment that has to abide by SOX or HIPAA—and everything must run with the minimum set of permissions—SQL Server Agent proxy accounts become very handy.

At one finance company, we ran all our SQL Servers under a domain account with minimum permissions. Because all the SQL Servers ran under

Continued

the same domain account, we didn't like giving SQL Server account rights to network shares for loading and exporting data. If any server became compromised, the data in the network share could then be accessed.

SQL Server Agent proxy accounts were a great solution to this problem. Each import and export process was set up with its own proxy account used for that one process. This kept unauthorized processes from having accidental access to network shares and data that they weren't supposed to have access to.

Error Logs

When you are troubleshooting problems with the SQL Server Services themselves, the event logs and SQL Server ERRORLOG are your best friends. SQL Server doesn't hide the problems it's having, and it is very good about placing exactly what is wrong with the database in these logs. What won't be in these logs, however, is information about database performance problems. If there are IO issues, they will be logged. Unfortunately, poorly performing queries and slow SQL statements aren't logged into either the event log or the SQL Server ERRORLOG.

Windows Event Log

There are several event logs on Windows Server. One of the most interesting for troubleshooting performance issues is the Application log where severe errors are logged. You can access the Application log via the Computer Management MMC snap-in or the Event Viewer MMC snap-in (see Figure 10.8). Each one is set up by default as its own icon within the System Tools folder.

Figure 10.8 Computer Management
MMC Snap-in Showing the Application Log

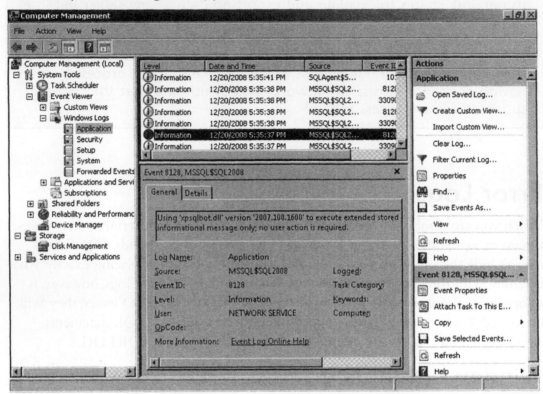

SQL Server Log

There are a few ways to access the SQL Server ERRORLOG file. The easiest way to access it is via SQL Server Management Studio. As shown in Figure 10.9, you can connect to the server within the Object Explorer and navigate to the **Management** folder, then the **SQL Server Logs** folder. Right click on the log that says **Current** and select **View SQL Server Log**.

Figure 10.9 Object Explorer

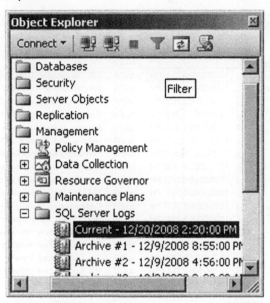

Because the error log displays in a separate window, as shown in Figure 10.10, you can view the current log as well as the six most recent error logs. To view the older log files, simply uncheck the current log and check the log file you wish to view. To view the details of a log entry, simply select the entry in the window on the upper right to view the details in the lower right pane. If you are unable to connect to SQL Server because it's down or too busy to allow other sessions to connect, you can access the log file directly on the hard drive.

Figure 10.10 SQL Server Error Log

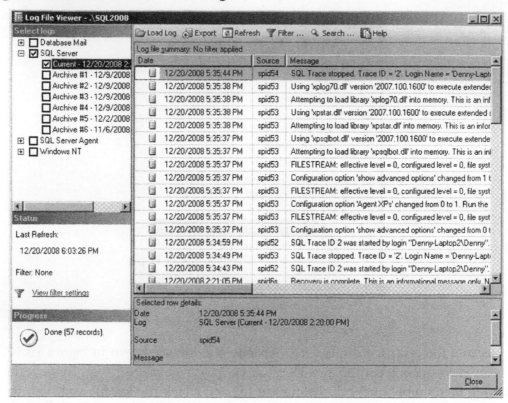

The SQL Server ERRORLOG file is written in plain text and can be opened in notepad, textpad, or any other text editor. By default, the ERRORLOG file is located in the C:\Program Files\Microsoft SQL Server\MSSQL\MSSQL\Log\ folder. If you are unsure where the log file is stored, you can look at the startup parameters of the SQL Server service. The easiest way to do this is to open the SQL Server Configuration Manager and select the properties of the service. Then select the **Advanced** tab as shown in Figure 10.11. In the Startup Parameters entry, you will see the -e parameter. This is the full path to the ERRORLOG file. As you can see in Figure 10.11, the ERRORLOG file for this instance is located at d:\mssql\MSSQL10.SQL1008\MSSQL\Log\ERRORLOG.

Figure 10.11 SQL Server Configuration Manager

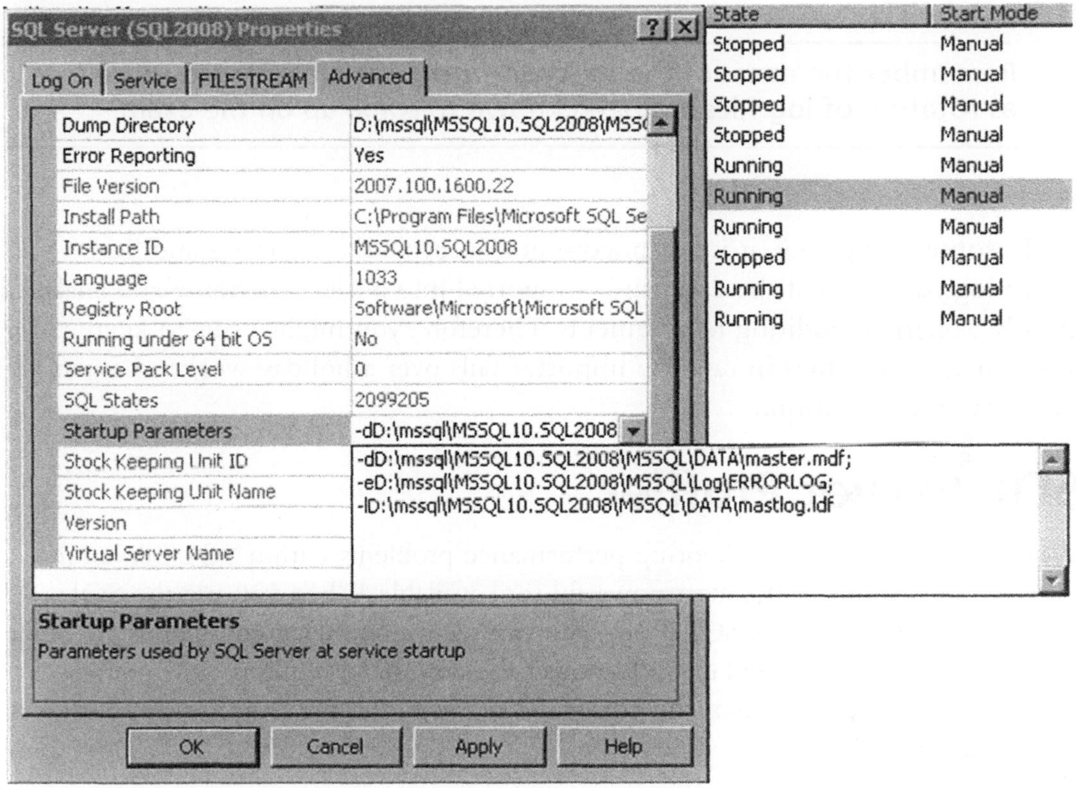

Every time the SQL Server service is restarted, the error log is cycled and the oldest log is deleted. By default, SQL Server keeps the six most recent copies of the ERRORLOG in files named ERRORLOG.1, ERRORLOG.2, and so on. You can adjust this by right clicking on the SQL Server Logs folder in the Object Explorer and selecting **Configure**. Change the default value to a value from 6 to 99. When the SQL Server service is restarted, logs will continue to be saved until the number of logs specified has been reached. This setting also affects the number of SQL Server Agent log files kept.

If your log file grows too large, you can use the **sp_cycle_errorlog** system stored procedure to cycle the error log. This procedure does not cycle the SQL Server Agent's log file. You can cycle this log file manually by using the **sp_cycle_agent_errorlog** system stored procedure.

In some companies, it is not uncommon to cycle the error log and SQL Agent log daily so that the data can be imported into a data warehouse and analyzed nightly as part of auditing requirements. Therefore, you might want to keep more than six log files in case the importer fails over a holiday weekend or an administrator's vacation.

SQL Server Profiler

When it comes to troubleshooting performance problems within SQL Server, the SQL Server Profiler is the most powerful tool available. When you use the SQL Server Profiler to create a SQL Trace, you can see exactly what commands are being run, how many millisecond of CPU power the command requires, how many IO read and write operations the command requires, and the length of time it takes for the command to be executed.

The key to successfully using SQL Server Profiler to monitor for performance problems is knowing what events to monitor. SQL Server Profiler has hundreds of events that can be monitored. Monitoring all of them is simply too much data to go through, and not all of these events are relevant to performance issues.

New & Noteworthy...

Using SQL Server Profiler to Monitor for Deprecated Features

One extremely useful feature of SQL Server Profiler is the ability to monitor your running code for deprecated features. This allows you to easily identify if any of your features are to be removed in future versions of Microsoft SQL Server.

There are two events that SQL Server Profiler can raise when you are monitoring for deprecated events:

- Deprecation Announcement
- Deprecation Final Support

The Deprecation Announcement is raised when the feature being used is to be removed in a future version of the SQL Server product after the Kilimanjaro release.

The Deprecation Final Support event tells you that the feature being used is to be removed in the next major release of the product. This means that the feature is scheduled to be removed with the Kilimanjaro release.

The default template is usually a good place to start when looking for performance problems as by default it includes the Start and Completion of each batch executed against the SQL Server instance (see Figure 10.12). It also includes a few events that aren't of much use when looking for performance problems.

Figure 10.12 Default SQL Profiler Event Selection

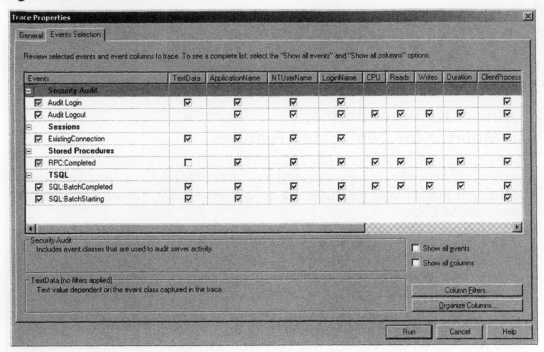

You can turn off the events in the Security Audit and Sessions sections by unchecking their respective check boxes. You can also uncheck the SQL:BatchStarting event because it only shows when commands are started not when they are completed. You will also want to check the box in the TextData column for the RPC:Completed event. This will leave the trace returning all the statements that are executed against the SQL Server instance (see Figure 10.13).

Figure 10.13 SQL Profiler Event Selection

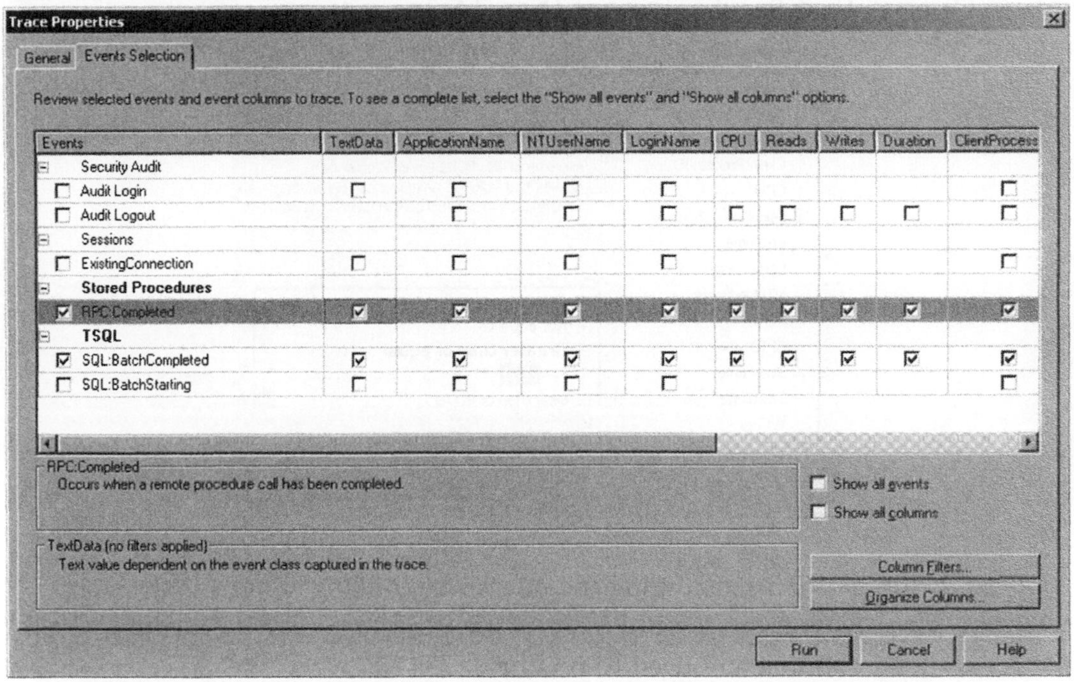

When you run the SQL Profiler Trace by clicking the **Run** button, every statement being executed against the database instance is returned to the SQL Profiler application. If you are monitoring a high load database server, this will quickly become more data than you can sift through. You can reduce the amount of data by clicking the **Column Filters** button. This allows you to return only certain rows back to the client.

By setting the trace to be filtered against the Duration column, you will see all statements executed against the database that take over 2.5 seconds (2500 milliseconds) to complete (see Figure 10.14). If this trace returns too much data, you can stop it, change the filter to a higher number, and then run it again.

Figure 10.14 SQL Profiler Trace Set to
Return Queries That Run for Longer Than 2.5 Seconds

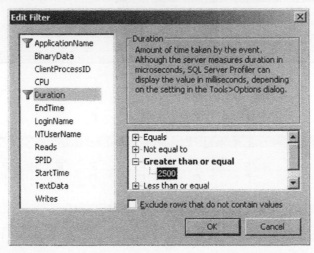

Next, begin performance tuning the queries by looking at your indexes and execution plans. As you can see in Figure 10.15, it becomes easy to identify which queries are long running and need to be tuned.

Figure 10.15 SQL Server Profiler Showing Long Running Queries

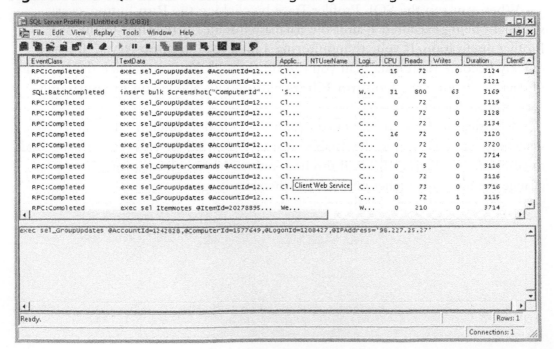

TEST DAY TIP

When using SQL Server Profiler, remember that times filters are done in milliseconds, not seconds, for greater control.

Performance Monitor

The Performance Monitor includes hundreds of performance counters related directly to the performance of the SQL Server instance. Like the SQL Server Profiler, you have to know which counters to look at depending on the data you wish to see.

If you want to look at memory issues, some counters to monitor are found under the SQLServer:Buffer Manager group. The buffer cache hit ratio and page life expectancy tells you how long the data is staying in the buffer cache and what the odds are that SQL Server will be able to find the data in memory. The higher the buffer cache hit ratio and page life expectancy, the better the chances that SQL Server will be able to find what it is looking for in RAM and will not need to read data from the disk. The less SQL Server needs to go to the disk, the better it will perform. Because the page life expediency data is in seconds, you may need to divide the value by 60 (for minutes) or 3600 (for hours).

EXAM WARNING

SQL Server 2008 has many new performance monitor objects. While not all of them are covered here specifically, you should familiarize yourself with them.

For disk issues, you can look at the physical disk counters. Some counters that give you the best insight are the following:

- current disks queue
- avg. disk sec / read
- avg. disk sec / write
- disk read / sec
- disk write / sec

The *current disks queue* counter records the number of operations currently queued and waiting for disks to become available. The *avg. disk sec / read* and / *write* tell you how long it's taking disks to respond to each operation. This number is critical to the health of your SQL Server. Any number over .01 seconds per operation is going to show as higher than normal CPU load and waits within the SQL Server. The read and write operations-per-second numbers tell you how much load is being placed on the disks by SQL Server and other operations. If the operations-per-second number is low and the seconds-per-operation number is high, you may have a disk performance issue that needs to be addressed.

If you think that another application on the server is causing high disk IO, you can use performance monitoring to look that data as well. Under the Process group, you'll find several counters including the IO Data Operations / sec counter. You can then select the application you think is causing the problem, as well as the SQL Server process, to see which is taking the IO. You can also add in all your applications to see which ones are taking the IO load.

TEST DAY TIP

There are many performance monitor counters with similar names. Pay careful attention when the exam refers to the *avg. disk sec / read* and *disk reads / sec* counters, for example, since these two counters have very different meanings.

When you are monitoring backup jobs, throughput to your backup devices is very important. However, monitoring the number of IOs per second doesn't give you a true idea of how fast your backup is taking. In addition, you also need to subtract the IO of anything else writing to the disk. Because of this, Microsoft has included the SQL Server:Backup Device counter, which has the Device Throughput Bytes / sec. Doing some math will give you the throughput in kilobytes or megabytes per second.

NOTE

Performance monitoring data can be scheduled and saved into a text file or database.

Summary of Exam Objectives

The key to not only passing the Microsoft exams but also being an excellent database administrator is your ability to troubleshoot a variety of problems that SQL Server might present. This means knowing the various locations SQL Server logs information and when it is logged.

With the newer edition of Microsoft SQL Server, we have several new features that present their own set of challenges. A key one is the ability to use proxy accounts when running job steps. While this gives you more flexibility, it can also give you more problems because of an added layer of complexity to the process.

While using third party tools can make tracking down issues easier, those tools may not always be available to you. Knowing how to use SQL Profiler and SQL Server Management Studio to capture data about the issues you are having is vitally important—especially because the Microsoft exams test your knowledge of the native tools not the third party tools.

Exam Objectives Fast Track

Service Troubleshooting

- ☑ Know how to start the SQL Service from the command prompt and what the various switches mean.

- ☑ Only members of the sysadmin fixed server role can connect when SQL Server is running in single user mode.

- ☑ Remember the location of the ERRORLOG file.

Concurrency Issues

- ☑ The key to fixing concurrency issues is to send in the difference not the new value.

- ☑ Transactions can also resolve concurrency issues. This technique must be used very carefully as it can cause its own problems.

- ☑ Most developers are aware of the concurrency issue and how to deal with it; however, there are some who do not.

Agent Issues

☑ Problems with the SQL Server Agent are logged in the SQLAGENT.OUT file and not the ERRORLOG file. This file is in the same location as the ERRORLOG file by default.

☑ Individual job steps can be setup to run under a specific SQL Server Agent proxy account. The entire job cannot be setup to run under a proxy account.

☑ The owner of the job must be allowed to access the proxy account, even if the owner of the job is the same Windows account that makes up the credential that makes up the proxy account.

Error Logs

☑ Error data is logged to both the Application log and the ERRORLOG file.

☑ SQL Server audit information such as login successes and failures are logged to the security log.

☑ SQL and SQL Agent logs can be viewed either from SQL Server Management Studio or by looking at the text files via the file system.

SQL Server Profiler

☑ SQL Server Profiler allows you to view commands executed against SQL Server in the order executed.

☑ You can filter statements returned by SQL Profiler by any of the columns displayed.

☑ Seconds are reported and input in milliseconds, not seconds, for greater precision.

Performance Monitor

☑ Performance Monitor has hundreds of metrics that report on a database instance.

☑ Several metrics have similar names.

☑ Performance monitoring can be scheduled and data analyzed after the fact.

Exam Objectives
Frequently Asked Questions

Q: I've messed up the path to my tempdb database, and now SQL Server won't start. How can I fix it?

A: Start SQL Server from the command prompt using the −c, −m, and −f switches, then correct the path to the tempdb database.

Q: Of the two resolutions to the concurrency issue shown, which one was the better solution?

A: The solution that requires more client code change is the better of the two solutions because it does not impact the cashiers' productivity.

Q: Can a SQL Server Agent proxy be created against a SQL Server login?

A: No, proxies can only be created against credentials not logins.

Q: Should I run SQL Server Profiler against the database all the time?

A: No, running a trace takes resources away from the database.

Q: If I just want to see the statements as they are completed, what SQL Server Profiler events should I monitor?

A: You will want to monitor the RPC:Completed and the SQL:BatchCompleted events. This gives you the completion of all statements being executed. If you want to see the statements being executed within stored procedures, monitor the SP:StmtCompleted event.

Q: Why do performance monitor counters with similar names give such different numbers?

A: With performance monitor counters, some counters with similar names have different numbers because they show very different information. The key to performance monitor counters is to look to the descriptions, which give a breakdown of the data actually being captured.

Self Test

1. What protocol and port number need to be open between the client machine and SQL Server for clients to resolve instance names to port numbers?

    A. TCP 1433

    B. TCP 1434

    C. UDP 1433

    D. UDP 1434

2. You have been informed that a job has been failing. Where should you look to see why the job has failed?

    A. ERRORLOG file

    B. SQLAGENT.OUT file

    C. Job history within SQL Server Management Studio

    D. Windows Application log

3. If the SQL Server service is not able to start, which log will contain the reason why?

    A. SQLAGENT.OUT

    B. Windows Security Event log

    C. Windows System Event log

    D. ERRORLOG

4. Your SQL Server will not start. You have been told by the systems administrator that they changed the permissions on the SQL Server folder tree. Where can you find information about why the SQL Server will not start?

    A. The SQL Server Agent log file SQLAGENT.OUT

    B. Windows Application log

    C. Windows Security log

    D. Windows System log

5. You are attempting to locate the path to the ERRORLOG file. You open the SQL Server Configuration Manager and edit the service. Which parameter of the SQL Server service should you look at?

   A. –d

   B. –l

   C. –e

   D. –t

6. Your company has a policy of rotating the SQL Server and Agent log files daily. You have configured a SQL Agent job to run daily and cycle the error log. You have found that the SQL Agent log is not being rotated as required. What stored procedure should be used to rotate the SQL Agent log?

   A. sp_cycle_errorlog

   B. sp_cycle_agent_errorlog

   C. sp_cycle_sqlagent_errorlog

   D. sp_cycle_agent_sqlagent.out

7. You are running a SQL Server trace looking for long running queries, but there is too much data to sift through. What filter should you apply to your trace to show only the long running queries?

   A. CPU

   B. Reads

   C. Writes

   D. Duration

8. You are setting up a trace and wish to filter the trace to show only statements that take over 5 seconds to complete. What value (in what unit) should you enter in the filter window?

   A. 5 (seconds)

   B. 50 (decaseconds)

   C. 5000 (milliseconds)

   D. .083 (minutes)

9. You are looking at a SQL Server that is having performance problems. You have found that the SAN storage is not working correctly. Which performance monitor should you look at to confirm that the storage is not writing data quickly enough?

    A. Current Disk Queue

    B. Avg Disk Sec / Write

    C. Avg Disk Write / Sec

    D. Avg Disk Queue

10. You wish to monitor the throughput of your backup operation to see if the backups are running at their full potential. What performance monitor counter should you monitor?

    A. SQL Server: Backup Device – Device Throughput Bytes / sec

    B. PhysicalDisk – Avg Disk Write / Sec

    C. PhysicalDisk – Disk Writes / Sec

11. You have a SQL Server Agent job configured to run T/SQL statements. The job runs under a domain account that is not a member of the sysadmin fixed server role. You wish to add a Command Exec job step to the job. The job fails on the step because the domain account doesn't have rights to run Command Exec job steps. What should you do to correct this issue without granting excessive rights to the instance?

    A. Make the logon a member of the sysadmin fixed server role.

    B. Make the logon a member of the Windows Administrators group on the server.

    C. Create a credential based on the Windows logon. Create a proxy based on the credential. Grant the logon rights to the proxy. Assign the proxy to run the job step.

    D. Create a proxy based on the Windows logon. Create a credential based on the proxy. Grant the logon rights to the credential. Assign the credential to run the job step.

12. You have a SQL Server with several instances installed on it. After the server reboots users are only able to connect to the default instance. What should to do to enable your clients to connect to the named instances again?

    A. Restart the SQL Server services for the named instances.

    B. Restart the SQL Server Agent services for the named instances.

    C. Restart the SQL Server service for the default instance.

    D. Restart the SQL Browser service.

13. While attempting to troubleshoot connection issues to your SQL Server, you need to identify the TCP port the SQL Server instance is listening on. You examine the SQL Server ERRORLOG as show in Figure 10.16. What ports are being used to connect to the instance?

Figure 10.16 A SQL Server ERRORLOG

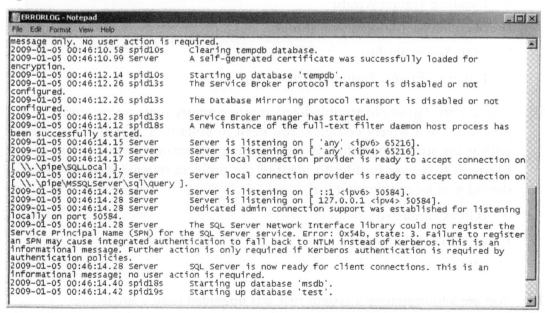

    A. TCP Port 65216

    B. TCP Port 50584

    C. UDP Port 65216

    D. UDP Port 50584

14. You have restarted your SQL Server in single user mode but are unable to connect to the SQL Server using the sqlcmd command line utility. The error message that you receive says that only one administrator can connect at this time. What does this error mean?

    A. The sqlcmd utility cannot be used when the SQL Server is in single user mode.

    B. Another login that is a member of the sysadmin fixed server role has connected to the SQL Server. Disconnect that login before you can connect.

    C. The SQL Server is not yet ready for connections. Wait for the SQL Server to complete its startup process before connecting.

15. You are attempting to troubleshoot a poorly performing stored procedure that is very complex. What tool should you use to identity the problem statement within the procedure?

    A. Database Tuning Wizard

    B. SQL Server Management Studio

    C. SQL Server Profiler

    D. Database Engine Tuning Advisor

16. You are attempting to troubleshoot another poorly performing stored procedure that is very complex. You need to determine which statement within the stored procedure is causing the performance problem. You decide to use SQL Server Profiler to identity the problem statement. What event should you be monitoring for?

    A. RPC:Completed

    B. SQL:Batch Completed

    C. SP:Stmt Completed

17. You are administrating a system that was upgraded from a single-user Microsoft Access database to a multi-user inventory application using SQL Server 2008 as the backend. Users are complaining that the inventory is no longer accurate. You examine the stored procedure that updates the inventory and you find the following stored procedure:

CREATE PROCEDURE UpdateInventory

@Sku VARCHAR(50), @InventoryAmount INT

AS

UPDATE Inventory

    SET Inventory = @InventoryAmount

WHERE Sku = @Sku

GO

How should you change this procedure in order to correct the problem?

A. CREATE PROCEDURE UpdateInventory

    @Sku VARCHAR(50),

    @AmountSold INT

    AS

    UPDATE Inventory

        SET Inventory = Inventory – @AmountSold

    WHERE Sku = @Sku

    GO

B. CREATE PROCEDURE UpdateInventory

    @Sku VARCHAR(50),

    @AmountSold INT

    AS

    UPDATE Inventory

        SET Inventory = Inventory + @AmountSold

    WHERE Sku = @Sku

    GO

C. CREATE PROCEDURE UpdateInventory

    @Sku VARHCAR(50),

    @InventoryAmount INT

    AS

    UPDATE Inventory

        SET Inventory = Inventory – @InventoryAmount

    WHERE Sku = @Sku

    GO

D. CREATE PROCEDURE UpdateInventory

@Sku VARCHAR(50),

@InventoryAmount INT

AS

UPDATE Inventory

   SET Inventory = Inventory + @InventoryAmount

WHERE Sku = @Sku

GO

18. You are the database administrator for Contoso, Ltd. Your company policy states that each employee uses a single workstation. The business unit uses a Win32 application on each workstation and a hard coded SQL Server login to connect to the database. You wish to monitor the activity of a specific user within the application by using SQL Profiler. What column can you use to filter against to restrict the data to only the one user in question?

A. TextData

B. LoginName

C. NTUserName

D. HostName

19. Suppose you are running a SQL Agent job with a command executable under a domain account that is not a member of the sysadmin fixed server role. If no proxy account is configured, what domain account would a job step be run under?

A. Users account

B. Sysadmin account

C. Account running the SQL Server Agent

D. Account running the SQL Server

20. A user who is not a member of the sysadmin fixed server role is attempting to create a job to call an SSIS package. This job step must be created under a proxy account, but the user reports that they do not have the correct proxy account listed in their drop down menu. What should be done to resolve the issue without granting the user unneeded rights?

A. Make the user a member of the sysadmin fixed server role.

B. Grant the user rights to the credential that the proxy is based on.

C. Grant the user rights to the proxy.

D. Add the user to the SQLAgentOperatorRole fixed database role within the msdb database.

Self Test Quick Answer Key

1. **D**

2. **C**

3. **D**

4. **B**

5. **C**

6. **B**

7. **D**

8. **C**

9. **B**

10. **A**

11. **C**

12. **D**

13. **A**

14. **B**

15. **C**

16. **C**

17. **A**

18. **D**

19. **C**

20. **C**

Chapter 11

MCTS SQL Server 2008 Exam 432

SQL Server XML Support

Exam objectives in this chapter:

- Working with XML Data
- HTTP Endpoints
- Web Services
- XQuery Explained
- XPath

Exam objectives review:

- ☑ Summary of Exam Objectives
- ☑ Exam Objectives Fast Track
- ☑ Exam Objectives Frequently Asked Questions
- ☑ Self Test
- ☑ Self Test Quick Answer Key

Introduction

This chapter will serve as an overview of XML for the database administrator (DBA). In this chapter, XML, XQuery, and XPath will all be covered in the context of what a DBA needs to know.

This chapter will also cover why you would set up HTTP endpoints, as well as aspects of HTTP endpoints and some of the uses for them.

Working with XML Data

When you are working with data that is semistructured, unstructured, or of an unknown structure, XML can provide platform-independence and ensure portability by using structural and semantic markup. SQL Server 2008 provides native XML features such as interoperability between XML and relational data, the ability to index XML data for efficient query processing and good scalability, SOAP, ADO.NET, and OLE DB access, in addition to the ability to back up, recover, and replicate XML data. We start reviewing these features by taking a look at XML indexing.

Understanding XML Indexing

SQL Server 2008 allows for the creation of indices only on the XML data type. Indices are used to optimize XQuery queries. They index all tags, values, and paths over the XML instances in the XML data type column. SQL Server provides two key types of indexing on the XML data type: *CREATE PRIMARY XML INDEX* and *CREATE XML INDEX*.

Exam Warning

The first index on the XML data type column must be the primary XML index.

The *CREATE PRIMARY XML INDEX* removes the need for SQL Server to shred your XML data during every query. It should be used when you store large XML documents in each row of a table. You cannot create a primary XML index on a non-XML column, and you can only create one primary XML index on a given XML column. Figure 11.1 presents the syntax for creating a *CREATE PRIMARY XML INDEX*.

Figure 11.1 *CREATE PRIMARY XML INDEX* Syntax

```
CREATE PRIMARY XML INDEX [index_name]
      ON table_name (xml_column_name)
```

New & Noteworthy...

XML Data Type

XML instances are stored in XML type columns as large binary objects (BLOBS). These XML instances can be large, and the stored binary representation of XML data type instances can be up to 2 GB.

Figure 11.2 shows the syntax you can use to create a table and insert some values into the table.

Figure 11.2 Sample XML Data

```
CREATE TABLE [dbo].[XML_Table](
      [pk] [int] IDENTITY(1,1) NOT NULL,
      [customerName] [varchar](255) NULL,
      [customerPhone] [varchar](255) NULL,
      [customerAddress] [xml] NULL,
CONSTRAINT [PK_XML_Table] PRIMARY KEY CLUSTERED
(
      [pk] ASC
))

INSERT INTO XML_Table (
      [customerName],
      [customerPhone],
      [customerAddress]
) VALUES (
      /* customerName - VARCHAR(255) */ 'Monica Banning',
```

```
        /* customerPhone - VARCHAR(255) */ '555-8746',
        '<customer><address1>123 Main Street</address1><city>Newark
        </city><state>DE</state><zip>14785</zip>
</customer>' )
INSERT INTO XML_Table (
        [customerName],
        [customerPhone],
        [customerAddress]
) VALUES (
        /* customerName - VARCHAR(255) */ 'Jennifer Liddle',
        /* customerPhone - VARCHAR(255) */ '555-2497',
        '<customer><address1>45 Andrew Street</address1><city>Clifton
        </city><state>AH</state><zip>18783</zip>
</customer>')
```

To create the primary key for this table, you will use the code shown in Figure 11.3.

Figure 11.3 Create Primary XML Index

```
CREATE PRIMARY XML INDEX [PK_XML_Data_customerAddress]
        ON XML_Table (customerAddress)
```

Secondary XML indexes are also created on a XML data type column. There are three types of secondary XML indexes (see Table 11.1).

Table 11.1 Secondary XML Index Types

Secondary Index	Description
PATH	XML index helps with queries that use XML path expressions.
VALUE	XML index helps with queries that search for values anywhere in the XML document.
PROPERY	XML index helps with queries that retrieve particular object properties from within an XML document.

To create a secondary XML index, you must use the *CREATE XML INDEX* statement. Figure 11.4 shows the syntax for the *CREATE XML INDEX*.

Figure 11.4 *CREATE XML INDEX* Syntax

```
CREATE XML INDEX index_name
      ON table_name (xml_column_name)
      [USING XML INDEX xml_index_name
         [FOR {VALUE|PATH|PROPERTY}]
```

Using the table you created in Figure 11.5, XML_Table, you will create a secondary XML index on the customerAddress column.

Figure 11.5 *CREATE XML INDEX* Usage

```
CREATE XML INDEX [SD_XML_Data_customerAddress]
      ON XML_Table (customerAddress)
USING XML INDEX [PK_XML_Data_customerAddress]
FOR VALUE
```

Along with creating primary and secondary indexes on XML data type columns, you can also modify these indexes. The *ALTER INDEX Transact-SQL DDL* statement can be used to modify existing XML indexes. In Figure 11.6, you will modify your secondary index, *DB_XML_Data_customerAddress,* to turn *ALLOW_ROW_LOCKS OFF.*

Figure 11.6 *ALTER INDEX* Usage

```
ALTER INDEX [SD_XML_Data_customerAddress] ON XML_Table
      SET(ALLOW_ROW_LOCKS = OFF)
```

XML indexes are *ENABLED* by default, but you can *DISABLE* an XML index. To do so, you set the XML index to *DISABLE.* You will *DISABLE* the secondary instance that you created (see Figure 11.7).

Figure 11.7 Using *ALTER INDEX* to *DISABLE* an Index

```
ALTER INDEX [SD_XML_Data_customerAddress] on XML_Table DISABLE
```

Of course you can drop XML indexes. You use the *DROP INDEX Transact-SQL DDL* statement. If you drop the primary XML index, any secondary indexes that are present are also dropped. In Figure 11.8, you will drop the secondary index.

Figure 11.8 Using *DROP INDEX* to *DROP* an XML Index

```
DROP INDEX [SD_XML_Data_customerAddress] ON XML_Table
```

HTTP Endpoints

In SQL Server 2008, HTTP endpoints provide SQL server developers with new capabilities for using Web Services within SQL Server. It is worth noting that Web Services are not new to SQL Server 2008. SQL Server 2005 introduced HTTP endpoints and allowed you to consume Web Services and map them to SQL Server objects.

EXAM WARNING

Native XML Web Services (SOAP/HTTP endpoints) has been deprecated in SQL Server 2008

Http Endpoints Defined

HTTP endpoint enables developers to expose stored procedures and functions within a database as methods that can be called from any application using SOAP. SQL Server listens for HTTP requests natively on the server and then processes them; this requires fewer outside components to administer and easy application development and deployment. HTTP endpoint supports protocols such as HTTP, TCP, and payloads such as SOAP, TSQL, SERVICE BROKER, and Database Mirroring.

EXAM WARNING

SQL Server HTTP endpoints are not supported on SQL Server 2008 Express Edition.

Endpoint Can Interface to a Stored Procedure

SQL Server stored procedures can be exposed to the HTTP endpoint, making any database object that can be executed or accessed in a stored procedure available to the endpoint. You will see an example of this in the next section. As always, it is very important to consider database security when setting up database objects to be accessed through an endpoint. Be sure to verify that the data that is being made available is safe for exposure to a web service. Underlying stored procedure calls or tables may inadvertently provide more access than intended. Always make sure that you are familiar with the data and any restrictions before providing access.

How to Create the Endpoint

To create an HTTP endpoint, you first need to determine what object you want to expose from SQL Server. You can expose stored procedures or user-defined functions as the endpoints for the mapping. In this example, you will create a stored procedure that will select against the tblhost table and tbl_host_thresholds table to return the first computer name in the results (see Figure 11.9).

Figure 11.9 *CREATE PROCEDURE* Code for spGetThresholds

```
CREATE PROCEDURE [dbo].[spGetThresholds]
AS
select Top 1b.csname from tblhost_thresholds a
inner join tblhost b on a.hostid = b.id
```

Next, you will create the endpoint for this procedure so that it can be used by an application. You can use the **Create a 10-point** command, as shown in Figure 11.10.

Figure 11.10 *CREATE ENDPOINT* Code for GetThresholds

```
CREATE ENDPOINT [GetThresholds]
     STATE=STARTED
AS HTTP
(
     PATH=N'/Thresholds',
     PORTS = (CLEAR),
     AUTHENTICATION = (NTLM, KERBEROS, INTEGRATED),
     SITE=N'W2K3SRVR',
```

```
        CLEAR_PORT = 80,
        COMPRESSION=DISABLED)
FOR SOAP
(
    WEBMETHOD 'Thresholds'(
        NAME=N'[MS70432].[dbo].[spGetThresholds]',
        SCHEMA=DEFAULT,
        FORMAT=ALL_RESULTS),
    BATCHES=DISABLED,
    WSDL=DEFAULT,
    SESSIONS=DISABLED,
    SESSION_TIMEOUT=60,
    DATABASE=N'MS70432',
    NAMESPACE=N'http://MS70432/Thresholds',
    SCHEMA=STANDARD,
    CHARACTER_SET=XML
)
```

The *CREATE ENDPOINT* has a number of key elements. You will see in your code that the *STATE* argument is set to *STARTED*, indicating that the HTTP endpoint listener is running. Review Table 11.2 for the options available for this argument.

Table 11.2 Settings Available for the *STATE* Argument

STATE Argument	Description
STARTED	Endpoint is started and is actively listening for connections.
STOPPED	Endpoint is stopped. In this state, the server listens to port requests but returns errors to clients.
DISABLED	Endpoint is disabled. In this state, the server does not listen to the endpoint port or respond to any attempted requests to use the endpoint.

Next, you will see that you specified the *AS HTTP* clause. The *AS HTTP* sets HTTP as the transport for the endpoint. The *AS HTTP* clause includes additional settings that you will find listed in Table 11.3.

Table 11.3 Settings Available for the *AS HTTP* Clause

AS HTTP settings	Value	Description
PATH	*URL*	Specifies the URL path that identifies the location of the endpoint on the host computer specified in the SITE argument. PATH is a logical partitioning of the URL namespace that the listener uses to route requests appropriately. PATH must be part of the URL that the client uses to send HTTP SOAP requests to an instance of SQL Server.
AUTHENTICATION	{ BASIC | DIGEST | NTLM | KERBEROS | INTEGRATED }	Specifies the authentication type that is used to authenticate users that log on to an instance of SQL Server. You can specify BASIC, DIGEST, NTLM, KERBEROS, or INTEGRATED, or a combination of these values separated by commas (,).
PORTS	{ CLEAR | SSL }	Specifies one or more listening port types that are associated with the endpoint. CLEAR and SSL can be specified at the same time. If only CLEAR is specified, the incoming requests must use HTTP. If SSL is specified, the incoming requests must be Secure HTTP (https://) requests.

Continued

Table 11.3 Continued. Settings Available for the *AS HTTP* Clause

AS HTTP settings	Value	Description
SITE	{ ' * ' | ' + ' | 'webSite' }	Specifies the name of the host computer. If SITE is omitted, the asterisk is the default. If sp_reserve_http_namespace was executed, pass <hostpart> to the SITE keyword * (asterisk) Implies that a listening operation applies to all possible host names for the computer that are not otherwise explicitly reserved. + (plus sign) Implies that a listening operation applies to all possible host names for the computer. webSite Is the specific host name for the computer.
CLEAR_PORT	clearPort	Specifies the clear port number. If PORTS = (CLEAR), this clearPort specifies the clear port number. The default port number is 80.
SSL_PORT	SSLPort	Specifies the SSL port number. If PORTS = (SSL), SSLPort specifies the SSL port number. The default SSL port number is 443.
AUTH_REALM	{ 'realm' | NONE }	If AUTHENTICATION = DIGEST, specifies the hint that returns to the client, which sent the SOAP request to the endpoint, as part of HTTP authentication challenge. The default is NONE.
DEFAULT_LOGON_DOMAIN	{ 'domain' | NONE }	If AUTHENTICATION = BASIC, specifies, the default login domain. The default is NONE.

Continued

Table 11.3 Continued. Settings Available for the *AS HTTP* Clause

AS HTTP settings	Value	Description
COMPRESSION	{ ENABLED | DISABLED }	If set to ENABLED, SQL Server will honor requests where gzip encoding is accepted, and return compressed responses. That is, if a request comes in with an HTTP header specifying GZIP as a valid "accept-encoding", the server returns the response gzip-encoded. Default is DISABLED.

Lastly, you will see in your *CREATE ENDPOINT* statement that you specify the *FOR SOAP* clause. Table 11.4 shows you the arguments that are supported by the *FOR SOAP* clause.

Table 11.4 Settings Available for the *FOR SOAP* Clause

FOR SOAP setting	Value	Description
WEBMETHOD	['namespace' .] 'method_alias'	Specifies the Web method used to send requests via the HTTP SOAP endpoint. You can declare multiple Web methods per endpoint. You need to specify the NAME setting for the WEBMETHOD setting. The name setting includes 'database.schema.name'
SCHEMA	{ NONE | STANDARD | DEFAULT }	(This option is for the WEBMETHOD clause.) Determines whether inline XSD schema will be returned for the current Web method in SOAP responses. NONE XSD schema is not returned for SELECT statement results sent through SOAP.

Continued

Table 11.4 Continued. Settings Available for the *FOR SOAP* Clause

FOR SOAP setting	Value	Description
		STANDARD XSD schema is returned for SELECT statement results sent through SOAP. DEFAULT Defaults to the endpoint SCHEMA option setting. If a schema is not specified or this option is set to DEFAULT, the SCHEMA option specified for the endpoint determines whether the SCHEMA for the method result is returned. To get a schema for the result of a SELECT query that uses the FOR XML option, you must specify the XMLSCHEMA option in the query, regardless of the setting of the SCHEMA option here.
FORMAT	{ ALL_RESULTS | ROWSETS_ONLY | NONE }	Specifies whether a row count, error messages, and warnings are returned with the result set. The default is ALL_RESULTS. ALL_RESULTS Returns a result set, a row count, and error messages and warnings in the SOAP response. ROWSETS_ONLY Returns only the result sets. Use this option with client applications that use the Visual Studio 2005 Web Services proxy class generator, if you want the results returned as a single data set (System.Data.Dataset object) and not as an object array. NONE Suppresses the return of SOAP-specific markup in the server response.

Continued

Table 11.4 Continued. Settings Available for the *FOR SOAP* Clause

FOR SOAP setting	Value	Description
		This option can be used as a mechanism to support applications that have a stored procedure in which the response will be returned as is, in raw mode, by the server. When this option is in effect, the application is responsible for returning well-formed XML. This feature can be used to control the response for a number of reasons, For example, it could be used to create a stored procedure that would return a WS-Policy. The FORMAT=NONE option has the following conditions for use:
		The method must be implemented by using a stored procedure without output parameters. User-defined functions are not allowed with this response format. Either the query must be a single-statement FOR XML query (Multiple FOR XML statements are not allowed with this response format); or the output must consist of a single column that has the name XML_F52E2B61–18A1–11d1–B105–00805F49916B and of the type nvarchar.
BATCHES	{ ENABLED | DISABLED }	Specifies whether ad hoc SQL requests are supported on the endpoint. The default is DISABLED. ENABLED allows SOAP requests for ad hoc queries that use the sqlbatch method to be sent to this endpoint.

Continued

Table 11.4 Continued. Settings Available for the *FOR SOAP* Clause

FOR SOAP setting	Value	Description
		If batches are enabled, ad hoc SQL requests can be executed on the endpoint by calling the sql:sqlbatch method. This method also exposes parameterized query functionality; therefore, it can take an optional list of SqlParameter elements that will describe metadata and values for the parameters of the specified query.
		Within the query, parameter names starting with the at sign (@) can be embedded. Matching parameter names must be supplied; otherwise, an error is returned for the request.
LOGIN_TYPE	{ MIXED | WINDOWS }	Specifies the SQL Server Authentication mode for the endpoint. If LOGIN_TYPE is not specified, the default is WINDOWS.
		LOGIN_TYPE can only be used to further restrict the authentication mode for endpoints that are based on the server global authentication mode that was selected when the instance of SQL Server was installed.
		MIXED Allows either SQL Server Authentication or Windows Authentication to be used to authenticate endpoint users.
		If MIXED is specified and the server is installed in Windows Authentication mode, an error is returned.
		When set to MIXED, SQL Server Authentication is supported on the endpoint, and the endpoint must be configured to use a Secure Sockets Layer (SSL) port.

Continued

Table 11.4 Continued. Settings Available for the *FOR SOAP* Clause

FOR SOAP setting	Value	Description
		WINDOWS Allows only Windows Authentication to be used to authenticate endpoint users.
WSDL	{ NONE | DEFAULT | 'sp_name' }	Indicates whether WSDL document generation is supported for this end-point. If NONE, no WSDL response is generated or returned for WSDL queries submitted to the endpoint. If DEFAULT, a default WSDL response is generated and returned for WSDL queries submitted to the endpoint. In exceptional cases, where you are implementing custom WSDL sup-port for the endpoint, you can also specify stored procedures by name that will return a modified WSDL document.
SESSIONS	{ ENABLED | DISABLED }	Specifies whether the instance of SQL Server allows sessions support. If set to ENABLED, SQL Server allows sessions support, whereby multiple SOAP request/response message pairs can be identified as part of a single SOAP session. The default is DISABLED.
SESSION_TIMEOUT	TimeoutInterval	Specifies time in seconds (as an integer) that is available before a SOAP session expires at the server when no further requests are received. The default is 60 seconds. This overrides the time-out value specified in the SOAP session header.

Continued

Table 11.4 Continued. Settings Available for the *FOR SOAP* Clause

FOR SOAP setting	Value	Description
		The time-out time that is initialized when the server finishes sending a SOAP response message to the client. If the time-out elapses before another SOAP request with the same session ID specified in its header, the session is terminated at the server.
DATABASE	{ 'database_name' | DEFAULT }	Specifies the database in the context of which the requested operation is executed. If database_name is not specified or if DEFAULT is specified, the default database for the login is used.
NAMESPACE	{ 'namespace' | DEFAULT }	Specifies the namespace for the endpoint. If namespace is not specified or if DEFAULT is specified, the assumed namespace is http://tempuri.org. You can overwrite the default namespace when you specify a specific method by using WEBMETHOD 'namespace'namespace.
SCHEMA	{ NONE | STANDARD }	Specifies whether an XSD schema is returned by the endpoint when SOAP results are sent. NONE Omits inline schema from SOAP responses. STANDARD Includes inline schema in endpoint responses.
CHARACTER_SET	{ SQL | XML }	Defines the behavior when the result of an operation includes characters that are not valid in XML. The default is XML.

Continued

Table 11.4 Continued. Settings Available for the *FOR SOAP* Clause

FOR SOAP setting	Value	Description
		SQL Encodes the characters that are not valid as character references, and then returns them in the result. In this case, an XML parser may reject the returned XML as not valid. XML Encodes characters according to the XML specification. Any characters that are not allowed in the XML character set will cause SQL Server to send an invalid XML error back to the client.
HEADER_LIMIT	N/A	Specifies the maximum size, in bytes, of the header section in the SOAP envelope. If the SOAP headers don't fit in this size, the server generates a parsing error. If not specified, a default value of 8 KB (8192 bytes) is assumed.

To ensure that your endpoint is configured correctly, you can submit an HTTP request to the server. You can do this by opening your web browser and navigate to http://w2k3srvr/thresholds?wsdl. If the endpoint is responding, it will return the WSDL for your service.

The screen shot in Figure 11.11 is the web reference dialog box from Visual Studio 2005. You will see that in the address bar, you typed in your URL (http://w2k3srvr/thresholds?wsdl), and it returned your method, Thresholds, which you specified in the *WEBMETHODS* setting in your *CREATE ENDPOINT* statement.

Figure 11.11 Add Web Reference Dialog Box in Visual Studio 2005

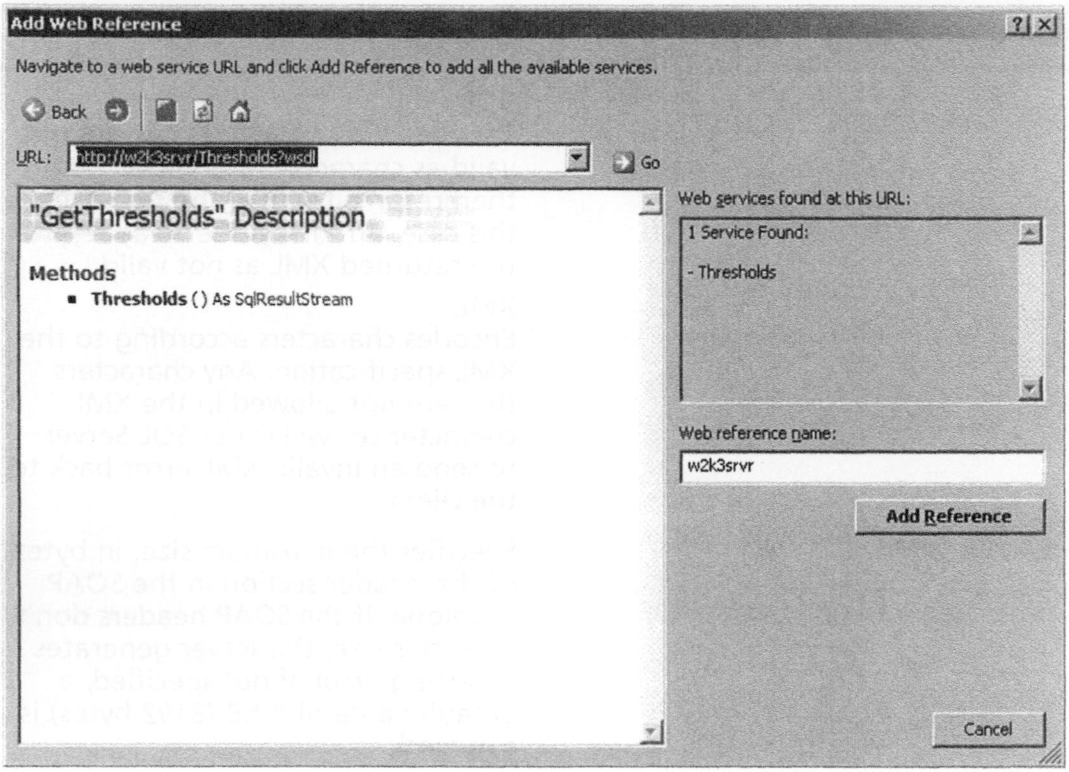

Web Services

Web Services is a simple platform–independent message framework that runs as a web service and is accessed by web platform elements such as SOAP, UDDI, and WSDL. Web Services uses XML as a base language so that a web service can be written in C++, VB.NET, or C#. Web Services is based on established HTTP protocols for transmitting messages. This is a major advantage if you want to build an Internet-scale application because most of the Internet's proxies and firewalls won't interfere with HTTP traffic.

So how does this all actually work? For example, let's say you own one of the biggest auction sites in the world and you want to expand your business to allow open-source developers to create open-source software that retrieves listings of auctions. You don't want to give them direct database access or have to maintain a set of APIs, so you create a web service. This web service contains functions that perform queries against your database. The open-source developer would call this function, via SOAP, and, presto, they have the information. So what happens during the process of requesting the auction information? We will use the diagram shown in Figure 11.12 to walk through the process.

Figure 11.12 Requesting Information via a Web Service

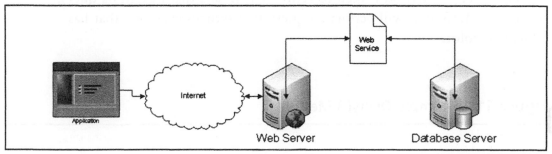

1. The "Application" creates a SOAP request and invokes the web service.
2. The SOAP request is sent over a network using the HTTP protocol. The "Web Server" receives the SOAP request, which then carries out the work it has been asked to do on the "Database Server."
3. When the work is completed, it is turned into a SOAP response.
4. The SOAP response is sent over a network using the HTTP protocol, and the SOAP request is processed by the "Application."

Web Services are being used by more and more companies worldwide as a mechanism to transfer data. It can bring together applications that are not written in the same programming language.

XQuery Explained

SQL Server 2008 supports a subset of the XQuery language as defined by the World Wide Web Consortium (W3C). The XQuery is a fully featured language that is used to query structured or semistructured XML data. Based on the existing XPath query language, XQuery adds support for better iteration, better sorting results, and the ability to construct the necessary XML. XQuery can be used to query and manipulate data from XML documents or data sources that can be viewed by XML. There are four simple methods for querying XML data with XQuery:

- Query( )
- Value( )
- Exist( )
- Nodes( )

The query() method is used to return XML data that matches a query. In Figure 11.13, you will perform a query that returns everyone that has a favorite color.

Figure 11.13 Sample Query( ) Method

```
DECLARE @xmlData XML
SET @xmlData = '<?xml version="1.0" encoding="UTF-8" standalone="yes"?>
        <employee>
            <person>
                <name>
                    <FirstName>Addie</FirstName>
                    <LastName>Banning</LastName>
                </name>
                <Age>21</Age>
    <FavoriteColor>Blue</FavoriteColor>
            </person>
            <person>

                <name>

                    <FirstName>Bill</FirstName>
                    <LastName>Bergen</LastName>
                </name>
                <Age>99</Age>
    <FavoriteColor>Green</FavoriteColor>
            </person>
            <person>
                <name>
<FirstName>Jennifer</FirstName>
                <LastName>Liddle</LastName>
```

```
                    </name>
                    <Age>9</Age>
      <FavoriteColor>Pink</FavoriteColor>
                </person>
             </employee>'
-- Here we create the table to hold the XML data
CREATE TABLE #tbl_xml (id INT IDENTITY PRIMARY KEY, employee XML)
-- Here, we insert the XML data into the xml column of the table
INSERT INTO #tbl_xml(employee)
VALUES (@xmlData)
-- Here, we perform our query
SELECT employee.query(
'for $p in //employee
where $p//FavoriteColor
return
    <employee>
        <name>{$p//FirstName}</name>
    </employee>
'
)
FROM #tbl_xml
DROP TABLE #tbl_xml
```

In Figure 11.13 you created a temporary table called #tbl_xml and inserted the XML data into that temporary table. The query shown in Figure 11.14 uses XQuery to *SELECT* the information in the XML data type to list everyone that has a favorite color. Let's take a look at this query in more detail.

Figure 11.14 Query( ) Method In-depth

```
SELECT employee.query(
'for $p in //employee
where $p//FavoriteColor
```

```
return
   <employee>
     <name>{$p//FirstName}</name>
   </employee>
'
)
FROM #tbl_xml
```

The first part of your query, *SELECT people.query*, uses a standard SQL Command, *SELECT*, followed by the column name in your #tbl_xml document, people. You then use the method, query(), to tell your *SELECT* statement that you will be querying against this XML data column. After that, you simply write out an *XPath* statement and close it with the *FROM* clause. XPath will be discussed in the next section.

EXAM WARNING

You need to follow some basic syntax rules when you write your code. First, XQuery is case sensitive. Pay close attention to this. Second, XQuery elements and attributes MUST BE valid XML names. Lastly, XQuery variables are always defined with a $ followed by the variable name (example: $name).

Table 11.5 describes the XQuery method argument.

Table 11.5 Query( ) Method Argument

Query() Argument	Description
XQuery	Is a string, an XQuery expression, that queries for XML nodes such as elements, attributes, in an XML instance.

The value( ) method allows you to extract a value from the XML document. This will allow you to compare XML data with data from non-XML columns.

For example, in Figure 11.15, you can use the following query to return the age of "Bill Bergen" to an integer.

Figure 11.15 Sample Value() Method

```
SELECT employee.value('/employee[1]/person[2]/Age[1][text()]', 'int')
AS Age FROM #tbl_xml
```

As you can see, the value( ) method requires arguments. The first argument is the XQuery expression, and the second argument is the SQL data type. Use Table 11.6 as a guide for the value( ) parameter.

Table 11.6 Value() Method Argument

Value() Argument	Description
XQUERY	Is the XQuery expression, a string literal, that retrieves data inside the XML instance. The XQuery must return at most one value. Otherwise, an error is returned.
SQLType	Is the preferred SQL type, a string literal, to be returned. The return type of this method matches the SQLType parameter. SQLType cannot be an XML data type, a common language runtime (CLR) user-defined type, image, text, ntext, or sql_variant data type. SQLType can be an SQL, user-defined data type.

The exist( ) method is used to check the existence of a value in a XML document. This method will return an integer value of 1 if the value returned is a non–NULL value and a 0 integer for a NULL value. In Figure 11.16, you will query the sample XML document, shown in Figure 11.13, to determine whether the specified values exist. Table 11.7 describes the exist() method argument.

This example checks to see if an employee with the first name of Jennifer exists.

Figure 11.16 Samples of the Exist( ) Method

```
SELECT pk, employee FROM #tbl_xml
WHERE employee.exist('/employee/person/name/FirstName[.="Jennifer"]') = 1
```

With a slight variation of this query, we will now search on the LastName.

```
SELECT pk, employee FROM #tbl_xml
WHERE employee.exist('/employee/person/name/LastName[.="Liddle"]') = 1
```

Table 11.7 Exist( ) Method Argument

Exist( ) Arguments	Description
XQuery	Is an XQuery expression, a string literal.

The last method for querying XML documents in an XML data type is the nodes( ) method. The nodes( ) method will return a rowset for each row in the query. This is helpful when you want to make your XML data type into a relational format. Every XML document has a node, and in the XML data type this is the document node. The document node is the node at the top of every XML data type. In Figure 11.17 you query the sample XML document, shown in Figure 11.14, to return rows for each person in your employee node.

Table 11.8 describes the nodes( ) method argument.

Figure 11.17 Sample Node( ) Method

```
SELECT T2.employee.query('.')
FROM #tbl_xml
CROSS APPLY employee.nodes('/employee/person') as T2(employee)
```

Table 11.8 Nodes( ) Method Argument

Nodes( ) Argument	Description
XQuery	Is a string literal, an XQuery expression. If the query expression constructs nodes, these constructed nodes are exposed in the resulting rowset. If the query expression results in an empty sequence, the rowset will be empty. If the query expression statically results in a sequence that contains atomic values instead of nodes, a static error is raised.
Table(Column)	Is the table name and the column name for the resulting rowset.

SQL Server 2008 provides extensions that allow XQuery to modify data using the modify() method. The modify() method includes three DML statements: *INSERT, DELETE*, and *REPLACE VALUE OF* (see Table 11.9).

Table 11.9 Modify( ) Method Argument

DML	Description
insert	Inserts one or more nodes as a child. INSERT allows you to insert XML before or after and existing XML node. You can also insert attributes.
delete	DELETE XML elements or attributes from your XML document
replace value of	REPLACE A NODE with a new value that you specify. The node you select must be a single node, not multiple nodes.

In Figure 11.18 you use your XML document, shown in Figure 11.13, to perform *INSERT, DELETE*, and *REPLACE VALUE OF...* This figure will insert the tag **<HireDate></HireDate>** for employee number 3, Jennifer. Notice that you use the *UPDATE* statement to perform this function and not the *INSERT* statement. The insert is performed in the XQuery command.

Figure 11.18 Insert DML for Modify() Method

```
UPDATE #tbl_xml SET employee.modify(
'insert <HireDate>5/5/1999</HireDate>
 as last into (/employee/person[3])[1]')
where pk=1
```

In Figure 11.19 you will update employee number 3's age from 9 to 10 using the replace value of DML.

Figure 11.19 Replace Value of DML for Modify() Method

```
UPDATE #tbl_xml
    SET employee.modify(
        'replace value of (/employee/person[3]/Age[1]/text())[1]
        with "10"'
        )
```

```
where pk=1
go
```

In Figure 11.20 you will use the delete DML. Here you will delete employee number 3's HireDate.

Figure 11.20 Delete DML

```
UPDATE #tbl_xml
      SET employee.modify(
              'delete /employee/person[3]/HireDate')
where pk=1
go
```

New & Noteworthy…

XML Modifications

XQuery, natively, does not support modifying XML data. This was a feature that Microsoft added with SQL Server 2005 and modified with SQL Server 2008.

XPath

XPath (XML Path Language) is a standard navigation language that is defined by the World Wide Web Consortium (W3C). The XPath query language is used to identify a set of nodes within an XML document. As implemented in SQL Server 2008, SQLXML 4.0 implements a subset of the W3C XPath specification. XPath can be used to compute values such as strings, numbers, or Boolean values from an XML document. It supports many different expression types. Table 11.10 describes each expression type and their description.

Table 11.10 Expression Types for XPath

Category	Function	Description
Numeric	Ceiling	Returns the smallest integer of the values passed
	Floor	Returns the largest integer of the values passed
	Round	Rounds to the nearest integer
Boolean	Not	True or False value
String	Concat	Concatenates the strings passed
	Contains	Returns a true value if the first argument contains the second argument
	Substring	Returns a portion of the first argument starting at the location of the second argument
	String-length	Returns back the length of a string passed
Node	Number	Returns a number for the value of the node passed
Context	Position	Returns an integer that is the current position in the sequence.
	Last	Returns an integer that is the count of the last item in the sequence
Sequences	Empty	Returns true if the argument passed, which is a sequence, is empty.
	Distinctvalues	Removes duplicates from your sequence
Aggregate	Avg	Returns the average of a set of numbers
	Count	Counts the number of items in the set and returns an integer
	Min	Returns the minimum value from a set of numbers

Continued

Table 11.10 Continued. Expression Types for XPath

Category	Function	Description
	Max	Returns the maximum value from a set of numbers
	Sum	Returns the sum of a set of numbers.
Constructor	Various	Allows you to create an XSD type from another type or literal
DataAccess	Data	Returns the typed value of the node
	String	Returns the value of the argument as a string

Now, let's explore some examples of how SQL Server 2008 uses XPath to calculate numbers, strings, and Boolean values. In Figure 11.21, you have created an XML document and stored that in your XML data type in the declared table @XMLTable.

Figure 11.21 Sample XML Document

```
DECLARE @xmlData XML
SET @xmlData = '<?xml version="1.0" encoding="UTF-8" standalone="yes"?>
    <product>
    <item>
        <name>BaseBall Gloves</name>
        <tagid>52487-1</tagid>
        <quantity>10</quantity>
    </item>
    <item>
        <name>BaseBall Bats</name>
        <tagid>52487-1</tagid>
        <quantity>15</quantity>
    </item>
    <item>
        <name>BaseBall Balls</name>
        <tagid>94235-1</tagid>
        <quantity>4</quantity>
```

```
        </item>
    </product>'
-- Create a new table
declare @XMLTable table (pk INT IDENTITY PRIMARY KEY, colxml XML)
--Insert data into the new table
INSERT INTO @XMLTable(colxml)
VALUES (@xmlData)
```

In Figure 11.22, you will use the XPath function, *count,* to count the number of item nodes in your XML document.

Figure 11.22 XPath Expression Count

```
-- Count the number of people
SELECT colxml.query(
'count(//item)
')
FROM @XMLTable
```

In Figure 11.23 you will use the XPath function, *contains*, to return the string that contains the word "BaseBall Bats."

Figure 11.23 XPath Expression Contains

```
SELECT *
FROM @XMLTable
WHERE
        colxml.exist('/product/item/name[contains(.,"BaseBall Bats")]') = 1
```

Now we will switch to showing basic examples of using the numeric and string functions.

Figure 11.24 shows an example of the XPath *number* function. This function can be used to convert a nonnumeric value to a numeric value. The result of this example query would return the employee where the EmployeeID is a number that is equal to 680.

Figure 11.24 XPath Expression Numeric

```
/Employee[number(@EmployeeID) = 680]
```

Figure 11.25 shows an example of the XPath *string* function. This function can be used to convert a non-string value to a string value. The result of this example query would return the employee where the EmployeeID contains a string value that is equal to 680.

Figure 11.25 XPath Expression String

```
/Employee[string(@EmployeeID)="680"]
```

These are just a few examples of all the XPath expressions that can be used. You can refer to Table 11.10 Expression Types for XPath to find more.

Summary of Exam Objectives

This chapter examined XML, XQuery, XPath, HTTP endpoints, and Web Services. You learned how to use XQuery to retrieve and modify data within an XML data type.

HTTP endpoints provide ways to allow developers to expose their code and access it using their SOAP client. You learned how to create an HTTP endpoint with SQL Server 2008 as well as how to secure it.

Lastly, we reviewed Web Services and how developers use Web Services to present data to their clients. Web Services uses XML as its base language so that all programming languages, whether written in C++, VB.net, or C#, can communicate with it.

Exam Objectives Fast Track

Working with XML Data

☑ The first index on the XML type column must be the primary XML index.

☑ An XML index cannot be created on an XML type column in a view, table value variable with XML type columns, or XML type.

☑ The stored representation of XML data type instances cannot exceed 2 gigabytes (GB) in size.

HTTP Endpoints

☑ Expose stored procedures and functions within a SQL Server 2008 database.

☑ Support two protocols, HTTP and TCP.

☑ Support payloads, *SOAP, TSQL, SERVICE_BROKER*, and *DATABASE_MIRRORING*.

☑ Use *CREATE ENDPOINT* to create an endpoint.

☑ Not supported in SQL Server 2008 Express Edition.

Web Services

☑ Web Services use XML as a base language and can be written in programming languages such as; C++, VB.NET, or C#.

☑ Web Services can be accessed by web platform elements such as SOAP, UDDI, and WSDI.

☑ Web Services enable programs written in different languages to communicate.

XQuery Explained

☑ XQuery is a language used to query XML documents.

☑ XQuery uses four methods for querying: query( ), value( ), exist( ), and nodes( ).

☑ XQuery is case sensitive.

☑ XQuery provides extensions for modifying XML, modify( ).

☑ Three DML statements are used in conjunction with modify( ), INSERT, DELETE, and REPLACE VALUE OF.

XPath

☑ XPath is a query language used to identify a set of nodes in an XML document.

☑ XPath computes strings, numbers, or boolean values.

☑ The four categories of XPath operators are Boolean, Relational, Equity, and Arithmetic.

Exam Objectives
Frequently Asked Questions

Q: Can the clustered primary key of a table be changed if an XML index already exists on a table?

A: No, all XML indexes must be dropped before a clustered primary key on a table can be modified.

Q: Are SQL Server HTTP endpoints supported in all SQL Server 2008 versions?

A: No, HTTP endpoints are not supported in the SQL Server 2008 Express edition.

Q: Can a stored procedure be exposed for endpoint mapping?

A: Yes, database objects such as stored procedures and user-defined functions can be exposed for endpoint mapping.

Q: Is the XQuery language case sensitive?

A: Yes, it is important to remember that XQuery statements are case sensitive when building queries.

Q: Which methods are available for querying XML data with XQuery?

A: The query(), value( ), exist( ), and nodes( ) methods are available when using XQuery.

Q: What language is used to select a set of nodes from an XML document?

A: The Xpath language is used to select a set of nodes from an XML document.

Self Test

1. Which of the following is a benefit of using XML data?

   A. Native to Windows

   B. Better performance

   C. Native to SQL Server

   D. Platform independent

2. Which of the following benefits can an XML index provide?

   A. Easy table access

   B. XML data type conversion

   C. Efficient query processing

   D. Access to ADO.NET

3. Which of the following is a SQL Server 2008 native XML feature?

   A. Ability to back up XML data

   B. Ability to set up server roles

   C. Ability to set up database roles

   D. Ability to set up SQL Agent proxies

4. Which of the following is the size limit of the XML data type?

   A. 2 MB

   B. 2 GB

   C. 2 KB

   D. 2 bytes

5. Which of the following data types is used in SQL Server 2008 to store XML data?

   A. Table

   B. bit

   C. XML

   D. Binary

6. When you use *CREATE XML INDEX( )* syntax, what type of index are you creating?

    A. A primary XML index

    B. A clustered index

    C. A secondary XML index

    D. A nonclustered index

7. You have a table containing columns with the XML data type. No primary key has been assigned yet, but indexes have been set up on a few of the other table columns, including columns defined with the XML data type. You want to define the primary key. Which of the following best describes what you can do?

    A. Use the *CREATE PRIMARY XML INDEX()* syntax to create the primary key.

    B. Drop all indexes on the non-XML columns.

    C. Drop all indexes on XML columns.

    D. Drop the table and re-create, defining the primary key on the XML column first.

8. Which of the following DDL statements will create a primary XML index?

    A. *CREATE XML INDEX()*

    B. *ALTER INDEX()*

    C. *DROP INDEX()*

    D. *CREATE PRIMARY XML INDEX()*

9. Which of the following DDL statements will disable a XML index?

    A. *CREATE XML INDEX()*

    B. *ALTER INDEX [SD_XML_Data_customerAddress] ON XML_Table*

    C. *DROP INDEX()*

    D. *ALTER INDEX [SD_XML_Data_customerAddress] ON XML_Table DISABLE*

10. What happens to secondary indexes if the primary XML index is dropped?

   A. Nothing happens to secondary indexes. They remain defined on the table.

   B. Secondary indexes will be dropped.

   C. Non-XML indexes are dropped.

   D. All XML and non-XML indexes are dropped.

11. What effect does dropping a secondary XML index have on a table that has a primary XML index defined?

   A. The primary XML index is automatically dropped and needs to be re-created.

   B. All secondary indexes will be dropped.

   C. Only the XML index defined in the DDL statement will be dropped. There is no effect on other indexes.

   D. All XML and non-XML indexes are dropped.

12. Which of the following has been deprecated in SQL Server 2008?

   A. HTTP endpoints

   B. Native XML Web Services (SOAP/HTTP endpoints)

   C. Web Services

   D. XML storage

13. Which of the following SQL Server 2008 editions does not support HTTP endpoints?

   A. Express edition

   B. Enterprise edition

   C. Developer edition

   D. Web edition

14. When creating the endpoint, what happens when the *STATE* argument is set to *STARTED*?

   A. The endpoint is started, and it is actively listening for connections.

   B. The endpoint will not start until after the database server has been restarted.

C. The endpoint will start when SQL Agent calls it.

D. The endpoint will start when a user requests it.

15. How can you easily test an endpoint to ensure that it is working?

A. Type the URL of the endpoint into a query window of the SQL Server Management Studio and click on **execute**.

B. Create a new test web service that consumes the endpoint.

C. Run the URL from the DOS command prompt.

D. Browse to the endpoint URL in the add web reference screen in Visual Studio.

16. Which of the following program languages can be used when creating Web Services?

A. BASIC

B. COBOL

C. Action Script

D. C#

17. What does the XQuery Query() method do?

A. Returns XML data that matches a query.

B. Returns the node of the query.

C. Returns an extracted value from an XML document.

D. Checks for the existence of a value in an XML document.

18. Which of the following are extensions of the XQuery modify( ) method?

A. Update

B. Delete

C. Exists

D. Nodes

19. If you want to identify a set of nodes within an XML document, which of the following is used?

A. SELECT

B. XQuery

C. EXISTS

D. XPath

20. Which of the following is an expression type for XPath?

A. Approximate

B. Binary

C. Unicode

D. Node

Self Test Quick Answer Key

1.	D	11.	C
2.	C	12.	B
3.	A	13.	A
4.	B	14.	A
5.	C	15.	D
6.	C	16.	D
7.	C	17.	A
8.	D	18.	B
9.	D	19.	D
10.	B	20.	D

Chapter 12

MCTS SQL Server 2008 Exam 432

Service Broker

Exam objectives in this chapter:

- The Queuing Concept Explained
- Service Broker Defined
- Message Types
- Contracts
- Queues
- Services
- Routes
- Sending a Message

Exam objectives review:

- ☑ Summary of Exam Objectives
- ☑ Exam Objectives Fast Track
- ☑ Exam Objectives Frequently Asked Questions
- ☑ Self Test
- ☑ Self Test Quick Answer Key

Introduction

This chapter will introduce the DBA to SERVICE BROKER. It will explain what SERVICE BROKER is, how to set it up, and how to test to be sure it's functioning. It will also educate the DBA on some of the uses for SERVICE BROKER. SERVICE BROKER is commonly used for asynchronous tasks.

The concept of messages and queues is explained in this chapter, along with contracts and message types.

The Queuing Concept Explained

The concept of message queuing has been around for many years. Microsoft has included message queuing as an available option within the operating system since Windows NT 4.0. Starting with SQL Server 2005, the SQL SERVICE BROKER (SSB) has been included within the database platform. SQL SERVICE BROKER, like all message queuing technologies, allows for asynchronous messages to be sent from one server to another with the receiving server processing that message and carrying out some predefined task.

A simple analogy is that one process within SQL Server is going to send an e-mail to another process within SQL Server. The second process will read the message and do something based on the contents of that message. The beauty of SQL SERVICE BROKER is that the something that it does is totally up to the developer of the stored procedure that is going to be run.

The beauty of message queuing in general is that message delivery is guaranteed in the order sent, as is the fact that a message can be received only once. What this means is that no matter how many people are sending messages to the receiving system the messages will always be processed in the correct order that they were sent, and the receiving system can receive them once and only once. This will prevent the system from reprocessing the same message twice and causing errors because of processing the same message twice. The only way a message can be processed twice would be if the sending system sent the same message text as two separate messages.

Whereas other messaging systems like Microsoft Message Queue (MSMQ) can be accessed directly by Windows applications or applications on other operating systems, SQL SERVICE BROKER does not currently support this. In order to send or receive a message you have to log in to the SQL Server database. Neither Microsoft nor any third party as of this writing has written a way to send or receive messages without connecting to the SQL Server database. Because of this, SQL SERVICE BROKER may not always be the correct solution for your messaging environment. If the messages are not going to be sent or received by T/SQL then SQL SERVICE BROKER may not be your best option.

Service Broker Defined

There are two main concepts within SQL SERVICE BROKER: sending and receiving messages. Any process can send a message, provided it has the required rights to do so. Messages can be received on demand—for example, through a SQL Server job performing a *RECEIVE* command on the queue or by a Windows application logging into the database and performing a *RECEIVE* command on the queue. Messages can also be received and processed automatically by using what is called an activated stored procedure. The activated stored procedure is a normal stored procedure that is started automatically by the receiving queue when a message is received. The procedure would then RECEIVE the message and process the contents of the message as needed (we will examine this more closely later in the chapter).

Any database within the SQL Server instance can use the SQL SERVICE BROKER including the system databases. It is recommended, however, that you not make any changes to the SQL SERVICE BROKER within the system databases because SQL Server uses the SERVICE BROKER for its own tasks. In fact, even if you have never used SQL SERVICE BROKER before, if you use SQL Mail to send e-mails from the SQL Server you are using SQL SERVICE BROKER, because SQL Mail uses the SERVICE BROKER to queue the messages for sending.

The SQL SERVICE BROKER is a collection of objects within the database that when configured can be used to send messages from one process to another. These messages can be sent within the same database, to another database within the same instance of SQL Server, to another database in another SQL Server instance on the same server, or to another SQL Server instance on another server either within your company's network or to another company's network.

There are a few Dynamic Management Views (DMVs) that are used to gauge the health and performance of the SERVICE BROKER system. Of these the most important when troubleshooting SQL SERVER BROKER issues are the sys.conversation_endpoints and the sys.transmission_queue. The sys.conversation_endpoints is used most often to troubleshoot issues when sending messages from one queue to another within the same database; the sys.transmission_queue is used most often to troubleshoot issues when sending messages from one database to another. With regard to the SQL SERVICE BROKER it is important to remember that when we speak of sending messages from one database we are talking about sending messages within the instance of SQL Server or across servers.

EXAM WARNING

Know the difference between the sys.conversation_endpoints and sys.transmission_queue catalog views; know when you should check each, and what information is in each one.

The sys_converstaion_endpoints contains information about each conversation that is in flight at the current time as well as the conversations that were closed most recently. The DMV contains a single row for each conversation regardless of how many messages are contained within the conversation. If there is a problem with a message moving from the source to the destination you can identify which end of the conversation is having the problem based on the state column of this DMV. It will also tell you the number of messages within the conversation as well as when the conversation will expire (if ever).

The sys.transmission_queue contains information about each message that is stalled for one reason or another. There will be one record in this DMV for each message that is stalled, as well as one record for each message that is in flight between databases. The most useful column of this DMV is the transmission_status column. This column tells you in plain, easy-to-read text what the cause of the problem is. Once this issue is resolved the message will either move on to its destination or another error will be displayed, which then needs to be resolved. If there is no value in the transmission_status column then the message is in flight and has not failed.

The SQL SERVICE BROKER is extremely flexible when it comes to the message body itself. You can send a single value as the message text, or a binary object. The most common way to send data, however, is as an XML document. This provides you the most flexibility when sending the message since you can send more than one piece of data within the same message. In fact, you can send several records' worth of data if you so desire, provided that you structure your XML document correctly. You can even send a blank message and have the receiving system execute a different branch of code based on the message type of the message being sent.

When messages are sent, they are sent within conversations. A single conversation can have messages of many message types, but a conversation exists between two services (and queues) only. A single conversation can contain a single message, or several messages. When people first start building SQL SERVICE BROKER applications they usually start out with a single conversation per message. However, as you get into larger and more complex SQL SERVICE BROKER applications you will begin to see that sending more than one message per conversation will increase your system performance. However, doing so does add another layer of complexity to the configuration.

Head of the Class...

Optimize Your Service Broker Conversations

The SQL SERVICE BROKER is a very well-written system. This can be shown by the fact that the SQL SERVICE BROKER has not had to change much between the SQL Server 2005 and SQL Server 2008 versions. Although I'm sure that there have been some backend changes to the system, there have not been any real new features added to the system since the SQL Server 2005 release. However, there are ways to optimize your SQL SERVICE BROKER system.

When you are working with a high load SQL SERVICE BROKER application you can increase the performance of your application by reusing the same conversation for many messages. Doing so will increase the performance of your application in a couple of places. By not creating a new conversation for each message you will increase the performance of your SQL SERVICE BROKER application by about 4x. By doing a receive on multiple messages at a single time the performance of your *RECEIVE* command will increase by about 10x.

There are a couple of different techniques that can be used to do this. The first, published by Remus Rusanu (found on his blog http://rusanu. com/2007/04/25/reusing-conversations/), uses a table that allows for a separate conversation per SPID. The second, published by Denny Cherry (found on his blog http://itknowledgeexchange.techtarget.com/sql-server/ improving-sql-service-broker-performance/), uses a table that allows for a single conversation handle per source and destination combination.

In Remus's technique he leaves it up to you to decide how to tell the SQL SERVICE BROKER when to close the conversations. You can use length of time, or the number of messages depending on your specific situation.

In Denny's technique a random number is used to determine whether the conversation should be closed. Although this solution takes away some

Continued

> control, you can increase or decrease the average number of messages per conversation by adjusting the multiplier against the RAND function. When the random value is 0 then a blank message is sent using a separate message type. Then a new conversation is created and the normal message is sent against the new message type. The receiving procedure then uses the separate message type to know when the conversation should be closed using the *END CONVERSATION* command.
>
> Either technique can be used equally well to tell the SQL SERVICE BROKER how often to close the conversations. Both blogs give full T/SQL source for both solutions.

The SQL SERVICE BROKER comes ready to use within all your databases, however, the databases must be configured to allow the SQL SERVICE BROKER to run. This is done with an ALTER DATABASE command with the NEW_BROKER switch being specified. If you ever have to restore a database that is using the SQL SERVICE BROKER you will need to turn the SQL SERVICE BROKER back on using the ALTER DATABASE command, but this time using the ENABLE_BROKER switch. If you use the NEW_BROKER switch on a database that is using the SQL SERVICE BROKER already all messages that are in flight or in queue will be lost. If you use the ENABLE_BROKER switch on a database that has never been set up to use the SERVICE BROKER before, it is the same as using the NEW_BROKER switch.

```
ALTER DATABASE AdventureWorks
    SET NEW_BROKER;
```

Exam Warning

Remember when to use the *NEW_BROKER* and *ENABLE_BROKER* switches. The exams like to show lots of options that look similar.

SQL SERVICE BROKER can be used to send messages from server to server. You can also configure SQL SERVICE BROKER to route messages through another server by routing the message to the second server, and having a route on that server, which then forwards the message on to a third server. This can be done with any edition of SQL Server 2008 with one requirement. Two SQL 2008 Express Edition instances cannot send messages directly to each other. In order for two SQL Server 2008 Express Edition instances to send messages to each other, the messages must route through another edition of SQL Server.

EXERCISE 12.1

SETTING UP THE SQL SERVICE BROKER

Check the sys.databases catalog view and if needed enable the SQL SERVICE BROKER using the ALTER DATABASE command.

Message Types

Message Types are the first of the types of objects that we will be looking at. The Message Type is simply a definition of the type of data that will be contained within the message. When you create a Message Type you define the type of validation that the SQL SERVICE BROKER will be performing on the body of the message. You have four options for this validation. They are NONE, EMPTY, WELL_FORMED_XML, and VALID_XML WITH SCHEMA COLLECTION, with NONE being the default. As with all other database objects Message Types are created under the ownership of a specific database user or database role. Although it is most common to create the objects under the ownership of dbo, any valid database user or role can be specified.

TEST DAY TIP

Make sure that you know the rules for each of the validation options of the MESSAGE TYPES.

Message Types are created using the *CREATE MESSAGE TYPE* command. Like all the other objects within the SQL SERVICE BROKER Message Type, objects are database specific. The name of the Message Type can be up to 128 characters in length. Although you can use any object name for any SQL SERVICE BROKER objects, since the messages can be sent between systems great care should be used when naming objects so as to ensure that there are no naming collisions when sending messages between servers. One technique is to use a UNC style naming convention, which helps keep SERVICE BROKER object names from colliding with each other when you start sending messages between servers. This technique is what will be used in all the sample code in this chapter.

The validation type NONE is used when you wish to put any type of data within the message body. This includes text, numbers, XML, or binary data. When using this validation type, you can send any data you like within the message body, except for a NULL value. If you want to ensure that an empty message is sent, you have to specify the validation type EMPTY.

The validation type WELL_FORMED_XML requires that the data you are inserting into the message is correctly formed XML. This saves you from having to write your own validation logic at the receiving side of the message to ensure that the data is a valid XML document.

The validation type VALID_XML WITH SCHEMA COLLECTION requires not only that your XML data be valid, but that it meets the requirements of the predefined XML schema collection. The XML schema collection should be an already defined XML schema definition created within the SQL Server database. Although the creation of XML schemas is outside the scope of this chapter, you can read more about it by referencing Books OnLine under the index heading "CREATE XML SCHEMA COLLECTION statement." When using this validation type, before sending the message SQL SERVICE BROKER will first check that the XML document you are sending fits the required XML schema definition; if it does the message will be sent. If the message does not fit the XML schema definition the message will not be sent, and an error message will be returned to the calling code.

The actual syntax for creating a Message Type is very simple and straightforward.

```
CREATE MESSAGE TYPE [YourApplication/YourMessageType]
       AUTHORIZATION dbo
       VALIDATION = NONE;
```

As you can see in the sample code, the name of the Message Type is *YourApplication/YourMessageType*. The Message Type will be owned by *dbo*, and there will be no validation performed. I most often use the validation of NONE or EMPTY because I prefer to have my own logic on the receiving side handle checking if the XML is correct. I also do not want the SQL Server engine to have to spend extra time checking that the XML fits the official definition of "well-formed XML."

If you wish to change the validation after you create the Message Type you can alter the Message Type by using the *ALTER MESSAGE TYPE* command. The authorization cannot be changed after the Message Type has been created.

EXERCISE 12.2

CREATING MESSAGE TYPES

Create four message types within the AdventureWorks database. Use the validation NONE for two of them and WELL_FORMED_XML for the other two. Create the Message Types based on the data shown in Table 12.1.

Table 12.1 Message Types and Their Validations

Message Type Name	Message Type Validation
MT _None	NONE
MT _XML	WELL_FORMED_XML

Contracts

Within the SQL SERVICE BROKER a contract defines what message types can be used on a single conversation and which side of the conversation can use which message types. Every conversation uses a single contract for the duration of the conversation. If you wish to use a different contract during an existing conversation you have to close the conversation and create a new one.

When defining the contract you specify which end of the conversation can use which message type. The initiator of the contract is the sender of the message, and the target of the contract is the receiver of the message. Like the Message Type, the name of the contract can be up to 128 characters and is created using the AUTHORIZATION statement to assign ownership of the object to a specific user or role within the database.

When naming your contract do not name the contract with the keyword ANY. If you create a contract using the keyword ANY as the name you will not be able to successfully assign priorities to the conversations using the CREATE BROKER PRIORITY command. The use of this command is outside the scope of this text; however, you can read more on this command in Books OnLine under the index setting "CREATE BROKER PRIORITY statement."

SQL SERVICE BROKER Contracts are created using the CREATE CONTRACT command. The CREATE CONTRACT command is very straightforward with few options when creating the contract.

```
CREATE CONTRACT [YourApplication/Contract1]
        AUTHORIZATION dbo
        (
        [YourApplication/YourMessageType] SENT BY INITIATOR,
        [AnotherApplication/AnotherMessageType] SENT BY TARGET
    );
```

When looking at this example code, you can begin to see why the naming conventions shown here can make it quite a bit easier to see which SQL SERVICE BROKER objects go with which Application.

EXAM WARNING

Pay special attention to the SENT BY options in the exam. The various options can get confusing during the exam. Also pay attention to the wording of the questions.

If you wish to create a contract that uses the same Message Type for both the initiator and the target either you can specify the Message Type twice as done above, or you can specify that the Message Type be sent by ANY as shown here.

```
CREATE CONTRACT [YourApplication/Contract1]
    AUTHORIZATION dbo
    (
        [YourApplication/YourMessageType] SENT BY ANY,
    );
```

Either syntax is perfectly acceptable, and neither is incorrect.

There is no ALTER CONTRACT command in SQL Server 2005 or SQL Server 2008; perhaps this command will make it into a future version. This prevents you from adding or removing a Message Type from the contract after the contract has been created. The only way to add or remove a Message Type from a contract is to create a new contract, modify all services that reference that contract to use the new contract, and then remove the original contract from the database using the DROP CONTRACT command.

There is no easy way to see after creating the contracts which Message Types are contained within the contracts. You can manually right-click on each contract in the object explorer and script each object out. In a large SQL SERVICE BROKER environment this could take hours or days to the SQL Server database. Because of this, having a good knowledge of the SQL SERVICE BROKER Catalog

Views is extremely important. You will find the meta data about the Message Types in the sys.service_message_types catalog view, and the meta data about the contracts in the sys.service_contracts catalog view. The linking view between these two catalog views is the sys.service_contract_message_usages catalog view. This view contains the id of the contract and the Message Type, as well as bit flags for which end of the conversation can use the message type.

In SQL Server 2008 a properties screen was introduced, which will allow you to view the contract and see what Message Types are bound to the contract. However, there is no way to view which contracts are bound to which Message Types.

EXERCISE 12.3

CREATING CONTRACTS

Create two contracts. Each contract should be bound to both message types. Use the chart shown in Table 12.2 when creating your contracts.

Table 12.2 Contracts and Message Types

Contract Name	Message Types
CT_Sender	MT_ None MT_ XML
CT_Receiver	MT_ None MT_ XML

Queues

The SQL SERVICE BROKER queue is where the messages are sent to and received from. You can think of them as kind of like tables, except that you cannot change the structure of them. Just like a table you can select data from the queue, and doing so will not affect the messages within the queue. However, because this is a SQL SERVICE BROKER queue and not a table you cannot INSERT, UPDATE, or DELETE any of the data within the queues. Because queues are physical objects created within the database, you can specify a database schema that contains the object, however, it is most common to leave the queue in the dbo schema. As the queue is a physical object that stores the messages that are sent to it, you will need to specify the SQL Server File Group that will store the data from the messages in it.

When creating the SQL SERVICE BROKER queues you have several options from which you can select. You can enable or disable the queue from receiving messages via the STATUS option. You can tell the SQL SERVICE BROKER to keep messages after they have been received or to delete them after they have been received via the RETENTION flag. You also have the option of having a stored procedure be run by the SQL SERVICE BROKER by using the ACTIVATION settings. By default the STATUS setting will be enabled, and the RETENTION setting will be disabled. The ACTIVATION setting will be enabled by default, however, without the procedure name set no action will be taken until you specify the name of the stored procedure to execute. This procedure, if specified, must exist. Therefore, it is recommended that you create the queue, then the procedure that will read from the queue, then use the ALTER QUEUE command to set the activation procedure. With the exception of setting the file group all options that are available in the CREATE QUEUE command are available in the ALTER QUEUE command.

Activated stored procedures are probably one of the most important parts of the SQL SERVICE BROKER system. They allow the SQL Server to automatically start a stored procedure when a message arrives so that messages can be processed as quickly as possible. You can even control how many copies of the stored procedure are running—from a single thread up to 32,767 threads. You will want to be very careful with how high you set this setting since setting it too high could cause your SQL Server CPU to increase as you add thousands of threads to the system.

Configuring & Implementing...

Message Queues in the Real World

SQL SERVICE BROKER is used by many companies in many different ways. Pretty much anything that doesn't need to give data back to the user can be set up to go through the SQL SERVICE BROKER. This gives the user a faster experience since the user interface does not have to wait for the process to be completed. Some of the various things that can be done with the SQL SERVICE BROKER include data logging, Windows service to Windows service messages, and physical file manipulation.

Continued

In systems where each record has a physical file assigned to it, you can set up a trigger, and when the records are deleted, a SQL SERVICE BROKER message is sent containing the files that need to be deleted. A Windows service can then receive the messages in the queue and delete the physical files. The same can be done when files need to be moved from one place to another. When the record is updated, an update trigger on the table fires and sends a message to the SQL SERVICE BROKER. The message is then downloaded by a Windows service, which then moves the physical file.

Many companies have all sorts of data logging going on either within the internal application, or within the web server to track site usage. This allows the web site to log data about the site usage, without having to wait for the database to process the insert or any rollups that are done based on the insert.

When you increase the number of threads that the Queue will run in parallel and there are already messages in queue, the new threads will normally start within a few seconds. When you reduce the number of threads, no threads are halted at that time. The threads must stop on their own by running out of messages to process. No new threads will be started, but there will be more threads running than are configured until those threads begin to end.

The same effect occurs if you stop the activation. No new threads will be started but the running threads will continue to process until they run out of messages to process. If you change the procedure name of the activated procedure then the new procedure name will not be used until there is room for a new thread to be started in the number of threads running. If you have the queue configured for five threads and there are five threads running when you change the procedure name, the new procedure will not be used until after one thread has stopped. At this time the new procedure name will be used when the new thread is started. If you need to stop all the activated procedures from processing any additional messages then you will want to disable the queue, which will prevent the activated procedures from receiving any new messages out of the queue, causing the procedures to exit after they have finished processing the current message.

Using an example let's look at how the queue is going to handle the activated stored procedure. First, we will make a few assumptions about the *dbo.YourProcedure* procedure and the queue.

1. The procedure *dbo.YourProcedure* contains a loop that will attempt to process all the messages in the queue in a single execution of the procedure.

2. The procedure *dbo.YourProcedure* takes one second to process each message due to the complex business logic within the procedure.

3. The queue *[MyApplication\ReceivingQueue1]* receives four messages per second at the peak load and one message every two seconds at the lowest load.

As you can see from the following sample code, we have configured the queue to run a maximum of two copies of the stored procedure at any one time. When the first message arrives in the queue, the SQL SERVICE BROKER automatically starts our stored procedure *dbo.YourProcedure*. When the second message arrives in the queue the first thread is still running, so SQL SERVICE BROKER spawns a new thread and starts another copy of the *dbo.YourProcedure* stored procedure. When the third message arrives in the queue, the SQL SERVICE BROKER already has two copies of the procedure running so it does not start a third one. Once one of the procedures finishes processing the data, the loop within the stored procedure tells it to check for another message. Since the third message has arrived in the queue, that message is received and the stored procedure begins processing the data within that message. As you can see you need to find a balance between processing all the messages as quickly as possible and keeping system resources free to complete other tasks.

```
CREATE QUEUE [MyApplication\ReceivingQueue1]
       WITH STATUS=ON,
             RETENTION=OFF,
             ACTIVATION (
                    STATUS=ON,
                    PROCEDURE_NAME=dbo.YourProcedure,
                    MAX_QUEUE_READERS=2,
                    EXECUTE AS dbo
             )
       ON YourFileGroup;
```

Test Day Tip

The process of setting up an activation procedure can get confusing. Be sure to remember that you need to create the queue, then the procedure, then set the procedure as an activation procedure.

Each queue you create to receive messages should have a queue that is used as the source of the message. After each conversation is closed the receiving queue will send a message back to the source queue telling it that the conversation has been closed. Although you can have these messages sent to the same queue, in a high-volume environment this will create extra load for the receiving queue to handle. Therefore, it is recommended that you always create a sending queue to which these acknowledgments can be sent. This sending queue, which receives the acknowledgments, should have an activated stored procedure that receives all the messages and ends the conversations.

EXERCISE 12.4

CREATING QUEUES

Create two queues within the AdventureWorks database. They should be named Q_Sender and Q_Receiver.

Services

Services are used to bind the queue to the contract. Remember where I said that messages are sent to the queue? Well actually they aren't. Messages are sent from a service to another service. The receiving service then delivers the message into the specific queue. Once all the messages on the conversation have been received and removed from the queue, the receiving queue sends a message back to the sending service acknowledging that the messages have been received and that the conversation can be closed.

Each service binds a single queue to one or more contracts. This allows you to have different contracts referencing different message types, all sending messages to the same service. Although this is allowed, it is most common to have a single service bound to a single contract.

The services are created using the CREATE SERVICE command. The CREATE SERVICE command is pretty straightforward, with no settings other than the queue and the list of contracts. Like the other objects within the SQL SERVICE BROKER the name of the service can be up to 128 characters. Like with contracts, you should not create a service with the name ANY because this will prevent you from using prioritization when sending messages. You cannot specify a schema name when creating a service, however, like the other objects (other than the queue) you can set the authorization to any user or group.

```
CREATE SERVICE [YourApplication\YourService]
    AUTHORIZATION dbo
    ON QUEUE [MyApplication\ReceivingQueue1]
    ([YourApplication/Contract1]);
```

In the event that you have created a source queue and a receiving queue, each queue will need a service binding it to the contract or contracts that you will be using. If you wish you can create a service with no contracts. This means that the service cannot receive any messages, it can only send messages to another service. Be very careful when you create your service names. Service names are case sensitive when you are sending messages from one database to another no matter the collation setting of the databases. If the case is not correct when you are sending the message then the message will fail with a service not found message.

TEST DAY TIP

Make sure that you are aware of which catalog view holds which data.

Like the contracts there is no easy way to see which services are bound to which queues and which contracts. As discussed earlier, the meta data for the contracts is found in the sys.service_contracts catalog view, the meta data for the queues is found in the sys.service_queues catalog view, and the meta data for the services in found in the sys.services catalog view. You can find which services are bound to which contracts in the sys.service_contract_usages catalog view, and you can find which queues are bound to which services in the sys.service_queue_usages catalog view.

EXERCISE 12.5

CREATING SERVICES

Create two services in the AdventureWorks database. Each service will be bound to its own queue and its own contract. Use the data in the chart shown in Table 12.3 when creating your services.

Table 12.3 Services, Contracts, and Queues

Service	Contract	Queue
SVC_Sender	CT_Sender	Q_Sender
SVC_Receiver	CT_Receiver	Q_Receiver

Endpoints

Endpoints are used to allow the SQL SERVICE BROKER within two instances to talk to each other. The SQL SERVICE BROKER has its own special Endpoint, which cannot be used for any purpose other than for the SQL SERVICE BROKER. At its most basic an Endpoint is a TCP port that is open for communication from another SQL Server's SERVICE BROKER.

Because Endpoints allow for access into the SQL Server you should be careful about when you create them, and what settings you use to create them. Setting incorrect settings on an Endpoint could allow a rogue SQL Server on your network to send SERVICE BROKER messages into your production system.

Each SQL Server instance can have one and only one SERVICE BROKER Endpoint. All databases within that instance will share the Endpoint. However, the databases within the instance will know nothing of the Endpoint because the Endpoint is used for allowing access into the SQL Server. Because of this you need to tell the SERVICE BROKER only about the remote Endpoints. This is done through Routes, which we will discuss later.

If you are sending messages between two SQL Server instances on a single server each instance will need its own Endpoint. Because you cannot share a TCP port between the two instances each instance will need its own TCP port number. Whenever possible it is much easier to use a single TCP port number for all the SERVICE BROKER Endpoints in your environment. Doing so will make it much easier to keep track of which server uses which port number since they are all using the same port number.

TEST DAY TIP

Pay attention to how many servers are involved in the questions. This will change whether the endpoints can be on the same TCP port number or not.

Of all the possible commands that we have used, the CREATE ENDPOINT command is probably the most complex because it allows for server-to-server communication, so you will need to know quite a bit about how the servers will be talking to each other, as well as have a decent knowledge of Windows Authentication architecture. There are many options available as part of the CREATE ENDPOINT command, which we will not be covering as part of this chapter.

If all you want to do is get an Endpoint up and running in a development environment, then this sample code will get you up and running. There is virtually no security on this Endpoint whatsoever, so it shouldn't be used for your Endpoints on your production systems.

```
CREATE ENDPOINT YourSSBEndpoint AUTHORIZATION sa
    STATE=STARTED
    AS TCP (LISTENER_PORT=5555, LISTENER_IP=ALL)
    FOR SERVICE_BROKER (AUTHENTICATION=WINDOWS,
    ENCRYPTION=REQUIRED ALGORITHM RC4,
    MESSAGE_FORWARDING=DISABLED);
```

As you can see from the sample code, we named our Endpoint. Any name is acceptable up to 128 characters. The authorization is the login that owns the Endpoint. Remember that Endpoints are server-wide, not database-wide, which is why the owner must be a login and not a user or role. The owner can be a SQL Login or a Windows Login, or is the login of the user creating the Endpoint by default.

EXAM WARNING

Pay attention to the authentication options. The questions will be specific about the requirements but they will have a lot of useless information that you will need to filter through to get to the correct information.

An Endpoint has three potential states that it can be in: Stopped, which is the default; Started; and Disabled. When an Endpoint is Started it accepts remote connections. When an Endpoint is Stopped it is listening for removed connections and rejects them with an error. When an Endpoint is Disabled the TCP port is closed and any attempts to connect to the Endpoint will fail, saying that the server could not be found.

There are two ways that SQL Server can listen for an Endpoint; those options are TCP and HTTP. SERVICE BROKER Endpoints require that the listener be a TCP endpoint. The LISTENER_PORT can be set to whatever TCP port number you wish to use to allow communication from other servers. It is recommended that you use a TCP port number over 1024 as most ports under 1024 are assigned to other services. Some key ports over 1024 that you do not want are:

- **1270** Microsoft MOM Agent
- **1293** IPSec
- **1311** Dell OpenManage
- **1433** SQL Servers Port Number
- **1512** WINS
- **1521** Oracle Default Port Number
- **2381** HP Insight Manager
- **3389** Remote Desktop's Port Number
- **3306** MySQL

If you are having trouble selecting a port number to use you can find the list of registered port numbers and the applications that claim them at http://en.wikipedia.org/wiki/List_of_TCP_and_UDP_port_numbers.

In the example shown I specify the LISTENER_IP of ALL. This allows a remote SQL Server's SERVICE BROKER to connect on any IP address that is assigned to the server. If the server has a DHCP address then this would be the setting you would want to use. If the server has multiple IP addresses then you will want to use this setting as well if you wish to have the remote system connect to any of the IP addresses. If you wish to have the remote systems connect to a single IP address only then specify the IP address there within single quotes. The IP address that you specify must be an IP address currently hosted by the SQL Server or the CREATE ENDPOINT command will fail with an error.

We then tell the CREATE ENDPOINT command that we are creating this endpoint FOR SERVICE_BROKER to use. We are then setting the Authentication to Windows Authentication. If you choose you can use Certification-based authentication. You can also specify whether NTLM or KERBEROS authentication should be used, in addition to being able to tell the Endpoint to NEGOTIATE the more secure connection. Because we do not specify which Windows Authentication protocol (NTML or KERBEROS) to use, NEGOTIATE is used by default.

When we create the Endpoint we can also specify if Encryption is DISABLED, SUPPORTED, or REQUIRED. In the example I selected REQUIRED, which prevents anyone from listening to the network traffic and seeing what data is being passed from server to server. This helps protect the databases from attack because we are encrypting the data as it flows between the two servers. REQUIRED is the default encryption setting when creating an Endpoint. You can also specify which encryption algorithm you wish to use when encrypting the data between servers. The default is the RC4 algorithm. The other options are AES, AES RC4, and RC4 AES. If you specify the AES RC4 or the RC4 AES algorithm this tells the Endpoint to use either algorithm, attempting the first one specified, and then falling back to the second one.

When specifying the encryption algorithm to use it is important to know the difference between the two. The AES algorithm is a much stronger encryption algorithm than the RC4 algorithm, but that increased level of protection comes at a cost of additional CPU power being needed to encrypt and decrypt the data. If security is a high priority for you it is recommended that you use the AES algorithm. If you have TCP encryption, offload chips on the network cards of your servers; then encryption can be disabled, because the network card will handle all encryption and decryption for you before the data leaves the server.

Routes

Routes are used to tell the SQL SERVICE BROKER that a message needs to be sent to another server on the network. The function of a route is pretty basic. When a message is sent to a service, before delivering that message to the receiving service the SQL SERVICE BROKER checks the routes table to see if there is a route defined on that service. If there is, then the route is used to send the message to the remote machine instead of delivering it to the local service.

When setting up a route to a remote instance of SQL Server you will need three pieces of information from the remote machine. The first piece of information you will need is the IP address of the remote machine. If the remote machine is at another company then you will need the public IP address that is being NATed to the SQL Server. The second piece of information you will need is the port number that was configured on the remote machine's Endpoint. If the Endpoint was set up a while ago, you can query the sys.service_broker_endpoints and sys.tcp_endpoints catalog views to get this information.

```
SELECT p.port
FROM sys.tcp_endpoints as p
JOIN sys.service_broker_endpoints as s ON s.endpoint_id = p.endpoint_id;
```

The third piece of information that you will need is the GUID, which uniquely identifies the remote database's SERVICE BROKER from other systems in your enterprise. This can be found by querying the sys.databases catalog view on the remote server. The value you are looking for can be found in the service_broker_guid column. If the value is all zeros then you will need to issue an ALTER DATABASE command against the remote database to configure the SERVICE BROKER.

Routes are created to the remote system by using the CREATE ROUTE command. The CREATE ROUTE command must be run on both servers so that each server knows about each other so that the messages can flow from the sender to the receiver, and so that the acknowledgements can flow from the receiver to the sender.

```
CREATE ROUTE YourRoute AUTHORIZATION dbo
WITH SERVICE_NAME = 'YourApplication\YourService',
     BROKER_INSTANCE='',
     LIFETIME=68400,
     ADDRESS='tCP://RemoteMachine:5555',
     MIRROR_ADDRESS='tCP://OtherRemoteMachine:5555';
```

The SERVICE_NAME is where the case sensitivity comes into play that was mentioned earlier. When the local server does its matching to see if the service name you are sending to matches that of the route it does a byte-by-byte comparison against the values. If there is any case sensitivity mismatch then the messages will not follow the route to the remote machine. You can also create a route with no service name. Doing this will cause all messages to follow the route, however, this will happen at a lower priority than if a route exists for a specific service. In other words, if you have a route to SERVER1 with no service name, and a route to SERVER2 for the YourApplication\YourService service, then messages to the YourApplication\YourService will be sent to the SERVER2 and messages to all other services will be sent to SERVER1.

The BROKER_INSTANCE parameter is also optional, however, it is recommend that you specify the value so that you can more easily control which database on the remote server receives the message. When the conversation is created you can also specify the BROKER_INSTANCE if you would prefer to specify it there.

The LIFETIME is another optional parameter. This parameter will allow you to set the time (in seconds from the time the route was created) that the route is valid. When the specified number of seconds has passed the route will automatically be deleted. If the LIFETIME is not specified then the route will never expire and will remain until manually deleted with the DROP ROUTE command.

The ADDRESS parameter is a required parameter that tells the route the name or IP address and port number of the remote machine to connect to. You can specify a local machine name as was done in the example, or the full DNS name of the machine, or the IP address of the machine if there is no DNS name or host name set up. The machine name is followed by a colon and the port number on which the Endpoint is listening.

The MIRROR_ADDRESS parameter is an optional parameter. If you are not using database mirroring on the remote database then this setting is not needed. If you are using database mirroring then it is strongly recommended that you provide the Endpoint information for the mirror server. If you do not, and the mirror fails over, then the SERVICE BROKER will not be able to send the messages to the remote machine until the mirror fails back. The MIRROR_ADDRESS parameter uses the same syntax as the ADDRESS parameter.

If you are sending messages to a clustered instance the MIRROR_ADDRESS is not needed, because when a cluster fails over, the same IP address is used on the remote machine. If you are using Windows 2008 clustering and have different IP address subnets on both sides of the cluster because you are clustering between data centers, you can specify the second subnet's IP address in the MIRROR_ ADDRESS field, but it is recommended that you instead use the DNS name of the SQL Server so that when the cluster fails over and updates DNS the connection simply is redirected to the correct host.

Like all the other SERVICE BROKER objects there is no easy way to see to which service a route is bound. The only way to view this information short of scripting out the route is to view the meta data for the routes in the sys. routes catalog view.

Sending a Message

Once the SQL SERVICE BROKER objects have been created you are ready to send a message. Sending a message is actually a two part process. First you must create a conversation upon which you can send messages by using the BEGIN DIALOG command. Then you can send your message using the SEND command.

When you begin a conversation with the BEGIN DIALOG command you must specify from which service you are sending the message, to which service you are sending the message, as well as the contract to which the messages will conform (remember that the contract contains a bunch of message types). When you specify the source of the message you will be formatting the name as a database object. When you specify the destination of the message you will be formatting the name as a text string. The contract will also be formatted as a database object. This means that you cannot use variables to define your source service or your contract.

```
DECLARE @conversation_handle UNIQUEIDENTIFIER

BEGIN DIALOG @conversation_handle
FROM SERVICE [YourApplication\YourService]
TO SERVICE 'YourApplication\YourService'
ON CONTRACT [YourApplication/Contract1]
```

You'll notice that the TO SERVICE line has the service name wrapped in single quotes, not square brackets, since it is a text string, not an object name.

The value now contained within the *@conversation_handle* variable will be used within the SEND command. Most typically the SEND command will be the next command in the stored procedure that is sending the message. When sending a message you have to provide the Conversation Id on which the message will be sent, the message type of the data in the message, as well as the data to be sent within the message. All fields are required with the exception of the data within the message, which is optional if the message type validation was specified as EMPTY or NONE. Sample code of a message with data in the message body would look like this:

```
DECLARE @conversation_handle UNIQUEIDENTIFIER
DECLARE @message_body XML

BEGIN DIALOG @conversation_handle
FROM SERVICE [YourApplication\YourService]
TO SERVICE 'YourApplication\YourService'
ON CONTRACT [YourApplication/Contract1]
SET @message_body = (SELECT * FROM sys.tables FOR XML AUTO)

SEND ON CONVERSATION @conversation_handle
MESSAGE TYPE [YourApplication/YourMessageType]
(@message_body);
```

At this point your message text has been sent. If you query the queue using the SELECT statement you should see the message in there. If not check the sys.transmission_queue and sys.conversation_endpoints DMVs and see if there are any errors that need to be resolved.

Now that you have sent the message, you need to be able to receive the message. Being able to look at the message using the SELECT statement is all well and good, but if you used the SELECT statement to get the values out of the queue you would be processing the same message over and over. This is where the RECEIVE command comes into play. The RECEIVE statement is what is used to get the messages out of the queue so that you can do something with the data in the message. The RECEIVE statement will look very similar to the SELECT statement. You can specify which columns you wish to receive and you can specify filters based on those columns if you so desire. A typical RECEIVE statement will look something like this:

```
DECLARE @message_body XML

DECLARE @conversation_handle UNIQUEIDENTIFIER

RECEIVE TOP (1) @conversation_handle=conversation_handle, @message_
body=cast(message_body as XML)

FROM [MyApplication\ReceivingQueue1];

END CONVERSATION @conversation_handle
```

You can also receive more than one message at one time. In order to do this you will need to receive the messages into a table, and change the TOP command to a different value. You will also need to configure your process to send more than one message per conversation as all messages that are received need to be part of the same conversation.

```
DECLARE @Messages TABLE

(@conversation_handle uniqueidentifier,

message_body varbinary(MAX))

INSERT INTO @Messages
RECEIVE TOP (100) conversation_handle, message_body
FROM [MyApplication\ReceivingQueue1];
```

At this point the message data has been received and the conversation closed. If you are sending more than one message on the conversation then you will want to put login within the receiving code so that you know when to issue the END CONVERSATION command. Once the END CONVERSATION command has been issued no new messages will be accepted on that conversation. The acknowledgment is sent to the sending service when the END CONVERSATION command is run, telling it that the conversation has been completed. That calling service should then complete an END CONVERSATION command on the conversation handle, which will complete the process of ending the conversation and tell the SERVICE BROKER to mark the conversation as closed and ready for the automated cleanup procedures to remove the final data from the sys.conversation_endpoints DMV.

EXERCISE 12.6

SENDING AND RECEIVING MESSAGES

Now that you have created the services, queues contracts, and message types try sending messages from the SVC_Sender Service to the SVC_Receiver Service. This will be done by first creating a conversation, then sending a message on that conversation. Create a small XML document and send the XML document as the body of the message. After you send the message query the receiving queue and see that the message arrived. Receive the message using the RECEIVE command and see that the message has been received. After you have received the message perform an END CONVERSATION on the conversation handle.

After you end the conversation you should query the sending queue. You will now see a message in the sending queue. Perform a RECEIVE command on the sending queue, and perform an END CONVERSATION on the conversation handle.

After you have processed the full round trip of the first message, create a new conversation and send two messages on the same conversation. After both messages are in the receiving queue, RECEIVE the messages and end the conversation. Then do the same to the sending queue to complete the closing of the conversation.

If the messages are not received in the receiving queue, check the output of the sys.conversation_endpoints and the sys.transmission_queue catalog views for specific errors.

Summary of Exam Objectives

Having completed this section you will have an understanding of the message queuing concept, as well as knowledge of the components of the SQL SERVICE BROKER. You will be able to create and manage SQL SERVICE BROKER objects as well as send messages using the SQL SERVICE BROKER and have those messages be processed automatically by an activation stored procedure.

By completing this chapter you will have an understanding of concepts of the technology being used by the SQL SERVICE BROKER; as well as when the SQL SERVICE BROKER is the correct solution and when it is not the correct solution to the problem. You will also know when to use the sys.transmission_queue and sys.service_endpoints DMVs to troubleshoot the SQL SERVICE BROKER.

Exam Objectives Fast Track

The Queuing Concept Explained

- ☑ SQL SERVICE BROKER, like all message queuing technologies, allows for asynchronous messages to be sent from one server to another with the receiving server processing that message and carrying out some predefined task.

- ☑ The beauty of message queuing in general is that message delivery is guaranteed in the order sent.

- ☑ Neither Microsoft nor any third party as of this writing has written a way to send or receive messages without connecting to the SQL Server database. Because of this, SQL SERVICE BROKER may not always be the correct solution for your messaging environment.

Service Broker Defined

- ☑ SQL SERVICE BROKER allows for asynchronous messages to be sent from one process to another, either on the same database, same instance of SQL Server, a different instance of SQL Server, or a different physical server.

- ☑ Any process can send a message, provided it has the required rights to do so.

- ☑ It is recommended that you not make any changes to the SQL SERVICE BROKER within the system databases because SQL Server uses the SERVICE BROKER for its own tasks.

Message Types

- ☑ Message Types are defined on the system, and are configured with either no validation, an empty message, well-formed XML, or a specific predefined XML schema.

- ☑ All messages are sent based on a specific type.

- ☑ If you wish to change the validation after you create the Message Type you can alter the Message Type by using the ALTER MESSAGE TYPE command.

Contracts

- ☑ Contracts are logical definitions that control which message type the sender and receiver can use.

- ☑ Within the contract you can specify if the message type can be used by the sender, receiver, or both.

- ☑ Each conversation uses a single contract for both sending and receiving the message(s).

Queues

- ☑ Queues are the physical database objects that contain the messages.

- ☑ Queues can have activated procedures that are run automatically when a message is received.

- ☑ When messages are sent they are delivered to a queue from where they are processed.

Services

- ☑ Services are the objects to which the message is actually sent. The service binds the queue to the contract.

- ☑ Endpoints allow the SQL SERVICE BROKER on a remote instance to connect to the local instance and deliver messages.

- ☑ When sending from one database to another the sending and receiving service must exist in both databases.

Routes

☑ Routes are bound to services and tell the SQL SERVICE BROKER to which remote machine and database to deliver the messages.

☑ When configuring the routes service names are case sensitive, regardless of the database collation.

☑ Routes can be configured to expire to prevent messages from being delivered after a specific date to the remote instance.

Sending a Message

☑ When sending a message, the message body cannot be NULL; blank messages can be sent, but the value may not be NULL.

☑ Messages are sent using the SEND statement after the conversation have been created using the BEGIN DIALOG statement.

☑ Messages are processed in the order they are received within the conversation.

Exam Objectives
Frequently Asked Questions

Q: What is the difference between asynchronous and synchronous processing?

A: Synchronous processing is when the client is waiting for a response; asynchronous processing is done after the client has stopped waiting for a response. An example of a synchronous process would be when a client application executes a normal stored procedure.

Q: Are routes required when using SQL SERVICE BROKER?

A: No. Routes are needed only when you are sending SQL SERVICE BROKER messages from one database to another. They are not required if the source and final destinations are in the same database.

Q: How can I add another Message Type to a contract?

A: There is no direct way to add a Message Type to a contract. You have to remove the contract and re-create it, which requires removing the contract from all services to which it is bound and then binding the new contract to the services before you can begin sending messages against the new Message Type.

Q: What is the easiest VALIDATION setting to use in the Message Type definition?

A: The VALIDATION setting NONE is the easiest to use since there are no requirements for the body of the message.

Q: In what data type is the message body sent?

A: Message data is sent in the *varbinary(max)* data type. You can use the CAST function to convert the data back to the expected data type.

Q: Does each database have its own Endpoint?

A: Endpoints are instance-wide, not database-wide. Each instance can have only a single SQL SERVICE BROKER Endpoint.

Self Test

1. You are working with a developer to design a message processing system. SQL Server SERVICE BROKER has been selected as the Message Queuing system. You are tasked with designing a solution that will allow for the fastest processing of messages while impacting the system with the lowest possible impact. You are expecting only a few messages to be received per hour, but these messages should be processed as quickly as possible. What should you do?

   A. Write a Windows Service that queries the queue every minute looking for new messages to process.

   B. Write a stored procedure that queries the queue, and schedule this procedure to be run by the SQL Server Agent every minute.

   C. Write a stored procedure that queries the queue, and set it as an activated stored procedure on the queue.

   D. Write a Windows Service that queries the queue every hour looking for new messages to process.

2. You are working with your database developer to design a SQL SERVICE BROKER application. The developer has a need to send a blank message as part of an existing conversation but he is receiving an error saying that the *message_body* cannot be NULL. What should you do?

   A. Delete the Service and the contract. Create a new Message Type with a validation of empty. Create a new contract containing both the new Message Type and the original Message Type. Re-create the service. Tell the developer to use the new Message Type when sending the messages with the NULL message body, and that the message body should be excluded from the SEND statement when the message body should be blank.

   B. Create a new Message Type with a validation of empty. Add the Message Type to the service using the ALTER SERVICE command. Tell the developer to use the new Message Type when sending the message with the NULL message body, and that the message body should be excluded from the SEND statement when the message body should be blank.

   C. Create a new Message Type with a validation of empty. Add the Message Type to the contract using the ALTER CONTRACT command. Tell the developer to use the new Message Type when sending the message with the NULL message body, and that the message body should be excluded from the SEND statement when the message body should be blank.

D. Delete the Service and the contract. Create a new MESSAGE TYPE with a validation of WELL_FORMED_XML. Create a new contract containing both the new MESSAGE TYPE and the original message type. Re-create the service. Tell the developer to use the new Message Type when sending the messages with the NULL message body, and that the message body should be excluded from the SEND statement when the message body should be blank.

3. A developer is attempting to delete some obsolete SQL SERVICE BROKER objects from the database as part of your annual database object cleanup project. However, each time he attempts to drop the contract (YourApplication/Contract1), he receives the error "The contract 'YourApplication/Contract1' cannot be dropped because it is bound to one or more service." How can you identify the service or services that are bound to this contract in the least amount of time?

A. Script out all the Services on the instance and read through them looking for the service or services that are bound to the contract.

B. Join the sys.services catalog view and the sys.contracts together in a SELECT statement and use the output to identify which services are bound to the Contract in question.

C. Join sys.services, sys.contracts, and sys.service_contract_usages together in a SELECT statement and use the output to identify which services are bound to the contract in question.

D. Use the object explorer to view the properties of the contract.

4. You work for Adventure Works LLC as a database administrator. Your order entry system uses SQL SERVICE BROKER to get orders from the web site into the database. A customer contacts your customer service department saying that their order is showing on the web site but has no order details. Your SQL SERVICE BROKER queue is configured with the RETENTION flag set to ON. You need to reprocess the SQL SERVICE BROKER message; what do you do?

A. Mark the message for reprocessing by using the UPDATE command against the queue.

B. Use the RECEIVE statement to receive the message a second time by putting the message handle in the WHERE clause of the RECEIVE statement.

C. Get the value of the message by using the SELECT statement against the queue and send a new message using the value from the old message.

    D. Use the ALTER QUEUE statement with the ALTER MESSAGE syntax to change the status of the message from processed to pending.

5. You manage a large SQL SERVICE BROKER system, which sends messages from server to server. You have restored your production database to your development environment. You need to ensure that messages are being sent from your development server to the other development servers in your environment and not to your production servers. Which method do you use?

    A. Use the ALTER ROUTE statement to change the ADDRESS and BROKER_INSTANCE values to those of the remote development server. Then use the ALTER DATABASE statement to change the local SERVICE BROKER GUID and enable the SERVICE BROKER with the ENABLE_BROKER syntax.

    B. Use the ALTER ROUTE statement to change the ADDRESS and BROKER_INSTANCE values to those of the remote development server. Then use the ALTER DATABASE statement to change the local SERVICE BROKER GUID and enable the SERVICE BROKER with the NEW_BROKER syntax.

    C. Use the ALTER DATABASE statement to change the local SERVICE BROKER GUID and enable the SERVICE BROKER with the NEW_BROKER syntax.

    D. Use the ALTER DATABASE statement to change the local SERVICE BROKER GUID and enable the SERVICE BROKER with the ENABLE_BROKER syntax.

6. You are setting up a new SQL SERVICE BROKER application and the application requires that messages be sent to a SQL Server Instance that is mirrored. You need to configure a new route and ensure that the route fails over to the mirror server. Which syntax will create this route correctly (assuming that the GUID provided is correct)?

    A.
```
CREATE ROUTE YourRoute
AUTHORIZATION dbo
WITH SERVICE_NAME='YourApplication\YourService',
BROKER_INSTANCE='721B1C8E-B314-4E73-A9ED-194CF1DA87EB',
ADDRESS='TCP://SQLServer4:8432',
MIRROR_ADDRESS='TCP://SQLServer4_Mirror:8432';
```

B. CREATE ROUTE YourRoute

   AUTHORIZATION dbo

   WITH SERVICE_NAME='YourApplication\YourService',

   BROKER_INSTANCE='721B1C8E-B314-4E73-A9ED-194CF1DA87EB',

   ADDRESS='TCP://SQLServer4:8432';

C. CREATE ROUTE YourRoute

   AUTHORIZATION dbo

   WITH SERVICE_NAME='YourApplication\YourService',

   BROKER_INSTANCE='721B1C8E-B314-4E73-A9ED-194CF1DA87EB',

   ADDRESS='TCP://SQLServer4:1433',

   MIRROR_ADDRESS='TCP://SQLServer4_Mirror:1433';

D. CREATE ROUTE YourRoute

   AUTHORIZATION dbo

   WITH SERVICE_NAME='YourApplication\YourService',

   BROKER_INSTANCE='721B1C8E-B314-4E73-A9ED-194CF1DA87EB',

   ADDRESS='TCP://SQLServer4',

   MIRROR_ADDRESS='TCP://SQLServer4_Mirror';

7. Your application has an XML schema that was defined at a prior time. You wish to ensure that the message sent by your application conforms to the defined XML schema. Which syntax should you use to enforce this with the least amount of T/SQL code when sending the message?

A. CREATE MESSAGE TYPE [YourApplication\YourMessageType] AUTHORIZATION dbo VALIDATION = NONE

B. CREATE MESSAGE TYPE [YourApplication\YourMessageType] AUTHORIZATION dbo VALIDATION = EMPTY

C. CREATE MESSAGE TYPE [YourApplication\YourMessageType] AUTHORIZATION dbo VALIDATION = WELL_FORMED_XML

D. CREATE MESSAGE TYPE [YourApplication\YourMessageType] AUTHORIZATION dbo VALIDATION = VALID_XML WITH SCHEMA COLLECTION YourXSDSchemaObject

8. You are configuring SQL SERVICE BROKER on a database that has never used SQL SERVICE BROKER before. What command needs to be used to set up the SQL SERVICE BROKER for use for the first time?

A. ALTER DATABASE YourDatabase SET NEW BROKER;

B. ALTER ServiceBroker ENABLE;

C. `ALTER DATABASE YourDatabase ENABLE BROKER`

D. `EXEC sp_enablebroker`

9. You have restored your production database after the database became corrupt. What needs to be done, if anything, to ensure that the SQL SERVICE BROKER works correctly after the database restore has been completed, without losing any messages that are waiting to be processed?

A. Use the ALTER DATABASE command with the NEW_BROKER switch to enable the SQL SERVICE BROKER.

B. Use the ALTER DATABASE command with the ENABLE_BROKER switch to enable the SQL SERVICE BROKER.

C. Use the ALTER DATABASE command with the RESTORE_BROKER switch to enable the SQL SERVICE BROKER.

D. Nothing needs to be done to enable the SQL SERVICE BROKER after a database restore is completed.

10. You wish to maximize the performance of your SQL SERVICE BROKER application. You have decided that you want to increase the number of messages sent per conversation. What technique should you use?

A. Create a conversation and send all messages to all services on that conversation.

B. Create a conversation for each destination service and send all messages on the corresponding service.

C. Send the messages with a NULL conversation handle.

11. You are managing a system that uses SQL SERVICE BROKER. You wish to pause the automatic processing of messages that arrive sporadically without stopping messages from being delivered into the queue. Which command should you use?

A. `ALTER QUEUE YourQueue`

   `WITH STATUS=OFF;`

B. `ALTER QUEUE YourQueue`

   `WITH ACTIVATION (`

   `STATUS=OFF);`

C. ALTER QUEUE YourQueue

   WITH ACTIVATION (PAUSE=TRUE);

D. ALTER QUEUE YourQueue

   WITH MAX_QUEUE_READERS=0;

12. You need to identify the TCP port number that your SQL SERVICE BROKER Endpoint is using. Which query will allow you to most easily identify the TCP port number of the SQL SERVER BROKER Endpoint?

   A. SELECT p.port

      FROM sys.tcp_endpoints as p

      JOIN sys.service_broker_endpoints as s ON s.endpoint_id = p.endpoint_id;

   B. SELECT p.port

      FROM sys.tcp_endpoints as p

      JOIN sys.endpoints as s ON s.endpoint_id = p.endpoint_id;

   C. SELECT p.port

      FROM sys.service_broker_endpoints p;

   D. SELECT p.port

      FROM sys.endpoints p

13. You are designing a new asynchronous messaging infrastructure for a new Enterprise level application that your team is developing. Under which circumstance should you not use SQL SERVICE BROKER?

   A. When both the sending and receiving processes are going to be T/SQL commands.

   B. When the sending process will be a T/SQL command, and the receiving process will be a Windows process.

   C. When the sending process will be a Windows process, and the receiving process will be a T/SQL command.

   D. When both the sending and receiving processes are going to be Windows processes.

14. You are designing a SQL SERVICE BROKER application that will be sending messages from instance to instance. Both instances will be running

SQL Server 2008 Express edition. The messages will be routed through a third instance of SQL Server 2008. What edition or editions can be used as the server that is forwarding the messages from one SQL Server 2008 Express instance to another SQL Server 2008 Express instance in your production environment? (Select all that apply.)

A. SQL Server 2008 Express Edition

B. SQL Server 2008 Web Edition

C. SQL Server 2008 Workgroup Edition

D. SQL Server 2008 Standard Edition

E. SQL Server 2008 Enterprise Edition

F. SQL Server 2008 Developer Edition

15. You are managing an OLTP database that makes heavy use of the SQL SERVICE BROKER. You have identified that an activated stored procedure is causing performance problems. You need to stop processing by the activated stored procedure as quickly as possible. What action should you take?

A. Use the ALTER QUEUE command and set the MAX_QUEUE_ READERS setting to zero.

B. Use the ALTER QUEUE command and set the ACTIVATION STATUS = OFF.

A. Use the ALTER QUEUE command and set the STATUS = OFF.

D. Use the ALTER QUEUE command and change the PROCEDURE_ NAME setting to an invalid stored procedure name.

16. You are creating new SERVICE BROKER objects for a new SQL SERVICE BROKER application. The IT department coding standards require that when contracts are defined you must specify the message type used for the source and destination. You are creating your new services and are defining your message types. Which code block is the correct code block to use?

A.
```
CREATE CONTRACT YourContract AUTHORIZATION dbo

SourceMessageType SENT BY ANY,

DestinationMessageType SENT BY ANY;
```

B.
```
CREATE CONTRACT YourContract AUTHORIZATION dbo

SourceMessageType SENT BY INITIATOR,

DestinationMessageType SENT BY ANY;
```

C. CREATE CONTRACT YourContract AUTHORIZATION dbo

SourceMessageType SENT BY INITIATOR,

DestinationMessageType SEND BY TARGET;

17. You are seeing performance problems on your SQL Server SERVICE BROKER application. Messages are taking too long to be processed by the activated stored procedure. The stored procedure itself is already fully optimized. What can you do in order to decrease the amount of time it takes to process messages with the least amount of effort?

   A. Increase the number of parallel processes that are run automatically by changing the MAX_QUEUE_READERS value via the ALTER QUEUE command.

   B. Increase the number of parallel processes that are run automatically by the receiving service by changing the MAX_QUEUE_READERS value via the ALTER SERVICE command.

   C. Reduce the number of messages by sending more data per message.

   D. Create more queues and send some of the messages to each of the queues.

18. You have two instances on a server that need to be able to send messages between the instances. Your corporate IT policies say that SQL SERVICE BROKER Endpoints must be created on TCP port 5600. You create and bring online the first Endpoint, but you cannot get the second Endpoint to come online. What should you do to correct the issue?

   A. Add a second IP to the server. Configure the first instance to use the first IP for the Endpoint, and the second instance to use the new IP for the Endpoint. Start the Endpoint on the second instance.

   B. Change the port number of the second instance to a different port number using the ALTER QUEUE command and bring the Endpoint online.

   C. Restart the SQL Server instance that has the Endpoint that will not come online.

   D. Use the ALTER ENDPOINT command with the FORCE_ONLINE switch to force the Endpoint to come online.

19. You are defining new SQL SERVICE BROKER objects. Your messages must contain XML data, but there are several different schemas that can be used that will be identified by the receiving process by querying the XML document

within the message body to identify which code branch to use. What validation method should you use when creating the Message Type?

A. NONE

B. EMTPY

C. WELL_FORMED_XML

D. VALID_XML WITH SCHEMA COLLECTION

20. You have a SQL SERVICE BROKER application that you wish to increase the performance when receiving messages. What changes should you make?

A. Change the receiving code to load the data into a table, increasing the number of messages being received at one time by increasing the value of the TOP parameter.

B. Change the sending code to send more than one message in the same conversation. Change the receiving code to load the data into a table, increasing the number of messages being received at one time by increasing the value of the TOP parameter.

C. Change the sending code to send more than one message in the same conversation.

D. Increase the number of activated procedures that can run at any one time.

Self Test Quick Answer Key

1.	**C**	11.	**B**
2.	**A**	12.	**A**
3.	**C**	13.	**D**
4.	**C**	14.	**B, C, D,** and **E**
5.	**B**	15.	**C**
6.	**A**	16.	**C**
7.	**D**	17.	**A**
8.	**A**	18.	**A**
9.	**B**	19.	**C**
10.	**B**	20.	**B**

Chapter 13

MCTS SQL Server 2008 Exam 432

Performance Tuning

Exam objectives in this chapter:

- Tracing
- Locks, Blocking, and Deadlocks
- Guide to Dynamic Management Views (DMVs)
- Partitioning
- Performance Data Collection (Data Collector)
- Resource Governor

Exam objectives review:

- ☑ Summary of Exam Objectives
- ☑ Exam Objectives Fast Track
- ☑ Exam Objectives Frequently Asked Questions
- ☑ Self Test
- ☑ Self Test Quick Answer Key

Introduction

This chapter will explain how to ensure SQL Server is performing optimally. It will cover the use of profiler and the DMVs to ensure optimal performance from your queries.

This chapter also covers setup and use of the data collector (performance data collection). This is an exciting and powerful new feature in SQL Server 2008 and should not be overlooked.

Using application pools and the resource governor will also be covered in detail in this section. Application pools can help you get control of your resources so that mission-critical processes get a higher priority than nonmission-critical processes.

SQL Server 2008 provides an excellent platform for scalable, multiuser data-driven applications that perform well on commodity hardware. SQL Server has enjoyed wide acceptance and holds a strong position as database platform of choice for Online Transaction Processing (OLTP) and Online Analytical Processing (OLAP) for small and medium-sized business around the world. Additionally, Microsoft has made significant progress in winning market segment share with enterprise customers as SQL Server features, performance, and reliability continue to improve. However, no matter how good any database product is, an inefficient query join structure, missing or poorly selected indexes, or badly designed storage subsystem can each cause significant problems.

Query response time can mean the difference between users who are content and users who consider an application unavailable when performance is so bad it affects their ability to do their job, or they receive an application timeout or disconnect. Adoption of 64-bit hardware, multicore systems and huge physical memory has afforded many SQL Server administrators to overlook performance troubleshooting. Administrators often address performance or scalability issues by migrating to bigger and faster hardware, however this approach is limited in its effectiveness.

Any complex product or solution provides many opportunities for failure, and performance within SQL Server is no exception. Applications based on SQL Server often consist of many moving parts and sometimes disconnected or loosely connected users, each of which can add complexity in identifying the root cause of performance problems. Fortunately SQL Server 2008 is provided with a comprehensive arsenal of tools to assist with performance troubleshooting and tuning.

Administrators of SQL Server 2008 need to be skilled and knowledgeable with the performance tools provided with Windows–System Monitor and with the SQL Server specific tools, such as SQL Profiler and DYNAMIC Management Views (DMVs). In addition to considering hardware resources, SQL Server has a finite number of internal resources, such as locks and latches. Problem queries can sometimes conflict with themselves or each other, or exhaust these resources and it's important to know how to identify problems such as these and options to resolve these problems.

Tracing

Half of performance tuning is finding the problem. System Monitor is the performance monitoring tool provided by Windows and this can be useful when measuring hardware performance or bottlenecks and useful in identifying the process on a server that is causing a slowdown. If users are complaining of poor response times and SQL Server is running on a shared server, perhaps with a third-party application or webserver such as Internet Information Services (IIS), System Monitor can help find the process consuming resources. If a server is dedicated to SQL Server, or investigation with System Monitor identifies SQL Server as the cause of the problem, a limited set of System Monitor counters are available to continue troubleshooting. System Monitor provides a serverwide overview and it isn't possible to see exactly what SQL Server is doing at any point in time, which becomes useful when tracing.

As the performance tuning exercise is refined, it becomes necessary to get visibility of activity within SQL Server, and this is when we need tracing. Tracing provides the ability to collect data about the Transact-SQL (T-SQL) commands and Multi-Dimensional Expressions (MDX) that are executed on a database server. Additionally it is possible to trace for information about events affecting system performance such as deadlocks, warnings, data and log file shrinks/grows, and blocked processes. Tracing can also gather information about the way SQL Server processes requests internally such as locks, lock escalation, and query execution plans.

SQL Server Profiler (known as SQL Profiler or simply as Profiler) is the graphic tool installed alongside SQL Server used to define, configure, and start/stop traces. SQL Server Profiler can be found at Start > All Programs > Microsoft SQL Server 2008 > Performance Tools > SQL Server Profiler.

Once Profiler is launched, a toolbar and grey background appears, and you'll first need to create a new trace. To create a new trace, either click File > New Trace or click the left-most icon from the toolbar. The next screen is the server connection dialog; here, specify the name of the server and SQL Server instance to be traced, and connection credentials.

After successfully connecting to an instance of SQL Server, the next dialog allows control over how trace data is stored and what data is captured. As shown in Figure 13.1, it's possible to provide a name that describes the trace.

Figure 13.1 Create a New Trace with SQL Server Profiler

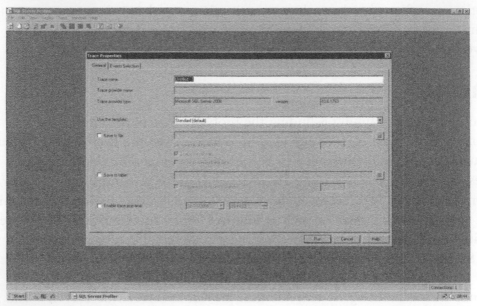

Trace Templates

The next configuration option is the trace template option, where the Standard template is selected by default. Trace templates provide a preconfigured trace definition for common trace scenarios. It is possible to create new trace templates, or modify those provided with SQL Server. It is usually possible to start with a template and adjust the events and filters based on your needs. Table 13.1 contains a summary of the trace templates, when you might use them, and the events captured.

Table 13.1 Trace Template Summary

Name	Description	Events
SP_Counts	Used to trace calls to start Stored Procedures.	SP:Starting
Standard	Captures data to provide instance overview, including T-SQL Statement and Stored Procedure Start and Completion.	Audit Login Audit Logout ExistingConnection RPC:Completed SQL:BatchCompleted SQL:BatchStarting

Continued

Table 13.1 Continued. Trace Template Summary

Name	Description	Events
TSQL	Captures T-SQL batch start times, useful for troubleshooting client application performance and correlating data captured from applications with SQL Server events.	Audit Login Audit Logout ExistingConnection RPC:Starting SQL:BatchStarting
TSQL_ Duration	Records all T-SQL Statements and the duration to complete.	RPC:Completed SQL:BatchCompleted
TSQL_ Grouped	Useful for capturing activity about a specific user or application, this template groups T-SQL commands by user or client.	Audit Login Audit Logout ExistingConnection RPC:Starting SQL:BatchStarting
TSQL_Locks	Captures all the Transact-SQL statements that are submitted to SQL Server by clients along with exceptional lock events. Use to troubleshoot deadlocks, lock time-out, and lock escalation events.	Blocked Process Report SP:StmtCompleted SP:StmtStarting SQL:StmtCompleted SQL:StmtStarting Deadlock Graph (Use against SQL Server 2005 or SQL Server 2008 instance.) Lock:Cancel Lock:Deadlock Lock:Deadlock Chain Lock:Escalation Lock:Timeout (Use against SQL Server 2000 instance.) Lock:Timeout (timeout>0) (Use against SQL Server 2005 or SQL Server 2008 instances.)

Continued

Table 13.1 Continued. Trace Template Summary

Name	Description	Events
TSQL_Replay	Use this template if the trace is to be replayed. Captures all events necessary to recreate statements/workload on a different server.	CursorClose CursorExecute CursorOpen CursorPrepare CursorUnprepare Audit Login Audit Logout Existing Connection RPC Output Parameter RPC:Completed RPC:Starting Exec Prepared SQL Prepare SQL SQL:BatchCompleted SQL:BatchStarting
TSQL_SPs	Useful for troubleshooting poorly performing Stored Procedures, this template will capture each step within the stored procedure to display execution duration.	Audit Login Audit Logout ExistingConnection RPC:Starting SP:Completed SP:Starting SP:StmtStarting SQL:BatchStarting
Tuning	Captures T-SQL completion times, used to pass to SQL Server Database Tuning Advisor for analysis.	RPC:Completed SP:StmtCompleted SQL:BatchCompleted

EXAM WARNING

Be sure you have a good idea of what's included in the trace templates. You should especially take note of the Replay template, which is used to make a trace capture for replaying on a test server.

After you choose a trace template, it's possible to click Run, and server activity will begin to fill the screen. This can be useful to verify the required events are being captured, or to monitor SQL instances where activity is low (a development workstation or test server where workload is restricted). However, reading and analyzing results captured through Profiler directly to the screen can become unwieldy on a server with even moderate load. In this situation, consider tracing to a flat file or database table, which will speed up the trace and allow for post-capture analysis.

Trace Events

Selecting the Events tab from the top of the trace properties dialog allows control of the event classes that will be captured when the trace is running. The events that are already selected are those specified in the trace template. Click Show All Events and Show All Columns to display all events and options available for capture. You can choose any events that are necessary to include these in the trace definition. Figure 13.2 shows some useful events to include in each trace, the Errors and Warning events. These will alert you to a number of conditions that you should be aware of when troubleshooting any SQL Server problem.

Figure 13.2 Select Show All Events and
Show All Columns to Display All Possible Events and Columns

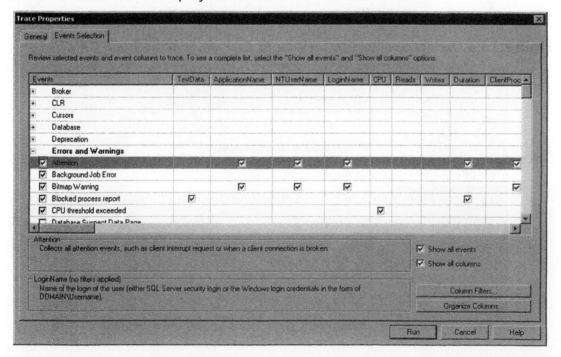

Configuring & Implementing...

Exercise Caution with LOCK Trace Events

SQL traces affect server performance. Trace as few events as necessary—you'll save overhead and capture less data to analyze! Exercise particular caution when capturing any events in the LOCK event class, since a busy SQL Server may acquire and release many thousands of locks per minute.

Trace Filters

Trace filters allow restrictions to be applied on the data that is captured by the trace. This can be useful on particularly busy or shared servers when filters can be used to capture activity for a single user, database, or application. Filters can be applied to include (Like) or exclude (Not Like) trace data.

To apply a filter, click Column Filters from the Trace Properties dialogue and select the Column on which to filter. In the example shown in Figure 13.3 all requests from server LONDBS1 are excluded from the SQL Trace.

Figure 13.3 Use Trace Filters to Include or Exclude Specific Trace Data

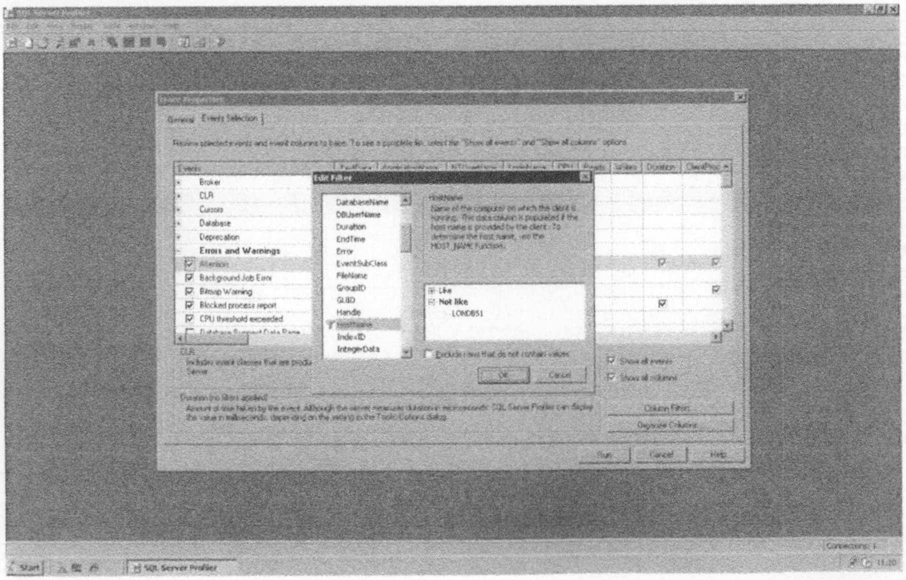

Server-Side Tracing

Server-side tracing reduces the impact of tracing and is recommended when tracing busy production servers or machines where system resources (memory, CPU, etc) are low. Additionally, when traces are run from the server itself there is no network time involved in reporting start times for query execution. Since network time can vary (e.g., latency due to traffic of other network users), tracing across a network can produce inconsistent results.

There are two methods to create a server-side trace. As always a family of stored procedures are provided, which can be cumbersome and difficult to translate to actual events and columns. It is possible to create a trace within Profiler and then script the trace definition. To script the trace definition, select File > Export > Script Trace Definition > For SQL Server 2005–2008.

Open the trace definition in SQL Server Management Studio, and you'll see the sp_trace_create statement to define the trace. Here you'll need to replace InsertFileNameHere with the path to the folder where trace files should be saved (see Figure 13.4). Try to avoid tracing to system drives, or those where data or log files are stored, since this will affect performance of the database server.

Figure 13.4 Trace Definition Created by SQL Profiler

Configuring & Implementing...

Avoid Tracing to System Drives

Try to place the trace files on a dedicated disk with enough capacity for the duration of the trace. Avoid storing trace files on system drives. If the drive does fill, recovering a server from a full system partition is more difficult and time consuming that if a nonsystem partition fills.

Once the destination is configured, run the script and make a note of the TraceID that is returned by the query. The trace is now defined on the server; however, there's an additional step required to start the trace. The system stored procedure sp_trace_setstatus is used to control the trace, and requires parameters TraceID and status. Table 13.2 shows the status parameters. In order to start TraceID 2, we'll need to run sp_trace_setstatus(2,1).

Table 13.2 Status Parameters to Control Server-Side Traces

Status	Description
0	Stop trace
1	Start trace
2	Close trace and remove trace definition

Finally, if you lose track of which traces are running on a server, run Select * from fn_trace_getinto(null) to return details of all traces. Remember that unless you've disabled it there's a default trace running at all times to populate the DMVs; this will be TraceID 1.

Combining System Monitor and Profiler Traces

First introduced to SQL Server 2005, this excellent feature of Profiler allows Administrators to combine a System Monitor (Performance Monitor) trace with a SQL Trace. This presents a single view of system resources (disk, memory, CPU)

with the statements executing at the time; for example, enabling Administrators to correlate high-CPU conditions with a specific stored procedure or T-SQL statement.

Figure 13.5 shows the timeline from System Monitor, which allows a view of hardware utilization. The red vertical bar allows administrators to jump to a particular point (e.g., a CPU spike), and the profiler trace will identify the T-SQL running at the moment of the spike.

Figure 13.5 Combining System
Monitor and Profiler Traces for a Single View

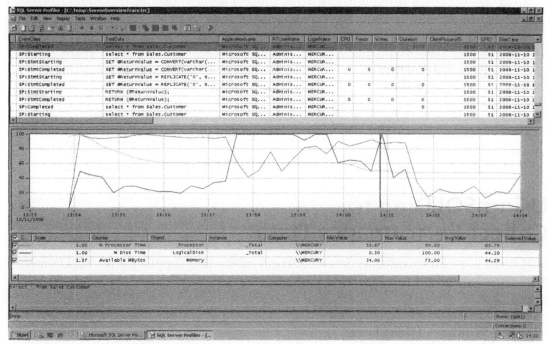

Replaying Traces

SQL Server provides the ability to replay traces; typical scenarios involve capturing a trace from a production server and replaying the trace against a test or preproduction server. This can help when evaluating changes and also with some troubleshooting scenarios. Each statement captured in the trace will be replayed against the target server; this can be helpful in verifying that a fix implemented on a test server does resolve a problem.

There are a minimum set of events required for trace playback; alternately use the Replay trace template. Not all servers can be traced and replayed; for example, if the server is participating in Transactional Replication trace replay isn't possible because of the way transactional replication marks transactions in the log.

Head of the Class...

Working with SQL Trace Data

Capturing trace data on a busy server many generate many gigabytes of data. Using a server-side trace to a file on a local disk will minimize the tracing overhead. However, unless you're looking for a specific event in the trace, often the best way to manage the data is to load the trace data from a flat file into a table. The following function will load trace data from a file into a table:

```
SELECT * INTO srv1_trace FROM::fn_trace_gettable('c:\temp\trace1.trc',
default)
```

Once the data is in a database, analysis with TSQL queries is much easier!

Using SQLDiag to Collect Performance Data

SQLDiag is a command-line, data–collection utility first supplied with SQL Server 2005 that can useful for collecting performance data. SQLDiag collects the following:

- Windows Event Logs
- SQL Server Configuration details
- System Monitor Performance logs
- SQL Server Profiler Trace data
- SQL Server blocking information

Essentially, SQLDiag doesn't do anything that couldn't be achieved separately—each of these tools could be run independently, however SQLDiag it makes it easier to start and stop data collection and ensures all relevant information is collected each time data capture is run.

EXERCISE 13.1

RUNNING A TRACE WITH SQL PROFILER

This exercise will demonstrate running a trace with SQL Profiler. Initially, you'll get started with a basic trace using SQL Profiler:

1. Launch SQL Profiler from Start > Programs > Microsoft SQL Server 2008 > Performance Tools.

2. Connect to a valid SQL Server instance.

3. Name the trace.

4. Select Standard template.

5. Click the Event Selection tab.

6. Check both Show All Events and Show All Columns check boxes.

7. Enable all events in the Errors and warnings Event Class.

8. Click Run to start the trace.

Next, you can fire an error message from a query window and then correlate this in the SQL Profiler trace:

1. Start SQL Server Management Studio.

2. Connect to the same instance SQL Profiler is monitoring.

3. In a query window, run the following command:
   raiserror('trace error text', 16,1)

Finally, validate the SQL trace has seen the error message:

1. Return to SQL Profiler.

2. Pause the trace to prevent any new events being added.

3. Locate the error (usually highlighted in red) with the text 'trace error text'.

Locks, Blocking, and Deadlocks

Concurrency control is a vital part of any relational database management system and in SQL Server this is implemented primarily through Locking. Locking involves reserving resources (usually data pages) for a particular purpose; this can affect the availability of those resources. When a single task reserves lots of resources or runs for an excessive time blocking can occur, which affects system performance. Deadlocks are a situation when two tasks each want to reserve a resource that the other already has locked—a vicious circle occurs where neither can complete without the other first releasing its locks.

Locking

Locking is responsible for ensuring database users don't interfere with each other, and is an essential component of any Relational Database Management system. Locking provides concurrency control within the database engine. A transaction is one or more actions, treated as a unit of work. There are a set of database properties that help understand transactions and the importance of locking:

- **Atomic** An atomic transaction must either complete or fail. No aspect of the transaction must be allowed to succeed or fail without all changes succeeding or failing. Should one modification fail, the whole transaction should be rolled back.

- **Consistent** Data must be consistent when a transaction completes. Data integrity must not be compromised by a transaction.

- **Isolated** User transactions should be isolated from each other. Data affected by one transaction can be accessed by other transactions only in the state it was before the transaction began, or after the transaction completes.

- **Durable** Once a transaction has completed the changes must persist, even if there is a crash or system failure.

SQL Server uses careful transaction management to enforce Atomicity and Consistency. The Transaction Log ensures transaction durability since all changes are first written to the transaction log. Finally, Isolation is provided by locking within the database engine.

Blocking

We should consider locking to be completely normal activity within the database engine. When there are lots of users working on a SQL Server database or in a situation with a poor index strategy or badly written queries there can be many thousands of locks. If a transaction holds many locks or holds locks for a long time, eventually this can cause blocking. Blocking occurs when a transaction is waiting for a lock on a resource, usually because a lock is already held by another task.

Deadlocks

Excessive blocking can significantly impact performance and as such, it's really important to get visibility of tasks that are blocking each other and investigate options to help them coexist. Severe blocking can lead to deadlocks, which will result in SQL Server ending one session, causing a rollback. In a deadlock situation a vicious circle can occur when two (sometimes more) tasks, each already holding locks, are waiting for locks that the other holds. Figure 13.6 shows an illustration. It's called a deadlock because both processes could wait endlessly for the other to release the locks it needs unless SQL Server intervened. There's a mechanism within SQL Server to detect and end deadlocks whereby SQL Server will end the task that is least expensive to rollback.

Figure 13.6 Deadlock Scenario

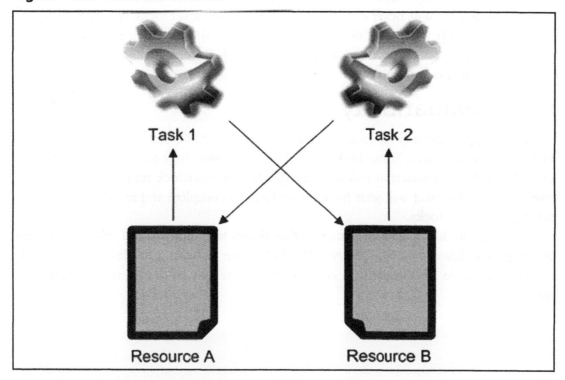

Transaction Isolation Levels

SQL Server provides five isolation levels for transactions, which include various pessimistic to optimistic locking strategies. These isolation levels provide control over a balance between concurrency and data integrity. Isolation levels may be selected based on application requirements for data consistency and user concurrency. Isolation levels may provide good concurrency (nonlocking), but may provide inconsistent data; this may be acceptable in some scenarios. In other cases, data consistency is important, as such performance may be sacrificed in favor of consistent data.

Lock Escalation

SQL Server always tries to lock the fewest resources possible to maximize concurrency. Fewer locks provides good concurrency but there is an overhead in system resources while managing locks. There are times when SQL Server is managing so many individual locks that it becomes more efficient to increase a single lock on an object at a higher level—this is lock escalation.

If a task holds a large number of row or key-range locks, these may be escalated to a table lock. If SQL Server initially takes page locks, these can be escalated to table locks. SQL Server will never escalate from row to page level locks. A new feature introduced in SQL Server 2008 is that with partitioned tables, lock escalation may occur to the partition level, instead of the table. SQL Profiler includes an event for lock escalation (Lock:Escalation).

Lock Compatibility

There are approximately 22 lock types in SQL Server 2008, each providing a different lock type for resources. Some lock types allow other processes to read the data, too (also depends on transaction isolation level), whereas other lock types require exclusive access to data and will wait for existing tasks to complete and release locks before taking their own locks.

There's a lock compatibility matrix that shows the logic around which locks can be taken simultaneously. SQL Server Books Online includes a full lock compatibility matrix, and Table 13.3 contains a compatibility summary of the six most common lock types.

Table 13.3 Common Lock Compatibility Matrix

	Existing Lock					
Requested Lock	**IS**	**S**	**U**	**IX**	**SIX**	**X**
Intent Shared (IS)	✓	✓	✓	✓	✓	✗
Shared (S)	✓	✓	✓	✗	✗	✗
Update (U)	✓	✓	✗	✗	✗	✗
Intent Exclusive (IX)	✓	✗	✗	✓	✗	✗
Shared with Intent Exclusive (SIX)	✓	✗	✗	✗	✗	✗
Exclusive (X)	✗	✗	✗	✗	✗	✗

Detecting and Resolving Locking Problems

SQL Server 2008 Management Studio has an Activity Monitor that shows sessions and their state (whether they're running, waiting, or sleeping). Activity Monitor is available by right-clicking the instance name within Management Studio and features a new look for SQL Server 2008 (see Figure 13.7).

Figure 13.7 Activity Monitor in SQL Server 2008 Management Studio

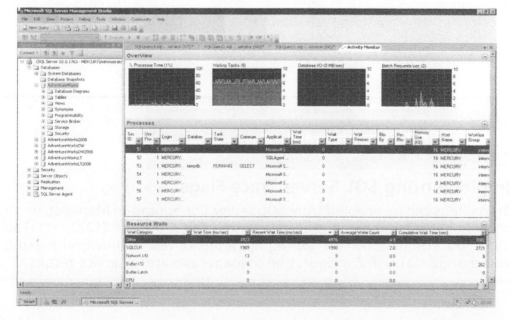

SQL Server Profiler provides good information; in particular, there's a blocked process report that can capture locking details for sessions exceeding the blocked process threshold (controlled by sp_configure). In situations where there's an intermittent performance problem and blocking is a suspect, the blocked process report can be useful. There are a number of DMVs that provide visibility of locks held by specific sessions and any blocked processes. The DMVs sys.dm_exec_requests shows sessions that are suspended waiting for a lock. Additionally, querying sys.dm_tran_locks shows more detailed locking information.

If blocking problems are serious there's a good chance deadlocks may also occur. SQL Server Profiler provides a good level of information, including Deadlock Chain (all sessions involved in the deadlock). Profiler can also capture a deadlock graph, which reveals the commands being executed, locks held, and the session nominated as the deadlock victim.

Sometimes deadlocks can be few and far between, but they can still cause problems and a continuous Profiler trace may seem excessive to identify the problem. In this scenario Trace Flag 1222 can be useful since this will output deadlock details to the SQL Server Error Log.

Once deadlock information has been captured in the SQL Server Error Log, review the processes that are conflicting. Sometimes they're different processes and at other times they're multiple instances of the same query or stored procedure. Try to rework the query or stored procedure to overcome the locking problem, perhaps reduce the size of the transaction, create a new index, or use an alternative join strategy.

Configuring & Implementing...

Implementing SQL Server Trace Flags

Trace Flags can be enabled from SQL Server Configuration Manager, using the –T1222 startup parameter or by using DBCC traceon (1222, –1). The DBCC traceon method will not require a service restart, however making the change through Configuration Manager requires a service restart.

EXERCISE 13.2

MONITOR DEADLOCKS

This exercise will demonstrate how to enable a trace flag to proactively monitor for deadlocks within SQL Server:

1. Start SQL Server Configuration Manager from Start > Programs > Microsoft SQL Server 2008 > Configuration Tools.

2. Select SQL Server Services from the left-hand pane.

3. Locate the SQL Server instance where the trace flag is to be added in the right-hand pane.

4. Double-click the SQL Server service.

5. Click the Advanced tab.

6. Locate the startup parameters field.

7. Move cursor to the right-most position.

8. Add a semicolon and T1222 to the end of the string—the command should finish up something like this:

    -dC:\Program Files\Microsoft SQL Server\MSSQL.1\MSSQL\DATA\ master.mdf;-eC:\Program Files\Microsoft SQL Server\MSSQL.3\ MSSQL\LOG\ERRORLOG;-lC:\Program Files\Microsoft SQL Server\ MSSQL.3\MSSQL\DATA\mastlog.ldf; -T8029; T1222

9. Click OK.

10. Restart the SQL Server service for the trace flag to take effect.

To view the output of the traceflag—that is, to monitor whether any deadlocks have occurred:

1. Start SQL Server Management Studio.

2. Expand the Management folder.

3. Expand SQL Server logs.

4. Double-click the log file.

    Alternately, run sp_readerrorlog from a query window to read the contents of the active error log.

Guide to the DYNAMIC Management Views (DMVs)

DMVs are almost certainly the single most useful tool for troubleshooting and performance tuning for SQL Server databases. DMVs and DYNAMIC Management Functions (DMFs) provide Administrators with a simple yet powerful insight into the workings of SQL Server and hardware resources (disk, memory, CPU). There were 89 DMVs introduced to SQL Server 2005 and 47 new DMVs released with SQL Server 2008. These can be grouped in two broad types:

- Server Scoped (require VIEW SERVER STATE permission on the server)

- Database Scoped (require VIEW DATABASE STATE permission on the database)

DMVs can be categorized as follows (there are others that don't fit into these categories):

- Common Language Runtime

- Cryptographic

- Database Mirroring

- Execution

- Extended Events

- Filestream

- Full-Text Search

- Index

- I/O

- Query Notifications

- Replication

- Service Broker

- SQL Server Operating System

- Transaction

As mentioned in the Profiler section earlier in this chapter, there's a SQL trace running continuously in the background and cycling itself while SQL Server is running. This trace gathers the data used by the DMVs; you should be aware of those that provide snapshot information and others that provide data cumulatively since the last service restart. The trace data is not persisted anywhere within SQL Server, although this is possible (covered in the Performance Data collection, later).

DMVs provide information that often could be reached only by querying metadata or system tables. SQL Server administrators often like a real-time view of current server activity, and they might use the Activity Monitor within Management Studio, or if they have a background with SQL Server 2000 or earlier. They'll probably use SP_WHO or SP_WHO2—both provide session level activity view. There are, however, a couple of DMVs in Table 13.4 that provide this information plus much more.

Table 13.4 Using DMVs to View Current Activity within SQL Server

DYNAMIC Management View	Purpose
sys.dm_exec_requests	Provides information about a request currently executed by SQL Server
Sys.dm_exec_sessions	An overview of all current sessions (SPIDs) within SQL Server

It's easy to SELECT all data within a DMV, however there are great opportunities to write useful queries to interrogate DMVs. One such example is sys.dm_db_index_physcial_stats. This DMV shows the level of index fragmentation. In previous versions this was available from the DBCC SHOWCONTIG command, however this was very intensive for Disk IO, and the results were cumbersome and difficult to manipulate without significant effort. The following example shows a query that categorizes index fragmentation as High (more than 30%), Medium (less than 30%), and Low (less than 5%), ordering the results by greatest fragmentation first since this is where we should pay most attention:

```
SELECT

    OBJECT_NAME(indstat.object_id, indstat.database_id) AS obj_name,
    QUOTENAME(sysind.name) [index_name],
    CASE

        WHEN avg_fragmentation_in_percent < 5 THEN 'LOW'
        WHEN avg_fragmentation_in_percent < 30 THEN 'MEDIUM'
        ELSE 'HIGH'

    END as frag_level,
    indstat.*
```

```
FROM sys.dm_db_index_physical_stats (DB_ID(), NULL, NULL, NULL, 'LIMITED')
AS indstat

INNER JOIN sys.indexes sysind ON indstat.object_id = sysind.object_id AND
indstat.index_id = sysind.index_id

ORDER BY avg_fragmentation_in_percent DESC
```

The output of the sys.dm_db_index_physcial_stats can be used as the input to an index maintenance job. In this scenario it is possible to build a SQL Server Agent job that takes action based on the output of the sys.dm_db_index_physcial_stats, such as an index reorganize (for indexes with low or medium fragmentation) or rebuilding indexes (for those indexes with heavy fragmentation).

Extending the idea of good indexing maintenance, SQL Server can also suggest indexes that would help improve query performance. This information is provided by a group of DMVs, the most useful of which is sys.dm_db_missing_index_details. Using the output from this DMV, we can generate the CREATE INDEX statement to add the new index and improve performance! However, there numerous limitations of the missing indexes feature; for example, it doesn't consider the cost of maintaining an index and it doesn't specify an order for columns to be used in the index.

There are DMVs such as sys.dm_os_* that reflect aspects of the SQL Server Operating System and can be useful barometers for understanding more about SQL Server Internals, system memory consumption, requirements, and the like. The following query uses the sys.dm_exec_query_stats to provide the top 10 queries consuming most CPU:

```
SELECT TOP 10

    SUM(qrystat.total_worker_time) AS Total_CPU_Time,

    SUM(qrystat.execution_count) AS Number_of_Executions,

    COUNT(*) as Number_of_Statements,

    qrystat.plan_handle

FROM

    sys.dm_exec_query_stats qrystat

GROUP BY qrystat.plan_handle

ORDER BY sum(qrystat.total_worker_time) DESC
```

EXERCISE 13.3

REVIEW USEFUL DMVS

Take a look at the following DMVs to become familiar with the contents:

`sys.dm_exec_requests`

`sys.dm_exec_sessions`

`sys.dm_exec_sql_text`

`sys.dm_exec_query_stats`

`sys.dm_os_wait_stats`

`sys.dm_db_index_usage_stats`

`sys.dm_db_index_operational_stats`

`sys.dm_db_missing_index_details`

Partitioning

Organizations collect more data and retain data for longer than ever before. The phenomenal growth of the storage manufacturing industry over the past 10 years is a testament to continually increasing data collection. Given adequate capacity, storing large quantities of data within SQL Server is no big problem, until we need to retrieve some data or perform any maintenance. New challenges arise from retrieving single rows or range searches of multiterabyte databases, while maintaining good response times.

Partitioning was first available in SQL Server 7.0, although in different versions this application logic was required to determine the partition holding a specific row. In SQL Server 2000 it was possible to define a view that unified the data and in SQL Server 2005 table partitions were completely transparent to applications. SQL Server 2008 Enterprise edition provides the next generation of table and index partitioning, which introduces a round-robin thread model to satisfy queries accessing multiple partitions. Additionally, SQL Server 2008 includes new level of lock escalation, which means locks can escalate from row or page locks to partition locks. This differs from SQL Server 2005, where row or page locks could be escalated directly to table locks.

Horizontal Partitioning

Horizontal Partitioning involves dividing a large table into a number of smaller tables, each containing all columns for a subset of rows. Dividing rows into separate tables means each table is much smaller and access times are typically more efficient, and therefore faster. Partitioning maintains data integrity, and it is possible to partition based on any column; however date ranges are most common for partitioning. This allows administrators to separate recent (usually more active) data from older archive data, improving the performance of data access to the frequently accessed data (usually recent rows).

Vertical Partitioning

This method splits a large table into a number of smaller tables; each table contains every row, but a subset of all columns. The database normalization process provides vertical partitioning by removing any attributes not dependent on the primary key, joining these with a primary key/ foreign key constraint. Consider this method with caution, since retrieving all columns for a given row will require a join between the tables, which could be expensive in terms of performance.

Filegroups

Successful implementations of table partitioning improve availability and performance of the entire table since many operations can be performed in parallel. Availability can be improved because backup and restore operations can be performed on an individual filegroup. Additionally performance can be improved because CHECKDB and regular scan and seek operations can be performed in parallel when partitions are implemented on their own filegroups.

It's common for SQL Server databases to grow to hundreds of gigabytes, and multiterabyte databases are no longer unusual. It's likely that the fastest disk storage and backup target full backups will take many hours to complete. Filegroups help by allowing partial backups, or by allowing backups to run in parallel. Every database has a primary filegroup, and if you're going to create multiple data files it's recommended to create these on a secondary filegroup.

Partitions can operate within a single filegroup, however it is recommended that to gain the full benefit of table partitioning, each partition reside on its own filegroup. This approach provides the benefit that each filegroup (therefore partition) can be stored on a different disk, meaning there are lots of benefits in I/O throughput and therefore database performance. The following example creates a new database with a primary filegroup (required) and four further filegroups, each with one data file:

```
CREATE DATABASE Orders
Create FILEGROUP OrdersGroup1
(NAME = OrdersGrp1Fi1_dat,
```

```
        FILENAME = 'F:\MDF\OrdersG1Fil_dat.ndf',
        SIZE = 5120MB,
        FILEGROWTH = 1024MB),
FILEGROUP OrdersGroup2
(NAME = OrdersGrp2Fil_dat,
        FILENAME = 'G:\MDF\OrdersG2Fil_dat.ndf',
        SIZE = 5120MB,
        FILEGROWTH = 1024MB),
FILEGROUP OrdersGroup3
(NAME = OrdersGrp3Fil_dat,
        FILENAME = 'H:\MDF\OrdersG3Fil_dat.ndf',
        SIZE = 5120MB,
        FILEGROWTH = 1024MB),
FILEGROUP OrdersGroup4
(NAME = OrdersGrp4Fil_dat,
        FILENAME = 'I:\MDF\OrdersG4Fil_dat.ndf',
        SIZE = 5120MB,
        FILEGROWTH = 1024MB)
LOG ON
(NAME = Orders_log,
        FILENAME = 'E:\LDF\Orders_log.ldf',
        SIZE = 5MB,
        FILEGROWTH = 1MB)
GO
```

The concepts and goals of partitioning are fairly easy to grasp; the hardest part is understanding the language around the implementation of table partitioning. Essentially, there are two concepts introduced by a comprehensive wizard and accompanied by corresponding T-SQL commands.

Selecting a Partition Key and Number of Partitions

Any column can be used as a partition key and this column is the logical division between partitions. The partition function implements the partition key, but not the data placement on disk. It's important to know the data and data access patterns since this knowledge will help select the partition and number of partitions. If there are logical boundaries or grouping to data, use these as the partition key; for example, if orders are typically queried by calendar months or fiscal quarters, these could be a natural choice as a partition key.

Partition Function

The partition function is used to map rows to partitions based on the partition key. The partition function specifies the boundary between each of the partitions. LEFT or RIGHT is used to determine in which partition the boundary value resides; LEFT is default. The following example creates a partition function that partitions orders based on order date:

```
CREATE PARTITION FUNCTION [pf_Orders](datetime) AS RANGE LEFT FOR
VALUES(N'2002-01-01T00:00:00',
N'2003-01-01T00:00:00',
N'2004-01-01T00:00:00')
```

This statement will create four partitions (despite only three values being listed). The boundary values are shown as "equal to or less than" since the partition is created with RANGE LEFT. The data is split between the partitions as follows:

Partition Number	Partition 1	Partition 2	Partition 3	Partition 4
RANGE LEFT	<= 2002-01-01	> 2002-01-01 AND <= 2003-01-01	2003-01-01 AND <= 2004-01-01	> 2004-01-01

Partition Scheme

The placement of data is determined by the partition function. The partition scheme controls mapping between partitions and filegroups. Performance gain can often be realized by using a 1-1 mapping between partitions and filegroups, and further by placing each filegroup on its own logical disk.

The following example creates a partition scheme, mapping each partition to its own filegroup:

```
CREATE PARTITION SCHEME [ps_Orders] AS PARTITION [pf_Orders]
TO ([fgSalesOrders1], [fgSalesOrders2], [fgSalesOrders3], [fgSalesOrders4])
```

The partition scheme definition will map the partitions to filegroups as shown in Table 13.5.

Table 13.5 Sample Partition Scheme

Partition Number	Partition 1	Partition 2	Partition 3	Partition 4
RANGE LEFT	<= 2002-01-01	> 2002-01-01 AND <= 2003-01-01	2003-01-01 AND <= 2004-01-01	> 2004-01-01
Filegroup	fgSalesOrders1	fgSalesOrders2	fgSalesOrders3	fgSalesOrders4

Moving Data between Partitions

Partitioning provides performance and manageability benefits and migrating to a partitioned table is relatively pain free. There are three options for moving data between partitions:

- Split Partition
- Merge partition
- Switch Partition

The Partition splitting is implemented with the partition function and alters the boundary between partitions to divide an existing partition. A split commonly is used when adding a new partition at the end of an existing range. Merge partition again is administered with the partition function and can be used to combine two partitions. Both merge and split use the ALTER PARTITION FUNCTION TSQL command:

```
ALTER PARTITION FUNCTION pQuantity()
SPLIT RANGE(500)
```

Finally, probably the most useful function is SWITCH partition, which is useful when moving a complete partition. Be aware that ALTER TABLE… SWITCH is considered schema modification, therefore requires schema modification (Sch-M) lock on the table. Using the SWITCH functionality, it's possible to implement a sliding window, whereby partitioning automatically manages the partitions. Here's an example of the sliding window:

- Partition 1 – Current week
- Partition 2 – Previous 2 weeks
- Partition 3 – Previous 3 months

- Partition 4 – Previous 3 to 6 months

- Partition 5 – Everything older than 6 months

In this scenario the partitioning functionality will provide automatic management for partitions and optimal performance for recent data. Older data is still available, however data retrieval times will likely be longer since there are large indexes.

Performance Data Collection

Performance data collection is one of the most significant new features for SQL Server Administrators. Performance data collection builds on the strengths of the DMVs to provide long-term data storage and reporting based on this data. Performance data collection will assist Administrators with troubleshooting, performance tuning, and capacity planning.

Performance Data Collection Explained

The performance data collector is a great new feature and really easy to get up and running in SQL Server 2008 to collect and store performance data, providing reports on the collected data. The data collector itself can be considered a SQL Server client consisting of data sources, an executable called dcexe.exe, data warehouse database, SQL Agent jobs, and Integration Services. Available sources include System Monitor (Perfmon) counters, DMVs, SQL Profiler traces, and application data/logs.

The performance data warehouse builds on the strength of the data provided by DMVs by collecting and reporting on this data. Performance data collection was designed to be used as an enterprise data repository, gathering data about all SQL Servers in an environment. Centralizing data collection and storage reduces the overhead on each monitored server and provides a single point for reporting. The reports provided by the performance data warehouse provide information useful when troubleshooting a problem (i.e., a system performance baseline that is self-documenting) and with trending and capacity planning. The data can be useful for retrospective troubleshooting as well as planning for the future.

The performance data collection feature consists of two distinct components, the Management Data Warehouse (MDW) and Data Collections (DC). The MDW is used to store the data used for reporting. Data Collectors are used to extract performance data from target SQL Server instances and to load this data into the MDW. The feature is disabled by default and both components require configuration prior to use. Data collection can be performed only by SQL Server 2008 instance and targets must be SQL Server 2008.

Management Data Warehouse

The Management Data Warehouse (MDW) is the relational database used to store the data collected from the monitored servers (data collection targets). The MDW is just a normal relational database hosted on SQL Server 2008 that needs to be configured by the Administrator before data collection can begin. The MDW can be used to capture data from the same instance, or from remote instances. In many deployment scenarios, it is intended that MDW is used as an enterprisewide repository for system and custom collection sets from many target servers. The management reports are produced using the data stored in the MDW.

Configuring MDW

The MDW must be set up prior to data collection being configured since the MDW must be supplied as the target for data collection. To launch the MDW configuration wizard within Management Studio, within the Management folder, right-click Data Collection and choose Configure Management Data Warehouse as shown in Figure 13.8.

Figure 13.8 Launch the Wizard to
Configure Management Data Warehouse

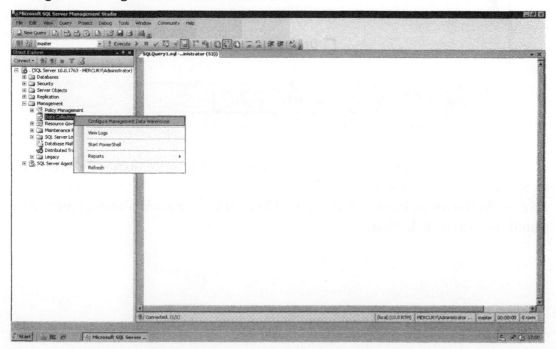

Launching the configuration wizard, the first screen displays a Welcome notice. Click Next to continue, as shown in Figure 13.9.

Figure 13.9 Welcome Screen for Data Management Warehouse

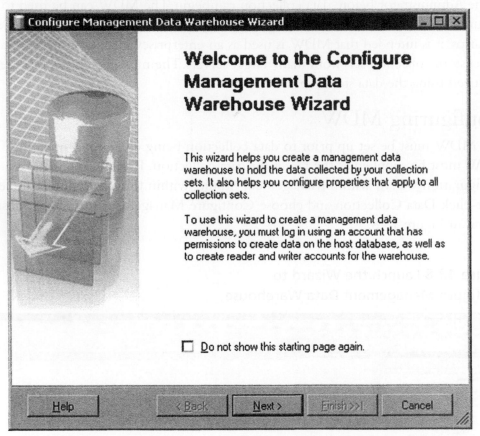

The next step in the wizard is to select either to Create or upgrade a MDW or to Set up data collection. Since data collection requires an MDW, it should be set up first. As shown in Figure 13.10, verify Configure or upgrade a management data warehouse, then click Next.

Figure 13.10 Select Configure or Upgrade an MDW to Set Up the MDW

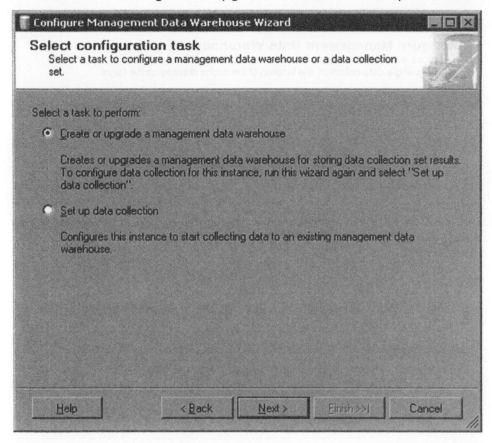

Next, the wizard requests details of the database to be used as the MDW. In most cases, we'll need to create a new database to use for this purpose; otherwise, choose an existing database from the drop-down list. Click the New button to create a new database (shown in Figure 13.11).

Figure 13.11 Configure the Database to Use as MDW

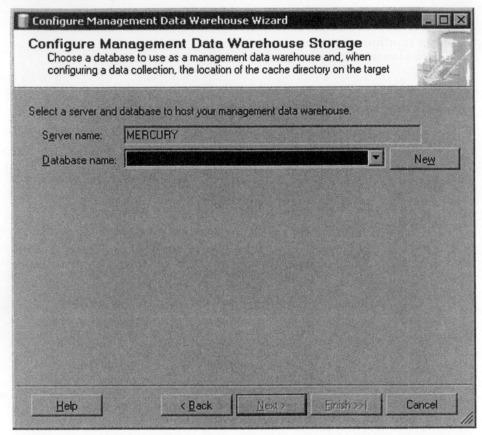

Configure the new database by entering a database name and configuring the locations for data and log files, if necessary (see Figure 13.12). It's worth mentioning that by default the MDW creates the new database in SIMPLE recovery mode, meaning transaction log management is not necessary. Administrators requiring point-in-time recovery for the MDW should change the database to FULL recovery mode and take regular transaction log backups.

Figure 13.12 Configure the Name and Location for the MDW Database

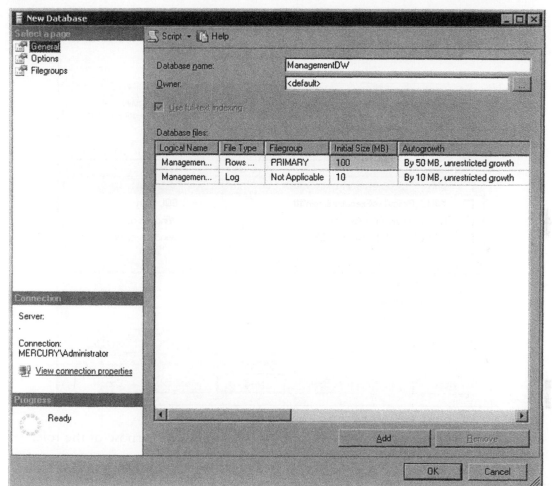

The next step in the MDW process is security configuration, where it is possible to map database users to MDW roles (see Figure 13.13).

Figure 13.13 Map Logins to MDW Roles

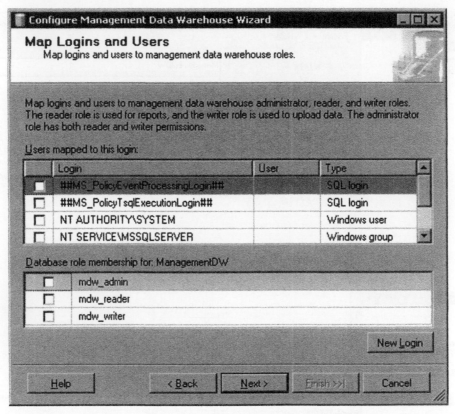

Table 13.6 summarizes each role and the permissions or purpose of the role.

Table 13.6 Roles and Their Permissions

Role	Permissions
mdw_admin	Read/ write/ update/ delete access to MDW
mdw_writer	Allowed to insert/ upload data to the MDW—required for data collectors
mdw_reader	Read access to MDW

To complete MDW configuration, verify the settings on the summary step of the wizard and click Finish. The MDW setup is now complete and we can progress to configure data collection.

Configuring Data Collection

Data collection is configured using the MDW as the target for collected data. Data collection is performed on every configured server using a usermode process called dcexec.exe. This standalone process is responsible for collecting data as defined in a collection set. Two types of data collections can be defined: System or Custom data collections. There are three system data collections listed in Table 13.7.

Table 13.7 System Data Collections

System Data Collection Set	Description
Disk Usage	Tracks disk space usage information for data and log files
Server Activity	Records systemwide performance data such as memory, disk, CPU, and data from the SQL Server operating system
Query Statistics	Stores queries and execution plans for frequently executed or resource-intensive queries

In addition, Administrators can define custom data collections. Custom data collections can consist of one of four collection sets (see Table 13.8). Custom collection sets can be useful to establish a complete system baseline.

Table 13.8 Custom Data Collection Sets

Set	Description
T-SQL Query	Runs a query defined by an Administrator and stores the result in the MDW
SQL Trace	Executes a SQL Trace; if configured will upload the trace data to MDW
Performance Counters	Used to collect System Monitor (Performance Monitor) counters related to SQL Server
Query Activity	Collects queries and execution plans; collects same data as Query Statistics

Configuring & Implementing...

Show Caution with Custom Collections Using SQL Trace

Misconfigured SQL Traces can harm server performance. SQL Traces can be very resource intensive when implemented in any form (e.g., SQL Profiler, server side traces, or custom data collectors). Be cautious when adding events and filters to the trace and be aware of the overhead to running a trace.

Data Collection Caching

Data collection can be configured in one of two caching modes: either cached or noncached. Depending on the scenario, a number of factors should be considered to decide which mode to configure:

- Cached mode: Data collection runs on one schedule and temporarily stores collected data on the server. Periodically (on a separate schedule) a different job will upload data from the temporary location to the MDW.

- Noncached mode: Data collection and data upload run on the same schedule. Data is collected and directly uploaded to the MDW.

These logins and roles are created on the server carrying out data collection (see Table 13.9).

Table 13.9 Data Collection Roles and Permissions

Role	Permissions
dc_admin	Complete administrative permissions (Create, Read, Update, Delete)
dc_operator	For Administrator running and configuring Collection Sets (Read, Update access)
dc_proxy	Required to list and view collector packages

Management Data Warehouse Reports

The real benefit of the performance data collection feature is reporting (see Figure 13.14). The reports present the data available in the MDW and reveal the true value of the feature. The three system data collections each have a predefined report available, and other reports can be built as required. The MDW reports can be useful for establishing a system baseline, troubleshooting, and capacity planning.

Figure 13.14 Reporting Available on MDW

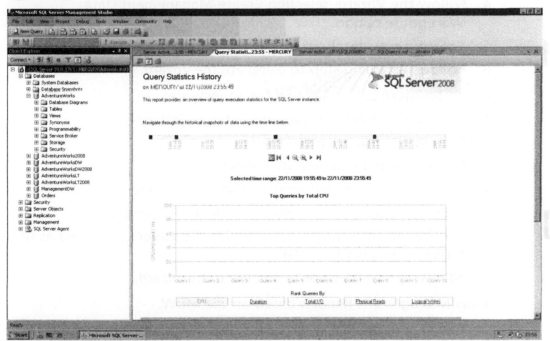

The performance data collection feature enables DBAs to monitor and report on system performance, availability, and capacity on a number of servers with relative ease and simplicity. The Performance Data Collection solution is flexible and adaptable with custom collections and reports configurable if required.

EXERCISE 13.4

PERFORMANCE DATA COLLECTOR

In this exercise you will configure the management data warehouse and performance data collector for a single server.

1. Start SQL Server Management Studio.
2. Expand the Management folder.
3. Right-click Data Collection and choose Manage Data Warehouse.
4. Follow the Wizard, selecting Create Management Data Warehouse option.
5. Create a new database for the MDW.
6. Follow remaining step to complete the wizard.

Now, configure data collection for an instance:

1. Start Management Studio on the target instance.
2. Expand the Management folder.
3. Right-click and enable Data Collection.
4. Right-click and choose Manage Data Warehouse.
5. Follow the wizard selecting Setup data collection.
6. Specify the name and credentials for the server configured as the MDW in the previous steps.
7. Follow remaining steps to complete the wizard.

View Management Reports based on the MDW:

1. Connect to the SQL instance hosting the MDW.
2. Expand the Management folder.
3. Right-click on Data Collection.
4. Choose Reports > Management Data Warehouse > Server Activity History.

Resource Governor

The Resource Governor is a much-awaited feature of SQL Server 2008 and will be one of a small number of features that is useful enough to be sufficient motivation for a number of customers. Server consolidation is more popular than ever with customers, realizing many benefits of better hardware utilization and more cost-effective database deployments. However consolidation does have some drawbacks. The most common objections to server consolidation is performance, because shared (multi-instance) servers and shared SQL Server instances can introduce challenges in ensuring consistent performance for all database users. Common problems arise from mixed users where regular OnLine Transaction Processing (OLTP) users mix with reporting users on the same instance; examples can be found where databases for the finance department combine with sales order databases. In this situation, normal database traffic consisting of inserts, updates, and deletes can conflict with the workload generated by reports run by finance users executing month- or year-end reports based on historic sales data.

The Resource Governor was introduced to SQL Server 2008 to provide predictable performance for mission-critical workloads. Resource Governor achieves predictable performance by monitoring and reserving minimum levels of critical resources such as CPU and memory for specific tasks or groups of tasks.

Resource Governor Concepts

The Resource Governor consists of three key concepts: Resource Pools, Workload Groups, and Classification Functions. The Resource Governor exists to manage minimum resources available for different groups of users or tasks. However the governor is more intelligent than simply dividing resources among users; if resources are unused elsewhere on a server, a given user can be permitted to use excess of their quota (up to a maximum allocation) until a time when another user or process requires the resource (memory or CPU).

This section introduces each concept and uses an example to illustrate the purpose and implementation of the concept. The example relates to a college whereby requests from lecturers should receive priority over requests received from students.

Resource Pools

Resource pools are used to manage minimum and maximum restrictions on physical server resources. Conceptually, Resource Pools enable multiple virtual SQL Server instances to operate within a single physical instance. Each pool (virtual instance) is allocated a minimum and maximum CPU and memory resources. There is a limit of 18 custom resource pools in addition to the two resource pools created when SQL Server 2008 is installed:

- INTERNAL: Use for SQL Server internal system processes
- DEFAULT: Used by workloads unassigned to any workload group

The combination of minimum values across all pools cannot exceed 100% and the maximum value can be anywhere between the minimum value and 100%. In addition to Min and Max settings, Resource pools have two further calculated values; Effective Maximum and Shared % (see Table 13.10). The Effective Maximum is determined by calculating the max value of a Resource pool and the minimum values of all other Resource pools. The internal pool has highest priority of all Resource pools since this is where internal processes are handled; it is not exposed to effective or share maximums.

Table 13.10 Resource Pool Calculated Values

Resource Pool	Min %	Max %	Calculated Effective Max %	Calculated Shared %	Effective Max Calculation Explained	Shared % Calculation Explained
Internal	0	100	100	0	Not applicable to internal pool	Not applicable to internal pool
Default	0	100	50	50	min(100, 100–50) = 50	50–0=50
Pool-A	10	100	60	50	min(100, 100–40) = 60	60–10=50
Pool-B	35	90	85	10	min(90, 100–15) = 85	85–35=10
Pool-C	5	70	55	50	min(80, 100–45) = 55	55–5=50

The following T-SQL can be used to create two resource pools, the first for lecturers and the second for students:

```
CREATE RESOURCE POOL rscpLecturers
WITH
( MAX_CPU_PERCENT = 100,
  MIN_CPU_PERCENT = 50)
GO

CREATE RESOURCE POOL rscpStudents
WITH
```

```
(MAX_CPU_PERCENT = 50,
MIN_CPU_PERCENT = 0)

GO
```

Workload Groups

The Workload Group makes managing the Resource Governor easier. The Workload Group makes it easier to assign user session requests to a specific resource pool. Workload groups also make it easier to monitor resource consumption within each Resource pool. Workload groups may be moved between Resource pools by the administrator if a particular Resource pool becomes too busy or overloaded.

Similar to Resource pools, administrators can create their own Workload Groups and there are two groups created when SQL Server is installed:

- INTERNAL: Use for internal SQL Server operations
- DEFAULT: All unassigned session requests are serviced by this workload group

Here's the T-SQL required to create a group for two workload groups:

```
CREATE WORKLOAD GROUP grpLecturers
WITH
(IMPORTANCE = MEDIUM)
CREATE WORKLOAD GROUP grpStudents
WITH
(IMPORTANCE = LOW)
```

Classification Function

The classification function is created to identify incoming requests to SQL Server and map these incoming requests to a workload group. The classification function is a user-defined function (UDF) and is created as a scalar valued function. The function can use any valid property to classify a new session, such as Username, Hostname, or IP address.

Only one UDF can be designated as a classifier at any one time. Consider performance of the UDF when creating the function since it will be used to evaluate every incoming session. The Dedicated Administrator Connection (DAC) is not exposed to classification; as such the DAC can be used to trouble-shoot performance problems relating to classification. Once the classifier function has been defined, it should be assigned to the Resource Governor, followed by the reconfigure statement:

```
ALTER RESOURCE GOVERNOR
WITH (CLASSIFIER_FUNCTION = dbo.func_Session_Classifier)
```

Configuring & Implementing...

Always Enable DAC When Using Resource Governor

All new sessions are subject to the classification function. Enable Dedicated Admin Connection to provide access for troubleshooting since this connection is not subject to classification.

Validate Configuration

The Resource Governor should be enabled before use (is disabled by default). Configuration changes can be made dynamically and don't require a service restart, however the following instruction should be used after any changes to bring these into effect:

```
ALTER RESOURCE GOVERNOR RECONFIGURE
```

Use the following DYNAMIC Management Views (DMVs) to verify configuration is as intended:

```
sys.dm_resource_governor_resource_pools
sys.dm_resource_governor_workload_groups
```

Resource Governor Summary

The Resource Governor is an important new feature to manage resource allocation among groups of users. The following simplified pseudo-steps illustrate the process an incoming session steps through in order to be allocated resources by the governor:

1. Session begins.
2. Classification function executes.
3. Workload Group membership determined; otherwise use Default.
4. Query executes within specified resource pool.

Summary of Exam Objectives

This chapter provided an overview of performance tuning in SQL Server 2008, including an introduction to tracing with SQL profiler, an overview of locking and blocking, the basics of Dynamic Management Views and Performance Data Collection. Additionally we looked at how the Resource Governor can be used to manage mixed workloads to ensure minimum resource availability.

We also looked at table partitioning – a technology useful when maintenance (backup, reindexing, checkdb) become cumbersome with particularly large tables. Partitioning provides the option to separate a large table into a number of smaller tables – which is completely transparent to the application.

Exam Objectives Fast Track

Tracing

- ☑ Use SQL Profiler to capture the statements being executed on a server for performance review/ analysis.

- ☑ There can be an overhead with running traces, consider how many events you capture, any filters you apply and where the trace is run.

- ☑ Trace data saved directly to a database or to a file then imported into a database for easier analysis.

Locks, Blocking, and Deadlocks

- ☑ Locking and blocking is normal in a database – but if frequency is excessive they can lead to performance problems.

- ☑ Deadlocks are always damaging for performance – use SQL Profiler to capture a trace or enable traceflag 1222 for more details about the processes involved in deadlocking, then address the cause.

- ☑ Consider the transaction isolation level and indexing to ensure processes use appropriate locking mechanisms based on their requirements.

Guide to the Dynamic Management Views

- ☑ DMVs and Dynamic Management Functions (DMFs) provide a view on SQL Server internals and can be used for troubleshooting and fault diagnosis.

☑ DMVs can be server-scoped or database-scoped reflecting the data tracked within the DMV.

☑ DMVs run continually in the background with a very low overhead, data provided is either cumulative (since last service restart) or a snapshot view.

Partitioning

☑ Partitioning can be used to split a large table into a series of smaller tables transparent to the application.

☑ Horizontal partitioning can be used to split a table into several smaller tables with all columns and a smaller number of rows (often by date).

☑ Vertical partitioning divides a large table into several smaller tables each with all rows, but a subset of columns.

Performance Data Collection (Data Collector)

☑ The Performance Data Collection allows collection of performance data from a number of servers to a central data warehouse for analysis and reporting.

☑ Performance data is stored in the Management Data Warehouse (MDW) which is a relational database intended to be an organization-wide repository for performance data.

☑ Data collection is the process of harvesting performance data from target servers to store in the MDW.

Resource Governor

☑ Resource Governor provides capability to identify inbound connections to SQL Server and provide these connections with minimum and maximum resource (Memory, CPU) allocation.

☑ Resource pools are used to control physical server resources, while workload groups map users groups to resource pools the classifier functions are used to assign users to workload groups.

☑ The Dedicated Admin Connection (DAC) is not subject to the resource governor.

Exam Objectives
Frequently Asked Questions

Q: What's happening when SQL Profiler reports missing events?

A: This happens occasionally with very busy servers when tracing to a table or to SQL Profiler. In this situation the SQL Profiler tool is unable to keep up with the volume of events that are generated. Consider using a server side trace and saving the trace to a flat file, local to the database server.

Q: How big will the trace file grow?

A: The size of trace files is determined by the workload, events, and columns included in the trace definition. A very busy server with only a few events defined can produce a file as large as a quiet server with many events included. Be sure to monitor the growth of trace files to ensure they don't fill any drives, and if you're leaving a trace unattended (e.g., overnight) ensure there is plenty of disk space to include activities such as nightly maintenance or data loads.

Self Test

1. You're the DBA for a sales and marketing organization that has a high rate of data change (lots of INSERTS and DELETES). Over the past few weeks the SQL server has gradually become slower. Which DMV could help identify the cause?

    A. Sys.dm_os_schedulers

    B. Sys.dm_os_slow_tasks

    C. Sys.dm_db_index_physical_stats

    D. Sys.dm_exec_requests

2. Which of the following could be used within a function by Resource Governor to classify incoming sessions?

    A. IP Address

    B. Username

    C. Server Role Membership

    D. Hostname

3. You've recently enabled Resource Governor to ensure the Finance and HR departments each receive a fair share of CPU and memory on a consolidated SQL Server. Since Resource Governor has been operating, some users have experienced connection timeouts and you suspect the classifier function may be the cause. How could you identify the cause?

    A. Run SQL Profiler

    B. Connect using Dedicated Admin Connection

    C. Capture Performance Monitor data

    D. Reboot the server and see if problem recurs

4. You're troubleshooting a slow running problem and you'd like to see which indexes, if any, are being used by the slow query. You're configuring a SQL profiler trace. Which events should you include to see the actual execution plan in XML?

    A. Showplan XML Statistics Profile

    B. SQL:BatchCompleted

    C. Showplan XML

    D. RPC:Completed

5. Users complain that the database server is slow to respond or causes timeouts, and you've been running a server-side trace capturing details of query performance. The server is busy and you've generated 10 × 1 GB trace files. What's the best way to find queries with the longest duration?

   A. Open each trace file in Profiler and find longest duration.

   B. Open the trace in Excel and sort by duration.

   C. Use fn_trace_gettable to load the data into a table, analyze with TSQL queries.

   D. Run the trace again with a filter.

6. You're responsible for maintenance for a mission-critical database that is 650 GB in size, with a particularly large sales order table. The nightly index maintenance scripts are fully optimized but regularly run longer than the maintenance window. How could you resolve this with minimal impact to the business?

   A. Delete old data from the sales order table.

   B. Separate sales data into separate databases, one for each calendar year.

   C. Don't carry out index maintenance.

   D. Implement table partitioning.

7. You're responsible for managing a database that uses table partitioning for a stock trading firm. Performance on the partition storing most recent trades has started to degrade and you'd like to begin a new partition. Which statement should you use?

   A. ALTER PARTION FUNCTION... SPLIT

   B. ALTER TABLE ... SWITCH

   C. ALTER TABLE ... SPLIT

   D. Denormalize the table to 5th Normal Form

8. When a new SQL Server session is started that meets none of the criteria defined in the Classifier function, to which resource pool is the session assigned?

   A. Internal

   B. Default

   C. Custom-1

   D. None

9. You're the Administrator for a SQL Server used by a number of departments within your organization. At the end of each month the Accounts department runs a number of reports that calculate complex ratios and analytics. During this time other users frequently receive timeouts and poor performance. What's the best solution to limit the impact of these CPU-intensive reports run by Accounts?

    A. Implement table partitioning.

    B. Separate data and log files.

    C. Use Resource Governor.

    D. Request Accounting users run reports only at night.

10. You're a Systems Engineer responsible for SQL Server, and a case had been escalated via the helpdesk where a user reported an exception in an application—the error included deadlock victim. You'd like to implement monitoring to capture details of the deadlocked processes and locks held with minimum overhead. Should you:

    A. Start a SQL Profiler Trace.

    B. Capture Lock\Deadlocks per second with Windows System Monitor.

    C. Enable trace flag 1222.

    D. Review the sys.dm_tran_locks DMV.

11. A developer is using locking hints within a stored procedure and has some questions about lock escalation. You describe lock escalation as the time when SQL Server:

    A. Changes down from table locks to row locks.

    B. Changes from SHARED to UPDATE locks.

    C. Changes up from row lock to table locks.

    D. Changes from an UPDATE lock to EXCLUSIVE lock.

12. You're working with an external vendor on a patch to their application. They've applied the patch to the test environment and would like to simulate some production-like workload to assess the success of the patch. You've decided to capture a SQL trace. Which trace template will you use?

    A. TSQL_Replay

    B. Tuning

C. Standard (default)

D. Capture_test_server

13. You're responsible for SQL Server in the organization and the IT Manager would like to forecast the remaining storage capacity that exists on the disk. Which SQL Server tools could help with capacity planning?

A. SP_spaceused

B. Resource Governor

C. SQL Profiler

D. Performance Data Collector

14. You're responsible for SQL Server performance and one of the developers reports INSERTS are particularly slow. You suspect that a previous developer has created some redundant nonclustered indexes and these are hindering INSERT performance. How can you tell if an index is used?

A. Sys.dm_db_index_usage_stats

B. Sys.dm_db_index_request_count

C. Sys.dm_redundant_indexes

D. Sys.dm_db_missing_index_details

15. There is blocking occurring on your production SQL Server, you've found the session at the head of the blocking chain, and retrieved the SQL_HANDLE. Now you need to find the query executed by the user. Which DMV can help?

A. Sys.dm_exec_requests

B. sys.dm_exec_sql_text

C. sys.dm_db_query_plans

D. sys.dm_stored_proc_text

16. Which SQL Server versions can be monitored by the Performance Data Collector?

A. SQL Server 2008

B. SQL Server 2005

C. SQL Server 2000

D. SQL Server 2005 Enterprise Edition

17. What's the best method to run a SQL Trace with minimum overhead on the server being traced?

    A. Run SQL Profiler from your desktop.

    B. Run SQL Profiler from the server.

    C. Run a server-side trace to a database on the server.

    D. Run a server-side trace to a file on a fast local disk.

18. Which of the following collections could be monitored by the Performance Data Collector?

    A. SQL Trace

    B. T-SQL Queries

    C. Query Activity

    D. Client Response Statistics

    E. Performance Counters

19. Which component of table partitioning determines the boundary between partitions?

    A. Partition function

    B. Partition scheme

    C. Partition index

    D. Partition view

20. Which transaction property ensures changes are still present following a crash or system failure?

    A. Atomicity

    B. Consistency

    C. Isolation

    D. Durability

Self Test Quick Answer Key

1. **C**

2. **A, B, C, D**

3. **B**

4. **A**

5. **C**

6. **D**

7. **A**

8. **B**

9. **C**

10. **C**

11. **C**

12. **A**

13. **D**

14. **A**

15. **B**

16. **A**

17. **D**

18. **A, B, C,** and **E**

19. **A**

20. **D**

Self Test Quick Answer Key

1. C	11. C
2. A, B, C, D	12. A
3. B	13. D
4. A	14. A
5. C	15. B
6. D	16. A
7. A	17. D
8. B	18. A, B, C, and E
9. C	19. A
10. C	20. D

Chapter 14

MCTS SQL Server 2008 Exam 432

Implementing Objects

Exam objectives in this chapter:

- **Understanding DDL and DML Language Elements**
- **Working with Tables, Indexes, and Constraints**
- **Viewing and Modifying Data**

Exam objectives review:

- ☑ Summary of Exam Objectives
- ☑ Exam Objectives Fast Track
- ☑ Exam Objectives Frequently Asked Questions
- ☑ Self Test
- ☑ Self Test Quick Answer Key

Introduction

SQL Server 2008 is a mature enterprise data platform, providing objects for storing, accessing, and modifying data. In this chapter you will discover how to create tables, indexes, stored procedures, functions, and triggers. Designing database objects and writing scripts for their creation is usually the role of database developers. However, database administrators must understand the concepts behind database objects and have the skills necessary to create and modify them. This chapter will provide you with these key skills.

Database objects are divided into two broad categories: storage and programmability. *Tables* are units of data storage, structured by *columns* and *rows*. Each column in a table stores data of a specific *data type*. Many built-in data types are available for you to choose from, or you can create custom *user-defined data types* if necessary. Tables can store large amounts of data, which can take a long time to query. To maximize query performance, you can create fast lookup structures known as *indexes*. Indexes are created on frequently searched on columns and enable quick traversal when looking for particular values within a table, similar to the index you will find at the end of a printed book. You can associate *constraints* with table columns. Constraints define the rules to which data in a particular column or columns must adhere. For example, you can use a constraint to specify that values stored in the **EMailAddress** field are of a particular format. Unique constraints ensure that data for a particular column is unique across the table. For example, you may enforce that product names are always unique in the Products table. Constraints can also define relationships between tables, such as the necessity to have a Customer entity associated with every Order entity. These are known as *foreign key constraints*.

Programmability objects allow you to define *Transact-SQL* statements that can be reused again and again. *Views* are based on *Transact-SQL SELECT* statements. They represent a way of viewing a data set and show data from one or more underlying tables. Views can be updated, allowing you to write data to the view and to update underlying tables. *Stored procedures* are compiled *Transact-SQL* statements that perform particular actions. Stored procedures can accept parameters and return values. *Functions* are similar to stored procedures, except that they always return a value and never update data. *Triggers* are actions defined on tables that will execute every time data in a table changes.

Together these database objects compose a database system. Techniques and best practices for designing a database system are beyond the scope of this book. However you must understand the concepts behind database systems so that you can maintain them correctly and effectively.

Understanding DDL and DML Language Elements

Transact-SQL is the language used to create objects and access data in SQL Server. Data Manipulation Language, (DML) is part of the Transact-SQL language that allows you to insert, modify, and delete data in SQL Server tables. The core statements that constitute DML are *INSERT, UPDATE, DELETE*, and *MERGE*. In this chapter you will only use these statements in a basic way, as they are outside the scope of this book and exam.

Data Definition Language (DDL) is a subset of Transact-SQL that deals with creating database objects such as tables, constraints, and stored procedures. You will examine these statements in depth as they are mapped directly to the exam objectives. SQL Server 2008 Management Studio provides a rich user interface for creating these database objects. However, not all functionality is available within the user interface, and often you will use DDL scripts to create your database objects. The SQL Server 2008 Management Studio user interface simply allows you to create an underlying *DDL* statement using the appropriate GUI component. Figure 14.1 shows the user interface for creating a table. The *DDL* statement for creating the same table is shown in Example 14.1.

Figure 14.1 SQL Server Management Studio User Interface

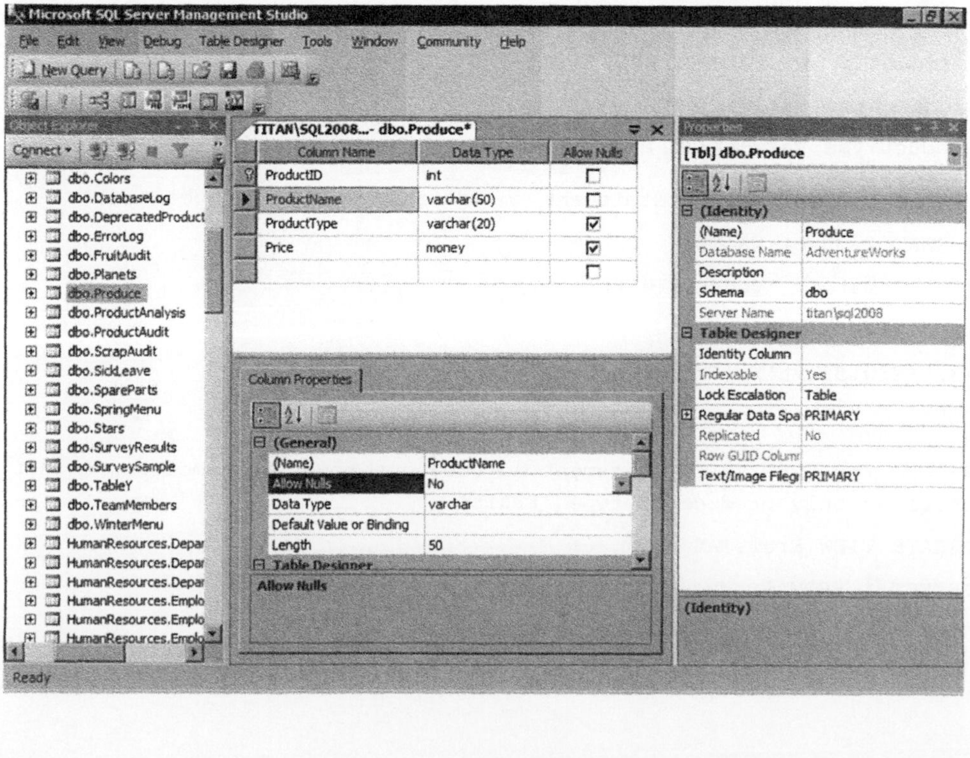

TEST DAY TIP

Remember that the user interface provided by SQL Server 2008 Management Studio allows you to visually design *DDL* statements. Any task that is available in SQL Server 2008 Management Studio can be completed using a DDL script, but not all options available within a DDL script are available within the user interface.

The key *DDL* statements are *CREATE, ALTER,* and *DROP.* The *CREATE* statement creates a SQL Server database object, like a table, view, or stored procedure. Example 14.1 creates a new table named Produce and a new view named Fruits. In this example we also use the *INSERT DML* statement to add three rows into our new table.

Example 14.1 Using the *CREATE DDL*
Statement to Create a New Table and View

```
USE AdventureWorks;
GO

-- Use the CREATE DDL statement to create a new table named Produce
CREATE TABLE Produce
(ProductID int PRIMARY KEY,
ProductName varchar(50),
ProductType varchar(20))

-- Use the INSERT DML statement to add rows to the Produce table
INSERT Produce VALUES
(1, 'Tomato', 'Vegetable'),
(2, 'Pear', 'Fruit'),
(3, 'Kiwifruit', 'Fruit');
GO

-- Use the CREATE DDL statement to create a new view named Fruit that
shows us only produce of type 'Fruit'
CREATE VIEW Fruit AS
SELECT * FROM Produce WHERE ProductType = 'Fruit';
GO
```

```
-- Use the SELECT statement to view the data in the Fruit View
SELECT * FROM Fruit
-- Results:
-- ProductID       ProductName    ProductType
-- ---------       -----------    -----------
-- 2               Pear           Fruit
-- 3               Kiwifruit      Fruit
```

The *ALTER DDL* statement changes an existing object and it can be used to add or remove columns from a table. You can also use this statement to change the definition of a view, stored procedure, trigger, or function. Example 14.2 adds a Price column to the Produce table we have created in Example 14.1. In this example we also redefine the view to include the new Price column. Do not confuse the *ALTER* statement, which changes an object definition, with the *UPDATE* statement, which changes data in a table.

Example 14.2 Using the *ALTER DDL* Statement
to Add a New Column to a Table and Redefine a View

```
-- Add a new column
ALTER TABLE Produce
ADD Price Money;
GO

-- Use the UPDATE statement to set prices
UPDATE Produce SET Price = 2.50 WHERE ProductID = 1;
UPDATE Produce SET Price = 3.95 WHERE ProductID = 2;
UPDATE Produce SET Price = 4.25 WHERE ProductID = 3;
GO

-- Redefine the view
ALTER VIEW Fruit AS
SELECT ProductID, ProductName, Price FROM Produce WHERE ProductType =
'Fruit';
GO

SELECT * FROM Fruit
-- Results:
```

```
-- ProductID      ProductName    Price

-- ---------      -----------    -----

-- 2              Pear           3.95

-- 3              Kiwifruit      4.25
```

The *DROP DDL* statement removes an object from the database. If other objects depend on the object you are attempting to drop, this statement will not succeed and an error will be raised. Example 14.3 deletes data from the Produce table, and then removes both the Fruit view and the Produce table from the database. In this example, we also attempt to drop the Person.Contact table. This operation will fail, as other objects depend on Person.Contact. Do not confuse the *DROP* statement, which removes an object from the database, with the *DELETE* statement, which deletes data from a table.

Example 14.3 Using the *DROP DDL*
Statement to Remove Tables and Views from a Database

```
DELETE FROM Produce;

SELECT * FROM Fruit;

-- Results:

-- ProductID      ProductName    Price

-- ---------      -----------    ------

-- (0 row(s) affected)

DROP VIEW Fruit;

GO

DROP TABLE Produce;

GO

DROP TABLE Person.Contact;

-- Results:

-- Msg 3726, Level 16, State 1, Line 1

-- Could not drop object 'Person.Contact' because it is referenced by
a FOREIGN KEY constraint.
```

When preparing for the exam, ensure you have practiced using the *CREATE, ALTER,* and *DROP DDL* statements and have achieved a good understanding of the DDL syntax. The AdventureWorks sample database is a great tool for learning Transact-SQL without the risk of damaging your live databases. Exercises in this chapter are based on the AdventureWorks database. Perform all exercises to get hands-on experience in writing and executing DDL queries.

Configuring & Implementing...

Minimally Logged Operations and the Database Recovery Model

Earlier examples in this chapter have made use of *INSERT, UPDATE,* and *DELETE DML* statements. These DML operations (as well as the *MERGE* statement) are logged operations. When an operation is logged, data about the operation is stored in the SQL Server transaction log. The transaction log files can be backed up and replayed into an earlier database backup. Although the log replay functionality is slow, it allows you to restore the database to the point in time when the database file was lost.

For performance reasons, some operations that affect SQL Server data can be performed as nonlogged or minimally logged. This means that the information about these operations is not fully recorded in the SQL Server transaction log. Nonlogged operations offer much better performance than logged operations. If a nonlogged operation occurs after the database has been backed up, you will not be able to replay the logs into the database after you have restored the database from backup.

The following DML operations are either nonlogged or minimally logged, depending on database recovery model:

- *TRUNCATE TABLE.*
- *WRITETEXT* and *UPDATETEXT.* These statements are deprecated and should not be used. Use *column.Write* instead.
- *SELECT INTO.*

Continued

You cannot use these statements when publishing tables as part of replication. The selected database recovery model determines what transactions are recorded in the transaction log. Three recovery models are available for SQL Server 2008 databases:

- Simple recovery model
- Full recovery model
- Bulk-Logged recovery model

When the database recovery model is set to Simple, log files are reused as soon as they become full. This means that the transaction logs use up very little space, and you don't need to worry about log file management. However, when a database is set to the Simple recovery model and the database file is lost, you will not be able to recover any changes made after the last full backup. You will also not be able to recover to a point-in time, as transaction details are stored in transaction logs that have been overwritten in this case.

The Full recovery model could be said to be the opposite of the Simple recovery model. Transaction logs are kept, and all transactions without exception are written to the logs. This includes nonlogged operations like *TRUNCATE TABLE* and *SELECT...INTO*. Although you lose the performance advantages of nonlogged operations with this recovery model, all data is recoverable provided transaction logs are intact. You can also restore to a point in time if necessary.

The Bulk-Logged recovery model is similar to the Full recovery model, except that nonlogged operations are performed as nonlogged. This provides a performance advantage for Bulk-Logged operations. If a Bulk-Logged operation has occurred since the last full backup, you will not be able to recover any changes made since the last full backup. The Bulk-Logged recovery model does not support point-in-time recovery.

In production environments, the full database recovery model is generally used, as it ensures maximum recoverability. If you wish to perform a high-performance nonlogged operation, you can temporarily switch the recovery model to Bulk-Logged, perform the operation, switch the recovery model back to Full, and perform a full backup. The Full recovery model is the default when creating databases in SQL Server.

Working with Tables and Views

Tables are the database objects that store data in a SQL Server database. Tables are structured as columns and rows, like a spreadsheet. The columns define the type and length of data they can store. Every table must have at least one column. Column names must be unique within a table; that is, you cannot specify ProductName column to appear twice in the Product table. Tables store the underlying data within the .MDF and .NDF data files as pages and extents. (These are discussed in more detail in Chapter 7.) Columns are sometimes associated with constraints, for example, *PRIMARY KEY, UNIQUE,* or *DEFAULT.* Types of constraints will be explained later in this chapter. You can also mark columns with the following special attributes:

- **Identity Columns** Values for these columns are generated automatically in sequence by incrementing every time a row is added. Usually, values 1, 2, 3, *n* are used, but you can define your own seed (starting value) and increment value for the identity column.

- **Computed Columns** These columns do not store any data; instead, they define a formula that calculates the column value at query time.

- **Timestamp Columns** These columns are used as a mechanism for version-stamping table rows and tracking changes.

- **Uniqueidentifier Columns** These columns store Globally Unique Identifiers (GUID). GUID values are used for replication and are guaranteed to be unique.

When defining columns for a new or existing table, you can specify column *nullibility.* A column is said to be nullible if it allows storing null (empty) values. You can choose to mark a column as not nullible. If anyone attempts to insert a *NULL* value into this column, an error will be raised, and the *INSERT* operation will fail.

Creating Tables

Tables can be created and modified using the SQL Server Management Studio table designer or the *CREATE TABLE* or *ALTER TABLE* statements. To access the SQL Server Management Studio graphical table designer, in Object Explorer expand the database in you wish to create the table. Then, right-click **Tables** and click **New Table**. To modify an existing table, right-click it and then click **Design**. The table designer shows the columns that will be created for your table at the top and the properties of the selected column in the **Column Properties** pane, usually located at the bottom of the screen. Figure 14.2 shows the use of SQL Server Management Studio to create a new table.

Figure 14.2 Using the SQL Server Management Studio Table Designer

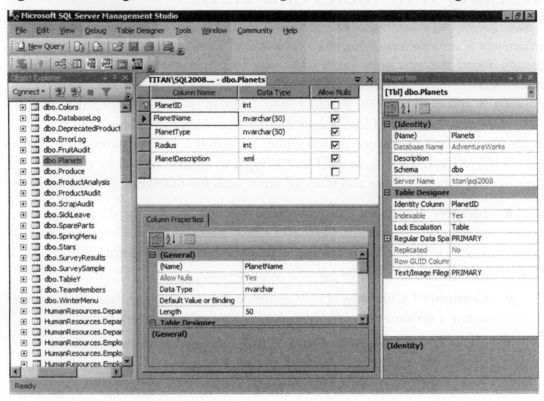

To create a table using DDL, use the *CREATE TABLE* statement along with the syntax shown in Example 14.4.

Example 14.4 *CREATE TABLE* Statement—Syntax

```
CREATE TABLE [database_name].[schema_name].table_name
(column1_name data_type [NULL | NOT NULL] | [PRIMARY KEY] | [IDENTITY],
Column2_name data_type [NULL | NOT NULL],
[<computed_column_definition>]
```

In this statement, the *table_name* is the name of the table you wish to create. When defining columns, you can specify whether or not they will allow *NULL* values. You can also state that a column will be designated as the *PRIMARY KEY* for the table and whether it will contain automatically incrementing values, known as *IDENTITY* columns. The *computed_column*_definition is the formula for a calculated column. When defining columns, you must designate a data type, like varchar or int, and in some cases a length.

Table 14.1 summarizes built-in data types that are available to you when you are defining columns.

Table 14.1 Built-In Data Types

Numeric	Character	Dates and Times	Other
Tinyint	Char	Datetime	Binary
Smallint	Nchar	Smalldatetime	Bit
Int	Varchar	Date	Cursor
Bigint	Nvarchar	Datetime2	Xml
Smallmoney	Text	Datetimeoffet	Smalldatetime
Money	Ntext	Time	Varbinary
Decimal		Timestamp	Uniqueidentifier
Double			Hierarchyid
Float			Rowversion
Real			Sql_variant
			Image

Some of the data types shown in the table also allow you to specify the length or precision for the data stored in the column you are creating. For example, a column of type char(1000) allows you to store up to 1000 characters per row. A column of type decimal(10) allows you to store up to 10 digits on either side of the decimal point, while decimal(10,5) allows you to store numbers of up to 10 digits with up to 5 digits to the right of the decimal point. Variable-length data types, like varchar, nvarchar, and varbinary, consume only the space that the characters stored in the column take up. Fixed-length equivalents of char, nchar, and binary consume a fixed amount of space regardless of the amount of actual data contained in the column. Data types prefixed with "n"—nvarchar and nchar—store Unicode text and can be used to store characters from multiple languages in one column.

Creating User–Defined Data Types

Sometimes you need to create your own data types that are based on the built-in data types introduced earlier. Custom data types are also known as user-defined data types (UDFs). UDFs are especially useful when you must store the data with the same length or precision over and over again. For example, you can create a new user-defined data type to represent people's names. This UDF can be based on nvarchar(50) and cannot contain nulls. This UDF can now be bound to any column that is to contain people's names and will be consistent throughout. Create your user-defined data types in the Model system database, so that it is automatically inherited by all new databases you create. User-defined data types are created using the *CREATE TYPE* statement. The syntax is shown in Example 14.5.

Example 14.5 *CREATE TYPE* Statement—Syntax

```
CREATE TYPE [schema_name.]type_name
{ FROM base_type([precision],[scale])
  [NULL | NOT NULL]
}
```

Example 14.6 shows the syntax used to create a user-defined data type named PersonName and to create a table that contains two columns of type PersonName.

Example 14.6 Using the *CREATE TYPE* Statement

```
CREATE TYPE PersonName
{ FROM varchar(50)
NOT NULL
};
GO
CREATE TABLE TeamMembers
(MemberId int PRIMARY KEY,
MemberName PersonName,
ManagerName PersonName);
GO
```

Use the *ALTER TYPE* statement to change the definition of your user-defined types. The *DROP TYPE* statement should be used to remove the user-defined data types you no longer need in the database. You cannot remove user-defined types from the database while there are tables with columns based on these types. If you attempt to use the *DROP TYPE* statement to remove a data type that is in use, you will get an error message similar to: "Msg 3732, Level 16, State 1, Line 1. Cannot drop type 'PersonName' because it is being referenced by object 'TeamMembers'. There may be other objects that reference this type."

Working with Constraints

Constraints are data validation rules that are bound to a column or a set of columns in a table. Constraints can also be used to enforce a relationship between two entities represented as two tables. The available types of constraints are as follows:

- **Check Constraints** These constraints validate the integrity of data in a column by checking it against a valid comparison. For example, you can use a *CHECK* constraint to ensure that no one in your Employees table has a Birth Date earlier than 01/01/1880. You can also use a *CHECK* constraint to validate that an e-mail address is always at least seven characters long.

- **Primary Key Constraints** PRIMARY *KEY* constraints represent the unique identifier column that will enforce the uniqueness of each row. For example, you can designate the CustomerID column as the PRIMARY KEY for the Customers table. If you get two customers that have the same values in the Name column and other columns, but represent different people, you will use the primary key to distinguish between them. It is a best practice to always have a primary key in each table and to use surrogate primary keys that have no meaning to the application.

- **Unique Constraints** These constraints are similar to *PRIMARY KEY* constraints, except that you can have more than one unique constraint per table. For example, you can designate that the combination of FirstName, LastName and TelephoneNumber is unique in the Customers table and that the EmailAddress column can only contain unique values.

- **Foreign Key Constraints** These constraints enforce a relationship between two tables. For example, you can use a *FOREIGN KEY* constraint to specify that any row in the Orders table must have a corresponding row in the Customers table, and that the tables are linked through the CustomerID column, which is included in both tables. Once this *FOREIGN KEY* constraint is enforced, you cannot delete a row from the Customers table that has related rows in the Orders table.

- **Default Constraints** Also known as "defaults," the *DEFAULT* constraints specify a default value to be inserted into a column if no value is inserted. Defaults can be bound to a column that is defined as *NULL* or *NOT NULL*. An example of a default is to use the value "Not Applicable" for the ProductColour every time someone adds a product to the Products table without specifying a color.

When you attempt to insert, delete, or modify data in a table that will result in a constraint violation, the statement will roll back. *DML* statements, like *INSERT, UPDATE, DELETE,* or *MERGE*, always succeed or fail as a whole. For example, if you were inserting 1000 records into a table, but one violated a *PRIMARY KEY* or *UNIQUE* constraint, all 1000 rows would roll back and nothing would be inserted. If a *DELETE* statement violates a *FOREIGN KEY* constraint, even on one row, the entire *DELETE* statement would fail and nothing would be deleted. You will never receive a partial result set from a *DML* statement. Example 14.7 shows the syntax used for working with constraints.

TEST DAY TIP

Remember that *DML* statements commit as a whole or not at all. A constraint violation will cause the entire statement to fail and roll back.

Example 14.7 Working with Constraints

```
CREATE TABLE Stars
(StarID int PRIMARY KEY,
StarName varchar(50) Unique,
SolarMass decimal(10,2) CHECK(SolarMass > 0),
StarType varchar(50) DEFAULT 'Orange Giant');
GO

INSERT Stars(StarID, StarName, SolarMass)
VALUES (1, 'Pollux', 1.86);

INSERT Stars(StarID, StarName, SolarMass, StarType)
VALUES (2, 'Sun', 1, 'Yellow dwarf');

SELECT * FROM Stars
-- Results:
-- StarID  StarName     SolarMass     StarType
-- ------  --------     ---------     ------------
-- 1       Pollux       1.86          Orange Giant
-- 2       Sun          1.00          Yellow dwarf

INSERT Stars(StarID, StarName, SolarMass, StarType)
VALUES (2, 'Deneb', 6, 'White supergiant');
```

```
-- Results:

-- Msg 2627, Level 14, State 1, Line 1

-- Violation of PRIMARY KEY constraint 'PK__Stars__06ABC647542C7691'.
Cannot insert duplicate key in object 'dbo.Stars'.

-- The statement has been terminated.

INSERT Stars(StarID, StarName, SolarMass, StarType)

VALUES (3, 'Deneb', -6, 'White supergiant');

-- Results:

-- Msg 547, Level 16, State 0, Line 1

-- The INSERT statement conflicted with the CHECK constraint "CK__
Stars__SolarMass__58F12BAE". The conflict occurred in database
"AdventureWorks", table "dbo.Stars", column 'SolarMass'.

-- The statement has been terminated.

INSERT Stars(StarID, StarName, SolarMass, StarType)

VALUES (3, 'Deneb', 6, 'White supergiant');

SELECT * FROM Stars

-- Results:

--DROP TABLE Stars

-- StarID      StarName      SolarMass      StarType

-- ------      --------      ---------      ------------

-- 1           Pollux        1.86           Orange Giant

-- 2           Sun           1.00           Yellow dwarf

-- 3           Deneb         6.00           White supergiant
```

Creating Indexes

An index is a lookup structure created on a table to optimize sort and query performance. Indexes are created on a particular column or columns, and store the data values for this column or columns in order. When raw underlying table data is stored in no particular order, this situation is referred to as a *heap*. The heap is composed of multiple pages, with each page containing multiple table rows. When raw underlying data is stored in order, sorted by a column or columns, this situation is referred to as a *clustered index*. For example, if you have a table named Customer, with a clustered index on the FullName column, the rows in this table will be stored in order, sorted by the full name. This means that when you are searching for a particular full name, the query optimizer component can execute the query more efficiently by performing an *index lookup* rather than a *table scan*. Only one clustered index is allowed per table; usually this is created on the column designated as the *PRIMARY KEY*.

You can also create additional *nonclustered indexes* on a table that is stored either as a heap or as a clustered index. A nonclustered index is a separate lookup structure that stores index values in order, and with each index value, it stores a pointer to the data page containing the row with this index value. Nonclustered indexes speed up data retrieval. It makes sense to create nonclustered indexes on all frequently searched on fields in a table. The trade-off with indexes is write performance. Every time a new row is inserted, the index must also be updated. When writing data to a table with nonclustered indexes, sometimes the pages within the table have to be rearranged to make room for the new values. In addition, indexes are storage structures that take up disk space. Indexes are created using the *CREATE INDEX* statement. Example 14.8 shows the syntax for creating an index.

Example 14.8 *CREATE INDEX* Statement—Syntax

```
CREATE [ UNIQUE ] [ CLUSTERED | NONCLUSTERED ] INDEX index_name
ON table_or_view ( column1 [ ASC | DESC ], column2, ...n)
[ INCLUDE (additional_column_name, ...n) ]
[ WHERE filter_clause]
[ WITH OPTIONS]
```

The *CREATE INDEX* statement creates a clustered or nonclustered index on a specified column or columns. You can choose to create the index as *UNIQUE*, which will enforce a unique constraint on the index columns. A *filter_clause* can be specified to create indexes only on a subset of data that meets specific criteria. This is useful for a very large table, where creating an index on all values of a particular column will be impractical. Table 14.2 summarizes index options that can be used with the *CREATE INDEX* statement.

Table 14.2 Index Options

Option	Explanation
PAD_INDEX = ON | OFF	When this option is ON, free space is allocated in each page of the index. Allows for new values to be inserted without rearranging a large amount of data. The amount of free space allocated is specified by the FILLFACTOR parameter. When this option is OFF, enough free space for one row is reserved in every page during index creation.
FILLFACTOR = fill factor percentage	Specifies the percentage of each page that should be filled up with data. For example, a fill factor of 80 means 20% of each page will be empty and available for new data. The fill factor is used only when you create or rebuild an index. Fill factor and index padding are discussed in detail in Chapter 7....
SORT_IN_TEMPDB = ON | OFF	Specifies whether the data should be sorted in the tempdb database instead of the current database. This may give performance advantages if the tempdb database is stored on a different disk to the current database.
IGNORE_DUP_KEY = ON | OFF	Specifies that duplication errors should be ignored when creating unique indexes.
STATISTICS_NORECOMPUTE = ON | OFF	Specifies that optimization statistics should not be updated at this time.
DROP_EXISTING = ON | OFF	Specifies that the existing index with the same name should be dropped and then be re-created. This equates to an index rebuild.
ONLINE = ON | OFF	Specifies that the underlying table should remain online and accessible by users while the index is being built. This option is only available in SQL Server 2008 Enterprise or Developer edition.
ALLOW_ROW_LOCKS = ON | OFF	Specifies whether locks should be held on each row, as necessary.
ALLOW_PAGE_LOCKS = ON | OFF	Specifies whether locks should be held on each page, as necessary.

Continued

Table 14.2 Continued. Index Options

Option	Explanation
MAXDOP = max_degree_ of_parallelism	Specifies the maximum number of processors that are to be used during the rebuild operation.
DATA_COMPRESSION = NONE | ROW | PAGE	Use data compression at row or page level of the index. Data compression is discussed in detail in Chapter 7.

Example 14.9 creates a clustered index (by star name) and a nonclustered index (by star type) on the Stars table we created in the previous example. Figure 14.3 shows how the *IX_Star_Name* can be created using the interface of SQL Server Management Studio.

Example 14.9 Working with Indexes

```
--Create the table specifying that the primary key index is to be
created as nonclustered
CREATE TABLE Stars
(StarID int PRIMARY KEY NONCLUSTERED,
StarName varchar(50) Unique,
SolarMass decimal(10,2) CHECK(SolarMass > 0),
StarType varchar(50) DEFAULT 'Orange Giant');
GO

CREATE CLUSTERED INDEX Ix_Star_Name
ON Stars(StarName)
WITH (PAD_INDEX = ON,
FILLFACTOR = 70,
ONLINE = ON);
GO

CREATE NONCLUSTERED INDEX Ix_Star_Type
ON Stars(StarType)
WITH (PAD_INDEX = ON,
FILLFACTOR = 90);
GO
```

Figure 14.3 Creating an Index Using SQL Server Management Studio

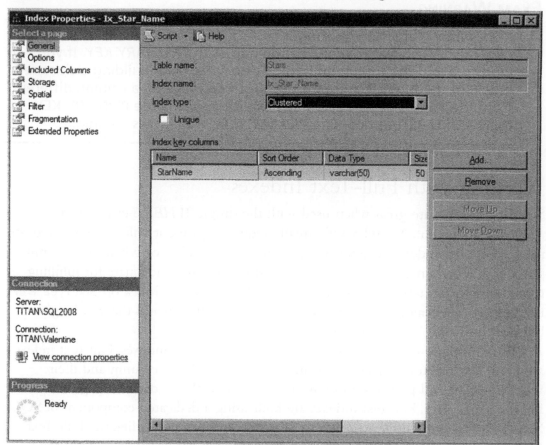

When you are creating a *PRIMARY KEY* constraint, an index on the column(s) designated as *PRIMARY KEY* will be created automatically. This index will be clustered by default, but this can be overridden when creating the index by specifying **PRIMARY KEY NONCLUSTERED** option. As a best practice, it is recommended that you accept the default of the clustered primary key column, unless you have a specific reason to designate another column as the clustered index key. Usually, the automatically created index is named *PK_TableName_<Unique Number>*, but this can be changed at any time by renaming the index. For example, a newly created Stars table with a *PRIMARY KEY* of StarID automatically has an index named *UQ__Stars__A4B8A52A5CC1BC92*.

Working with Full-Text Indexes

Standard indexes are great when used with the simple *WHERE* clause of the *SELECT* statement. An index will greatly reduce the time it will take you to locate rows where the indexed column is equal to a certain value, or when this column starts with a certain value. However, standard indexes are inadequate for fulfilling more complex text-based queries. For example, creating an index on StarType will not help you find all rows where the StarType column contains the words "giant," but not the words "supermassive".

To fulfill these types of queries, you must use full-text indexes. Full-text indexes are complex structures that consolidate the words used in a column and their relative weight and position, and links these words with the database page containing the actual data. Full-text indexes are built using a dedicated component of SQL Server 2008—the *Full-Text Engine*. In SQL Server 2005 and earlier, the Full-Text Engine was its own service, known as full-text search. In SQL Server 2008, the Full-Text Engine is part of the database engine (running as the SQL Server Service).

Full-text indexes can be stored on a separate filegroup. This can deliver performance improvements, if this filegroup is hosted on a separate disk from the rest of the database. Only one full-text index can be created on a table, and it can only be created on a single, unique column that does not allow null values. Full-text indexes must be based on columns of type char, varchar, nchar, nvarchar, text, ntext, image, xml, varbinary, and varbinary(max). You must specify a type column, when creating a full-text index on a image, varbinary, or varbinary(max) columns. The type column stores the file extension (.docx, .pdf, .xlsx) of the document stored in the indexed column.

Example 14.10 amends the Stars table to include a *Description* column and creates a full-text index on this column. The *FREETEXT* function allows us to search on any of the words specified using the full-text index. This yields a similar user experience as using an Internet search engine.

Example 14.10 Creating and Using a Full-Text Index

```
ALTER TABLE Stars

ADD Description ntext DEFAULT 'No description specified' NOT NULL ;

GO


CREATE FULLTEXT CATALOG FullTextCatalog AS DEFAULT;

CREATE FULLTEXT INDEX ON Stars(Description)

KEY INDEX PK__Stars__06ABC6465F9E293D;

GO


UPDATE Stars SET Description = 'Deneb is the brightest star in the
constellation Cygnus and one of the vertices of the Summer Triangle.
It is the 19th brightest star in the night sky, with an apparent
magnitude of 1.25. A white supergiant, Deneb is also one of the most
luminous stars known. It is, or has been, known by a number of other
traditional names, including Arided and Aridif, but today these are
almost entirely forgotten. Courtesy Wikipedia.'

WHERE StarName = 'Deneb';

UPDATE Stars SET Description = 'Pollux, also cataloged as Beta
Geminorum, is an orange giant star approximately 34 light-years away
in the constellation of Gemini (the Twins). Pollux is the brightest
star in the constellation (brighter than Castor (Alpha Geminorum).
As of 2006, Pollux was confirmed to have an extrasolar planet orbiting
it. Courtesy Wikipedia.'

WHERE StarName = 'Pollux';

GO


SELECT StarName

FROM Stars

WHERE FREETEXT (Description, 'planet orbit, giant');

GO

-- Results:

-- StarName

-- -----------------------------------------------------

-- Pollux
```

EXERCISE 14.1

CREATING TABLES, CONSTRAINTS, AND INDEXES

In this exercise, you will use *Transact-SQL* statements to create a table named Planets. You will create constraints and indexes on the table to enable fast search and data validation. You will also create a full-text catalog on the TeamMembers table.

Before you begin, you must have the following software installed on your computer:

- SQL Server 2008—a free trial is available for download
- AdventureWorks sample database

1. Open SQL Server Management Studio. To do this, click **Start | All Programs | Microsoft SQL Server 2008 | SQL Server Management Studio**.

2. Create a new query against the AdventureWorks database,

3. Create the Planets table and insert three rows of data into it using the following statement.

```
IF Exists(SELECT * FROM sys.tables WHERE name = 'Planets')
DROP TABLE Planets;
GO

CREATE TABLE Planets
(PlanetID int IDENTITY PRIMARY KEY NONCLUSTERED,
PlanetName varchar(50) NOT NULL,
PlanetType varchar(50) NULL,
Radius int CHECK (Radius > 1000),
PlanetDescription varchar(max));
GO

INSERT Planets (PlanetName, PlanetType, Radius) VALUES
('Earth', 'Terrestrial Planet', 6371),
('Jupiter', 'Gas Giant', 71492),
('Venus', 'Terrestrial Planet', 6051);
GO
```

4. View the data in the Planets table using the following statement.

```
SELECT * FROM Planets
```

5. Create a unique clustered index on the PlanetName column with 80% FILLFACTOR using the following statement.

```
CREATE UNIQUE CLUSTERED INDEX Ix_Planet_Name
ON Planets(PlanetName)
WITH (PAD_INDEX = ON,
FILLFACTOR = 80);
GO
```

6. Update the table to include planet descriptions. Create a full-text index on the PlanetDescription column.

```
UPDATE Planets SET PlanetDescription = 'Earth is the third planet
from the Sun. Earth is the largest of the terrestrial planets in
the Solar System in diameter, mass and density.' WHERE PlanetName
= 'Earth';

UPDATE Planets SET PlanetDescription = 'Jupiter is the fifth
planet from the Sun and the largest planet within the Solar
System.' WHERE PlanetName = 'Jupiter';

UPDATE Planets SET PlanetDescription = 'Venus is the second-
closest planet to the Sun, orbiting it every 224.7 Earth days.
It is the brightest natural object in the night sky.' WHERE
PlanetName = 'Venus';
GO

CREATE FULLTEXT CATALOG PlanetsFullTextCatalog AS DEFAULT;
CREATE FULLTEXT INDEX ON Planets(PlanetDescription)
KEY INDEX IX_Planet_Name;
GO
```

7. Use the FREETEXT function to locate the planet that contains the words "sky bright in the night."

```
SELECT PlanetName
FROM Planets
WHERE FREETEXT (PlanetDescription, 'sky bright in the night');
GO
```

8. Do not delete the table, for you will use it in the next exercise.

Viewing and Modifying Data

A view is a database object that represents a saved *SELECT* statement. Views are also referred to as virtual or logical tables. Views can be queried in the same way as tables, and some types of views can be updated, too. Using views instead of tables can greatly simplify data access and decouple client applications from the underlying tables containing actual data. With appropriate use of views, it is possible to completely change the schema of the database and redesign the tables without breaking any client applications. Think of views as an abstract interface between your physical database tables and the people or applications querying them.

Creating Views

SQL Server 2008 allows you to create views of the following types:

- **Standard View** This view is based on one or more base tables. The view may include joins, filter restrictions (using the *WHERE* clause), and row count restrictions (using the *TOP* and *ORDER BY* clauses). You cannot use the *ORDER BY* clause in a view without specifying the *TOP* clause as well.

- **Updateable View** A view that is based on a single underlying table can be updated directly. Executing *INSERT, UPDATE, DELETE,* and *MERGE* statements on this type of view will affect the data in the underlying table. You can also define an *INSTEAD OF INSERT, INSTEAD OF UPDATE,* and *INSTEAD OF DELETE* triggers on any view, which will perform a particular action when you attempt to insert, update, or delete data in the view.

- **Indexed View** Sometimes it is valuable to create one or more indexes on a view in order to optimize the time it takes to query the view. Indexes can be created on views using standard *CREATE INDEX* syntax.

- **Partitioned View** A partitioned view joins data that is spread across a table partitioned horizontally—for example, if you have partitioned a table by OrderDate to store orders from five years ago and earlier in one partition, orders created within the last five years in another partition, and orders created this year in yet another partition. A partitioned view will join all the partitions together into one Orders virtual table containing data from all three partitions.

To create a view, use the *CREATE VIEW* statement syntax shown in Example 14.11.

Example 14.11 *CREATE VIEW* Statement—Syntax

```
CREATE VIEW [schema_name].view_name[(column_names)]

[ WITH ENCRYPTION | SCHEMABINDING ]

AS select_statement

[ WITH CHECK OPTION ]
```

Specifying the *column_name* in a view definition allows you to assign names to computed columns or to rename columns produced by the *SELECT* statement. This is useful for calculated columns and columns that may have ambiguous names. If you don't specify explicit column names, the view columns will inherit the same names as the columns in the *SELECT* statement.

Specifying the WITH ENCRYPTION option encrypts the view definition. This also prevents the view from being used in replication.

Configuring & Implementing...

Using the SCHEMABINDING Option to Lock in a View's Underlying Schema

Views are named *SELECT* statements and include one or more columns from one or more tables. What will happen if a column or table referenced by a view is dropped from the database? The view will become invalid and will return an error the next time it is queried. To lock the view into the schema objects it relies on, add the **WITH SCHEMABINDING** option to your *CREATE VIEW* statement.

This option enforces that any table or column referenced by this view cannot be dropped or altered, until the view itself is dropped. This applies only to columns referenced by the view. You can freely add and remove columns from underlying tables, as long as they are not used in the view.

Only specify the **SCHEMABINDING** option when the view references tables from a single database.

Example 14.12 creates a view based on the Stars table using the **SCHEMABINDING** option. We then attempt to alter the underlying structure of the base table but receive an error. Figure 14.4 demonstrates how the same view can be created using the graphical view designer in SQL Server Management Studio.

Example 14.12 Working with Views

```
CREATE VIEW MyStarsView WITH SCHEMABINDING
AS SELECT StarName, StarType FROM dbo.Stars
WHERE SolarMass >=1;
GO

SELECT * FROM MyStarsView;
-- Results:
-- StarName        StarType
-- --------        ----------------
-- Deneb           White supergiant
-- Pollux          Orange Giant
-- Sun             Yellow dwarf

ALTER TABLE Stars
DROP COLUMN StarType;
GO
-- Results:
--Msg 5074, Level 16, State 1, Line 1
-- The object 'MyStarsView' is dependent on column 'StarType'.
-- Msg 5074, Level 16, State 1, Line 1
-- ALTER TABLE DROP COLUMN StarType failed because one or more objects
access this column.

-- This view is updateable, as it is based upon only one base table
UPDATE MyStarsView
SET StarType = 'White Supermassive Giant'
WHERE StarType = 'White supergiant'
GO

SELECT * FROM MyStarsView;
-- Results:
```

```
-- StarName        StarType

-- --------        -----------------------

-- Deneb           White Supermassive Giant

-- Pollux          Orange Giant

-- Sun             Yellow dwarf
```

Figure 14.4 Creating a View Using SQL Server Management Studio

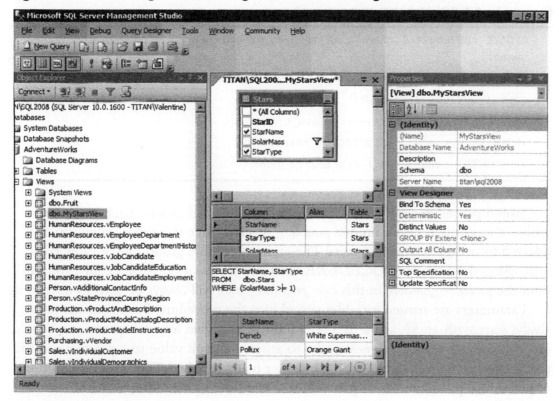

Creating Stored Procedures

Stored procedures are *Transact-SQL* statements that perform one or more actions and are saved in the database with a name. Stored procedures, used widely to encapsulate the logic of your database system, can accept parameters and return values. Stored procedures are the only database object that can update data by executing *DML* statements. For example, you may write a stored procedure named AddCustomer that accepts a CustomerName, EMailAddress, and PhoneNumber parameter. The logic within this stored procedure can check that the potential customer's details are valid, insert a new row into the Customers table using parameter values supplied, and then return the CustomerID of the newly created customer.

To create a stored procedure, use the *CREATE PROCEDURE* statement syntax shown in Example 14.13. The *CREATE PROCEDURE* keywords can be shortened to *CREATE PROC*. To change the definition or options of a stored procedure, use the *ALTER PROCEDURE* or *ALTER PROC* statement.

Example 14.13 *CREATE PROCEDURE* Statement—Syntax

```
CREATE PROCEDURE [schema_name].stored_procedure_name[; procedure_
number]

[@parameter1_name parameter1_data_type [=default_parameter_value]

[OUT | OUTPUT] [READONLY]

[@parameter2_name parameter2_data_type...]

[WITH ENCRYPTION | RECOMPILE | EXECUTE AS]

AS [BEGIN] transact_sql_statements [END]
```

Stored procedures can be grouped into logical named groups. Each procedure within a group will have a unique *procedure_number*, while the entire group can be referred to using the *procedure_name*. The entire procedure group can be dropped at once using the *DROP PROCEDURE* statement. To use a single procedure, you can omit the *procedure_number*. In this case *procedure_name* will always be used to refer to it.

Parameters are named variables passed into the procedure. Parameter names always start with an @, and a data type must be specified for each parameter. You can also use the *default_parameter_value* to assign a default value to a parameter if the procedure was called without this parameter being supplied. The most common use of procedure parameters is to pass values to the stored procedure, so that it can use these values within the *Transact-SQL* statements that comprise it. Sometimes you must return values back to the caller of your stored procedure. To do this, mark each parameter you wish to return to the caller as *OUTPUT* or *OUT* (the two are equivalent). If the parameter is not to be updated within the stored procedure, you can specify it as *READONLY*.

Similar to defining views, specifying the **WITH ENCRYPTION** option encrypts the stored procedure definition. Specify the **WITH RECOMPILE** option to instruct the database engine never to cache the execution plan for this stored procedure. Instead, the optimal execution plan will be calculated every time the procedure is called. The **EXECUTE AS** option allows you to run the procedure as an alternative set of user credentials, different from those of the caller.

Example 14.14 creates and executes a stored procedure to add a new row into the Stars table. The procedure accepts parameters for the star name, star type, solar mass, and description; and returns the ID of the newly created star.

Example 14.14 Creating and Executing a Stored Procedure

```
CREATE PROC AddNewStar
@ID int OUT,
@StarName varchar(50),
@SolarMass decimal(10,2),
@StarType varchar(50),
@Description ntext = 'No description provided.'
AS
BEGIN

  DECLARE @NextStarID int
  SET @NextStarID = (SELECT MAX(StarID) FROM Stars)
  SET @NextStarID = @NextStarID + 1
  INSERT dbo.Stars(StarID, StarName, SolarMass, StarType, Description)
  VALUES(@NextStarID, @StarName, @SolarMass, @StarType, @Description)
  SET @ID = @NextStarID

END;

DECLARE @NewStarID int
EXECUTE AddNewStar @NewStarID OUT, 'Sigma Octantis', 5.6, 'Giant'
SELECT @NewStarID as NewStarID
SELECT * FROM Stars
-- Results:
-- (1 row(s) affected)
-- NewStarID
-- -----------
-- 4
-- (1 row(s) affected)
```

```
-- StarID  StarName     SolarMass    StarType       Description

-- ------  --------     ---------    --------       -----------

-- 3       Deneb        6.00         White Supermassive Giant   Deneb is the…

-- 1       Pollux       1.86         Orange Giant              Pollux,also…

-- 4       Sigma        5.60         Giant                     No description…
            Octantis

-- 2       Sun          1.00         Yellow dwarf              No description…

--(4 row(s) affected)
```

Creating Functions

Functions, like stored procedures, are saved *Transact-SQL* statements. Unlike stored procedures, functions cannot perform actions by executing *DML* statements. Functions always return a single value or a single table-valued expression. They are used by database developers to encapsulate and reuse calculations. For example, you may create a function to calculate the tax amount given a particular salary or to determine whether an e-mail address that has been provided is valid.

It is possible for a function to take no parameters, but often functions accept multiple input parameters and use the parameter values in the calculation which the particular function represents. Unlike stored procedures, functions do not support output parameters. The following types of functions are available within SQL Server 2008

- **Scalar functions** These functions return a single value of any data type.

- **Single statement table-valued functions** These functions execute a single *SELECT* statement and return the result of this statement as a table-valued expression.

- **Multiple statement table-valued functions** These functions return several table-valued expressions created by one or more *SELECT* statements.

- **Built-in Functions** SQL Server provides many built-in functions to perform common tasks. For example, the *GETDATE()* built-in function returns today's date and time. The *AVG()* function returns the average value across a column.

You can use the *CREATE FUNCTION* statement to create new functions using the syntax shown in Example 14.15. You can use the *ALTER FUNCTION* statement to change the function's definition.

Example 14.15 *CREATE FUNCTION* Statement—Syntax

```
CREATE FUNCTION [schema_name].function_name (

[@parameter1_name parameter1_data_type [=default_parameter_value],

[@parameter2_name parameter2_data_type...] )

RETURNS data_type

AS

transact_sql_statements
```

Example 14.16 demonstrates how to create and use scalar and table-valued functions.

Example 14.16 Working with Functions

```
CREATE FUNCTION ConvertKilogramsToPounds

(@Kilograms decimal(18,2))

RETURNS decimal(18,2)

AS

BEGIN

DECLARE @Pounds decimal(18,2)

SET @Pounds = @Kilograms * 2.21

RETURN (@Pounds)

END

PRINT dbo.ConvertKilogramsToPounds(5)

-- Results:

-- 11.05
```

Creating Triggers

Triggers are stored procedures that are bound to a table or view. They run when a *DML* statement is executed on the table or view. You can specify triggers as *FOR UPDATE, FOR INSERT,* and *FOR DELETE.* These triggers will execute immediately after *INSERT, UPDATE,* or *DELETE* operations. You can also create *INSTEAD OF UPDATE, INSTEAD OF INSERT,* and *INSTEAD OF DELETE* triggers. These triggers will execute without the data being actually inserted, updated, or deleted.

A trigger can query tables and views, execute *DML* statements, and include complex Transact-SQL logic. The trigger and *DML* statement that caused the trigger to fire occur within the context of a single transaction. It is possible to roll back *INSERT, UPDATE,* and *DELETE* statements from within a trigger. This is useful for complex data validation purposes. You can use triggers to manually cascade changes through related tables; to guard against malicious or incorrect insert, update, and delete operations; and to enforce other restrictions that are more complex than those defined by using *CHECK* constraints.

EXAM WARNING

Triggers should be used sparingly because they have severe performance implications. In addition,, triggers can be difficult to maintain.

Unlike *CHECK* constraints, triggers can reference columns in other tables. For example, a trigger can use a *SELECT* statement from another table to compare to the inserted or updated data and to perform additional actions, such as modifying the data, or displaying a user-defined error message. Triggers can evaluate the state of a table before and after a data modification and take actions based on that difference. Multiple triggers of the same type (*INSERT, UPDATE*, or *DELETE*) on a table allow multiple different actions to take place in response to the same modification statement. Triggers also allow the use of custom error messages.

Triggers can be specified as *FOR, AFTER,* or *INSTEAD OF.* The trigger action will fire during the *DML* statement, after the *DML* statements, or in place of the *DML* statement, respectively. Triggers can be specified for *UPDATE, INSERT, DELETE,* or any combination of these.

How do you know what data the user is attempting to insert, update, or delete within a trigger? The trigger can access special tables called *INSERTED* and *DELETED.* These virtual tables exist only while the trigger is executing. The *INSERTED* table contains the new values you are attempting to insert into the table, or new values of the row when you are attempting to update data. The *DELETED* table contains the row you are attempting to delete or old values of the row when you are attempting to update data. Make use of these tables by querying them to determine old and new values of the data being affected. To cancel the *DML* statement from within a trigger and roll it back, use the *ROLLBACK TRANSACTION* statement.

Example 14.17 demonstrates how to create triggers, and the effect they take after a *DML* statement is executed on the table to which the trigger is bound.

Example 14.17 Creating a Trigger on the Stars Table

```
CREATE TABLE StarHistory
(StarHistoryId int IDENTITY PRIMARY KEY, StarName varchar(50), OldType
ntext, NewType ntext, DateChanged DateTime);
GO

CREATE TRIGGER UpdateStarHistory
on dbo.Stars
AFTER INSERT, UPDATE
AS
BEGIN
    INSERT StarHistory (StarName, OldType, NewType, DateChanged)
    SELECT INSERTED.StarName, DELETED.StarType, INSERTED.StarType,
GETDATE()
FROM INSERTED LEFT JOIN DELETED on INSERTED.StarID = DELETED.StarID
END
GO

UPDATE Stars SET StarType = 'Burnt out' WHERE StarName = 'Sun';
GO

SELECT * FROM StarHistory
-- Results:
-- StarHistoryId StarName   OldType          NewType      DateChanged
-- ------------- ---------- ---------------- ------------ ----------------
-- 1             Sun        Yellow dwarf     Burnt out    2009-01-21
                                                          11:56:29.530
```

TEST DAY TIP

You don't need to be able to write a trigger for the exam. Make sure that you understand the concepts behind triggers and why you may wish to use them. Remember that triggers can be defined on views as well. Creating *INSTEAD OF* triggers on a view that is not updateable will allow you to perform actions when a user attempts to insert, update, or delete data in the view.

EXERCISE 14.2

WORKING WITH VIEWS AND STORED PROCEDURES

In this exercise, you will use *Transact-SQL* statements to create views and stored procedures that show and modify data in the Planets table that you created in Exercise 14.1. Make sure that you have completed Exercise 14.1 before proceeding with this exercise.

1. Switch to **SQL Server Management Studio**.

2. Create a new query against the AdventureWorks database.

3. Create a view named **TerrestrialPlanets** that shows planet name and planet description for only those planets where the type is "Terrestrial Planet" and insert a new row into the view. View the data in the underlying table to ensure the new row has been inserted. Use the following statement.

```
CREATE VIEW TerrestrialPlanets AS
SELECT PlanetName, PlanetDescription
FROM Planets
WHERE PlanetType = 'Terrestrial Planet'
GO

SELECT * FROM TerrestrialPlanets;

INSERT TerrestrialPlanets
VALUES ('Mars', 'Mars is the fourth planet from the Sun in the
Solar System.')
SELECT * FROM Planets
```

4. Create a trigger that will update the PlanetType to "Terrestrial Planet" when a new row is inserted into the **TerrestrialPlanets** view. Use the following statement.

```
DELETE FROM Planets WHERE PlanetName = 'Mars';
GO
CREATE TRIGGER UpdatePlanetType
on dbo.Planets
AFTER INSERT
AS
```

```
BEGIN

   UPDATE Planets SET PlanetType = 'Terrestrial Planet'

   FROM Planets join INSERTED ON INSERTED.PlanetName = Planets.
PlanetName

END

GO


INSERT TerrestrialPlanets

VALUES ('Mars', 'Mars is the fourth planet from the Sun in the
Solar System.')

SELECT * FROM Planets
```

5. **Create and test a stored procedure that will update the radius for a given planet. Use the following statement.**

```
CREATE PROCEDURE UpdateRadius

@Radius int,

@PlanetName varchar(50) AS

BEGIN

   UPDATE Planets SET Radius = @Radius WHERE PlanetName = @
PlanetName

END;

GO

EXECUTE UpdateRadius 3376, 'Mars';

GO

SELECT PlanetName, Radius FROM Planets
```

Summary of Exam Objectives

In this chapter you have learned about creating database objects. As a database administrator, you must understand the types of objects that comprise a database system. Database objects are divided into two broad categories: storage and programmability. Tables store data and are created using the *CREATE TABLE* statement. For each column in the table you must select a built-in or a user-defined data type. Indexes are created on tables to maximize query performance. Constraints are associated with table columns and define the rules to which data in a particular column or columns must adhere. Constraints can also define relationships between tables, like the necessity to have a Customer entity associated with every Order entity. These are known as *foreign key constraints*.

Programmability objects allow you to define *Transact-SQL* statements that will be reused over and over again. *Views* are based on *Transact-SQL SELECT* statements. They represent a way of viewing a data set, and they show data from one or more underlying tables. Views based on a single underlying table can be updated. Specifying the **WITH SCHEMABINDING** option when creating a view prevents the underlying table from being modified, if the modification will affect the view. *Stored procedures* are compiled *Transact-SQL* statements that perform particular actions. Stored procedures can accept parameters and return values. *Functions* are similar to stored procedures, except that they always return a value, and they never update data. *Triggers* are actions defined on tables that will execute every time data in a table changes. Triggers can be created *FOR UPDATE, FOR DELETE,* and *FOR INSERT.* You can also create triggers for *AFTER* and *INSTEAD OF DML* operations.

Exam Objectives Fast Track

Understanding DDL and DML Language Elements

- ☑ Data Definition Language (DDL) contains statements used to add, modify, and remove objects from the database. The *DDL* statements are *CREATE, ALTER,* and *DROP.* These statements can be used to create and manipulate tables, data types, indexes, views, stored procedures, functions, and triggers.

- ☑ Data Manipulation Language (DML) is a part of the Transact-SQL language that allows you to insert, modify, and delete data in SQL Server tables. The core statements that comprise DML are *INSERT, UPDATE, DELETE,* and *MERGE.*

- ☑ DDL manipulates database structure, while DML manipulates actual data stored in tables.

Working with Tables, Indexes, and Constraints

☑ Use the *CREATE TABLE* statement to define a table by listing columns in the table along with corresponding data types.

☑ Indexes are useful for fast searching and sorting data. One clustered index is allowed per table, and the underlying table data is stored in the order of the clustered index. Nonclustered indexes are separate lookup structures that point to the table heap or the clustered index.

☑ Full-text indexes are used for specialized querying using functions like *FREETEXT*. Only one full-text index is allowed per table.

☑ Indexes and constraints can be defined separately and are bound to an existing table.

Viewing and Modifying Data

☑ A view is a *SELECT* statement saved with a name. A view can be updated if it is based on a single table, or if it has *INSTEAD OF* triggers defined on it. Indexes can be created on a view as well as on a table.

☑ A stored procedure is any *Transact-SQL* statement saved with a name. Stored procedures can update data by using *DML* statements.

☑ A function is a *Transact-SQL* statement that usually performs a calculation. Functions must return a value. Functions that return a single value are known as scalar functions, whereas functions that return a table-valued expression are known as table-valued functions.

☑ A trigger is a statement that runs automatically, when data in a particular table or view is modified. Triggers can cancel transactions by using the *ROLLBACK TRANSACTION* statement. Triggers can be specified as *FOR, AFTER,* or *INSTEAD OF.* You can access special *INSERTED* and *DELETED* tables within the trigger to find out the old and new values of rows that are being updated.

Exam Objectives
Frequently Asked Questions

Q: When should I use the *TRUNCATE TABLE* statement rather than the *DELETE* statement?

A: You should use the *TRUNCATE TABLE* statement if you want to quickly and indiscriminately empty the table. A performance advantage is achieved with the *TRUNCATE TABLE* statement when the database recovery model is set to Bulk-Logged. The *DELETE* statement allows you to restrict the data you will be deleting using a *WHERE* clause.

Q: Does the *TRUNCATE TABLE* statement remove the table from the database?

A: No, the *TRUNCATE TABLE* statement removes all data from the table, but the table structure and its definition remain intact.

Q: What is the best indexing strategy?

A: Indexing strategies vary depending on your data access pattern and parameters such as the size of your table. As a rule of thumb, it is recommended that you create a clustered index on the *PRIMARY KEY* column and multiple nonclustered indexes for other frequently searched-on columns.

Q: When should I use **FILLFACTOR** and **PAD_INDEX** options?

A: Use these options when creating or rebuilding an index. Bear in mind that **FILLFACTOR** and **PAD_INDEX** optimize write performance, but slightly decrease read performance because more data pages have to be accessed. Do not bother padding indexes based on identity columns. In these cases, new values will never go in the middle of a page, always at the end.

Q: Why would I use the *FREETEXT* search function instead of multiple *LIKE* '%value%' comparisons?

A: Using *LIKE* comparisons is a highly time- and resource-consuming operation that always requires a table scan. The *FREETEXT* utilizes the full-text index structure and delivers much better performance than the *LIKE* comparison.

Q: What is the advantage of using an updateable view over updating the table directly, given that the updateable view will by definition always be based on a single table?

A: A view is more flexible. For example, you may wish to restructure the underlying tables without the need to change your client applications. You will only need to update the view in this case, not everything that referenced the tables being restructured.

Q: Why should I use stored procedures in preference to functions?

A: Stored procedures are usually used to perform an action, like update, insert, or delete, whereas functions are usually used to perform calculations. Functions cannot be used to execute *DML* statements.

Q: If I define multiple triggers on a single table, what is the order of the triggers firing?

A: The triggers will execute in random order; you cannot rely on the order of triggers firing.

Self Test

1. You are creating a view named WeeklySales. This view is used to create a sales report that is presented to management at the beginning of each week. You want to ensure that the underlying tables on which this view is based are not accidentally modified causing the report to break. What is the easiest way to implement this?

   A. Use a *CREATE VIEW WITH CHECK* constraint to create a view.

   B. Use a *CREATE VIEW WITH SCHEMABINDING* statement to create the view.

   C. Do nothing. When a view is based on a table, the underlying table cannot be modified until the view is dropped.

   D. Use a DDL trigger to roll back any statement that attempts to modify the table that the view depends on.

2. You have a view named YearlySales that lists all sales for the year. The reporting application your organization uses allows you to query the YearlySales view by CustomerName or by OrderDate. You receive unfavorable feedback from users that report generation is painfully slow. What is the best way to optimize report performance?

   A. Create indexes on CustomerName and OrderDate columns.

   B. Create a *UNIQUE* constraint on CustomerName and OrderDate columns.

   C. Create a *DEFAULT* constraint on CustomerName and OrderDate columns.

   D. Create a full-text index on CustomerName and OrderDate columns.

3. You have a very large table containing documents stored as a column of varbinary data type. The table is named Documents and is not referenced by *FOREIGN KEY* constraints. What is the most efficient way of removing all records from this table, while leaving the table ready for inserting new records (select all that apply)?

   A. *TRUNCATE TABLE* Documents

   B. *DELETE* Documents

   C. *DELETE FROM* Documents

   D. *DROP TABLE* Documents

   E.   Set the Database Recovery Model to Full

   F.   Set the Database Recovery Model to Bulk-Logged

4. You have a table named Products, which contains the ProductID, ProductName, Model, and Color columns. The ProductID is marked as *IDENTITY*. You wish to ensure that there are never two products with the same combination of name, model, and color. What is the easiest way to achieve this?

   A.   Create a *PRIMARY KEY* constraint on the ProductName, Model, and Color columns.

   B.   Create a *DEFAULT* constraint on the ProductName, Model, and Color columns.

   C.   Create a *UNIQUE* constraint on the ProductName, Model, and Color columns.

   D.   Create a trigger *FOR INSERT* that checks that there is not already a combination of name, model, and color in the table.

5. You have two tables: PrizeDraw and Employees. Both tables have a PersonName column. You must ensure that employees cannot enter the prize draw. A record with the name that already exists in the Employees table cannot be inserted into the PrizeDraw table. What is the best way to achieve this?

   A.   Create a *CHECK* constraint on the PrizeDraw table.

   B.   Create a *CHECK* constraint on the Employees table.

   C.   Create a trigger on the Employees table.

   D.   Create a trigger on the PrizeDraw table.

6. You are tasked with creating a Reseller table, with the Commission column containing the commission percent. When a new reseller is added, the default commission level is 30%. What is the easiest way to implement this rule?

   A.   Create a *FOR INSERT* trigger on the Reseller table.

   B.   Create an *INSTEAD OF INSERT* trigger on the Reseller table.

   C.   Create a *DEFAULT* constraint on the Commission column.

   D.   Create a *CHECK* constraint on the Commission column.

7. You have a table named EmployeePhoto. This table is not referenced by any *FOREIGN KEY* constraints. What is the most efficient way of deleting the EmployeePhoto table entirely, including data and structure?

    A. *TRUNCATE TABLE* EmployeePhoto

    B. *DELETE* EmployeePhoto

    C. *DELETE FROM* EmployeePhoto

    D. *DROP TABLE* EmployeePhoto

8. The HR manager has asked you to create a table that will store candidate resumes. These files are created using Microsoft Word 2003 or Microsoft Word 2007, and the HR manager wishes that they are stored in this format. It is a requirement that the HR representatives are able to query the table using search engine style syntax. How should you create the table?

    A. *CREATE TABLE* Resumes

        (ResumeID int *PRIMARY KEY NULL,*

        ResumeFile varbinary(max),

        FileType varchar(10))

    B. *CREATE TABLE* Resumes

        (ResumeID int *PRIMARY KEY,*

        ResumeFile varbinary(max))

    C. *CREATE TABLE* Resumes

        (ResumeID int *PRIMARY KEY,*

        ResumeFile varbinary(max),

        FileType varchar(10))

    D. *CREATE TABLE* Resumes

        (ResumeID int UNIQUE NULL,

        ResumeFile varbinary(max),

        FileType varchar(10))

9. You have a table named TeamMembers containing the data shown in Table 14.3.

Table 14.3 TeamMembers Table

MemberName varchar(50) PRIMARY KEY
Valentine
Hayden
Matthew

MemberName is the *PRIMARY KEY* for the table. You execute the following statement:

```
INSERT TeamMembers Values ('Phil'), ('Valentine'), ('Peter')
```

Which team members will be present in the TeamMembers table after the statement executes?

A. Valentine, Hayden, Matthew, Phil

B. Valentine, Hayden, Matthew, Phil, Peter

C. Valentine, Hayden, Matthew, Phil, Valentine, Peter

D. Valentine, Hayden, Matthew

10. You have created a Customers table and an NZCustomers view using the following definitions....

```
CREATE TABLE Customers
(CustomerID int IDENTITY PRIMARY KEY,
CompanyName varchar(50),
Country varchar(50),
Notes varchar(max));
GO

CREATE VIEW NZCustomers AS
SELECT * FROM Customers WHERE Country = 'New Zealand';
GO
CREATE TRIGGER Trig_NZCustomers
ON dbo.NZCustomers INSTEAD OF INSERT
AS
BEGIN
   SELECT CustomerID FROM INSERTED
END
GO
```

You notice that when you insert data into the NZCustomers view, no error occurs, but the data does not appear in the table. What is the cause of the problem?

A. The *Trig_NZCustomers* must be dropped because it is preventing the insert operation.

B. The view cannot be updated because of the *WHERE* clause. Remove the *WHERE* clause from the view.

C. The *IDENTITY* column is preventing new CustomerIDs from being generated. Redefine the column not to use the *IDENTITY* attribute.

D. You must explicitly call **COMMIT TRANSACTION within Trig_NZCustomers**.

11. You are adding a Notes column to a table named Customers. You are instructed that the *Notes* column must always contain a value, even if the value is "No notes available." Unfortunately, many stored procedures you use to add data to the Customers table omit the Notes column, and it is impractical to redesign the stored procedures. What is the easiest way to ensure that the *Notes* column in the Customers table always has a value assigned?

A. Define the Notes column as *NULL*. Create a default constraint on the Notes column with the default value of "No notes available."

B. Define the Notes column as *NOT NULL*. Create a default constraint on the Notes column with the default value of 'No notes available'.

C. Define the Notes column as *NOT NULL*. Create a check constraint on the Notes column.

D. Define the Notes column as NULL. Create a check constraint on the Notes column.

12. You have a view that displays records from multiple tables within the same database. These tables are managed by different team members. Frequently, your view is inaccessible, when someone modifies the underlying tables. You are instructed by management that the view must work and be accessible at all times. You wish to prevent people from deleting or modifying the tables your view relies on. What is the best way to achieve this?

A. Use an *ALTER TABLE WITH SCHEMABINDING* statement to update each of the source tables.

B. Use an *ALTER TABLE WITH CHECK* statement to update each of the source tables.

C. Use an *ALTER VIEW WITH SCHEMABINDING* statement to create the view.

D. Use an *ALTER VIEW WITH CHECK* statement to create the view.

13. You have a large table named CustomerEnquiries. There is a clustered index on the CustomerName column. Unfortunately, your users inform you that it

takes an excessively long time to add a new customer to the table. How should you resolve this issue?

A. Use the *ALTER INDEX* statement with the **FILLFACTOR** and **PAD INDEX** options.

B. Use the *DROP INDEX* statement to drop the index.

C. Use the *ALTER INDEX* statement with the **NONCLUSTERED** option.

D. Use the *ALTER INDEX* statement with the **REBUILD** option.

14. You have a table named Customers. When a new customer is added, you must check the CreditRating table for the proposed customer's credit rating. If the credit rating is below a certain value, you must not allow the customer to be added to the Customers table. What is the best way to achieve this?

A. Create a *FOR INSERT* trigger.

B. Create an *AFTER INSERT* trigger.

C. Create an *INSTEAD OF INSERT* trigger.

D. Create a *CHECK* constraint.

15. You must create a stored procedure that adds a row to the Customers table and returns the ID of the newly inserted customer. Select the statement that will declare the procedure parameters correctly.

A. CREATE PROC AddNewCustomer

@ID OUT,

@CustomerName varchar(50),

@Notes varchar(max)

AS...

B. CREATE PROC AddNewCustomer

@ID int OUT,

@CustomerName varchar(50),

@Notes varchar(max)

AS...

C. CREATE PROC AddNewCustomer

@ID int,

@CustomerName varchar(50) OUT,

@Notes varchar(max) OUT

AS...

D. CREATE PROC AddNewCustomer

ID int OUT,

CustomerName varchar(50),

Notes varchar(max)

AS...

16. You have a table named Orders that contains the OrderID, CustomerID, Amount, and OrderDate columns. You must retrieve all orders placed in the last seven days. What criteria should you use with the *WHERE* clause (select all that apply)?

   A. *WHERE DateDiff*("week", OrderDate, *GETDATE( ))* <= 1

   B. *WHERE DateDiff*("day", OrderDate, *GETDATE( ))* <= 7

   C. *WHERE GetDate*("day", OrderDate, *DATEDIFF( ))* <= 7

   D. *WHERE GetDate*("day", OrderDate, *DATEDIFF( ))* >= 7

17. You have a table named Orders. You must make sure that the order date for each order occurs before the ship date. What is the best way to achieve this?

   A. Create a *CHECK* constraint using *CHECK* (OrderDate > ShipDate) statement.

   B. Create a *CHECK* constraint using *CHECK* (OrderDate < ShipDate) statement.

   C. Create an *INSTEAD OF INSERT, UPDATE* trigger.

   D. Create a *FOR INSERT*, UPDATE trigger.

18. You always allow 50 Unicode characters for names of people, and you never allow names to be null. You wish to create a user-defined data type that will be used whenever a person's name must be stored. How should you create the data type?

   A. CREATE TYPE PersonName { FROM varchar(50) NOT NULL }

   B. CREATE TYPE PersonName { FROM nvarchar(50) NOT NULL }

   C. CREATE TYPE PersonName { FOR varchar(50) NOT NULL }

   D. CREATE TYPE PersonName { FROM nvarchar(50)}

19. In your database system, you must frequently convert from EURO currency to USD currency, using the exchange rate stored in the ExchangeRates table. What is the best way to achieve this?

    A. Create a function that accepts an @EURAmount parameter and returns the USD value.

    B. Create a stored procedure that accepts an @EURAmount parameter and selects the USD value using the *SELECT* statement.

    C. Create a view that accepts an @EURAmount parameter and selects the USD value.

    D. Create a stored procedure that accepts an @EURAmount parameter and returns the USD value using the *SELECT* statement.

20. You wish to add a new column to an existing view object. What are some of the ways to do this? (Select all that apply)

    A. Use Visual Studio object designer.

    B. Use the SQL Management Studio object designer.

    C. Use the *ALTER VIEW* statement.

    D. Use the *ALTER COLUMN* statement.

Self Test Quick Answer Key

1. **B**

2. **A**

3. **A, F**

4. **C**

5. **D**

6. **C**

7. **D**

8. **C**

9. **D**

10. **A**

11. **B**

12. **C**

13. **A**

14. **A**

15. **B**

16. **A, B**

17. **B**

18. **B**

19. **A**

20. **B, C**

Index

Printed and bound by CPI Group (UK) Ltd, Croydon, CR0 4YY

03/10/2024

01040343-0015